MULTIMEDIA

Concepts and Practice

Upper Saddle River, New Jersey 07458

ACQUISITIONS EDITOR: David Alexander
EDITOR-IN-CHIEF: Mickey Cox
DEVELOPMENTAL EDITOR: Rebecca Johnson
ASSOCIATE EDITOR: Kyle Hannon
EDITORIAL ASSISTANT: Erika Rusnak
DIRECTOR, STRATEGIC MARKETING: Nancy Evans
SENIOR MARKETING MANAGER: Sharon Turkovich
MANAGING EDITOR, PRODUCTION: Sondra Greenfield
PRODUCTION EDITOR: Michael Reynolds
MANUFACTURING BUYER: Lisa Babin
SENIOR MANUFACTURING SUPERVISOR: Paul Smolenski
MANUFACTURING MANAGER: Vincent Scelta
SENIOR DESIGNER: Cheryl Asherman
DESIGN DIRECTOR: Patricia Smythe
INTERIOR DESIGN: Lee Goldstein
COVER DESIGN: John Romer
COVER ART: Steven Lyons
SENIOR PRINT/MEDIA PRODUCTION MANAGER: Karen Goldsmith
PRINT PRODUCTION MANAGER: Christy Mahon
PRODUCTION SERVICES: Elm Street Publishing Services, Inc.

Library of Congress Cataloging-in-Publication Data

McGloughlin, Stephen,
    Multimedia : concepts and practice / Stephen McGloughlin.
      p. cm.
    ISBN 0-13-018830-1
      1. Multimedia systems.   I. Title.

    QA76.575 .M335 2001
    006.7--dc21   00-062367

Microsoft Excel, Solver, and Windows are registered trademarks of Microsoft Corporation in the U.S.A. and other countries. Screen shots and icons reprinted with permission from the Microsoft Corporation. This book is not sponsored or endorsed by or affiliated with Microsoft Corporation.

Photo and screen capture credits appear before the index

Prentice-Hall International (UK) Limited, *London*

Prentice-Hall of Australia Pty. Limited, *Sydney*

Prentice-Hall Canada Inc., *Toronto*

Prentice-Hall Hispanoamericana, S.A., *Mexico*

Prentice-Hall of India Private Limited, *New Delhi*

Prentice-Hall of Japan, Inc., *Tokyo*

Prentice-Hall Pte Ltd., *Singapore*

Editora Prentice-Hall do Brasil, Ltda., *Rio De Janiero*

12919373

10 9 8 7 6 5 4 3 2

ISBN 0-13-018830-1

Dedicated to my wife,
Bre,
without whom this wouldn't have been possible.

BRIEF CONTENTS

CONTENTS

3 Getting Started in Multimedia   41

Part 2 MULTIMEDIA GRAPHIC DESIGN   67

4   Multimedia Building Blocks: 2D Graphics   67

Part 5   DIGITAL SOUND AND MUSIC

Part 6   MULTIMEDIA INTEGRATION, AUTHORING, AND APPLICATION DEVELOPMENT   301

14   Multimedia Integration and Authoring   301

16 Creating Awesome Multimedia Applications on the Web 374

PREFACE

[A computer is] like an Old Testament god; lots of rules and no mercy.

Joseph Campbell

As a teacher, I like quotations. They can provide a succinct perspective that would take paragraphs to spell out.

You'll agree that the usability and reputation of computers have advanced considerably in recent times—especially in contrast to Joseph Campbell's opinion of some years ago. Computing today is a much better state of affairs, a fact attributable almost entirely to developments in and use of multimedia technology. We, as humans, like things elegantly simple, but computers are inherently complex. To bring together these opposing forces we use the art of multimedia and the interface.

Everything should be made as simple as possible, but not simpler.

Albert Einstein

Without an easy-to-use interface for your computer application, you would be propelled back to those difficult early years of text-based computing technology, and you would most likely share the sentiments of Joseph Campbell. To use modern fast and powerful computers and software applications without the benefit of multimedia technology is inconceivable. If you doubt this premise, then take a look at the Internet, for instance. It had been around for many years, unknown and in everyday use in governmental and educational institutions, as a text-based communications tool, until an easy-to-use interface in the form of the Internet browser unlocked the immense potential of the media-rich World Wide Web. The rest is unquestionable history. The Internet's success is just one example of the power of multimedia. Today, multimedia capability and enhancement are a basic expectation of every new computer purchaser—and at the turn of the last century, over 11,000 new computers were purchased every hour of every day!

I think there is a world market for maybe five computers.

Thomas Watson, chairman of IBM, 1943

See what I mean about quotations?

WHAT IS *MULTIMEDIA: CONCEPTS AND PRACTICE?*

Any sufficiently advanced technology is indistinguishable from magic.

Arthur C. Clarke

This book is designed specifically to guide you through the many, and often complex, technologies that collectively come together to create multimedia applications. Multimedia really refers to the creation and bringing together of many media elements and components into a computer-based presentation or application.

The skills and technologies of computer graphic design, 3D modeling and animation, digital sound recording and editing, digital video capture and manipulation, Internet content and application development, multimedia application authoring, and a little computer programming are all required of the complete multimedia developer. Above and beyond these hands-on skills, the multimedia creator also needs project management skills of greater depth than most computer-related development projects require. While a broad and all-encompassing field, multimedia is also fun and exciting, and it can provide the developer with both a lucrative source of income and a tremendous sense of creative accomplishment.

In this book you will find a good introduction to the creative and application-development technologies that fill the multimedia producer's toolbox. It is important to note that in-depth coverage of any one of these tools could fill a book equal to the size of the one you're reading. The intent of this book is not to make you an expert in using each of these tools, but to give you a good start in the right direction for each technology. It is intended to show the new multi-media developer how these tools work together in a harmony that can produce a product greater in value than the sum of it's individual parts. Thereafter it is up to the multimedia developer to use those resources provided by this book, its companion CD-ROM, its Web site and other publications to peruse more specialized knowledge in those areas that are of most interest.

As an instructor, I have found that students in my introductory multimedia courses always seem to gravitate toward one or two technologies in the multi-media range that most appeals to them. They may be more turned on by computer 3D modeling and animation. Perhaps their passion lies in digital video editing and in morphing. In any case, their further pursuit and specialization in these interests always provide a more rewarding and more rounded experience in the context and understanding of the other technologies that comprise multi-media. I have designed and built this book to fulfill that need and to provide a good and solid springboard from which to jump into the chosen deep end.

HOW TO USE THIS BOOK

I choose a block of marble and chop off whatever I don't need.
François-Auguste Rodin, when asked how
he managed to make his remarkable statues

Multimedia: Concepts and Practice is cumulative. It presents in six parts a progressive journey through the world of multimedia development. Principles and some history of the field first provide a sense of place in Part 1. In Part 2, the theory of interface design is then illustrated with actual hands-on interface creation through image editing and graphic design tools and techniques. The creation of 3D imagery using common graphic design tools segues into computer 3D modeling and animation in Part 3. Manipulating digital video follows in Part 4, which brings up the technology of special effects and morphing. Digital sound editing, required of most digital video products, is covered in Part 5, just before Part 6, Multimedia Integration, Authoring and Application Development, which brings it all together.

Once you have created your media components for your production, you will need to assemble them into the final multimedia product. After the final product is created, the question "What can I do now with my newfound skills?" remains. This question is answered in the final chapter for this book, Multimedia as a Way of Life, found on the book's Web site at http://www.prenhall.com/mcgloughlin.

Besides providing a progressive path through the field of multimedia, this book has also been structured to provide a valuable reference on which you can depend throughout your multimedia career.

Exercises and critical thinking challenges at the end of each chapter are designed to reinforce the chapters subject matter. As the book progresses, so does the Master Project—a cumulative "big picture" project that follows the cumulative learning and adds sequentially towards a final multimedia production for the reader.

WEB SITE (http://www.prenhall.com/mcgloughlin) AND SOFTWARE USAGE

It would appear that we have reached the limits of what it is possible to achieve with computer technology, although one should be careful with such statements, as they tend to sound pretty silly in five years.

John Von Neumann (ca. 1949)

Since multimedia encompasses so many technologies, the number of software applications and tools required of the complete multimedia developer is large. In recognition of the limited resources of most readers, especially those starting out in this field, you will find throughout this book tremendous emphasis on multiple software options. While some recognized (and expensive) "industry standard" applications are discussed, much effort has been put into providing instruction and guidance on more affordable but equally suitable alternatives.

The software industry is fast paced and ever changing. It is inconceivable that this book in print only could maintain a complete current version set of the many software tools described herein. Therefore great care has been taken to write this book to the fundamental features and capabilities of each application. Even though versions of the software may change, the instruction will continue to be sound and current. The processes used with these applications are emphasized along with step-by-step instruction. These taught skills transcend software versions and are often valid for, and common to, many brands and manufacturers. Because this book addresses so many different software applications, you are encouraged to use the book's Web site—http://www.prenhall.com/mcgloughlin—for resources and references about the latest versions of these applications.

The Web site is designed to complement and add value to the text. It also provides links to download demonstration versions of the software applications used throughout the book. Both as the author and as a multimedia instructor, I do not usually encourage the use of demonstration versions of software applications other than for evaluations of their purchase-worthiness. Every demonstration version of every software application is restricted in one way or another. Some are tremendously restricted, as in the case of Adobe's Photoshop, where the ability to save your work is disabled, and some are less so with Jasc's Paint Shop Pro, where some features are disabled, but the "evaluator" is provided with a working version for a defined time period. None of these demonstration versions are suitable tools for the serious multimedia developer. Once you evaluate and compare them, be prepared to invest in the full product, both to gain the most value from this text and for use as professional tools in your multimedia development endeavors. Please note that this book is written for those using the full versions with full capabilities.

The dynamic companion Web site to *Multimedia: Concepts and Practice* is referenced throughout the text with a Web icon. The Web site features the following:

- Chapter 17, Careers in Multimedia
- Chapter objectives, software demos and updates, online magazines, online digital portfolios, bibliography, chapter specific URLs, and additional exercises
- Chat facilities, including Message Board and Live Chat. Message Board allows users to post messages and check for responses. Live Chat allows users to discuss course topics in real time and enables professors to host on-line classes.
- A secure, password-protected Instructor's area featuring a download of the Instructor's Manual

THE CD-ROM

It's hard to make a program foolproof because fools are so ingenious.

Unknown

What would a book about multimedia be without its own CD-ROM! A bit like a resume attached to an empty portfolio, I would think.

Like this book's Web site, the CD-ROM is designed to be complementary to *Multimedia: Concepts and Practice*, not a repetition of its contents. In itself, it is a terrific example of a multimedia application at work. Within the CD-ROM you will find not only the sample files referenced in the text, but also worked examples of exercises to guide users through any areas they may find difficult to understand. In addition, the CD-ROM contains sample applications and multimedia mini-tutorials to walk the reader through those concepts that are difficult to describe adequately in text alone.

ACKNOWLEDGMENTS

All parts should go together without forcing. You must remember that the parts you are reassembling were disassembled by you. Therefore, if you can't get them together again, there must be a reason. By all means, do not use a hammer.

IBM maintenance manual, 1925

This book has been challenging in many ways. That you are actually reading a published copy is in no small way due to the hard work and efforts of the publishing teams at QUE E&T originally, of Prentice Hall, and of Elm Street Publishing Services. A special thanks goes to Rebecca Johnson, whose editorial skills and hard work (and patience with the author) kept us all sane and on schedule. Thanks also to David Alexander for his support and belief in this book, to Rick Hornor for a great technical editing job (thanks, Rick!), and to Michele Heinz for her terrific work bringing the final stages together. To Jon Phillips, Randy Haubner, and Songlin Qiu, thanks for allowing me to sow the seed on this one and for providing me with the opportunity to see it through. I would also like to thank Linda Behrens and the team at University of California Davis Extension. While I was director of Interactive Media Development there, they stuck with and supported me during the times when this project seemed overwhelming. Thanks, guys!

I especially want to thank my wife, Bre, and our kids, who not only supported me on this project but also made it possible for me to spend countless antisocial hours locked away on the computer, researching, writing, designing, and producing what you hold in your hands. This book would not exist without their incredible patience and tremendous personal sacrifice. This book is really for them.

For the many other individuals who devoted their time and energies to this book who I haven't mentioned by name, you are much appreciated.

I am grateful for the following reviewers whose excellent feedback helped refine and evolve this challenging project:

Donna Mitchell Austin, Louisiana State University

Linda Ericksen, Lane Community College

Bruce Gibbs, Art Institute of Atlanta

Matthew Goddard, New Hampshire Community Technical College

Dennis Jones, Tarleton State University

Cathie LeBlanc, Plymouth State College

Dave Pickens, Alexandria Technical College

David J. Rosser, Essex County College

Steve Schwab, Art Institute of Florida

Nancy Stern, Hofstra University

Yixin Zhang, McNeese State University

This book was developed with the technical assistance and support of:

Adobe Inc. (www.adobe.com)

Black Knight Productions, Greg Bassett (www.just3d.com)

Caligari Corp. (www.caligari.com)

Clickteam, in particular Yves, whose support with Multimedia Fusion went far beyond the call of duty (www.clickteam.com)

IMSI USA (www.imsisoft.com)

JASC Software Inc. (www.jasc.com)

Macromedia Inc. (www.macromedia.com)

MetaCreations Inc. (www.metacreations.com)

Microsoft (www.microsoft.com)

Sonic Foundry Inc. (www.sonicfoundry.com)

Template Graphics Software Inc. (www.tgs.com)

And finally…

A computer terminal is not some clunky old television with a typewriter in front of it. It is an interface where the mind and body can connect with the universe and move bits of it about.

Douglas Adams, Mostly Harmless, 1992

MULTIMEDIA

Concepts and Practice

One

MULTIMEDIA
CONCEPTS

A BRIEF INTRODUCTION TO MULTIMEDIA

Chapter Outline

Chapter Objectives

After completing this chapter, you will be able to:

- Define the term *multimedia* and the concepts surrounding this technology.
- Discuss the evolution of multimedia technology.
- Describe the important role multimedia plays in the progress and evolution of modern computing and digital devices.

Chapter Overview

To understand multimedia, it is important to define it and to consider its technological evolution. To this end, you will read a brief history of the main milestones in the development and evolution of multimedia. Having developed a "sense of place" for multimedia, you will then understand the exciting potential it holds for us all.

A CONCISE DEFINITION OF MULTIMEDIA

Multimedia is one of those terms that can mean many different things to different people. Because so many computer disciplines come together under the heading of multimedia, it is difficult to know exactly where the definition begins and where it ends. Jeff Burger, columnist for *NewMedia* magazine, once wrote:

> Defining multimedia reminds me of an ancient proverb about the three blind men, each encountering an elephant for the first time. One, touching the tail, said it was like a rope. Another, embracing the beast's leg, described it as a tree. The third, holding the elephant's trunk, likened it to a snake. Multimedia can appear to be different things, depending on whom you ask.

Yet it would seem that most everyone knows what you mean when you use the term. It is arguably the most widely used buzzword in computing history. I recently made a trip to Dallas, Texas, and on leaving the airport I could see a large and brightly lit billboard from the freeway on-ramp. It displayed just two words. The first word, in huge letters was the brand name NEC, and beneath it was nothing but the word *Multimedia*. It seems that nothing more was needed to get the message across. The word *multimedia* alone suggests technological capability and promise.

So is multimedia a theatrical play in which colorful props mingle with live actors, and where music and sound effects abound? This would certainly describe an event in which *multiple* forms of *media* work together. To some, it could be. However, this definition could place the origins of multimedia back a few centuries more than one would probably be comfortable with. How about a special-effects motion ride at an amusement park? Again, multiple forms of media are involved, but would you consider this a multimedia product?

Most people you ask would not consider these examples of multimedia. So what is multimedia?

Multimedia is the presentation of a (usually interactive) computer application, incorporating media elements such as text graphics, video, animation, and sound, on a computer. It is the melding of the sensory power of television with the data manipulation and interactive capabilities of the computer (see Figure 1.1).

The word *multimedia* was coined quite some time ago and has evolved and expanded to encompass the latest technologies as they developed. What was considered multimedia in the late 1970s would most likely fall short of today's definition. Technology specialists estimate that you will see more technology advancement in the next five years than you have seen in the last fifteen (roughly since the PC revolution took hold). Multimedia is an integral part of

multimedia

The presentation of a computer application, usually interactive, that incorporates media elements such as text graphics, video, animation, and sound on a computer. Multimedia melds the sensory power of television with the data manipulation and interactive powers of the computer.

Figure 1.1
The modern capabilities of the personal computer system have fueled a multimedia revolution.

today's computing technology; in five years you will look on multimedia as an entirely different beast.

To understand the context of this technology, you need to consider multimedia's history.

THE HISTORY OF MULTIMEDIA

"Computer years" and "dog years" are synonymous. Each year in the life of a human can be seen as at least seven years in the life cycle of a computer—and often more. Now you know the secret as to why computers become obsolete so quickly. They simply grow older sooner.

In the context of computer years, our history of multimedia brings us back to 1972, about 200 "computer years" ago! This seems like a long history, doesn't it? That was the year when the first video game was launched upon an unsuspecting consumer population. The world has never been the same since.

A GAME OF PONG, ANYONE?

In 1972 the game Pong was the latest and greatest. It provided many hours of addictive fun, and launched both the computer game arcade and interactive media industries with a bang.

Pong is generally considered the first commercial multimedia product, as it combined graphics, sound, animation, and interactivity in a widely available commercial computer product (see Figure 1.2).

PONG, ANYONE?

For those of you who do not remember Pong, it was a simple electronic table tennis game in which by turning a control, you could move your paddle (shown as a vertical white bar on your side of the screen) up and down the screen to intercept the small square ball as it bounced its way toward your side of the court. If you hit the tiny ball, you'd get a simple *boop* sound effect and the ball would be bounced back toward your opponent, who then had to return it to you. Just like Ping-Pong. If you missed, your opponent scored a point, and vice versa. You can still play Pong on the Web!

Figure 1.2
This illustration of Pong is from a modern revival of the game on the Web.

game cartridge
An electronic device that stores game software and data. Many home entertainment video game consoles use game cartridges, which typically fit into a slot in the game console to provide the player with a new game to play.

interactive kiosk
A self-contained multimedia application provided in a public-display case in a format that users can interact with. Interactive kiosks usually take the appearance of arcade video game consoles or automated teller devices.

ATARI

The interactive laser disc debuted in 1973. This device stored digital data on a large plastic disc resembling a 12-inch CD; when connected to a personal computer, it allowed the user to interact with the software application stored on it. After 1973, all was relatively quiet on the multimedia front until 1977, when a small company called Atari brought the fun of the fledgling video arcade into the home with the Atari 2600; the toy industry has never been the same since. At its peak, popular Atari 2600 game cartridges were selling more than three million copies per year. In that same year, IBM launched the first multimedia interactive kiosk products, called DiscoVision. Interactive kiosks used interactive multimedia technology to provide information services to the public.

In the Multimedia Museum section on the enclosed CD-ROM, check out the video clip advertisement for the Atari 2600.

MULTIMEDIA IN THE TWILIGHT ZONE?

Multimedia has been applied in some strange ways over the years. One of the most bizarre was a product for the Atari 2600 called MindLink. At the time, Atari executives thought it was possible to control your computer with brainwaves. The product was not a success except as a curiosity in the archives of bizarre computer applications.

APPLE, IBM, AND THE PC REVOLUTION

So far you have progressed 35 "computer years" into the emerging field of multimedia, with not a lot to show for it.

In 1977 a tiny startup company began selling a unique product designed and prototyped in the garage of one of its founders, Steve Jobs. By 1978, the Apple II with floppy drive became an overwhelming success, and for many years brought affordable computing to homes, schools, and businesses throughout the world. The Apple II launched what we now call the personal computer revolution.

Not to be outdone, IBM joined forces with a small company called Microsoft in 1981 to create another small computer called the IBM PC. Though it was very expensive, and quite limited in its capability (the first IBM PCs used tape recorders to load and save software), IBM's name and credibility made it (and Microsoft) an overnight success. The following year, the Apple II had voice synthesis capability. Computers could now "talk," though it would be many years before personal computers could "listen" (interpret and respond to human spoken instruction) as well.

Christmas 1981 almost saw the bubble burst on the whole concept of multimedia. The video game business was a complete and unexpected flop, with too many games of poor quality flooding the market. Kids grew bored with playing the poor quality games, while parents grew impatient with the unavailability of new ones. If not for a new company called Nintendo with a better-quality product and strict quality control over the games themselves, the video game industry might have disappeared. Nintendo went on to sell more than 30 million machines to date, and over 80 percent of U.S. families with children own one. Quite a comeback, don't you think?

THE MOUSE THAT ROARED

During the late 1970s and early 1980s, researchers for Xerox Corporation in Palo Alto, California, were developing a completely new way of interacting with a computer. Central to this development was a small plastic device they called a *mouse*, named after its unusual appearance. This pointing-device technology, along with what was becoming known as a *graphical user interface* (GUI), found a home in the vision of Steve Jobs and Steve Wozniak, founders of Apple. The GUI gave users a fluid, easy, graphical way to control their computer, and therefore make it a productive tool. By representing computer programs and data files as small pictures, and by giving users a way to point at those pictures and drag them to wherever they needed to go, the GUI allowed users to intuitively get their work done visually, without typing in complicated lines of instructions. This was quite a revolutionary concept at the time.

During the 1984 Super Bowl, Apple aired a now-famous TV commercial that unveiled its Macintosh computer to an unsuspecting world. It portrayed a lone woman athlete breaking through the gray stone facade of an oppressive "Orwellian" society. It's difficult to explain in just text (for this we need multimedia!), but you can see this commercial in the Multimedia Museum section of the enclosed CD-ROM. Simply click on the Macintosh ad button. This commercial fired the imagination and buying enthusiasm of millions, and it didn't even show the computer! Yet the Macintosh and its easy-to-use operating system and interface opened the doors to accessible computing for millions who couldn't comprehend the complex text-based instructions typical of all other systems. It truly was an inspirational machine, and made it easier for users to unleash the power of the personal computer.

But to correctly address the history of multimedia and the place of the Macintosh, one must also reference the ill-fated Lisa computer. When the Lisa was launched on an unsuspecting market, a mouse was a novelty that many traditionalists often scorned. But the almost complete sales failure of the Lisa nearly

voice synthesis
A computer technology that can generate sounds that closely resemble human speech and that can interpret recorded human speech.

operating system
The program that is first to load on a computer and that sets up the computer system, its peripheral devices, and services to be ready for the user to run a specific software application.

mouse
A computer data input device that can sense the directional hand movement of the user as it is moved around on a flat surface. This positional and movement data are translated into positional coordinates for an onscreen pointer, which follows the movement. In this fashion a user can use the mouse to "point" at objects on the screen.

saw the demise of the mouse as an integral part of a computer's interface. Imagine computers today with no mouse! And while the Lisa was not a successful product, its successor was Steve Jobs's compact and feature-rich (in those days) Macintosh—one of the computer industry's all-time success stories.

The entire multimedia revolution has been founded on the intuitive interface and graphical abilities of the GUI. In the early 1980s, many people already familiar with computers resisted using a mouse because removing one's hands from the keyboard represented to them a loss of control. There was a certain amount of arrogance involved, too. At that time I thought that the designers, teachers, and small-businesspeople who owned Macintoshes had it too easy, but I could not see that they were more effective than I in getting the same job done.

It took traditionalists time to resist their urge to use the keyboard and to appreciate this technology's potential to make computing not only easier, but more efficient. It took time for them to accept this complete paradigm shift and to realize that they could achieve far more if they didn't have to type a large set of complex instructions to get the job done. The fact that most GUI applications worked in the same fundamental way reduced what had previously been a challenging learning curve and allowed users to concentrate on the task at hand. Though many initially resisted the GUI, try purchasing a personal computer today without a mouse and a GUI. It's almost impossible.

Now apply the GUI's history to the multimedia interface. Focusing on the job at hand and removing the distraction of the operating system makes the multimedia interface perhaps *the* next revolution in computer usage. Just look at the World Wide Web to see just how much the interface has changed the way we use our computers, and how multimedia technology is the fuel driving such technology advances. In Chapter 2, you will examine why this is so in more depth.

MULTIMEDIA IN THE 1980s

In the same year as the Macintosh's birth, another technology was quietly born from a research project at NASA and developed with parts purchased at local Radio Shack stores. Virtual reality (VR) was invented, with both the head-mounted display and the dataglove as integral parts.

Virtual reality is the penultimate multimedia interface. Using an intuitive control (the dataglove) the user can interact with the computer through a visual environment that not only is depicted in 3D, but also is designed to appear remarkably similar to the real world we live in.

While the Xerox-developed GUI provided a more "natural" way to use and manipulate computer programs and files by clicking and dragging them, VR provides an even more natural operating environment. VR tries to replicate the real 3D world and use it as a way to interface with our computer. Why? Because we as humans are designed to function at our best in a three-dimensional environment—that's why we have stereoscopic vision to perceive three dimensions, for instance. The more closely an operating system can simulate that real-world experience, the greater the productivity it can extract from the human user.

With a dataglove, users can appear to grab, hold, and manipulate virtual objects that appear on a head-mounted screen so close to them that they believe they are "inside" that VR environment. To be able to write a document by using a virtual pen, or shop for products in a virtual store, or search for files in a virtual filing cabinet allows us humans to harness the computational power of the computer in a way that feels natural to us. Without multimedia technology facilitating this interface, it couldn't possibly work.

Meanwhile . . . In 1985, Marc Canter borrowed money from his in-laws to found a new company called MacroMind and to sell his new software product, VideoWorks. VideoWorks later evolved to become what we now know as Director from Macromedia—the most widely used cross-platform multimedia *authoring* tool on the planet. Figure 1.3 shows Macromedia's Web site. Today

virtual reality

A computing technology that attempts to simulate a "natural" 3D interactive environment for the user.

head-mounted display

Used in virtual reality applications, a computer screen display in a device that is worn on the head. Because of its proximity to the wearer's eyes, the display fills the user's complete field of view.

dataglove

A device resembling a glove covered in wires and electronic components, worn on the hand, that transmits data from an array of movement and position sensors. This data can be converted by a virtual reality software application into positional information to use as an onscreen pointer.

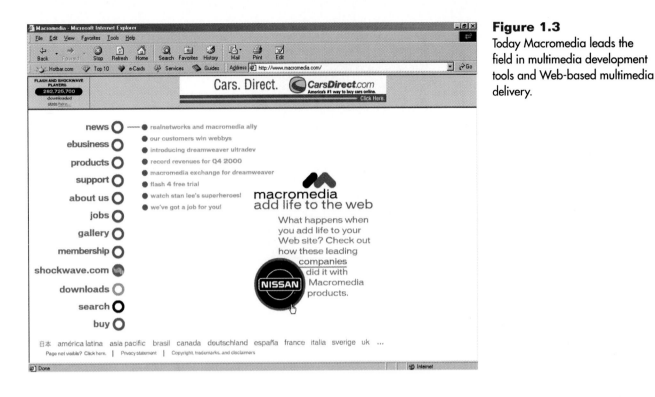

Figure 1.3
Today Macromedia leads the field in multimedia development tools and Web-based multimedia delivery.

Macromedia leads the field in multimedia development tools and Web-based multimedia delivery. Later in this book you will use Macromedia products, especially Director, and then you will see what a significant product Marc hatched way back then.

In this same year, Intel launched its 386 (short for *80386 series*) family of processors. The 386 processors finally made enough computing power available to handle multimedia applications and efficiently use the new CD-ROM devices launched that same year (see Figure 1.4). To enhance the new computing performance, Microsoft brought Windows 1.0 to the PC. While it was a good start in bringing the GUI to the PC platform, Windows 1.0 was crippled by an Apple lawsuit against Microsoft over this operating system being too "Macintosh-like." This was to be the first blood drawn in the never-ending platform rivalries between Windows and Macintosh systems that continue to this day.

Figure 1.4
A CD-ROM drive with a CD-ROM (bottom), a DVD player (center), and a rewriteable CD-ROM drive (top).

Figure 1.5
It was Apple's early advancements in the areas of graphics and video display performance that gave the Macintosh a head start in the graphic design and video production industries.

CD-R
A *Recordable* version of the CD-ROM format.

sound card
A device in a computer system for generating, recording, and playing hi-fi sound from sound data.

MIDI
A technology and data protocol specifically designed for the computer control of electronic musical instruments. MIDI stands for *Musical Instrument Digital Interface.*

joystick
A computer data input device that can sense the position of a stick as it is manipulated by the user.

World Wide Web (www)
A version of the original Internet that supports graphics and multimedia technologies to enhance user experience and ease of use on the Net.

MPC
An early defined set of standards for a multimedia-playing computer system. MPC stands for *Multimedia Personal Computer.*

The year 1986 saw the first electronic encyclopedia from Grolier; Harvard Graphics, the first presentation package; the first International Conference on Multimedia; and the first CD-ROM. Commodore Computers launched the Amiga computer, which offered a new standard of graphics, sound, and video capabilities well beyond that available to date. The Amiga system was so advanced for its time that it inspired the creation of innovative multimedia companies such as NewTek (Video Toaster and LightWave 3D) and Play Inc. (Trinity and Snappy). These companies build hardware and software products that capitalize on the graphics and multimedia capabilities of the "host" computer to perform amazingly creative tasks, such as capturing, editing, adding special effect, and recording digital video. Truevision's Targa video interface cards, though primitive by today's standards, gave the PC its very first video capturing and video printing capabilities.

In 1987, the Mac II, shown in Figure 1.5, brought color to the GUI. A software product called HyperCard, included free with Macintosh systems, enabled users to develop rudimentary but graphical applications for presentations, educational programs, reference programs, and the like.

In 1988, CD-R (CD-Record) technology enabled ambitious computer users to create their own CD-ROM or music CD, though this technology didn't become affordable for most consumers until the mid-1990s.

In 1989, NewTek's Amiga-based Video Toaster changed the way we watch television and movies. This product brought affordable video special effects, computer animation, and graphics to both video producers and hobbyists alike. In the same year, the Sound Blaster sound card for PCs from Creative Labs made audio on the PC affordable. Sound Blaster cards also play MIDI music, provide a joystick game port, and have set computer sound capability standards that other manufacturers follow to this day.

THE 1990s: A MULTIMEDIA EXPLOSION

With all of the enthusiasm for the final decade of the twentieth century, multimedia exploded with Compton's Interactive Encyclopedia and Grolier's competing Multimedia Encyclopedia in 1990. Debate also erupted over who had rights to the digital form of media, just as news broke that Bill Gates, chairman of Microsoft, was buying the electronic rights to every major art piece around the world.

In the 1990s, Adobe released Photoshop, a photo editing and graphic design application that set the standard for such products to this day (see Figure 1.6).

Figure 1.6
Adobe's Photoshop alone started a revolution in the digital tools available for graphic designers.

Also, Microsoft launched multimedia-enabled Windows 3.0, which finally brought a usable GUI (there were previous poor attempts at this from Microsoft and others) that also supported the new multimedia devices (sound cards, CD-ROM, and so on) coming onto the market for the PC platform.

The first publicized interactive multimedia "pitch" was developed for the city of Atlanta, which helped it secure the rights to host the 1996 Olympic Games. A video clip showing this presentation is available in the Multimedia Museum section of the enclosed CD-ROM.

NewMedia, the first real magazine devoted to multimedia, was launched in 1991. Later that year, a small but incredibly significant announcement went mostly unnoticed—the unveiling of the multimedia-capable version of the Internet called the World Wide Web (www). Perhaps the reason the Web and its supporting Internet saw little attention initially was because they were brought out during a year crowded with technological releases. Adobe's Premiere (software for editing digital video that you will become familiar with later in this book), Silicon Graphics's powerful Indigo computer system, Apple's QuickTime digital video format, the MPC and MPEG standards, and CD-I players were all released to enthusiastic and insatiable consumers in 1991.

In 1992 the first children's interactive book title, *Just Grandma and Me*, was launched at about the same time as the first gory "shoot-'em-up" game, Wolfenstein 3D. This game later evolved into the megahit game titles Doom and Quake—each adding its own new level of realistic mayhem. Incidentally, the immensely prosperous company Id, which produced these games, has grown completely from earned revenue of these products and without a single dollar of outside investment money—a rarity for this industry. Windows version 3.1 fulfilled the multimedia promises of version 3.0, and Kodak and others developed the Photo CD format for high-definition digital images on CD-ROM. Late in 1992, the interactive multimedia travel journal *From Alice to Ocean* was released to rave reviews and set new standards for multimedia design quality.

In 1993, the hardware platform for the new multimedia revolution got a boost with the adoption of double-speed CD-ROM drives as a multimedia standard (a little slow compared to twenty-first–century CD-ROM speeds, in excess of 48X, don't you think?); graphically impressive new CD-ROM titles such as

MPEG

A set of digital video formats that provide high-definition and frame rate performance with very high levels of data compression. This format results in quality digital video files that retain good quality and long playing time in a small file size. MPEG stands for *Motion Picture Experts Group.*

CD-I

A mildly successful version of the standard CD-ROM format. A CD-I (for *Interactive*) device, looking much like a hi-fi CD player, could be hooked up to a TV and could display a multimedia application that provides the user with a high level of interaction with the product without the need for a computer system.

Photo CD

A format of image storage data designed by Kodak Corporation to store high-definition images on a CD-ROM.

browser

A software application designed to allow the user to connect to, navigate, and view the World Wide Web.

Mosaic

The very first graphical browser application.

The 7th Guest and Myst brought photographic-quality computer 3D imagery and animation to the forefront of gaming technology (see Figure 1.7). Doom was a phenomenal gaming success, and the movie *Jurassic Park* devastated similar movies before it with unequaled special effects and computer animation, most of which were created on consumer systems such as Silicon Graphics and Apple Macintosh computers. The technology and power was finally coming into the hands of the people. The invention of the graphical Web browser brought that realization even closer. Mosaic was the first such browser, developed with taxpayer-funded grants from the National Science Foundation and released in 1993. The world was never the same again.

In 1994, ratings were instated to indicate a computer game's suitability for minors, and a new Web browser called Netscape, from a spun-off group of Mosaic developers, was making waves. The Internet and the World Wide Web were attracting interest among computer users other than college "nerds" and scientists (stereotypical original users of the Internet).

Probably the capstone year for multimedia was 1995, because it was about this time that the growing affordability and accessibility (available in department stores as well as the specialized computer stores) of the multimedia PC was so

Figure 1.7

With its photo-realistic computer graphics, sound effects, and well-designed virtual world, Myst remained at the top of the best-selling games list for over four years. Since its release in 1993, Myst sales have topped 2.5 million.

I don't think anyone would argue that the Internet has not been the single biggest influence on increased computer use in recent years. Internet and Web buzzwords often overshadow multimedia. I occasionally hear arguments such as, "Multimedia is dead, and now the Web is the only way to provide an application." How might the Web provide anything of value *without* multimedia? Such arguments confuse the term *multimedia* with the physical device, such as a CD-ROM. As a technology, multimedia is now pervasive. It is incorporated into almost everything we do each day. Unless you live in the wilderness or are a hermit (in which case, if you are reading this book, I am indeed impressed), you can't avoid the influence of multimedia or the Internet.

When you consider how much our society depends on digital communications, it is scary to think of what would happen if it all disappeared! Once it almost did.

In mid-May 1998, the primary satellite that carried more than 80 percent of the United States' pager communications (along with TV channels and some cellular phone services) went out of orbit, and suddenly millions of pagers went dead silent. This made headline news for days; emergency services stopped, doctors couldn't receive calls, stockbrokers missed lots of business, and commerce nationwide was affected—just because one piece of equipment failed.

I use this as an example of a digital technology, such as multimedia and the Internet, that has had so much impact that we don't realize just how much so until it is gone. You will read later about the convergence of technologies such as multimedia and the Internet and see that one is equally dependent upon the other.

---

very well complemented by the new 32-bit, high-performance Windows 95 operating system. Previous versions of Windows were slow 16-bit software programs that ran in the computer's primary operating system, called MS-DOS. Windows 95 used the 32-bit processors in the then-current computer systems and provided highly integrated multimedia capabilities in an easier-to-use operating system, especially for first-time buyers who had little or no computer experience. This plentiful supply of inexpensive, powerful computers loaded with sound and video capabilities, supplied with speakers (as much an essential hardware add-on by then as a mouse) and a host of other multimedia goodies, further fueled a surge in multimedia hardware and software product development—so much so that the intervening years since 1995 are a blur of multimedia and Internet innovation and product releases. Since then Windows 98 and Windows 2000 have further built upon the multimedia foundation of Windows 95, perhaps the most significant product of that year.

Since 1995 the world of multimedia has exploded, most significantly with Web-related technology and features taking top billing on most new product launches. Digital video capturing and editing is inexpensive and has become widely available; CD-ROM burners are small and affordable enough to have in your home system; digital cameras, make the acquisition of images a snap; and inexpensive, high-performance, multimedia-loaded computers are widely available. Standard computer systems now possess sufficient computing horsepower to develop impressive multimedia products, and the software tools to build them are more plentiful than ever. The fine art of Web publishing is becoming available to everyone, much as desktop publishing became commonplace in the late 1980s. Now anyone can create his or her own professional and entertaining multimedia products, whether they be CD-ROM-based or Web-based.

In summary, multimedia is one of those technologies that work best when they are unnoticed. The best multimedia products, as you will read later in this chapter, use this technology to make the application more efficient by rendering the underlying technology invisible.

MS-DOS

A text-based operating system that set the standard for personal computer usage before the invention of the graphical user interface. MS-DOS stands for *Microsoft Disk Operating System*.

WHERE IS IT ALL GOING?

As an instructor of multimedia and the related technologies that make up most multimedia applications, I am often asked where I think multimedia is taking us. Let me give you my educated opinion of where I see multimedia's future. If I'm anywhere close, this future promises you, the multimedia developer, a fun and rewarding ride.

TECHNOLOGY CONVERGENCE

We have seen incredible advances in many areas of computer-related technology: the Internet and the World Wide Web, distance learning, digital photography, integrated television services, and computer-based telecommunications, to name a few. Have you noticed how all of these technological advances are overlapping more and more? Telephone calls are now frequently made over the Internet, education uses more and more multimedia, your home TV is becoming a computer terminal for the Web, and TV cable services companies are competing with telephone companies and satellite dish companies to provide faster Internet access. Manufacturers of DVDs are hoping that the DVD player in your computer and on top of your TV will both do the same job of providing high-definition movies or interactive multimedia applications at the touch of a mouse or remote control. Soon there will be little difference between a TV, a hi-fi/boombox audio system, a home office fax/copier, a telephone system, and a personal computer.

All of these technologies are coming together to create the "Super Appliance." The glue that holds them together is multimedia. Consider the following scenario, and watch for the asterisks (the asterisks indicate where multimedia is a core technology).

Imagine a device as portable as today's pocket computers or even a pager. It would take still pictures,* scan a document* or capture video,* connect to any other computer system* through a wireless connection, send and receive e-mail and faxes,* play any multimedia application* from its own internal storage or from the communications link, and enable you to reach anyone via video phone.* On top of this, it also would look after your business,* records,* creativity,* and recreation.* The same system could incorporate health sensors* to correlate how your body is functioning with a fitness- and diet-planning application.* Your spending and income could be managed by a personal finance application* through a connection to your bank account, and all shopping could be truly "cashless." You could download your favorite artist's CD* and listen to it through headphones while you get some work done reading e-mail on your head-mounted display.* When you tire of reading e-mail, change TV channels* to your favorite talk show. Of course only you could operate your device, as voice printing* and retinal eye scanning* are also part of the system. This whole system could be voice-operated, negating the need to use a keyboard for input.

This is not a device from the latest sci-fi movie. This list of features represents inexpensive technologies that are already available. The parts exist. You can buy pocket computers that run most of the common business applications used on desktop systems. You can buy Walkman-size digital music players that download, for a small fee, your favorite music. Some digital cameras are designed to plug directly into your computer interface slot (no cable). You can get wearable computers that use head-mounted display glasses. Wireless communications allows you to access your e-mail and the Internet from anywhere you please. Digital wristwatches monitor your heart rate and other vital signs as you exercise. Online banking is one of the fastest-growing technologies in the

DVD
A data storage disk device, resembling a CD, that can store large capacities of data—up to 14 GB. Originally meaning *Digital Versatile Disk*, DVD has come to mean *Digital Video Disk*, an incorrect term that was widely used.

---

*Multimedia technology required.

banking industry. Computer security systems incorporating fingerprint readers, eye scanners, and voice recognition are becoming commonplace.

But how long before they converge? I suspect not long; again, multimedia is the essential ingredient that makes such a device possible.

THE APPLIANCE FOR THE MASSES

Just recently I went into a Sam's Club discount warehouse store and was amazed with what I found in the computer section. There was a top-brand, hot-off-the-production-line, superfast-processor, multimedia PC system with DVD, loads of RAM, 3D 32-bit graphics, 64-bit sound, 56K modem, video capture, vast monitor, huge speakers with subwoofer, microphone, integrated phone management system, and more goodies and software than I had seen in one place since the previous year's COMDEX computer show in Las Vegas! I had just read, drooling, about this latest processor a couple of nights before, and it wasn't supposed to be released yet! After I picked my jaw up off the floor and checked this baby out, I almost fell over when I saw the price—$1,500. For all that! Not only were systems like this unavailable yet in "conventional" computer stores, but they were also much more expensive. Had my wife not been with me, I would have been $1,500 poorer but the proud owner of one humdinger of a system for all my multimedia development work (and play).

The most significant thing about this experience was *not* the amazing specification of the system, nor the price, but that it was available at Sam's Club. In between the microwave ovens, car tires, and bulk dog food was the most powerful Pentium computer system you could get—anywhere! There's no technical support from Sam's Club and you'll have a tough time getting most technical questions answered. Did this bother anyone? Not at all. In fact, several of these systems were lined up in the carts of drooling consumers at the checkouts.

The personal computer has truly become just another appliance. That doesn't mean that it's as crude as a dishwasher, but that it's an accepted tool for use in our everyday lives. Imagine the market for your multimedia work that this acceptance creates!

Consumers are more technically savvy and more comfortable with computer technology than ever before. Through the power of multimedia, these systems are now very user-friendly and intuitive to use—to the extent that one is willing to spend an additional few thousand dollars during a trip to the local warehouse club.

Furthermore, when you consider the multimedia and Web capabilities of such a loaded system, can you imagine users' expectations for it? You don't bring such a system home to an excited family just to do word processing and spreadsheet analysis. It is no longer acceptable *not* to include multimedia elements in what once were considered "boring" applications. For example, personal finance applications such as Intuit's Quicken and Microsoft's Money all use multimedia to make the task easier and more effective, as shown in Figure 1.8.

As multimedia developers, our job is to meet and even exceed those expectations by providing the multimedia products that sophisticated consumers demand. Thankfully, we can accomplish this using systems much less powerful than the one just described.

EDUCATION AND ENTERTAINMENT

Through multimedia the barriers between education and entertainment are steadily eroding. Multimedia-based education titles often include content usually considered entertainment, whether in the form of short movies, games, or simulations. Figure 1.9 shows a multimedia software product called Virtual Corporation from Microfocus that blends a business simulation with an entertaining futuristic game and voice-activated control. In the next section, you will

Figure 1.8

The multimedia front-end interfaces for products such as Microsoft's Money 98 (top left) and Intuit's Quicken (bottom right) make financial planning and accounting easier than ever before.

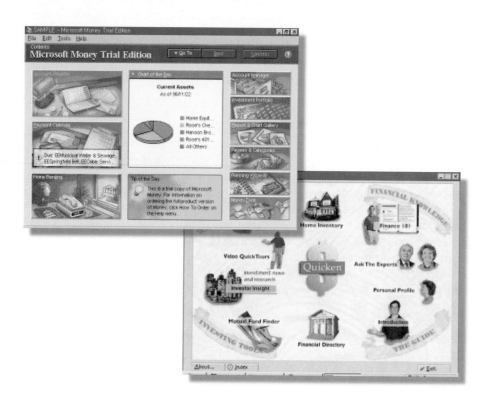

learn more about multimedia's benefit to self-paced education and why it is one of the fastest-growing areas in the multimedia industry.

The modern entertainment industry relies on multimedia technology. Whether you purchase the latest game title or tickets to the latest amusement park ride or movie, multimedia is everywhere. The convergence of sensory experience (such as motion rides), 3D visual technologies, superlarge screen formats, high-definition images, and 3D surround sound has transformed the entertainment experience. While there will always be those who enjoy a warm evening's

Figure 1.9

In Microfocus's Virtual Corporation, the user operates the software by "talking" to the simulated characters on the screen.

round of miniature golf, the cutting edge entertainment products, whether in the theater or in the home, are taking center stage.

In the home, educational products will gain the sophistication of entertainment titles and incorporate a more engaging experience for the user. Even products that present large quantities of data, such as encyclopedias, can become very entertaining with a good dose of multimedia in the mix. Simulations and role-playing applications will provide a richer educational experience. In the next chapter you will see just how to apply multimedia to achieve such objectives.

THE "OTHER" APPLIANCES

Light switches, washing machines, cookbooks on CD-ROM or DVD, lawn mowers, and automobiles will all be transformed by multimedia. They may not look that different, but they will operate more easily and include more capabilities. For example, in 1998 Intel announced its Car Chip. This chip is a Pentium-level microprocessor that's used in automobile control systems to provide functions such as engine monitoring, antilock braking, e-mail, telecommunications, Web access, navigation assistance, TV, entertainment, and more (see Figure 1.10).

When you consider that the Mars Pathfinder Lander (see Figure 1.11) used an off-the-shelf PC as its brains and operated flawlessly over 33 million miles from home, you begin to realize how we are only scratching the surface of this technology's potential.

Home networks are already making home management easier. Computers can adjust your lighting and music/entertainment patterns to preset combinations to suit your moods. The more sophisticated systems can sense the identity of each individual in each room and adjust environmental settings, such as lighting, temperature, and music to match that person's personal settings. Given this technology, such a house management system could provide users with their favorite movie or TV channel in whichever room they move to, or route a telephone call directly to where they sit.

Software companies are providing products that connect your home computer to receive special signals over the Internet. These signals can instruct your computer, through a special interface for this purpose, to activate your lawn's sprinkler system depending on weather patterns in your location. Try using that application without multimedia!

Figure 1.10
Intel's Connected Car PC technology brings multimedia into the automobile.

SOFTWARE

Now that you have a sense of the magical capabilities of complete multimedia computer systems, let's look at what's really driving these capabilities "under the hood." Underlying all of this technology is software. Software is the life force that makes the computer do something useful.

What we once considered purely functional software applications, such as word processing and spreadsheets, are now being spruced up with multimedia and given a new lease on life.

In the next chapter you will read how and why this injection of multimedia into common software applications has become so important to modern computing technology. The key to more efficient and easier use of increasingly sophisticated technology is in the multimedia interface.

In summary, what does multimedia mean for us? The answer is simple. It means lots of opportunity for us to feed the growing appetite this technology creates with excellent multimedia products!

KEEPING AN OPEN MIND

At this initial stage of learning about multimedia, the best way to avoid problems is to avoid strong or polarized opinions or definitions of this technology. As this chapter demonstrates, there can be as many definitions of multimedia as the number of people you ask to define it. It can be easy to get "locked" into one narrow way of seeing multimedia and become blind to its other aspects.

Keep an open mind and develop your own personal definition and sense of this amazing technology. Be warned that a narrow or polarized view or definition is usually a biased one.

Be wary of those who purport to be multimedia experts. Examine their work and don't rely on what they tell you. The real experts in multimedia will be pleased to show you their accomplishments.

Likewise, be aware of those who preach the one-product approach to multimedia development. True multimedia development requires many products in your development toolbox, and those who advocate just one approach (whether it be a computer or software brand) are most likely biased.

Chapter Summary

- Multimedia means quite different things to many people. A clear definition of multimedia as a technology is an essential starting point.

- To fully understand multimedia it is important to gain a context for the evolution of the collection of technologies that make multimedia possible.

- Given the history of multimedia, and its close ties with the development of the personal computer in recent years, you can appreciate multimedia's potential in the future.

- When it comes to defining multimedia, keep an open mind. A narrow view or definition is usually a biased one. Be wary of those who preach the one product approach to multimedia development. True multimedia development requires many products in your development toolbox.

Key Terms and Concepts

browser, 10
CD-I, 9
CD-R, 8
dataglove, 6
DVD, 12
game cartridges, 4

head-mounted
  display, 6
interactive kiosk, 4
joystick, 8
MIDI, 8
Mosaic, 10

mouse, 5
MPC, 9
MPEG, 9
MS-DOS, 11
multimedia, 2
operating system, 5

Photo CD, 9
sound card, 8
virtual reality, 6
voice synthesis, 5
World Wide Web
  (www), 9

Checking Your Knowledge and Skills

The following questions will help you assess how well you have learned the lessons of the chapter you've read. These questions are designed to make you think and to form new connections between the new topics you have just reviewed. By completing these exercises, you will have a better understanding of the material and its real-world application.

1. Define multimedia according to what you have read and learned in this chapter. Try to be clear and concise and avoid simple verbatim copying of the chapter text. Develop a definition that best says, for you, what multimedia is all about.

2. What, in your opinion, would be the best application of multimedia? Support your answer with examples.

3. Describe the ideal computer system of the future, and specify how many features of this system would require multimedia to function.

Critical Thinking Challenges

1. Can you write a better definition of multimedia than that given in this chapter? Without the constraint of limited page space, you should be able to expand the definition of multimedia so that it is clear to absolutely anyone, including someone who has never seen a computer!

2. Given the main components of a multimedia presentation, such as sound, graphics, video, animation, interaction, and so on, produce a list of these elements in order of importance, and then decide which multimedia component you could most afford to drop from the list. Why? Which multimedia components are must-haves? Why?

3. In the previous exercise you were asked to remove the least important multimedia element from a multimedia presentation. What effect would such a move have on one of your favorite multimedia applications? Describe your answer in a "before-and-after" scenario.

4. Assuming multimedia was never invented, plot the evolution of the personal computer from the 1980s to today, but without incorporating multimedia technologies. What assumptions and conclusions do you form from this exercise?

Hands-on Exercises

CREATING A MULTIMEDIA TIMELINE

1. On a large sheet of paper (such as a flip chart page or poster board), carefully draw a multimedia timeline depicting the history of multimedia. Keep the line to scale, and clearly label each event and milestone in each year.

2. To this multimedia timeline, add other events and discoveries in the world of technology that share this time period.

3. Expand your timeline to include world events (perhaps using a different-color pen for clarity) such as space missions, Desert Storm, presidential elections, movie releases, the Kosovo crisis, and so on. Try to imagine the computer systems people were using back in the days surrounding such events.

Master Project

WHAT IS A MASTER PROJECT?

Throughout this book, you will complete a master project that will develop and evolve as you progress through successive chapters. Each chapter will introduce new knowledge and skills to your portfolio of multimedia abilities, and you will be required to apply these skills to the master project.

The master project requires you to create your own multimedia resume that showcases your skills and abilities as a multimedia producer. While this may seem a little daunting now, remember that you will build this master project as you progress through the book. As your skills grow, you will have a terrific opportunity to practice them on this master project.

For now, just be aware of this project, as you have not yet covered any of the skills required to start it. You will begin to acquire those skills in Chapter 2.

2

WHY MULTIMEDIA?

Chapter Outline

Chapter Objectives

After completing this chapter, you will be able to:

- Discuss why you would apply multimedia technology to a software application
- Understand the importance of the interface to a computer software application
- Describe the benefits of multimedia that are evident in this chapter's review of leading multimedia titles
- Understand the persuasive case for multimedia by studying "before" and "after" examples

Chapter Overview

In Chapter 1 you learned the history of multimedia and how this technology evolved into what we almost take for granted today. In this chapter you will learn why this technology is so important. You will also see examples of how computer use can be transformed by multimedia.

WHY APPLY MULTIMEDIA TECHNOLOGY TO SOFTWARE ANYWAY?

You might wonder why you would want to apply multimedia to software. This question is important. Applying multimedia technology to any computer application is neither easy nor inexpensive. It usually requires considerable up-front investment of time and money—but since it is more and more commonly done, it must be worth it, right? You can be the judge of that—but as you'll discover, the benefits of applying multimedia are many.

EASE OF USE

The purpose of applying multimedia to any computer-based application usually revolves around making the application easier to use. The productivity benefits of making work easier are enormous. By applying an intuitive and easy-to-follow front end to an application, you can increase the user's effectiveness considerably. For example, as the program becomes easier to operate with a multimedia interface, the user becomes less dependent on instructions. Figure 2.1 shows the

Figure 2.1
The Microsoft® Money 98 interface has many multimedia enhancements that improve the usability of the product.

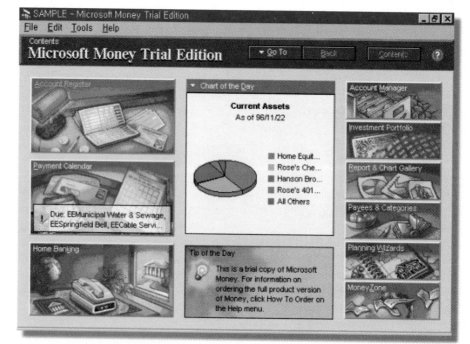

One of the easiest traps to fall into when designing multimedia applications is to overdo the interface. Keep the requirement for an intuitive design in mind, coupled with the adage, "Simpler is better." You will read later about multimedia design criteria, but now is a good time to start thinking this way. Otherwise, you run the risk of creating an elaborate product that places bells and whistles above function, and you get what we call "feature creep"—as the design progresses, unnecessary additional features and elements creep in. Having too many features detracts from the program's function and irritates the user. This is particularly true of Web applications. As a multimedia developer, you must guard against feature creep in your own work, and also in that of anyone who works for you and your client.

multimedia interface used for Microsoft Money 98, a financial-planning application that will be the subject of a case study later in this chapter. Money 98 represents a significant move by Microsoft toward the use of multimedia-enhanced products.

INTUITIVE INTERFACE

It is not sufficient to simply apply multimedia elements to an interface and expect to reap the benefits without some strategic planning. To succeed, a multimedia interface must be intuitive, which means that the choice of images, icons, visual and audible responses, and reaction to user input are obvious. The user knows to choose the correct control (button) for a function simply because the control looks like what it's intended to do. A button that looks like a filing cabinet might access records; a camcorder icon might access a video clip. For example, users expect the ▶ button to play a media piece, or the 🏠 Home button to bring them back to a "home" page or the first screen in the application. Should a graphic depicting an electric toaster represent employee records? Of course not, because it wouldn't make sense and therefore wouldn't be intuitive.

intuitive

A concept of computer software interface design in which users can determine the function and capabilities of the application and its controls through their own intuition. An intuitive interface designer uses icons and imagery taken from common life-experience objects and how they function to guide users to similar functions within the software application. For example, using an image of a magnifying glass to identify the control that provides the application's search function would be considered intuitive.

EVOLUTION OF THE INTERFACE. If you look at the development of software applications not usually associated with multimedia, such as accounting or payroll programs, you have some idea of how the interface has developed and where it is headed.

Back in the late 1970's and early 1980's, accounting software consisted mainly of a numbered series of options on the screen, called a *menu*. Options such as "Customer Data," "Balance Sheet," "Invoicing," and so on were accessed by pressing an option's number on the keyboard. This menu was completely text-based and there was no such thing as a mouse (see Figure 2.2).

With the advent of the Macintosh, Microsoft Windows, and Windows-type operating environments for computer systems, initial conversions of the old text-based software applications still retained these numbered menus down the center of the main screen. But now the option to click them with a mouse, as well as pressing the keys, was available. As users became more familiar with these Windows-type operating systems, menu choices moved to the top menu bars on the screen, and each menu item could be clicked to present drop-down lists of submenu choices. The process of clicking choices and then selecting specific operations was far more intuitive than the older text-based keyboard-operated interfaces, and resulted in a great productivity boost. The drop-down menu structure afforded a greater number of choices, which were arranged by topic at the top of the screen. And almost every software application in these

Figure 2.2

An original text-based menu interface often looked like this.

Windows-type operating environments worked the same way and soon became familiar to users. Software was becoming more friendly (the term *user friendly* was coined about then), easier to use, and more productive, even though the capabilities of these software applications had become more complex (see Figure 2.3).

The computer's multimedia capabilities and mouse-driven interface allowed the development of innovations such as interactive online help files, voice notations, animated logos, and highly intuitive graphical interfaces. The intuition built into a well-designed pictorial interface eliminated the need to understand the textual jargon of older menu systems. If you didn't exactly know what was meant by "Create two-year amortization profile for nonliquid assets," would you be inclined to use that menu option, or would you wade through a manual or try to contact an expert in the software first? Using multimedia to provide intuitive controls and explanations to assist the user through particularly difficult sections of the task have provided even further productivity gains (see Figure 2.4). Compare Figure 2.3 with Figure 2.4 to get a sense of this multimedia interface advantage.

It's interesting to note that the fundamental software behind these products hasn't changed in any major way throughout the years. The software required to

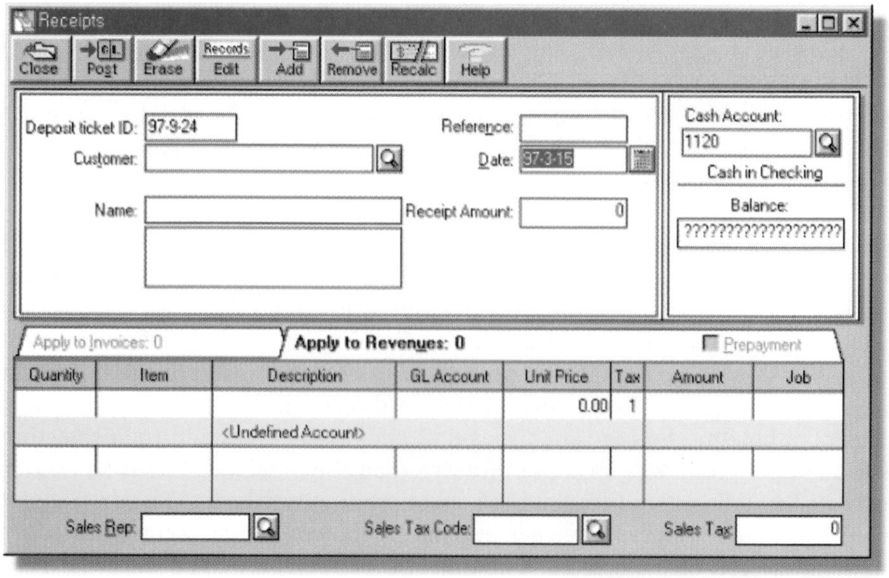

Figure 2.3

Peachtree's Windows-based accounting package is a vast improvement over the old text-based versions.

balance a balance sheet, create a profit and loss statement, or create a statement of account for customers remains fundamentally the same. The math required to perform these calculations also remains the same. The primary difference between these applications over the years is in the user interface and in how much easier it has become to use these products. Multimedia is at the heart of these evolutions.

IMMERSIVE EXPERIENCE

An *immersive experience,* in software interface terms, exists when the software application takes over the entire computer screen and provides the user with a customized, intuitive interface with which to operate the program. Creating an immersive experience with multimedia usually requires removing the distraction of the computer's operating system. The objective is to almost convince users that they are no longer using a computer but rather a customized machine to achieve the goals of the application. Many multimedia applications use the entire screen and provide buttons and controls in the interface that are customized for that application alone, which draws the user into direct one-on-one operation, makes the software easier to use, and eliminates the distraction of the operating system. Compare the two screens in Figures 2.5a and 2.5b. Both illustrations show the same application at work, but which is less distracting and easier to focus on? This method of focusing the user's attention exclusively on the software application's interface provides a higher level of productivity.

SELF-PACED INTERACTION AND BETTER RETENTION

The notion of self-paced learning is an old one, but it thrives most in the world of multimedia, especially in computer-based training (CBT). Many studies have been done on the benefits of user-controlled presentation of media and information. Perhaps you have heard the story of the kid at the back of the classroom who always seems behind the rest of the students. It turns out that many of these "slow" kids have been, in fact, far brighter than their classmates, but had

Figure 2.5a

The visible desktop around the application's edges distracts the user and is a reminder of the operating system running in the background.

Figure 2.5b

Simply by "taking over" the entire screen, the program creates a sense of focus and comfort for the user.

simply tuned out an educational pace that didn't keep up with the speed of their intelligence. This is a common problem in many areas of life where passive information is relayed at a predetermined pace and not everyone can operate at that pace.

Enter interactive multimedia applications; the ability to process information at one's own pace is crucial to their success. You can spend twelve hours with a multimedia encyclopedia or just twelve minutes; it's your choice (see Figure 2.6). You can have the narrator repeat a message a dozen times so that you clearly understand it. Try doing that with a teacher or a presenter at a seminar, or a salesperson demonstrating a new product. These people would get very irri-

Figure 2.6

A multimedia encyclopedia such as Microsoft Encarta allows self-paced investigation into many multimedia-enhanced topics.

PricewaterhouseCoopers (PwC), a large international accounting and business consultancy firm, uses multimedia to train its auditing staff and keep them current on new regulations, legislation, and industry developments. More than seven thousand employees in fifty countries have used PwC's multimedia-based program. In a multiyear study, PwC found that the time needed to train each employee using multimedia, compared to a traditional classroom method, was about 50 percent less. The cost per student using multimedia was $106, compared to $760 for their classroom-bound colleagues. Students using multimedia also had better retention of the material. Add to that the logistical benefits of not needing a set class schedule or a physical room and you have a win-win situation.

The experiences of PricewaterhouseCoopers are quite common. These findings are quite typical for other organizations applying CBT as their training method. Although much more expensive up front to develop and implement, multimedia-enhanced CBT costs far less in the long term and provides much better results in terms of the educational outcome for the student.

tated with you fairly quickly. Ask them to speed up or slow down, or to give a twelve-hour presentation instead of the twelve-minute one that they had planned on, and they would probably, at best, politely refuse.

The benefits to the user of a self-paced multimedia presentation include better retention and application of the information presented. An example of these benefits is demonstrated in the sidebar about multimedia's return on investment in the realm of CBT.

BETTER UNDERSTANDING OF THE CONTENT

Multimedia-enhanced CBT enables the student to better comprehend the material. Concurrent presentation of text, images, animation, video, and sound complement each other to provide a richer and broader range of information. Many studies have shown that students learn better and more easily when information is presented in ways that stimulate several of the student's senses concurrently. The human mind "tunes out" after a while if the information is presented in only one homogenous format. For instance, you might consider the task of reading through a large encyclopedia tedious and perhaps overwhelming. You can only take in so much text before feeling the effects of "information overload." However, convert that text into a synopsized form on a computer screen, presented concurrently with a narration of the details, and include an animation of the concept being presented, and you not only stimulate your many senses simultaneously, but you also make the task of assimilating that information easier and faster. If you just listen to a narrator, or just read a textbook, you have just one "information stream" in which to assimilate the information at the most comfortable reading or listening pace that you can muster. However, if the narrator shows slides during the presentation, or if the book is accompanied by an audiotape, then more information streams are available and you can absorb more information in the same time. Figure 2.7 shows an example of such a multimedia encyclopedia software application.

COST EFFECTIVENESS

Applying multimedia technology to software applications and software development produces a more cost-effective product. When you consider not having to print a costly, in-depth training manual and not requiring as much technical support as you would need for a nonmultimedia application, the cost-saving benefits become apparent. In addition, users who enjoy using the software and find

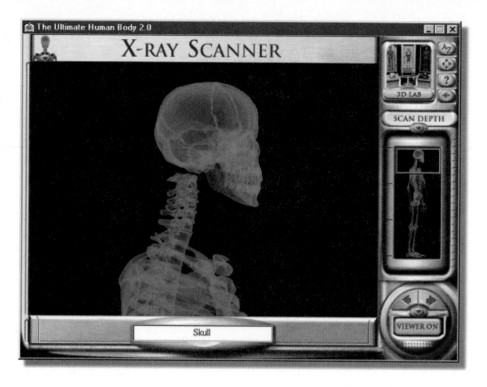

the interface intuitive and engaging are more likely to upgrade to the next version and purchase more products from that company.

MORE FUN = GREATER EFFICIENCY

By making a multimedia application more fun to use, you can also make it more
efficient. Some cultures have difficulty with the concept of associating fun with
efficiency, but take a good look at the way we can use fun to our advantage.

Current office productivity software suites, such as Microsoft Office 2000,
use "fun" elements to accomplish goals. Software wizards (programs that take
you through a series of prescribed steps to quickly accomplish a job) and digital
assistants (programs that catch errors or suggest better methods) are efficiency-
enhancing features that can be fun to use (see Figure 2.8).

With multimedia products we have ample opportunity to introduce fun
elements to help users feel more at home with the application and to guide
them to a more efficient way of doing the job. Dorling Kindersley's multimedia-based encyclopedia Virtual Reality Bird is chock-full of fun elements that
enhance the transmission of the information about birds and related topics
(see Figure 2.9).

wizards

A feature of a software application
that automates the steps of a
complicated process; similar in
concept to *digital assistants*. For
instance, for a program that
calculates your income taxes, the
data needed can be quite involved
and complicated. Instead of filling
out an onscreen form similar to a tax
return, the user enters each element
of the information needed in
response to a question from the
program. In this way the process is
broken down into a sequence of
wizard questions and user responses.

digital assistant

A type of software application, or
part of a software application,
designed to guide you through a
process. Such programs are often
characterized as the user's *personal
assistant* and are depicted as a
person, animal, or cartoon character.
Not to be confused with *personal
digital assistant (PDA)*, which is an
electronic device.

THERE IS SUCH A THING AS TOO MUCH FUN!

It probably goes without saying that if you're not careful, you can overdo some of
these elements, especially the "fun" aspect. This is why it is so important to ask others to test your product for you during and after the development process. Too many
fun features could distract users from the core purpose of the application, rather
than assist them in using it. Remember that simpler is usually better, and the fun
elements should be applied only insofar as they benefit the program's operation.

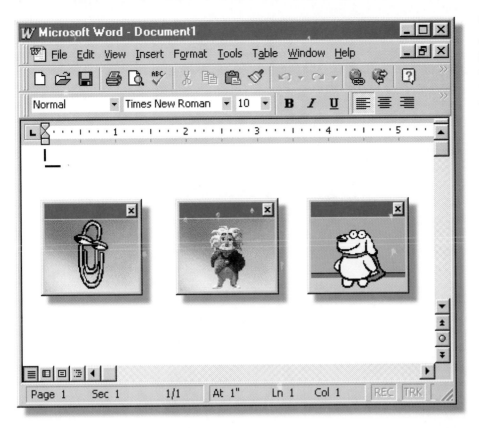

Figure 2.8
Microsoft Word 2000 provides a personal digital assistant to make suggestions and to catch your mistakes. This figure shows a few of the many forms this assistant may take, although you use only one at any given time.

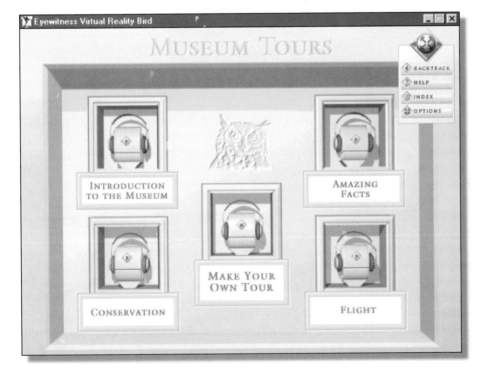

Figure 2.9
In Virtual Reality Bird you can take an audio tour of the museum, which is, in effect, an automated digital assistant.

THE DASHBOARD PHILOSOPHY

The parallels between automotive technology and computer technology are worth closer inspection, and there is much to learn from comparing them. For instance, in the early years after the invention of the automobile, cars were

Figure 2.10a
These old photos show early automobiles from the turn of the century being followed by their full-time mechanics. Thankfully cars in those days couldn't travel any faster than the mechanic could jog! *From the collections of Henry Ford Museum and Greenfield Village.*

Figure 2.10b
ENIAC, one of the first electronic computer systems, occupied a whole building and was difficult to maintain. Replacing a bad tube meant checking the computer's nineteen thousand possibilities.

expensive and were owned only by those who could afford to employ a full-time mechanic to keep them going. They were big, noisy, terribly unreliable machines that required pampering and constant attention (see Figure 2.10a). Sound familiar? Early computers had many of the same requirements and characteristics (see Figure 2.10b). Did you know that early computers were so big and clunky that insects and small animals used to nest in them, and often caused the machines to have errors or fail completely? This is how the term *bug* (computer error) was coined.

Both the automobile and the computer have evolved into user-friendly machines. If you drive, then you can appreciate how you can get into your car, start the engine, and drive tens or hundreds of miles to your destination with little regard for the technology you are using. While you drive, if you're like me, you're probably eating a rushed breakfast, mulling over the events of the day, or simply taking in the music or conversation on the radio. Driving has become second nature for most of us; we completely fail to appreciate the technology behind the dashboard. We propel over a ton of metal, glass, plastic, and various fluids at about sixty-five miles per hour down a freeway within inches of other similarly huge obstacles of similar mass at similar speeds. We weave and bob in between each other on the roads without concern for the mere few square inches of rubber that suspend us above the pavement and for the large tank of explosive fuel behind us. We don't consider the detonations that drive each piston, or the carburetion process that mixes just the right amount of fuel and air to respond to

Note that the automobile has primarily one function: transportation. In contrast, the computer is a multifunction machine that provides whatever function the software it is running was designed for. This often results in a different interface (dashboard) for different applications. If the interface is intuitive, then users will have a sense of what they should be doing, and can get the job done.

The way you or I can jump into a Volvo or a Volkswagen and instantly drive it away should also apply to using the same software application on a Macintosh or on a PC, providing it's the same product. The interface should be the same regardless of the platform (computer) on which it is run. For example, Adobe products, such as Photoshop and Premiere, both of which you will have opportunity to use later in this book, look and operate the same on many platforms (see Figure 2.11).

the many sparks per second right on cue. The electronics in modern cars contains more computing power than it took to place humans on the moon. Cars not only have become far more reliable with age but also behave in a predictable and controllable manner—much like current computers.

The computer interface is like the automobile's dashboard. It is the way we communicate with the device and how it communicates with us. We don't need to comprehend the technology that makes the machine work. By watching a few simple gauges and lights on the car's dashboard, we have at our fingertips all the information and all the controls we need to drive effectively—so much so that we forget that operation and simply do what needs to be done without a second thought. Did you ever notice, especially when parking, that you could "sense" the extremities of the car, and could "feel" when the fender was getting too close to something? This is simply the result of a high level of familiarity with your vehicle. Nonetheless it shows how "tuned in" one can be to a piece of equipment.

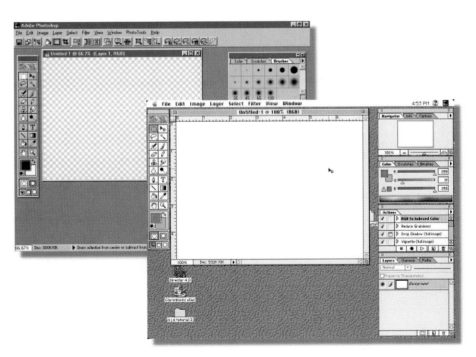

Figure 2.11
The Windows version of Photoshop at the top uses the same interface as the Macintosh version.

The computer interface has a responsibility to provide the same intuitive level of operation to the user while removing the need to comprehend or understand the technology behind it. This is the epitome of "user friendly." An intuitive interface allows the user to do the job without that second thought. No pause is needed to figure out what the computer is actually doing in response to that button click—you just move on to the next task. Multimedia is our computer's dashboard.

REVIEW OF LEADING MULTIMEDIA TITLES

The following examples of multimedia software titles have been chosen to represent the primary multimedia interface types. By studying these examples you will get a sense of the many interface design possibilities available to the multimedia developer, and a sense of which interface is best suited to which application. If you would like to get one or more of these fun titles, check out this book's Web site for the latest availability information and details on where to acquire them.

DORLING KINDERSLEY'S VIRTUAL REALITY BIRD

The whole concept of an immersive and intuitive interface is well demonstrated in Dorling Kindersley's wonderful product Virtual Reality Bird. The interface is a 3D rendering of a museum, and the changing shape of the mouse pointer guides you where to click and hints at the expected result. For example, when you move the mouse pointer over a central area of a room view, the pointer changes into a forward arrow, suggesting that you might move forward if you click there (see Figure 2.12). This visual suggestion is sufficient to guide you through this in-depth product.

Figure 2.12
The main interface screen of Dorling Kindersley's Virtual Reality Bird shows an arrow mouse pointer indicating the direction in which you would likely move if you clicked the mouse button.

Arrow mouse pointer

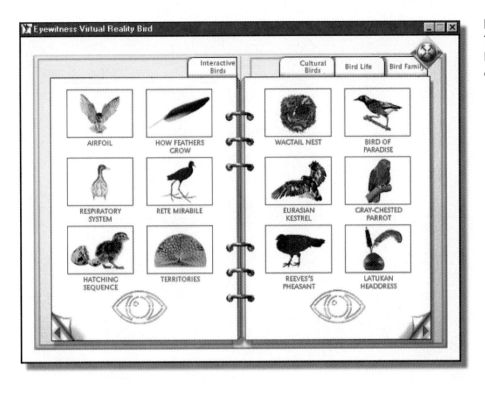

Figure 2.13
The visual index in Virtual Reality Bird is designed to look just like a ring-binder notebook.

Any encyclopedia, by definition, is a complex reference product providing vast quantities of information related to a given topic. Likewise, Virtual Reality Bird provides a vast amount of information, but the intuitive 3D interface makes it easy to digest, navigate, and cross-reference. This representation of a 3D world as an interface, called a *spatial environment,* works well in most applications. If you know how to navigate through a building by walking from room to room, then you already know how to use this kind of interface.

If you don't want to tour the museum, you can bring up the contents index (see Figure 2.13). This simple menu of topic choices is designed to look and operate like a ring-binder notebook. If you know how to use such a book, you already know how this interface works.

LAUNCH E-ZINE

Launch, an electronic magazine or e-zine, is available in the magazine section in most good bookstores. It comes in a magazine-sized cardboard folder with a CD-ROM enclosed; the entire contents of the e-zine are on the CD-ROM. The folder is a throwback to the paper format used for most magazines. Without the folder, you probably wouldn't notice the e-zine on the shelf.

Figure 2.14 shows the primary interface for *Launch,* offering several menu options in the form of buildings. Clicking any building takes you inside that building to the magazine content it contains. Billboards in the city display continual video clips and advertising.

Launch depends heavily on the use of digital video, and characters are bluescreened (a technique you will explore in Chapter 10) onto the background graphics. The interiors use a large amount of 3D computer-modeled art (which you will get to try out in Part 3) and are graphically intuitive. Again, a spatial environment, though not as extensive as in Virtual Reality Bird, is used here.

Launch includes hot spots, which are graphical areas of the interface that become highlighted when the mouse pointer moves over them to indicate importance. These hot spots, in conjunction with the changing mouse pointer, are the only feedback you need to explore the e-zine.

hot spot

An area of a software application's interface that visually changes when the mouse pointer moves over its surface. This visual "reaction" draws attention to that screen area and indicates intuitively to the user that this is an important element of the interface that should be clicked.

Figure 2.14

The *Launch* interface is a 3D representation of a town. Note the billboards playing video advertisements.

INTEL'S DISCOVER THE BENEFITS OF GENUINE INTEL BUILDING BLOCKS DEMONSTRATION CD-ROM

Intel's Building Blocks CD-ROM, which I was involved in developing with the team at Anderson Solone in Sacramento and their partners for Intel Corporation, was intended to demonstrate the new AGP graphics technology of Intel's Pentium II line of processors. The challenge was to make a new and complex technology understandable to Intel dealers who would sell it.

As shown in Figure 2.15, the interface is designed in a hierarchical menu format where selecting one menu option brings you to a submenu of information and presentation pieces. The border of the interface provides primary navigation controls; the content is kept within the borders.

The presentation of text with graphics, animation, video, sound, and even links to the Web are demonstrated in the Intel CD-ROM. By combining these elements to transmit its message, Intel provided a richer information source to

Figure 2.15

The primary interface of Intel's technology showcase product is easy to navigate. Each menu item is a hot spot that reacts to the mouse passing over it.

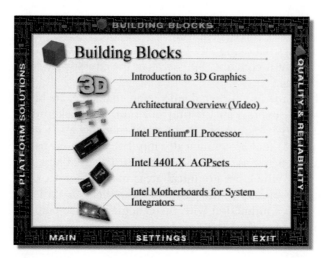

its dealers around the globe, including access to the details of the new technologies Intel was launching at the time. Multimedia made Intel's task of bringing its customers up to speed on new developments much easier and less expensive than alternative methods.

REALITY INTERACTIVE'S ISO 9000 REGISTRATION AUDIT PREPARATION SOFTWARE

When tackling complex topics, such as training employees to be compliant with ISO 9000 manufacturing standards (such standards are sometimes required of industries to ensure quality and compatibility in that industry), multimedia can make the whole imposing process simpler and easier to comprehend and apply later. Reality Interactive's ISO 9000 software uses multimedia to break this process into simple, easier-to-absorb sections.

Figure 2.16 shows the primary interface of this product; the main sections are represented by the primary "buttons" on the screen. Notice the use of drop shadows (the shading around and beneath the graphics to give visual depth) and 3D beveling to highlight the interface's primary controls. Important buttons stand out more against the foreground, while the background graphic is muted to ensure that it is no more than a background.

In this instance, multimedia makes the preparation for a standards audit more manageable and easier for employees to achieve. Reality Interactive's ISO 9000 software uses many videos and simulations to provide realistic, self-paced training for employees who are preparing for this audit. These simulations reproduce the actual audit process. The benefit? Employees can make mistakes

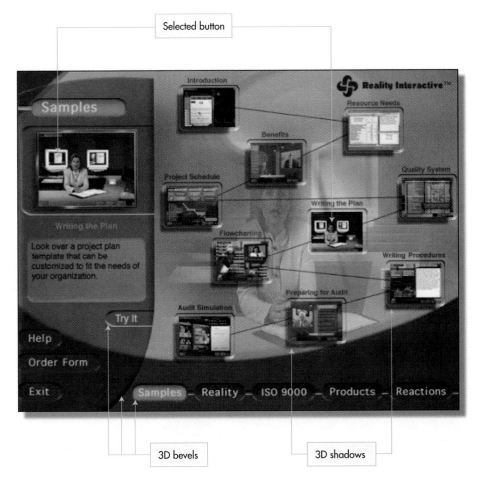

Figure 2.16
The main screen of Reality Interactive's ISO 9000 training software shows how 3D bevels and shadows bring the most important controls to the foreground. Note how the selected button stays depressed.

and learn from them without suffering the dire consequences such mistakes would have in the actual audit.

NEC'S MULTIMEDIA STORY AND WALL DATA'S SALSA STORY

NEC's Multimedia Story and Wall Data's Salsa Story have one goal in common: to harness the persuasive powers of multimedia to invoke emotions from the users. NEC's Multimedia Story brings the world of multimedia to life in a ninety-second animation that peaks with a display of NEC products (see Figure 2.17). Wall Data's Salsa Story portrays a customer's dim and bleak office existence before purchasing Salsa software, and then the exciting and much improved lives of Salsa users thereafter. While I cannot personally vouch for the validity of this message, it is a terrific example of how multimedia's multiple sensory streams can invoke feelings. Figure 2.18 shows the "before" and "after" Salsa imagery.

INTEL'S 3D TECHNOLOGY WEB SITE

Intel's 3D technology Web site has been enhanced with 3D graphics and 3D technologies to show customers that Intel's new line of 3D graphics products are as good as they get. This is a very difficult thing to achieve on the Web for many reasons. First, Intel is trying to show customers who don't have its new 3D technology what it looks like and what its benefits are. It's like trying to sell color TV with an ad viewed on a black-and-white set.

Second, Intel is trying to demonstrate graphics performance over a medium that is at best slow with graphics that are intended to impress the viewer. Typically, these files are large and slow to transmit. Who is patient enough to wait for the images to load unless there is a reward for doing so?

When we developed this Web site, the team at Anderson Solone and I wanted the site to have visual impact and easy-to-navigate interfaces that would allow the user to "drill down" to the core details. The result was an online village—the "spatial environment" concept—and for this we used a technology

Figure 2.17
NEC's emotive Multimedia Story ends in a crescendo of visual impact.

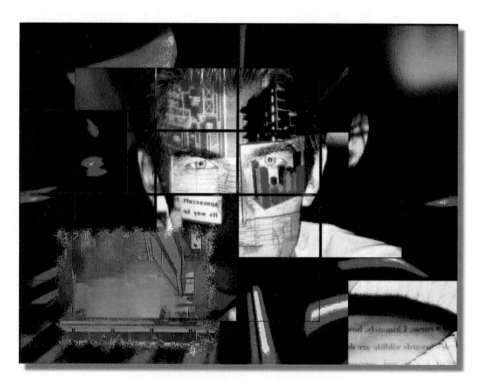

Figure 2.18
The opening animation sequence of Wall Data's Salsa demonstration invokes feelings of officeplace doom, followed by cheerful imagery of office life after installing Salsa. Note the use of drab colors for gloom and bright colors for positive feelings.

called Surround Video (see Figure 2.19). This technology is similar to Apple's QuickTime technology, but offers more features and clarity for this particular project.

The first page, as shown in Figure 2.20, inquires whether a customer's browser application has the required plug-ins and, if not, provides a link to download the appropriate software.

The Intel Web site is a good example of applying a heavily graphical interface to transform a Web site into a more usable and navigable product. You will

Figure 2.19
The Intel 3D technology Web site provides an easy-to-follow interface, with the primary images and environments appearing above the navigation console.

read more about this Web site in the next section of this chapter and also throughout this book.

MULTIMEDIA MAKEOVERS

The following are two examples of how applying multimedia to a product transformed how the product operated and how, in one of these cases, the application of multimedia affected sales in the marketplace.

MICROSOFT MONEY

Microsoft Money has always been an easy-to-use and capable financial-management software package. Its origin dates back to the days of Windows 3.0 and it is interesting to see how it has evolved.

The evolution of Microsoft Money into Microsoft Money 98 is really a story about interface design and software industry politics. Years ago Money was competing fiercely against Quicken from Intuit Corporation, which enjoyed the lion's share of the market, mainly due to its early market entry and maintaining customer loyalty thereafter. Because Quicken had a large loyal following of users, it was recognized as the market leader. If you wanted to trust your personal financial records to a piece of software, wouldn't you choose the established market leader in the field? Well, most consumers thought this way and continued to buy the more expensive Quicken in droves, passing over the equally capable Money.

Then Microsoft wanted to purchase Intuit and was stopped by federal legislators. The option of simply acquiring the competing product was gone, so what could Microsoft do to win more market share? The answer lay in multimedia.

Figure 2.21
Screens from the old (top left) and multimedia-enhanced (bottom right) versions of Microsoft Money.

As you can see in Figure 2.21, the "before" and "after" screens for Money tell quite a tale. The original Money interface looks just like most Windows plain-vanilla products (as did Quicken's at the time), relying heavily on an understanding of the financial terminology used in the pull-down menus. However, in Money 98, maintaining your financial accounts was a snap, and the interface had become intuitive (no pun intended, Mr. Intuit) and easier to follow. Throughout the program, wizards assist you through complex transactions and processes by asking questions and making changes based on each response. Using easy-to-follow graphics, animation, video, and sound effects, Microsoft transformed Money into a user-friendly product and increased its market share in most areas where it competes against Quicken. While Quicken still tends to dominate (Intuit also followed suit with a multimedia makeover for Quicken), Money 98 helped Microsoft gain significant market share and user acceptance over Quicken.

It is interesting to note that Money 98 actually performed *fewer* functions than the original version. Microsoft's engineers removed unnecessary and superfluous features and focused on making the core operations of managing one's finances as easy to use as possible. Meanwhile, while the interface has changed dramatically, the basic accounting number-crunching that the software does hasn't changed much. The magic is in the interface.

INTEL'S 3D TECHNOLOGY WEB SITE

Figure 2.22 shows the "before" and "after" design of Intel's 3D technology Web site. The original site looks like many Web sites—nice design but mostly uninspiring. This was not the message or image Intel wanted to convey, so we set about transforming the front end to represent what a 3D technology showcase Web site should look like.

By providing users of this online resource with an intuitive and high-tech interface, two primary objectives were met. First, users were presented with an interface that uses imagery and design elements that reflect the 3D nature of the site content. The site itself became a living, breathing example of the technologies being presented. Second, the navigability and ease of use of the site

Figure 2.22
The "before" (top left) and "after" (bottom right) views of our 3D multimedia enhancement.

increased tremendously. Users could get to the information they needed without having to wade through pages of dry text, and without getting lost in the process. For Intel, the investment of considerable time and money into the project was far outweighed by the benefits of this multimedia approach.

AVOIDING PITFALLS

There are two problems you should avoid during this early stage of your discovery of the world of multimedia. The primary problem to avoid is the "feature creep" trap. When multimedia is new to you, it can be completely absorbing. You're like a kid at Christmastime, wondering which toys to play with first. One of the transitions you will have to make when moving from *beginner* to *novice* and on through *accomplished* to *expert* in this field is to let go of the toys and focus on the functionality of the work at hand. Just because you have learned a new technique doesn't mean you have to use it. First, determine whether your product will benefit from using the new technique, rather than creating a feature that sticks out like the proverbial sore thumb. Worse still, using too many features may make your product a cacophony of special effects. Use the bells and whistles in moderation—and then only when it is beneficial to do so. You will have many opportunities to flex your creative muscles and use those features in other products. If you're still not convinced, take some time to create a project simply for your own gratification, using as many the features as you'd like. Afterward, cast a critical eye over the results and see how many of those features could be removed without detracting from the usability of your product.

The second problem to avoid is dependence on one platform. At this stage, if you are an exclusively Macintosh or Windows user, take some time to play with the other platform to get familiar with it. The best multimedia developers use both systems without much thought to switching between them to get the job done in the most productive way possible. In the next chapter we will analyze the platform issues in detail, but for now, it's critical to gain some exposure to the other system.

Chapter Summary

- Multimedia technology can be used to make computer applications easier to use, more efficient, and more enjoyable.

- An intuitive interface is essential to a good multimedia product. It also brings the added benefits of less reliance on (or elimination of) a user manual and technical support for the product.

- A multimedia interface provides an ease of use and a level of software application control and comfort for the user that is otherwise unattainable. It is the natural next step in the evolution of how we use computers.

- The win-win promise of multimedia offers users faster assimilation, longer retention, and better application of the information content, as well as tremendous cost savings over the more traditional methods of information presentation.

- The "dashboard philosophy" shows us how an intuitive interface can make complex computer technologies manageable and usable. The same principle has made automotive technology intuitive and easy for us to use over the last hundred years.

Key Terms and Concepts

digital assistants, 26   hot spots, 31   intuitive, 21   wizards, 26

Checking Your Knowledge and Skills

1. List eight reasons for using multimedia technology in a computer-based application.
2. Of the eight reasons you listed for using multimedia technology, rank them in order of importance and write a short paragraph explaining your chosen order.
3. History has seen many technology-driven surges in civilization, from the invention of the wheel to the invention of electricity. Following the correlation of the automobile and the computer as developing inventions that have become more an integrated part of society and easier to use in the process, correlate the evolution of the computer software interface with another technology of your choice.
4. Armed with the information in this chapter, create a promotional flyer for your fictitious or actual company that persuades your client to adopt multimedia as a technology for effective promotion, information dissemination, and training.

Critical Thinking Challenges

1. Determine, from the examples in this chapter and those referred/linked to this book's Web site, which of these multimedia products you consider your favorite, and why. Analyze your answer for insight into what features and aspects of that product make it your favorite.
2. Reflect on the CD-ROM and Web-based examples described in this chapter and analyze the pros and cons for each. Assume you have a product to develop for a client, who asks your advice on which way to deliver it—on CD-ROM or from a Web site. Which would you choose for your client and why?
3. If a multimedia product was created for both Macintosh and Windows platforms and looked and operated the same way on both, which would you prefer to run it on and why?
4. If you have a clear platform preference, examine the basis for your preference and determine what software developers could do to make the less-preferred system just as appealing as your preferred choice. Does this exercise give you any insight into either your preference or into the task of a developer?

Hands-on Exercises

MULTIMEDIA DEVELOPMENT PROPOSAL

Find a software product or Web site that, in your opinion, would benefit from a multimedia makeover. Write a persuasive report on the product that you would present to convince the product's manufacturer that:

1. They should convert their product to a multimedia format.

2. They should employ you to take on the task.

Master Project

GETTING STARTED WITH A CONCEPT

Chapter 1 introduced the Master Project that you will complete. Here is the first step in that project.

Your Master Project is to create a multimedia résumé. This digital portfolio, if done well, will be a tremendous asset to you as you pursue a career in multimedia. You need to set the groundwork for this project.

From the multimedia examples described in this chapter, and given the large array of technology "toys" available to you as a multimedia producer, draft a project proposal, detailing in a few short paragraphs what you envision your portfolio will look like. You will want to define your concept at this point, which is best done by identifying the content that you want to present in your digital portfolio and then mapping it out on paper. A flow chart is always helpful for visualizing such a plan. A simple diagram and a written concept of your goals is the best starting point.

Figure 2.23, which shows a few screenshots from a digital portfolio by designer Joe Mack, is a good example of how an attractive interface can be designed to present what may otherwise be ordinary and perhaps uninteresting information. Such a digital résumé certainly stands out from the paper-based applicants. How better to show a command of the technology?

This book's Web site has a page dedicated to a list of links to online digital portfolios—both good *and* bad. Use it as a resource to find your own style.

Figure 2.23

Several screenshots of Joe Mack's digital portfolio from his Job Seek Interactive project.

3

GETTING STARTED IN MULTIMEDIA

Chapter Objectives

After completing this chapter, you will be able to:

● Describe what is required of those who work in multimedia and find your own place in this exciting field.

● Identify the various hardware and software tools of multimedia development and determine which workstation configuration is best suited to your needs.

● Determine which type of computer system, Mac or PC, is best for your needs.

● Describe the stages in the multimedia production cycle and discuss how to plan for a multimedia project to achieve the best outcome.

● Apply the technique of storyboarding to the planning and design process.

● Plan for different multimedia delivery systems.

● Discuss the significance of and immense opportunity for multimedia development on the Internet.

● Identify with one of the many multimedia job prospects.

Chapter Overview

In this chapter you will become acquainted with the tools of the trade, and will start to determine which products will best work for your multimedia development projects. You may even form an opinion about your place in this field and the career path you would like to take. Don't worry if your goals are still not clear to you by the end of this chapter. By the end of this book, you will have addressed your role in multimedia development. This chapter also introduces you to the multimedia project planning process and provides a template project plan you can apply to your subsequent projects.

FINDING YOUR OWN PLACE IN THIS FIELD

As you read in Chapter 1 and 2, multimedia is a vast field encompassing many areas of expertise and crossing many technology boundaries. A multimedia producer could develop a career solely on CD-ROM-based promotional or Web-based distance learning applications. Either of these two positions would be considered a very fulfilling and lucrative career in multimedia. Both specializations require the same fundamental knowledge and skill set. The question you must ask (unless you already know the answer) is, "Which path should I take?"

The best way of dealing with this dilemma now is simply to forget about it. No, really. Chapter 17, which is available at this book's Web site, discusses multimedia career opportunities, and by the time you read that chapter you will know so much more about multimedia that this may no longer be a valid question for you. By then you will probably have determined your multimedia niche. You will have ample opportunity to test the tools and technologies of multimedia and will discover for yourself answers to the following questions:

- What area of multimedia am I really good at? Am I a better 3D animator or a better graphic interface designer? Can I create better digital video sequences or better multimedia Web pages?

- Which tools do I have the most fun with? Which applications are the most rewarding for me?

- Of the creative areas that I am good at and enjoy the most, which am I most productive at?

- Do I want to be a hands-on creative producer or a manager of those who do the hands-on work?

- Of the areas that I'm good at, which command the better salaries?

So to truly find your place in the field of multimedia really requires an understanding and experience of the possible areas in this field from which to choose.

If you're curious about multimedia careers, Boston College has a terrific Web site, shown in Figure 3.1, with a lot of information and job descriptions for the many career possibilities in multimedia.

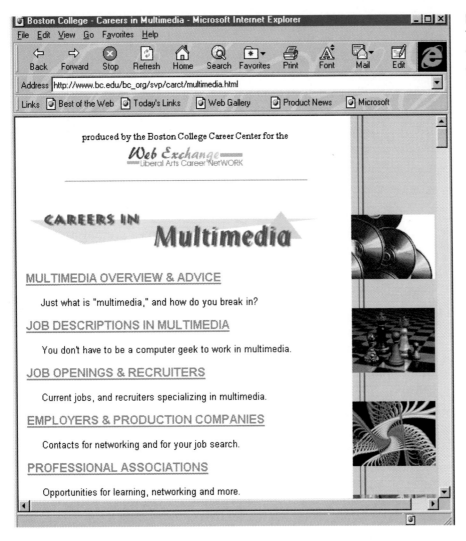

Figure 3.1
The Boston College Liberal Arts Career Network Web site is a great place to learn more about multimedia careers.

TOOLS OF THE TRADE

To develop multimedia content and applications, you will need a fast, multimedia-capable computer system incorporating *at least* the following:

- High-resolution graphics and a large monitor
- A good video display card capable of displaying 24-bit color
- A CD-ROM or DVD drive
- Stereo 16-bit sound capabilities with amplified speakers
- A high-speed modem, at least a 56Kbps model
- An Internet access account from an Internet service provider (ISP) or equivalent
- As much RAM as you can afford (absolute minimum of 32 MB for PCs and 64 MB for Macintoshes)
- A color printer

Depending on which area of multimedia you will specialize in, optional equipment may be required, such as the following:

- A removable large-capacity storage device, such as a rewriteable CD-ROM (CD-RW), Zip or Jaz drive
- A CD-ROM or DVD-ROM burner for creating your own master CD-ROM or DVD-ROM
- A digitizing tablet, which is an input device that can read the precise position of an electronic pen over the surface of an electronic tablet
- A flatbed scanner (may incorporate the ability to scan 35mm slides and film negatives)
- A good-quality digital camera
- A video capture/video printing card
- A good-quality computer microphone
- A hi-fi VCR compatible with your video capture/video printing card

The required software set for the multimedia producer includes the following:

- A graphic design photo editing application (such as Adobe's Photoshop, Jasc's Paint Shop Pro, or Corel's Photo-Paint)
- A 3D modeling and animation application (such as Caligari's TrueSpace, MetaCreations Ray Dream Studio, or NewTek's LightWave 3D or Inspire 3D)
- A morphing application (such as ScanSoft's Kai's Super Goo, Gryphon Software's Morph, or Ulead/Softkey's Morph Studio)
- A digital sound editing application (such as Sonic Foundry's Sound Forge or Macromedia's SoundEdit 16)
- A nonlinear digital video editing application (such as Adobe's Premiere, Ulead's VideoStudio Pro, or Lumiere)
- At least one multimedia authoring application (such as Macromedia's Director or Authorware, Clickteam's Multimedia Fusion, Astound Incorporated's Astound, or Asymetrix's ToolBook). Authoring refers to one's ability to create a software application or Web page without using, or even understanding, a computer programming language.
- A good Web page authoring/design tool (such as Macromedia's Dreamweaver, Adobe's PageMill, Netscape's Gold versions of Navigator or Composer, Corel's Web Designer, or Microsoft's FrontPage)

Optional software for the multimedia producer includes the following:

- A batch media file format conversion tool for creating uniform palettes and file formats across all the media content of your production (such as Equilibrium's DeBabelizer Pro, Jasc's Image Robot, or Alchemy Mindworks's Graphic Workshop)
- A Web animation and multimedia applet development tool (such as Macromedia's Flash or Microsoft's Liquid Motion)
- A Web-specific graphics design tool (such as Adobe's ImageReady or Macromedia's Fireworks)
- A good presentation tool for quick prototype presentations (such as Microsoft's PowerPoint or ScanSofts Kai's Power Show)
- A collection of stock images, video, animations, and clip art (from companies such as Corel, MetaCreations, PhotoDisc, Photodex, and so on). Such a library will prove invaluable for generating quick projects. You can also subscribe to such libraries online.

digitizing tablet

An input device that can read the precise position of an electronic pen over the surface of an electronic tablet; also known as a graphics tablet. Data about the pen's location are then translated into the onscreen position of the mouse pointer. In this way, artists, drafters, and others who prefer the feel of a pen over a mouse can use this device to draw more "naturally."

authoring

The process of creating a software application or Web page without the need to use, or even understand, computer programming. An authoring program provides the user with an intuitive design tool that will do the work of programming the end product to match the visual design of the author.

Figure 3.2
A TeleVideo SuperView Pro 260 17-inch monitor with .25 dot pitch and 1,600 × 1,200-pixel display capability. This monitor is typical of the type suitable for multimedia development.

- A multimedia-project-planning tools and prototyping application (such as Allen Communication Designer's Edge or Microsoft's PowerPoint)

On this book's Web site, you will find links to the Web sites and resources for all of these software applications so you can examine them yourself, and in most cases, download evaluation copies.

Several hardware devices deserve particular notice. They include monitors, sound cards, scanners, digital cameras, video capture cards, hard disk drives, and CD-ROM burners.

MONITORS.   Multimedia design and development is such a visual pursuit that a monitor is an important but often overlooked element of any multimedia development system. Computers tend to be priced without a monitor included, and because there is such a wide range in monitor prices, it's often easy to afford a terrific system with a "cheap" screen.

Buy the biggest and best monitor you can comfortably afford. You will need at least a 17-inch screen (a measurement of the diagonal viewable distance between opposite corners of the screen) and a dot-pitch value of .28 or smaller. Dot pitch is the distance in millimeters between each of the red, green, and blue dots etched into the phosphor of the inside of the screen; the smaller the number the finer the image (see Figure 3.2).

A *multisync* monitor allows you to change screen resolutions without having to reset your system. If you are using development tools that require a lot of screen real estate, such as Director or Premiere, then being able to switch to a larger screen resolution on the fly can be very beneficial.

Special (expensive) video display interface cards for your computer allow you to use two monitors on your computer and split the desktop display between them. Windows 98 and later versions can provide the ability to drive two video cards at the same time, and split the desktop display without the need for an expensive specialized dual-display video card. These devices are terrific for spreading out cluttered screens, as shown in Figure 3.3.

SOUND CARDS.   Sound capability on your computer is very important when it comes to developing multimedia products. Who would be interested in a mute multimedia application? Compatibility in sound playing is also very important. The original sound card for the PC platform, Sound Blaster, has established an industry set of standards to which other sound card manufacturers try to

dot pitch
The pitch at which successive dots used to create an image are spaced. The dot pitch value refers in millimeters to the space separating adjacent dots.

> **Why doesn't my screen always look just like the book's?**
> You might notice that your screen doesn't always match the screens in the text. You can expect to see slight variations sometimes—your system preferences could be set up differently, or your version of the software may be slightly different. These variations aren't important to learning how the software works. The general steps and your results will be virtually the same.

Figure 3.3

Companies such as Matrox produce special video cards that can use dual monitors. Shown is the Matrox G400 AGP dual display control panel and examples of dual-display monitor configurations.

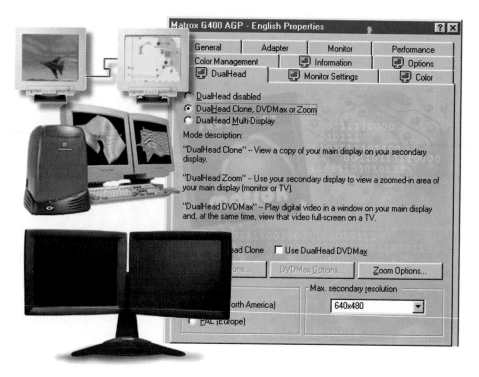

conform. By using a Sound Blaster–compatible card, your software applications will most likely run well without sound incompatibility issues.

Since the de facto standard in the PC world is Sound Blaster compatibility, then it is usually best to purchase a system with an actual Sound Blaster sound card from Creative Laboratories. Then you don't have to worry about how compatible your non–Sound Blaster product is, since it will be the definition of the standard.

While some non–Creative Labs sound interfaces are more compatible than others, the chance of any degree of incompatibility is not a risk you want to take. If you are going to use a non-Sound Blaster product, at least test it thoroughly and read some independent magazine reviews of the product.

Macintosh systems come with factory-designed sound capability built in, so compatibility should not matter as much on Macs.

SCANNERS.   A flatbed scanner can be an invaluable tool for the multimedia producer. However, there are a large range of scanners to choose from, ranging in price from about $50 to several thousand dollars.

Keep in mind that most multimedia products are designed to run with computer display devices, such as monitors, LCD panels, and perhaps computer video projectors. Dot resolution and color depth (number of colors used to display an image. See Chapter 4) are critical factors when choosing a scanner. Since computer displays use a 72 or 75 dots-per-inch (dpi) dot resolution, values anywhere above this are usually well within the quality requirements for multimedia work. A 300-dpi scanner can provide more definition and image quality than you probably need, and more than 300 dpi is usually overkill. Scanners offering higher scanning resolution are primarily intended for printing-press output—which may require images with up to 2,540 dpi! For multimedia development this is not necessary.

Figure 3.4 shows two blowups of an image detail showing screen gray-scale pixels and printer black dots. Note that the computer can use many shades of gray and pixels that can touch edge-to-edge to represent the image. However, your printer has no gray ink, and relies on how closely packed together black dots are to represent levels of gray, as seen in the bottom blowup. The more dots

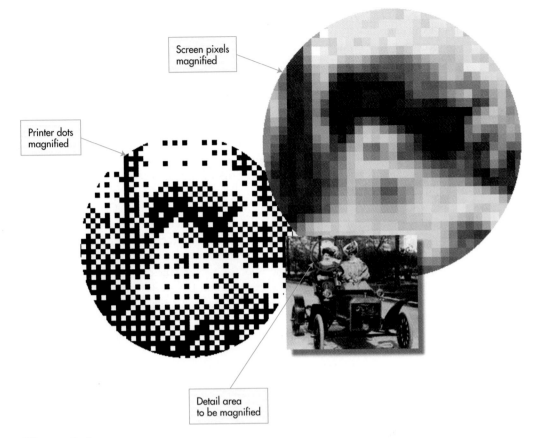

Figure 3.4
A detail magnification of a photograph. The top blowup shows a magnification of the pixels used on the screen, while the bottom blowup shows those dots as they appear on a black-and-white printer.

it can squish into this area, the finer the image. The difference between screen and printer resolution is that the printer needs far more dots per inch to match the visual detail that a screen provides.

Most scanners quote an optical resolution and an interpolated resolution. The optical resolution is how fine the device can scan the image; the interpolated resolution is the best resolution that the scanning software supplied with the scanner can extract from the optically scanned image. In other words, if your scanner is rated at a 300-dpi optical resolution and a 1,200-dpi interpolated resolution, then the scanning software can average the 300 dots per inch that it scans in, and insert four times as many dots in between them in the same image dimensions. This gives an impression of a finer detailed image and aids scaling and image manipulation work you may wish to do later.

With regard to color depth, you need to distinguish between multimedia development needs and those for printing-press output. For multimedia use, 24-bit color depth is ample color detail for your needs. At 24-bit color depth you have a range of over sixteen million color values to choose from. When you consider that the human eye can distinguish only ten million different colors and tone, you can see that 24-bit color is more than sufficient. Scanners offering 32-bit and higher color provide the color data required for CMYK-format images. CMYK format is required for printing equipment that separates the image into the four *process colors* that create what we know as full color.

As with the scanner's dpi specification, it is easy to spend an unnecessary amount of money on a product that is overkill for the job. More is not always better.

optical resolution
The level of resolution at which a device can scan the image.

interpolated resolution
The best resolution that the scanning software supplied with a scanner can extract from the optically scanned image.

CMYK
An acronym used in the printing industry to describe the four-color printing process. CMYK stands for Cyan, Magenta, Yellow and BlacK. In computer terms, this format is often used to describe 32-bit color formats.

DIGITAL CAMERAS. The selection of inexpensive high-quality digital cameras has never been better. By the time you read this it can only have improved. The technology, convenience, and the price of digital cameras has made them affordable and fun to use.

Before purchasing a camera, check out magazine and online reviews of the available products and comparison-shop on the basis of performance and best value *before* stepping into a store. Your primary source of information should never come from a sales clerk, even in a store that stocks all of the competing models. In my experience, the efforts of the sales staff in the very competitive world of consumer electronics tend to be driven more by sales commission and current must-sell models than by the needs of the consumer. While this is not always true, and there are very capable sales personnel out there, it is always best to do your own homework before venturing into the store. Online magazine Web sites, such as those found at ZDNet (www.zdnet.com), will guide you.

For the multimedia producer, quality is the key factor in choosing a suitable digital camera, followed by performance and convenience. The prime factor that determines quality in digital cameras is the image size captured by the device. Do not consider a camera that makes less than 640-x-480-pixel images, as the images will be too small for many applications, and scaling up the images will make them blurry and pixilated.

A camera that includes a display panel to preview the images you've taken is a must-have. When you're in the field taking photos, you need to be able to review them to make sure you got what you needed for that project. When you get the camera home and upload the images, it will most likely be too late to discover a finger over the lens!

Most digital cameras connect into your computer via a cable, but some have better connection methods. Cable transfer of images can be slow and error-prone, and can devour expensive batteries while the camera is connected (unless you have a power adapter for it or use rechargeable batteries). Look for cameras that use disks or cards that can be brought to the computer for uploading. The convenience and speed of this method in a production facility will be well worth it. Try to get a camera that can accept a rechargeable battery, as store-bought camera batteries can be very expensive—and digital cameras consume them like crazy.

My recent favorite digital camera, and the one I use daily, is from the Sony Mavica series. My Mavica has a display panel viewfinder so that I know exactly what I am shooting. It stores the images (up to forty-four in standard resolution) on a standard 3.5-inch floppy disk that I can read on my system back at the studio and has a 10X magnification optical zoom. The images are great-quality in fine mode, and the rechargeable battery lasts three hours before needing another charge. This camera cost me less than $500 and will probably cost even less by the time you read this book. There are more models in the Mavica series that offer far higher performance, higher resolution, and even MPEG video and sound recording, but for a higher price tag.

VIDEO CAPTURE CARDS. There are many video capture cards available for both PCs and Macs that offer various levels of sophistication, features, capabilities, and prices. Look for a product that offers full-screen (640 × 480), full-motion (30 frames per second) video capture and playback.

If you want your video editing work (or your pilot for a sci-fi animation series) to be viewable on videotape, you must make sure that the video capture card you buy has the ability to print to video. Too often I have counseled students who have spent a lot of money on a video capture card and have expended lots of time and effort on a video project to discover that they have no way to get the final product back onto videotape. In such circumstances, especially if the new video card cannot be returned to the vendor, this necessitates purchasing a video output card just to complete that project. Many video capture cards offer full-screen, full-motion video output as well, so try to identify a product that suits your needs with that feature.

When capturing video on someone else's video capture system, be sure to save the captured video file in a standard format. You will read more about this in Chapter 10; for now, know that most video capture cards do their work by creating a digital video file in their own proprietary format. This is usually a format that works hand-in-hand with the hardware of the capture card to get the best quality and fastest capturing possible. However, if you do not convert the file to a standard format before taking it away, it may not be viewable on another computer that doesn't have the same video capture card installed.

Some companies, such as Pinnacle Systems' Miro (www.pinnaclesys.com), manufacture their video capture cards for both PC and Macintosh. This can be a real benefit if you're collaborating with someone who uses a different platform, yet you want seamless transfer of your video work between you both.

HARD DISK DRIVE SPACE AND REMOVABLE LARGE-CAPACITY STORAGE. The rule with hard disk drive space is the more, the better. Multimedia is a ravenous consumer of drive space. It takes but a few video files and image libraries to gobble up your free space on your hard disk drive. Buy big.

In addition, if you are looking to do a lot of video capture and output-to-tape work, you will need a hard disk drive capable of sustained fast data-transfer rates. The video interface you purchase should come with requirement specifications for the hard disk drive needed. Some also come with software to test your existing hard disk drive and assess its ability to perform as required. Keep this in mind, as you may have to add a second fast video-serving drive to your system.

The important issue with removable large-capacity storage devices is compatibility with wherever you wish to transport your data. If your colleagues use Zip drives and you have a SyQuest device, then you'll have no luck getting that 80 MB video clip to them easily. The most commonly used disk format is Iomega's Zip drive. This 100-MB or 250-MB format can be a savior, especially when taking work home for the weekend. While the new 120-MB floppy disk format seems to be gaining acceptance, it has a long way to go before displacing Zip drives.

Iomega (www.iomega.com) also manufactures a 2-GB Jaz drive, but be sure that your colleagues also use this format before committing to one. The blank disks are pricey, but well worth the ability to transfer or archive up to two whole gigabytes of data.

Rewriteable CD-ROM drives may seem like a good idea, but unless those with whom you wish to share your work have a compatible CD-ROM drive, they won't be able to read your disk.

CD-ROM BURNERS. CD-ROM burners, as opposed to rewriteable CD-ROMs, can be a valuable asset in your array of multimedia development tools. These devices can make a standard (now multi-session) CD-ROM readable on any system with a CD-ROM drive. While they have been dropping in price in recent years, they still represent a significant investment for the multimedia developer. Blank CD-R disks have become very inexpensive too. My first CD-ROM burner was a Kodak model that I bought in 1994 for almost $8,000. Then the blank CD-R disks were over $10 each! It was slow, was prone to errors, and took up as much desk space as my computer did. My current burner from Hewlett-Packard is built into a drive bay in my system, costs about $180, and operates much faster and more reliably than its predecessor. The blank disks can now be bought for under a dollar a piece on special!

One of the keys to owning a good CD-ROM burner is to get good, stable, CD-R software to complement it. Adaptec produces Easy CD Creator Deluxe software, which is an excellent and stable product for this purpose. One of the

multi-session

The designation for CD-R devices that can record more than one block of data, or session. You can record several sessions on a multi-session CD-R, provided there is enough space. Multi-session CD-Rs can be read only on compatible multi-session CD-ROM devices.

most frustrating things about burning CD-ROMs is that the process can take some time. If an error occurs in midburn, you are left with a useless CD that cannot be reused, and the prospect of starting the process over again in the hope that the error won't reoccur! Easy CD Creator Deluxe seems to have fewer crashing problems than most of the many similar applications I have used in the past. When looking for this software product, don't be fooled by the advertising. It is for some reason promoted more as a product for creating music CDs and for converting your old vinyl LPs to CD than as a CD-ROM creator. While it can create music CDs very well, it can also create terrific CD-ROMs.

While this list may seem imposing, you do not have to acquire everything at once. Most software companies provide free evaluation copies of their products so that you can select the most appropriate product. Starting with a basic multimedia computer system and some inexpensive software, you can get off to a productive start, and add more items to your toolbox as your needs dictate.

Here's the good news. These hardware and software tools are both freely available and inexpensive, especially compared to what the professional studios had to pay for similar power and performance just a few years ago. Today a digital video system requires a personal computer, two monitors, and digital video editing software to more than replace the capability of what used to occupy a whole room. Everything on one desk!

For most multimedia production needs, a multimedia computer system designed for the home will provide the power and services you need to create engaging multimedia applications. With a few small add-ons (for example, a CD-ROM burner) you can configure a capable multimedia development workstation from your local discount store or office supply warehouse.

THE MULTIMEDIA COMPUTER—THE PROMISE FULFILLED

As you learned in Chapter 1, you can walk into many noncomputer stores and purchase a system that will more than meet your multimedia development needs. The inexpensive availability of such sophisticated tools is a great boost to your productivity.

The question now is, which brand of computer and how fast a system do you need? More often than not, the multimedia product you produce will have to run on either a Windows or Macintosh system. If you need to use another type of computer, such as an SGI or Sun system for instance, then you will need to find an expert in that particular system platform. This person will help you identify the availability and cost of the software tools and hardware add-ons you will need to support that computer.

MAC OR PC—DOES IT REALLY MATTER?

The answer to this question is a resounding "NO!" There may be reasons to consider one above the other, but both do a terrific job as a multimedia producer's tool. I am asked this question often by my students and in class I tell all students to leave favoritism at the door. The bottom line is that the differences between PCs and Macs are few when compared to the overlooked similarities between them.

Selecting a Mac or a PC usually boils down to familiarity. Which system do you already know and want to continue using? The best multimedia producers own and use both Mac and PC systems and interchange them for many tasks on the same projects. This is the best of both worlds!

Table 3.1 lists the pros and cons of using a Macintosh or a PC system for multimedia production. You can use these points to weigh your choice.

Historically the Macintosh has taken hold in the creative industries such as graphic design, advertising, multimedia production, animation, and movie production. In the early to mid-1980s the Macintosh offered a friendlier system for nontechnical professionals who knew nothing of computers. The Mac had a credibility problem as a serious business tool, but designers appreciated the easy-to-use mouse and graphical interface. This often resulted in creative companies having a fleet of Macintoshes out back in the production rooms, while a few PCs held down the front office, the accounts, the payroll, and other "business" functions. In that era, the Mac provided productivity right out of the box. With the graphic design tools and video processing applications that started on the Mac for the same reasons, this system quickly gained a loyal following. Unfortunately, some people became zealots in their defense of one platform over the other.

Today, more and more Windows-based PCs are being used in what has been traditionally considered Mac territory. This trend will most likely result in a homogenous mix of both systems being used, which would provide more value and computing power to those who use both platforms to get their work done than to anyone who exclusively uses just one platform.

TABLE 3.1	Macintosh vs. PC for Multimedia Production
Point	**Counterpoint**
PCs are often less expensive than Macintosh systems, as are their peripherals and software.	Macintoshes have less variation in quality and reliability, which can often be an issue with cheaper PC systems
Macintosh peripherals are easier to install and use.	PC systems provide more options for troubleshooting and fixing if something goes wrong.
Macintosh systems require less technical knowledge and experience than PCs.	For technically oriented users, the PC platform offers more configuration options, add-ons, and extras, which are also upgradable when technology changes (as it always does).
PC systems with Windows NT have become the animator's system of choice.	Macintosh systems are often the graphic designer's system of choice.
PCs offer Zip, Jaz, SyQuest, and many other large storage removable disk options.	So do Macintoshes. In fact, the disks can be used in both systems as long as they are formatted as a PC disk.
Macintosh systems do a terrific job of video processing and editing.	So do PCs! Most industry-standard digital video nonlinear editing systems are available for both PC and Macintosh platforms.
More multimedia is produced on Macintosh systems than on PCs.	This **used** to be true. Those producing early multimedia came from a graphic design background, where the Macintosh has always had a firm foothold. Familiarity rules!
Most multimedia is produced to run on PCs.	True, but only because there are so many more PCs installed than Macintosh systems. One of the driving forces behind developers' using PCs to create multimedia instead of Macintosh systems is to be compatible with the target platform for the products.
Macintoshes are easier to use.	True—if you are a Macintosh user! In reality, the ease-of-use ratings of Windows 98 and later versions and Mac OS 8 and later versions are almost identical.
PCs need less RAM and are less costly.	True, but the Mac allows for the management of the amount of memory required to run each application. Macs do tend to need more RAM, but also tend to be more stable when using it heavily.

TABLE 3.2 Absolute Minimum System Requirements for Multimedia Development	
Windows System	**Macintosh**
200 MHz Pentium MMX processor	Macintosh Power PC 9600/200 604e processor
32 MB of RAM	64 MB of RAM
32X CD-ROM drive	32X CD-ROM drive
16-bit sound card and amplified stereo sound speakers	Amplified stereo sound speakers
3 GB hard disk drive	3 GB hard disk drive
Accelerated video card with at least 2 MB of video RAM	Accelerated PCI graphics card with 2 MB of video RAM
17-inch SVGA monitor with .28 dot pitch	17-inch multisync monitor
56K internal fax/modem	56K internal fax/modem
Internal Zip drive (external Zip drives are too slow)	Internal or external (SCSI) Zip drive
Internal CD-ROM burner	Internal or external (SCSI) CD-ROM burner
Color inkjet printer with 600-dpi resolution or better	Color inkjet printer with 600-dpi resolution or better
24-bit 300-dpi flatbed scanner	24-bit 300-dpi flatbed scanner
	Extended keyboard and mouse

I would suggest that you evaluate your budget and determine how much system you can get for the money. If you already have one platform, that's a good reason to stick with a similar system to take advantage of the software and peripherals you already have. If you can afford it, get both! Over the years I have accumulated five PCs and two Macs for my multimedia consultancy and development work. All but one of the PCs (an old 486SX laptop) and one of the Macs (an old Mac Classic) are in daily use.

Table 3.2 lists two comparable starter systems for multimedia creation and development.

While you can purchase much more powerful systems at a favorable cost, Table 3.2 provides an absolute minimal basic system for multimedia production. If you can afford to buy something better, then by all means do so! Your multimedia development and production experience will be all the more enjoyable for it.

THE MULTIMEDIA PRODUCTION CYCLE

With tools in hand, you are ready to tackle your first multimedia project. Well, not so fast. One of the most frequent sob stories I hear is of the student or budding multimedia producer who takes on a project and jumps into the deep end without prior project planning and organization. It happens all the time and creates far more damage to the startup developer than you might think. In the early days of your multimedia career you will be in reputation-building mode. It can take about seven good projects to erase the bad reputation of one failure or dissatisfied customer. A little foresight and planning can go a very long way.

MULTIMEDIA PROJECT PLANNING

Planning a multimedia project is quite similar to most any project-planning task. The primary difference is planning for technology. A seasoned and highly skilled classical project planner would have a difficult time planning for a multimedia project simply because of the complexity of the many technologies required. If you can master and appreciate the technologies required and can anticipate and plan for their implementation, then what remains is planning for the developmental and business functions of the project.

Thankfully there is a software application that can greatly assist the multimedia developer in this task. Allen Communications's Designer's Edge is a multimedia project organizational and planning tool that collects and sorts the many aspects and issues surrounding a multimedia project (see Figure 3.5). Designer's Edge will help you produce and track project documentation as well as help you produce visuals for the client that can be later exported into one of many multimedia authoring tools. You can find a link to Allen Communications online from this book's Web site, and from there download an evaluation copy of this product. Products like Designer's Edge allow you to enter the project details as you learn them, including graphics and sketches, and formulate all the proposal, specification, and planning documentation. This can save a huge amount of time and effort, produces professional-looking reports for your client, and makes you look very organized!

The problem with planning and then following that plan is that it can take all of the spontaneity out of the work. That's the whole point. Another term for spontaneity in a development project is *feature creep*—in which the enthusiasm of the developer and/or the client gets out of hand and new innovations and ideas start to creep into the specification. Of course, this happens without any adjustment to the original price for the project. Why wouldn't the client be excited about getting more work for the same fee? A little planning at the outset would have produced a specification document for the project that would have shown the extras to be chargeable extras, or at least features to be considered for a possible "Phase 2" of the project.

It really doesn't take too much time to plan and organize a project. The benefits include time and money savings and enhancing your credibility with the client. It is always best to document the project and ask the client to sign a specification sheet that describes to everyone's satisfaction the scope, extent, and expected results. Also include deadlines and, if suitable, a few midproject milestones—points in the development process where you can meet with the client

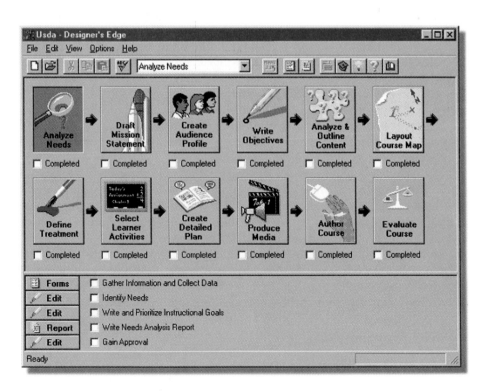

Figure 3.5
Allen Communications's Designer's Edge 2.0 Pro is a tremendous asset to the multimedia producer. It can help you plan, organize, and track your project and save you a great amount of effort in the process.

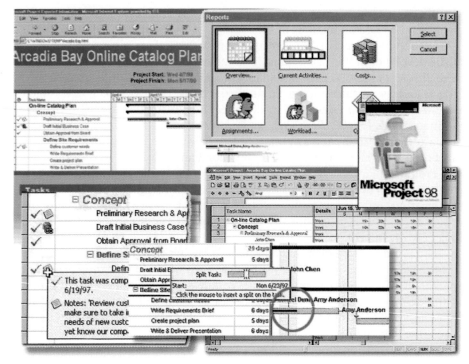

to review the work. Project-planning software applications such as Microsoft's Project 98 and Project 2000 are excellent products for helping you organize a multimedia development project over a project timeline. Such products help you track resources, costs, responsibilities, review milestones and deliverables, and monitor the project timetable. Figure 3.6 shows some screenshots of Microsoft's Project 98. Project 98 can produce many views of your project data to best help you and your client understand and control the development process.

Usually you will require a commencement fee, typically one-third of the project bill, to start work. This is important to get client "buy-in" on the project. If clients are financially committed from the outset they are more likely to see projects through. If you start with no financial commitment from clients, you run the risk that they are just testing to see if you can do the job. Without any financial commitment there is no loss for the client if they should pull the plug on the project, but you have at that point already invested quite a lot. Get the commencement fee. You will be pleasantly surprised at how willing and understanding clients are to pay this. This is simply good business practice. Once you develop an ongoing relationship with a repeat client, you can forgo the commencement fee as an indication of mutual trust.

Thereafter, set and meet your milestones in the project timeline. Always plan a little padding into the timeline to accommodate unforeseen problems, and if you can beat the deadline, then the client will be impressed. Don't complete the project too early because this can give those who do not comprehend what's involved the impression that you overcharged them.

A good first milestone is the visual interface design, followed by a partial working prototype milestone, followed by the first-release test version milestone, followed by the completed master copy on CD-ROM or a Web site. The following sections deal with the components and milestones of the multimedia project.

STORYBOARDING

The term *storyboarding* refers to the visual layout of a production story line in a comic-strip fashion. Figure 3.7 shows part of a typical storyboard in the making.

Figure 3.7
On a recent project I used this storyboard. It was created using storyboarding sticky notelets (supplied by MarkerTek, www.markertek.com) on a cork board.

A storyboard allows the developer to test the overall concept for completeness and visually define all the aspects of a project that can be anticipated. It also allows for good visual communication among development team members so that all understand the parameters of the project. Storyboarding is also the time to make changes and discuss the more difficult aspects of the project.

This technique enables the developer to see the extent of the project and keep a "visual map" of the project in mind when in the thick of the development process. When you're deep into the project, the pressure will seem much less oppressive if you know what's on the other side of the development hill you're climbing.

Additionally, a good storyboard is an invaluable tool for communicating with clients and getting their input. It is better to get this feedback early, at storyboard time, than toward the end of the project. You don't want to discover, after having invested large amounts of time and effort, that the client had changes to make.

Common tools for storyboard creation are pen and paper, whiteboards, Post-it storyboard notelets, and presentation products such as Microsoft's PowerPoint. PowerPoint allows you to create each storyboard panel and then edit and rearrange them to your heart's content.

MEDIA COMPONENTS

If you can view each of the pieces that go together to make a multimedia product as components, then life suddenly becomes easier. The media components of your project, such as video clips, interface backplate, button graphics, sound bites, animations, or applets, are just building blocks for the whole application you are creating. They are the pieces of the puzzle that you will finally assemble into an application that is far greater in value than the sum of the individual parts.

If you can think in terms of media components and their design, creation, and assembly, then you can approach the project in a phased and manageable way. In other words, try to eat the project in small bites rather than swallowing the whole thing in one gulp. Otherwise, chances are you'll choke.

By classifying your media components and listing them, you can then judge which items are sequential and depend on another item being completed before you can work on it. For instance, a video clip that incorporates an animation sequence cannot be done until the animation is completed. Designing

Figure 3.8

On drive D I have a directory layout that organizes my files into a combination of media component types and projects.

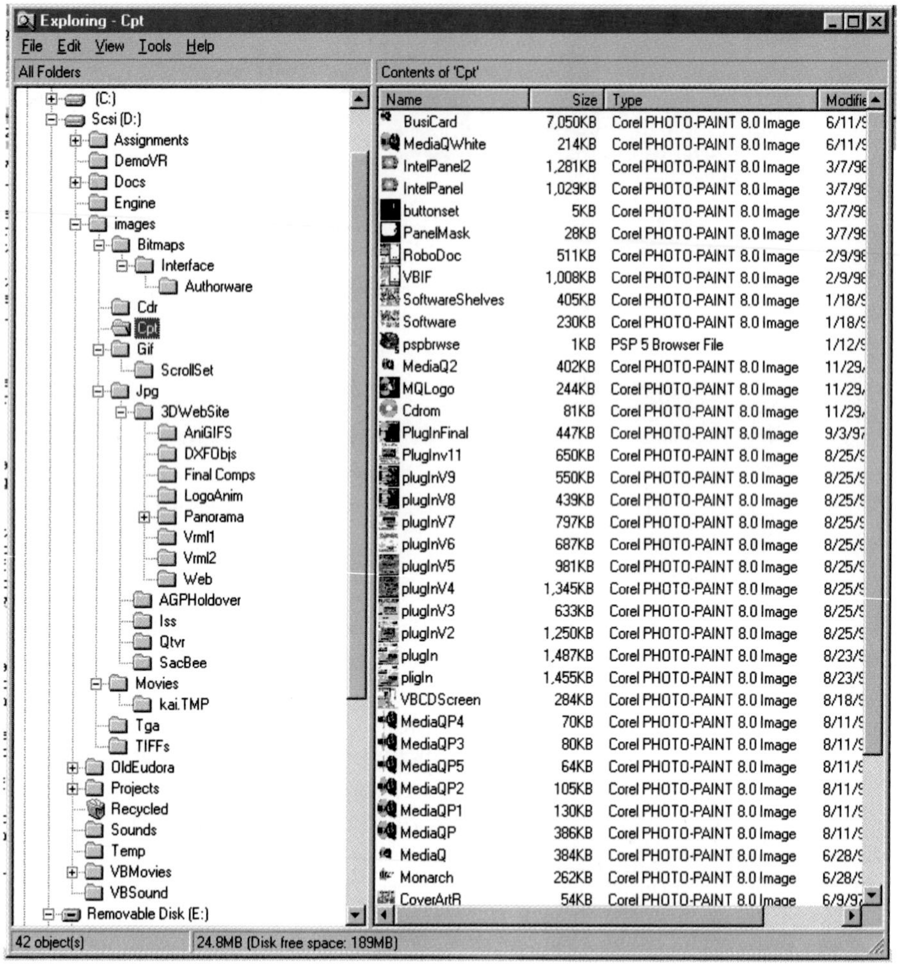

interactivity usually requires the controls and buttons to be designed first. Gather the pieces in separate directories on your hard drive (or removable drive), as shown in Figure 3.8, and when you have collected the pieces you need to begin assembly, then do so. Once I have completed a project, I archive that project's files to a CD-ROM and free up the space for the next one. Your system may be quite different, but it is important to develop an organized structure so that you can easily locate and sort your media files.

Starting the authoring process and creating the media pieces on the fly is an inefficient way to operate. Chances are you'll need to redo work on the early pieces because the last piece you created doesn't match them anymore.

Think of the multimedia project as one of those plastic models you may have created as a kid. Before you started to build your model plane, boat, or car, you had all the pieces laid out on a table; you had purchased your glue, paint, and brushes; and you had everything ready to assemble. Imagine if you had to fetch or even sculpt each piece as you went along, following only a design in your head!

Multimedia projects are not any more suitable for such an approach than are plastic models. A little patience at the beginning in collecting the required pieces will save a lot of time and grief later on.

PREPRODUCTION

Preproduction is preparing to produce the media component in question. Perhaps an image has to be converted to 24-bit color to accommodate the special effects you wish to apply, and then has to be converted back to 8-bit color depth.

An animated object may require a special material or logo painted on its surface in the animation, and these images may have to be created before the animating can start. If sound files are supplied on videotape, they will need to be digitized before you can edit them and crop sequences to suit the application.

Try to evaluate in advance as best you can the extent of such work. It may seem obvious at first, but a little quiet thought and evaluation of the project specifically for such preproduction effort will help prevent deadline and milestone overruns. Without such preparation work, much time can be lost and squandered through a lack of foresight.

Thinking in terms of what you need to prepare for each media component will prove a valuable exercise. In time, and with experience, this process will become second nature once you become familiar with the processes required to create each media component.

PRODUCTION AND POSTPRODUCTION

The rest of this book is dedicated to the production process and the skills required to create impressive multimedia content for your projects. There is often more to the production process than just using the software tool to get the job done. The best multimedia creators use the tools interchangeably to create greater works than using any of the tools on their own could produce.

For instance, you may be animating a space scene that shows a spacecraft flyby and then docking into a rotating space station. For this example, the same principles apply whether you are creating a forensic animation to recreate an auto accident or animating a box of soap for a commercial.

What if after animating the space flyby, it looks too clinical, that is, fake? Using a video editing product, you can apply postproduction techniques to the animated clip and turn a clinical scene into a realistic one. Postproduction techniques involve using another application to add additional features and effects to the media component after it has been created. In our example, you could apply camera blur to simulate actual film recording; particle effects and lens flares to simulate the rocket flames; perhaps some debris; and other subtle touches such as camera movement and some bright fades to simulate the docking impact and smoke billows.

In the interactive version of this book you can find an example of such a "before and after" postprocessed animation sequence in the Gallery section.

The same techniques apply to all of the media applications you will learn to use as a multimedia producer. A video sequence can be "painted on" using a technique called *rotoscoping* with Photoshop or Photo-Paint; a morphed sequence can be enhanced in a video editing application; a morphing program can be used to create a fill-in sequence between video clips or a special effect for use in a video editor; a sound editing application, such as Sound Forge, can be used to modify the soundtrack for a video clip and merge it with another from a different source. As your skills grow as a multimedia developer, you will find yourself jumping back and forth between your applications to create layered and sophisticated effects.

As your knowledge of these applications deepens, you will find yourself analyzing television and movie special effects to determine how you could reproduce those special effects on your development system. It will be the techniques that you can't figure out that will impress you!

TESTING

Your job is not done when you finish the last element of your multimedia project. The testing phase of any project is *critical*. It absolutely cannot be overlooked. In some circumstances, depending on the clients and your relationship with them, the clients can do the testing on their time. Usually, however, you

postproduction technique
A process applied to a multimedia piece to produce the final effect, once the raw media content is first produced, such as a computer animation file, or a digitized video clip from a camcorder. For example, a live-shot video clip may have 3D titles superimposed onto it and perhaps a shooting star particle trail may be added. These treatments of the raw materials are postproduction techniques.

morphing
A visual animation technique that distorts the shape of one image to match that of another while fading between them.

don't want to allow this, as you will be exposing your flaws to clients, which is never a good idea.

Always allow a nice chunk of time toward the end for testing, revision, and repair of any problems that testing exposes. Once a bug is encountered and fixed, it must be tested again to verify that it is fixed at the point in the application where it was encountered and anywhere else in the product. Sometimes repairing one bug introduces a different bug, and then that one has to be fixed. Cycling through the debugging process can take quite some time, especially when it depends on outside testers to get back to you in a timely manner.

It is very tempting, especially if you work alone, to do the testing yourself. This will never do. As the developer you will subconsciously anticipate what should happen when a particular button is pressed, or when another video clip comes up. This is akin to proofreading your own writing. Not only are you too close to it to be objective, but you subconsciously read ahead and fill in the blanks in the script when you should be identifying and fixing such errors.

You cannot predict how someone who has never seen your product before will use it. What you consider intuitive controls may look foreign to others simply because they don't have the insight you have into the design of the piece to correctly interpret the images! Independent testing can really help create a robust, bulletproof, easy-to-use product.

Independent testing also gives you feedback on how your product performs on a variety of computer systems. Whether your product is a CD-ROM or a Web site, you would like it to behave the same way for all users, and the testing process will prove this and/or indicate where you need to make changes to achieve this design goal.

PRODUCT DELIVERY

Up to the point of wrapping your multimedia project for delivery, the development processes required for the media components of your multimedia application, whether it is to run on a CD-ROM, on a DVD-ROM, on a Web site, or over an intranet, are by and large the same. Consider your multimedia development skills interchangeable over projects. Whether you are creating a Macromedia Director interface for a CD-ROM product or a Director Shockwave interface for your Web site, the development skills, knowledge, and techniques are fundamentally the same. Planning, storyboarding, collecting content, and developing and editing that content is the same process for most all multimedia product development, irrespective of the chosen delivery format. Deciding on your delivery format will determine the final authoring and wrapping up of the project. Subsequently, this delivery format choice may require specialized skills, techniques, and content formatting for the chosen delivery vehicle. The nice thing about this common early-development approach to multimedia production is that if you wish to produce the same product in another delivery format (say a CD-ROM-based product you would like to modify for the Web), you will only have to reformat some of the content and re-author to suit the new final location.

The delivery system will also have performance considerations that you will have to plan for. For example, a DVD-ROM will do a far superior job of presenting video than will a Web site. Plan for the delivery system you intend to use, and format your media components to suit. As you read through subsequent chapters and learn the skills needed to use these creative tools, pay attention to references to the different delivery formats—especially to Web considerations.

MULTIMEDIA DELIVERY SYSTEMS

A *delivery system* is the medium or data storage device used to deliver your multimedia application. This could be a CD-ROM, a floppy disk, a DVD-ROM, the

TABLE 3.3	Comparison of Performance and Capabilities of Various Storage Devices			
Description	**Capacity**	**Speed**	**Easily Updatable?**	**Easy to Create Applications?**
Floppy disk	1.44 MB	Very slow	Yes	Yes
Hard disk	Whatever free space is available; most commonly ranges up to 20 or more gigabytes.	Very fast. The fastest performance of all.	Yes. Data can be overwritten.	Yes
CD-ROM	650 MB	Fast	No. Once a CR-ROM is created, the contents are set. Multisession CD-Rs allow writing to the free space, but to read such a CD-R, the user must have a multisession-capable drive.	Yes, once a CD-ROM writing drive and software are purchased.
DVD-ROM	Up to 14 GB in the best format.	Fast	No. Once a DVD-ROM is mastered (a process available only from service bureaus at this point), it can't be updated or changed.	No. Currently a master DVD-ROM's content must be shipped to a third party to create a master for testing, and later to create production quantities of the DVD-ROM.
Internet, Web servers	Infinite. The capacity of a Web server is limited only by the storage capacity of the system, or the number of servers providing the service.	Variable. The current standard modem speed to design for is 28.8 Kbps. The speed (bandwidth) is as good as the *pipe* (Internet connection) the data are pushed through.	Yes. Media and data residing on a Web server are as changeable as any data on your hard disk. Once your ISP provides access to your Web server space, you can make any changes you want, whenever you want. If you own your own server, updates can be instant.	Yes. Any connected computer system, even an old system that has been written off, can be turned into a Web server with appropriate software.
Intranets (local-area and wide-area networks)	Same as for the Internet.	Variable. Bandwidth is usually not a problem; most intranets run on local-area networks, with cables connecting each system.	Yes. Same as for the Internet.	Yes. Same as for the Internet.

Internet, or an intranet. The primary multimedia delivery systems are compared in Table 3.3.

THE INTERNET

The Internet deserves special mention because the World Wide Web (the graphical form of the Internet) has been the greatest technological advance since the invention of the computer itself. Figure 3.9 shows a map of primary global Internet backbone connections. From these primary circuits, mostly fiber-optic connections, branch out all of the smaller connections that reach the hundreds of thousands of Internet service provider companies, which in turn reach your home and business personal computers. If you have ever browsed the Net, you have sent and received data over these circuits.

Figure 3.9

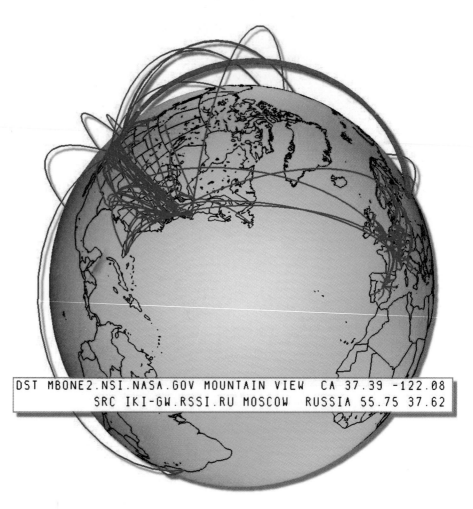

Figure 3.9
The primary international Internet backbone. These connections do not actually loop in the air between continents, but they do illustrate the Internet's complexity. It promises only to get bigger and more complex.

DST MBONE2.NSI.NASA.GOV MOUNTAIN VIEW CA 37.39 -122.08
SRC IKI-GW.RSSI.RU MOSCOW RUSSIA 55.75 37.62

The Internet provides the multimedia user with the following capabilities:

- *The connected PC.* The Internet connects your computer to millions of other computers to share information and data at will. Intel, a leading developer of computing technology, has been pursuing the goal of the *visually connected PC.* This is their concept of a multimedia-based computing system that can connect to other similar computers using the Web and other forms of telecommunications to share data, video, images, and other forms of multimedia. The Internet and multimedia provide the foundation for this vision.

- *Infinite storage and retrieval capacity.* When connected to the Net, you have a vast virtual disk drive of unfathomable capacity attached to your system. This is why *thin client PCs* are coming of age. These bare-bones systems need only minimum hard drive and peripheral capabilities and a connection to the Net, and they can function as well as the best loaded systems out there. Why purchase expensive system hardware and software when all you need to do is surf the Net and run online applications?

- *A uniform graphical environment.* Using a graphical browser application, you can access almost anything on the Web, use most any Web-based application, and view most any online data and images. You can communicate and interact with others online and share and find new data at will. This standard interface still allows quite a lot of design latitude for the creative developers among us, but the great thing is that within these parameters there are no limits to what you can achieve as a multimedia applications developer.

- *Platform independence.* As long as your clients use a graphical browser, such as Microsoft's Internet Explorer or Netscape's Navigator/Communicator, it doesn't matter what computer system they are using. Whether they are using a Mac, a PC, or a DEC Alpha or Amiga, they will all be able to view, use, and interact with your online application. This is the nearest thing we have as multimedia developers to true cross-platform compatibility.

- *Publishing power in the hands of the masses.* Companies quickly realized that entrepreneurs who possessed a little creativity, some initiative, and the right tools could create their own Web presence to compete with the big guys. When you view a Web site you get an immediate impression from its design about the caliber of the company behind it. But you really don't know whether this is a teenager's creation or a Web site created at great expense for a Fortune 100 corporation with annual revenue in excess of that of most small countries. What you see is what you get. What you do know is that you'd kill for the Fortune 100 company's Web design contract, but the teenager may have a better chance of getting it!

- *Multimedia on tap.* The Web has matured to the point that providing true multimedia applications over the Net is easier than ever. Media streaming technologies advance continuously and provide greater media performance through slower connection speeds. Products like Macromedia's Flash provide interactive graphical interfaces along with sound effects, audio and video streaming, and multimedia performance from a Web page.

- *Built-in redundancy-proofing.* The problem of computers and software becoming out-of-date so quickly does not necessarily apply to the Web. The latest versions of the browser applications that drive the Internet are free downloads. These browser applications are designed to accept technology advances in the form of plug-ins that upgrade the browser with whatever capability it needs to access the latest Web multimedia developments. And since these upgrades are usually free downloads, users can keep up with technology advances quite easily.

For you, the multimedia producer, the Internet represents a vast, insatiable, high demand for your work. While you may do work for distribution on CD-ROM or DVD-ROM, you will find a large proportion of your work will be Web-based.

This opportunity is yours to grasp. Given time, the Web may settle down, but at current growth rates the online population of those needing multimedia-enhanced Web sites to promote their goods, to fill orders, or to communicate with their customers will only grow.

THE INTERNET AND INTRANETS

All of the characteristics for the Internet apply to Intranets, which after all, are just private Internets within a company. Intranets are, by quite a margin, the fastest growing area of Internet technology sales. More Intranet servers are installed than Internet servers by two to one. This activity is creating a demand for multimedia applications to take advantage of these installations. You can have great multimedia applications over such a system without worrying about what speed your users will connect at and what system configuration they have. It's a controlled environment where these factors are predetermined.

WORKING IN THE INDUSTRY

The concept of a multimedia "industry" is a recent one. Other industries have dipped into the multimedia pot and have extended their work to encompass multimedia projects. Advertising agencies, video studios, graphic design shops, software developers, and educational institutions all applied multimedia to their existing work in response to client demand and competitive needs to add extra-special "dazzle" to their work. Some early multimedia productions show how bad the marriage of one of these traditionally nonmultimedia fields with the technology of multimedia can be when done in a haphazard fashion.

In 1996 Toyota Motor Corporation (www.toyota.com) released a multimedia CD-ROM advertising its automobile lineup. Even though this product was produced by one of the largest advertising agencies in the world, it proved how those not familiar with multimedia technology and concepts can get it wrong. The finished product was slow and unmanageable on even the fastest systems, mixed control visuals and metaphors, and included a mishmash of conflicting technologies. This resulted in a difficult and frustrating product to use.

In recent years, there has been an upsurge of companies whose sole purpose has been to develop multimedia solutions. The Internet has provided a needed boost for multimedia developers, and the advances on the Web have fueled this emerging industry.

WHERE ARE THE EXCITING JOBS?

You will read more about finding a job in multimedia in Chapter 17 (on the Web site), but you should keep the points raised in the following paragraphs in mind as you begin to learn and develop your multimedia skills. The Web site for this book also provides up-to-date information about jobs in this field, including salary surveys, job expectations, and job descriptions.

Multimedia development tends to fall into the following broad categories, though the cross-fertilization that goes on between these areas blurs the boundaries.

- *Promotional CD-ROM production.* Developing CD-ROM-based multimedia is a lucrative business that has increasing demands for products in this format. The competition from Web-based multimedia has almost settled down, and the increased volume in both industries more than compensates for any CD-ROM development work that has been converted to Web-based delivery. The trick in this field is to build a CD-ROM-based portfolio of your best work and list references once you have them. When Joe Mack wanted a job in multimedia development, he created his JobSeek CD-ROM (see Figure 2.23 in Chapter 2). He received thirteen job offers after sending out his CD-ROM portfolio. You will find a short movie on the creation of JobSeek in the interactive version of this book on the accompanying CD-ROM, in the Gallery section.

- *Multimedia Web site development.* Multimedia Web sites are in increasing demand. To tap into this market you will need to master the online multimedia tools and have your own showcase Web site to refer potential clients to. In this field more than any, work references are very important. Link your best work to your promotional site.

- *Multimedia supplement to the creative industries.* Many ad agencies, video production studios, and graphic design companies are looking for talented employees to bring them into the multimedia age. Their clients are becoming more sophisticated and demanding and want the level of technology and flair that they see in other digital formats. You'll be surprised with what happens when you drop off a résumé and a digital portfolio at these kind of companies.

- *Working for a multimedia company.* You may have difficulty identifying a multimedia company and then finding one that has an opening. The high-profile companies tend to be inundated with employment requests and the smaller, less conspicuous outfits tend to have all the help they need. However, an entry-level position in a small to medium-sized firm is not that difficult to come across, as those companies tend to be in a growth mode. Be sure to check them out, though, as not all companies can survive in this competitive field. You may have to start as a hands-on entry-level technician, but advancement tends to be fairly easy for those who are skilled (and patient).

GOING IT ALONE?

Have you thought about being a freelance multimedia developer? There is a lot to be said for going it alone in this field. Getting work as a freelancer depends on the credibility of your work and your commitment to getting a quality job completed on time.

To make it as a freelancer, you will have to be able to demonstrate good examples of your work. If you can show good references, and there is demand for your services, you can build a small and lucrative clientele that will come back again and again for your business. Many video production studios, graphic design shops, and advertising agencies are on the lookout for a good, reliable multimedia producer that they can partner with to compensate for their lack of skills in this new area. A business card, a CD-ROM portfolio, and a Web site will go a long way in getting business.

By providing an invaluable service to your clients, you can achieve a lot with just a modest investment in a multimedia development system at home. Multimedia development has got to be one of the best cottage industry opportunities of the century!

AVOIDING PITFALLS

Many issues were covered in this chapter, and here we highlight the pitfalls you should avoid at all cost. First, when setting up your multimedia development system or studio, you will have many brands and products to choose from, and all claim to be the best choice! What should you do?

You will need impartial advice—which is very difficult to find in this industry, mainly because many developers advocate their personal choice of system as some sort of justification for their investment. If you ask the advice of a multimedia developer, then you place him or her in a position of "expert." From there, how can such people recommend anything other than what they currently use? If they do so, then they are also saying that the tools they use are inadequate for the job and that their choices of equipment were wrong! This is not likely the case.

The best solution is to get the advice of several developers and weigh their recommendations. If there are common recommendations from developers in different organizations and fields, then you will begin to see a winner among the many offerings. A good source of impartial advice is your local college or university extension if either offers multimedia courses. Often instructors will be willing to talk with you about buying or upgrading a system as long as you don't take too much of their time.

Magazines are the best source of product recommendation. Their frequent product review articles usually recommend a clear favorite and rank the available products on a feature-by-feature basis. This book's Web site has a section offering links to online magazines and product reviews for you to use.

Second, planning your multimedia project in advance will help you avoid a multitude of potential problems. This cannot be overemphasized. Not only can you "see" the whole project at once, but so can your client, and this shows control over the project that can only inspire confidence in your skills.

Third, when considering a career in multimedia, look beyond the horizon at possibilities that may not seem obvious. Some friends of mine develop multimedia titles for a local cable TV company. Their training products are used nationwide and are well sought after. Not the sort of work you'd expect from your cable guy, is it? Multimedia is such a pervasive collection of technologies that it is possible to find an element of it in most any industry. And that's where the new opportunities for multimedia developers will come from. Companies that now farm out their multimedia development may hire these skills to produce their multimedia applications in-house under tighter control. There's another job opening!

Chapter Summary

- Getting started in multimedia requires not only that you develop a familiarity with the many technologies that make up multimedia, but that you also find your own strengths and weaknesses therein. You must determine your "place" within the realms of multimedia.

- Most currently available personal computers make terrific multimedia development workstations with a few software and hardware add-ons.

- Both Macintosh and Windows-based systems make sound multimedia development systems, and anyone who tells you otherwise is biased. The most versatile and proficient multimedia developers use both platforms.

- The multimedia production cycle should be followed carefully. Using the multimedia production cycle as a road map for development can save you much grief later and help you avoid missing crucial steps.

- There are several ways to deliver your multimedia product, and you must determine which one works best for you and your client. Consider the pros and cons of delivery via CD-ROM, DVD, the Internet, an intranet, and maybe even floppy disk.

- There are many ways to achieve gainful employment in this field. Determining your position and role in this field is an important step. When considering a career in multimedia, look beyond the horizon at possibilities that may not seem obvious.

- When setting up your multimedia development system or studio, seek the advice of several developers and weigh their recommendations. A good source of impartial advice is your local college or university extension.

Key Terms and Concepts

authoring, 44
CMYK, 47
digitizing tablet, 44

dot pitch, 45
interpolated
  resolution, 47

morphing, 57
multi-session, 49
optical resolution, 47

postproduction
  techniques, 57

Checking Your Knowledge and Skills

1. What do you consider to be the most important aspect of multimedia project planning, and why? Explain your answer.

2. List the primary requirements of a multimedia development computer workstation and describe how each feature of such a system is used in the multimedia development process.

3. Given your requirements for a multimedia development system as you defined them in question 2, develop a budget for the purchase of this system. Obtain a quote for an exact matching system, either from a magazine, online, at a local computer store, or using a combination of sources, and see how well you did in keeping to your budget.

4. List and rank in order of importance six primary reasons why the Internet has been such a resounding success. Explain the relative importance of each reason.

5. Design a concept for a multimedia product and storyboard your ideas. Explain the benefits of having a storyboard, and describe how the process of storyboarding your idea helped (if it did) your development of the concept.

6. Find a Web site that in your opinion is a terrific example of a multimedia product. How do you think it would convert to a CD-ROM-based multimedia product, and what in your opinion would be the advantages of doing so?

Critical Thinking Challenges

At this stage, you have developed a sense of the initial starting processes for a multimedia development project and have seen some of the possible jobs where these skills can be applied. Now consider the following:

1. If you are currently a dedicated PC or Macintosh user, draft a persuasive case for the adoption of the other platform as the best multimedia development system available, whether you personally believe it or not. Use current technology offerings to support your argument. Did this exercise change your mind, or did it give you any insights?

2. Describe your ideal multimedia development workstation, including software and peripherals, from currently available technology (no dreaming up new and futuristic toys). Summarize why this is the best system for you. If you had to sacrifice three hardware and three software elements, what would they be, and

why? Why did you keep those that you did? Could you still develop multimedia titles with the remaining system?

3. Which would you prefer, the multimedia job of your dreams, starting at minimum wage, or a lower managerial position in a multimedia production company with no hands-on work at all for an attractive salary? Why?

4. If a client came to you with a project to promote her chain of car dealerships, and she wanted to project an upbeat image (her company used the term "MTV" in their description), would you recommend a CD-ROM or Web site approach? Keep in mind that the purpose of the project is to attract customers, to coax them into signing away a large chunk of change for the shiny new vehicle on the lot, and to project that trendy image. Justify your recommendation.

Hands-on Exercises
PROJECT PLANNING

Using the evaluation copy of Designer's Edge available as a download via a link on this book's Web site or another planning tool, develop a proposal for a multimedia product for a local business. Designers Edge provides step-by-step guidance and a sequence of questions and phases for you to complete to execute this exercise. A tutorial is available on Allen Communications Web site at www.allencomm.com/software/designer/index2.html.

1. Collect all of the information about the project you can at the beginning.

2. Install Designer's Edge and input all of the factors and information you have collected.

3. Information that Designer's Edge asks for, which you have not yet collected, must be determined and entered at this stage. Determine the missing data through research and/or client interviews. If a required information item is inappropriate to your project, then you may skip it, but be careful to review it again toward the end. Often the need for missing information becomes apparent after the other elements of the project are all in view and are organized.

4. When you have completed this exercise, print out the reports provided by Designer's Edge and ask a col-

league, an instructor, or a friend who was not part of the development process to review it.

5. Having created a persuasive proposal for the project, decide how you would present it to the client. Offer a choice of a CD-ROM or a Web site–based product and detail the pros and cons of these options.

Describe the benefits to the client in hiring you to create this product.

6. Use a storyboard to present a visual of the project and to invite the client's input. Use this input to revise the project parameters and represent your revised version.

Master Project
THE PLAN

In Chapter 2 you developed the concept for the master project. You have, at this stage, developed a good idea for the concept and layout of your digital portfolio (if not, this would be a good time to go back and check out the master project instructions in Chapters 1 and 2). Now it is time to start planning and documenting this project and preparing for the next stage—the actual design.

Develop a description of the multimedia résumé you wish to produce. Design a storyboard and a flowchart of the navigation that the user is expected to take through the product. Begin collecting the materials and content for the project and assess the size and scope of the task. Define your audience and what platform(s) your product will be able to run on. Find examples of multimedia port-folios that you admire and use them to formulate your design. You will find links to suggested examples of online digital portfolios on this book's Web site.

Develop a timeline for the development of your digital portfolio, and set milestones and deadlines for yourself. Give yourself ample time to complete the project, allowing enough time for testing and revision.

Create a binder for this documentation and screen-shots of digital portfolios your admire. You will be referring to it as your master project develops.

This book's Web site has a page dedicated to a list of links to online digital portfolios, good *and* bad. Use this as a resource to finding your own style.

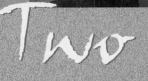

MULTIMEDIA

GRAPHIC

DESIGN

4

MULTIMEDIA BUILDING BLOCKS: 2D GRAPHICS

Chapter Outline

Chapter Objectives

After completing this chapter, you will be able to:

● Discuss the significance of graphic design and image choices for your multimedia project's interface.

● Define the concept of resolution and explain why resolution takes on many different meanings when applied to different images and devices.

● Describe the role of computer input, display, and output devices and their quality identifiers and characteristics.

● Discuss the relationships between image quality, size, and performance factors in a multimedia application, and describe how to adjust these properties to achieve your design goals.

● Describe the concept of color depth for both computer displays and digital images.

● Define the concept of image color palettes and describe how to manipulate them to avoid associated display problems.

● Distinguish between line art and bitmapped images in a computer context.

● Acquire the image resources you will need to design your interface and characterize the elements of good multimedia interface design.

Chapter Overview

As you have learned, the interface is the most important element of any multimedia production. In this chapter you will learn the principles and processes that are applied in the creation of an interface, which will prepare you for this book's hands-on component. While this chapter may get a little technical, bear with the details and try to get your mind around them. They will be of tremendous benefit to you when you are working with your media components and need to manipulate them to fit your multimedia CD-ROM or Web page production.

Probably the most significant component of any multimedia production is its graphics. Where would any multimedia piece be without graphics? No photos, no interface, no buttons, no toolbar, no pleasing images or visual icons? Good graphic design is as crucial to a multimedia product as the combination of all the remaining elements of the work. The other media components may be more conspicuous, but not as much as poor graphic design would be.

Imagine entering a well-designed and nicely decorated room like one of those picture-perfect rooms you see in the home decor magazines at the store. You can "feel" that this room is well designed because it appeals to you. You see the furniture and the fixtures, the drapes and the pictures on the wall. Now imagine all those elements in the same room, but there is no room! No walls, just the same collection of elements in the middle of a parking lot somewhere. Sounds nasty, doesn't it? The graphic design of your multimedia project is the walls, the wallpaper, the flooring, and the ceiling of your multimedia "room." You may not notice them, but they support all of the other elements. A good interface design works best when not noticed as being significant.

To create an easy-to-use and well-received multimedia product, you must pay close attention to the look, feel, and performance of each graphical element in the product. It is not enough to create stunning designs. You must also format these digital components in the most efficient and streamlined way.

In this chapter you will learn about graphic file formats, how and why they work, and how best to optimize them to suit your multimedia project. You will learn the technical principles behind these graphic elements. In Chapter 5 you will begin to apply these principles in your graphic design.

RESOLUTION

color resolution
The number of colors displayable in any image file format or computer screen display setting.

The term *resolution* is most often associated with an image's degree of detail. It can also refer to the quality capability of a graphic output device (monitor) or input device (scanner), and is sometimes used to refer to the number of colors that an image can display. Confusing? Don't worry. You will learn how to distinguish between these meanings and understand what resolution is all about.

COLOR RESOLUTION

bit
The smallest piece of computer data available. In the same way that letters are used to make words, which are used to make sentences, bits (*binary digits*) are assembled to make "words" of eight bits, called *bytes,* and multiple bytes are used to form the instructions used by computers to get their work done.

Color resolution, also called *color depth,* specifies the number of bits used in an image file to store color information. A bit, or *binary digit,* is the smallest unit of data in the computer world. Computers use a counting system called *binary,* from the Latin word for "two." This means that computers can understand only two values: on and off, much like a switch (see Figure 4.1). When a computer counts, it can do so only with the two digits, 1 and 0.

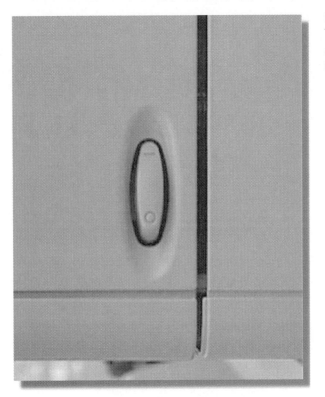

When we count, we use ten digits—the numbers 0 through 9. To go any higher in counting, we use combinations of these ten symbols to represent larger numbers. For example, 10 is a combination of the symbols 1 and 0. We call this the *decimal* system, from the Latin word for "ten."

With only two digits, the computer runs out of numbers after 1. Remember, it has only 0 and 1 with which to count. To go any further, it needs a coded combination of 1's and 0's to be able to understand values greater than *on* and *off*.

To this end, computer scientists gave the computer an ability to count in coded groups of eight 1's and 0's. This 8-bit code can represent a number value by the combination of 1's and 0's. So the values from 00000000 through 11111111 include, for example, 01001101, 00000100, 10000001, 10100011, and any other combination. Starting at the code representing zero (shown as 00000000), this system can represent as many values as there are combinations of eight 1's and 0's, up to the highest value of all 1's (11111111). A combination of eight bits is called a byte.

There are only 256 possible combinations within an 8-bit byte. Using this binary method, as seen in Figure 4.2, 00000000 would add to zero, 00100000 would add to 4 (as only the 4 was switched on), 1010000 would add to 5 (1 and 4 are switched on), 01001100 would add to 50 (sum of 2, 16 and 32 being switched on as shown) and 11111111 would add up all number values to give 255.

This is why an 8-bit system is also called a 256-value system. And since you start counting at zero, the biggest value you can count to is 255. "But you said there were 256 values!" There are. If you started counting from 1, then you would reach 256. But since you have to include a zero value, and it takes up the first combination, then there are only 255 combinations left, and that's the maximum number you can reach before running out of combinations.

Obviously, computers can count higher than 255. Combinations of bytes achieve this. The more 8-bit groups ganged together, the bigger the number of combinations you can achieve.

Since the computer has to store all these values, it uses a byte to store one number or character, and combinations of bytes to store more complicated data.

byte

A piece of computer data made up of eight bits in a specific order. Much as the dots and dashes of Morse code are arranged to describe letters and words, bits are arranged in groups of eight to form bytes.

Figure 4.2

The way the 8-bit code of a byte is evaluated is by assigning a value to each bit position in the group of eight as shown. If the switch is "on" (value shown as 1), you count that number as being present and then add up all numbers present from left to right.

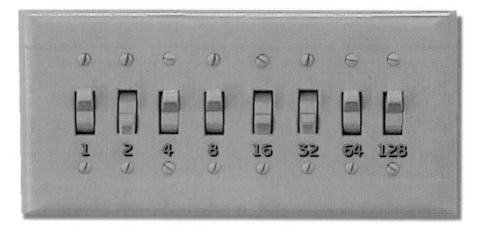

Soon you will need thousands (kilobytes), millions (megabytes), and billions (gigabytes) of bytes to be stored on your system. That's where your big hard drive comes in.

So when a computer video display card is called an 8-bit or 24-bit display, you now know that this is a reference to a one-byte or a three-byte display system, respectively. Now they are never described in bytes, but if you keep that notion in mind you can figure out easily how many colors can be displayed by the video display card and roughly how much memory the image will take up.

For instance, take an 8-bit display as shown in Figure 4.3. The maximum number of colors that such a system can show is 256. That's why it is also called a 256-color display. Why only 256? Because it uses eight bits (one byte) to display each dot of color (called a *pixel*). Since we know that there are only 256 values

Figure 4.3

The same image at different color resolutions. Both the 8-bit and 4-bit images have been forced to accept the system palette of colors to illustrate the image differences and to show the dithering (random pattern of dots) in the image.

24-bit, 16 million colors

8-bit, 256 colors

4-bit, 16 colors

1-bit, 2 colors

that a byte can represent, then that is the limit of the different color combinations that such a display system can show at any time.

With a 24-bit display, there are three bytes (3 times 8 bits equals 24 bits) available to store color values. You could also look at this from the perspective of an 8-bit display multiplied by three ($256 \times 256 \times 256$ colors). This gives a 24-bit display sixteen million (actually 16,777,216) color value possibilities for each pixel on the screen. With such a huge combination, or *palette,* to choose from, such a display system is often also called *true color.*

IMAGE RESOLUTION

Image resolution is quite a different beast from color resolution. It refers to the number of pixels (*picture elements,* or dots) used to represent the image. It also has a relationship to *device resolution,* namely the screen's display resolution.

Every computer image is displayed as a series of pixels arranged in rows and columns. In particular, bitmapped images are stored as a large array of colored dots that from a distance (the distance from your normal viewing position to your monitor screen) seem to merge together to give a recognizable picture. The effect is much like the dots you see when looking at a newspaper or magazine photo under a magnifying glass—when you view the picture normally you no longer see just dots, but rather a detailed picture. Your eyes compensate for the lack of visual information between the dots, and your brain's visual interpretation of the image fills in the missing spaces. Figure 4.4 illustrates this process.

Because image resolution refers to the width and height of the image in pixels, and because each pixel needs a certain amount of memory space to store the color of each pixel, you can determine the memory required to display and store an image with just these two pieces of information.

For example, a 100-x-100-pixel image has a total of 10,000 pixels (100 multiplied by 100). If this is an 8-bit color resolution image, then you know that one byte (eight bits) is required to store the color information for each dot. 10,000 one-byte dots gives you a memory requirement of 10,000 bytes, or about 10 KB (kilobytes). If this is a 24-bit color image, then 24 bits is the same as three bytes (if one byte equals eight bits), and 3 bytes times 10,000 pixels is a total memory requirement of 30,000 bytes, or about 30 KB. Note that there is a threefold memory cost to using 24-bit color compared to 8-bit color. If you can get away with 8-bit color resolution, then the performance of that image in your multimedia piece will be better.

If you find this difficult to digest, give it a little time and try again. It helps to know the basis for, and the relationship between, these different forms of resolution.

image resolution

The number of pixels used to display an image—usually given by pixel width times pixel height (such as a 640×480 image). The greater the number of pixels used to display an image, the better the image detail definition will be, but the file size will also increase.

pixel

A dot of colored light that, when grouped together with many other pixels in a large array, represents an image on a computer screen.

bitmapped images

An image displayed on a computer screen as an array of colored dots, called *pixels.* When viewed at normal viewing distance from the computer screen they give an impression of an image.

Figure 4.4
A 320-x-240-pixel-resolution image. The smaller image to the right is a 100-x-100-pixel piece of the larger image. The smaller inset at the bottom is a 30-x-33-pixel piece of the above images (can you find it in the larger images?). When magnified, this small image shows the array of 30 pixels across by 33 pixels down as individual dots of color.

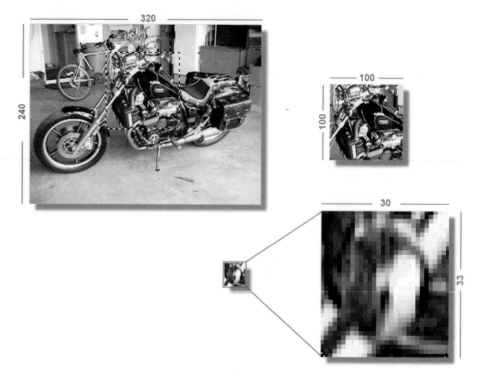

The next section shows the relationship between image resolution and the resolution of the device displaying, printing, or scanning the image.

DEVICE RESOLUTION

The resolution of your hardware device will be stated as part of the product's specification. It should be apparent on the packaging, in the manuals, and in the literature for the device. The primary devices to be aware of are input devices such as scanners; display devices such as your computer display adapter (also known as a video card) and monitor; and your output device, which is usually your printer.

INPUT DEVICE (SCANNER).   Your scanner will specify two key resolutions from which you can assess its capabilities: scanning resolution and the color resolution.

scanning resolution
The resolution in dots per inch at which you choose to scan an image.

Scanning resolution is defined in dots per inch (dpi). This is the number of discrete points of color information the scanner can "see" in a given inch. If your scanner is rated for 300-dpi resolution, this means that to scan a square-inch picture, it will create a digital image that is 300 × 300 pixels in dimension. It can "see" down to a 300th of an inch. While this is quite impressive, most scanners now have a resolution of 600 dpi.

As discussed in Chapter 3, a scanner's resolution specification is often given in an optical resolution and a higher interpolated resolution value. So a scanner with an optical resolution of 600 dpi and an interpolated resolution of 2,400 dpi will scan at only 600-dpi resolution, but the images can be converted into a 2,400-dpi image by the scanning software. This is useful for projects that are to be printed by a printing bureau or company. High-quality full-color printing—of the caliber you would find in a glossy brochure, for instance—requires at least a 2,400-dpi-resolution image. Since scanners that can optically scan at that definition are extremely expensive, a good alternative is a less expensive scanner with software that can interpolate a higher image resolution to compensate for the lower optical resolution. The result, to the eye, is a high-definition image that looks darn-near perfect.

Scanner color resolution is the same as image color resolution, which was explained in the previous section. Many scanners offer 32-bit color resolution; again, this seemingly excessive value (billions of colors when our eyes can deal with only ten million) is to cater to those who want to do full-color CMYK work for professionally printed end results. There is even a 48-bit color resolution for really high-end work.

DISPLAY DEVICE (DISPLAY ADAPTER AND MONITOR).   So far you've read about the resolutions that refer to image size. The display adapter/monitor combination brings additional definitions into the mix that affect the way you view the images.

The color resolution and pixel dimensions that are used for images, as you have seen, also are used to describe a computer's onscreen display. If a computer displays a full screen (called the *desktop*) that is 640 × 480 pixels in dimension, this means that the biggest image the computer can *completely* show while using those settings is one that is also 640 × 480 pixels. If your image is larger than that, then you must either live with seeing only a 640-x-480-pixel piece of it, or change your desktop resolution to a higher setting, as shown in Figure 4.5. The most common PC desktop resolutions for a computer display are 640 × 480, 800 × 600, 1024 × 768, and 1280 × 960. These values are the desktop size shown by the video display card, and have no bearing on the physical size of the screen used to view it on.

For example, whether you view the evening news on a 60-inch big-screen projection television or on a tiny 9-inch screen, the images you view are exactly the same and always fill the screen. On the bigger screen you do not see the news presenters at the same 9-inch size as on the tiny screen. If this were the case you would conceivably see around the edges of the set and see all of the crew, the cameras, the microphone boom, and the lighting in the ceiling! The actual broadcast images always scale themselves to fit the dimensions of the TV device you are using. Likewise, whatever resolution you set your desktop display to on your computer, the image will fill the monitor screen no matter what size the monitor is. A larger monitor, however, makes it easier on the eyes to view detail, just as it is easier to see detail on a large-screen TV.

Figure 4.5
An 800-x-600-pixel image as it would be displayed on a system with a desktop size setting of 640 × 480. Whether shown on a 14-inch or a 21-inch screen, the image remains the same, as the desktop resolution settings haven't changed. Monitors are measured by the diagonal distance between opposing corners.

Figure 4.6

The red, green, and blue dots etched into the phosphor coating on the inside of your TV screen are much easier to see than those on a computer monitor because the TV screen has a much coarser dot pitch. The dot pitch shown is the distance between two of the same color dots expressed in millimeters.

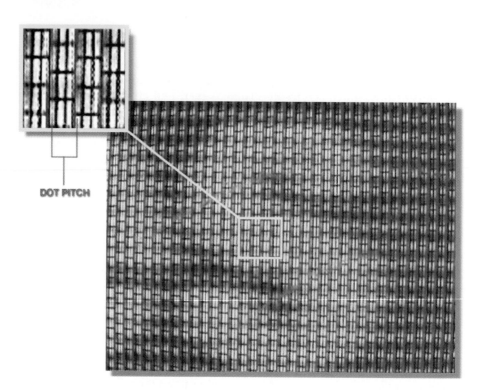

DOT PITCH

However, a measure of monitor device resolution that determines the quality of the picture is the dot pitch of the screen. Dot pitch is the distance in millimeters between dots of the same color. The monitor, just like a television set, displays images by adjusting the intensity of red, green, and blue dots on the inside of the screen. Figure 4.6 shows a close-up of the letter s as shown on a TV screen, and the top left inset image shows a further magnification of those red, green, and blue dots.

For computer monitors, the dot pitch has to be much finer. You can see the red, green, and blue dots of a TV screen with the naked eye. On a computer monitor, the smaller dot pitch makes the dots far less obvious. Typical computer screens have a .28 dot pitch. This means that there are .28 millimeters between dots of the same color. Figure 4.7 shows an image we have already encountered as it is displayed on my 17-inch computer monitor in a graphics program. The larger image on the right shows a close-up of a small detail of the screen. You can just about begin to see the individual red, green, and blue dots. This close-up is at the same magnification as the close-up of the TV screen (Figure 4.6), where you have no trouble distinguishing individual red, green and blue dots. The smaller the dot-pitch value, the better the resolution of the monitor.

The display adapter's resolution is usually 72 dpi. This means that the screen will show 72 dots of image information for every visual inch of image. So if you scan an image at 300 dpi, and then show it on a 72-dpi display, it will appear huge, because an image that has 300 dots in every scanned inch needs approximately 4.17 inches of 72-dpi screen to display each inch of the original image. (300 / 72 = 4.17). The net result is that the image will appear about four times bigger than it did on the scanner bed. You will have to scale it down to 25% zoom to be able to see it.

When scanning or creating an image for a multimedia product, an image resolution of 72 dpi is usually sufficient; bigger than that is overkill. Again, the higher dpi ratings are intended for printed output. A 72-dpi image printed on a 600-dpi laser printer would look coarse and bad. Therefore, you would like to match an image resolution of 600 dpi with that of your printer to get the best

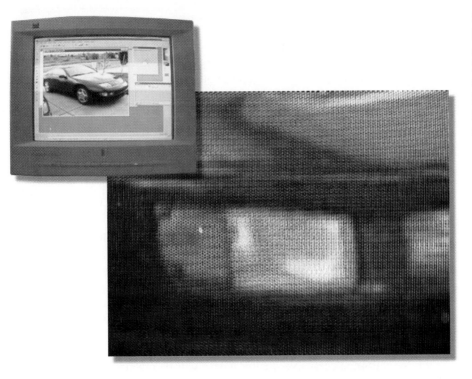

Figure 4.7
My 17-inch computer monitor
displaying a picture of a car. The
image on the bottom right shows
a close-up of a detail of that
image, and you can begin to see
the individual dots of the screen
resolution appear.

quality from that device. For a 72-dpi display, however, it will have to be reduced to match that screen resolution to look right.

Display adapters also have a color resolution setting. What happens if you have a 256-color display and want to show an image that has sixteen million colors? The display adapter will automatically do a "best fit" of the 256 colors available in its palette to show the image. Often the display adapter will introduce image dithering to increase the apparent color range by mixing dots of colors to approximate shades of colors that it doesn't have available. Figure 4.3 shows how the 256-color image uses dithering to smooth out the shades of colors.

In multimedia, it is best to design your application to work on the lowest-specification system, which is a 640-×-480, 256-color display. If it works well on such a system, it will work well on any other system. Keeping your graphic content within this size and optimized for an 8-bit palette has great advantages, though it may take extra work to compress your work to this level. We will have more discussion on that later.

image dithering

A process of displaying images using a random dot pattern to give the viewer an impression of more detail and colors than the file format or computer display can actually support.

OUTPUT DEVICE (PRINTER). The printer's resolution is a simple dots-per-inch relationship between the data being sent to it and the printer's dpi capabilities. The printer device places that many dots of ink onto the paper. A 600-dpi color printer will print best an image that also has 600-dpi resolution. If the image is a 72-dpi image, the printer will either print it very small (at 600 dots per inch, 72 dots don't come even close to covering an inch) or fill in the required dots with approximated values. Sometimes this gives an image a "pixilated" (blocky) appearance. Usually the graphics program figures all of this out for you, but if you want to get a precise image out of your printer, it is a good idea to match resolutions.

To gauge the quality of a printer, watch primarily for the dpi value. Furthermore, be aware that there are special papers that can, especially in inkjet printers, enhance the quality of the printout. They don't affect the device resolution, but simply do a better job of handling the ink dots and prevent them from *wicking* (soaking) into the paper and blotching and fading.

SIZE VERSUS RESOLUTION VERSUS PERFORMANCE

As you have already learned, there is a direct relationship between the quality of an image file and the amount of memory required to store and display it. The higher the definition and the more colors you wish to display in any image all increase (often dramatically) the size of the image data.

With multimedia applications, there is an inverse relationship between an image's size and its performance. The bigger the file, the more data the computer has to get to the screen to display it. Take our previous example of a 100-×-100-pixel image weighing in at 10 KB for an 8-bit color version and at 30 KB for a 24-bit version. The poor old computer has to work three times as hard to display the 24-bit image which may look just as good in 8-bit mode. If all of your graphics are this "fat," it may compromise the overall performance of the multimedia piece.

You could end up with a beautiful-looking multimedia application that irritates users because it is slow and unresponsive. In the case of video, where the computer may have to display thirty versions of the image in succession every second to show motion, these size issues can quickly bog down the performance of the application. Figure 4.8 illustrates this balancing act you must follow to squeeze the best possible performance out of your multimedia CD-ROM, DVD-ROM, or Web site.

There are many ways to adjust your image's size and performance characteristics while retaining acceptable quality. These will be discussed in detail in the next chapter. For now you should keep in mind the options that follow.

resizing

Changing the pixel width-by-height size of an image.

resampling

The process of converting a digital image to a different resolution (also used in the context of digital video and digital sound).

RESIZING AND RESAMPLING. While *resizing* and *resampling* both refer to creating a different-sized image from the original, they do their job quite differently. Resizing simply expands or contracts an image to the new required size, while resampling actually rebuilds a new pixel pattern for the same images at the new size. The visual difference between these two processes is that resampling gives an even, smooth image in the new dimensions, while resizing, having stretched or compressed those pixels into the new dimensions, can introduce interference patterns if the pixels no longer align as they should.

Figure 4.8

The inverse relationship between image quality and performance is a balancing act. You have to balance what you believe to be acceptable quality for the piece with its performance capabilities.

Figure 4.9
This cropped image, bottom left, shows only the rev counter, which is the subject matter required for the application—the rest of the image is superfluous. Cropping created a 76 KB 164-x-160 image from the original 480-x-360 image shown, weighing in at 506 KB. The cropped image was further optimized by reducing the color depth to 256 colors. Notice the comparable visual quality.

Either way, the resulting image can perform better if you resize or resample it to a smaller format. Be careful, however, because these terms can get mixed up in different graphic design applications. Test them to see for yourself what they are doing before committing to the changes they will make to your work.

CROPPING.   By cropping (trimming) an image in size and removing unnecessary edges from around the main subject of the image, you can shed quite a few bytes. If there is any opportunity to crop your image and still retain its intended purpose, then do so. It all adds up. Figure 4.9 shows how a cropped image displays the subject matter far better than the complete image.

cropping
The process of trimming the image size and removing unnecessary edges around the main subject.

FILE FORMATTING.   As you will read later in this chapter, there are many formats in which to save your image file. Some do a better compression job than others, creating smaller file sizes on disk as a result. By experimenting with these formats, you will quickly develop a sense for which format is most appropriate to your needs.

COLOR-DEPTH ADJUSTMENT.   Color-depth adjustment is the same as adjusting the color resolution. As you can see in Figure 4.9, the reduction in this instance of the cropped image to a 256-color image not only reduced the image size by 430 KB, but didn't really affect image quality. Because of the small range of different colors in the cropped image, an optimized (specially chosen) palette of 256 colors was enough to go around and not cause any dithering. Reducing the color overhead of your images can save a lot of disk and display memory space. Figure 4.10 is similar to Figure 4.3, but it shows actual file sizes for this image at 640-x-480 resolution. Smaller file size means greater performance.

COLOR PALETTES

Remember how each of the image color resolutions also could be described in terms of a set number of colors? The number and choice of colors is called a palette. Just as a painter uses a wooden palette, the computer graphic artist chooses colors from a digital palette (see Figure 4.11).

palette
The entire collection of all individual colors used to display a digital image.

Figure 4.10

This illustration, similar to the one shown in Figure 4.3, shows the actual image file sizes for this image at 640-x-480 resolution. Note that the 256-color version does not use an optimized palette, and if one were applied, the difference between the top two images would be difficult to discern, as you can see in Figure 4.12.

Color palettes become a design issue when you drop down to 8-bit color images and when you run your product on 8-bit color displays. For displays above 8-bit, the computer display adapter can automatically sort out any palette problems you may encounter. Depending on the color resolution, your images may have different palettes, and when you get into 8-bit palettes and below, there can be a marked difference between using predefined set palettes, such as the system palette, and a palette specifically optimized for that image.

Figure 4.12 shows several images and their different palettes. Notice the high quality of the 8-bit image using an *optimized color palette*. When an opti-

Figure 4.11

Artists have been using wooden palettes for thousands of years (shown at left). Computer artists use digital palettes, which operate on the same principle. The digital palette shown at right as a rectangle of 256 colors is from an 8-bit, 256-color image.

Figure 4.12
Several variations of the same image, converted to different color resolutions, provide for those images different color palettes, as shown beneath each image.

mized color palette is used, the small range of 256 colors can be chosen to best suit the color range of the image. The example shown in Figure 4.12 uses an optimized palette of mainly reds, greens, and grays. Apart from a few blues and an orange or two (for the other car's lamp, which peeks into the image on the bottom left), all other colors are missing. The 256 available color "slots" have been given to colors that the image can best use to give a good-quality image. Compare this to the palette and image quality of the center-top image, which is forced to use the system-set 256-color palette. Since this image can use only those colors that suit, and must ignore the colors in the system palette that don't occur in the image, the result is a quality compromise as the image does its best to dither the usable colors to display the picture.

A problem can arise when you use a nonstandard 8-bit palette on an image and then present it on a 256-color computer display. Since 8-bit displays can show only 256 colors at a time, using a 256-color image with an optimized custom palette is not usually a problem, as the display adapter shifts its selection of 256 colors to match those required of the image. However, when two 8-bit color images are shown at the same time, and they have different custom palettes, then which selection of 256 colors is the 8-bit display supposed to show? Quite a dilemma.

What will happen is that the display adapter will simply adopt the custom palette of the last image to be displayed, and ignore the other images. So if your multimedia product has an 8-bit background and interface, and the user selects a button that displays a new 8-bit image with a different palette, things go awry. The new image will display well but the interface will shift the palette to match the new image and, as a result, will show a psychedelic combination of colors that would nauseate even the worst designer. When one image's custom palette is forced onto another image, the results can be very nasty, as shown in Figure 4.13. In this figure, the two top images are shown with optimized 8-bit palettes. Their respective palettes are shown beneath them in the center row. The bottom row shows what happens when the palette from one image is forced onto the other image. If both images are shown on a 256-color display, when the top image's palette is used, then the bottom image would be forced to look like the illustration.

This phenomenon is known as "palette switching" and results in false coloring of some images. The resulting "posterized" effect can be quite disturbing.

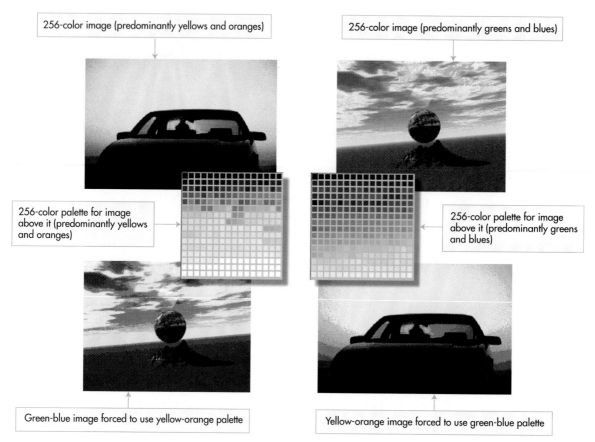

256-color image (predominantly yellows and oranges)

256-color image (predominantly greens and blues)

256-color palette for image above it (predominantly yellows and oranges)

256-color palette for image above it (predominantly greens and blues)

Green-blue image forced to use yellow-orange palette

Yellow-orange image forced to use green-blue palette

Figure 4.13
This illustration shows what can happen when another custom palette is forced onto an image.

The solution to this problem is to create a *super-palette,* which is one 256-color palette designed to suit all the images in your project. This will be a compromise palette, since sharing one palette will require some images to make do with fewer than 256 usable colors. It can be better than using a system palette and forcing that into all images, however. Products such as Equilibrium's Debabelizer Pro are a tremendous tool for creating super-palettes for batches of images.

LINE ART VERSUS BITMAPPED IMAGES

There is a difference between line art (also known as *vectored images*) and bitmapped images that is rather important. With line art images, the image data are stored in the form of data points that describe the collection of lines, curves, circles, ellipses, text, polygons, and other shapes and their characteristics such as line type and fill/shading specifications. This information can be stored as coordinates and property data. The computer can then faithfully recreate the image by reading through these instructions and redrawing the image.

A bitmapped image, as you have read earlier in this chapter, is an array of color dots that when looked at from a distance forms an image. You can represent a photograph as a bitmapped image, but not as a drawn image. You can scale a drawing up and down with no loss of image quality, but not so with a bitmapped image. This is shown in Figure 4.14, where a drawing of a face retains detail and sharp edges when zoomed in, while the photo of the child gets grainy and pixilated when zoomed in. When seen close up, the bitmapped image breaks down into individual pixels, while the drawing still retains smooth edges and curves.

Vector-based drawn image

Magnified section of vector-based drawn image

Magnified section of bitmapped image

Pixel-based bitmapped image

Further magnification of vector-based drawn image

Figure 4.14
The different effects of zooming in on a bitmapped image (middle left) and a line art drawing (top right).

The bottom detail image in Figure 4.14 also shows bezier curve control handles as they are used to draw smooth curved edges. To draw a smooth curve freehand would be quite difficult, but bezier curves allow you to bend and flex the curvature of the line by dragging control handles on the end of dotted lines when editing.

FILE FORMATS AND CONVERSION

You can save your graphics work in many file formats. These file formats are also called codecs (from the words *c*ompression and *dec*ompression), and they are, in a sense, drivers that can compress an image file into a small on-disk file, and later decompress that image file on demand for viewing on screen.

Some formats, such as Windows Bitmap format, retain the full quality of the original image as raw data in an uncompressed file. Some file formats, such as JPEG (short for *Joint Photographic Experts Group*), offer a choice of the percentage of full quality that you'd like to store the image in and very good file compression. File compression allows you to store the image data in a smaller disk file. The amount of video memory required to display the image does not change, as the JPEG codec uncompresses the file back to its original size in memory.

There are many file formats to choose from and you will read about the appropriate format for the job when you read the appropriate chapter. For now you may want to experiment with these formats. See "Checking Your Knowledge and Skills" at the end of this chapter for an exercise on graphic file formats.

bezier curve

A method of drawing a smooth, curved line on a computer screen. Bezier curves provide draggable handles on the ends of the curve to allow the adjustment of the degree of curvature.

codecs

Derived from the terms *c*ompression and *dec*ompression. This term describes the file compression formats used to store audio and video data.

JPEG

An acronym for *j*oint *p*hotographic *e*xperts *g*roup, the name of a common file format that supports high color and image resolution while consuming relatively little file space.

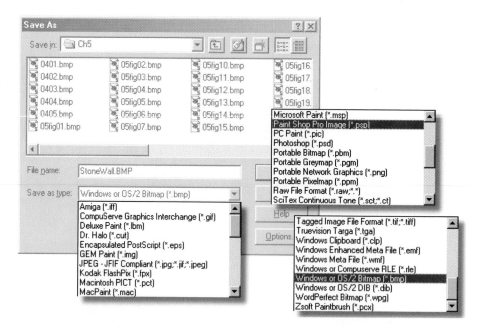

Figure 4.15

The Save As function of all professional image editing applications (Paint Shop Pro is shown here) offer a multitude of file formats for saving your image files.

Converting from one file format to another is quite simple. Any good graphic design software will have a Save As option under the application's File menu. In the Save As dialog box, you should be offered all of the many file formats supported by that product. Figure 4.15 shows the many file format choices available when saving your work. Converting your file from one format to another can be as simple as loading the file and saving in the new required format. If you would like a simpler solution or if you have a batch of files to be converted all at once, software packages are available to do this for you. Some graphic design products, such as Corel's Photo-Paint, have batch processing options. Some batch processing applications, such as Graphics Workshop for Windows, are free downloads as shareware and do a terrific job of multifile conversion. Others, such as Debabelizer Pro for both Windows and Macintosh, offer a multitude of processes for images (and even video) but can be expensive. These applications can make the production process of a large multimedia project a lot easier.

IMAGE SOURCES AND INPUT

In the next chapter you will read learn how to create your own graphics for your multimedia product. You will receive hands-on instruction on the major graphic design techniques to complete the job. But since you usually start out with an image or a design that you will modify to suit your needs, where do you get such raw materials? The following sections address this very question.

SCANNERS

A flatbed scanner is one of the most useful peripheral pieces of hardware you can attach to your computer for this work. Simply having the ability to digitize an image opens up a world of graphic sources. You can scan an image of a floppy disk for graphics; you can use photographs taken last summer; you can use any newspaper or magazine as a source of materials (though you do need to check out the copyright issues of using someone else's work); and you can digitize your own sketches and artwork, which is very helpful for prototyping and storyboarding.

DIGITAL CAMERAS

Digital cameras can be a terrific source for images. I use mine all the time and have used it for many of the illustrations you see throughout this book. Taking a photo and including it in your multimedia product within minutes is a terrific asset and it also helps you be dynamic and responsive to your clients' needs. If you can put a crisp photo of the client into his or her prototype quickly and easily, you look good and your product prototype looks more custom-made for the client.

THE WEB

The World Wide Web provides a vast source of images and content. While most Web content belongs to those whose permission you should secure before using it, the debate over Internet copyright and how to enforce it still rages on. While you could conceivably download and modify an image beyond the owner's recognition, you should probably not take this risk with a professional product. Generally, using such images is permitted for personal products, but if you make any money with the product, you enter "commercial use" territory and need to have your permissions in hand and documented.

To take an image from the Web, simply right-click it (for Mac users, hold down the mouse key for a second) and select the Save Image option from the shortcut menu. It's that simple. Many of the illustrations for this book were acquired this way, with the permission of their owners.

CLIP ART

Clip art includes clip photos, video clips, and animation clips. Most computer stores carry CD-ROMs packed with stock images for you to use. Before you buy these products, make certain that the formats of the images suit your needs (video clips may not suit your need for a background pattern, for instance) and check on the box for royalty conditions. You will need to find products that explicitly offer *royalty-free use*. Beware of those that offer royalty-free use as long as it's for your own personal use. If this is in fact the case, then that's okay, but you don't want to produce a product for a client only to learn later that you now owe significant royalties to the company that provided the images.

Good sources of clip images are Corel's Professional Photos CD-ROM series and Photodex's Picture Factory series. MetaCreations and PhotoDisc have a series of high-quality images on CD-ROM. Some companies, such as Artbeats, specialize in patterns and textures. Companies such as SoftKey and Walnut Creek supply shareware CD-ROMs with large libraries of such content at low cost. Check this book's Web site for links to suppliers of clip image collections.

CREATE YOUR OWN

While there are no permission issues with creating your own images, it can be time-consuming. Use a scanner to digitize your own artwork and a digital cameras to take your own photos. You can use any graphics package to create your own graphics.

THE POSSIBILITIES FOR MULTIMEDIA USAGE

Graphics in a multimedia product are used primarily for background and button interface work. In addition, images can be used to display content, catalog products, show places, diagram processes, or simply enhance the other content surrounding the message. Figure 4.16 shows a computer application for cataloging

Figure 4.16
A multimedia-enhanced interface using quite a bit of graphic design to make it more fun.

products that uses multimedia elements to make the process fun. Notice the patterned background image that incorporates embossed and recessed panels to frame the buttons and application components. The theme buttons are simply fun and attractive for the Ty Beanie Baby collector.

In the next section you will learn about building an interface and what design considerations you should take into account.

GRAPHIC DESIGN AND THE INTERFACE

The whole purpose of creating a graphical interface for your multimedia product, whether it be on CD-ROM, on DVD-ROM, or Web-based, is to make your product easy to use and more intuitive. The following pointers will help you develop your multimedia interface design:

1. *Define a control area and a stage area.* The multimedia interface needs to provide the user with navigation and application controls, and an area within which to present the primary content. Figure 4.17 shows an example of a multimedia interface and identifies the control and stage areas. In this figure the diagram below the image shows the stage area as a green box. This is where the changing content is displayed. The red rectangles indicate control areas that provide buttons and feedback to the user.

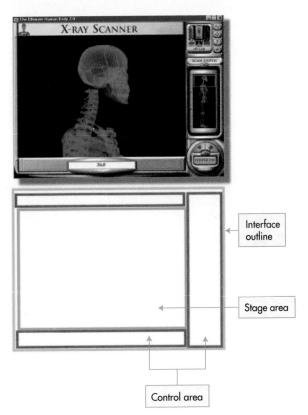

Figure 4.17
This interface design from Dorling Kindersley's Ultimate Human Body identifies the control and stage areas.

Defining control, feedback, and stage areas in the planning and storyboard phases of your project is very important. A good goal is to always leave sufficient stage area to display your content, while using margin area for controls and banners. Note how this was done in the example shown in Figure 4.17.

2. *Choose muted background images and appropriate button graphics.* A background image should not impose on or distract from the main focal point of the multimedia presentation. Figure 4.16 shows a background that is subtle and not visually distracting to the user.

Button design can be critical to a multimedia interface design. Buttons either should look like appliance buttons—like those on a TV remote control—with appropriate text, or, if completely graphical, they should visually represent their function. The best and most intuitive buttons are those that "tell" the user their function. The button icon can be supported by text when the mouse pointer moves over the button, as shown in Figure 4.18. Note how the background image does not impose on the screen content and offers embossed frames in which to view that content.

3. *Use visual depth to indicate importance.* A sense of visual depth can be achieved by representing dimension and depth in the interface. To accomplish this, you can use graphical techniques such as drop shadows, embossing, lens effects, and 3D images. The user perceives controls that appear "closer" as being more important and more significant. The psychological effect of "lifting" an image off the background image can be quite powerful. Figure 4.19 shows the exact same application but one version has had the background image removed. The background image's purpose is to frame the content and give the appropriate emphasis to it. Note the difference in both designs. Can you see the benefit of applying visual depth to controls? You can make an application "come alive" by simply adding

Figure 4.18

This interface design relies on the user's intuition to know what the images on the controls mean, and on the text that appears when the mouse pointer moves over the button face.

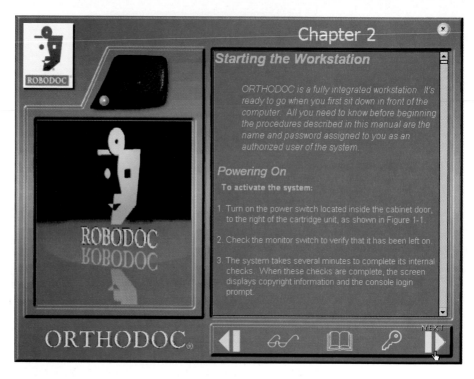

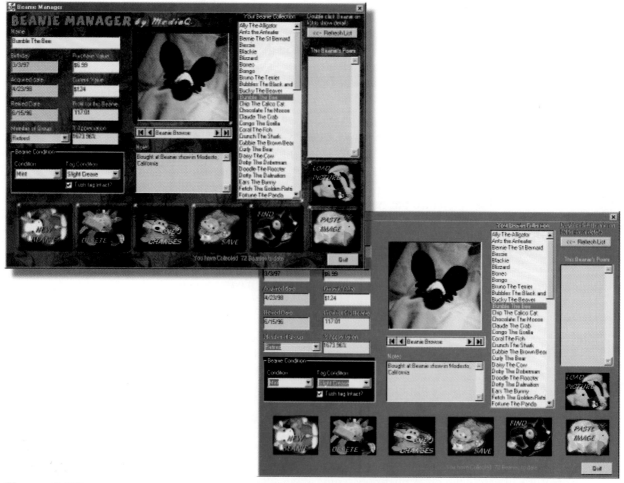

Figure 4.19

Beanie Manager without the background graphic (bottom right) looks a bit static.

> If you want to apply a filter or special effect to your design, such as a drop shadow or embossing, and that feature seems unavailable in your graphic design application, don't panic. There is probably not sufficient color depth in your image to allow for the mixing of colors to create the new visual effect. Increase the image's color resolution to 24-bit, create the special effect, and then reduce the number of colors back down again.

shading and highlights to imitate depth. Note the subtle but powerful effect that adding a little perspective and depth can achieve. Also note how the drop shadow around the top left image gives it more significance than the one in the bottom right. Drop shadows can have a powerful effect in getting your attention.

4. *Keep it simple.* When you first encounter the terrific special effects and graphical toys available to you, you'll probably want to use them all. This would be inappropriate. The best graphical effects are those that are unnoticed. Special effects that give users a good feeling about the interface and direct them to the most efficient operation of the product are the best graphic design for an interface. Those that do not will hamper the application's performance.

AVOIDING PITFALLS

When designing graphics for your multimedia application, the easiest way to avoid falling into problems that will cost you time and effort later is to plan ahead. Decide at the outset the specification of the system your least-equipped user will be using. Set this, and state this, as the minimum system requirements to run your product. The lower you set the standard, the more users will be able to use your product, but the less sophisticated it will be in terms of design and visual appeal. If you are working on contract, have the client specify the minimum system requirements for the product and stick to that.

When you are designing for the Web such considerations become surprisingly easier, but more complicated when deciding what plug-ins to use. (We will discuss that further in later chapters.) For the Web, the selection of graphic formats is restricted and those formats are designed to work on even the oldest, clunkiest systems, as long as they have a browser application and are connected to the Web.

Map out the basic layout of your interface and prototype it. You can prototype it by creating a mockup and showing it to your client and your colleagues. Do not get too complicated or ornate in your design—remember simpler is better.

Watch for palette issues in your design. If you are designing for an 8-bit display computer system minimum requirement, then create a super-palette for your images so that you don't get palette switching.

Chapter Summary

- There is an interdependent relationship between the factors that affect a media component's file size, its viewable size, its quality and resolution, and its performance characteristics within the multimedia application. The multimedia developer must balance the opposing demands and effects of these factors to achieve the performance and presentation goals of the piece.

- While color resolution, image resolution, and device resolution factors can be quite technical in nature, a basic understanding of their interactions can provide you with insight and intuition into how they operate and how they can be controlled.

- Of the many types of image data and file formats, you can choose the formats most suited to your needs.

- There are many sources of images for your multimedia product. By manipulating them effectively you can make them part of your multimedia production.

- Designing a multimedia interface is a very important step-by-step process.

Key Terms and Concepts

bezier curve, 81
bit, 68
bitmapped images, 71
byte, 69

codecs, 81
color resolution, 68
cropping, 77
image dithering, 75

image resolution, 71
JPEG, 81
palette, 77
pixel, 71

resampling, 76
resizing, 76
scanning resolution, 72

Checking Your Knowledge and Skills

1. What do you consider the most important aspect of multimedia interface design, and why? Explain your answer.

2. Using a 24-bit image, such as one of those provided in the Samples folder of this book's CD-ROM, create a series of identically sized images and save them in different color resolutions. Look at the file sizes and compare them. Did the image file format you chose to save them in have any bearing on this exercise?

3. Using a 24-bit image, such as one of those provided in the Samples folder of this book's CD-ROM, create a series of identically sized images and save them in different file formats. Save one file for each format available in your image editing application's Save As menu options. Compare the on-disk file sizes of the images and determine which format you would most likely use for a multimedia project, and why.

4. Using colored block diagrams, design an interface that you believe would work well for your choice of multimedia application. Then design one that would *not* work for the same application. Explain your reasoning for both diagrams.

5. Analyze your favorite multimedia application's interface design, and explain why you believe it works so well.

Critical Thinking Challenges

Given the design considerations that you now know are important to multimedia graphics and interface design, answer the following questions and challenges:

1. Find a multimedia application and a similar Web-based application and examine their respective interfaces. List their commonalties and their differences, and explain which of the two you believe works best.

2. Describe what would be for you the absolute perfect multimedia interface design. Summarize why this is the best design for you. Is this design best suited for a CD-ROM or Web application, and what would you do to make it more suitable for the delivery system it's less suited to?

3. If you had a choice of selling your multimedia product to 200 million users worldwide based on a 256-color palette, or to only 60 million (out of the 200 million) customers using a 24-bit color system, which design would you opt for? Why?

4. Create a diagram that shows the relationship between input image resolution, display image resolution, actual image file resolution, and output image resolution. Describe the decision process you need to go through to match resolutions across this process for both a printed brochure project and for a digital CD-ROM-based multimedia project.

Hands-on Exercises

INTERFACE DESIGN

Using a conventional paper sketchpad and colored pencils or pens:

1. Design an interface for a multimedia product.

2. Design for your interface intuitive buttons in appropriate control areas.

3. Design feedback areas.

4. Design a primary stage area.

5. Be sure to use a background scheme that is not imposing or distracting.

6. Provide visual depth to the project that supports the intuitive nature of your interface.

Master Project

DESIGNING AN INTERFACE CONCEPT

So far you should have created a binder for the project that documents your project concept and shows a project plan and timeline for the project.

Add to this binder your diagrammatic design for your product's interface, explaining the choice of button designs and background images. Create a series of sketches of your concept that you can refer to later when you approach the actual creation phase of the interface. Use these sketches to get feedback from your peers, colleagues, and family. Evaluate and document their comments and adjust your design to accommodate what you thought to be good suggestions or criticism.

GRAPHIC DESIGN TOOLS

Chapter Outline

Chapter Objectives

After completing this chapter, you will be able to:

- Use the features of most any photo/image editing software application.

- Use Paint Shop Pro, a popular photo/image editing software package, to accomplish fundamental multimedia design functions such as using masks and selections, adjusting color, working in layers, and applying special-effect plug-in filters.

- Use Painter, a popular natural-media painting software package, to accomplish fundamental multimedia design functions such as using masks and selections, using layers, using natural media tools, using image hoses, and applying special-effect filters.

Chapter Overview

This chapter will bring you up to speed on popular image editing tools as quickly as possible by helping you become familiar with their operation before applying them to actual multimedia production (in Chapter 6). There is no substitute for the practice and time spent using these techniques and procedures. It is very important that you spend quality time getting familiar with these programs.

In this chapter you will be introduced to two applications: Jasc's Paint Shop Pro 6, an image and photo editing tool, and Corel's Painter 6, a natural-media painting tool.

An image and photo editing software application provides tools for manipulating and editing a digital bitmapped image. Such an application is ideal for editing a digital photo or scanned image, or for creating graphic elements for a Web page. Photo editing tools allow you to create a digital image from scratch, or edit and manipulate an imported image from another source.

A natural-media painting tool's primary function is to try to replicate the look and feel of using real-life paints, brushes, pencils, chalks, and other drawing and painting tools. These applications use a software technology called fractals that can create natural-looking images by introducing those fine details and imperfections found in real life, which removes that clinically clean "computer" look. Such products can help the artist create awesome art with the appearance of media such as watercolor or oils, for instance, with all the advantages of a digital image editing program.

The principles and processes you will learn should apply to similar applications of different brands. You will use these tools to perform the graphic design and interface creation for your multimedia work; as such, they represent vital assets in your multimedia production toolbox.

Paint Shop Pro offers phenomenal value at the recommended list price of $99 (direct from Jasc's Web site at www.jasc.com or follow the link from this book's Web site). While no one will dispute that Adobe's Photoshop is the industry leader in image editing software, its retail price of $609 can sometimes be a disincentive to the beginner in this fun field. Furthermore, you can download a functional demonstration version of Paint Shop Pro from Jasc's Web site. Adobe offers a demonstration version of Photoshop, but at the time of writing this, it is a "crippled" version, disallowing the saving of your work, rendering it ineffectual for use in following the examples in this book. Therefore I have chosen Paint Shop Pro as the image editing application for examples and direction in this book. However, for those of you who already have Photoshop, there are Photoshop-specific tips throughout this text. Painter was chosen as a prime example of a natural-media graphic design tool and its application in the creation of impressive multimedia. While not as inexpensive as Paint Shop Pro, it is still not in the same price bracket as Photoshop. With Painter you will experience a very different and less technical way of creating outstanding imagery for your multimedia development. Painter can also be downloaded in demonstration version through a link on this book's Web site. The demo version of Painter may be restricted in features. See this book's Web site for details.

natural-media painting tool

An image editing tool, or graphic design software application, that is used to simulate natural drawing and painting tools and media, such as pencil, chalk, oil paints, and watercolors.

fractals

Pattern detail in an image generated with a mathematical algorithm. Viewed from a distance, the edges of fractal images seem smooth. Zooming into a fractal image shows increasingly complex detail.

JASC'S PAINT SHOP PRO 6 PRIMER

Paint Shop Pro 6 from Jasc is an amazing product for many reasons. First, it offers a remarkable array of features and capabilities for a fraction of the cost of products such as Adobe's Photoshop and Corel's PhotoPaint. Second, included among those capabilities are features that exceed those of the more expensive "professional" products, or features for which you would have to buy additional expensive plug-ins for the more "mainstream" products. However, I will be comparing Photoshop to Paint Shop Pro in this section of the chapter, for those of you who would like information specifically on Photoshop. But for the vast majority of your multimedia graphic design needs Paint Shop Pro will meet (or exceed) your needs.

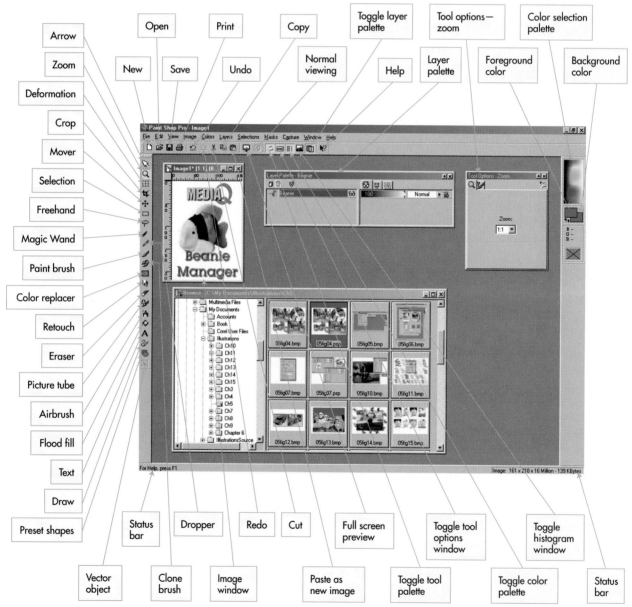

Figure 5.1

Paint Shop Pro's interface is quite straightforward. Note that the Tool Options dialog box shows the settings available for the selected tool.

Extended options for Photoshop tools are available in the Options dialog box. The Options are viewed by clicking on the Options tab, which is next to the Navigator and Info tabs.

Paint Shop Pro's interface is quite straightforward. It uses toolbars on the top and left sides of the screen, as shown in Figure 5.1. If you let the mouse pointer pause over these buttons, the function of that button will be described in a small pop-up label. Each time you select one of the tools on the left side of the screen, the Tool Options dialog box, as shown in Figure 5.1, shows details and options available for adjusting that tool. To keep the tool options and dialog box open at all times, click the small button to the left of the *x* button at the top-right corner of the panel. Click it again to revert the panel to its "hide-away" mode.

Paint Shop Pro supports layering, as do Adobe's Photoshop and Corel's PhotoPaint. Layering is a technique used to separate pieces and elements of your graphic onto separate layers in the image. It's as if each element is painted on its own sheet of celluloid or thin glass and then stacked with the rest of the image layers. When viewing from above, it looks like one complete image, but each layer can be moved and edited separately from the rest of the composite image. Figure 5.2 shows how an illustration was put together using layers. This illustration also shows the Paint Shop Pro Layer Palette. Each element of this illustration has its own layer, which is capable of being edited separately. You will read more about layering in Paint Shop Pro later in this chapter.

layering

A process that keeps elements of an image separate and editable independently from the rest of the image. Components of a layered image overlap in what appear to be layers. The layer that contains a particular element can be selected and the element edited without affecting the rest of the image.

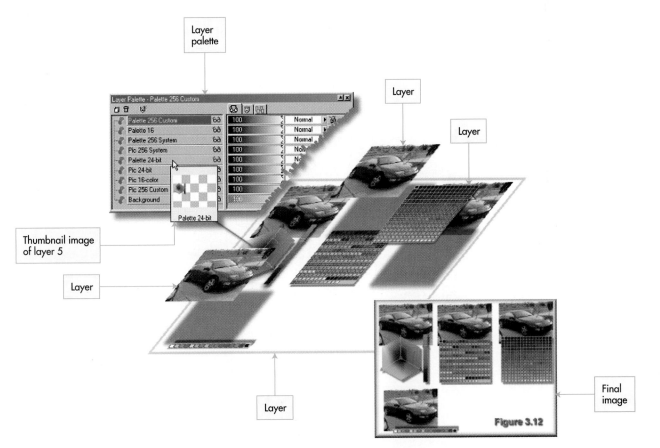

Figure 5.2
Paint Shop Pro's layering capabilities make creating and editing a complex composite image much simpler.

To open a file in Photoshop, procedures 1 and 2 will work. Photoshop does not have a Browse feature like Paint Shop Pro's. However, Photoshop has an additional Open As . . . command that allows you to open a graphics file in whatever format you wish to edit. This means that Photoshop automatically converts the image file to your format choice as you open it, regardless of what format the file was stored as.

OPENING AND VIEWING FILES

Paint Shop Pro offers three primary ways to open and view an image file:

1. From the File menu, choose Open. Locate the file you wish to edit by using the Open dialog box.
2. If the file you want to open is one you recently edited, choose its name, which appears as a menu option at the bottom of the File menu.
3. From the File menu, choose Browse. This command displays a visual catalog of the images in any folder on your hard disk drive. Figure 5.3 shows the Browse function in use. This feature of Paint Shop Pro provides an excellent way to view your work. Double-clicking the cataloged image opens it for editing. When you pause the mouse pointer over the thumbnail image in the catalog, an image information pop-up window appears.

SELECTIONS

As with any image editing program, Paint Shop Pro provides a range of selection tools with which to select the precise part of the image you wish to edit. When an area of the image is selected, a marquee selection border appears around the selected area (this is sometimes called a marching ants border, describing its

marquee
The animated border that appears around the selected area of an image, which can then also be used as a mask.

marching ants border
A cute descriptive term used sometimes to describe a selection marquee.

Figure 5.3
Paint Shop Pro's Browse feature provides an excellent visual catalog of your images, allowing you to choose an image file visually, as opposed to remembering the filenames of your work.

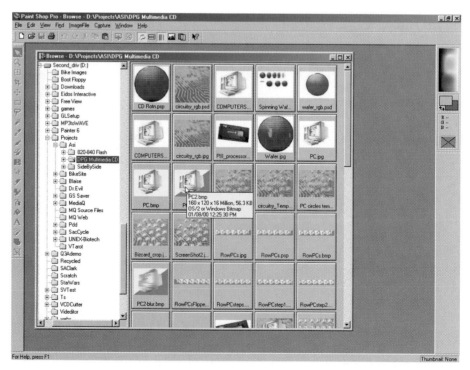

PHOTOSHOP SELECTION TOOLS

Photoshop provides the same selection tools as Paint Shop Pro, and then some. In the Photoshop toolbar, some tools have a small "tick" in the bottom right corner of the button. This indicates that if you hold your mouse button down on that tool, additional options will appear, as shown in Figure 5.4.

appearance). Once an area is selected, it can be copied and pasted as a new selection or layer, to its own image or to another open image.

A range of set selection shapes, such as rectangle, square, ellipse, and circle are available in Paint Shop Pro to assist you in selecting the area you desire. You can select them in the Tool Options dialog box when you choose the standard Selection tool.

The Lasso tool allows you to draw a freehand selection marquee around any area of your image. Figure 5.5 shows an irregular selection to which a drop shadow has been applied. In this illustration, the original image is shown at top left. The motorcycle was selected from the background using the Lasso tool. The bottom right image shows the motorcycle with the selection marquee around it and a detail of the image showing the marquee border. The selected motorcycle image with drop shadow is shown at bottom left.

The Magic Wand tool allows you to select an area of the image based on the color of that area. The Magic Wand tool selects all like colors in the image adjacent to the point where you clicked. The tolerance for how close the adjacent color has to be to be included in the selection is determined by settings in the Tool Options dialog box. The Magic Wand tool is great for selecting a piece of the image from a uniform background.

Lasso tool
A free-hand image selection tool used to select an image area.

Magic Wand tool
An image selection tool that is used to select contiguous areas of the same or similar color.

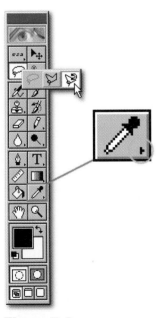

Figure 5.4
Photoshop's extended toolbar is accessed by holding down the mouse button on any tool showing the small "tick" in the bottom right corner, as shown.

Figure 5.5
By using the Lasso tool to select the image of the motorcycle from the busy background, you can set it apart as shown.

MODIFYING SELECTIONS

When selecting areas of the image with these tools, you can add to or remove from an existing selection by holding down the Shift key to add and the Ctrl key to subtract. This can be very helpful if you want to modify or extend the selection or if you want to trim the selection down.

FINE TUNING ADJUSTMENTS

The majority of Paint Shop Pro's color adjustment features affect only an area within a selection border on a selected layer. In the absence of a selection border, the color effect will be applied to the entire layer or image. Use the Selection tool and the Layer Palette panel to fine-tune your adjustments.

COLOR

Paint Shop Pro provides a multitude of color-related tools and options. Figure 5.6 shows the primary options in the Color menu. As you can see, these options are quite extensive and offer the multimedia developer many creative possibilities.

In addition to adjusting and changing colors in your image, you can select the colors in use for drawing, painting, and text.

On the right side of the Paint Shop Pro screen is a color selection panel, as shown in Figure 5.7. Also shown are the color swatches (small samples of color) representing the foreground and background colors currently in use. In this figure, the foreground color is gray and the background color is blue. Notice how the foreground color is shown overlapping the background color. The swatch with the X through it shows the color beneath the tip of the eyedropper mouse pointer when the eyedropper passes over a color. Clicking the green color with

swatch

A small representative piece of an image or of a color, which gives an impression of the larger overall image or color.

ADJUSTING COLOR IN PHOTOSHOP

Photoshop's color adjustment options are located on the Image menu in the Mode and Adjust menu options.

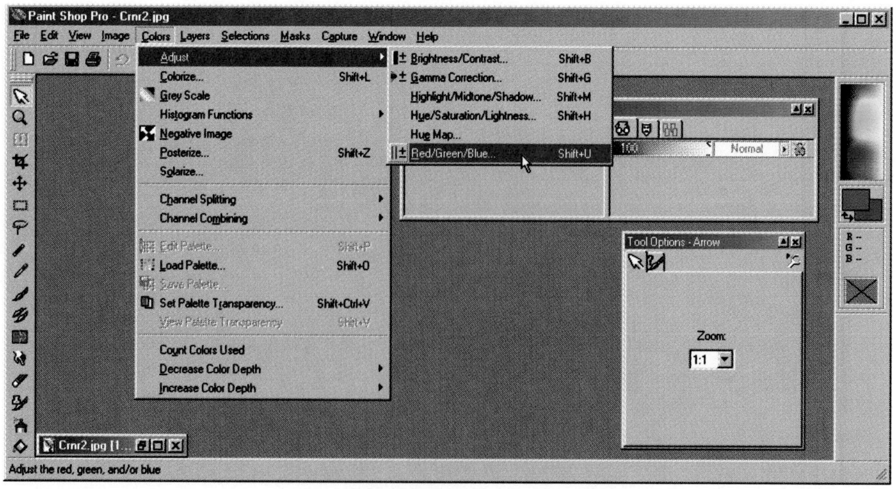

Figure 5.6

Paint Shop Pro's color adjustment and manipulation options are extensive.

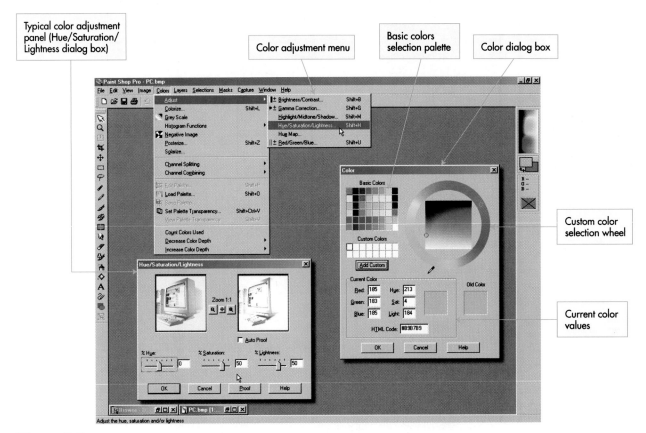

Typical color adjustment panel (Hue/Saturation/Lightness dialog box)

Color adjustment menu

Basic colors selection palette

Color dialog box

Custom color selection wheel

Current color values

Figure 5.7
Paint Shop Pro's Dropper shows a color-picking eyedropper mouse pointer. You use this to choose the desired foreground or background color.

FOREGROUND AND BACKGROUND COLORS

Some of Paint Shop Pro's special effects, such as the Buttonize feature, use the foreground and background color selections to create the desired effect. You may want to experiment with these colors to get a feel for their impact on the special effect.

The foreground and background colors can be quickly interchanged by clicking on the small right-angled arrow beneath the foreground swatch.

Buttonize

A special effect in which the edges of the image, layer, or selected portion of an image are shaded to look as if they are beveled, resulting in an appearance similar to that of a raised button.

the left mouse button would set this color as the foreground color, and that green would appear in the foreground color swatch. Likewise, the background color is selected by clicking the right mouse button.

Double-clicking the color swatches invokes the Color dialog box, which allows you to be more precise in your color choice. This dialog box is also shown in Figure 5.7.

SIZE AND RESOLUTION

Often you will need to resize an image or a layer to suit your needs. The simplest way to resize an image is to use the Resize command found on the Image menu. Figure 5.8 shows the Resize dialog box. You will want to specify the new size either as a percentage of the original image size, or as absolute pixel dimensions.

The aspect ratio of an image is the ratio of the image's width to its height. It is a convenient description of the shape of the image rectangle. As long as

aspect ratio

The ratio of an image's width to its height. A 640 × 480 image has an aspect ratio of 1.33:1, or 4:3—its width is 1.33 times its height. 4:3 is the same ratio in round numbers. When scaling an image, if you maintain the aspect ratio, you prevent distortion of the image as it is scaled.

Figure 5.8
Paint Shop Pro's Resize dialog box, showing the many resizing options available.

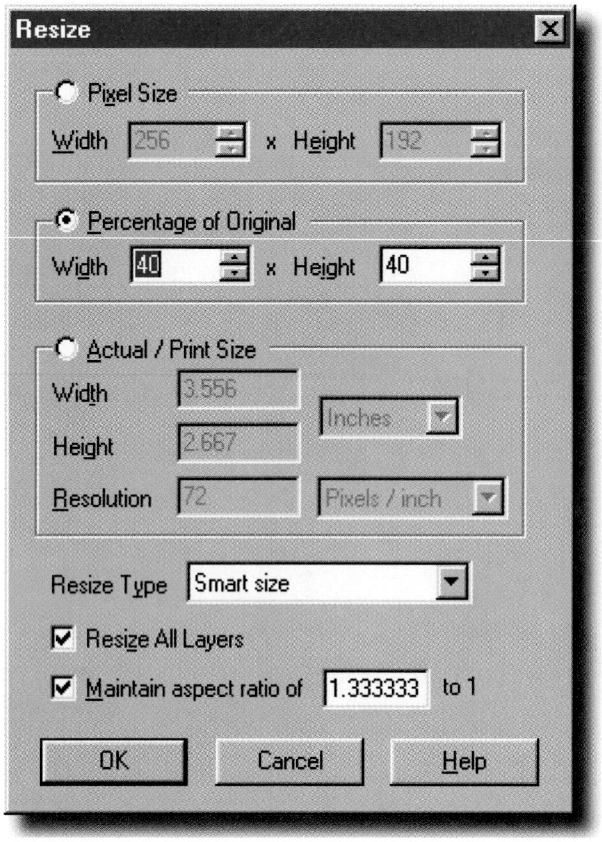

Resize

○ Pixel Size
Width [256] x Height [192]

◉ Percentage of Original
Width [40] x Height [40]

○ Actual / Print Size
Width [3.556]
Height [2.667]   [Inches ▼]
Resolution [72]   [Pixels / inch ▼]

Resize Type [Smart size ▼]

☑ Resize All Layers

☑ Maintain aspect ratio of [1.333333] to 1

[OK]   [Cancel]   [Help]

RESIZING IMAGES IN PHOTOSHOP

To resize images in Photoshop, use the Image Size . . . menu option on the Image menu. The Image size dialog box provides for either exact pixel dimension changes or percentage resizing.

you have the Maintain aspect ratio box checked (as shown in Figure 5.8), the resizing will be a direct scaling of the picture without distortion. If you want to change your image to a specific width and height that is a different aspect ratio to that of your image, you will have to uncheck this option.

Try resizing a few images with different settings to see the results.

LAYERS

One of the most powerful functions of image editing software in recent years has been the use of layers. This feature, pioneered by Adobe's Photoshop software several years ago, is now an essential tool in the modern image editing application.

Layering allows you to separate pieces of your image for individual editing while still viewing the composite results of your work. Figure 5.2 illustrates how you can visualize each piece of your image as floating on its own layer, in between the other layers. When you think about it, this technique is not that much different from creating a collage image from magazine cutouts. Each cutout image can be moved separately and brought to the front, or placed behind other cutouts. In the same way, layering allows us to deal with one piece at a time.

When you open an image in Paint Shop Pro, it is usually a flat image, meaning that it contains no layers, and can be considered as a single background-

flat image

An image without layers. An image whose layers have been merged is referred to as a flattened image.

LAYERING IN PHOTOSHOP

Layering in Photoshop is accomplished in much the same way as in Paint Shop Pro. Photoshop's layering commands are all available on the Layer menu. A subset of this menu is available in pop-up form when you click on the arrow in the top right corner of Photoshop's Layers dialog box.

NAMING LAYERS

You can use the Layer Palette to give each layer a meaningful name. This will assist you greatly in editing multilayer images. You will know which layer to select from the list in the Layer Palette because you will recognize it by name.

layer image. This is apparent in the Layer Palette in Paint Shop Pro. When there are multiple layers, the Layer Palette lists them. Figure 5.9 shows the Layer Palette and its functions. Note in this figure the thumbnail image of the layer contents that pops up when you pause the mouse pointer over the layer button. Also shown is the shortcut menu you can use for each layer by right clicking the layer button.

If you are copying image data from one image to another, you have the option of pasting it to your work as a new layer. This is often the better way to add new pieces to your image, because you can move, edit, and apply special effects to it separately from the rest of the image. You can always merge the layer with the image background later.

The Promote To Layer command on the Selections menu allows you to select pieces from a flat image and make new layers from these pieces at will.

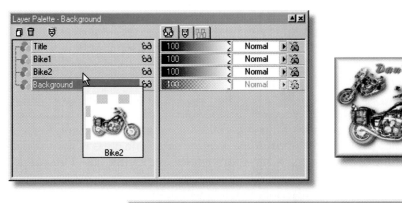

Figure 5.9
The Layer Palette for the image shown at top right.

PROMOTING TO LAYER IN PHOTOSHOP

Photoshop can also "promote" a selection to its own layer by using the Layer Via Copy or Layer by Cut commands. You can access these commands by clicking the New menu and choosing Layer, or by right-clicking the selected area of your image.

This can be very helpful if you want to edit only one piece without affecting the rest of the image.

The layered features of an image can be stored only in a file format that supports layering. If you try to save your layered work in an image file format, such as JPEG, that doesn't support layering, then your image editing software warns you that you are about to lose the layering information needed to recreate the layered image when next opened. Therefore, to be able to later access those image layers, it is important to save the file in a file format that supports layering. Photoshop file format (PSD) is one such format that has become an accepted file format standard for layered images. Your image editing software will most likely have a native file format (for Paint Shop Pro, this is PSP) that will also store layered images.

MASKS AND COLOR REPLACEMENT

mask

The area of an image selected using a marquee, which then prevents editing of the non-selected area of the image. The selected area is said to be masked off from the rest of the image.

You have read what a selection is in an image editing program. Sometimes these selections are also called masks because they effectively mask the part of the image not enclosed by the selection marquee from the effects of your editing. It's as if you applied masking tape over the entire surface of a photo and left exposed only the area you were about to work on. You could then spray-paint that section of the image without worrying about damaging the masked-off areas. This painting technique has been used for hundreds of years. Its digital counterpart, you will find, is even more versatile.

Figure 5.11 shows a section of a photo of my pet iguana's leg. A section of his forearm has been masked off using the Lasso tool. You can see the dashed line of the selection marquee indicating the perimeter of the masked area.

Airbrush tool

A painting tool, available in most image editing and graphic design software applications that is used to simulate the use of an airbrush, providing a fine, faded painting effect.

Using the Airbrush tool, I sprayed red all over the image, but only the area within the mask was affected. The area outside the mask marquee was protected from the red paint.

The Color Replacer tool is another easy way to make complex changes to your image. This tool replaces any instance of the current background color that appears in your image with the current foreground color. In Figure 5.11, I used the Color Replacer tool to paint the green color only in areas where the red showed, resulting in the green stripes through the red swirls. The foreground and background color settings for this process are also shown. Notice how the mask restricted my color replacement to only within the masked area.

Color Replacer tool

An image editing tool that is used to replace a color or specified range of colors with the foreground color.

MASKING IN PHOTOSHOP

Photoshop uses mask selections in the same way as Paint Shop Pro. In addition, Photoshop has a feature that shows you the unmasked area on screen by turning all masked parts of your image a pink color. The area left untinted is available for editing. This is achieved by clicking the button showing a dotted circle on a gray rectangle located toward the bottom of Photoshop's toolbar (see Figure 5.10).

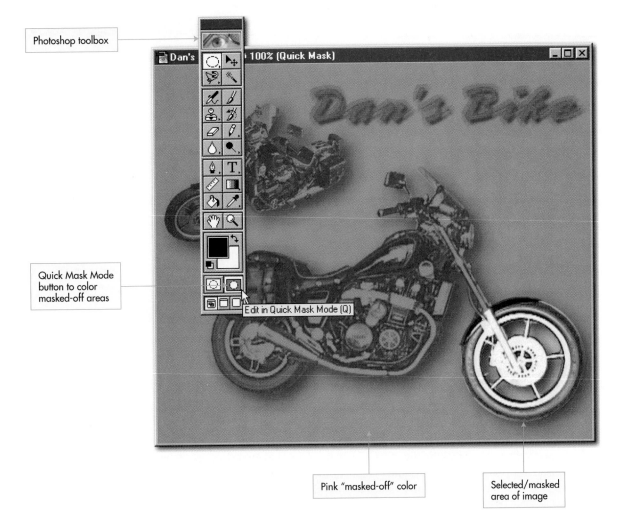

Photoshop toolbox

Quick Mask Mode
button to color
masked-off areas

Edit in Quick Mask Mode (Q)

Pink "masked-off" color

Selected/masked
area of image

Figure 5.10
The front wheel of the motorcycle is masked off using Photoshop's circle selection tool. Clicking the button indicated enters Quick Mask Mode.

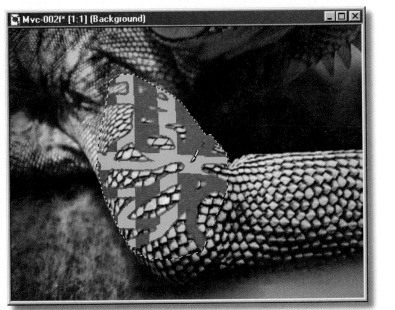

R 119
G 252
B 66

Figure 5.11
The masked area restricts the airbrushing of red swirls to the masked area. The replacement of some of that red with green using the Color Replacer tool is also confined to the masked area.

Figure 5.12

The masked area restricts the effect of a special-effect filter, such as the Hot Wax Coating filter shown.

COLOR REPLACEMENT RANGE

When using the Color Replacer tool you can adjust the range of colors replaced by adjusting the tolerance value in the Tool Options dialog box. This value allows you to include similar colors in the replacement, or restrict the replacement to just one specific color value. You'll find this setting by clicking the middle tab at the top of the Tool Options dialog box when the Color Replacer tool is selected.

Masked areas can also be used effectively to confine the effects of a special-effect filter. Figure 5.12 shows the effect of applying the Hot Wax Coating filter to the image. Notice how the changes to the image are confined to the masked area. Paint Shop Pro has over forty standard special effects. As with Photoshop, Painter, PhotoPaint, and others, Paint Shop Pro can use additional plug-in filters that you can buy separately at your computer store.

PAINTING AND RETOUCHING

In addition to editing images and applying special effects, applications such as Paint Shop Pro can also help you "paint." By using either the Paint Brush or Airbrush tool, and selecting the brush and texture properties you require, you can get quite artistic!

Figure 5.13 shows some of the selection of textures with which you can paint in Paint Shop Pro. This figure also shows the control panel for this tool, allowing you to choose from a large array of brush types and settings—whether you want to use a brush that resembles a crayon or charcoal.

Often you will want to touch up an image, or perhaps copy one section of an image onto another. To this end, Paint Shop Pro provides you with a cloning brush. Later in this chapter when you read about Painter, you will see that it too has a similar tool.

The Paint Shop Pro Clone Brush tool is quite versatile. It allows you to "paint" one image onto another. When you right-click the source image (the one

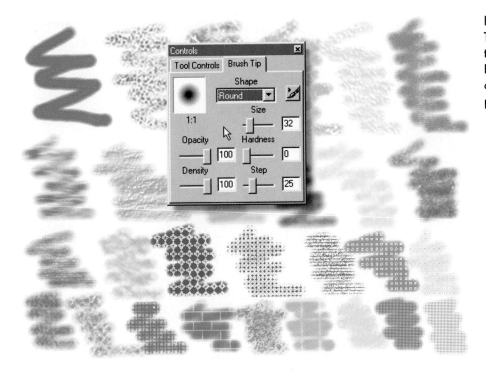

Figure 5.13
The Paint Brush and Airbrush tools are quite versatile. The Brush Tip control panel is shown on top of a selection of the many painting effects available.

you want to replicate part of), you set the starting point from which to copy. Then when you paint on the second image (the image to clone ONTO), the source image begins to appear from that starting point. As you paint on the destination image, you can see the clone source image beginning to appear. Take great care with the placement of your first right-click source point, or where you start cloning in the destination image. A little practice will be required to get the feel of this. Remember to use the Undo button as required.

A crosshair cursor moves around the source image, indicating the point from which you're cloning. Figure 5.14 shows the right-hand image being cloned onto the left-hand image. If you look closely you can see the crosshair

Clone Brush painting image

Clone Brush reference cross-hair pointer on source image

Figure 5.14
The Clone Brush tool "paints" the image of the bike from the right-hand source image onto the left-hand destination image.

CLONING IN PHOTOSHOP

Photoshop's Rubber Stamp tool does the same job as Paint Shop Pro's Clone Brush tool. You must hold down the Alt key (Option key for Macintosh users) on your keyboard and click the source image to set the cloning starting point.

cursor in the clone source right-hand image (on the bike's gas tank), and the cloning tool pointer in the left-hand image as it paints the image of the bike being cloned.

Cloning can be done within one image. You can right-click any part of the image you wish to replicate, and then paint that part elsewhere in the image. This is a terrific way to touch up images and hide flaws (or that ugly cousin you didn't want in the photo in the first place!). Figure 5.15 shows how seamlessly you can modify an image using this tool. I used elements of the existing sculptures to add the extra president at Mount Rushmore!

PICTURE TUBES

Paint Shop Pro has an interesting tool called a Picture Tube. This tool "spits" small images onto the page as you drag your mouse pointer over it. You really have to play with this tool to get a feel for how it works.

Using a library of small images oriented (facing) in different directions, the Picture Tube brush can draw them in a curvy line and the small pictures will face the direction of the curve. Figure 5.16 shows butterfly images created with the Picture Tube. Alternatively, you can paint the images at random for the desired effect. Paint Shop Pro comes with quite an array of Picture Tube image libraries.

Figure 5.16
The Picture Tube tool was used here to "paint" butterflies onto a scene I created in an application called Bryce. The effect is surrealistic.

ADDING TEXT

Using text in Paint Shop Pro is quite simple. Select the Text tool and click with the text pointer in the image where you wish to place the text. In the Text Entry dialog box that appears, you can enter your text and select your font parameters; when you're done, click the OK button. The fonts currently installed on your system will be listed in this dialog box, with a preview of the text in the selected font and style.

Once you have finished with the Text Entry dialog box, you can go back and edit the text by clicking it with the Text tool. As soon as the Text tool mouse pointer turns into a small letter A in square brackets (looks like [A]), then clicking will invoke the Text Entry dialog box again to edit the selected text. To set the text as an ordinary layer so that you can apply special effects and the graphics tools, right-click the text layer in the Layer Palette and choose Convert to Raster from the shortcut menu (see Selected Text tip box on page 106). This converts your text element from editable text into an image layer.

The color of your text will be the currently selected foreground color. You can change the color of the text while editing it in the Text Entry dialog box by clicking the color swatchbox. If you end up with the wrong color text, you will have edit the text again as described previously and change it to the correct

ADDING TEXT IN PHOTOSHOP

Photoshop adds text to an image similarly to Paint Shop Pro, but automatically places the new text on a new layer. In addition, right-clicking the text displays a shortcut menu that allows the text to be edited, even after it has been placed on the image.

When you place text on your image, it is at that point editable text on its own layer. This means that you can move it around and edit it until you wish to drop and merge it with the rest of the image. *Hint:* Watch for the mouse pointer changing to the movement crosshairs over your text before trying to drag it to another location. You can also convert it to its own image layer (called a *raster layer*) for image editing later if you wish. Most important, you can apply special effects to a raster layer. This means that after you convert your text to a raster layer, you can apply a drop shadow, cutout, or similar special effect.

color. Once you convert the text to a Raster layer, you cannot re-edit it and will have to start over to change the text attributes.

FILTERS AND SPECIAL EFFECTS

One of Paint Shop Pro's most powerful features, and the reason it is such a tremendous value at its price, is its built-in list of more than 40 special-effect filters. For more expensive photo editing tools such as Adobe's Photoshop, these special effects are often an additional purchase.

It is well worth your time to experiment with Paint Shop Pro's special effects. Use the Selection tool or the Mover tool to select areas or a layer of an image and apply each of the special effects, such as Hot Wax Coating, Drop Shadow, or Buttonize, to see what they do. You should adjust the filter's properties in the control panel provided to vary the effects.

In addition to the many standard special effects in Paint Shop Pro, this product also accepts third-party filter plug-ins for Adobe's Photoshop. This ability to extend the capabilities of the product makes your life as a multimedia designer much easier. If you need to include some special effect not available in Paint Shop Pro, simply buy it!

FILTERING IN PHOTOSHOP

Photoshop provides two types of filters: those that are used for layer contents, and those that are used for general application. These filters are located on the Layer menu under the Effects command and on the Filter menu, respectively. General filters are applied to selected areas (or the whole image in the absence of a selection); Layer Effects are applied to the contents of layers. Drop Shadow is one of the Layer Effects, for example.

PHOTOSHOP PLUG-INS

One of the most commonly used Photoshop filter plug-in sets comes as a product called Eye Candy, from the company Alien Skin. In your local computer software store, or in online catalogs (such as www.publisherstoolbox.com), check out the many other companies, such as Extensis, Corel and MetaCreations, that provide these add-ons for Photoshop and similar software image editing tools.

COREL'S PAINTER 6 PRIMER

Corel's Painter is known as a "natural-media" graphic design tool. This means that Painter's painting tools can create what visually looks like work created with actual artist's materials, such as oil paints, charcoal, pastels, watercolors, and so on.

The power of such a tool can be tremendous for both creating your own original work from scratch and for using these natural-media tools to reproduce and/or modify another image, such as a digitized photo. Painter can do this in a way that makes your image look as if it were painted or drawn by hand, as shown in Figure 5.17. Painter is also a useful tool for creating simple animations, background patterns, and special effects.

MOUSE VERSUS DIGITIZING TABLET

Some products like Painter do a terrific job of recreating onscreen the sort of work you would expect from actual artist's materials, with the additional magic of digital manipulation built in. Imagine actually painting an oil portrait of an individual on a canvas. If you made a mistake, wouldn't you just love to be able to grab the canvas and shake off the mistake, and continue painting? The Undo functions of such digital products provide these magical options.

While you may think that Painter and its cousin products are in fact better than natural media, a real paintbrush or pencil gives you aspects such as dexterity and tactile feedback that you cannot reproduce with a mouse. In fact, Painter and similar products will probably cause you to get very frustrated with your mouse.

Therefore you may want to consider acquiring a digitizing tablet. This device looks like a thin plastic rectangle; a cord connects it to your computer. An electronic pen digitizes your movements on the tablet and reproduces them on the screen. These devices do a far better job of mimicking the dexterity of your hand movements that is often needed when drawing, painting, or sketching. Think of signing your name with a pen or with a mouse. The difference is the same control difference between a digitizing tablet and a computer mouse.

Figure 5.17
Painter's cloning, natural-media, and paint nozzle features provide a multitude of creative options and techniques for the digital artist. These seven renditions of the original piggy bank picture (shown at top left) only scratch the surface of this software application's potential.

The following sections describe how you might use Painter. By reading through this section, you should become familiar enough with Painter to use it to create your multimedia content elements.

Products like Painter take a bit of getting used to and a bit of patience. The only real way to become familiar and comfortable with Painter (as with any complex computer software product) is to play with it. Take time to experiment and use its many features and tools. The more time you spend with Painter, the easier it will be to use and the more easily it will grow on you.

PAINTER'S UNIQUE INTERFACE

Figure 5.18 shows Painter's interface and controls. Take a moment to study this screen in detail. It is a good idea to review this figure while actually trying these controls with Painter on your computer.

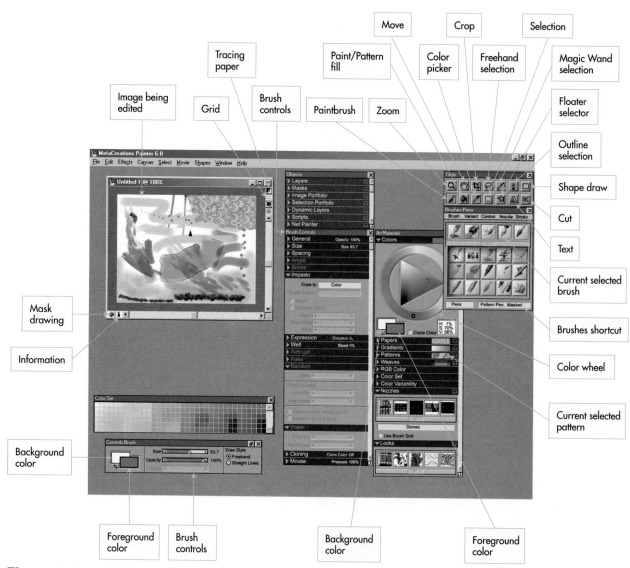

Figure 5.18
Painter offers quite a sophisticated interface, but one that makes intuitive sense once you learn its controls.

Did you ever notice how some tools have a little tick in the bottom corner of the button? This means that if you hold down your mouse button, additional options will appear. This enables the designers of this particular product to group more functionality into one toolbar. However, you will need to become familiar with those hidden tools and remember that they are there.

BRUSHES

Painter's brushes offer quite a range of different renderings of natural media. Figure 5.19 shows some of the variety available. By first selecting the appropriate brush type from the selection of icons in the Brushes dialog box (shown at top left), you can then select from further variations of that brush type. Just click in the text box in the Brushes dialog box, which in the figure reads "Big Dry Ink," and select the brush type of your choice from the menu shown. In the bottom left corner you can see a small image created by using the Image Hose brush to paint clouds, trees, and tall grass behind a stone wall (each type of image set available for the Image Hose is called a *nozzle*). Figure 5.19 also shows each of the brush types used with red ink, and the Controls dialog box, which allows size, opacity, and grain adjustment of the brush type.

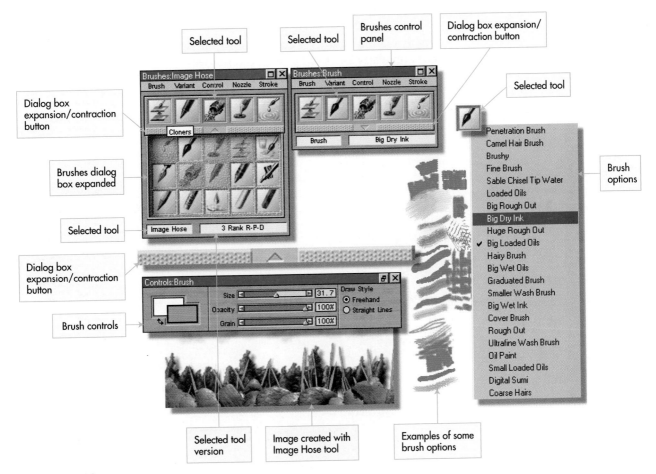

Figure 5.19
Painter's brush options are many and varied. Note the small image at the bottom, which was drawn using the Image Hose.

In Figure 5.19 you can see the Brushes dialog box in both expanded and retracted mode. By clicking the blue bar with the small arrow in the center, you can "open" a drawer containing many different brush options. Those already selected are shown as dimmed in the drawer. The text box shown at the bottom right of the Brushes dialog box lets you know what variation of the selected brush type you are using.

For example, if you select a regular brush option, shown as ▨ in the figure, and then click the bottom right text box, you are presented with additional brush options shown in the menu. To the left of the menu are shown the various brush types as they paint a stroke in red.

Each of these brush types offers a large variety of choices in brush subtype selection. But even then, the Brushes dialog box allows finer adjustment of the size, opacity, and grain characteristics of the brush selected. This combination of controls offers an infinite variety of painting tools to the digital artist.

One of the more valuable, but also more complex features of Painter's brushes is the set of controls available to build custom brushes. Figure 5.20 shows all of the dialog boxes available for creating your own custom brush type. Once you have adjusted the parameters you need, you can click the Build button (shown in the Brush Controls: Size dialog box), and Painter creates a new brush type to suit your parameters and stores it for you as a new brush type. While there are no set values for these dialog boxes—you simply adjust the parameters to suit your needs—a few pointers will help you become familiar with these controls.

- You can access the dialog boxes from the text menus at the top of the Brushes dialog box, namely the Brush and Control menu. The menus match the dialog box titles, as shown in Figure 5.19.

- When creating your own custom brush, it is usually best to modify one of the supplied brushes rather than creating your own from scratch. Select the nearest match to what you'd like the brush to do and start from there.

- Use a large blank new page, test your brush again and again and tweak it until you're satisfied with it. Take your time to experiment with custom brushes until you are satisfied with the results.

Figure 5.20
Painter's editable brush properties are quite extensive.

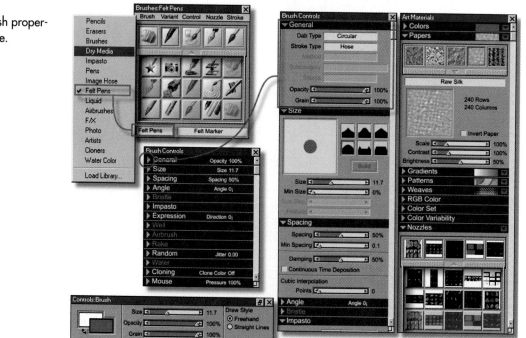

- You don't have to create a custom brush if you don't want to. Painter supplies a tremendous amount of variety in its stock brush options, so be sure that what you're looking for in a brush effect is not already available as a variant of a stock brush.

CLONING AND NOZZLE TOOLS

Of particular note are the cloning and nozzle tools. The cloning tools allow you to "trace" over an existing photo or image using a variety of different styles and brushes. The results of just a few of these cloning brushes were shown in Figure 5.17.

The cloning tools provide a valuable way to use an image in your multimedia product that just doesn't look right as a photographic picture. Perhaps you want to give it an artistic treatment, or you may want to trace most of the image and finish your own custom version with your own drawing. You may want to incorporate two images in the one by cloning one onto the other.

For example, say a family member was missing from a big reunion. Why not clone a picture of the missing relative behind the photo of the gathered crowd? There are an endless number of applications for this versatile tool.

Painter offers an Auto Clone process that creates a cloned image automatically for you, but does so in a smooth, orderly fashion. In Figure 5.17, the bottom left and third in from the left in the top row cloned piggy banks are auto-cloned. You can tell by how uniform the brush strokes are. This auto clone may be a suitable effect for you, or you may want to hand-clone your image; it's your choice. To access the Auto Clone function, on the Effects menu, choose Esoterica, then Auto Clone.

The Image Hose is one of Painter's great innovations. This brush allows you to "paint" a series of small images (using a *nozzle*) onto the page, as if you were spraying a confetti of small picture cutouts. Figure 5.21 shows a picture drawn completely with the use of the standard Image Hose nozzles that are supplied with Painter (you can purchase additional nozzles). You can use the Clouds, Trees, Mediterranean Houses, Poppies, Stones, and English Ivy nozzles to create a quite pleasing effect.

Here's how it works. I started with a gradient blue fill for sky and a green shape, then added successive rows of increasingly larger trees. This technique, along with increasing the brightness of the image with each row of new trees, gives a visual impression of distance. Next I used the Cumulus Cloud nozzle for clouds, and painted a few poppies into the foreground in different sizes. Then I "hosed" some houses onto the hillside and placed a few trees in front of them to embed them into the hill. Finally, after I added a few rows of stones, some different-sized English ivy leaves, and a text title, the image was complete.

CLONING

When using a cloning tool to trace over an image, you must open that image in Painter and set it as the Clone Source. You will find the Clone Source command on Painter's File menu. Once you have set the clone source image, create a new blank image with the same pixel dimensions as the clone source. This image will have a small tracing button ▣ at the top of its right margin.

Clicking this button will show and hide a "ghost" image of the clone source. You can then trace over this image with the brush of your choice; as your work progresses, you can hide the clone source image to get a clearer view, and then turn it back on to continue tracing.

Figure 5.21

Figure 5.21
Painter's Image Hose brush is a
fun tool, and this illustration
shows just some of the results
possible.

Some more conventional (non-natural-media) image editing products, such as Paint Shop Pro, have in recent years introduced similar cloning and image hose tools of their own, as described earlier in this chapter (see Figure 5.22). This is a good example of the overlapping features of these products. While they all have somewhat similar tools and techniques, they do differ considerably in the final results and how easily you can achieve those results. You should spend some time with these products in order to assess which one (or combination) best suits your needs.

Figure 5.22
This strange image shows a collection of images created with
the Paint Shop Pro Picture Tube,
which operates on the same
principles as Painter's Image
Hose.

Figure 5.23
Painter's Image Hose created an interesting background for this catalog cover design, which was finished in Corel PhotoPaint.

The best way to learn about Painter's Image Hose is to play with it for a while. Figure 5.23 shows a graphic design job I did a while ago using Painter's Image Hose.

COLOR

To choose colors in Painter, select the primary color of your choice from the color wheel, and then the shade of that color you are looking for from the shading triangle in the center of the wheel, as shown in Figure 5.24. In this way you can choose from an almost infinite variety of colors. The colors shown in the two examples here are painted to the left of the color chooser showing the color used. They were painted with the Watercolor brush, shown at top center. At the bottom right of the Colors dialog box is the Clone Color check box. This shows the color used in the tracing process using the Cloning brush. The top right Colors dialog box shows the RGB color selection panel, if you choose to dial in RGB color value to get the color you're looking for.

In the bottom right corner of the Colors dialog box is a text box that displays the HSV (Hue, Saturation, Value) or RGB (Red, Green, Blue) values for that color. Clicking this text box switches the display between these two options.

In the bottom left corner of the Colors dialog box are the color swatches for the foreground and background paint colors. In Painter, the foreground color is the one you usually paint with. Some brushes use additional colors to get their

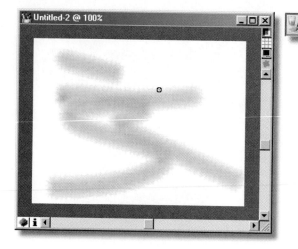

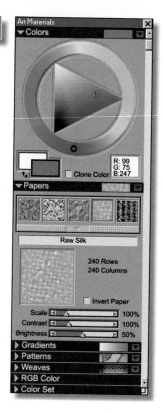

special effect and use this background color to develop the range of colors in the multicolor brushwork.

Beneath the Colors dialog box is the Papers dialog box, which contains buttons from which to choose the paper textures, gradients, patterns, and weave. Each of these parameters has additional effects on the appearance of your work. If you are using a chalk brush, and change the paper from a plain setting to a rough-texture setting, the resulting effect will be quite different. The effect should appear the same as if you went from drawing on smooth paper to drawing on rough paper.

The many possible combinations of these options make Painter a powerful tool for the digital artist. Again, it's important to spend time with this product, playing with the many options and getting a feel for how they interact, to become familiar, productive, and comfortable with Painter.

TEXTURES, PAPERS, AND PATTERNS

Painter gives you the ability to adjust and modify the textures of the "paper" you are painting on, which in turn affects the way the brushes behave when you paint. The center area of Figure 5.25 shows a series of blue crayon brush marks, each with a slightly different paper texture. In addition, you can apply texture effects by choosing Surface Control from the Effects menu, and then choosing Apply Surface Texture; the effects of this are shown at left in the variations of the piggy bank image we have been using. Paper textures are demonstrated in Figure 5.25 by the way the blue crayon brush strokes change appearance in the center of the illustration. At right are rectangles filled with some of the pattern fills available with Painter.

You can choose paper textures from the Art Materials dialog box by clicking the Paper button (click the arrow to the left of "Papers" to expand the Papers dialog box); you can choose gradients, patterns, and weaves the same way. Figure 5.26 shows each of these panels expanded to show the contents of each

Figure 5.25
A selection of some of Painter's texture special effects.

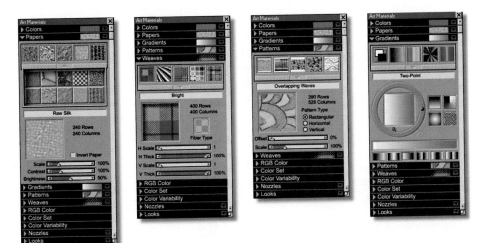

Figure 5.26
Painter's Art Materials dialog box, showing the Papers, Weaves, Patterns and Gradients dialog boxes expanded.

dialog box. Note that each dialog box is accessed by clicking the arrow to the left of the box title.

To select any one of these features, simply click the arrow to the left of the title, then select the flavor of the function you choose and apply it to your work. It is with combinations of these features and settings that you can most easily vary the effect of your brush.

SELECTIONS, MASKS, AND FLOATERS

Painter offers a range of selection and mask tools that can turn a selected piece of your graphic into a floater.

Once an element is a floater, it can be managed separately from the rest of the image, analogous to cutting magazine photographs to paste together in a montage. Until you paste down the cutting, you can move it and play with it until you're satisfied.

floater

A layer, in some image editing applications; also, a moveable selected piece of an image.

Floater is Painter's terminology for what is sometimes called a layer in Photoshop and Paint Shop Pro and an object in Photo Paint. It refers to a piece of the image that is not embedded within the entire image, but can be moved, scaled, manipulated, and worked on as a separate entity. It is called a floater because it appears to float above and among the background and other elements in the image, and is not incorporated into the rest of the picture (in a step called *defloating*) until you intentionally do so.

When you select part of an image in Painter, that selection can be promoted to a floater. In addition, the selected section is also masked off from the rest of the image, so any work you do within the selection will not spill over into surrounding areas; it is bound within the selection marquee.

This masking effect can be very useful when you want to modify or adjust a small part of the image. You can mask off that part and not worry about over-painting surrounding image areas.

To select or mask a section of an image, several selection tools are available:

- *The Shape selection tool* : This tool has a little tick in the bottom right corner of the button. If you hold down your mouse button, additional options will appear.

The Shape tool allows you to select a rectangular or elliptical section of the image. Once selected, the image piece shows a selection marquee around it. Moving the mouse pointer into this selection changes its shape to a moving crosshair, allowing you to move the selection area around until you are ready to use it. The selected area determines the "piece" of the selected layer that you will copy, cut, or float. Choosing Float from the Select menu converts the selection to a floater and sets it up on its own layer. Now the piece is movable and editable, independent of the rest of the image. Figure 5.27 shows an elliptical section of an image now converted to a floater and moved

Figure 5.27

The image of the bike has had a circular section selected using the elliptical selection tool. It's been converted to a layer by choosing Float from the Select menu.

Figure 5.28
The image of the car has had a freehand section drawn around the edge of the hood, and then converted into a floater.

slightly. The Layers dialog box indicates that this is the current floater selected. Also shown is the control panel for the selection tool when in use.

- *The Lasso selection tool* 🔲: The Lasso tool allows you to draw freehand a selection marquee or mask onto your image.

The trouble with this tool is the requirement for a steady hand to complete a nice smooth selection. To this end, you can do a couple of things to make this process easier.

First, you can use the Magnifier tool 🔲 to zoom in on the area to be selected and get a better view of your work.

Second, you can add to or take from the selected area by holding down the Shift or Ctrl key on your keyboard, respectively. When you do this, the Lasso mouse pointer has a little plus or minus symbol beside it, indicating that you are adding to or taking from the selection. This means that if you don't get the selection right the first time, you can always trim it and add to the edges until you consider it perfect.

Figure 5.28 shows an image of a car after converting the hood of the vehicle into a floater with the Lasso tool. Now that it's a floater, it can be moved up, a drop shadow added, and the space left filled with a pattern. The Lasso tool is also shown. Interesting effect, don't you think?

AVOIDING PITFALLS

Many issues are covered in this chapter, and with them are associated traps that you should avoid falling into.

You should take some time to become familiar with these image editing tools, their relative pros, and their relative cons. Spend just enough time to become familiar enough to decide which is the most appropriate tool for your needs. The more versatile multimedia developers will actually own and use most of these applications, and use each one for its best features. Often you can develop this level of familiarity with these products by using the freely available demonstration version of each application *before* you invest your hard-earned money. See the links to demo downloads at this book's Web site.

With a little research you can quickly become familiar with the range of plug-ins and additional add-ons for these software applications. Some of the special effects that you can apply are simply amazing. Spend some time researching these tools, as later you may save considerable valuable time on a project by being able to buy and use a set of plug-ins that could create a special effect that would otherwise take you many hours to complete manually.

When using image editing tools to create your multimedia application components, be sure to store those components in their own directory. Not only is this good file housekeeping, but some multimedia application authoring tools can load the contents of a directory in one step, saving you time and energy.

When creating images for your multimedia product, you will most likely develop images using layers or composite images. Your final result will be in the form of a flat image file, most likely in JPEG, BMP, GIF, or TIFF format. Since these formats do not support layer information, unless you save a layered version of the image, you will not be able to return to it for editing later. The simple solution is to create a subdirectory where you store these pieces of your future multimedia application. Name it "Scratch." In it, save the original layered versions of the images in the image editing application's own native format.

Chapter Summary

- Image editing and graphic design software applications are extremely useful tools in the development of multimedia application content.

- Paint Shop Pro and Photoshop are image editing applications whose special-effect plug-ins and editing tools can be put to great use when you design your multimedia application's interface and contents.

- While Photoshop and Paint Shop Pro are different software applications, their purpose and use are quite similar. The process of image editing is fundamentally universal across such programs. There are more similarities than there are differences between these products.

- All graphic design tools have a collection of selection and masking tools that enable you to precisely determine the area of your work you wish to edit and change, while protecting the surrounding image.

- Image editing tools allow you to save your work in a digital image file. This file can be in one of many formats, each with its own benefits and disadvantages. When saving in the application's native format, you also save additional image information, such as what parts are on what layers, which pieces are floaters, and so on, that is lost in a flat file format. However, this native format is usually usable only by the application from which it was saved (an exception to this is the Photoshop file format, which can be opened with many other image editing applications, provided that the version of the Photoshop format used is compatible with the other application).

- Painter is a natural-media graphic design tool that mimics the artistic effects of many forms of natural art tools and materials. Painting with digital materials such as digital oil paint, digital watercolor, digital charcoal, and other media provides many features unavailable with real-life materials, such as Undo and digital masking. However, the resulting artwork is remarkably similar to the real thing.

Key Terms and Concepts

Airbrush tool, 100
aspect ratio, 97
Buttonize, 97
cloning brush, 102
Color Replacer tool, 100

flat image, 98
floater, 115
fractals, 91
Lasso tool, 95
layering, 93
Magic Wand tool, 95

marching ants border, 94
marquee, 94
mask, 100
natural-media painting tool, 91

swatch, 96
tolerance value, 102

Checking Your Knowledge and Skills

1. Layering Exercise: Using a sample image, such as one of those provided in the Samples folder of this book's CD-ROM:
   - Open the image file in Paint Shop Pro or Photoshop.
   - Select elements of the image and promote them to their own layer.
   - Apply a different special effect to each layered element.
   - Save your work as a JPEG file of a different name.

2. Cloning Exercise: Using two sample images, such as those provided in the Samples folder of this book's CD-ROM:
   - Open both image files in Paint Shop Pro or Photoshop.
   - Using Paint Shop Pro's Cloning tool or Photoshop's Rubber Stamp tool, clone elements of one image onto the next to give a seamless composite effect.
   - Save your work as a TIFF file of a different name.

3. Text Application Exercise: Using a new blank image:
   - Type "Welcome to My Multimedia World" in the font and color of your choice using the text tool.
   - Create a nice soft shadow for your text using the drop shadow special-effect filter in your photo editing application.
   - Create a subhead in a smaller font beneath the heading you just created that says "Enter Here," and use your choice of special-effect filter to make this subhead stand out and highly legible.
   - Save your work as a Windows Bitmap (BMP) file with a different name.

4. Painter Exercise: Using your choice of Painter brushes and paper texture, create a drawing that demonstrates Painter's many brush possibilities.

5. Image Hoses Exercise: Using either Painter's Image Hose or Paint Shop Pro's Picture Tube, create a frame around the edge of your image using the "hosed-on" images.

Critical Thinking Challenges

Given the design considerations that you now know are important to multimedia graphics and interface design, answer the following questions and challenges:

1. Compare a photo editing application to a natural-media painting application. Which do you believe is most appropriate to your work as a multimedia designer? Do you think that they can be used together on a project? Explain your answers.

2. Create a prototype interface design for a multimedia product, using what you have learned to date. Use the drop shadow effect to emphasize the banner text and controls in your interface. Create an identical interface without the drop shadows. Which would you prefer for an interface, and why? Use these two images to describe, to someone who knows little about multimedia, the effect that using drop shadows has on the user.

3. From what you know so far, what advantages and disadvantages would there be in saving your work in that application's own native file format (for example, in Photoshop format or Paint Shop Pro format)?

4. With a photo image file of someone you know, use Painter's cloning technique to create a version of a photo image file that looks hand-drawn. Is there an advantage in using such an image in a multimedia presentation over the original photo? What sense or feeling does the viewer get from the natural-media image that is not conveyed by the original image?

Hands-on Exercises
IMAGE EDITING

Using a conventional paper sketchpad and colored pencils or pens:

1. Draw a picture of your choice of subject matter.

2. Scan the image into your computer system and bring it into a photo editing program.

3. Using the photo editing application, clean up the image and adjust the image attributes (brightness, contrast, luminance, saturation, and so on). Apply special effects to create a background for a multimedia application. Remember, you want a subdued and subtle image that will not impose on the focal points—the controls—of the interface.

4. Using Painter, draw as best you can an identical image using Painter's drawing tools. Feel free to enhance the image if Painter's tools offer more possibilities than your physical tools did.

5. Using Painter, adjust this image to create a similar background image for your multimedia production.

6. Choose your favorite of the two images by either printing them or displaying them both on the screen. Which method of creating the background image did you prefer?

7. Ask an impartial observer to select a background image. Which did he or she choose?

Master Project
PREPARING FOR THE INTERFACE PROTOTYPE

So far you should have created a binder that documents your project concept and shows a plan, timeline, and design documentation for the project.

Collect images and samples of work that you admire in preparation for the next step of creating your interface. You may want to include an image you can transform into a background for your product. You may want to collect a series of images of objects that could be made into button faces. You may have some images and media content you want to include in your work. Now is the time to collect this material and digitize those pieces that are not already digital. Use a Zip disk or similar storage device to keep your raw materials together.

An idea at this point is to collect images that reflect in abstract terms the section of your digital portfolio you wish to present. For instance, you may have a photo of your college or high school, or perhaps an image of some other college, that would make a great background. Such an image modified by "bleaching out" the image and softening it, would do well as a background for the section about your educational history. Alternatively, the same image converted to a black-and-white photo on a blue background would contrast well with primary yellow text with red bullets!

6

USING THE TOOLS

Chapter Outline

Chapter Objectives

After completing this chapter, you will be able to:

- Discuss the significance of graphic design and image choices for your multimedia project's interface.
- Apply techniques and methods for creating an intuitive multimedia application interface.
- Create a suitable background image (stage) for your interface.
- Create buttons, controls, and hot spots for your interface.
- Design appropriate visual and interactive responses for users.

Chapter Overview

In this chapter you will use some of the graphic design software tools you have just learned about to create a professional interface for your multimedia applications. This chapter takes you step by step through the process of creating a multimedia application's interface and controls. The processes and techniques described are useful for all aspects of image processing in the development of a professional multimedia application.

CREATING THE MULTIMEDIA PRODUCT'S IMAGE AND MOOD

As you read in Chapter 2, a multimedia product is a very visual one, and often an emotional one too—not to the extent that you are moved to tears, but certainly the content evokes within you a certain response to its visual design. For instance, you would not create a multimedia piece with neon colors and dance music for a funeral home, any more than you would use a predominantly black and gray design with somber music to promote a party services company. There is a lot to be said for choosing the appropriate "mood" design for your multimedia product.

Creating the appropriate image for your multimedia product involves both your ability to design to suit a purpose and common sense. There is no "magic formula." If you find this aspect of multimedia design particularly challenging (or if you simply don't think you can achieve these design goals), don't worry. The best way to create an appropriate design is to solicit assistance from others. For this review process, clear illustrations will suffice (as opposed to a completely assembled functional interface). In this instance a color printer can be invaluable. Create a mock-up interface, print it in color, and provide copies to your reviewers.

Find some people willing to spend a little time with your interface design and get their feedback about how they think it fits your design goals. While not all criticism will be appropriate (or even helpful), if you collect a good-sized sample of respondents (usually eight or more) then you can weigh the polarized and extreme responses and get a consensus. This feedback can be invaluable, especially when you consider it as insight into what will be going through the minds of those who will actually use your final multimedia product. Use your reviewers' comments to modify and improve your design, and be sure to show your test team the resulting changes. You will probably go through several rounds of such review before developing a perfect interface.

Take some time to think through your interface design and its tone. Do you want to create a professional product for business use or something with a wacky MTV flavor? Use the interface design and layout techniques you read about in Chapter 4 to map out your design. Get feedback, refine, and start to build.

CREATING AN INTERFACE

Creating an interface involves designing a layout and "look" and then creating the background image and the matching controls. In this chapter you will learn how to methodically create background and control graphics.

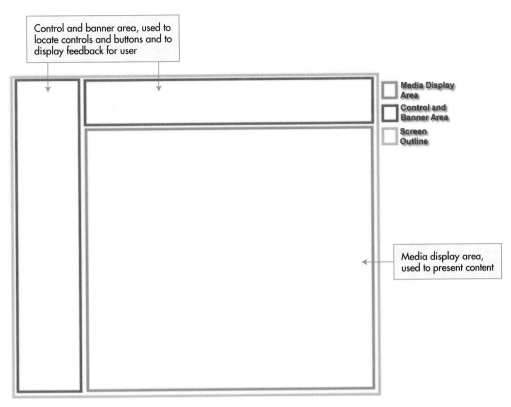

Control and banner area, used to locate controls and buttons and to display feedback for user

Media Display Area

Control and Banner Area

Screen Outline

Media display area, used to present content

Figure 6.1
This design layout uses the techniques presented in Chapter 4 and provides a typical plan for building the interface.

PLANNING FOR USABILITY

If the interface for your multimedia product is anything, it has to be functional. Functionality for a multimedia piece is not just that the buttons actually operate as they are supposed to; they also should look as if they'll do what they're supposed to do when you click on them. Their visual appearance should hint at their intended function.

Using the interface design and layout techniques you learned in Chapter 4, you should create a design that will provide appropriate control and display surfaces for your product's operation. The design should also provide sufficient display area for showing your media content. Figure 6.1 shows a typical multimedia design layout, and the one that will be "fleshed out" in this chapter. You, as the designer, should feel free to flex your creative muscles when building the functional interface for *your* application.

When planning your interface, be sure to select a background graphic that is suitable and representative of the product subject matter (for example, the logo of the company you are creating the product for, or a photograph of the subject matter faded out) and one that echoes the topic without imposing on the primary interface. For now, select a good topic image.

Another function of usability is designing appropriate button size. When designing your layout, focus on the proportions of your control areas (shown in red in Figure 6.1) to your media display area (shown in green). Your buttons and controls will have to fit within your control area, and this space will affect the possible sizes of your buttons. The object of determining button size is to design a control that is large enough to clearly display the icon, text, picture indicating its function, but not so large as to consume too much screen "real estate." Buttons that are too large can look crude, while buttons that are too small can be difficult to operate with accuracy. You must find a compromise size that fits your product's needs.

MIMIC REAL LIFE

As you have learned, it is more effective to provide users with buttons and controls that are pictorial and intuitive, rather than those that use text to indicate their function. It often helps to imagine six-year-olds using your multimedia product. If they can figure out the functions of your controls, then you can be sure that adults can too.

Whenever possible, use images for controls rather than text. Text causes users to pause for an instant and interpret the words. If the words are not crystal clear, they may hesitate even longer before clicking on the button. Hesitancy is intuition's worst enemy!

There is an exception to this general rule. When users pass their mouse pointer over a particular button, they may see text that describes that button's function. Sometimes that text will be in the form of a small pop-up panel showing a description or name for the button. This feature is called a ToolTip. Sometimes the button's appearance changes dramatically when the mouse pointer is moved over it. This is to draw the user's attention to the button's function. This button effect is called a hot button. A hot button effect can include a textual description of the button's intended function. Hot spots are described later in this chapter.

In this initial stage of your design, volunteer testers can help refine a good interface.

CREATING VISUAL IMPORTANCE AND DEPTH FOR IMPORTANT CONTROLS

As you read in Chapter 4, using techniques (such as drop shadows) that give 3D depth to important controls and buttons helps draw users' attention to them. Controls that appear physically closer to users have more psychological and visual importance. To this end, the multimedia interface designer uses embossing and drop shadow special effects to make those controls appear raised up off the interface background, and, therefore closer to users.

When you design a button or control, you have to create a separate image for each state of the button. A typical set of button states includes the following: an image for the *up* state of the button, when it is ready for a click; an image for the *roll over* state, which appears when the user passes the mouse pointer over the button (this image is often referred to as the "hot" button); and an image for the *clicked/depressed* state, which appears when users click the button and gives the animated impression of responsive movement of the control.

If you have a raised button using an emboss or drop shadow to indicate that it is in the ready-for-a-click up state, then users expect to see that button depress when they click it. To achieve this effect requires you to create an up button graphic, and then a depressed button graphic, which appears when you click the up version. Most authoring applications accommodate the building of such graphical and custom buttons by allowing you to assemble theses image sets into a button control.

If your button also acts as a hot spot (also referred to as a *rollover state*), then a third button image is required.

To show the button's transition from raised to depressed, you need to account for the users' perspective. If the up button is shown floating above the interface and casting a shadow below it, then you can see some of the background slightly beneath it (you can peek under it), and it obstructs some of the background behind it (blocking the view), as shown in Figure 6.2. When the button is depressed and against the background, you can't see any background beneath it (because it's flat to the background), and you can see all of the background that had been hidden behind the raised version, because it is no longer raised and obstructing the view. This is illustrated in Figure 6.2, where you can

ToolTip

The pop-up text message that appears when the mouse pointer is paused for more than a second over an interface control.

hot button

Similar in function to a hot spot, this is a button image (or state) that changes dramatically when the user passes the mouse pointer over it, to emphasize its importance to the user, sometimes also referred to as a "rollover."

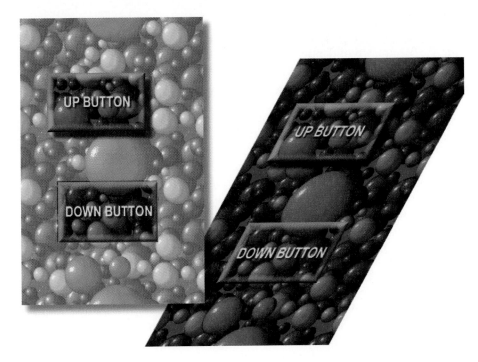

see how the raised button hides some of the background behind it, and how you can see some of the background beneath the raised button.

Because these images are two-dimensional, there is no real elevation and depression. This is an optical illusion. The illusion is achieved by first moving the button face up and to the left on the background (Figure 6.3, Step 3), and then applying a drop shadow special effect, as shown in Figure 6.3, Step 4. This sliding of the button graphic up and over gives the illusion of perspective, which is further enhanced by the drop shadow.

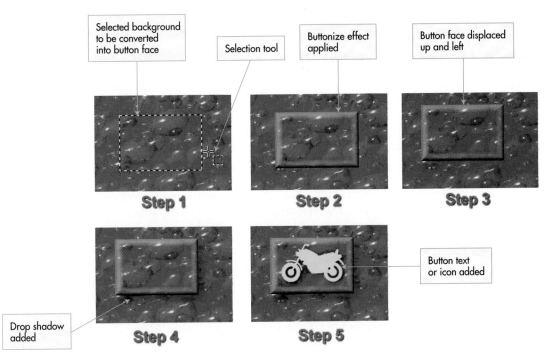

Figure 6.3
The illusion of a 3D elevated button can be created in five easy steps with any graphics software.

The five-step button creation process shown in Figure 6.3 illustrates how moving the button before applying the drop shadow is an essential aspect of creating the 3D illusion of depth.

DESIGNING HOT SPOTS AND VISUAL RESPONSES TO ACTION

Hot spot images can be very useful for your users. Providing visual response and feedback from a simple mouse movement over the control is a very intuitive action. It also removes some of the uncertainty users may have before clicking on a control. With additional information about a button's function, users are more likely to use the button freely. You can remove a lot of user hesitancy with hot spots. You have read previously the significance of a hot button; hot spots are simply an equally dramatic visual response to the mouse pointer moving into an area of the interface to which you wish to draw attention.

Hot spots do not have to be button images. Any area or element of your interface can be a hot spot. A hot spot can also be indicated as simply as a mouse pointer change. Often in spatial environment applications (as discussed in Chapters 1 and 2), users know that they can navigate in a certain direction because as they move their mouse around in the scene, the mouse pointer changes into an arrow that points in a particular direction.

You will want to experiment with hot spots. You can make any area of a graphic into a hot spot by having the graphic (or the mouse pointer) change when the mouse moves over it. Typically a hot spot incorporates a "glowing" effect, or a different picture when the mouse moves over the designated area.

Create hot spots with purpose. A hot spot is an intuitive way to encourage users to click on that area or control. Be sure to provide an appropriate response and function for that click. Otherwise you'll make your users nervous if they believe that your hot spots will not function as expected.

The primary purpose of the graphical techniques discussed in this chapter is to catch users' attention and to provide them with information. You want to guide them to choose the correct control for the correct purpose. You want them to be able to distinguish a control or button from the background instantly without giving it any thought. Once you have achieved this, follow through and give users the response they expect.

CREATING A STAGE FOR YOUR MAIN CONTENT

While it can often be the least noticed aspect of your multimedia production, the background or "stage" is perhaps the most important. It defines the look and feel of the whole product. Sometimes your project's background can be a simple plain color, and sometimes an elaborate but muted image. The intended feel of your final product will determine the type of background you use.

When building the interface components (including your background image) for your multimedia product, you will need to create individual graphic elements that you will assemble later into your multimedia authoring application. Typically you will collect the following components:

- A background image with pixel dimensions (width and height) that match the intended application size. Some applications show variants of the background on different screens. In this case you will need a background image for each screen.

- A banner graphic (if one is used) for displaying text, headings, and messages. It could be blank for the framing of text that's entered later in the authoring phase, or the graphic could incorporate the appropriate heading text and be created, text and all, in your graphic design application.

- For each button or control you will need at least two images: a raised image and a depressed image. If your button includes a hot spot response to a mouse pointer rollover (when the mouse pointer passes over the control), you will have to create and store a third image for that button. Later in the authoring application, each set of these button state images will be assembled into functional user controls.

- Most other elements and components fall into the category of content unless you have designed some hot spot effects or screen panels that are not common throughout. These too will have be stored in preparation for the authoring phase later.

In the following steps, you will use Paint Shop Pro to create a simple background image to match the interface plan shown in Figure 6.1 (you can always jump ahead occasionally to Figure 6.17 to see the final production). Once you have created the background image, you can then design buttons that will work with it. For this example the product subject matter will be an interactive guide to motorcycle maintenance. You will find the image used to create the background and controls shown in the illustrations for this application in the SAMPLES folder of this book's CD-ROM. It's called Dan's Bike.jpg. For Photoshop users, Photoshop tips will address what specific differences Photoshop may have.

1. Load Dan's Bike.jpg into Paint Shop Pro or your photo editing application.

2. Using the selection tool ▣ , select an area of the background image that corresponds to the display banner area in your plan (refer to Figure 6.1). Figure 6.4 shows the banner area selected on the background image.

3. The selection marquee outlines an area of the background that you can copy and then paste as a separate new image for later use. You are creating a banner-shaped section of matching background to work on later. From the Edit menu, choose Copy. From the Edit menu again, choose Paste, then

Figure 6.4

The selection marquee outlines the banner display area for the interface. Copying and pasting this part of the background and saving it to a separate file stores this image for later work.

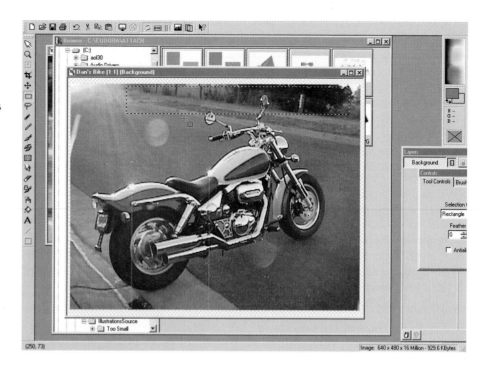

choose As a New Image (you can also use the Ctrl-C and Ctrl-V keyboard shortcuts to copy and paste). Note that when you paste to a new image the new image may appear larger than the original. The original may be at a different zoom factor than the new pasted image.

4. Save this banner image to your hard disk drive (don't forget where you save it) as a JPEG file and name it Banner. If you are presented with a message box indicating that the saved image will be a flat file and its layers will be merged select OK. (Usually image formats such as JPEG, PICT, or Windows Bitmap (BMP) do a fine job of storing the image in excellent image quality and are acceptable to most authoring applications.) Do not close this image yet.

5. Using the selection tool ▢, select an area of the background image that corresponds to the button toolbar area in your plan (refer to Figure 6.1). Figure 6.5 shows the toolbar section of the background selected.

6. Lighten and fade out the background image everywhere *except* in the toolbar area that you have selected. To achieve this, *invert* the selected area, so that everything but that area becomes selected by choosing Invert from the Selections menu. Now all areas of the background other than the toolbar area should be selected and ready to be faded out.

7. From the Colors menu, choose Adjust, then choose Brightness/Contrast, and use the Brightness/Contrast dialog box to fade the background to your liking, as shown in Figure 6.6. The object here is to create a faint image of the background that is recognizable, but is not distracting from the primary media and controls of the multimedia product.

INVERTING A SELECTION IN PHOTOSHOP

In Photoshop, the command to invert the selection is very similar: choose the Inverse command from the Select menu.

Figure 6.5
Using the selection marquee, select an area for a toolbar. By then inverting this selection, you select the background area to be faded out.

Resulting effect

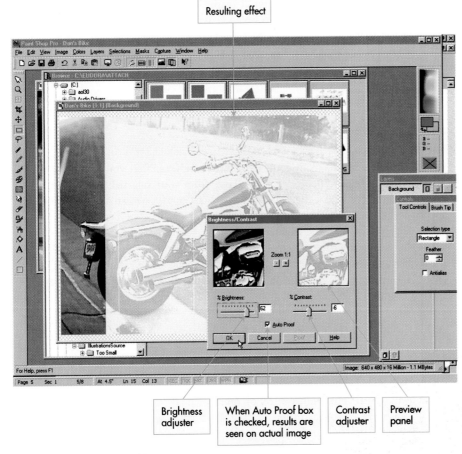

Brightness adjuster

When Auto Proof box is checked, results are seen on actual image

Contrast adjuster

Preview panel

Figure 6.6
In the Brightness/Contrast dialog box, use whatever settings you wish to fade out the background image to suit your needs.

ADJUSTING BRIGHTNESS AND CONTRAST IN PHOTOSHOP

To adjust the brightness and contrast settings of the selected area of the image in Photoshop, click the Image menu, choose Adjust, then choose Brightness/Contrast. When you have selected the settings of your choice, click OK to apply them.

8. Using the Invert command, invert the selection once again to reselect the toolbar section of the image. Now you are ready to turn it into a suitable toolbar.

9. To distinguish the toolbar from the background, buttonize it and give it a nice drop shadow. Both of these operations are done while the marquee surrounds the unfaded toolbar area. To buttonize the toolbar area, make sure that the background color, as shown in the background color square, is a light color. This is the highlight color used when the Buttonize special effect filter creates the 3D beveled button effect. If your background color is unintentionally dark, then the highlighted sides (top and left) of the buttonized panel will appear shaded and ruin the visual effect. You always can Undo such a mistake and do it over correctly.

10. From the Image menu, choose Effects, then Buttonize, and adjust the Buttonize parameters until they match those shown in Figure 6.7. Click OK to apply the changes.

    To emphasize the 3D effect you will also create a soft drop shadow for the toolbar. This will give the visual impression that the toolbar is floating above the background. Also, it gives visual importance to the toolbar.

11. While the toolbar area still has the selection marquee around it, click the Image, choose Effects, and then choose Drop Shadow. Set the Drop Shadow

BUTTONIZING IN PHOTOSHOP

Photoshop does not have an equivalent Buttonize filter that you can apply to a selection. However, if you create a new layer from your selected piece (from the Layer menu, choose New, then choose Layer Via Copy), you can apply one of the special layer filters available under the Effects command. The Bevel and Emboss effect works well using the Inner Bevel setting. Third-party filters for Photoshop usually include a filter that creates button edges that would work. Alien Skin's Eye Candy has a filter called Inner Bevel that does a terrific job of creating buttons. You can, of course, use one of the many standard filters that come with Photoshop to give your button face a look that distinguishes it from the background.

DROP SHADOWS IN PHOTOSHOP

If you have placed your toolbar selection on its own layer, as described in the previous Photoshop tip, you can then use the Drop Shadow command to create the desired effect. Click the OK button to apply your drop shadow.

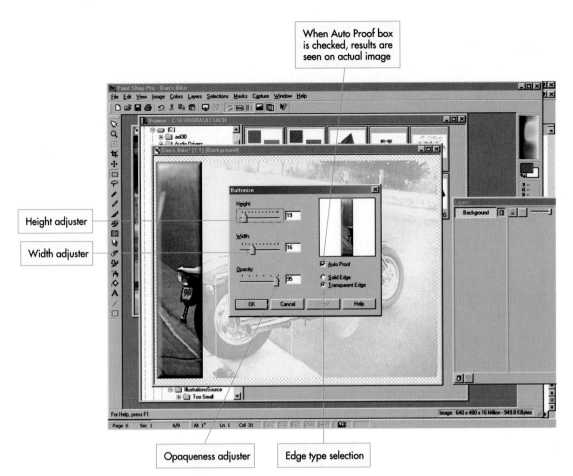

When Auto Proof box is checked, results are seen on actual image

Height adjuster

Width adjuster

Opaqueness adjuster

Edge type selection

Figure 6.7
Adjust the Buttonize dialog box parameters until you are pleased with the results. Using the Auto Proof option, you can preview the results of this operation.

dialog box parameters to those shown in Figure 6.8. You now have an attractive 3D toolbar and background.

12. Save this background image as Background.jpg. Save it to the same location on your hard disk drive as the other elements of this exercise.

13. Click the banner graphic, which should still be in an open window. Since this image has no area selected with a selection marquee, you can apply the Buttonize special effect and it will apply to the entire image. From the Image menu, choose Effects, then choose Buttonize, and adjust the Buttonize parameters to match those shown in Figure 6.7. If you want to match the appearance of the toolbar, those settings (providing you have not changed them since you buttonized the toolbar) should still be stored in the Buttonize dialog box. Click the OK button to apply your buttonizing effect.

14. Using the Text tool, type the following: The Interactive Guide to Motorcycle Maintenance. Select the font of your choice.

15. Save the banner image. You should now have a background image and a banner image for your interface.

The next step is to create your interface buttons.

Color of shadow (usually black or dark color)

Opaqueness adjuster

Blur (softness of the shadow edge) adjuster

Offset (direction of the shadow) adjuster

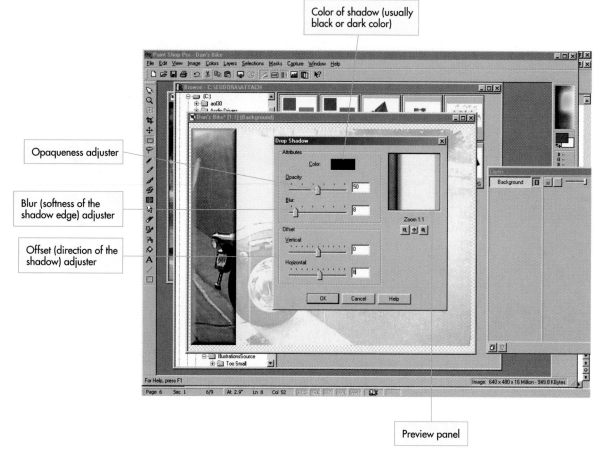

Preview panel

Figure 6.8
Using the Drop Shadow special effect, create a drop shadow that gives visual relief to the toolbar.

CREATING BUTTONS AND VISUAL CONTROLS

Creating 3D buttons is quite a simple methodical task. The important part is to plan the steps for each phase of the button (raised, depressed, and hot) and ensure that they all exactly match each other and the background they sit on. To accomplish this, you create each button phase on the same small piece (swatch) of the background, as shown in Figure 6.3. This swatch is cut from the background using the selection tool.

When the resulting button phases are built into a button control in an authoring application, you can be confident that they will match that background because you cut them from it in the first place! If you accurately place the matching swatch showing the image of the button on the background, the edges of the swatch should merge with the background pattern and all you will see is the button itself.

The magic of 3D-interface button creation becomes more apparent when you actually create a few.

 You will find the images used to create the background and controls for this application in the SAMPLES folder of this book's CD-ROM. The images are named Dan's Bike.jpg and ButtonBits.psd.

Continuing with our motorcycle maintenance application interface exercise, perform the following steps *for each button*:

1. From the toolbar area of the background graphic, select an area for the position of your first button. Figure 6.9 shows a section of the toolbar marked

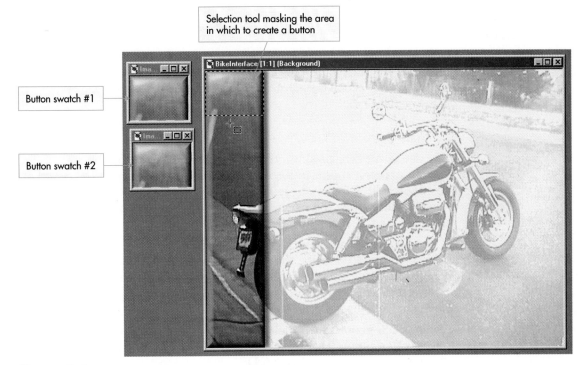

Selection tool masking the area
in which to create a button

Button swatch #1

Button swatch #2

Figure 6.9
Select a section of your toolbar to create a set of three swatches, one for each phase of the button you're about to create.

with the selection marquee. Your next step will be to copy this selected area and paste it into three new images, two of which are shown in Figure 6.9 to the left of the main interface image.

2. From the Edit menu, choose Copy. Then click again on the Edit menu, choose Paste, then choose As New Image. Paste two more images for a total of three new swatches as shown in Figure 6.10. Each swatch will be used for a different phase of our button.

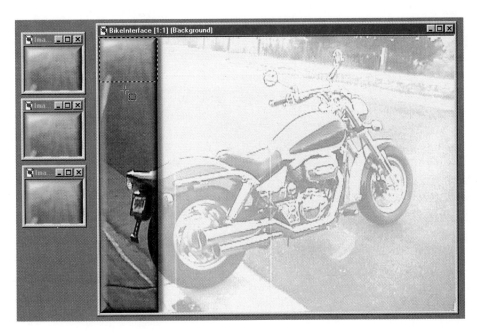

Figure 6.10
After pasting three swatches as new images, you are ready to begin creating your depressed button.

In Photoshop once you have selected the button face area using the selection tool, click the Layer menu, choose New, then choose Layer via Copy to create a new layer with a copy of the button face. Then the layer effects for drop shadow and beveling will be available to you.

3. On one of the swatches, use the selection tool to mark off the area of the button as it will appear in the depressed state. Try to keep to the center of the swatch. It is important to start with the depressed button, as this will enable you to copy the newly designed button face to the other swatches and continue designing the additional button phases.

4. Using the Buttonize command, create a beveled button face design to your liking. If you do not like the Buttonize command, feel free to try other effects, such as changing the luminance, brightness, or hue of the section selected. Whatever you do, make the selected button face look distinctly different from the background.

5. From the Selections menu, choose Promote to Layer. This creates a new layer with a button face on it, ready to edit in all phases. Your depressed button should look like Figure 6.11.

6. Now you will create the images for the button faces that will represent their intended function. You will find a selection of suitable images in a layered Photoshop image file called ButtonBits.psd, as seen in Figure 6.12. This

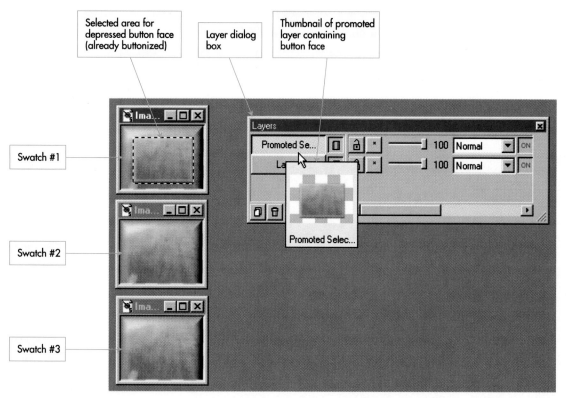

Figure 6.11
The swatch with the depressed button, showing the button face as a separate layer.

Figure 6.12
The ButtonBits image contains multiple layers, each of which has a different motorcycle component to use as a button face image.

image is provided in a Photoshop-format file so that whether you are using Paint Shop Pro, Photoshop, or another image editing application that supports layering, you will be able to load this image. Each of these images is on a separate layer that you can copy onto your new button faces.

7. Your first button will be for Scheduled Maintenance. You will use the Speedometer image for this button's picture because it shows the odometer, which is the primary indicator of when scheduled maintenance is due. To create a separate image of the speedometer from the layered ButtonBits.psd file, open the file in Paint Shop Pro, select the Speedometer layer using the Mover tool, and copy it. (Simply click the speedometer with the Mover tool, and that layer should show as selected in your Layer Palette.)

8. From the Edit menu, choose Paste, then choose As New Image to paste the copied image to a new image. You should now have a new image of the speedometer to size to fit your button, as shown in Figure 6.13.

9. Resize that new image using the Resize command (on the Image menu), and select a percentage reduction that will result in an image small enough to fit comfortably on the button face. In the example shown, a 25% reduction was used. Your reduction value will vary to suit your button size. Don't forget that you can always use Undo if you don't get it exactly right the first time.

10. Copy the resized speedometer image, and paste it onto the button face layer.

11. From the Image menu, choose Effects, then choose Drop Shadow to create a soft drop shadow beneath the speedometer, as shown in Figure 6.14. The button layer on this image should now have a button-with-speedometer

RESIZING IN PHOTOSHOP

Use the Image Size command (on the Image menu) in Photoshop to resize your images.

Figure 6.13
After pasting the copied speedometer layer as a new image, you can now resize it to fit your button face.

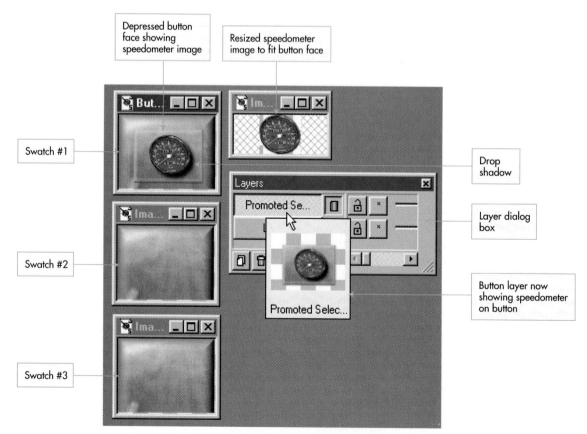

Figure 6.14
The Scheduled Maintenance button in the depressed state. Note the size of the speedometer and the drop shadow on the button.

Since you will most likely need a "flat file" format for your authoring application (where presumably your images will finally end up), you will lose the layering of the image elements once it is saved in such a format. This will prevent you from editing individual layers of that image later. If you think that you might like to edit the image again later (or if you're not sure whether you absolutely won't need to), then save a layered file that you can later edit in layers. If it turns out that you don't need it, you can always delete it. Recreating the file's layers because they were not preserved can be a frustrating task.

image for you to copy to the other blank button swatches. Save this complete image as a JPEG file, and call it MaintDn.jpg. Do not close this image, as you still need to access the button layer. If you need to close the program, save this image as a native Paint Shop Pro (or Photoshop) format image for later editing. This format will preserve the separate layers.

12. Now you will create the elevated button. From the depressed button image (MaintDn.jpg), hide all but the button and speedometer icon layers. Copy the visible layers, and then paste into the next blank button swatch as a new layer by clicking the Edit menu, choosing Paste, then choosing As New Layer. This second swatch should now look exactly like the depressed button.

13. Using the Mover tool , move the button face so that it is above and to the left of the location occupied by the button face in the depressed image.

14. Using the Drop Shadow command, give your elevated button a soft drop shadow that visually indicates that it is raised off the background, as shown in Figure 6.15. You now have a raised button. Save this image as MaintUp.jpg.

15. Now we move on to the hot button image. As with the raised button, you will need to copy the depressed button face from that image, and paste it into the remaining blank swatch. Do not copy the new raised button, as it has a drop shadow that will interfere with the hot button's glow effect.

16. Position the button face in the same location in the swatch as the raised button. Use the Drop Shadow command to create a glow around the button. To do this, set the shadow offset values to 0 (a shadow is directional, while a glow tends to radiate in all directions) and choose the color of your glow, such as red. Increase the blur value until you have a suitable glow around the button face. Keep the opacity value to 100%, as you want a strong glow. Learning to use the Drop Shadow effect to create a glow means that you do not have to depend on your image editing application having such a specialized feature.

17. If you choose, you can use the hot version of the button to place a textual prompt on the button that describes its function. This feature enables users to read the button's function when they move the mouse over it. Use Paint

CREATING A GLOW IN PHOTOSHOP

Photoshop has a layer special effect called Outer Glow that will work well here.

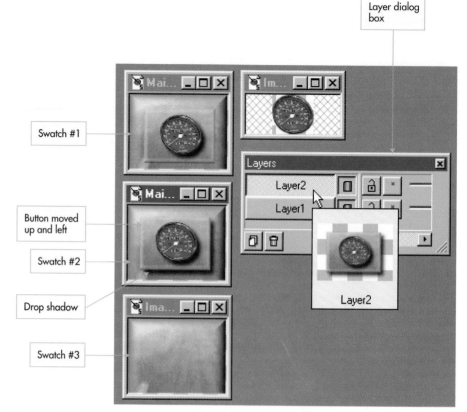

Swatch #1

Button moved
up and left

Swatch #2

Drop shadow

Swatch #3

Layer dialog
box

Figure 6.15
The raised button, showing the placing of this button up and to the left of the depressed button location, and the adding of a drop shadow.

Shop Pro's text tool **A** to place the text on the "glowing" button face.
Select a readable font of your choice and use a contrasting color such as yellow so that it is readable. Type the following: Scheduled Maintenance.
Figure 6.16 shows text on the hot version of the button; in this example, a
slight drop shadow is used to make the text more legible. Save this button
as MaintHot.jpg.

Save your new three-phase button set, along with the interface, and repeat
these techniques to create additional buttons on the interface. In Part 6 of this
book you will read how to assemble such image sets into a multimedia application, and turn them into functional and interactive controls and interface
components.

MORE GLOW, ANYONE?

To intensify the glow around an object, use the zero-offset drop shadow method to
repeat the same glow a second time (or more) over the first one. Alternatively, it is a
terrific investment to purchase plug-in special effect filters sets from companies
such as Alien Skin. Their Eye Candy plug-in set has a specialized glow filter that
offers more control than the zero-offset shadow. Alien Skin's plug-ins work well in
both Paint Shop Pro and Photoshop.

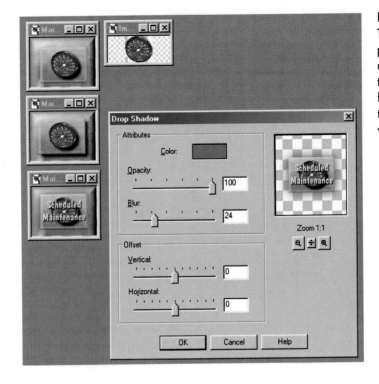

Figure 6.16
The hot button shows the textual prompt that appears when the user's mouse pointer hovers over the button face. Compare this figure to Figure 6.8, as both use the same special effect to achieve very different results.

If you would like to see what your button effects have turned out like, and cannot wait until Chapter 15 of this book, you can "assemble" your background, banner, and button images as layers in your image editing software. If you place the button-state images on top of each other in the correct location on the background, then switch on and off the visibility of the button layers, you can simulate the animation that takes place when users activate these controls. Figure 6.17 shows the completed interface at work. For this technique, place the button

Figure 6.17
The complete application interface at work.

images in the following layer order, topmost first: up state, hot state, depressed state. To see the "clicking" action, make the hot state button invisible and switch the up state button's visibility on and off to simulate its click operation. Repeat this technique with the hot state button visible to simulate the mouse rollover operation.

This chapter brought together the principles of interface and multimedia design in a practical and hands-on way. Now you should be able to create interfaces similar to the one shown, and, more important, you should be able to apply these techniques to creating your own unique control environment for your applications. Knowing the principles and reasons behind doing these things in the first place will guide you when you unleash your experimental creativity.

AVOIDING PITFALLS

As mentioned in the last chapter, and again in this one, planning ahead will help you avoid most obstacles. Create a sketch and do not be afraid to show it around and solicit feedback and comments. You can better solidify a design at this stage than after much work at your computer workstation.

multiple undo

A software application's ability to Undo a series of previous tasks, not just the most recent.

Remember the Undo button in your graphic design software. It will save you again and again. There is no need to worry about making mistakes when you know you can undo them. Most modern applications have multiple undo, which means that they can undo changes several steps back. Some applications, such as Corel's PhotoPaint and Jasc's Paint Shop Pro, provide a list of previous operations from which you can choose what to undo.

Remember that objects in your design that appear closer to users are perceived as more important.

When designing your raised button, do not forget to provide the perspective expected of a 3D button. Place the raised button above and to the left of the depressed button.

Do not overdo the hot spots and 3D effects. They often work better when there are few of them and they stand out. If you bury them among many similar 3D controls, they lose emphasis. Remember, simpler is better.

Chapter Summary

- To create the appropriate image for your multimedia product, you need to be able to design to suit a purpose and you need common sense. The best way to create an appropriate design is to solicit feedback from others.

- Creating an interface involves designing a layout and tone and then creating the background image and matching controls. Be sure to select a background that is representative of the subject matter.

- A background image should have pixel dimensions that match the intended application's size. Some applications show variants of the background on different screens. In these cases, you need a background image for each screen.

- When designing your layout, focus on the proportions of your control areas to the media display area. Buttons and controls need to fit within the control area. They should be large enough for users to see clearly and operate effectively, but not so large that they consume too much screen space.

- Controls that appear closer to users have more psychological and visual importance. To create this optical illusion, you can use embossing and drop shadow effects.

- When you design a button or control, you have to create a separate image for each phase. Each control has at least two images: a raised image and a depressed image. If your control has a rollover hot state, a third image will be required.
- Whenever possible, use images for controls rather than text. Text can be used quite effectively in a button's hot state, which can incorporate text describing a control's function. The text is visible only when users pass the mouse over the control, and therefore the interface "at rest" is unencumbered with a lot of textual messages. Hot spots can alleviate some of the uncertainty users may have about a button's or control's intended function.
- A banner graphic can be used to display text, headings, and messages.

Key Terms and Concepts

hot button, 124   multiple undo, 140   ToolTip, 124

Checking Your Knowledge and Skills

1. Find a photograph and create an interface design concept from it. Show the "before" photo, the scanned digital version of the photo, and the interface you designed around it. How did the subject and appearance of the image influence your interface design?

2. Using a 24-bit image, such as one of those provided in the SAMPLES folder of this book's CD-ROM, create a series of button controls, showing their raised, depressed, and "hot" states. Did the image file format you chose to save them in have any bearing on this exercise?

3. Using a 24-bit image, such as one of those provided in the SAMPLES folder of this book's CD-ROM, create a series of button controls for an interface. Create one set using text on the button faces to indicate the buttons' functionality. Create another set using icons or images on the button faces to indicate the buttons' functionality. Which button set would you most likely use for a multimedia project, and why?

4. Using a digitized photo of your family or a group of friends, create a series of hot spot graphics for each person in the photo. The purpose of the hot spot graphic is to encourage users to click that person in the photo to learn more about him or her. Provide a written description with your images explaining the intended function of this interface.

5. Create a screen capture of your favorite multimedia application and save it as an image file. Use your graphic design software to recreate the buttons and hot spots from this image, as if you were designing this interface from scratch, to match the "prototype" from which you took the screenshot. *Hint:* Most graphics packages, such as Paint Shop Pro, have a screen capture function to help you complete this exercise with ease.

Critical Thinking Challenges

Given the interface design considerations that you now know are important to multimedia graphics and interface design, answer the following questions and challenges:

1. Find a multimedia application you admire and examine the interface. What would you do to make it better? Pretend that the company that created this application has contracted you to design the next version of the product for imminent release. What would you design and why?

2. There are many multimedia (and Web) interfaces that do not use any 3D effects at all, and yet are quite effective. What do you think makes them so good, and how do they indicate visual significance for their controls? Macromedia Inc.'s Web site at www.macromedia.com is a good example of a well-thought-out 2D interface.

3. If you had to choose between using 3D controls with no hot spot reactions and 2D controls with only hot spot reactions for your interface, which would you choose? Why?

4. As mentioned in this chapter, it is not necessary to use the same interface throughout your application; you could use different interface controls and backgrounds in different areas of your application. What reason can you think of for doing this, and what would be the pros and cons of such an application design?

Hands-on Exercises
INTERFACE DESIGN

With a friend, colleague, or fellow student, select a multimedia application topic that you would like to design an interface for. Together, brainstorm the concept and create sketches of the design. Assign one of you to create the background and banner graphics, and the other to create the toolbar and button sets. Once you've done this, meet and see how these elements fit together. How effective was your planning session and to what extent did it help or not help with a successful design creation?

Master Project
BUILDING THE INTERFACE COMPONENTS

So far you should have created a binder for the project that documents your project concept, a project plan and timeline, and sketches and visuals for your design.

Now it is time to start building. With the concept sketches you have created so far, select a suitable background and create an interface image file set. Be sure to create a set of button images for each button or control along with your background and banner graphics. Save your work to a Zip disk (or equivalent) and keep it with your project binder.

CHAPTER

7

MULTIMEDIA BUILDING BLOCKS: 3D MODELING AND ANIMATION

Chapter Outline

Chapter Objectives

After completing this chapter, you will be able to:

- Discuss how subtle visual elements such as perspective, depth perception, shading, lighting, and shadows all give the visual impression of a 3D image.

- List the various output formats available from a computer 3D graphics and animation application and distinguish them from the saved 3D data file.

- Discuss how 3D graphics can greatly enhance a multimedia user interface and explain why they should be used in moderation.

- Describe how computer-generated animation video and keyframed animation are created.

- Discuss the role of 3D animation on the Web and why caution is required when implementing it.

- Describe the rendering process and how computer animation applications create their output images and animations.

Chapter Overview

In Part 2, you learned to create 3D effects. Buttons and toolbars that seem to stand out from the page give a visual emphasis that's difficult to miss. You view objects that appear closer to you as being more important because they are more noticeable.

This chapter will introduce you to the world of 3D computer modeling and animation. With these tools you can create computer "objects" that appear to have form and perspective through a process called modeling. You can think of this as similar to modeling with clay—you take a primitive shape of clay and mold, carve, whittle, and bend the shape into the required object. With digital tools, you accomplish the same tasks on screen, but with much more precision and far more tools than are available to the sculptor. These software applications, such as Caligari's trueSpace; NewTek's LightWave 3D and Inspire 3D; Kinetix's 3D Studio; MetaCreations's Infini-D, Ray Dream Studio, and Carrara; EIG.Sys's Poser; Corel's Bryce; and Template Graphics's 3Space Publisher, provide modeling and animation tools in one software product. Once you have created your 3D object, you can then have your application animate it based upon your instruction and input. You become the director of a virtual stage production. The objects are characters in the scene, whose composition and lighting are arranged and designed to your liking and behave completely under your control.

Not so long ago, animators had to physically draw and paint each frame of an animated movie by hand. Each image (called an animation "cel," named after the material—celluloid—that they were drawn on) was then photographed onto film so that you could view it on TV or in the movie theatre. At 30 frames per second, a typical 90-minute animated feature movie would require a team of animators to create 162,000 individual cels and then photograph them in the correct order!

Today modern computer animation software does most of this laborious work for us while also opening up tremendous possibilities for additional special effects and techniques. It's funny to think that animation cels are now expensive collector's items—often considered antiques!

WHAT IS 3D?

3D on a computer screen is, perhaps, a misnomer. The next time you use your computer, go ahead and touch the screen. It is flat. It's not really three-dimensional, is it? So what are we really talking about here?

Computer-generated 3D images, animations, and objects are all illusion. The multimedia producer creates images that look as if they are in 3D, even though they are on a flat surface. A good analogy would be that of a building. The architect's drawings are 2D plans of the structure. While a photograph of the building is actually 2D (as it's printed on a piece of paper), it shows a 3D image. Our brains perceive perspective and depth, but you cannot see parallax—you cannot tilt the picture to get a better look around the side of the building. Yet the photo has enough visual information to give the impression of a large mass with dimension and depth.

Figure 7.1 shows the progression from the 2D drawing of a building model through solid modeling, the addition of shadows, and the final addition of mate-

---

modeling

The processes used to create a 3D object in a computer 3D modeling and animation application.

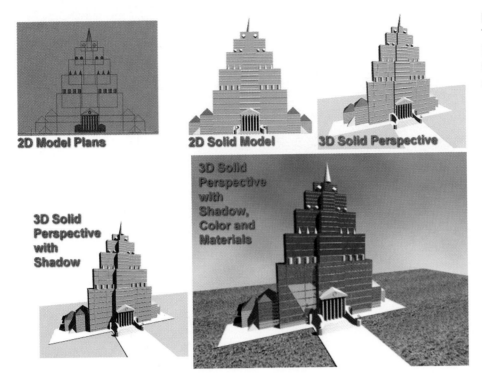

2D Model Plans

2D Solid Model

3D Solid Perspective

3D Solid Perspective with Shadow

3D Solid Perspective with Shadow, Color and Materials

rials and colors. In this illustration you can see how the visual sense or "realism" builds from step to step. With the addition of trees, a few hills, people, and perhaps vehicles, this scene begins to become more and more lifelike. Yet it is all illusion. Your task is to become a master of that illusion by using computer animation tools.

By providing the viewer with visual information about shape, lighting, shading, shadows, and perspective, you can create an image or an animation that has all the visual elements of a true-to-life scene. In multimedia you will use these elements to create 3D graphics, animations, and special effects.

DEPTH PERCEPTION

Figure 7.2 shows those elements that make a 2D image look like a 3D image. Notice how the tiled floor and the rectangular object in Figure 7.2 get smaller

CAN YOU SPOT THE WIRES?

You have seen the new generation of computer-based special effects in movies, whether you have realized it or not. Today most computer-generated special effects are so well done as to render themselves unnoticeable. The best special effects are those that you don't see! Gone are the days when, if you looked closely, you could spot the wires suspending Superman as he soared through the New York skyline.

Jurassic Park was among the first of this generation of movies to seamlessly integrate live and computer-generated elements into the movie. Other movies, such as *Toy Story* and *Antz*, are completely computer-generated and are prime examples of the level of sophistication to which computer animation tools have progressed. The best news is that these same software tools are available to you, the multimedia producer, for a modest investment.

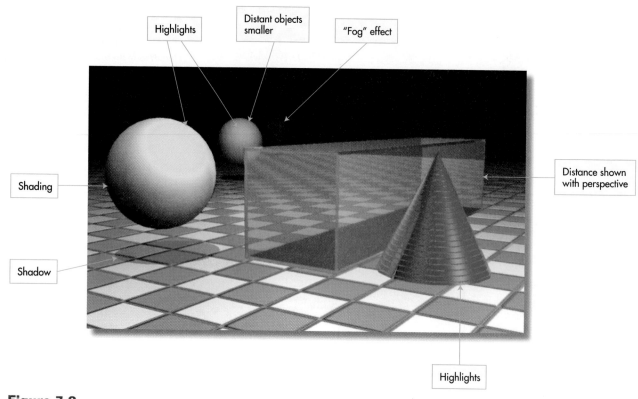

Figure 7.2
A few simple visual techniques give a realistic sense of 3D to a flat, printed image.

as they stretch into the distance. Just as you would expect from a real photo, no? Yet there is no actual distance on a printed image—just the illusion of distance.

The process of creating depth perception can be summarized in four easy steps. Refer to Figure 7.3 for an illustration of each step. These steps relate to any computer 3D modeling software; in the next chapter you will learn how to do this using a specific software application. For the moment, try to focus on the evolving steps, rather than the actual tasks used to get there.

1. Create a shape.

2. Apply shading to the shape to show the 3D form of the model. This is usually done with the 3D modeling software's *materials tool*. Many 3D modeling and animation programs combine steps 1 and 2 as one step when you create your original shapes, in a process called *solid modeling*.

3. Introduce lighting and shadows. Shadows are just as important as shading in providing 3D information about an object's shape and form. Shading and shadowing are two distinctly different things in a computer-generated 3D scene and should not be confused.

In real life, shadows and shading of actual objects are virtually the same thing: They result from a lack of illumination because the object's body is blocking the light. However, the computer treats shading and shadows in entirely different ways.

shading

A process in which the computer paints darker colors on the surfaces of an object that are farther away or obstructed from the light source.

On the computer, shading is a process in which the computer paints darker colors on the surfaces of an object that are farther away or obstructed from the light source. So it's really the computer "figuring out" which areas on the surface should be painted darker, rather than which areas are reflecting

less light. The computer does such a good job of this that you don't notice that it's "fake" shading. It's similar to applying eye shadow—painting a darker color to make a surface look shaded.

In contrast, shadows are created when an object obscures the light from a light source that has been explicitly told to cast shadows. The computer has to deduce, through a process called raytracing, which determines where every single ray of light goes after that ray leaves the light source, what the ray hits, what the ray bounces off (*reflection*), and what the ray is bent through (*refraction*). By figuring out which rays are blocked and which are not, the computer calculates a precise shadow in the shape of the object. Of course, you need to have a surface on which the shadow is projected. An object suspended in midair that casts a shadow is somewhat visually ineffective if you cannot see the shadow cast on something.

4. Add materials such as clouds, sky, or other appropriate images. One of the best ways to create a more realistic 3D scene is to use background graphics and object materials. Figure 7.4 shows two versions of our sample scene that use these materials to give the image a more realistic (though surreal) look.

By applying these steps you can create a convincing 3D scene for your interface background, corporate logo, Web page graphic, or controls for your multimedia piece.

In Part 2 you used some graphic design techniques to give an impression of visual depth. You will use the same techniques in computer 3D modeling to create similar effects. The difference with using a computer 3D modeling application is that most of this is done automatically for you by the software. However, the process of actually creating and manipulating the 3D objects in a 3D modeling application is completely different from creating these 3D scenes in a 2D graphic design package. While the learning curve with these types of computer creativity tools can be quite steep, the results can also be extremely rewarding.

shadows

Shadows are created when an object obscures the light from a light source that has been explicitly told to cast shadows.

raytracing

The process whereby the 3D modeling and animation software traces each virtual ray of light from a light source and follows it as it bounces, reflects, refracts, and is blocked by objects in the 3D scene. The result is a rendered scene showing a high degree of correctness in the way its lighting interacts with the objects in the scene.

Figure 7.4

Applying materials, textures, and backgrounds can create a more realistic look. The magic is in the details.

OVERVIEW OF COMPUTER ANIMATION AND VIDEO FILE FORMATS

Computer modeling and animation applications use two primary file types for their operation: (1) the output file, which is the final media piece that can be created in many still and moving picture file formats, and (2) the 3D data storage file, which is the 3D application's own data file that stores all of the information about the 3D scene so that you can later use and edit it again and again.

OUTPUT FILE

The output file type (rendered still-image output and rendered digital-video animation output) is the image or animation file that results from all of your work with your 3D modeling and animation application. It is the image or animation file that you can use in your multimedia authoring application. It is also stored on the disk in a standard data format that the other tools in your multimedia development toolbox, such as video editing, image editing, and authoring applications, can use.

If you want a "snapshot" of the 3D scene you're working on, computer animation applications can provide you with a single image file in a standard flat-file format. This still image can be stored in the standard image flat-file formats discussed in Chapter 5. The most common formats include JPEG, Windows Bitmap (BMP), Targa (TGA), and TIFF.

If you want to record animated motion, then your computer animation program can provide you a digital video file in a format such as Window's AVI or Macintosh/Windows QuickTime. There are also other digital video formats, such as AutoDesk's FLI, but AVI and QuickTime formats are by far the most widely used and will be supported by your authoring application. For Web animations there is also the Animated GIF file format, which you will read more about in Chapters 9 and 16. Only these file formats can store moving picture data.

In addition to using a video file to store your animated work, most animation applications can store the animated sequences as a series of individual images—one for each frame of animation. A three-second animation recorded at 30 frames per second will create 90 individual images, each showing the next incremental change in the animation. Such a collection of images can be useful for postprocessing of the animation in a digital video editing application and for using the animation in some multimedia authoring applications, but is not commonly used. Be careful with this format, as you can easily consume even the largest disk drive storing individual images for each frame of your animation!

3D DATA STORAGE FILE

This file type is used to store the 3D data that describe the objects and/or the scene. You can reload these files later for editing. This file type enables the 3D application to recreate your work and return all objects to the positions they occupied when they were last saved. This file contains the raw data that describe mathematically all of the geometry required to draw the scene on your screen for editing. It has no image content and is not viewable or usable by another noncomputer modeling and animation application. Typically, such a saved 3D file is in a proprietary format (specific to the program). However, a few 3D file formats are shared by such applications (and are referred to as interchangeable 3D object formats), typically are AutoDesk DXF, 3D Studio 3DS, Alias Wavefront OBJ, and increasingly in recent times VRML WRL files. These formats are generally interchangeable among the most commonly used 3D modeling and animation programs.

interchangeable 3D object formats

Some standard file formats used to store 3D object and 3D scene data that are recognized and used as standard formats in most 3D modeling and animation applications.

In contrast to these 3D data file types, output file types are merely images and do not contain any dimensional data to allow you to recreate and manipulate the 3D objects contained therein. For instance, you cannot load a digital video file into your 3D modeling and animation application and expect to be able to edit the 3D objects. However, the 3D data file stored by your application, when you use its save options, is a data file that mathematically describes the 3D scene and/or object. Using this file, you can reload and rearrange the scene and your view of it and create more output files in image or video file formats.

Table 7.1 summarizes the file formats usually available to these types of computer 3D modeling and animation applications.

REMEMBER TO SAVE!

With any 3D modeling application, be sure to save your work to its own native file format so that you can load that file again whenever you need to do additional work with it. Recall that when you render an output file, the image/video file you make will not recreate your 3D scene for you for further editing, no more than the program's native data file will be viewable in a digital image or video editing program. It is vital that you save your work and do not confuse rendering an output image/video file with the task of saving your work.

You can always reload your data file and render from it as many images and animation video clips as you wish. If you do not save your work's data file, you will have to rebuild it from scratch.

TABLE 7.1	Summary of Common File Formats Used by Most Computer 3D Modeling and Animation Applications.	
File Format		**File Extension**
Rendered Still-Image Output		
JPEG		.jpg
Windows Bitmap		.bmp
TIFF		.tif
CompuServe GIF (can also be an animation format, as shown below)		.gif
Targa		.tga
Macintosh PICT		.pct
Z-Soft Paintbrush		.pcx
Rendered Digital Video Animation Output		
AVI		.avi
QuickTime		.mov
AutoDesk Flick		.fli or .flc
Animated GIF		.gif
Interchangeable 3D Object Formats		
AutoDesk AutoCAD DXF		.dxf
AutoDesk/Kinetix 3D Studio		.3Ds
Alias Wavefront object		.obj
Virtual Reality Modeling Language (VRML)		.wrl

TIPS FOR EFFECTIVE 3D GRAPHIC GENERATION AND MANIPULATION

For your multimedia production you will often need a 3D element, or a logo, or a special visually effective control element. Perhaps you wish to design a complete 3D interface, or a spatial 3D environment within which to present your content. Using a 3D application can be a very technical and difficult task. The following tips will help you develop 3D content for your multimedia application.

- *Know what format your development tools can use.* It can be extremely frustrating to find that the other software tools you will use in your multimedia project do not recognize the beautiful 3D images and animation sequences you have invested many hours in creating. Take a little time at the outset to learn what formats they require.

- *Decide whether to model your own objects or use someone else's.* The modeling process can be time-consuming. Creating a 3D model of a recognizable object that looks real and correctly proportioned is a complex task. Often you can find usable objects in clip-model libraries. Most 3D modeling and animation software products come with a small library of objects you can use. Some manufacturers offer such libraries as an incentive for registering your product. Much as with clip-art libraries, you can use these models in your 3D scene without having to create them from scratch. People, vehicles, equipment, and so on are all available in 3D libraries (see Figure 7.5). The company that created your 3D modeling software will be the best source of information about where you can find such models. As you become more

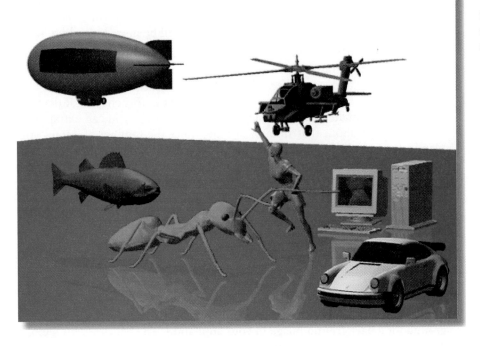

and more involved in developing multimedia content, you will most likely build a collection of such libraries.

- *Make sure that your computer system has ample resources to do the job.* Of all software tools available to the multimedia producer, computer modeling and animation tools are among the hungriest of them all when it comes to memory resources and processor speed. And they will not tolerate being put on any form of digital diet! These applications will gladly make use of whatever memory you make available, especially system RAM. The more RAM you can provide, the easier the rendering job will be for both you and the computer. The rendered image files and video segments that you create need storage space, and they too can gobble up your hard drive resources quickly. Be prepared to expand if your system is already a little cramped.

- *Allow enough time to get the job done.* Both the modeling and rendering processes can take extraordinary amounts of time to complete. For a recent project I completed for Intel Corporation, the opening animation sequence took over 100 computer hours to render! Build enough time into your project plan to accommodate the workload.

- *Don't overcomplicate the scene.* A fun software application may tempt you to create complex scenes with lots of reflective and transparent materials and lots of lights and shadows. Sometimes you can give the poor computer so much work to do that it can take more time than you have to complete the task. Every object, its material properties, and every light adds to the complexity of the scene, and it is easy to overextend the computer's resources and create a scene that you must wait many hours for the computer to render. If you find that a scene has a mistake in it that shows up only after a long render, you'll have to correct it and commit to another long rendering session just to see whether the changes you made work!

- *Practice, practice, and then practice some more.* You cannot spend too much time with any of the professional computer modeling and animation packages. The more experience and familiarity you have with these applications, the easier your next project will be. It all comes down to experience, which is a factor of how much time (and patience) you have for the software. Try some small projects and practice your techniques. Many small projects will teach you more than one big project, and they will be more rewarding, too.

- *Rendering animation requires the rendering of many individual images.* The computer has to "draw" each individual frame of an animation in a process called *rendering* and stack them all into a digital video format file. You will read a more detailed explanation of rendering later in this chapter. If the rendering of an animated scene is taking a long time, then you can extrapolate that it will take about that amount of time, times the number of frames you plan to animate. Keep this in mind as an indicator of how complex your animation is becoming as you build it. You can always reduce the level of ray-tracing and/or of anti-aliasing (an edge-smoothing process), or any of the other quality factors that you can adjust to hasten the rendering process.

- *Keep it small and simple.* With all the fun animation tools at your disposal, there is tremendous temptation to create the most elaborate masterpiece of all time. However, your authoring and development application may not be able to cope with the resulting huge files, and the performance of your entire multimedia project could be compromised. The best animations are elegantly simple. Keep the resulting animation video file small in terms of screen size and use tricks such as using a piece of your application's background for a background image in your animation. The backgrounds should match if done carefully, and you can create the illusion of your animation "floating" above your interface.

FEEDBACK ANIMATION

As you learned in Chapter 6, it is important to provide your users with a visual response (and, in some cases, an audio response) to the correct use of your interface controls. This assures users that they have correctly operated that control, and that the system is responding to their input by interacting with them. Without visual feedback to a correct action, users may think that the multimedia program is unresponsive and/or has crashed. This is especially true if the program needs a little time to load a large media element in response to a click, such as a video segment. Providing a visual indication that the buttons are working reassures users that all's well and adds to their sense of comfort with your product.

3D modeling and animation applications provide you with additional tools to take this feedback animation for controls to a new level. Instead of having a two-frame animation for a button—an up frame and a down frame—you can introduce multiple-frame animations and create button controls, such as levers, that have many frames in their animation as they move in response to the user's input. Figure 7.6 shows such a lever action in two forms: a two-frame switch-throw action, and an animated smooth switch movement that's created by using multiple frames. The visual effect of a smooth response to a click can be quite engaging for the user. It also demonstrates (if not overdone) a high level of sophistication and professionalism in your work. The animation need not be a button or switch. It could be an object or character that animates when you click on it—much like poking the Pillsbury Dough Boy!

The way to create such interactive animations is to choose, when rendering your animation, the option to save the frames of the animation as individual images instead of a video clip. Figure 7.6 shows individual frames of the animation that were rendered as a series of sequentially numbered images. You can then build these frames into a responsive animation in your multimedia application.

Multi-frame smooth button animation

UP   DOWN

Two-frame button animation

UP   DOWN

Figure 7.6
A multiframe animated control on your multimedia interface can often be more effective than a simple two-frame on/off button.

COMPUTER-GENERATED VIDEO

Typically, computer 3D modeling and animation applications output your final work in two broad classifications of output formats: either as a digital video clip or as a series of individual images, one for each frame of the animation. With the prevalence of the Web as a multimedia presentation platform, such applications are also providing Animated GIF file format as an option. You will learn more about this special Web format in Chapter 9.

It can be helpful to think of digital video in terms of a succession of frame images, each showing an incremental change in the motion being portrayed. As with a strip of film, we need an image for each individual frame of the movie. The animation software application creates (renders) an image for each frame of the resulting movie. (Part 4 of this book will cover in detail digital video and its various formats and video editing.) The following is a synopsis of the process.

Once you have collected the 3D models you want to animate, you need to set a series of animation keyframes (as the name suggests, these are key frames that define the animation) the application will use to create its animation. Here's what happens.

On the basis that your animation happens over time, the computer counts that time in frames per second (fps), starting at frame zero. While the most common setting is 30 fps, you can set the frame ratio to any value you wish. At a speed of 30 fps, the 30th frame represents the way your objects should look one second into the animation (strictly speaking, the 1-second point would be the 29th frame, since you start at frame number zero, but for clarity we will use frame

animation keyframe

A milestone frame in an animation sequence that sets the animation parameters that the 3D modeling and animation application uses to extrapolate the required animation over the previous frames leading up to that milestone frame.

MANY FORMS OF KEYFRAMING

Keyframing also is used in digital video editing and multimedia authoring, as well as computer animation generation. In each case it refers to setting special frames that represent milestones in the progress of the animation/video/multimedia product. However, the function and purpose of keyframing is quite different for each of these technologies. Keep an eye out for this term again in later chapters and be careful not to confuse them.

Figure 7.7

When you set the start frame object position and the end frame object position, the 3D modeling and animation software extrapolates all of the intermediate phases of a smooth motion between those two keyframes. This process is called tweening.

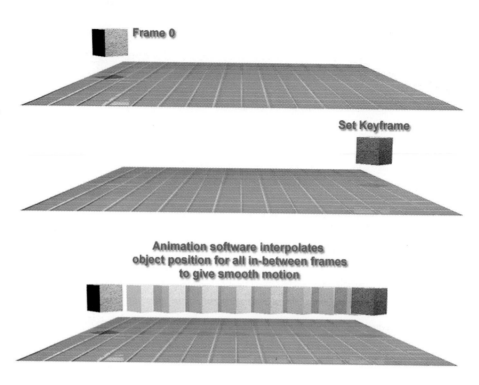

tweening

The process of extrapolation of animated frames between set keyframes. When the computer animator sets the keyframes, the intervening frames are tweened to provide smooth overall animation.

number 30). The 3D modeling and animation program allows you to jump directly to that 30th frame and move or change any object in the scene at that 30th frame. The 3D modeling and animation application takes these changes as keyframe instructions—meaning that it knows that you are arranging the objects in the scene as they should look one second into the animation. It then figures out the smoothest way to effect (animate) those changes in the 29 frames in between. This process is often called tweening (from the word *between*). So a keyframe can be viewed as an instructional milestone that "tells" the application where it has to be in the animation when it reaches that point at 30 fps. By setting successive keyframes over the animation timeline, you can have the 3D modeling and animation software fill in the gaps and create a smooth animation.

If you were to take a simple object such as a cube (see Figure 7.7) and place it at the left-hand side of your scene as a starting point (frame 0), then you could go to a specific frame number ahead and record changes that you would like the 3D modeling and animation application to animate. If you went to frame 60 and placed the cube at the right-hand side of the scene and recorded a keyframe, the 3D modeling and animation software would extrapolate all of the required positions for that cube for each frame of the two seconds of animation to show smooth motion. Figure 7.7 illustrates this process.

INTERNET CONSIDERATIONS

Though Chapter 9 and Chapter 16 will address the use of 3D graphics and animation on the Internet in detail, it is worth mentioning that the Web represents a phenomenal demand for the skills of multimedia developers and their ability to create 3D graphics and animation.

Because the Web is viewed through a common interface (the browser application), those competing for more attention on the Web are employing multimedia to grab and hold that attention. The ability to use a 3D modeling and animation application to create Web content quickly is a valuable one.

However, multimedia on the Web has some special considerations, among which the primary concern is file size and its resulting performance impact. Because any animation requires multiple frames to display the animated piece, the performance penalty of displaying that animated clip is roughly equivalent to having to download each frame of the animation as a separate image on the Web page. It can take a considerable time to do so. While often a Web animation is streamed (begins playing the initially downloaded frames while the rest are being downloaded), it still can take quite a while to display and play as intended on the user's computer.

The bottom line is this: For Web content, especially animation, keep it short and simple.

RENDERING AND RENDERING OPTIONS

The process of creating a 3D image from a 3D model or scene is a time-consuming task called rendering, in which the 3D modeling and animation program "paints" the photorealistic image of your 3D scene that you can use elsewhere, such as in your multimedia project. The application calculates how the scene should look given the scene's objects, their position, their surface materials and properties, the lighting of the scene, and what rendering options you have chosen. Every feature you add to your 3D scene adds to the work required of the computer to render the scene for you. The faster your processor (CPU) and the more memory (RAM) your computer has, the faster this task will be.

Typically the 3D modeling and animation application paints the scene from top to bottom, one line at a time, to create the type of image you expect from your design. When raytracing and calculating the lighting and shadow information for the scene, the computer will take quite a lot of processing time to complete the task. The following are some other rendering options that take additional time and processor horsepower:

- *Motion blur.* This technique is used to digitally create the visual effect of blurring caused by objects moving past the "camera." If you were to record a video sequence of a busy park or a racetrack, fast-moving objects would appear blurred if you froze the video on any frame. However, when the computer renders each frame as a still image, each frame is crisp and detailed, giving a clinical "computerized" feeling to the resulting animation. By rendering several frames before and after the actual frame being recorded, and then blurring them all together, the animation application incorporates an amount of blurring into the frame that relates to the amount of motion between that frame and its adjacent frames in the animation (see Figure 7.8). Typically the application renders and blurs together three frames before and three frames after the one being recorded. In this case your rendering time is increased sevenfold. The effect is to provide you with supersmooth, realistic animation, and is often worth the rendering time cost.

- *Depth-of-field rendering.* In this process, the computer renders a scene in such a way as to simulate the focusing characteristics of an actual camera

streaming

Refers to a special form of media delivery, typically used on the Web, that allows the first part of the media file to begin playing while the remaining part of the file is still downloading in the background. This eliminates the long waiting period that would be required if the file had to be completely downloaded before it could start playing.

Figure 7.8
Motion blur provides a real visual sense of motion.

Figure 7.9
The depth-of-field settings create a sense of camera lens focus in a rendered scene.

lens. Objects can become blurred and out of focus in the foreground and background, which adds greatly to the image's realism (see Figure 7.9). This feature, along with motion blur, gives that extra sense of realism in your animation. As with motion blur, there is a significant rendering time cost associated with this option.

- *Special-effect plug-ins.* As with image editing tools, such as Photoshop, most current 3D modeling and animation applications allow you to use special-effect plug-ins that you can apply to your 3D scene. Often they can be applied to one object at a time. Special effects such as lens flares can bring a rich feeling of realism to your work (see Figure 7.10). Imagine modeling a bowl of fruit, selecting one object in the middle of the basket, and applying a blur filter to it. You now have a realistic bowl of fruit with one blurred object nested in the center of the bunch no matter what angle you viewed it

Figure 7.10
Special-effect plug-ins, such as the lens flare effect shown, can greatly add to the sense of realism in a 3D image or animation.

from. While there may be no practical reason to do such a thing, being able to apply visual-effect plug-ins to individual 3D objects opens up endless creative possibilities. However, these features require much time to render your scene, so use them with care.

When outputting your work to a still or animation file, always leave time at the end for the computer to do its work. Often it is only after a multihour render that you spot a mistake. Having fixed the error, you will require another multihour render to see whether the correction fixes the problem!

I once created a very complex animation for the Sacramento Symphony that required the animation to be created on my computer, recorded on film, and projected onto a theater screen as the symphony played beneath it. That project had some animation sequences that required more than 80 hours to render all frames of a four-second segment! When your work gets that involved, it is time to consider a second computer devoted solely to the job of rendering so that you can continue to work on the other system.

AVOIDING PITFALLS

In this chapter, the section titled "Tips for Effective 3D Graphic Generation and Manipulation" lists a series of tips that will help you avoid problems when creating your own computer 3D graphics and animations.

In computer modeling and animation, the more computing resources you can provide, the better. Be sure that you have the recommended amount of RAM and better than the recommended processor to get the job done.

Remember to allow for rendering time at the end of your project. Creating the best animation the world has ever known, and not leaving enough time to render it to a digital video file, certainly defeats the purpose of all your hard work.

When evaluating 3D modeling and animation applications for purchase, do not be taken in by the cost of the application, on either end of the scale. You can easily pay $3,000 to $6,000 (and more) for this type of software, and often the additional features of these expensive software packages are few when compared to the $500 to $600 products. Furthermore, these applications often offer add-on software and special-effect plug-ins, which can cost more than many of the competing animation products. Watch your budget. Look at the product's capabilities and, most important, look at how easy or difficult it is to use. Some applications are more intuitive than others (a relative term in a very complex field). Magazines in this field often feature shoot-out comparison articles on these products that are worth paying attention to.

Chapter Summary

- Computer-generated 3D images and animations are optical illusions. The combination of perspective, shading, lighting, and shadowing in a scene gives the visual illusion of 3D.

- Raytracing is a process in which the path of each ray of light from each light source in a 3D scene is calculated and interacts with surface and material characteristics of each object in the scene. It is a computationally intensive process that can often increase the rendering times considerably.

- Rendering is the process by which the computer figures out how the 3D scene you designed should look and paints it so.

- Computer 3D animation applications can produce rendered image output in a variety of standard flat-image and digital-video formats. The output files are the files that are used in your multimedia applications. The 3D scene data must be saved in the 3D application separately from the output image rendering.

- It's important to provide users with a visual response to the correct use of your interface controls. This assures them that they have correctly operated the controls and that the system is responding to their input.

- A computer animation is created by setting keyframes over time and having the animation application create all of the intermediate frames of the animation.

- When you design for the Internet, it is very easy to overdo animation. Realize that the animation has to be downloaded to users' systems. At slow modem speeds, this could turn them away from your Web site.

- When finalizing your animation and rendering your final output, be sure to allow for sufficient rendering time, especially if you are applying special effects, motion blur, or depth-of-field features.

Key Terms and Concepts

Checking Your Knowledge and Skills

1. Find a photograph of a common scene, such as the inside of an office or house, or perhaps a landscape (magazine ads are great for this), and analyze the visual elements that tell you that it is a 3D picture. List those elements and compare them to the elements that make a computer-generated 3D scene look 3D.

2. Find a 3D animation on the Web and download it (use the Save As option from the shortcut menu that appears when you right-click the image—Mac users, hold down your single mouse button for the same shortcut menu). Use an image editing application such as Photoshop, Corel's PhotoPaint, or Animation Shop (which comes with Paint Shop Pro) to view the individual frames of the animation. Use that application to copy and paste each frame of the animation to a new image and show them as a list of the animation's frames. Identify the visual elements in this animation that make it look 3D.

3. Check out the Web sites of companies that produce 3D modeling and animation applications (www.caligari.com and www.newtek.com are two such sites). They may have showcase galleries of the work created with their products. Do a comparison of these applications based *solely* on the gallery content. Does the quality of work as shown in their gallery reflect the capabilities of the software?

Critical Thinking Challenges

Given the parameters for computer 3D design that you now know are important to multimedia content and interface design, answer the following questions and challenges:

1. Find a multimedia application you admire and examine its interface and content. What role does 3D imagery play in the interface and content of this piece? Given what you now know about 3D modeling and animation, what would you change in this product and why?

2. Having checked out the Web sites of 3D software application producers in exercise 3 of the previous section, how do you think these companies applied 3D imagery to their own Web sites, and do you think it is effective? Who uses 3D imagery more effectively?

3. If you had to choose between using 3D animated controls (such as a moving lever) or a simple up/down visual response for the controls of your product's interface, which would you choose? Why? What performance impact would implementing animated controls have on your work?

4. There are opinions for and against using a constantly visible running animation in an interface, such as a rotating logo. What reason can you think of for doing this, and what reasons can you think of for not doing this? List the pros and cons of this design feature.

Hands-on Exercises

CREATING A 3D INTERFACE

With 3D images you collect from the Web, magazines, photographs, and other multimedia applications, create a mock-up interface using as many computer-generated 3D elements as you can. You can do this easily in your image editing application by pasting these images onto an interface background of your choice. You may have to scan some of the photos or magazine images, and then cut the parts you want to paste onto your interface design. When you have finished your work, show it to others for critical review. Ask them whether they like your use of 3D graphics. At what point do you think that you would have too much 3D imagery?

Master Project

DETERMINING 3D EFFECTS

So far you should have created a binder for the project that documents your project concept, a project plan and timeline, and your sketches and visuals for your design. You should also have a collection of graphic elements and a background on a disk.

With the interface work you did in Chapter 6, print out these elements and assess which 3D effects you will want to implement. Make a note and create a concept sketch of what you would like to change. Keep the note and sketch for the next step in your Master Project in Chapter 8, creating 3D elements and animations.

Save your work to a Zip disk (or equivalent) and keep it with your project binder.

3D MODELING AND ANIMATION WITH INFINI-D AND TRUESPACE

Chapter Outline

Chapter Objectives

After completing this chapter, you will be able to:

- Understand the process of creating computer 3D models and animation using two state-of-the-art applications, Infini-D and trueSpace.

- Describe how to manipulate and edit 3D objects.

- Describe how to use 3D world and object axes and coordinate systems.

- Discuss how to combine objects in groups and describe how to use object hierarchies.

- Discuss how to use digital lighting to illuminate your 3D scene.

- Apply background images in your 3D scene.

- Describe how to create keyframed animation.

Chapter Overview

In this chapter you will learn how to do basic computer 3D modeling and animation in two popular animation applications, MetaCreations's Infini-D and Caligari's trueSpace. Both of these applications are sophisticated full-featured software tools capable of professional 3D graphics and animation. Both cost about $600 (if you're a student, check for educational pricing), and both are intended for multimedia content development work. trueSpace is currently a Windows-only product, while Infini-D is available for both Windows and Macintosh PowerPC systems. While these two products look quite different, the same processes and tasks are used to get the rendering job done—they just locate their controls in different places!

You will learn how to create a 3D model or animation, and then walk through the specific techniques required in both of these applications. This will give you a solid foundation in how the technology works and how to use it.

While the field of computer 3D modeling and animation is far greater in scope than one chapter could cover, this chapter will give you a good starting point for further study. This book's Web site provides suggested further reading in this field.

INTRODUCTION TO COMPUTER 3D ANIMATION: METACREATIONS'S INFINI-D AND CALIGARI'S TRUESPACE

You will find demonstration versions of Infini-D and trueSpace linked to the Downloads page of this book's Web site. They are functional demonstration versions, expiring after a set trial period. You should install these programs before progressing through this chapter because you'll comprehend more if you can use the actual program and see it operate on your screen as you read. While the free download demo versions of these applications can be quite helpful, they will not substitute for the full package. If at all possible, use the full software application. If not, then the demo versions will suffice until you can obtain the complete product.

You can also download the most up-to-date trial versions of these packages and learn more about them directly from www.metacreations.com and www.caligari.com, where you will find much more information about and examples of these products at work. If you're a student, look for deep educational discounts on these products, which are usually available directly from these companies and from educational software vendors such as www.creationengine.com. These Web sites also have gallery sections where you can view work created by other users of these software tools. These galleries are often inspirational and always fun to browse.

Both Infini-D and trueSpace enable you to create your own 3D objects from a series of primitive shapes, load object files, and place objects into a 3D scene. When you have arranged the objects in a scene, you can render a 3D image file, or you can animate the objects and save an animation video file or series of animation frame images to disk. These applications may do these tasks in different ways, but the process for both is fundamentally the same. In some of the demo versions of these products you may be prevented from saving the applications data file.

As computer applications go, those that enable us to create 3D imagery and animation are among the most complex available. Of those complex applications, trueSpace and Infini-D are relatively easy to use. Nevertheless, they are incredibly complex software tools and users must face steep learning curves before the tools can truly be considered "easy to use."

The primary difference between trueSpace and Infini-D is that trueSpace provides modeling, scene building, and rendering tools all in one interface, while Infini-D uses two separate applications, one for object modeling and one for animating and rendering. For users new to these kinds of applications, trueSpace's interface is often easier to use once they become familiar with the icon imagery used for the button faces. Infini-D's interface is less immediately intuitive, but follows a more traditional CAD (computer-aided design) screen format, similar to those used by other 3D modeling and animation applications, such as Inspire 3D and 3D Studio Max. However, compared to similar applications available on the market, both trueSpace and Infini-D rank among the easiest to learn and use.

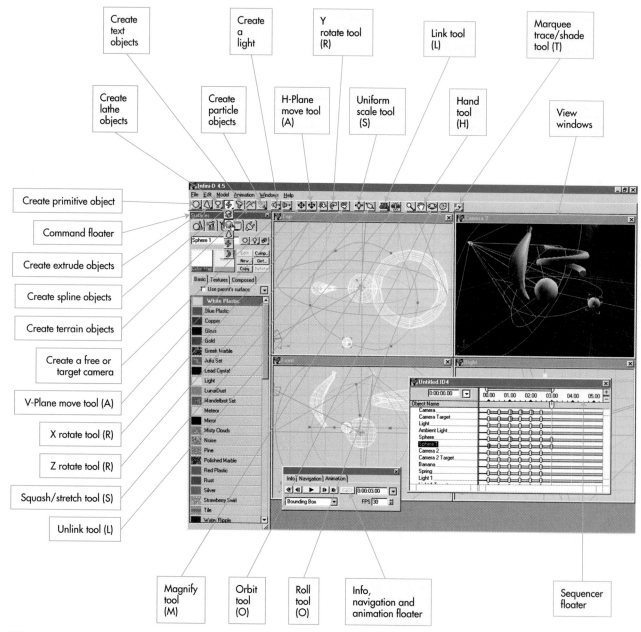

Figure 8.1
Infini-D's interface is controlled by selecting buttons in the toolbar margins.

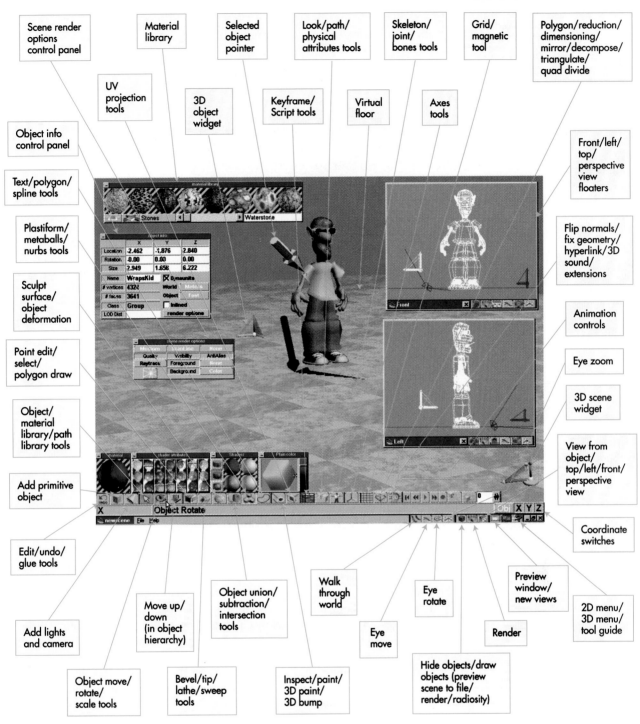

Figure 8.2
trueSpace's interface, showing some of the additional control panels activated.

Figure 8.1 shows the Infini-D interface and Figure 8.2 shows the trueSpace interface (Figure 8.3 shows trueSpace with the control panels turned off). Study these illustrations, and refer to them when using these software applications. You will find these "maps" quite handy when navigating through these products.

The next two sections describe the fundamentals of each product's interface. Each has its own way of doing things, so be careful not to confuse them.

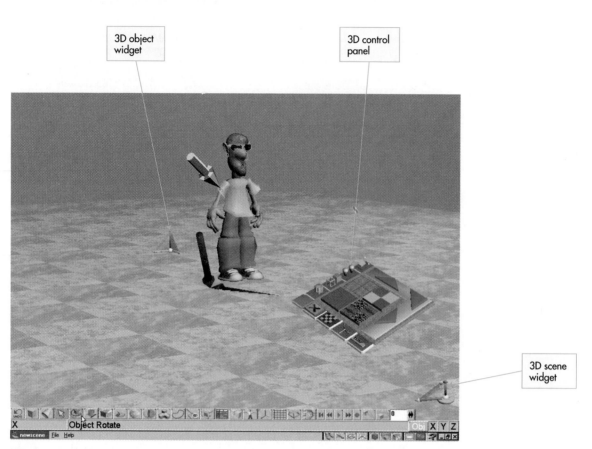

Figure 8.3
trueSpace's interface with the additional control panels of Figure 8.2 turned off.

NAVIGATION AND LEARNING AIDS

Both Infini-D and trueSpace (full purchased versions) come with quick-reference charts to assist users with interface navigation. These cards can be invaluable to first-time users.

Furthermore, both products use ToolTips extensively. These are the small prompts that appear when the mouse pointer pauses over an interface control. trueSpace also has an online help feature that provides tool information in the application's status bar.

Paying close attention to these prompts, especially when learning the interface for the first time, can greatly assist you in climbing that steep "learning curve."

HOW INFINI-D WORKS

Most of Infini-D's controls are accessible from the main screen, as can be seen in Figure 8.1. The following sections summarize the primary functional areas of the Infini-D interface.

TOOL GROUPS

At the top of the screen are the primary control buttons. These buttons display the Objects, Terrain, Particle, Lights, Cameras, Object Manipulation, Object Linking, View Manipulation, and Marquee Rendering tool groups, respectively.

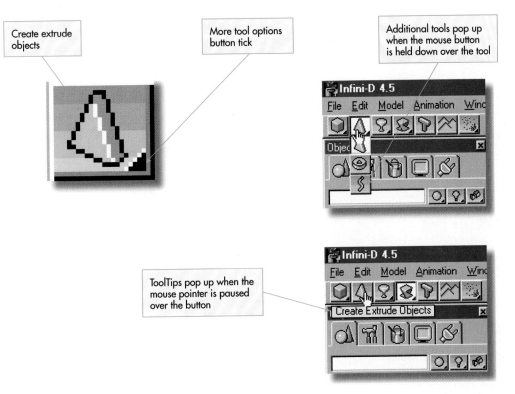

Figure 8.4
Infini-D's tool groups appear when you hold your mouse button down over any tool with a black tick in the bottom right corner.

You will notice two helpful features about Infini-D's tool groups. First, when you pause your mouse pointer over any tool, a description of that tool appears. Second, whenever a tool button has a small black tick, or triangle in the bottom right corner, this indicates that more tool options are available when you hold your mouse button down over this tool. Figure 8.4 shows the Extrude Object tool group that appears when you hold your mouse button down over the displayed tool from this group. Figure 8.4 also shows the ToolTip description of the control's function along with the indicator telling you that there are more options in this group.

COMMAND FLOATER

When you first open Infini-D, you'll see the Command Floater panel on the left side of the screen. This panel displays the information particular to the selected object in the scene, and allows you to modify those parameters as needed.

You can see this in effect in Figure 8.1, where the selected object is a small sphere called "Sphere 1." The surface material properties are displayed for that object in the Command Floater's Surfaces panel.

Figure 8.5 shows a selection of the Command Floater's panels. Note that when the panels' displays extend beyond the bottom of the Command Floater frame, you can drag them up or down within this frame to view the hidden panels.

INFORMATION, NAVIGATION, AND ANIMATION FLOATER

The Information, Navigation, and Animation floater provides you with important controls and information about the scene and the objects selected within it (see Figure 8.6). This is where you can finesse your objects, scene, and animation with precise control by entering exact coordinate and numeric values. For

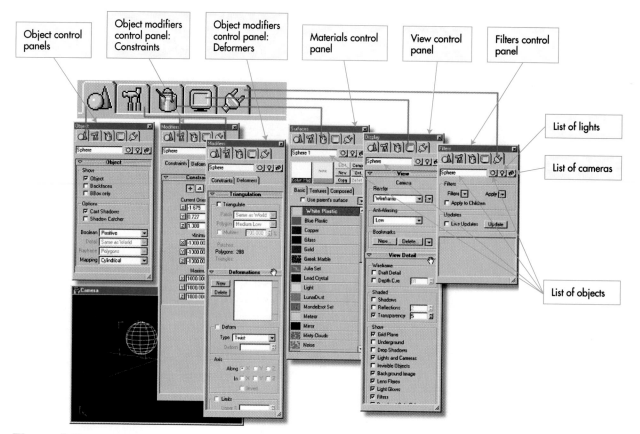

Figure 8.5

Infini-D's Command Floater panels provide practically all of the information that you need on the currently selected object. You can also modify these parameters as necessary.

instance, after dragging an object to an appropriate location in your scene, you can change its discrete location coordinates on the Navigation tab to fine-tune its position with greater accuracy than dragging with your mouse can provide. Similarly, you can also fine-tune the object Information and Animation parameters to obtain absolute precision. The Information, Navigation, and Animation floater is available from the Windows menu.

The Information tab, as seen at the top of Figure 8.6, displays the positional, rotational, and scaling coordinates of the selected object.

The Navigation tab provides a control console for moving within your scene. These controls seem to replicate the navigation controls at the top of the screen in functionality, but provide much finer control and precision.

The Animation tab provides the animation properties for your scene, and gives you precise control over the animation parameters.

THE SEQUENCER PANEL

The Sequencer panel (available from the Windows menu) provides access to all aspects of your scene's animation on a timeline (see Figure 8.7). Each object is represented in the left-hand list of objects, as is each aspect of that object's animation. The sub-elements for each object combine to create the animation for that object. If an object has sub-elements in its animation, a small arrow appears to the left of that object's name in the list. To review and edit these sub-elements, simply click the small arrow to reveal the sub-elements as an indented list beneath that object's name.

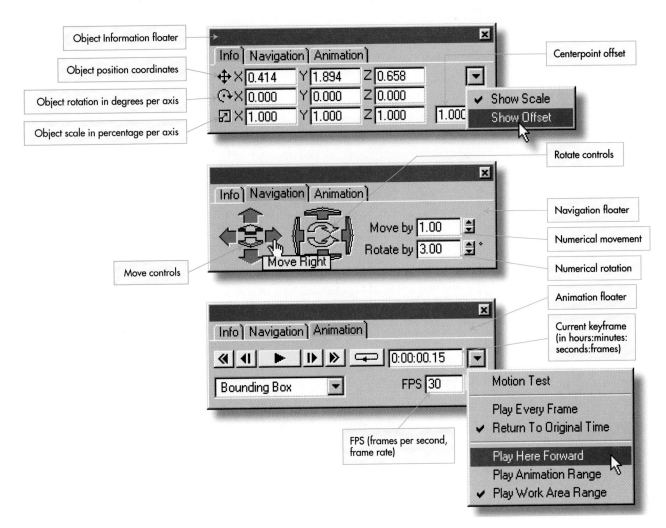

Figure 8.6

Infini-D's Information, Navigation, and Animation panel enables you to precisely control the object, scene, and animation parameters.

The start time, duration, and end time for each object's animation are displayed as a horizontal bar with control handles on each end. These control handles allow you to change the start time, end time, and duration of the animation for that object.

The Scene Time Marker indicates where in the scene's animation (as indicated by the timeline ruler) you are currently located. This is an important control, as any changes you make in the animated scene will be recorded as part of the animation at the time indicated by the Scene Time Marker.

The Sequencer is a good place to view any audio that you may have imported into Infini-D as a sound track for your animation. It gives you a good overview of a scene's animation parameters, and also allows you to edit those animation parameters while you check to see how those edits work within the overall animation.

SCENE VIEWS

The View windows are in the central part of the Infini-D screen and are clearly seen in both Figures 8.1 and 8.8. These windows provide multiple views on the same scene, which are crucial to any 3D modeling program. To fully appreciate

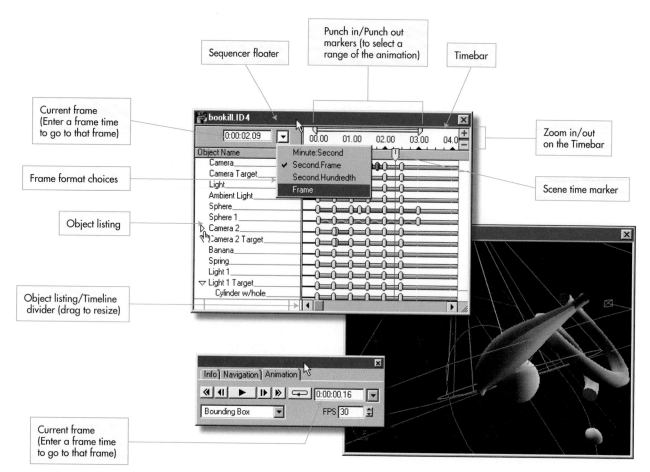

Figure 8.7

Infini-D's Sequencer panel provides a complete overview of all aspects of your scene's animation over a timeline.

Figure 8.8

Infini-D's View windows are set and changed through the Windows menu as shown.

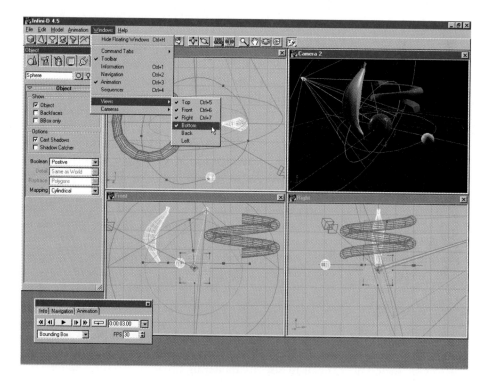

the positional relationships between the various objects in your scene, which appears on a two-dimensional screen, you will need to be able to view them from various angles. It's analogous to sculptors who need to move around their work to get a better view of a particular detail. If you strapped sculptors to their chairs and told them to do their work, it would be impossible for them to create a three-dimensional sculpture from just one view position. Likewise, it would be impossible for you to create a 3D scene on your computer without the ability to view that scene from many angles. The View windows provide simultaneous views from your choice of angles.

Figure 8.8 also shows how the View windows are set using the Views command on the Windows menu. Selecting a different point of view from this menu affects the currently selected View Window.

RENDER MODE

Infini-D uses a separate *mode* or screen to do its rendering. (This method is typical of many 3D applications; Caligari's trueSpace is an exception in that it renders the scene or object in the modeling and scene-building screen.) While Infini-D uses a separate screen, it is still within the primary application window. This means that when you're done rendering a scene, exiting Render mode restores the scene-building and animation screen. In this way you toggle back and forth between scene building and rendering. Figure 8.9 shows the Render mode screen for Infini-D.

You enter Render mode from the scene-building screen using the Render command on the File menu. On the way to the Render mode screen, you will be presented with numerous options to choose from that affect the rendering process, the image quality, and the way your animation is rendered to a digital video file or sequence of images. Figure 8.10 shows the Render Setup dialog box and describes some of the functions of the various options.

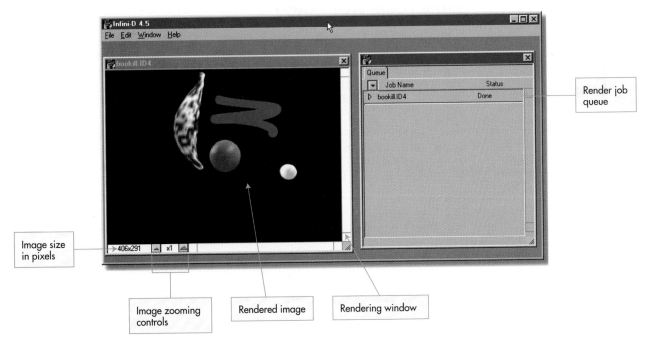

Figure 8.9
Infini-D's Render Mode is separate from the scene design screen; it renders your scene to a still image or an animation format.

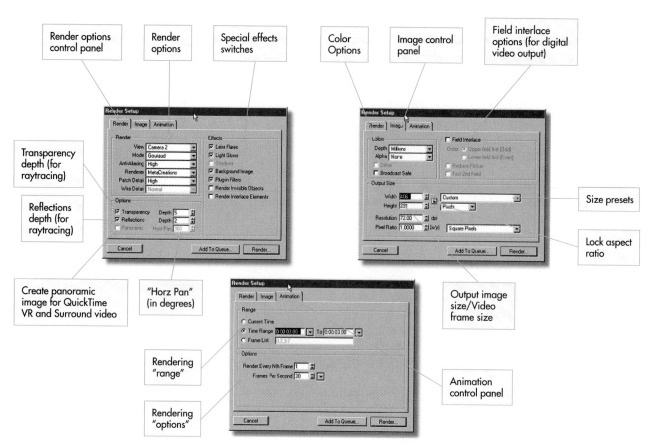

Figure 8.10
Infini-D's Render Setup dialog box provides numerous adjustable parameters that affect the final rendering of your scene or animation.

SPLINEFORM WORKSHOP

Infini-D provides a separate object-modeling mode called the SplineForm Workshop. In this mode you can create custom objects and shapes, as shown in Figure 8.11. This figure shows how a simple spline ("shaped line") can create a complex shape through the SplineForm Workshop's lathing (forming symmetrical 3D objects by spinning a spline around an axis). After you draw the right-hand curve (indicated by the small square handle or nodes at each joint), the curve is spun around the vertical axis to give a mirrored profile line in the left-hand Path Front window and a solid model of the resulting lathed object in the right-hand Object window.

You can insert a lathed object into your scene by selecting a lathed object from the Create Lathe Objects button group. Once the object is in your scene, select the object and right-click it. From the shortcut menu that appears, choose Edit, which is shown in Figure 8.12.

spline

Similar to a bezier curve in a drawing program, a spline ("shaped line") is a line that, when attached to other splines (with joints called *nodes*) forms the surface of a 3D model. Think of a spline as the line that forms the loop of a bubble wand. In the same way that soap film forms a surface in a bubble wand, the 3D object surface fills in any space enclosed by a spline or group of splines.

lathing

A process of forming symmetrical 3D objects by spinning a shaped line (*spline*) around an axis. Changing the spline changes the form of the 3D object. Lathing 3D objects in a 3D modeling and animation application works much like the way a potter creates a vase or goblet on a potter's wheel. The outline shape the potter creates with his or her hands is transferred to the 3D form by the spinning wheel.

DO YOU HAVE MORE THAN ONE MOUSE BUTTON?

The right mouse button is a very useful tool for PC users. In Infini-D (and more so with trueSpace), clicking an object, a control, or a scene window with it often invokes a shortcut menu with additional commands or commands you can access elsewhere but in a more convenient location.

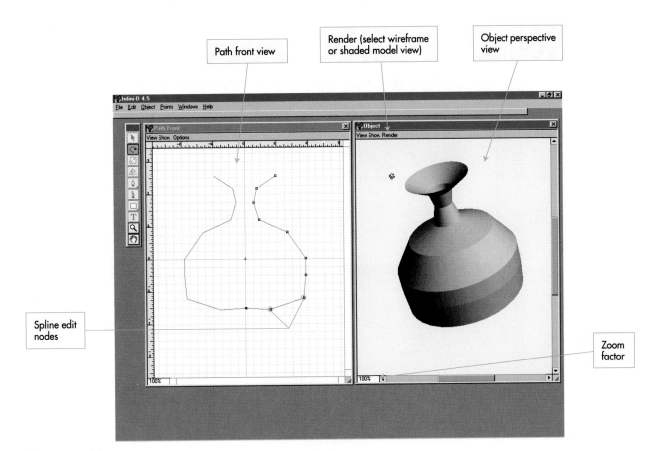

Path front view

Render (select wireframe or shaded model view)

Object perspective view

Spline edit nodes

Zoom factor

Figure 8.11
Infini-D's SplineForm Workshop allows you to create your own custom 3D models.

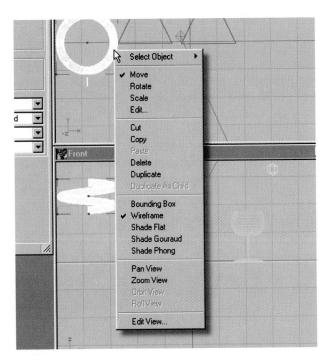

Figure 8.12
Clicking the right mouse button provides a shortcut menu offering many object manipulation options, including the Edit command.

Figure 8.13 shows the SplineForm Workshop in Freeform Vertical mode, and the Object window showing the object in wireframe form. This illustration also shows the menu options from which you can choose the various model editing modes. For example, in Freeform Vertical mode you can edit each

nodes

The joints at which splines are connected. Nodes provide handling lines that can be dragged to alter the direction and amount of curve in a spline.

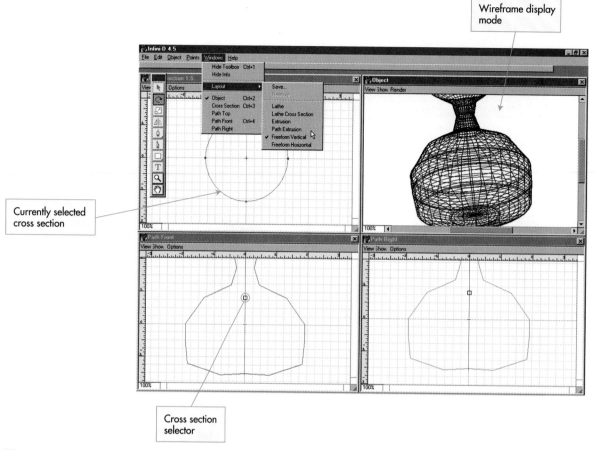

Figure 8.13
Infini-D's SplineForm Workshop is shown here in Freeform Vertical mode. It is selected from the Windows menu, as shown.

cross-sectional profile created by each node of the original spline that you saw in Figure 8.11. The small rectangular handle on the vertical red line, as seen in the bottom left Path Front window in Figure 8.13, indicates the position of the cross-section that you can edit. The slice through the model at that point is shown in the Cross Section view above it. Selecting the cross-section you want to edit is as simple as dragging the handle up and down the red line.

You can create complex and detailed custom objects for your 3D scene when you use the object modeling tools provided in the SplineForm Workshop.

HOW TRUESPACE WORKS

trueSpace locates all of its controls and functions on one screen. This can be beneficial and also confusing at the same time, as the benefit of having all controls available in one place can be offset by the number of controls to become familiar with and the resulting complexity of the interface. However, when you become familiar with and get a sense for the imagery used for the button icons, you will find this interface relatively easy and fluid to use.

Figure 8.14 gives you a quick color-coded overview of the imagery used in the trueSpace interface. Note that common icons are used for things such as objects, screen view, faces, and splines, and that the movement, rotation, and scaling operations are indicated by a common arrow motif. By studying this illustration while experimenting with the trueSpace interface, you can quickly get up to speed with the tools available.

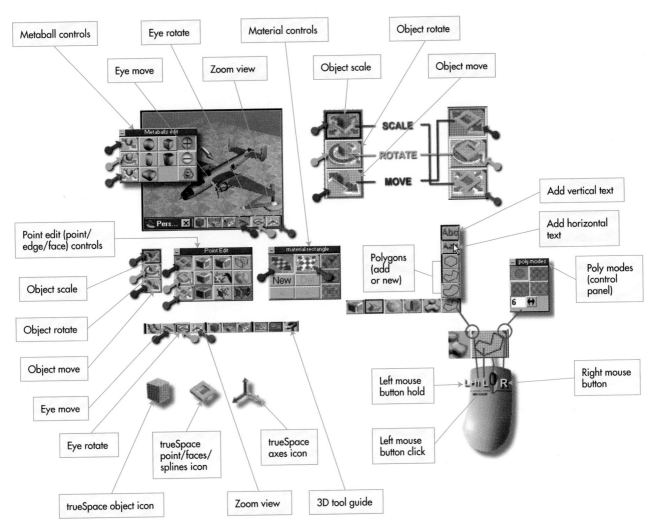

Figure 8.14
trueSpace has a complex interface (as do most 3D modeling and animation products) that becomes easier to understand when you become familiar with the imagery used in the tools and controls.

Most trueSpace control buttons have one or two small marks on the top corners of the button, as seen in Figure 8.14. The left-hand mark and the right-hand mark indicate that there are more features associated with that button when you hold down the left or right mouse button. All button functions are selected by clicking them using the left mouse button. If there is a small green mark in the top left corner of the button, holding down the left mouse button for a second invokes additional functions or tools, which are usually additional variations of that tool. Likewise, a small red mark on the top right corner of the button invokes additional information and controls for that button, usually in the form of a dialog box.

In trueSpace, you will find that right-clicking the scene or an object causes a 3D control panel to appear, as shown in Figure 8.3. Moving your mouse pointer over the buttons on this panel displays their function in the trueSpace status bar.

Likewise, the control widget (also shown in Figure 8.3) provides functions as described in the status bar when you move the mouse over the widget.

INSTANT HELP

Probably the most useful assistance you can get with trueSpace operations is from the 3D Tool Guide (see Figure 8.2). When the 3D Tool Guide is selected, you can click most trueSpace features, controls, or tools with the question mark mouse pointer and get an interactive animated tutorial on its function. This can be invaluable for the beginner.

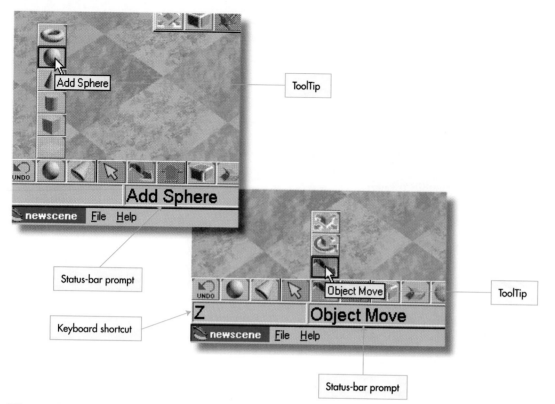

Figure 8.15
To help you remember the purpose of a tool, trueSpace provides prompts in the status bar and pop-up ToolTips.

Another very important feature of the trueSpace interface is the tool descriptions. As you can see in Figure 8.15, when you move your mouse pointer over the tool, a description of the tool appears in the status bar at the bottom of the screen. If there is a keyboard shortcut for this function, it appears to the left of the description. When selecting from a pop-up group of tools, a pop-up ToolTip indicates the functionality of the tool in question.

SCENE VIEWS AND FLOATING VIEWS

The first thing you'll notice when you open trueSpace is a fine marble-tiled "floor" stretching into the distance (see Figures 8.2 and 8.3). This floor gives you a better sense of where you are in this simulated 3D world and where your objects are placed in this scene. It also helps you figure out which way is "up."

Using the view selection tool, you can select this perspective view (the floor) or any one of three other orthogonal views. For the latter, this button, shown in Figure 8.16, uses an image of a house to represent the view you will choose. This is quite clever because we all know when we look at a conventionally styled house whether we are looking at the front, at the side, from above, or at an angle. You can easily choose a front, left, top, or perspective view of your scene by choosing that same type of "view of the house" icon. Holding down your left mouse button activates the available view selections.

Figure 8.16 also shows a series of smaller floating views. These floating views are invoked by selecting the series of new view buttons. They look exactly like the view-changing buttons for the main screen but have a thin border around the icon of the house. The border indicates that the view will be in its own window.

You will use these multiple concurrent views to look at your 3D scene from different angles. This will help you gauge the relative positioning of the objects in 3D space. This is similar to operating a robotic arm by remote control with

perspective and orthogonal views

When you are viewing a 3D object or scene, an orthogonal view looks straight-on at the scene and gives a 2D view of the model or scene without any perspective or depth. Such a view looks like a technical drawing or blueprint. A perspective view, however, gives a 3D view and shows perspective and depth for the 3D model.

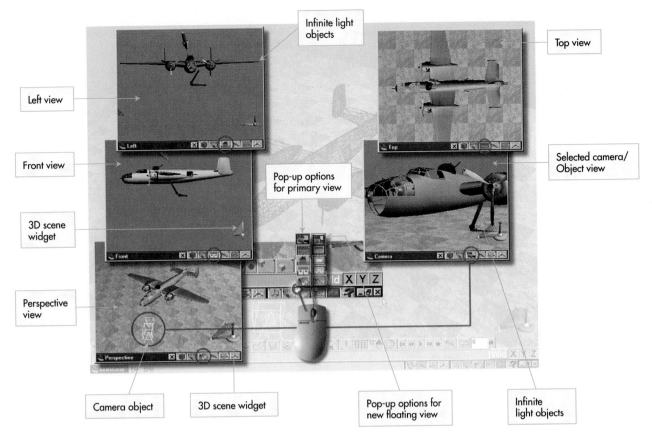

Figure 8.16
trueSpace uses a house image to indicate what view of the scene you can choose.

only closed-circuit TV monitors to see what you are doing. By glancing across multiple angle views, you can figure out precisely where the robotic arm is located and what it is picking up and moving. When an object obscures the work viewed from one angle, you can glance at another view for more visual feedback. Think of the floating view windows in trueSpace as closed-circuit monitors of the scene you're building.

To navigate within a scene, you use the series of Eye buttons, as shown in Figure 8.14. The Eye Move, Eye Rotate, and Zoom View buttons all have the motif of the move, rotate, and scale arrow, upon which is shown the scene axes icon.

NAVIGATION TIPS FOR TRUESPACE

Using your right mouse button to perform move, rotate, or zoom operations provides additional control axes or functions. For example, in perspective view, using the Eye Move control slides your view around on a plane parallel to the floor. Doing the same operation with the right mouse button moves you in the vertical plane, allowing you to raise and drop your viewpoint in the scene.

Use the navigation tool for the view window you wish to navigate within. Each view, whether the main view or any floating view, has its own set of tools that apply *only* to that view. In other words, if you select Zoom in the main perspective view, and then drag the mouse pointer in a floating view to effect the zoom, you may be disappointed with the results. You will be operating whatever navigation tool has already been selected in that floating view, not the main view.

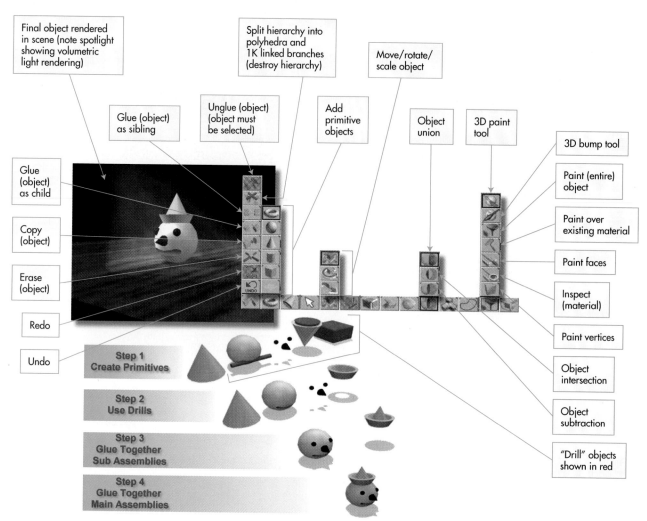

Figure 8.17

In four steps, modifying and gluing together some simple primitive shapes can easily create a recognizable model. The tools used are also shown as found on the toolbar.

gluing

The process of joining two or more 3D objects together as one larger combination object that, if desired, can be later broken down into its discrete pieces and unglued.

boolean object combination procedures

A process of adding, subtracting, and finding the difference between two 3D objects. Unlike gluing, when two 3D objects are added together in this way, the resulting object becomes a new single object without any of the information stored that would allow for a reversal of this process or a separation of the original two objects. A boolean object combination process results in one object.

When you select any of these scene navigation buttons and drag the mouse pointer in that scene, you can move, rotate, and zoom the scene to your needs.

OBJECT LOADING AND CREATION

You can load ready-to-go objects into your scene by choosing Load Object from the File menu and opening the Objects folder. trueSpace comes with a small library of already-modeled objects that you can place in your scene. However, you will most likely want to create your own models. There are many ways to create your own model with trueSpace, and the following refers only to the simplest methods.

trueSpace includes a selection of six *primitive objects:* cube, plane, cylinder, cone, sphere, and torus (or doughnut). Using a combination of these shapes, you can create quite complex models. These primitive shapes can be combined in a process that behaves like its name, gluing, and in a series of boolean object combination procedures, which will be described later in this chapter and shown in Figure 8.17.

Just as an engine is assembled from its component parts, you can build complex 3D objects by creating pieces and assembling them later into the complete object. Figure 8.17 shows how a series of simple primitive shapes can be combined into a recognizable, more complex object. By using a series of techniques such as object rotation, object scaling, object subtraction, and object gluing, the model shown in Figure 8.17 can be easily created.

In Figure 8.17, red objects were used as virtual drill bits to remove a section of the object being worked on. For example, the red elongated cylinder was subtracted from the sphere of the head to leave a mouth-shaped hole behind. When the cylinder is subtracted from the sphere, the space the two objects shared where they intersected is removed, leaving behind the elongated hole.

OBJECT MANIPULATION AND DISTORTION

In trueSpace you move, rotate, and scale objects using the buttons provided for this purpose (refer to Figure 8.14). When you use these tools, the mouse button you hold down can have a different effect depending on which tool you use and which view you use it in.

Depending on how you use them, the many variations of object manipulation tools available to you are best experienced hands-on. Practice with a primitive object and see how quickly you develop a "feel" for how these objects respond to your control. Don't forget to practice the various techniques in the different views to see how they respond.

The techniques for moving, rotating, and scaling an object will also apply to the movement, rotation, and scaling of splines, metaballs, and other objects (refer to Figure 8.14). A metaball is a special kind of 3D object that has additional properties that make it attract or repel other metaball objects.

WHICH MOUSE BUTTON DO I USE?

When you use the Object Move tool, the object's movement will be different if you're dragging it around in an orthogonal view, as opposed to the perspective view. Using the right mouse button in perspective view also moves the object up and down vertically in 3D space.

Similar to the way the Object Move tool operates, the Object Scale tool will have different effects in the 3D perspective view as opposed to any of the 2D orthogonal views. In the 2D views you only have two dimensions in which to scale your object, while in the 3D perspective view, using your right mouse button provides control over the additional (up and down) dimensions. In the perspective view, the right mouse button scales only in the vertical axis. Holding down both mouse buttons at the same time while using the scale tool gives uniform proportional scaling in all axes. Test these operations to get a feel for how they work.

When you rotate the object using the Object Rotation tool, a rotation in a 2D orthogonal view with the right mouse button gives you controllable rotation around an axis following your line of sight into the view. It's like pushing a pin through the object in that view and spinning the object around on the pin. Try this to see how it works. Rotating an object in the 3D perspective view using the right mouse button spins it on the spot around its vertical (2) axis, as if your "pin" has fixed it to the "floor."

Rather than using the object manipulation by dragging on the object itself, it is better to use these tools in trueSpace by first selecting the object (it will turn white if in wireframe mode) and then using them (holding down the appropriate mouse button and dragging) in the empty airspace AWAY from the object. They work just as well this way, and once you already have the object you want to manipulate selected, it will respond as expected. You don't have to touch the object with the pointer to make this work. When you have many objects close together this technique will prevent you from accidentally selecting the wrong object in the foreground when you try to click on the object you want.

virtual drill bit

An object used to remove its shape from another 3D object (used like a drill bit or a router) in a boolean subtraction process.

metaball

A special kind of 3D object with additional properties that makes it attract or repel other metaball objects. The surface of a metaball moves and flexes in response to that attraction or repulsion. The result is that metaballs can behave like beads of mercury, for instance, and produce very organic animation.

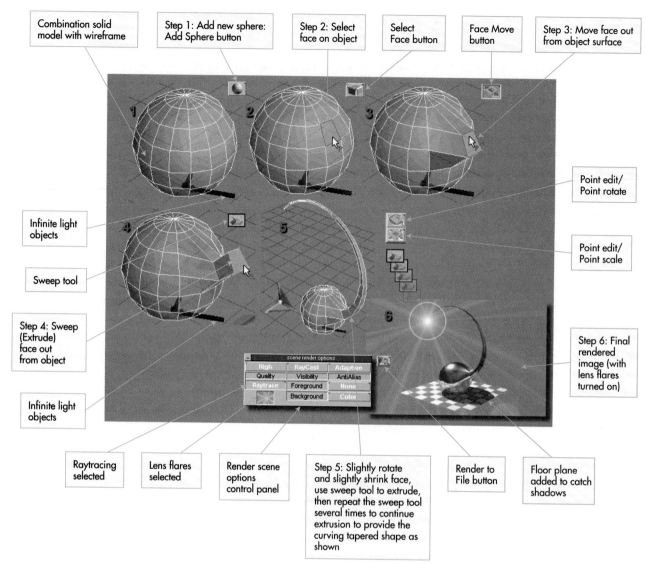

Combination solid model with wireframe

Step 1: Add new sphere: Add Sphere button

Step 2: Select face on object

Select Face button

Face Move button

Step 3: Move face out from object surface

Point edit/ Point rotate

Infinite light objects

Sweep tool

Point edit/ Point scale

Step 4: Sweep (Extrude) face out from object

Infinite light objects

Step 6: Final rendered image (with lens flares turned on)

Raytracing selected

Lens flares selected

Render scene options control panel

Step 5: Slightly rotate and slightly shrink face, use sweep tool to extrude, then repeat the sweep tool several times to continue extrusion to provide the curving tapered shape as shown

Render to File button

Floor plane added to catch shadows

Figure 8.18
A complex organic shape can easily be created in six steps. Step 6 shows the final object rendered with a light source showing a lens flare.

SHAPE MANIPULATION

trueSpace has many tools that distort and mold the shape of your objects, right down to the point-by-point surface level. Figure 8.18 shows the distortion of a simple primitive sphere into an organically shaped complex model. It is created with the following steps. Each tool used is shown next to the object in each stage of the project. This example is a good introduction to the primary object manipulation tools in trueSpace. These steps will be easier to comprehend as you follow along with the application.

- Step 1: Place a sphere primitive shape in the scene.
- Step 2: Using the Point Edit: Faces tool, select one of the faces on the surface of the sphere as shown.
- Step 3: Using the Point Move tool, pull the selected face out of the object surface. This is probably easier to do in a floating top view.

- Step 4: Use the Sweep (Extrude) tool to "grow" the face out of the sphere surface.

- Step 5: Use the Point Rotate tool and then the Point Scale tool to slightly rotate and then slightly shrink (using both mouse buttons at the same time with the Point Scale tool) the selected face. This will taper the extruded segment and tilt the end face. Each time you use the Sweep tool to extrude the face thereafter, the rotation and scaling are advanced incrementally. This gives the tapered spiral effect you see.

- Step 6: Paint the object with the material of your choice and then render the scene. The example shows a local light object placed at the tail tip. Lens flares were turned on for the rendering. A small plane primitive object was added to the final scene (and a "tile" material—shown later in Figure 8.21—applied as described in the section titled "Paints and Materials" that follows) to provide a "floor" onto which shadows could be cast for effect. In this example the tailed sphere was given a "chrome" material from the standard material library.

This simple technique was used to create the poster shown in Figure 8.19.

In addition to the object manipulation tools just mentioned, animation object deformation tools in trueSpace are used to deform an object while it is being animated. In trueSpace this tool is called a *stand-alone deformation object*. For instance, if you wanted to animate a model of a car being squished through a keyhole, you would use a stand-alone deformation object to accomplish this. A stand-alone deformation object distorts another object that is in contact or proximity to it.

Figure 8.20 shows how a *deformation pipe* can be used to distort an animated object. The airplane is animated along a path through the deformation pipe. As the airplane passes through the deformation pipe, it is shaped and distorted along the pipe to the same extent that the pipe itself has been deformed. This

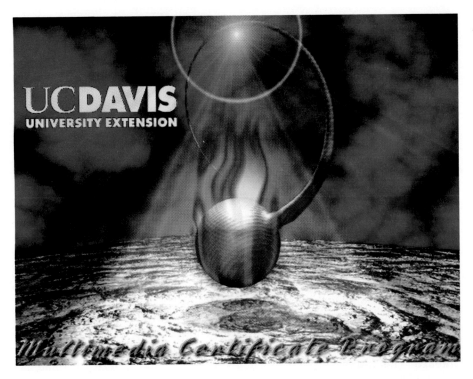

Figure 8.19
This poster was created using the same techniques described in Figure 8.18. trueSpace's volumetric lighting (ability to render light beams through "dusty" air), lens flaring, and procedural background cloud creation are also shown.

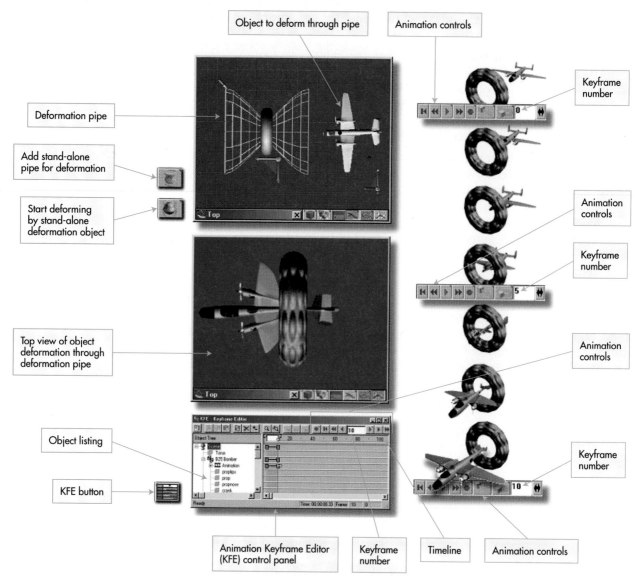

Figure 8.20

In this simple animation, the deformation pipe deforms the airplane as it passes through the pipe.

means that you can warp and deform the pipe in advance and then distort the object later as it passes through the pipe, much as water conforms to the inside shape of a tube.

AXES

As with all 3D modeling and animation applications, all work in trueSpace revolves around the use of axes for both the object in question and the scene you're working in. The ability to restrict, or "switch" these axes on or off, is a tremendous benefit to the 3D modeler and animator. When you switch off an axis, you eliminate its use for movement, scaling, and rotation of the object or scene.

In the bottom right corner of the trueSpace interface are three small buttons with the legends X, Y, and Z (refer to Figure 8.2). When these buttons look as if they're "pressed down," then they are selected and active. To turn off an axis, simply click the appropriate button; it will pop up and the axis legend will be dimmed. This can be very useful when you want to move, scale, or rotate an object with precision.

As you read earlier in this chapter, different views provide different results when moving, rotating, and scaling objects. In addition, by switching the axes on or off you can gain greater control over the manipulation of these 3D objects. With a little practice, you can become adept at using these features to your advantage.

Watch for the keyboard shortcuts available for switching axes on and off. They are the letters *A*, *S*, and *D* on your keyboard. These letters are located directly above the keys *Z*, *X*, and *C*, which select the object movement, rotation, and scaling tools, respectively. Practice will make you quite fluid and proficient in modeling with trueSpace.

Note that when you switch axes off for one tool, it is "remembered" when you use that tool again and doesn't apply to the use of the other object manipulation tools. Select and set each tool separately.

For example, if you were creating a face like the one shown in Figure 8.17, you would create one eye, copy it, and move it to the other side of the face. To ensure that the copied eye was level with the original, you would view the face in Front View, turn off the Y axis (to eliminate vertical movement), and drag the eye horizontally across to the correct position. No matter how much you move your mouse button in this instance, you cannot move the eye up and down—it is locked into horizontal movement only. In this way you can gain more control over the movement. Similarly, if you wanted to use the scale tool to turn a cylinder primitive object into a long pole, you would restrict the X and Z axes so that the only way the scaling tool could operate would be in the Y axis. This would cause the cylinder to shrink or grow in length, without a fear that it would become distorted in the other axes.

To the left of the three axes buttons is the coordinate system selector (also shown in Figures 8.2 and 8.3 with the Object coordinate system selected). By holding down the mouse button over this control, you can select from Object, World, or Screen coordinate systems. This choice becomes most important when moving, rotating, or zooming your view. For instance, in the World coordinate system, when you rotate your scene, you do so around a virtual pivot point at the center of the scene. This is the same place where new primitive shapes are placed when they're created. When you use the Eye Rotation tool, you "fly" around this point to get a better view. However, if the object you're trying to see better is way off the end of the scene, then this is not of much help. When you select the Object coordinate system, your scene rotation revolves around the center of the selected object. This makes it much easier to view the object.

You will develop a feel for the best time to use the coordinate system choices, and when to switch the axes on and off. This is best achieved by playing with the tools provided. Remember, the 3D Tool Guide is always available to assist you with these new tools. Take the time to practice with these features until you become comfortable with their operation.

PAINTS AND MATERIALS

trueSpace gives you a large array of material and painting tools for "coloring" your 3D objects. Figure 8.21 shows the primary material controls, including the Material Library. The Material Library is invoked by holding down the mouse button over the Object Tool arrow and selecting the Material Library from the pop-up tool options. You can add or delete materials in any library by using the Add Material and Remove Material buttons in the bottom left corner of the

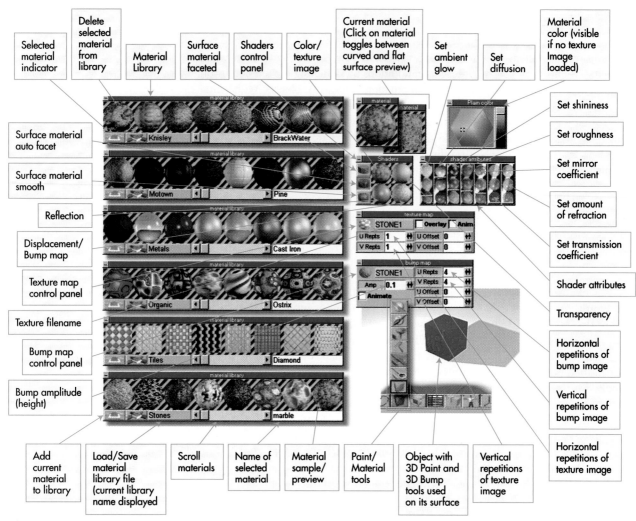

Figure 8.21

The material libraries and painting tools in trueSpace.

Material Library panel. The button to the right of the Add and Remove buttons, showing the name of the currently loaded library, allows you to load material libraries provided and save material libraries that you have modified. Figure 8.21 shows some of the standard material libraries that come with trueSpace along with the material editing tools, which are invoked by clicking the paint tools with the right mouse button. Clicking on the spheres in the Shaders panel will invoke a control panel for that shader. Figure 8.21 shows two of those control panels, for controlling texture maps and bump maps.

You use the Paint Object tool (which fills the object with the selected material), the Paint Faces tool (which paints one face at a time), and the Material Replacement tool (which replaces all instances of the material you clicked with the selected material) to exert complete control over your object's appearance. The Material Inspect tool lets you pick a material from the surface of an object and make it the currently selected material.

The 3D Paint and 3D Bump tools (refer to Figure 8.2) allow you to paint directly onto the object's surface. You can paint graffiti on the side of a 3D car model! The 3D Bump tool enables you to crease the surface of the 3D model, allowing you to further vandalize the 3D car! Figure 8.21 shows a blue cube with the word *Hi!* painted and etched onto the surface with the 3D Paint and 3D Bump tools, respectively.

While the autorecord feature for creating keyframed animation is beneficial, sometimes it can work against you. You must remember that any changes you make to an object, light, or scene in any frame other than frame 0 is recorded as a keyframe.

When you create an animation, always be conscious of the current frame number. For example, if you decide to introduce raytracing, but happen to be on frame 134 at the time, then trueSpace assumes that you are *intentionally* turning on raytracing at that keyframe. Likewise, when previewing an animation, you may decide to change the background color from white to blue. If you are not on frame 0 when making such a change, trueSpace will animate as many shades of white-through-blue as it can between frame 0 and the frame on which you told it to change the background to blue.

While this may be a pleasing effect, often it's not what you had intended. Be aware of what frame you're editing and always keep that Undo button in sight.

ANIMATION

At the bottom of the trueSpace interface is the animation controls group (refer to Figure 8.2). These VCR-like buttons allow you to record, rewind, and play your keyframed animation.

Creating keyframed animation is simple. (1) Select the object to animate. (2) Type in the required keyframe number to record on in the Current Frame Number box. (3) Press Enter to move to that frame. (4) Change the object as you would want it to appear on that keyframe. (5) Repeat from step (1) until you are happy with your animation. With the autorecord feature turned on (by default), everything you change on an object in any frame other than frame 0 is recorded as an intentional keyframed element of the animation. You'll remember that these key frames define milestones in your animated sequence, which the animation application uses to tween the intervening frames from.

By adding sequential frames in the Current Frame Number box and changing the object to show how and where it should appear at that keyframe, you can build quite a sophisticated animation. Figure 8.20 shows the Animation Controls group in action over ten keyframes as the aircraft passes through the ring.

Similar to the Sequencer in Infini-D, the Keyframe Editor shows the progression over time of each element of an animation (refer to Figure 8.20). In the left-hand panel listing the objects in the scene, each object listing can be expanded to show its component pieces. When you click on the small plus symbol, you can modify, delete, extend, or shorten the animation of each object over time.

autorecord

When autorecord is turned on, all changes made to a scene are automatically recorded as keyframe animation instructions unless the current frame number is 0.

RENDERING

All 3D modeling and animation applications, including trueSpace, enable you to render the scene from the view of your choice. With trueSpace, the rendering process happens in the view where you're editing. While this is unusual for such applications, in trueSpace it works well and is a tremendous asset when you fine-tune the final rendered image.

There are several levels of rendering in trueSpace, and you can change many rendering parameters in the Scene Render Options panel (refer to Figure 8.18). Furthermore, if you are rendering an animation, additional parameters come into play.

Figure 8.22 shows some of those parameters and how they interrelate. Each view has its own set of rendering tools. The Render a Portion of the Screen button (labeled 8) and the Radiosity button (labeled 7) are located only on the main

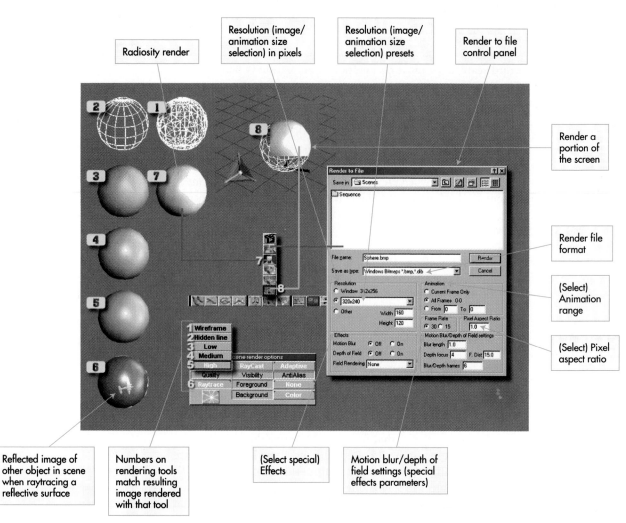

Figure 8.22

The many rendering options of trueSpace, each numbered and shown with a like-numbered example. Note that other objects in the scene become reflected in sphere number 6, the raytraced example.

screen but can be applied to all views. In radiosity rendering, the application calculates not only the lighting effects of the specified lights, but also the effects of light reflecting off surrounding objects and the scene's environmental parameters. In short, it is a computationally intensive process that provides more realistic lighting. The other rendering options are labeled 1 through 6 as they are found in the Scene Render Options panel; they give the corresponding results as numbered in Figure 8.22.

When you're rendering an animation, remember that there are effect options available such as motion blur, depth of field, and field rendering, described in Chapter 7. By selecting the correct combination of rendering options, you can achieve the desired effects for your 3D scene.

MORE MODELING: LATHE, PIPELINE, AND EXTRUSION METHODS

In addition to the processes described for Infini-D and trueSpace, you should be aware of some additional techniques that are common to all 3D modeling and animation applications.

Motion blur simulates the blurring effect seen in film or video recordings of live action. When you render sequential frames of an animation, the application draws a perfectly still image for each frame, which, when viewed in sequence, gives the illusion of motion. The frames can look a little "clinical" unless you simulate the blurring found in actual footage of live events. This is achieved by blurring together a few frames before and after the frame being rendered. The Blur Length/Depth Frames sets how many frames to blur together to achieve the desired effect. The more frames you include (to a point), the more realistic the effect, but this factor also multiplies the rendering time by the number of frames to blur together. A blur length of six frames requires the program to render six frames and blur them together for each actual frame of animation. A 30-frame sequence will therefore require the time to render 180 frames to achieve a motion blur depth of six frames.

Lathing is a process in which a drawn curve can be spun around an axis to produce a 3D form, much as a potter spins a lump of clay into an elegantly symmetrical vase. (Having done some clay throwing in my day, I can assure you that digital lathing is far simpler than using a potter's wheel. The potter's wheel has no Undo button!) In addition to lathing, there are two additional methods of extrapolating a complex shape from a cross-sectional curve: the pipeline and extrusion methods.

The pipeline method uses a spline curve to draw out the cross-section and have it follow the curve path, much as a fluid flows through a hose. This method can be used to form complex elongated shapes along a specified curve.

The extrusion method takes the cross-section and pushes it out a predetermined distance in a straight line. If you could take a printed letter of the alphabet and pull the face of the letter up off the page to create a 3D letter with sides extending back to the surface of the page, then you would in effect be extruding that letter.

Figure 8.23 shows examples of extrusion, pipeline, and lathing modeling methods. Figure 8.23 also shows flat and extruded text side by side. The extruded text has depth, while the flat text is just that—flat.

pipeline
A process whereby a shape is extended along a curved guideline path.

extrusion
A process whereby a 2D plane or face is given 3D depth or "thickness."

COORDINATES IN 3D SPACE

As mentioned before in this chapter, working in 3D space requires constant attention to the axes and coordinates used to define and place 3D objects in this space.

Every scene has its own coordinate system and set of axes. Both Infini-D and trueSpace provide you with a virtual floor, a visible grid in the scene. This grid lets you know which way is "up," where the foreground ends, where the background begins, and what relative scale you're working with. Figures 8.1 and 8.2 show these grids in action. Without these visual guides you could easily get lost.

In addition to using the scene X, Y, and Z axes to place and position objects, each object has its own unique set of object axes. The X, Y, and Z axes of an object determine which way it should be oriented in the scene (so that it stands on its feet and not its head) and which way is considered "forward" for that object. If, for instance, the coordinates for an object were incorrect, a 3D model of a car could conceivably stand on its tailpipe when at rest, and drive with its tires forward, as shown in Figure 8.24. While we know this is a ridiculous way to drive a car, the computer doesn't know any better; it only knows to apply

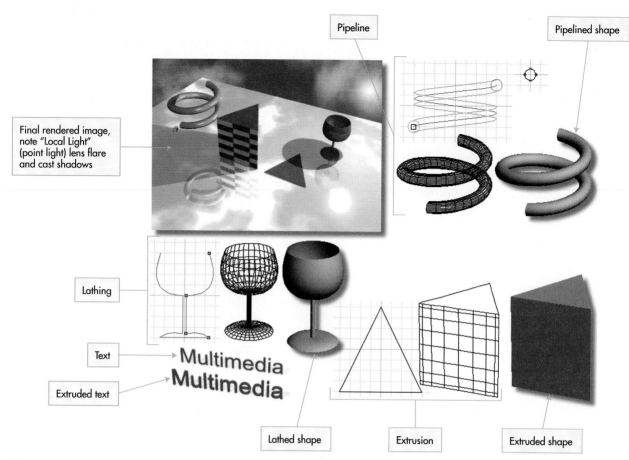

Figure 8.23
Modeling techniques such as lathing, pipeline, and extrusion are very useful in creating 3D models.

whatever coordinates it has been given for the object. This is illustrated in Figure 8.24 where the axes for the car have been rotated by 90 degrees to point the X axis downward. The resulting orientation of the object when it's next loaded into the scene or animated along a path will be as shown—sitting on its tailpipe! The button used to reveal the axes of an object is shown for trueSpace. Once visible, the axes can be moved and rotated exactly as you would move and rotate an object.

Note that the "location" in the object of the point where the axes meet determines that object's central pivot point. The pivot point is important, as it is the point around which the object will rotate. For example, the hands of a clock need to rotate to function, but their pivot point must be down at one end of the hand. This enables them to sweep around the face of the clock (as opposed to spinning around a point in the center of the hand). For a clock hand object, the pivot point would have to be moved down to one end so that when rotated, the hand works as a clock hand is expected to work. Likewise, if you were to model a person, the arm object would pivot around a point at the shoulder. If the pivot point for the arm object was where the elbow is located (the center of the arm object), then in order to rotate, the arm would have to detach from the shoulder to spin around the elbow point like an airplane propeller. Not a pretty sight!

Also shown in Figure 8.24 is trueSpace's Object Info panel, where you can edit and alter all coordinate aspects of the selected object. It is invoked by right-clicking the Object Tool. Infini-D's Object Info panel provides the same function (refer to Figure 8.6). This is where you can fine-tune the coordinates

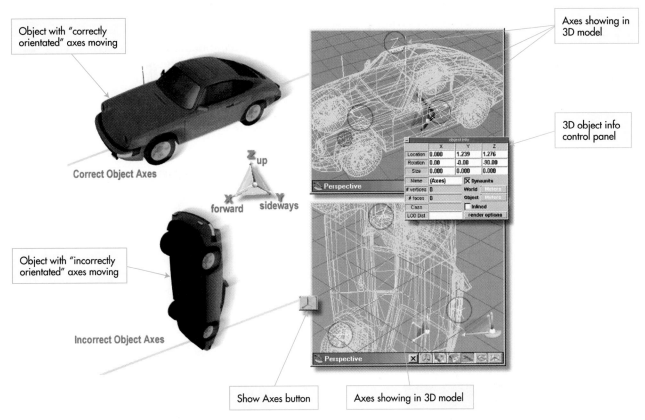

Figure 8.24
If the object axes are not correctly oriented, you won't achieve the desired results.

of your object that determine its location, rotation, and scale within the scene and animation. You will not often need such precise control over your 3D object, but if you do (such as if you need two objects to touch and want to avoid a gap between them), you know where it is and what it's for when you do. However, you may find that specifying the degree of your object's rotation can be useful.

TO WIREFRAME OR NOT TO WIREFRAME?

In most 3D modeling and animation applications, you can choose to view your scene in either a skeletal wireframe format or in a solid model format. This feature has appeared within only the last three to four years on personal computer–based 3D modeling applications with the advent of technologies such as OpenGL, 3DR, and DirectX/Direct3D 3D graphics drivers.

The benefit to you, the 3D modeler, is that in the solid model format, you view the scene in a way that looks more like the final rendered scene. The wireframe format can become confusing when there are a lot of complex objects side by side. The scene starts to look like a jumble of splines and object outlines. Distinguishing objects is often easier in solid model format, as you can tell which object is in front and which object is behind.

Surface and lighting characteristics show better in solid modeling format, and this may help you design your scene. Some solid modeling formats, such as the 3DR version used in trueSpace (trueSpace allows users to select among 3DR, OpenGL, and Direct3D), can also show a good rendition of the surface texture.

Viewing your models in wireframe mode usually makes it easier to see which object is selected, as it changes color and stands out from the other objects in the scene. Additionally, it is easier to select, manipulate, and paint faces on your wireframe model, as the objects are individually visible and identifiable.

As a 3D modeler, you can select the format you'd like to use while viewing and editing your scene. Some applications, like trueSpace, offer a combination view of solid model with a visible wireframe, as seen in Figure 8.18. Chose whichever format suits your needs at the time.

3D TEXT FOR YOUR MULTIMEDIA APPLICATION

Creating 3D text for your multimedia application is a simple task in most all 3D modeling and animation programs. Usually it is as easy as selecting the text tool, typing in the text, and letting the program render it. In trueSpace, however, you type your text straight onto the scene, while in Infini-D, you type the text in to a text entry box, and then it is placed in 3D form into your scene.

Figure 8.25 shows the text creation process in both trueSpace and Infini-D. Both text models have been created from the same font and both have been beveled for effect using the standard bevel settings. Once the text is in your scene it can be treated as any other 3D object.

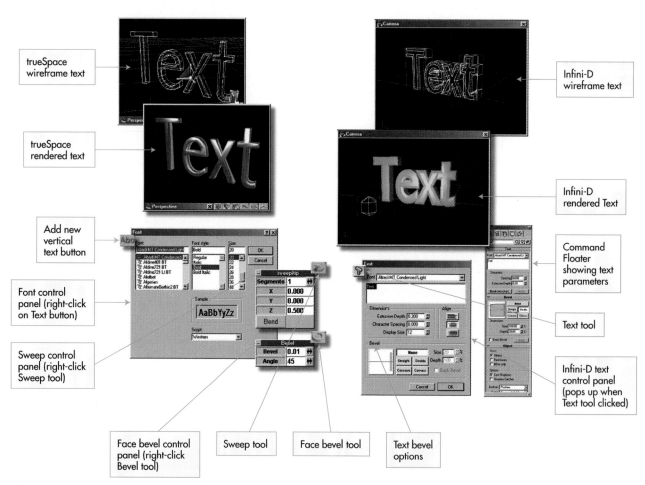

Figure 8.25
The 3D text creation process in both trueSpace and Infini-D.

If you want to animate your text, keep two things in mind. First, note where the text object's pivot point is located. Often the default location is at one end of the text object. This may have to be changed to achieve the required motion and rotation.

Second, note that the text object is a collection of letter objects (unless it's just one letter to start with) that can be separated into individual objects and edited or animated separately.

OBJECT GLUING/LINKING AND OBJECT HIERARCHIES

While the complex topic of gluing objects together in a hierarchical structure goes beyond the scope of this book, it is important to know the basics and the process of gluing together individual objects.

When you glue any two or more objects together, you combine them into a new single object whose components are objects that you have glued together. This new compound object can be manipulated in the same way as any other object, and all components are equally affected by your edits. You can still, however, break down that object and navigate through the subcomponents to select any component or subgroup and edit it separately.

This is similar to the way your hand consists of a palm, a thumb, and four fingers "glued" together. Each subcomponent is identifiable and movable, but when you move your hand you move all of the parts as well. Similarly, your hand is a component of your arm, along with your wrist, forearm, elbow, upper arm, and shoulder. Your hand "object," which itself is a group of objects, becomes a subcomponent of the arm. This dictates a hierarchy of the parts, as the fingers belong to the hand object, and indirectly to the arm object. The "ownership" tells us that the fingers may belong to the hand, but as the hand belongs to the arm, the arm can claim overall "ownership," and the hand no longer can be moved as an independent object. To separately identify the finger, you have to locate and select the hand and then subdivide the hand into its parts to reach the finger.

Once a 3D model's arm is glued together, moving the arm forces the hand and all of its fingers to follow the movement. Otherwise, if the fingers were separate objects, moving the arm would leave the fingers behind, dangling in 3D space. This would appear unnatural.

Figure 8.26 shows how these composite objects can be navigated when you want to select a subcomponent and edit it separately. In addition, both sets of controls for Infini-D and trueSpace are shown.

Also shown in Figure 8.26 are virtual bones and joints (shown in green and yellow respectively) within the humanoid model. These bones and joints can be used to create more lifelike movements with an object. Joints can be given characteristics that mimic the movement of real-world joints. For instance, an elbow joint would allow for 180 degrees of rotation of a "forearm" that would be restricted from moving beyond the extended straight-out position, and from rotating left or right. A hip or a shoulder joint would have its own set of axes and rotational restrictions. By defining a complete virtual arm using these special joints, the final result is a model that moves like a real arm. This technique of defining the joint motion characteristics in order to create realistic movement is called inverse kinematics.

Figure 8.26 illustrates the technique of using inverse kinematics and "bones" to create an articulated hand model that can be animated to move like a real hand. When such a bone-and-joint structure is established, simply dragging

inverse kinematics

A system of virtual bones and joints in a 3D modeling and animation application that provides lifelike animated movement of multi-jointed objects.

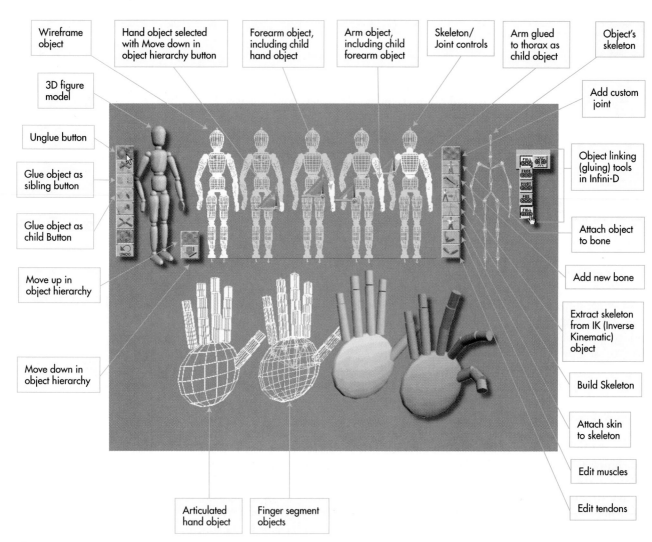

Figure 8.26
Objects made up of subcomponents can be glued together to create a hierarchy. This hierarchy is useful when later animating a linked articulated object.

the end of the model (in this case a finger) and moving it around provides life-like movement in your animation.

When gluing objects together you must decide whether to glue the selected object as a *child* object or a *sibling object*. When an object is glued as a child object, the parent object has precedence for all movement and editing of the combined object, much in the way the hand object would be considered a child object to the wrist and forearm. The subset group of the hierarchy is called the child object. In Figure 8.26, the hand is glued to the forearm as a child object. The resulting arm object is glued as child to the upper arm, creating the complete arm object, which is then glued to the chest and shoulders as a child object. Rotating the chest moves the arm with it. However, if you select the forearm group, it can be rotated without moving the chest or upper arm, but the hand moves with it. When moving, rotating, or scaling an object, you move, rotate, or scale its children objects along with it.

A sibling object is given the same hierarchy status as the object it is glued to. Both are considered equal subcomponents, much as each arm would be if an object's two arms were glued together. When glued as siblings, there is no need to navigate down the hierarchy to a subgroup, as the sibling objects have no parent relationship to each other. If the component parts of the arm in Figure 8.26 were glued together as siblings, then rotating just the forearm would do exactly that, but the other objects, such as the wrist and hand, would not rotate along with it. Take some time to experiment with object gluing. Line up a row of sphere objects, and glue each one in turn as a child to the next. Then try selecting just one of the spheres to manipulate it. Do the same for an identical group glued together as siblings, and repeat the exercise. By doing experiments like this you will develop a familiarity with object gluing.

LIGHTING YOUR SCENE

Lighting is a very important task in achieving the desired visual results in your scene, and it can be simple or complex.

The good thing about digital lighting in a 3D scene is that you have to "tell" a light to create shadows. Unlike real stage or movie production, you will not be driven crazy trying to arrange lighting to eliminate unwanted shadows in the scene. You simply pick a light and tell it to create shadows. Unless you select Shadow Mapping in trueSpace, you will need to make sure that you are rendering with raytracing to see the effects of the shadows.

The controls for doing this are always located in the lighting control panel. In Infini-D the Command floater (refer to Figure 8.5) provides lighting controls once you select the light you wish to change. In trueSpace, the lighting control panel appears automatically once you select a light object.

The primary forms of light are infinite light, point light, and spot light.

INFINITE LIGHT

Infinite light shines in parallel rays in the direction specified by the rotation of the infinite light object. This light doesn't have a "light source" but represents the effect of sunlight as it strikes the earth. Such light rays are all traveling in the same direction at that point as they cast a shadow on the ground.

POINT LIGHT

A point light source (called a Local Light in trueSpace) is located at a specific point in the 3D scene, and it emits light rays in all directions from that point, much like a light bulb dangling at the end of a cord. Figures 8.18 shows an example of point lighting.

SPOT LIGHT

A spot light object throws a cone of light much like a spotlight. You can change the shape of the cone by scaling the spotlight object to suit. Spotlights can be made to "look at" an object, which can be very handy if you want an object to remain under the spotlight no matter where you move it. Figures 8.17 and 8.19 show examples of spotlighting.

OTHER LIGHT FORMS

trueSpace provides area lights, projector lights, and skylights to simulate the special lighting qualities of each lighting form. The projector light can project an image or silhouette onto a scene, which can be a very nice effect. Infini-D provides tubular lighting as well as ambient light objects.

When using lighting, it is usually good to have one directional light to cast shadows, one foreground point light to fill in a little luminance, and additional lighting to suit. Remember that the more lighting you apply, the longer the rendering process will take, especially when using raytracing. The rays from each light have to be traced throughout the 3D scene.

BACKGROUND IMAGES

One of the most effective ways to visually enhance your rendered scene is to use a background image. In Infini-D, select a background image in the Environment panel. You can invoke this panel by choosing Environment from the Edit menu. In trueSpace, the background image is loaded by using the Scene Render Options panel.

Figure 8.27 shows the difference between using and not using a background image. Also shown in this illustration are the panels for both Infini-D and trueSpace from which you can load a background image.

If you are creating 3D content for a multimedia application or Web site, you may want to use a piece of the application's interface background as a background image for your 3D model. In this way you can place the rendered 3D image onto your project's interface and the background should blend in. This is similar to the way you created the 3D buttons in Chapter 6. Be careful to note the pixel dimensions of the piece you cut from your interface background, and render your 3D work to an image file dimensioned exactly the same. If you do this precisely, you should not be able to see the edges of the 3D image when it's positioned on the interface.

ANIMATING AND KEYFRAMING

The principles and techniques used to create a 3D computer animation have been covered in Chapter 7 and in this chapter. In Chapter 9 you will follow

Figure 8.27
The visual effect of adding a background image to a scene can be quite dramatic.

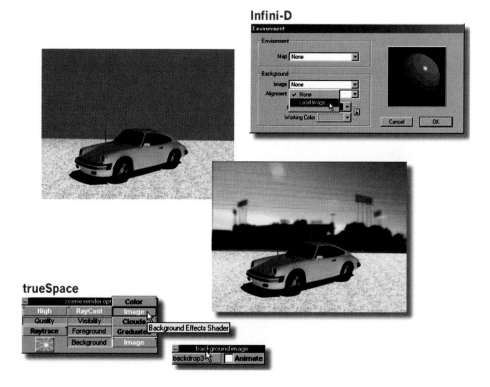

hands-on steps to create an animation in another 3D modeling and animation product, 3Space Publisher, and render it to one of several animation and video file formats.

As mentioned in Chapter 7, the most straightforward method of creating animation is to change the current frame number to the number of a desired keyframe. Change objects in the scene to where you would like them to be in that keyframe, and let the 3D modeling and animation application figure out how to animate them into those keyframe positions.

Figure 8.6 shows the Infini-D Animation floater panel, and Figure 8.20 shows the trueSpace Animation panel. By typing in the keyframe you want to animate and changing the objects in the scene at that keyframe, you can build, keyframe by keyframe, a complex animation. The application extrapolates the smoothest animation to get you from keyframe to keyframe.

Experiment a little by importing an object into either trueSpace or Infini-D, typing in a keyframe number or time respectively, and moving the object. Scale it at this keyframe and rotate it a little, too. Then click the play button and watch your animation unfold.

By using variations of this simple technique you can build complex animations for your multimedia application or Web page.

AVOIDING PITFALLS

By keeping an eye on pop-up ToolTips and prompts, and by using help features (especially trueSpace's 3D Tool Guide), you can familiarize yourself with the tools and their operation. The learning curve for 3D modeling and animation applications is steep, so take it slowly, experiment, and spend lots of time practicing.

Pay attention to your multiple floating views. A different view of the scene may show you a misalignment of objects not apparent in the 3D view. Also remember that the object-manipulation tools behave differently in different views. This is an advantage when creating your 3D scene.

On Windows systems, experiment with the multiple mouse buttons to get a feel for their additional functionality.

If you try to move, rotate, or scale an object and it appears stuck, check to make sure that you haven't inadvertently turned on the snap-to-grid functions of the application. Chances are that unchecking this feature will restore control for you.

When trying to precisely align objects, switch off an object's axis of movement. For additional control, use the Object Info panel.

When raytracing a scene, keep in mind that many factors can slow down this process, even on today's fast systems. Don't use too many lighting features, too much reflective or refractive material, or too many special effects, such as radiosity. If you don't like the results of the rendering and want to tweak an element, you will have to endure the rendering time all over again until you get it right. If draft modes will give you a good enough view of your scene, try to reserve the time-consuming features for the last rendering.

Although most 3D modeling and animation applications are very stable software products, especially considering the task that they perform, it is always important to save your work. Many hours of work can be lost if your system crashes, the power fails, or your cat takes a stroll across your keyboard. Keep backups of the scene data. You can always render the scene again once you have a good data file. If you lose the scene data, you have no recourse but to start over.

Chapter Summary

- Despite operational and superficial differences, good 3D modeling and animation applications, such as trueSpace and Infini-D, are remarkably similar in their functions and results.

- Computer 3D modeling and animation applications, while quite sophisticated and complex, can make a 3D designer's and animator's job very easy.

- Using a combination of simple primitive shapes, you can create complex 3D models.

- Object axes and coordinates are very important parameters of any 3D object. In particular, correct orientation of the object's axes is very important for believable animation.

- Creating computer animation can be as simple as entering in the desired keyframe number or time location and changing the scene objects to appear as you'd like them to at that point in the animation. It is the application's job to figure out the best way to extrapolate the smoothest path between keyframes.

- By adjusting rendering parameters, you can enhance a rendered scene to provide stunning visual effects.

- You can create objects easily from primitive shapes using the techniques of lathing, extruding, pipelining, and object face manipulation.

- When glued together, objects become sub-objects of the new combined object. These components can be selected individually again by navigating through the object component hierarchy.

- Lighting can greatly enhance your 3D scene. These applications provide several light types from which to choose. To cast shadows, the light must be told to cast shadows, and often raytracing must be used to determine and render shadows.

- A suitable background image can greatly enhance the appearance of a rendered 3D scene.

Key Terms and Concepts

autorecord, 183
boolean object
    combination
    procedures, 176
extrusion, 185

gluing, 176
inverse kinematics,
    189
lathing, 170
metaball, 177

nodes, 171
perspective and
    orthogonal views,
    174
pipeline, 185

spline, 170
virtual drill bits, 177

Checking Your Knowledge and Skills

1. Create a group of six primitive objects (you choose the objects). Using your 3D modeling and animation application's gluing tool, glue one to another as a child object. Glue the remaining objects in turn as children to the combination object until all objects are glued in turn as children.

2. Using the glued complex object created in exercise 1, use the hierarchy navigation tools (refer to Figure 8.26) to navigate up and down through the hierarchy. Use this exercise to become familiar with this technique. Select each subcomponent in turn, copy it, and move the copied object away from the combination object.

3. Using the copied object elements in exercise 2, glue each one to the next as siblings until all are glued together as one combination object. Using the hierarchy tools, navigate up and down through the subcomponents to get a feel for this form of object combination.

4. Refer to Figure 8.18 and create a spherical object with two spiraling "horns" coming out of both sides of the sphere. Once it is completed, create facial features from additional primitive objects, and render your final scene to a JPEG-format image.

5. Create a simple scene with a plane object for a floor and a cube object rotated to stand on one corner and floating above the floor object. Place a light into the scene to cast a shadow beneath the floating cube onto the floor. Import a background image to complement the image and render the scene to an image file.

Critical Thinking Challenges

Given the prevalence of digital 3D imagery in all aspects of media, whether it be the cover of a catalog or an ad on TV, answer the following questions to the best of your ability:

1. Find an example of digital 3D imagery that you admire and determine what elements make it so appealing. Is it the complexity or the elegant simplicity? Perhaps a stunning special effect caught your eye. Can you determine from what you have read so far how the digital artists may have created this work? What would you do to make it better? Pretend that the company that created this 3D imagery has contracted you to design the next version of the piece. What would you design and why?

2. There is a point where too much 3D imagery can look unpleasant. At what stage would you consider 3D digital content to be bad design? Can you discern a "happy combination" of 2D and 3D elements in an image? Do the illustrations in this book help you answer this question?

3. If you were to create a multimedia application that teaches users the basics of digital 3D design, how would you go about it, and why? Provide your answer in the form of a concept proposal for a prospective client who is willing to pay a ridiculous amount of money to have this done.

4. Of the two modeling formats discussed in this chapter, which do you prefer: modeling in the scene or modeling in a separate application window? Why?

Hands-on Exercises

JACK-IN-THE-BOX

Using the modeling steps illustrated in Figure 8.17, create a 3D model exactly like the one shown in the illustration. Having glued the model together, create a 3D box, and have "Jack" jump out of it in a simple animation by setting and resetting the required keyframes, and playing back the animation until you are pleased with the results.

Master Project

CREATING 3D CONTENT

So far you should have created a binder for the project that documents your project concept and includes a project plan, a timeline, and sketches and visuals for your design. You should also have begun the process of building your content and storing it on disk.

At this stage, determine what elements of your project would benefit from 3D modeling. Perhaps a 3D text banner? Maybe a rotating logo if your digital portfolio is for your business. Develop a wish list and begin thinking about how you might achieve it, knowing what you have learned so far about 3D modeling and animation. If you feel so inclined, begin to create your 3D content. This is also a good time to start building your gallery section if the portfolio is to present your digital artistry.

Save your work to a Zip disk (or equivalent) and keep it with your project binder.

USING 3D ANIMATION IN A MULTIMEDIA APPLICATION OR WEB SITE

Chapter Outline

Chapter Objectives

After completing this chapter, you will be able to:

- Determine which animation file formats and parameters are most suitable for which delivery system
- Distinguish between the animation format requirements of disk-based and Web-based multimedia applications
- Discuss the role of animation postprocessing and the application of video special effects and sound
- Use TGS's 3Space Publisher to create 3D animation for use in your Web page
- Create a 3D spinning-logo animated GIF
- Apply Active Styles in 3Space Publisher for 2D artistic animation effects

Chapter Overview

In Chapters 7 and 8 you were introduced to the magic and science of computer 3D modeling and animation. In this chapter you will create 3D content for your multimedia application, whether it be on CD-ROM, DVD-ROM, or the Web.

This chapter emphasizes the application of 3D graphics, regardless of the application they were created in. While trueSpace and Infini-D are both good programs for creating stunning 3D imagery, you can achieve similar results with many other fine applications. This chapter will emphasize the techniques and considerations involved in implementing this 3D content into your multimedia projects.

In addition to the examples of mainstream 3D modeling and animation applications you have seen, there is a new breed of specialized 3D graphic applications specifically designed for 3D Web content creation. These products provide a simpler way to create quick 3D images and animations for Web pages. While they usually do not have the range of tools, features, or capabilities of Infini-D or trueSpace, they also do not have the steep learning curve of such applications. You will see one such application, 3Space Publisher, in this chapter in a special section focused on quick and easy solutions for 3D Web content creation. While trueSpace, Infini-D, and other full-featured 3D applications can also create 3D Web content, you may want to use a program that is easier to learn and also less expensive.

3D GRAPHICS AND ANIMATION FILE FORMATS: WHAT'S SUITABLE?

As you learned in Chapters 7 and 8, the rendered 3D output file formats fall into the same categories as those of still digital images and digital video file formats. Depending on the required output (still image, digital video, image sequence) from the 3D application and the intended use of that output, you will narrow down those formats to the one or two most suitable format options.

With the advent of Web multimedia came the need to distinguish among CD-ROM-, DVD-ROM-, and Web-delivered multimedia applications. While a multimedia application, if so designed, can work very well in any form, some important technical considerations must be addressed. In the next section you will learn about the 3D file format considerations for disk-based and Web-based multimedia applications.

DISK-BASED APPLICATION AUTHORING CONSIDERATIONS

While the impact of media file size on application performance is not quite as critical with disk-based applications as it is on the Web, it is important to get the smallest file sizes you can without compromising the quality of the piece.

STILL DIGITAL IMAGES.   Multimedia authoring applications (such as Director, Authorware, Multimedia Fusion, and so on) usually compress and store still digital images internally when you create the final executable version of your product. They effectively do the image format selection for you!

Figure 9.1

Macromedia Director's import
file formats.

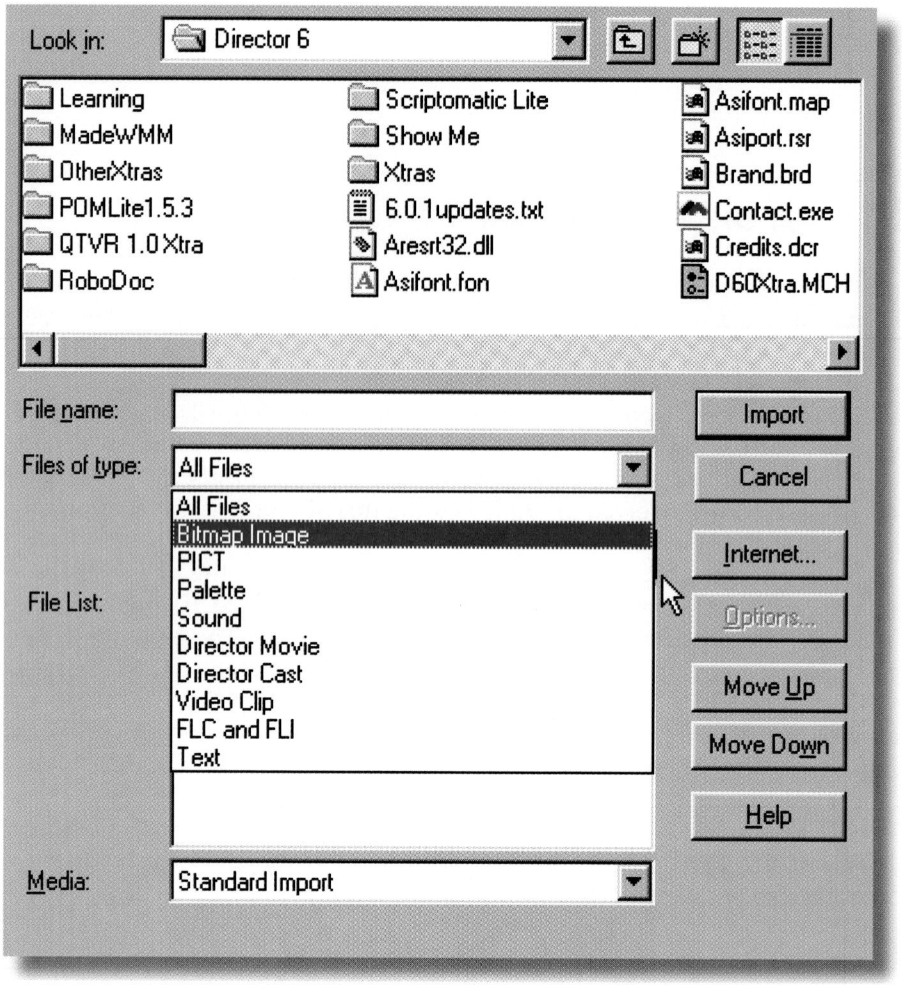

Therefore, your main consideration is what image formats your multimedia application will accept or import, and which of these formats provide the image fidelity and quality you are looking for. Figure 9.1 shows Macromedia Director's image import format options. Since the image will end up being optimized and compressed to the authoring tool's native format, you can concentrate on the visual quality issues. If you choose, however, to use external image files (not embedded in the executable when finished, but rather pulled in from a disk file when needed) you must then choose a format acceptable to your authoring tool that gives the smallest file size with the best quality. An external file is best used when you need the ability to change an image after the authoring and development has been done (an example would be a visual multimedia catalog of products that change seasonally). You will read more about this option in Chapters 14 through 16.

In addition, most authoring applications allow you to copy an image (or part of an image) and simply paste it into your project, as illustrated in Figure 9.2. This can often be the best approach. Not only do you avoid the intermediate steps of having to save the file and then import it into the authoring tool, but you can also try several image designs before committing to any one.

Most authoring tools will accept JPEG as a good universal image format. If you use this format, be careful to save the image at 100% quality settings or else you will see some pixelation and image deterioration.

For Windows systems, both Windows Bitmap (BMP) and TIFF formats offer noncompressed, full-quality formats that are good for maintaining fidelity of the

pixelation

Distortion of a computer image when the quality of that image is reduced to the point where it becomes coarse and "grainy."

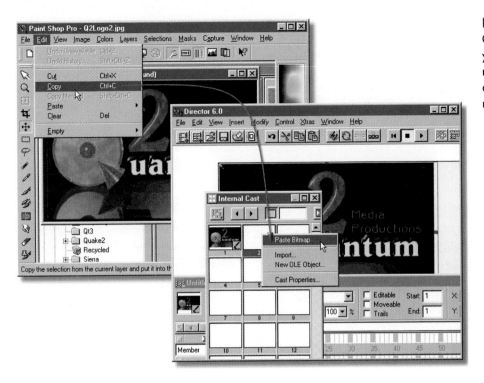

Figure 9.2
Copying and pasting between your image editing and multimedia/Web page authoring applications can make development work a lot easier.

image on the way to your project. For Macintosh users, Macintosh PICT or TIFF formats work well for the same reasons.

DIGITAL VIDEO AND ANIMATION FORMATS. Two basic animation formats are available to you in multimedia authoring: digital video and image frame sequences.

For digital video, your 3D application can render your animation to the digital file format of your choice, usually either Windows AVI format or Apple QuickTime format. At this stage most 3D applications do not render directly to any of the MPEG digital media formats.

Your choice of video file format will be governed primarily by whether this will be a cross-platform product when completed (will run on both Windows and Macintosh systems). If so, you will most likely choose Apple's QuickTime format as this format is supported on both Windows and Macintosh systems. If you do so, you must remember to provide your Windows users with the QuickTime for Windows drivers and Macintosh users with the correct version of QuickTime in case they do not already have these installed. The ability to

Keep in mind that whatever digital video file format you decide to render your animation in, you can always edit, modify, and convert that file format in a digital video editing application, as you will see in Part 4 of this book. By using such an application and because digital video files are always external files to the authoring tool, you can later change your mind about the best format to use.

PASTING AND SAVING IMAGES

Even though you copy and paste into your authoring tool, always save a backup file copy. If you are pasting a file that you may want to modify later, especially if the image contains layers, you will also need to save that file for later editing. The pasted image in the application can often be copied back to your image editing application (such as Photoshop), but since this will be a flat file, you may find yourself having to redo the image to rebuild the lost layering.

Use the pasting-to-the-authoring-tool technique to see various versions of an image, but remember that it is good practice to always save a copy of the image at the end.

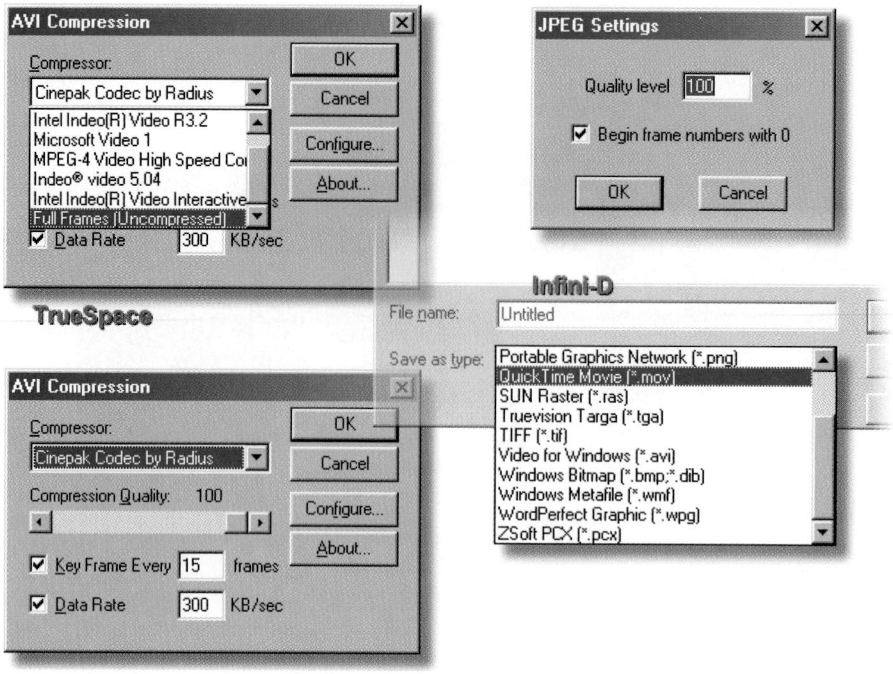

Figure 9.3

Caligari's trueSpace and MetaCreations's Infini-D provide many digital video and frame sequence image format options.

play QuickTime movies is not an inherent feature of the Windows operating system, but Windows does a marvelous job of playing QuickTime movies once the drivers are installed.

If your multimedia product will run on only one platform, then choose QuickTime as the suitable format for the Macintosh version, and Windows AVI for the Windows version. That way you can run the multimedia application on the appropriate system without having to guide your users through determining whether their system supports the nonstandard format and/or the installation of any additional driver software other than perhaps the correct version to run your product.

Thereafter, the type of data compression (*codec*) you use to format your AVI or QuickTime movie will be determined more by your own performance considerations than by the authoring tool. Since almost all multimedia authoring tools use external video files (the video file is included on the disk as a separate file linked to the executable file), their format support issues usually relate to the "brand" of digital video format rather than the codec used for that format. So if your authoring tool supports AVI, then it is usually your choice as to whether a Cinepak, Indeo, or other codec is best for your project. The codecs supported by your user's computer are determined by the version of the drivers installed on that system. You will learn more about codecs in Part 4. Figure 9.3 shows the Windows AVI and QuickTime codecs available for rendering from trueSpace and Infini-D.

Your authoring tool will usually provide additional information about what video formats it supports and what special handling and implementation considerations may exist.

FILM LOOPS

film loop

An element of a multimedia presentation that independently displays a looping animation in the application.

The term film loop is a specific reference from Macromedia's Director multimedia authoring tool. It refers to a technique in which a series of animated frame images can be stacked together into an object that can be placed anywhere in the application. When that object is encountered in the multimedia piece, it will animate all on its own, independently of any other animation on the screen. The concept is quite similar to that of an animated GIF image. When displayed on a

> You must check out either Microsoft's or Apple's Web site for information on redistributing their driver software to your users. There are simple and usually free or inexpensive licensing arrangements for doing this, but it is critical that you abide by the licensing conditions of the software you intend to distribute.

Web page, an animated GIF automatically animates by showing the frames of the animation stored in it in sequence. A film loop does the same thing. As an example, one of the most common uses for 3D film loops is for animated and spinning 3D logos and icons.

The technique used to create film loops will be addressed in Part 6. From the point of view of creating the series of animated frame images with which to assemble the film loop, the process is identical to that of building the content for an animated GIF file.

Having built your animation in your 3D application, you can choose to render the animation to a series of individual image files, each image in the sequence representing the next frame in the animation. That series of images is imported into your authoring application for assembly into a film loop. Some multimedia authoring applications, such as Multimedia Fusion, have the ability to import an animation, such as a GIF or AVI file, and convert it automatically into an internal film loop–type object.

WEB-BASED APPLICATION AUTHORING CONSIDERATIONS

In contrast to creating an executable disk-based multimedia product that can store image data internally, a Web page locates and loads externally stored image files when viewed in the user's browser application. Therefore, the Web page has to contend with downloading whatever file format you saved the file as it "builds" the Web page product on the user's screen. Figure 9.4 shows the components of a Web page and how the images that make up a Web page are really individual image files that are referenced in the page's HTML instructions.

In order for you to view the Web page on your browser, each image must be individually downloaded to your computer. This external storage of the images on the server and the need to download them enables you to save a copy of the image to your own disk. This is done by selecting the "Save Image to File" option from the shortcut menu that appears over the image when the right mouse button is clicked (or when a Macintosh mouse button is held down for a moment over the image).

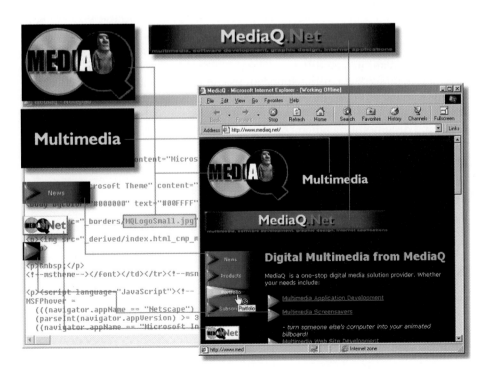

Figure 9.4
This Web page displays each visible individual image. The primary logo is called MQLogoSmall.jpg and can be seen referenced in the page's HTML.

Web pages have no internal image storage format or capabilities. The one exception to this is when you embed multimedia applications in your Web page, using technologies such as Macromedia's Shockwave. Even then the embedded media component is still a linked file. These embedded Web multimedia applications will be discussed in detail in Part 6.

STILL DIGITAL IMAGES. Your 3D imagery and content for Web page usage is restricted to only a few image file formats. Primary among these are GIF and JPEG. In addition to the advantages and disadvantages of these formats discussed in Chapter 4, you should be aware that GIF format (specifically version 89a or later) can support animation.

When your 3D image is intended for display purposes (perhaps a background image or interface button) and you do not require either animation or transparency, then JPEG is usually the best option. It can provide a high-definition 24-bit color image of your 3D work in a highly compressed, small file size. It also provides for progressive downloading, which shows a progressively less-blurred image as the data is downloaded. Progressive downloading is a better option for large images, as your users will more likely be engaged by the progressive *"resing-up"* of the slow-loading image than they would be if it appeared on their screen one line at a time as it downloaded.

DIGITAL VIDEO AND ANIMATION FORMATS: ANIMATED GIF VERSUS VIDEO. While there is probably no easier way to show animation on your Web page than by using an animated GIF, be aware that these files can get very large very fast. Animated GIF format is best used for small images that are animated in a perpetual loop—meaning that the animated sequence is played repeatedly. For a longer, bigger, or more sophisticated animation, you should consider embedded digital video or a multimedia applet to provide this content. Later in this chapter you will learn how to create such content from Template Graphic Systems's 3Space Publisher.

If your 3D animation program does not support animated GIF format, you will have to render your animation as a sequence of frame images and then import them into an animated GIF image creation tool. Microsoft's GIF Animator, Jasc's Animation Shop (shown in Figure 9.5), and TGS's 3Space GIF Animator are typical of these GIF animation creation applications (the latter two are supplied with Paint Shop Pro and 3Space Publisher respectively, demo versions of which are available as downloads from this book's Web site). In the case of Animation Shop, you can additionally paint, write text, and edit each individual frame of an animated GIF.

Often digital video editing applications can export to animated GIF format, but pay attention to both the visual quality of the output file and its size. Since GIF format uses a 256-color, 8-bit palette, your nice-looking video could appear grainy and disappointing when converted to animated GIF. It is easy to export a video sequence to animated GIF format and end up with a large-file-size image that drags down the loading time of its Web page.

PALETTE ISSUES

Setting and maintaining an 8-bit, 256-color palette for the digital graphic content of your multimedia project is, thankfully, becoming less and less necessary as time progresses. Maintaining a set palette is more important for Web content where many users from all over the globe may be accessing your Web site using old computer systems with 8-bit color displays.

To accommodate such users, a Netscape 216-color palette provides a standard set of colors that will always work on Macs, PCs, or other flavors of personal computers. If you choose to maintain a set palette, then you will have to

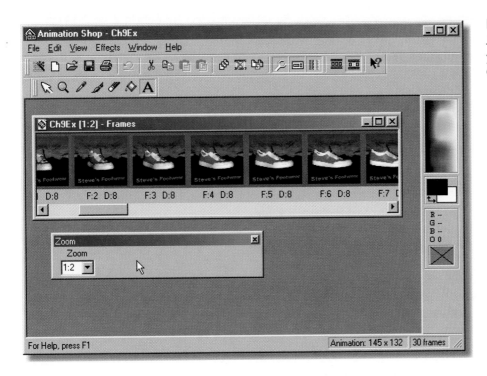

Figure 9.5
Jasc's Animation Shop enables you to create and edit animated GIF files.

apply that set palette to all of the graphic content of your project. This means that all interface images, button images, displayed images, animated sequences, and digital video content must all use the same palette.

Most authoring tools such as Macromedia's Director and Multimedia Fusion provide for the implementation of a set palette for 8-bit color content, but in the case of Web graphics, you must modify each image and media component separately to use that one palette. Graphic design tools such as Photoshop and Paint Shop Pro can load and apply a set palette to an image, though they do it one image at a time. Products such as Graphics Workshop and DeBabelizer use batch processing to convert all images and content to one palette in one go. Products such as DeBabelizer can create a custom super-palette that is best suited for all images in the batch.

If you want to create multimedia applications for those using limited computer systems, then you will have to either apply a standard palette (such as the Netscape palette) to your work, or use a product such as DeBabelizer to convert your content to use a custom super-palette across all images in your project.

ANIMATION POSTPROCESSING

Unless your animation is simple, perhaps a logo or short sequence, then you will probably want to edit further. For example, you may want to splice it together with other rendered animations "shot" from different views, or you may want to add a soundtrack, titling, or special effects. A must-have tool in the digital multimedia producer's arsenal is a digital video editing tool. These applications can cost as little as $50 and as much as tens of thousands of dollars. In any case, such an application enables you to do much more with your rendered animation after it has been rendered. I personally cannot remember the last time I rendered an animation that I didn't postprocess in some way with a digital video editing tool—and I create a lot of computer animation.

The techniques used to edit and manipulate digital video are exactly the same as those used to edit and manipulate digital animation—after all, they are

If your product is intended for mass circulation or for public consumption on the Web, then it is very important to adopt an 8-bit color palette for your content. In these circumstances you cannot determine whether your users will have better than an 8-bit display, and you may be causing many 8-bit-display users undue grief by not catering to them. If you decide not to adopt an 8-bit palette for a mass-distribution product, then be sure to print a "minimum system requirements" specification on the product wrapping or, in the case of a Web site, on the site entry page.

usually the same format anyway. These techniques will be discussed in detail in Part 4, but for now, consider what you can do to your animation with a digital editing tool. You can do the following:

- Add titles
- Reverse the animation's direction
- Turn it to black and white or posterized colors
- Emboss the image
- Add lens flares
- Add a soundtrack
- Splice it with live video
- Superimpose it over live video
- Remaster it in a different format or size

Often you will want to copy an animation sequence or simply add special-effect sounds. While animation tools such as Infini-D and trueSpace can incorporate sound into your animation output, a digital video editing tool gives you far more control over editing it.

SPECIAL APPLICATIONS: ANIMATING FOR WEB CONTENT USING 3SPACE PUBLISHER

As mentioned earlier, you can find 3D modeling and animation applications that have been specially designed for a specific application. Such programs, while not having the same breadth of features as a "generic" animation program, do perform their specific tasks very well, and can often reduce that steep learning curve associated with other 3D animation packages that have more tasks to perform. One such program is Template Graphics Software's 3Space Publisher. Figure 9.6 shows the main features and functions of the 3Space Publisher interface.

3Space Publisher scores highly on its ability to drag and drop 3D objects into the scene from a visual model library; render directly to animated GIF format (in addition to the conventional animation formats); create animation Java applets; create HTML content or complete Web pages to display the rendered work or to copy into an existing Web page project; and apply simple animation, such as spinning, by pointing and clicking.

This section is not intended to be a comprehensive guide to 3Space Publisher. Instead, it will give you a specific example of how this versatile program can enhance your Web page creation productivity.

CREATING A SPINNING-LOGO ANIMATED GIF

The following steps demonstrate how 3Space Publisher can be used to quickly and effectively create a spinning logo and render it to an animated GIF–format file for inclusion in a Web page (or in a multimedia program if you wish). Refer to Figure 9.6 for guidance on where to locate buttons and controls.

1. Start a new animation project in 3Space Publisher by clicking the New button.
2. Select the 3D object of your choice to represent your spinning logo from any gallery group of the 3D Clipart library. Drag it to one of the scene views.
3. Orient your 3D object in each view so that it appears as you would like it to in the final animated GIF, as shown in Figure 9.7. Use the Change Camera

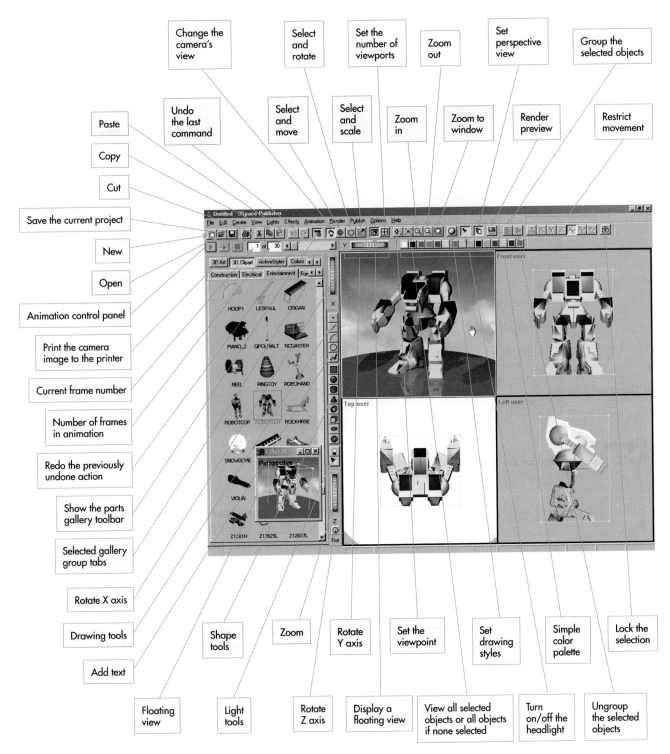

Figure 9.6
3Space Publisher is a terrific product for creating effective 3D imagery and animation for your Web pages.

View tool in the Perspective view to arrange the way you'd like the object to be seen. The X, Y, and Z thumbwheel tools will help you achieve this. Using the Change Camera View tool while holding down the Shift and Ctrl keys on the keyboard will slide and zoom the Perspective view, respectively.

4. Now it's time to add your company's name in 3D text. As you might guess from Figure 9.8, in this example I chose to add "Steve's Footwear" as my

Figure 9.12
3Space Publisher's Active Styles
feature provides an infinite
source of 2D drawing styles.

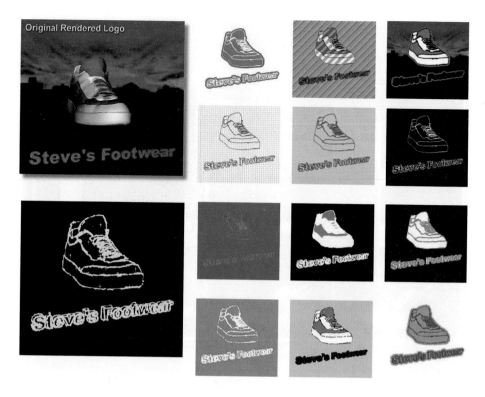

ACTIVE STYLES IN 3SPACE PUBLISHER

One of the gallery group buttons is Active Styles. This tab provides you with a library of special-effect styles that you can apply to your 3D animation by simply double-clicking the style you want. Your scene is automatically updated with that Active Style.

This unique feature of 3Space Publisher allows you to render your 3D animation in what looks like a hand-drawn 2D cartoon format. It provides an infinite range of artistic styles that can apply to your animation. This feature gives you all the benefits of easily created, keyframed 3D animation in a 2D format. If you're rotating a 3D model, for instance, the Active Style version provides the realism of rotating 3D geometry and perspective you would expect from a 3D application, while rendering the animation in a way that makes it look hand-drawn. Figure 9.12 shows the rotating shoe logo animation in a variety of Active Style treatments.

This Active Styles feature is especially cool when you consider that the stylized drawing modes can be applied to animation as well as still images (see Figure 9.12).

AVOIDING PITFALLS

The final destination for your animation file should be foremost in your mind when building your animation. Render it to the format needed—if you don't know what it is, find out, because different delivery systems have their own special requirements. You don't want to create an animated GIF for a multimedia CD-ROM authoring application that doesn't import such a file format. While you can always edit the file and convert it to a more suitable format, creating it in the correct format from the outset will save you a lot of unnecessary work. You also stand to have a better-quality end product if it doesn't have to go through multiple format conversions to get the desired results.

Often it may be easier to create the desired animation in a specialized application rather than in one of the mainstream comprehensive animation applica-

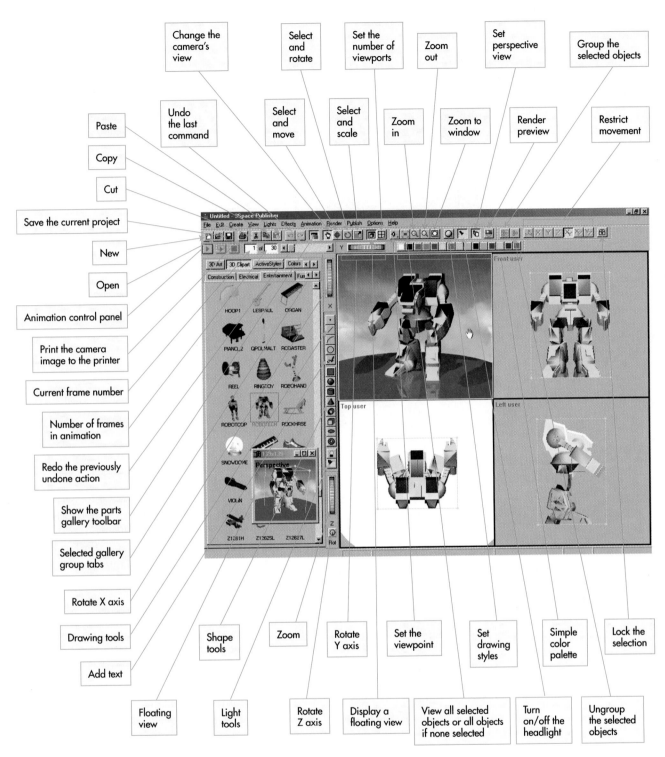

Change the camera's view

Select and rotate

Set the number of viewports

Zoom out

Set perspective view

Group the selected objects

Paste

Undo the last command

Select and move

Select and scale

Zoom in

Zoom to window

Render preview

Restrict movement

Copy

Cut

Save the current project

New

Open

Animation control panel

Print the camera image to the printer

Current frame number

Number of frames in animation

Redo the previously undone action

Show the parts gallery toolbar

Selected gallery group tabs

Rotate X axis

Drawing tools

Add text

Floating view

Shape tools

Zoom

Rotate Y axis

Set the viewpoint

Set drawing styles

Simple color palette

Lock the selection

Light tools

Rotate Z axis

Display a floating view

View all selected objects or all objects if none selected

Turn on/off the headlight

Ungroup the selected objects

Figure 9.6
3Space Publisher is a terrific product for creating effective 3D imagery and animation for your Web pages.

View tool in the Perspective view to arrange the way you'd like the object to be seen. The X, Y, and Z thumbwheel tools will help you achieve this. Using the Change Camera View tool while holding down the Shift and Ctrl keys on the keyboard will slide and zoom the Perspective view, respectively.

4. Now it's time to add your company's name in 3D text. As you might guess from Figure 9.8, in this example I chose to add "Steve's Footwear" as my

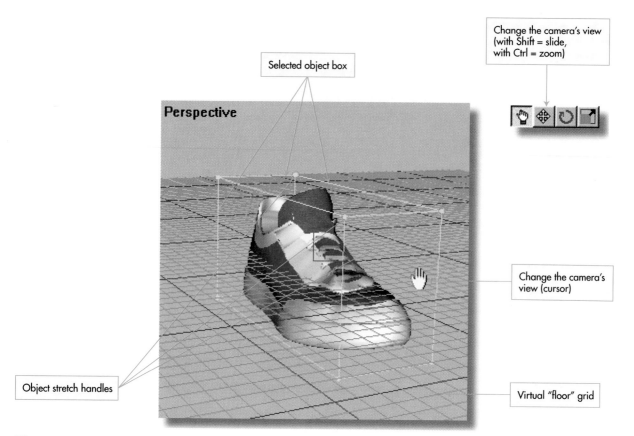

Figure 9.7
The 3D object selected for the rotating logo is oriented and awaiting text.

3D text. You can add whatever name you'd like. Click the Add Text button, type in your company name, and select the text properties you wish. Note that 3Space Publisher has no font size option, as in 3D space this has no real meaning; you scale letter objects to whatever size you want.

5. When you click the OK button, your mouse pointer changes to an X, as seen in Figure 9.8. Your first click with this pointer in any scene view will determine the location of the bottom left corner of the 3D text object you're creating. Thereafter, any mouse movement scales the text up and down, and the second mouse click sets that object size and finishes the text creation process.

6. You may want to arrange your view of the text with the logo object at this point. Since you will want to determine the final size of the rendered animated GIF, this is best done in a floating view, as shown in Figure 9.8. The

SIZING THE FINAL RENDERED PRODUCT IN 3SPACE PUBLISHER

3Space Publisher provides the floating view mode to allow you to size the final output of your rendered image or animation. You can, of course, render from any of the other scene views, but they are fixed in size and are rather large for Web page use. If you would like more precision in determining the size of your final output, you can stop (if playing) animation and right-click on the floating view, choose the Floating View command, and then choose the Size command from the shortcut menu. This will allow you to type in the precise pixel dimensions that you need.

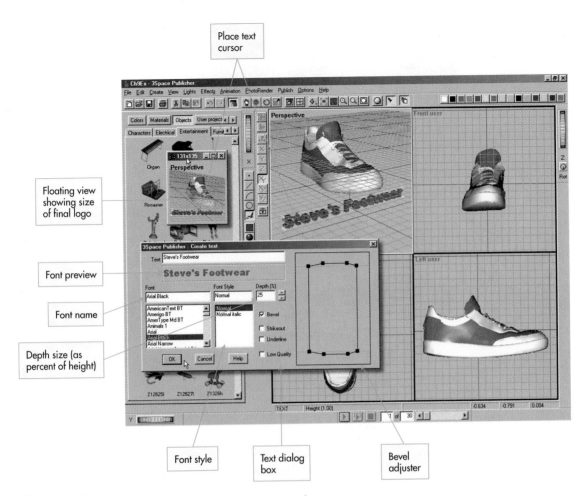

Figure 9.8
Adding, placing, and scaling text.

floating view is accessed with the Floating View command on the View menu. To see what a rendered version of your work to date looks like, select the render option of your choice from the Render menu.

7. With your logo object and company name in 3D text in the scene, it is time to set the materials of the scene objects. Select the object whose material you want to change and drag the material of your choice from the material gallery group on to that object; the selected object is painted in that material. By selecting the background (the empty space behind your objects), you can drag a material or image and drop it as a background image. The effect of the combination of materials dragged and dropped into the scene can be seen in Figure 9.9.

8. You should be ready to animate your spinning logo (in my case, the tennis shoe). Select the object to animate, and choose Spin Selected from the Animation menu. The spinner animation control panel, shown in Figure 9.10, will appear. The default settings will work for a full rotation of your object around its vertical axis. To apply this animation to your object, simply click the OK button. You may want to experiment with the settings again to see the different effects you can apply.

9. When you click the OK button, the animation instructions are transferred to the object and the bounding box surrounding it turns green (indicating an animated object). Also, the animation control panel at the bottom of the screen will show the number of frames you chose from the spinner control

Figure 9.9
The materials shown were dragged and dropped on to the appropriately selected object and background.

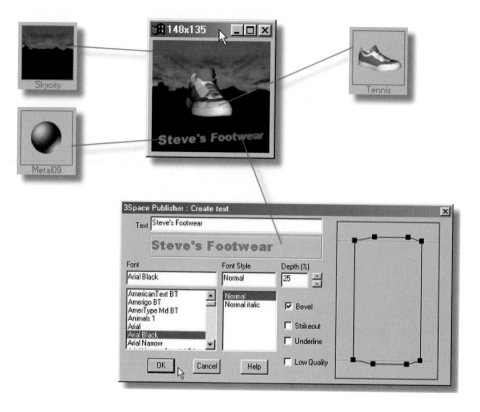

panel. To test the animation, click on the play or looped-play button in the animation control panel. Be sure to save your work as you go.

10. Rendering an animated GIF image is the simplest part of the whole operation. Make sure that the floating view is the one selected (you can do this by clicking in the scene shown in that view). Choose Animated GIF from the

Figure 9.10
The spinner animation control panel shows the default options selected.

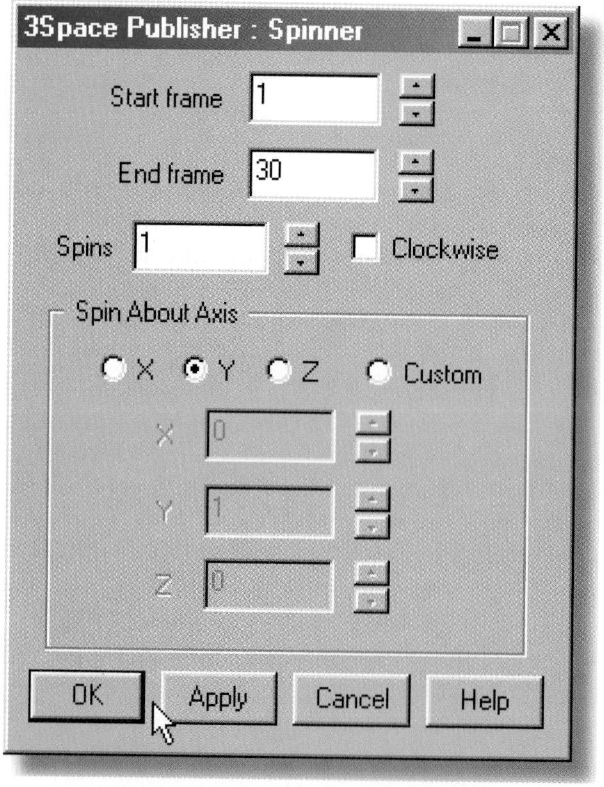

Figure 9.11
3SpaceGifAnimator is launched
by 3Space Publisher once the
animation is rendered.

Publish menu. Specify the location and name of your animated GIF image, whether you want it to be animated indefinitely, and what quality rendering you want, and click OK. 3Space Publisher will render and store each frame of your animation to the specified filename and location.

11. Once the rendering process is completed, 3Space Publisher will run the 3SpaceGifAnimator program. Clicking the play button will display your final animated GIF shown running in Figure 9.11. You can also use your Internet browser application (such as Netscape Navigator or Microsoft Internet Explorer) to view your new animated GIF by opening it as you would a HTML document.

Congratulations on your animated GIF logo! Now that wasn't too difficult, was it?

ANOTHER WAY

You've just created a spinning animation using an automated spinning animation feature of the animation application.

As discussed in Chapter 8, you can always create your own animation by typing in a specific keyframe and then changing the animated objects in the scene to whatever positions you would like them to be in at that frame when the animation plays. You can do this with as many keyframes as you wish. In this way you can incrementally build a sophisticated animation, having the animation software do all the hard work of figuring out how to animate the frames you don't specify.

The very best way, and realistically the only effective way, to become familiar with this keyframing technique is to experiment and practice it.

Figure 9.12
3Space Publisher's Active Styles
feature provides an infinite
source of 2D drawing styles.

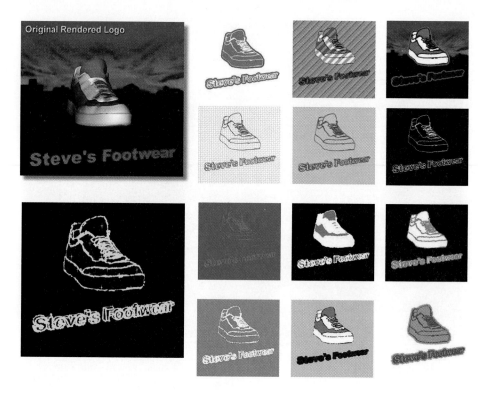

ACTIVE STYLES IN 3SPACE PUBLISHER

One of the gallery group buttons is Active Styles. This tab provides you with a library of special-effect styles that you can apply to your 3D animation by simply double-clicking the style you want. Your scene is automatically updated with that Active Style.

This unique feature of 3Space Publisher allows you to render your 3D animation in what looks like a hand-drawn 2D cartoon format. It provides an infinite range of artistic styles that can apply to your animation. This feature gives you all the benefits of easily created, keyframed 3D animation in a 2D format. If you're rotating a 3D model, for instance, the Active Style version provides the realism of rotating 3D geometry and perspective you would expect from a 3D application, while rendering the animation in a way that makes it look hand-drawn. Figure 9.12 shows the rotating shoe logo animation in a variety of Active Style treatments.

This Active Styles feature is especially cool when you consider that the stylized drawing modes can be applied to animation as well as still images (see Figure 9.12).

AVOIDING PITFALLS

The final destination for your animation file should be foremost in your mind when building your animation. Render it to the format needed—if you don't know what it is, find out, because different delivery systems have their own special requirements. You don't want to create an animated GIF for a multimedia CD-ROM authoring application that doesn't import such a file format. While you can always edit the file and convert it to a more suitable format, creating it in the correct format from the outset will save you a lot of unnecessary work. You also stand to have a better-quality end product if it doesn't have to go through multiple format conversions to get the desired results.

Often it may be easier to create the desired animation in a specialized application rather than in one of the mainstream comprehensive animation applications. The specialized application enables you to create good work as easily as possible. Professional animators always have several animation applications in their arsenal with which to complete the project as quickly and efficiently as possible.

Likewise, professional animators use several animation and digital video editing applications to achieve desired special effects and to create novel styles and "looks" for their clients. Postprocessing your animation in a digital video editing product opens a multitude of additional creative possibilities for your work. More important, a good digital video editing program can also help smooth out mistakes and fix errors in the original animation. By changing the speed and order of images and eliminating offending frames, you can repair many problems in an animation that would otherwise take considerable rendering time to rebuild.

Chapter Summary

- Rendering the final animation file in the correct format is a very important consideration. Different multimedia delivery methods will have their own special file format requirements.

- Two distinct multimedia delivery systems are disk-based (CD-ROM/DVD-ROM) and Web-based (Internet/intranet) multimedia products. There are specific factors to consider when authoring for either format.

- The video format you choose for your animation sequence will determine what driver software your users may need to install.

- Animated GIF file format is a common way to display animation on a Web page.

- Palette issues are an important consideration for multimedia production, especially for Web-based products.

- The animator's job is not done when the animation sequence is finally rendered from the 3D animation application. Often animation sequences will have to be spliced together, and sound effects will have to be added along with visual effects and perhaps titles. These postprocessing tasks are all best done in a digital video editing application.

- Specialized 3D applications can provide a simple and quick method for creating impressive 3D and 2D animation for your multimedia product or Web page. 3Space Publisher is one such tool.

Key Terms and Concepts

film loop, 200
pixelation, 198

progressive
downloading, 202

Checking Your Knowledge and Skills

1. Use a 3D modeling and animation program to create a spinning-object logo video clip for inclusion in a CD-ROM multimedia application authoring tool.
2. Use a 3D modeling and animation program to create a spinning-object logo animated GIF for inclusion in a multimedia Web page.
3. Find a Web page that includes an animated GIF that you like. Right-click the image (Mac users, hold down

your mouse button over the image) and use the Save As command on the shortcut menu to save this image to disk. Then, using an application such as Jasc's Animation Shop, Microsoft's GIF Animator, or TGS's 3Space GIF Animator, open the file and view its individual frames. Use that application to modify the file and make it your own (Animation Shop is particularly good for this).

4. In your 3D modeling and animation program, create a small animation and render it as a sequence of individual images. Using Jasc's Animation Shop, Microsoft's GIF Animator, or TGS's 3Space GIF Animator, import the sequence of images, set the timing and looping parameters, and save as an animated GIF. Load the file into your browser application to view your work.
5. In your 3D modeling and animation program, create a small animation and render it as a video clip and as an animated GIF (if your application doesn't output to animated GIF, use the technique mentioned in exercise 4). Compare and contrast the two formats. Which one is the larger file, and which is easier to implement into your Web page? Which would be the better choice for your Web page and which would be the better choice for a CD-ROM–based multimedia application?

Critical Thinking Challenges

Given the prevalence of digital 3D imagery in all aspects of multimedia, answer the following questions:

1. Find a Web site that uses a 3D animation that you admire. How is it implemented? One way to determine whether it's an animated GIF is to right-click the image (Mac users, hold down your mouse button over the image) and see whether the shortcut menu gives you the option to save the image. This will indicate that it is a GIF. If choices like "Play," "Stop," and "Rewind" pop up, then it's most likely an embedded video clip. If nothing pops up, then it's most likely an embedded applet, such as a Java or Shockwave applet. What do you think of the choice of format for that animation, and could it be done better in a different format? Why?
2. Review a selection of CD-ROM or DVD-ROM multimedia applications (at least four) and make a list of the 3D animation used in each case. Demonstration CD-ROMs from software manufacturers are very useful for such critiquing. Determine which applications from your sample group seem to make good use of 3D animation, and which overdo or underdo it. Rank them in order from best to worst in your opinion, and try to determine common factors that make them good or bad.
3. If you were to create a multimedia application that made heavy use of 3D animation, what parts of the project would rely on 3D animation, and what would be the purpose of using 3D animation as opposed to static imagery or straight video?
4. In the example you gave in the previous exercise, did you intend to create a disk-based or Web-based multimedia application? Explain why you chose that delivery system, and what conditions your choice places on you at the development and design phases.

Hands-on Exercises

CREATING A SIMPLE ANIMATION

Create a simple animation, no longer than three seconds in duration, and incorporate a background image and both static and moving objects in the scene. A spinning logo would be a good example of such an animation. Make sure to save your animation data file. Render the animation in "best quality" as a digital video file (one for each flavor of video format available to your 3D animation application), as an animated GIF, and as a sequence of frame images. If you don't change the screen size or the parameters of the animation, then you should end up with a collection of files showing the identical animation in a range of available formats. Compare and contrast the resulting file sizes, create a list of the various formats you created, and try to determine the most suitable formats for disk-based and Web-based multimedia.

Master Project

ANIMATION FOR YOUR PROJECT

So far you should have created a binder for the project that includes your project concept, a project plan and timeline, and your sketches and visuals for your design. You should also have begun the process of building your content and storing it on disk.

In the last chapter you determined what 3D content you would like to incorporate into your digital portfolio. Begin by storyboarding and sketching your animation concepts on paper and then, using the animation product of your choice, build the animation. Determine as early as you can what delivery system you intend to develop this project for. Render your animated content to the appropriate format and store it on your project disk. This would also be a good time to gather 3D animation examples of your work for your portfolio's gallery while you experiment with these applications.

Save your work to a Zip disk (or equivalent) and keep it with your project binder.

Four

DIGITAL
DESKTOP
VIDEO

10

MULTIMEDIA BUILDING BLOCKS: VIDEO

Chapter Objectives

After completing this chapter, you will be able to:

- Identify the special considerations required for online video streaming
- Discuss video data compression technology, formats, methods, and their application
- Describe the process of morphing and how morph videos are created
- Identify the complexities and parameters involved in purchasing, implementing, and using video capturing hardware and software, and the pros and cons of associated equipment
- Identify digital video editing methods

Chapter Overview

If you have been reading this book sequentially, you already know quite a bit about digital video. However, if you haven't read the sections on 3D animation, this may be a good time to do so because it will give you a better context for this chapter.

As with almost everything to do with multimedia, these chapter topics are interrelated and often indistinguishable. Graphic design and photo editing applications and techniques use 3D effects. 3D applications depend heavily on digital video effects. Digital video editing processes depend heavily on the use of still images and computer-generated animation, and bring us into the new arena of digital sound.

In this chapter you will learn the skills of digital video editing and manipulation.

OVERVIEW OF COMPUTER VIDEO FILE FORMATS AND SPECIAL EFFECTS

Digital video editing can appear to be quite a daunting and complex field, but once you master some basic techniques and learn some terminology, it becomes remarkably easy. In this chapter and the next, you will learn how to edit digital video using a nonlinear digital video editing application.

The final intended delivery system for your multimedia product incorporating the video clip is of prime importance, especially for digital video. A broad distinction can be made between disk-based and Web-based delivery of digital video. Disk-based digital video has the benefit of high data transfer rates from hard drive to processor within the computer system. In contrast, Web-based digital video has to contend with the data transfer rate of your connection to the Internet to get to your system's processor. The bottleneck with Web-based digital video is almost always the connection speed (also known as *bandwidth*) at which it is downloaded. Though technology is catching up to this problem, delivering digital video over the Web is challenging.

The technology of video streaming (playing a video clip while it is still downloading) for the Web has been improving steadily. Recent new MPEG digital video formats (MPEG-4) and codecs are providing full-screen, full-motion video supplied at dial-up modem connection speeds. While everyday usage of online video is a few short "computer years" away, the technology is there in bits and pieces waiting to be conglomerated into an elegant and easy-to-use solution. Microsoft's MPEG-4 format as used in NetShow (see Figure 10.1) currently offers one of the best quality and performance formats available. Companies such as Microsoft (www.microsoft.com) and RealMedia (www.real.com) are constantly driving up the performance standards for Web-based video. Check out their Web sites for the latest developments in this exciting field.

In the following descriptions of the various terms and formats associated with digital video, you will see the distinctions between disk- and Web-based delivery. Since a lot of these formats are determined and applied upstream in the digital video editing process, it is important to resolve your delivery requirements at the outset. This will save you a lot of reworking later on.

video streaming

A technology that compensates for slow connection speeds to the Internet by allowing a video clip to begin to play as the remaining part of the clip is still downloading. As long as the section playing does not catch up with the section being downloaded, the user should be able to view the video as it is downloading, as opposed to having to wait for the entire clip to download before viewing.

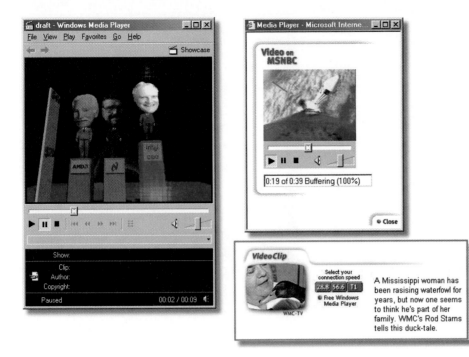

Figure 10.1
Microsoft's NetShow/Media
Player offers the latest in quality
and performance for streaming
video delivered over the Web.
Note the bandwidth options
provided for the "duck tale."

This said, one of the tremendous benefits of digital video editing applications, such as Lumiere and Adobe's Premiere, are that they enable you to change the digital content and remaster it again and again without significant quality loss (when you do it correctly). So do not worry if you find that you've been working on a format not suited for the intended use. You can always go back and rework it. However, you can save on that reworking time by planning correctly from the get-go.

FRAMES AND FIELDS

Digital video, as with film and analog (taped) video, is based on a frames-per-second linear presentation format. This means that a video segment plays, at a defined speed and frame rate, from start to finish. Each frame is an individual image, much like a still photo, that shows the next incremental change in movement of the clip's subject matter. When stacked one after another and then played back in quick succession, the frames give the illusion of motion. Figure 10.2 illustrates this process.

How many of these frames are displayed per second determines the "smoothness" of the motion viewed. This parameter is referred to as frames per second, or fps. The more frames displayed for each second of video, the smoother the video appears.

The human eye starts to see discrete frames (can determine individual frames from just jerky video) at about 12 fps. Typical computer animation sequences, especially for older computer systems, are rendered at a rate of 15 fps. The frame rate for your domestic (non-HDTV) TV is 29.97 fps (rounded up to 30 fps for computer applications). Typically, 24–30 fps is the frame rate used for digital video and animation to provide smooth and nonjerky digital video.

Not only do IMAX theaters use nine-story-high screens and superwide film, but their movies are shot at an incredible 60 fps. This exceedingly high frame rate provides a powerful sense of realism and removes the flicker sometimes seen in the corner of the eye. Since the IMAX screen occupies the whole field of view, such a frame rate virtually eliminates flicker in the viewer's peripheral vision.

frames per second

A numeric value that specifies the number of video frames displayed in quick succession for each elapsed second of playing video.

Figure 10.2

A series of images (frames) displayed in quick succession provides the illusion of a "moving picture," in this case a man sitting down.

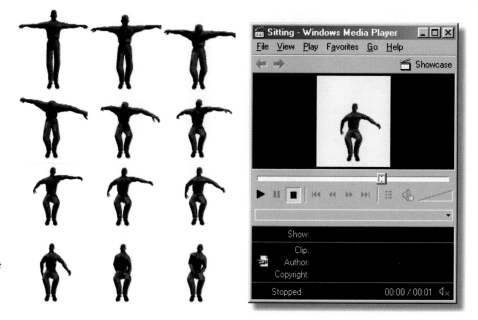

interlacing

A technique used for video broadcast that displays each frame of video by first displaying the first scan line and all odd-numbered lines thereafter in the frame, and then displaying the second line and all even-numbered lines of the frame. This is done faster than the eye can detect and is a technique that was originally introduced as a way to prevent the top part of a video frame from fading by the time the scanning electron beam reached the bottom of the frame when all scan lines were scanned in succession.

field

A set of odd or even scanned lines used for interlacing.

field rendering

Since digital video played on a computer screen does not need interlacing, digital video editing applications (and some 3D modeling and animation applications) provide the option to create interlaced video, which is then suitable for broadcasting. This digitally created interlacing is called field rendering.

A significant difference between video/television and computer displays is that video/television always uses interlacing, while computer displays usually do not. A brief history is necessary to understand the concept of interlacing. In the 1940s and 1950s, the challenge to television set designers was to overcome the problem of phosphor fade on television display tubes. The electron beam that scanned the TV image onto the inside of the TV screen was slower than the fading rate of the coating that made the scanned electron beam glow. By the time the full screen (484 scan lines) had been "drawn" from top to bottom, it was already beginning to fade from the top down. At the frame rate of the time, this fade at the end of each frame scan caused an annoying and distinct flicker.

To work around this problem, the clever engineers first scanned all of the odd lines and then backed up and scanned all of the even lines of the frame's image before advancing to the next frame. This technique spread the fading over the whole image and virtually eliminated the flickering problem. Quite clever, don't you think?

Each of these sets of lines is called a field (hence the terms "odd field" and "even field"). The technique of mixing the two fields together to create one image is called interlacing. Figure 10.3 shows the effect of interlacing. This is why in computer animation and digital video editing applications you will see a reference to field rendering, usually offering a choice of Odd, Even, or No Field Rendering.

WATCH OUT FOR THAT TIGER!

The peripheral vision of your eye can perceive frame flicker at 30 fps. This area of your vision has been fine-tuned by evolution for spotting small subtle movements in the extreme edges of your field of view—just in case you need to jump out of the way of that saber-toothed tiger about to ambush you as you amble through the forest in your loincloth! While you seldom view a TV from the corner of your eye, try this sometime while slightly moving your head, and you'll begin to see a frame-rate flicker.

As a multimedia developer you need to be aware of this since your user will no doubt be viewing your work head-on on a computer screen.

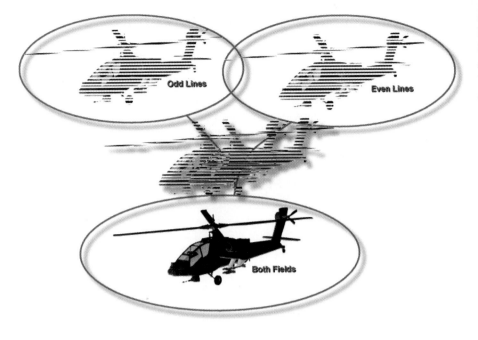

Figure 10.3
By interlacing odd with even television scan lines, engineers could compensate for the failings of early television technology. Merging the odd and even lines gives the complete image.

When video was established, a frame rate of 30 fps (29.97 fps actual) was chosen, with two interlaced fields per frame. This gives a field rate of 60 (59.94 actual) fields per second.

field rate
The number of fields per second displayed when applying interlaced video. Typically this number is twice the frame rate (fps × 2).

VIDEO ON THE WEB AND VIDEO STREAMING

The concept of video streaming was conceived to work around a serious restriction inherent in Internet communications technology. The speed of data transfer (bandwidth) available to most Web users with dial-up modems is far too slow to play video data. At speeds where you have to wait for each image to be displayed on your screen, you can imagine the problem if each image is a frame of video, and the requirement was to display fifteen of those each second!

The initial solution to this problem was to not even consider playing the video directly over the Net. Users would download the video file to play later on their own systems. However, this solution proved to be next to useless, since the time required to download small and short video clips of poor quality were more than most users would tolerate. Users lost patience and simply went to another site on the Web and didn't bother with the lengthy download.

To aggravate this problem, users' modem connections could quickly become swamped with downloading the video file so that browsing the Web was effectively suspended until the download was complete. This was too much of a commitment on the part of typically impatient Net surfers just for a poor-quality video file at the end of the download.

Some innovative companies, notably RealMedia, Intel, VXtreme, and Vivo, developed new video file formats and codecs that went a long way toward meeting the obvious demand for easy-to-view video over the Web with the less-than-ideal connection technology of the time. They adopted very high compression methods to get a large amount of video into a tiny file size, and developed the process of video (and other media) streaming.

In video streaming, the video file format supports the viewing of the initial part of the file that has downloaded while the remainder of the file is still downloading. Rather than waiting for the whole file to reach your hard drive, you can begin to watch the video clip while it is downloading. If the downloading data stream can match or exceed the data rate required of this very small version of the file, then users can view the video clip as they download it.

Such encoding typically allows for several versions of the video clip to be created, each best suited for a different modem connection speed. This gives users a choice of viewable video that best matches their modem's performance. However, the slower your modem speed, the poorer the quality of the video clip. And some of the video clips encoded for slow modems, such as 14,400 Kbps modems, can be really awful.

While current streaming video technology still has a way to go to provide TV-quality video over the Web at dial-up speeds, there have been tremendous advances in recent times. RealMedia's G2 technology and MPEG-4 from Microsoft are getting very close to the ideal (as shown in Figure 10.1). Current versions of both AVI and QuickTime format support video streaming in some form for Web-based applications, but the purpose-built Web codecs do a far better job.

Check out this book's Web site for links to examples of video streaming and content on the Web, and decide how well the best of current technology is measuring up.

VIDEO ENCODING: CODECS

Most computer systems cannot cope with displaying a full frame image in one-thirtieth of a second if that frame is an individual, uncompressed image file. To continue to display 30 of those images per second for an extended period will overtax even the highest-performance systems. A single uncompressed 640 × 480 (about full-screen video size), 24-bit color image can be as large as a megabyte in file size. For your computer to throw 30 of these onto the screen for every second of video (a data rate of 30 MB per second) is a daunting task. Although a 32X CD-ROM drive can push out an optimal 4.8 MB per second of data, this device would fall quite short of such a demanding video clip.

Thankfully you do not have to worry about this too much, because you are provided with integrated software applications, or drivers, called *codecs*. These drivers compress the video file into small, compact, and highly usable file sizes, often with little compromise on screen size or image quality. They effectively reduce the amount of data needed to represent the video images on the screen.

spatial compression

A digital compression of video data that compresses the size of the video file by compressing the image data of each frame.

lossy

A term used to describe a codec that loses video quality with higher data compression.

temporal compression

A digital compression of video data that uses similarities of sequential frames over time to determine and store only the image data that differs from frame to frame.

SPATIAL COMPRESSION AND TEMPORAL COMPRESSION.   In broad terms, there are two types of compression. Spatial compression compresses the space required to store each individual image. This is like the compression used to make a JPEG-format image much smaller than its uncompressed counterpart while retaining much of the visual fidelity of the image (as described in Chapter 4). Spatial compression works by making each individual frame's image smaller, and usually results in a lossy compression (one that loses image definition). With spatial compression you trade small file size for image quality.

Temporal compression (also known as frame differencing) uses the similarities of individual frames over time to remove repetitive data. Only the changes between sequential frames are stored.

For instance, if the video clip is of a person talking against a blank background, with no head movements, then the only differences between subsequent frames would be the movement of the mouth as the person talks, and perhaps a few eye or expression movements. If the computer displays just the first full frame of the sequence, and then only changes the facial features as they change from frame to frame, then you would see the complete video clip without needing to store each individual frame of the segment. By storing one reference frame and then only those changes from that frame for the remaining sequence, the file size of the digital video clip can be drastically reduced without apparent loss of image fidelity.

The reference frame is referred to as a *keyframe*. The frequency of when a keyframe is stored—and therefore the number of frames extrapolated between

keyframes—will affect the size and quality of the digital video file. Typically keyframes are stored every half or whole second of video. The more stored, the bigger the video file, but the better the quality of the extrapolated in-between frames, as they get refreshed with a new reference frame more frequently.

Depending on the codec employed, selecting too infrequent a keyframe will cause image deterioration in one of two ways. A too-distant keyframe may cause the displayed frames to deteriorate as they look less and less like the original reference frame. Then the changes between the current frame and the reference frame may have no bearing on the differences between that frame and the one before it, which is what gives us the illusion of motion. Another problem occurs when the differences are so great from that distant reference frame that the codec is effectively storing and displaying each complete new frame, since each is different from the last keyframe. In this case, storing all individual frames again defeats the purpose of compression.

Usually when selecting your codec, you will be prompted with the best keyframe frequency for that codec. You will also have the opportunity to specify your own custom keyframes. This is most important when there is a drastic change in the displayed image. In such an event, the keyframe would not be at all similar to the current frame and your codec would be compromised until the next scheduled keyframe is captured. In this case you could place a marker at this transition and force a correct keyframe to be stored, and then resume the periodic keyframing from that point on.

FLAVORS OF FORMATS AND CODECS.

When you render your edited video to a digital video file, you will choose a video file format in which to store the video clip. For computer use, the primary choices are Microsoft's AVI format, Apple's QuickTime format, and some versions of MPEG. Additionally, there are other formats, such as AutoDesk's FLC format, but most digital video falls into the MPEG, AVI or QuickTime camps. Consider these formats the "brand" of video file format. To get the job done, these codec flavors use either symmetric compression, in which the time needed to compress the video is the same as that needed to decompress it for display, or asymmetric compression, where compression takes longer than decompression. Each of these brands offers several codec compression formats, which can be considered the "flavor" of that brand of video file format. Figure 10.4 shows some of the video brand and flavor options available from Adobe's Premiere.

The following summary may help you decide which file format brand to choose:

- *AVI*. Microsoft's AVI format, while not the best performer, is supported on all Windows systems, which is by far the bulk of personal and business computer systems installed. Of the 11,500 personal computers sold worldwide every hour as of mid-1999, most are Windows systems. Know who your user is. No additional software is required of a Windows 95/98/NT4/2000 system to play AVI files. Extensive codec support also can provide good compression and performance. Non-Windows systems, such as Macintosh computers, do not support AVI format and will require special software (available from Microsoft) installed to view the video. Be sure to supply such software to these users if you use AVI format.

- *QuickTime*. A very good video format (version 3 or higher), QuickTime is widely supported on Macintosh and Windows systems. Most Windows 95/98 systems will play QuickTime video but may require the installation of driver software if the version of QuickTime required to play your video is a more recent one than that supported. While you will have to provide your users with the necessary QuickTime software installers, QuickTime still remains the brand of choice for cross-platform multimedia development.

The term *keyframe* has two distinct meanings in computer animation and in digital video. In developing computer animation, the keyframe is a snapshot of the animation at that point over time. The animation application's task is to animate the parameters of the object or scene for each frame of the animation to smoothly arrive at the designated keyframe looking exactly as the animator designed it.

In digital video, the keyframe is the periodic full reference frame stored and used for temporal compression of that video sequence.

symmetric compression
A codec that compresses the video data in the same amount of time as it takes to decompress it for playback uses symmetric compression.

asymmetric compression
A codec that compresses the video data in more time than it takes to decompress it for playback uses asymmetric compression. Asymmetric compression usually provides greater compression, resulting in smaller file size.

Figure 10.4

Adobe's Premiere's selection of video output format brands and codec flavors is vast. Each General Settings File Type has its own selection of codecs, as shown.

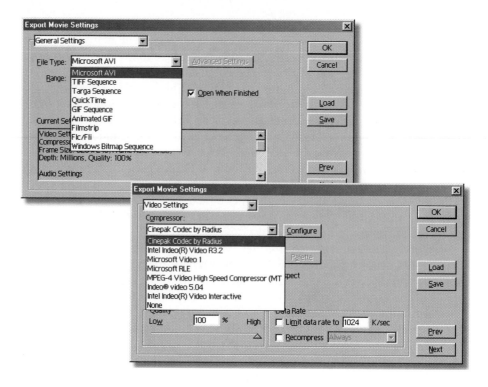

QuickTime drivers also support QuickTimeVR format. (VR stands for Virtual Reality—a format that provides a 360-degree image that the user can rotate and view as if he or she were in the scene depicted.) QuickTime is available free from Apple—if you don't mind that your users see an advertisement from Apple each time they use it. To get a version without advertising, you can pay a fee per every copy you distribute.

- *MPEG.* MPEG is growing in popularity as computer system performance improves. MPEG-1 encodes a video clip in 352×240, 320×240, 176×112, or 160×112 screen size only, but can be played full-screen at 30 fps with a smooth frame rate at acceptable image quality. The original MPEG-1 format was designed to give VHS movie quality at CD-ROM data rates. It is also a true cross-platform format, supported in both Windows and Macintosh systems. The problem with MPEG is that its compression is highly asymmetric and usually requires expensive hardware to encode in this format. While inexpensive ($100–$200) hardware encoding devices and some software encoding products are available for creating MPEG-1 (and some MPEG-2) format files, the quality of these "domestic" encoders is not terrific, and often results in jerky playback when played full-screen on medium-performance systems. The new MPEG-4 format promises good quality at low data rates, and the ability to encode for different playback data rates. Adobe's Premiere 5, which you will read about later, supports MPEG-4 format encoding. Before using MPEG, check that your intended users' systems can support the version you will adopt. As with AVI and QuickTime formats, you may have to supply a driver installer, and in some versions of MPEG (namely MPEG-2), your users may have to have decoding hardware installed in their computer systems.

The following summary may help you decide which codec to choose. Most of these codecs offer a quality choice for the final video image, allowing you to get additional compression in exchange for some visual quality:

- *Microsoft Video 1.* The original AVI compressor from Microsoft is quite lossy, but its quick compression times make it ideal for rough rendering to gener-

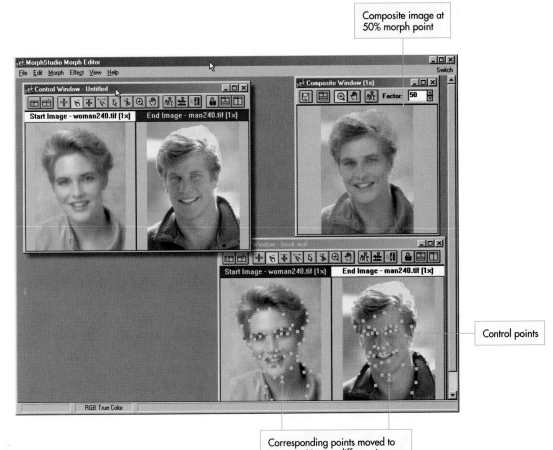

Figure 10.7
Ulead's Morph Studio in action, showing the first and final images with their reference points clearly visible.

selling software, for about $12), Elastic Reality from Avid Technology, and others. When choosing a morphing application, look for those that can morph video clips together as well as still images. This can be a very useful tool for creating movie special effects.

MORPHING TIPS

First, whenever possible, try to morph between images that have identical (or at least similar) backgrounds. Since it is the subject matter of the image you're morphing, and not the background, the first background will fade into the second one. If the backgrounds are different, the fading of the backgrounds will distract the viewer from the morphing of the subject matter. If necessary, use a photo editing tool to create the same background on both images.

Second, try to get all of the noticeable points of both images included in the morph. If the second image doesn't have particular features, such as visible ears, but they are visible on the first image, then provide reference points for them anyway, and move those points into where you'd expect those ears to be on the second image. One of the most common mistakes in morphing is to omit a feature when placing reference points. The result will be the fading of that feature without any movement. This can detract from, if not ruin, the visual effect of morphing.

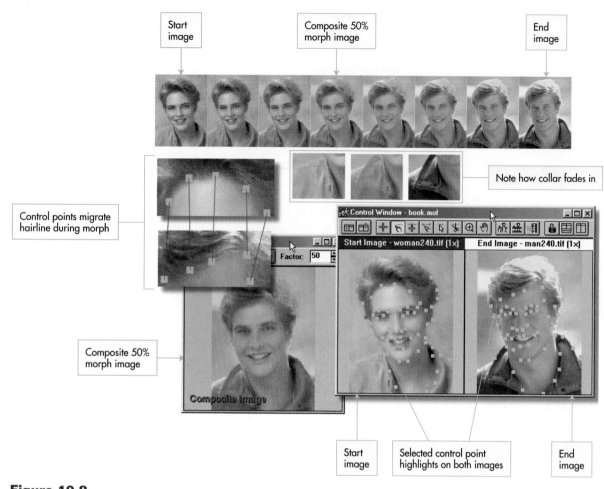

Figure 10.8
The anatomy of a typical morph.

DIGITAL VIDEO HARDWARE AND SOFTWARE CONSIDERATIONS

When working with digital video, you will need to consider adding some additional products and programs to your multimedia development workstation.

ANALOG AND DIGITAL VIDEO CAMERAS

The object of editing digital video is first to get the video you want to edit into a digital format. If you intend to create video footage to incorporate into the editing project, then you will have to consider whether to use a conventional analog video camera or a digital video camera.

Video cameras come in all shapes, sizes, and formats. Analog video camcorders can be purchased for a few hundred dollars and can do a terrific job of capturing video for later digitizing for digital editing. These "domestic" cameras tend to provide far better image quality when connected directly to your digitizing workstation and the video is captured live. There can be quite a bit of image quality loss when the video is first recorded to videotape and then digitized later. More expensive camcorders, however, especially those that use professional Betacam-format tape, and even some Hi-8-format tape camcorders, retain good image fidelity even after taping. Providing you have a good-quality video capture board in your workstation, you can expect to capture video of at least as good a quality as that you see on a screen connected directly to the camcorder.

Digital video cameras are becoming more common and more affordable every day. While still quite expensive for quality units when compared to their analog cousins, they do offer excellent quality with no degradation of captured quality. Some digital camcorders can plug directly into your computer system for fast and easy downloading of the recorded video. Products that incorporate Sony's FireWire technology are simple plug-and-download devices that avoid the complications of conventional video capturing and digitizing. In recent months, computer systems have been showing up in computer stores with FireWire ports sold as a standard feature.

For quality of video and ease of importing that video into your video editing application, it's difficult to beat a good digital video camera. If your budget is the main consideration, then an inexpensive domestic analog camcorder and an inexpensive video capture interface card for your video workstation will do a terrific job.

VIDEO CAPTURING HARDWARE

Video capturing hardware options fall into two main categories: those for capturing analog video and those for capturing digital video. Since products for capturing digital video are simple and straightforward devices (plug into your digital camera and download), I will focus here on devices used for capturing analog video.

A video capture interface card is designed to convert an analog video signal connected to it into a digital video file in real time. This is quite a daunting task when you consider that the device must record 30 full-screen frames of an image per second and store them in a disk file without missing a beat. This is such a demanding process that it requires dedicated hardware devices to do this conversion for you—hence the video capture interface.

Considerations when choosing a video capture device include the following:

- *Does it capture full-motion video?* Many "video capturing" devices look like a terrific value until you realize that they simply capture still images from a video feed. Make absolutely sure that the product you invest in captures full-motion video at 30 fps.

- *Does it capture at 640 × 480 image size or greater?* If you intend to do broadcast work or create a video project that will end up on videotape, then 640 × 480 is the smallest capture size you should consider. For purely digital multimedia work, you can often work in resolutions down to 320 × 240, but bigger is still better in this regard.

- *Does it also capture sound?* While this feature is not essential (as your system's own sound card can be used to capture a video segment's soundtrack when digitizing), some video capture cards provide sound capturing features that are more flexible and often result in better-synched and better-quality sound for your video. Such a feature on a video capture card can be a tremendous asset, but beware that it also costs more than buying a video capture card with no sound recording capability.

- *Can it "print to video"?* Most video capturing products do just that—capture video. However, what if, having created your masterpiece, you would like to create a videotape of your work? Or what if you would like to make a videotape of that excellent computer animation you created in the last chapter? Be absolutely sure that your video capturing interface has the ability to output to videotape, and if it doesn't, that you do not foresee a need for such a feature. This is probably the most commonly overlooked feature when it comes to purchasing video capturing hardware, and often the most frustrating, since the lack of such a feature is usually only discovered after many hours of video editing and creativity.

Because video capturing devices use dedicated custom hardware to perform the arduous task of converting a video signal to a digitized video file in real time, such systems usually use their own proprietary digitizing software and codec. The net result is that the captured video segment, while it looks and performs well on the system with the capturing device installed, will not be viewable on another computer system unless it too has the same proprietary codec (and probably the same hardware) installed.

This is not a problem once you take an additional step before bringing your captured video file to another system. By using your digital video editing software to create a new movie in a standard AVI or QuickTime format, you create a version that can be brought to other systems. This process is referred to as "flattening" the video clip.

This problem most often occurs when you have someone else digitize video for you, or you use a digitizing system in, say, a school's computer lab. Remember to create a version of the video clip in a format you know your system will recognize and you won't fall into this trap.

- *Does it support both AVI and QuickTime formats?* For multimedia development, it is very important to be able to work in both of these primary digital video formats. Without one or the other you will be locked out of a significant number of multimedia development opportunities. Make sure the device supports both formats.

Once set up, you should be able to connect your video camera or videotape player to the back of the interface. From within your video editing software (a version is often supplied with the hardware), simply select that application's video capture feature and watch the magic unfold. You are ready to digitize!

While this may sound oversimplified, the trick with these devices is to achieve a clean and solid installation. Once they are correctly set up, they work well and repeatedly so. Therefore, it is very important to follow each step of the installation instructions to the letter.

Some manufacturers (Apple Computers is particularly well known for its AV line of Macintosh systems) create complete turnkey video workstations, with video capturing, editing, and printing hardware and software preinstalled. Such systems can often represent tremendous value and a quick and painless way to begin digital video editing. However, they often use proprietary hardware and software that may not be compatible with other systems. Check out the specifications carefully before investing.

Be careful of manufacturers who, to sell off stock of a soon-to-be-outdated system, bundle the systems with video capturing hardware and sell them at an apparently low price. These systems can become very confining very soon. If you are attracted by such a ready-to-go system, a good bet is to stick with well-known brand names and purchase only from either the manufacturer or from reputable vendors.

GETTING YOUR VIDEO ONTO VIDEOTAPE

As mentioned in the previous section, if you want to create a videotape of your work, it is important to make sure that the video capturing hardware you purchase can output to videotape. The process of recording your desktop video project onto tape is called "printing to video" and requires special hardware to

Often the videotape recorder in a camcorder is of superior quality to that of a VCR, especially Hi-8-format units. Consider connecting to the camcorder if it supports a video signal input, and create the master on the camcorder's format tape. Thereafter, use this tape to make duplicates. If you already have a camcorder, you could save money on not having to purchase a VCR for your video editing workstation.

accomplish. Assuming that you have such hardware, there are some additional considerations to make sure that you get the best possible quality recording of your work. Here are a few pointers:

- *Make sure that you have the correct connections between your computer video output port and your videotape recorder.* It still surprises me how many multimedia developers, especially when backed up against a deadline, jeopardize their project by not having the correct cables to connect to their VCR. Determine this well before you get to the point of actually needing these connections.

- *Make sure that your video editing workstation has a suitably fast hard drive.* You'll need a high-performance hard drive to sustain a constant data flow to support outputting your edited video at full-screen 30 fps. The hard drive should sustain the data rate recommended by the manufacturer of your video output hardware for extended periods of time. The video capture/printing interface manufacturer will recommend the specification of the hard drive, and often will name compatible drive models needed to perform this demanding job. This role of video server drive has traditionally been the domain of SCSI hard drives, as they both have offered the required performance and can sustain it for the duration of the video clip. They are, however, relatively expensive when compared to other types of hard drives. In recent years IDE hard drives have met these stringent performance demands for video serving, but some forms of IDE drives cannot sustain the required data rates for more than short bursts at a time. Again, check the recommendations of the video capture/printing interface device. Often this product will come with a software utility to test your existing drive's performance. If not, phone the manufacturer's technical support line to see whether it can recommend the drive that your system uses.

- *Record your video on a suitably good-quality VCR and tape.* When you create your master tape, don't scrimp on the tape quality. For a few dollars more, you can get a far better tape to make your master copy with. Thereafter, use less-expensive tapes to distribute the next-generation copies. Likewise, record to the best-quality VCR or videotape recording deck you can beg, borrow, or steal for the project. While a domestic VCR can do an excellent job of recording your video output, the lower quality begins to show up dramatically after a few generations from this master version. At least use a four-head recorder, if not a six-head unit. If possible, connect your system to a Betacam tape deck for best results.

CAPTURING STILLS

There are several ways to capture still images for inclusion in your video production:

- *A scanner.* Perhaps the simplest way is to scan the image file. A good flatbed scanner is an invaluable tool for the digital video producer. Since most scanners have scanning resolutions that are best suited for printed output, the scanning resolution will most likely be in excess of your needs for video work. A 300-dpi, 24-bit color or greater scanner will do a terrific job of capturing a still image for inclusion in your video project.

- *35mm slides.* For capturing images on 35mm slides, a scanner that has a slide-scanning attachment, a purpose-built slide scanner, or a slide attachment for your video camera are appropriate options. All do a terrific job, though the camera attachment can be prone to light variations.

- *A digital camera.* This is a must-have for the serious digital video producer. It enables you to quickly and easily capture and import still images. Be sure that the resolution of your camera meets or exceeds the screen size of your intended video project. For example, if your video project includes a 640 × 480 video clip, then to achieve best fidelity from your camera's images they should also be at least 640 × 480 when taken. The current multi-Megapixel cameras all offer image resolutions in multiples of 1,024 × 768 pixels—suitable for most video work.

- *Photo processing services.* Most photo processing services can provide (for an additional fee of course) a digital version of your photographs, typically on diskette or Photo CD. While this service is very convenient, check the resolution (screen size) of the images produced by the service to see whether they match your intended usage.

- *A video capture card.* As mentioned previously in this chapter, all video capture devices will capture still images from your video camera or videotape deck. Some of the less expensive video capture devices will capture only still images, and are often purchased by unsuspecting consumers who thought that capturing "video" implied full-motion video. Not so. Be careful to read the fine print on the box when investing in any video capturing device. In any case, for capturing still images, setting a video camera up on a tripod and pointing it at a picture or an image you wish to capture as a still can be an easy way to input still images with existing equipment. A video camera with a macro lens can be particularly beneficial for such close-up work.

EFFECTIVE VIDEO MANIPULATION FOR MULTIMEDIA

In the next chapter you will learn how to edit and manipulate digital video to create your own custom masterpiece. The following is an overview of this process.

JUST AN EDITING INTERFACE

An important point to remember when using any digital video editing application is that you are using a pictorial interface that visualizes for you the intended edits, sound tracks, and special effects that you intend to build into your final video project. The frame-by-frame pictures of the various clips that make up your work are simply a diagram. The application does not store the video, no more than saving your project file does any more than create a simple data file listing the locations of the clips and images you want to incorporate into the final video.

Only when you have taken the last step of building your new video piece will your work actually exist in any cohesive form. When the application begins the rendering process and shows a rendering progress bar, it is creating a new video piece based on the instructions given in the "diagram" you view on screen.

It is simply fetching all of the components you have specified from all over the computer's disk drive(s) (and network, if located on one) and recompiling them together into one video file. What you see on the construction window of your video editing application is a very sophisticated flow chart.

The upshot of all of this is that the project file you save from such an application is not enough to recreate your work on another system. It is only the *listing of the location* of content you specified for the video project, not storage of that content.

If you are working on a video project at work and save the project and take it home, you will most likely get an error message stating that the application cannot find the required video files for your project in their appropriate locations. Unless you have all of the components indicated in the construction window on your home system, and located in the same directories as your project data file expects, you will not be able to work any further on the project. You will have to bring it back to your work system, where all of the original content is accessible. When moving between systems, you must move the saved project file *and* all of the video clips, images, titles, sound files, and whatever else you have decided to use in the project.

ORGANIZING YOUR PROJECT

Digital video editing applications work best when all of the contents of your project are located in the same directory on your hard drive. Not only can you then import a complete directory at a time, but when faced with the common problem of working in more than one location, you do not have to find and gather the content. Simply copy the working directory to a Zip disk, Jaz disk, or CD-ROM.

Additionally, the digital video editing application will create its own subdirectories to store temporary and previewing files. By working out of one directory, and saving your project to that directory you ensure that these files also are transferred between systems when you move the project around.

ALLOW TIME

The process of building your new video file can take quite some time, especially if you use a very asymmetric codec, as you read earlier in this chapter. I have seen many of my projects and those of my colleagues and students get into trouble because the time required to compile the movie at the end of the day was not adequately factored into the project timetable.

It can take many hours for the application just to complete the final video product. For example, I recently finished a 30-second animation video clip for Intel Corporation that took over 30 hours for the animation to render, and only then did I have my animation video clip "raw materials." The video editing, manipulation, and compiling of the final piece took another twelve hours, three of which were taken by the video editing application building the final video piece. And the system I used was a 450 MHz Pentium II with 128 MB of RAM—no slouch!

The critical mistake occurs when, having compiled and rendered the video project to the final video file, you play it back and spot a glitch. Perhaps the special effect you applied is not showing as intended. Maybe the sound effects are not synchronized with the action. In any case, the problem will require reworking, and usually there is not enough time left to do it.

An easy solution is to frequently preview your work, especially the critical sections. Make occasional test clips just of those areas you expect may be off. Your test clip can be small, low-quality, and created with a codec that is quick to render.

STORYBOARDS

Whenever possible, use storyboarding to design and conceptualize your project. It is easier and quicker to complete a project when you have a crystal clear picture of the extent and requirements of the work. Often, those "artistic souls" among us believe that such organization cramps creativity. Not so! You can still be creative while fabricating a professional and accurate video product to the specification of those who have consigned you to do this work. Even if there is no client, a storyboard can avoid the problem of "painting yourself into a corner," or developing a project to the point where you get stuck and cannot find an elegant way to end it. A storyboard maps out the beginning, middle, and end, so you can set up each section to smoothly transition into the next. Figure 3.9 in Chapter 3 illustrates a simple storyboard.

It's your time and frustration after all, but a little (enjoyable) time spent conceptualizing and brainstorming at the beginning can often make the difference between a smooth or frustrating project. If you are working in a team, this step in the development process becomes a critical communication tool to ensure that everyone is "on the same page" and working toward a common finale.

AVOIDING PITFALLS

When assembling the content you intend to include in your video project, keep it all in one directory for easy access by the editing application and for easy transportation between editing systems. If you are a student, losing track of your video project elements is a particularly important pitfall to avoid.

Be careful when purchasing a digital video workstation or the components to create one. Determine the features that you will need and then evaluate the available products on how best they meet those needs. You can often find good value in ready-to-go digital video editing systems, but be wary of the confines and lack of expandability of such systems.

Based upon your intended use of the digital video file you're creating, you will need to choose the most appropriate video file format and codec to meet those needs. Each codec has its own pros and cons, so choose wisely. If encoding for Internet deployment, then use one of the Web-specific streaming codecs. Be aware that some encoding can be very asymmetrical and therefore can take considerable time to render to your new video file. Always factor in a large time buffer toward the end of your project to allow for re-rendering. This will eliminate mistakes that are apparent after you see the rendered product.

Don't go overboard with transitions and special effects, as they can add considerably to the time required to render the video. Filters, especially, can be layered, and each additional filter multiplies the time taken to render out that clip in your video project. Run a test render to see how slow it may be getting and judge from there.

Keep your soundtrack file size as small as possible without compromising your quality. In Part 5, you will learn how to create quality sound for your video or multimedia product in the smallest possible file size. Video that looks and performs wonderfully can suddenly grind to a halt with the data-rate overhead of the soundtrack.

When morphing, make sure that the backgrounds of both images are both plain and as close to identical as you can get them. Otherwise your morph may lose its visual impact with a changing background that can distract the viewer.

Before running out to your local electronics store, see whether the equipment you have will fit your needs. Run a test clip and judge the quality. At that point you will know whether an additional expenditure is required.

If you are capturing or digitizing on a system other than the one you will be editing on, remember to flatten the video file to a standard format. A digitized video file captured in the proprietary codec supplied by the capture interface manufacturer will not be viewable on another system that does not have the same video capture system installed.

Chapter Summary

- The world of digital video is a minefield of buzzwords and special terminology. Often, words such as *frames* and *fields* can have a different meaning for digital video than when used elsewhere in the multimedia production process. It is important to become familiar with these terms and what they represent.

- The video format "brand" you select and the codec "flavor" you choose to compress your video with will determine what quality you can expect, how long it will take to create, and what computer systems you can use to play the final video piece. For video delivery over the Web, a codec and format that support very high compression and streaming and provides your users with a plug-in for their browser will be required.

- Digital video editing is often referred to as non-linear video editing because when you use dig-

ital video files, you don't need to fast-forward or rewind a tape to locate an edit point. Any section of a digital video file can be accessed randomly. Conversely, a linear editing system must seek the appropriate spots on the linear videotape to be able to "splice" scenes together.

- Using a digital video editing application provides a multitude of video special effects previously available only to video editing production facilities at tremendous expense.

- Morphing is a simple and fun process you can use to create a stunning visual effect.

- Shooting, capturing, editing, and printing digital video can require quite a lot of equipment, software, and significant investment of both time and money. Choose wisely when building your digital video editing workstation.

Key Terms and Concepts

Checking Your Knowledge and Skills

1. List the features you would need in a digital video workstation. Go to an online store (or to an actual store, if more convenient) that sells digital video editing equipment and software, and configure a digital video development workstation to suit your perceived needs. DV Direct (www.dvdirect.com) and Micro-Warehouse/MacWarehouse (www.microwarehouse.com, www.macwarehouse.com) are two such online vendors. Others are listed on this book's Web site. Find out what the least expensive, but complete, system you can assemble would cost. Create a shopping list and write a system specifications and features list for your custom system.

2. Having created a specification, a list of features, and a budget for your ideal digital video workstation in exercise 1, search for a comparable ready-to-go system that matches your specification, and see how the cost of such a system matches your budget. An Internet search will help with this, as will this book's Web site. Apple Computers (www.apple.com), Media 100 (www.media100.com), and Avid (www.avid.com) are such vendors, but don't restrict your search to just these sites, as more are available.

3. A suitably comparable ready-to-go digital video workstation will most likely be PC- or Macintosh-based. Perhaps you found another system. In any case, locate

another turnkey system based on a different platform from that of your original choice and compare both pricing and specification. Include ease of use in your evaluation of which system you think is better.

4. Review and compare the specifications and prices of several video capturing hardware devices. Determine the best of the selection, and review its specification against the following checklist:
   - Can it capture 640 × 480 size frames at 30 fps?
   - Can it capture audio?
   - Can it print to video?
   - Does it come with digital video editing software?
   - Is it compatible with a system you own?
   - Does it require special memory, hard drive, or video capabilities?
   - Does the manufacturer supply installation software to test and configure your system to suit?
   - What video inputs does it support?
   - Is it compatible with standard video editing applications such as Adobe's Premiere?
   - How many special effects and transitions does it provide?
   - Does it support both AVI and QuickTime digital video file formats?

5. Choose an application for which you need to create a video segment. It may be part of a multimedia CD-ROM, a lesson on an educational Web site, or a videotape. Create a storyboard for the video piece and, given your design, determine what file format "brand" and what codec "flavor" you would chose. Explain why. How much time would you allot to this project?

Critical Thinking Challenges

Given the prevalence of digital video in all aspects of multimedia, answer the following questions to the best of your ability:

1. Find a Web site that uses digital video content that you admire. Can you determine what format the site developers chose? What do you think of the choice of format for the video, and could it be done better in a different format? Why? Does the presence of video enhance or detract from the Web site's design?

2. Review a selection of CD-ROM or DVD-ROM multimedia applications (at least four) and make a list of the digital video used in each case. Demonstration discs from software manufacturers are very useful for such critiquing. Determine which of your sample group make good use of digital video and which could use improvement. Rank them in order from best to worst, and determine common factors that make them "good" or "bad." Kinetix Inc., manufacturer of 3D Studio Max animation software (www2.discreet.com), produces an excellent sample/demo CD-ROM you should check out.

3. If you were to contract an individual or a studio that purports to be a digital video master, what would you look for in that person or organization to satisfy you that they could do a professional and competent job?

4. Go to a multimedia magazine Web site (such as www.newmedia.com or www.avproducer.com) and search for digital video applications for the Web. Create a report of your findings and decide which technology and development strategy you would adopt for your own multimedia Web site project that incorporated digital video.

Hands-on Exercises

PLANNING AND STORYBOARDING FOR VIDEO

It is commonplace to purchase time on a video editing system from a video editing bureau. Those who do this for a living do much preparation before they arrive at the facility they have hired for the job. The preparation involves collecting all the media and video clips, sound bites, and images that these professionals compile together in their final work. Such preparation also helps prevent cost overruns from extending the booked studio time (if even money is available to do so). In such circumstances it's a "get it right the first time," one-shot deal, so thorough preparation is essential. While good preparation comes from having done several projects and from knowing what to prepare for, this exercise will help you get a feeling for this process.

In preparation for the next chapter, design a storyboard for an advertising video you wish to produce. It can be for a product or a service, or even just an informational advertisement, which will eventually be aired on TV.

Once you have a storyboard, begin to collect the footage, images, sound effects, music, and video files that you will need to edit together on a digital video editing system. Include in your storyboard SMPTE time codes for the sequences you want to use and filename references for any digital content you have. Content that is not yet digital should be converted or captured at this point.

You should end up with a project kit, ready to edit.

Master Project

PREPARING FOR DIGITAL VIDEO

So far you should have created a binder for the project that documents your project concept and includes a project plan, a timeline, and your sketches and visuals for your design. You should also have started to build your content and store it on disk.

An example of some digital video work that you have done would be an essential component of your multimedia digital portfolio. To prepare for creating such examples, follow the instructions in this chapter's Hands-On Exercises and create a ready-to-edit package of storyboard and digital content with which to create your working example piece. However, the final video clip you will create will be a digital video file, not a master videotape.

As you may have guessed, in the next chapter you will create your video masterpiece from the content package you create in this exercise. Save your work to a Zip disk (or equivalent) and keep it with your project binder.

11

HANDS-ON NONLINEAR VIDEO EDITING

Chapter Objectives

After completing this chapter, you will be able to:

- Use two competent digital video editing software applications: Lumiere and Adobe's Premiere

- Describe the digital video project production process and discuss how to manage your own video production

- Describe the digital video editing process and apply special-effect filters, transitions, soundtracks, and more

- Create your own digital video product using almost any digital video editing application

- Identify the many video output options available to you, including videotape, and how to use them to finish your digital video editing project

Chapter Overview

In the previous chapter you learned about the technology of digital video editing and some of the techniques involved. Now it's time to try your hand at this fun and creative process.

As you have learned, there is often a full-featured, less expensive alternative software tool that can help you accomplish your objectives. This is very much the case with desktop digital video editing. In this chapter you will learn about the leading application in this field, Adobe's Premiere. You will also learn about Lumiere, another full-featured digital video editing product that comes with oodles of clip art, clip photos, clip video, clip sounds, and a full copy of Corel's PhotoPaint (comparable to Photoshop in graphic editing features). Although Lumiere is a Windows-only product, at about a tenth of the price of Premiere, it is well worth checking out and is available in most computer stores. Check this book's Web site for links to more information about these products.

Many other digital video editing applications are also available, among them Ulead's Media Studio (www.ulead.com) and complete systems from companies such as Media 100 and FAST. They all operate under similar principles and use similar techniques. Once you understand the operation of a digital video editing suite, this knowledge will transfer well to other brand systems.

Editing digital video is useful well beyond straightforward video production. In the multimedia world, digital video editing is also used to add titles and special effects to animation, create Web animations, postprocess and integrate morphs into a larger production, and bring still images to life. It will also unleash the creative monster within you, so stock up on food and sleep, and prepare to be absorbed.

INTRODUCTION TO DESKTOP DIGITAL VIDEO EDITING: LUMIERE AND ADOBE'S PREMIERE

Both Premiere and Lumiere operate on very similar principles. Their similarities can be seen in Figures 11.1 and 11.2, which show the interface and operating environment for both applications. See how many common features you can spot.

In the following sections, you will have an opportunity to use these digital video editing products. You will find links to demonstration copies of these applications linked to this book's Web site. You can also download the latest demonstration version of each of these products directly from their manufacturer's respective Web sites. This book's Web site also includes further links to other manufacturers of similar products. Note that these demo versions are restricted in their capabilities and features. To fully appreciate both the information in this book and the amazing abilities of these products, you should invest in the full versions.

The primary function of the digital video editing application's interface is to provide you with a graphical representation of the editing you are applying to your video project. You can import the video clips, sounds, and images that you want to incorporate into your video project, and then drag and drop them into the Timeline/Project window. In effect, you can "assemble" a new video segment at will. You can apply special video effects to each clip, create titles, superimpose one clip onto another, apply engaging transitions between clips, and much more.

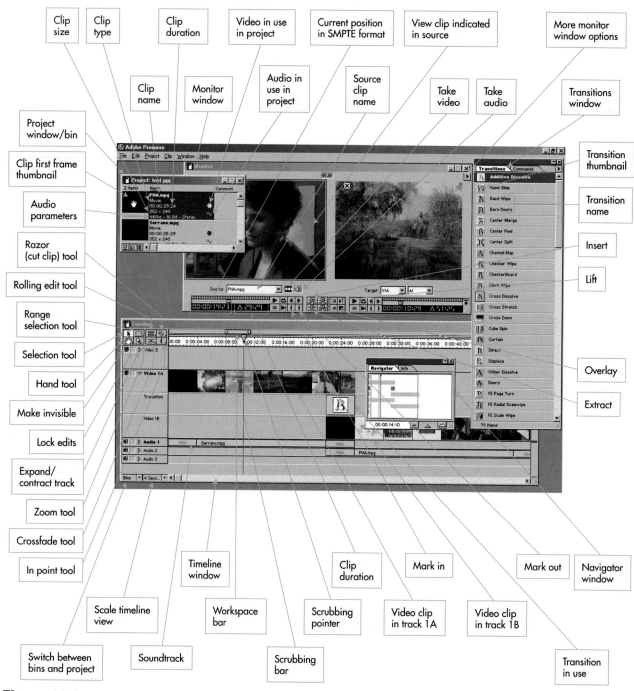

Figure 11.1
Digital video editing with Adobe's Premiere 5.

You can preview your work at any time. At that point, the program creates a temporary low-quality version of your work for you to see the effect of your editing in real time. Until you build your final video project, however, the edits shown in your Timeline/Project window are only an indication of what the final project will entail. When you build the final output video segment, the application goes through your Timeline/Project window "map," assembles frame-by-frame all of the content you indicated on that screen, and compiles it into one continuous video clip. This is your final product.

Until you complete that building process, saving your project only saves a data file storing a location and reference to all of the components, identifying

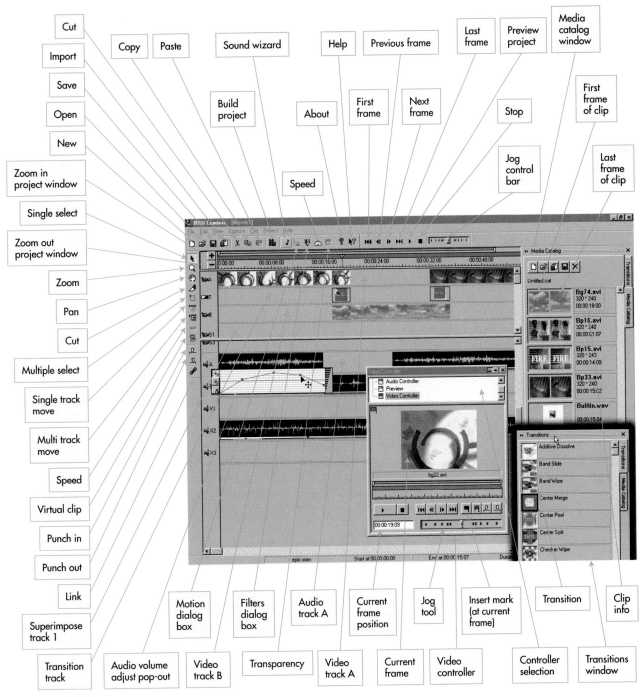

Figure 11.2
Digital video editing with Lumiere.

how they are laid out in the Timeline/Project window, and describing what edits and effects have been applied to them. This data file does not store your content components, only references to them. For instance, if you are importing video clips from a CD-ROM, then the next time you load your project to do further editing, unless that CD-ROM is available, your project will not be able to locate and load that clip and will fail to reassemble itself.

It is important to make a clear distinction between saving this data file and creating the final, newly edited digital movie when you "build" your project. Once built, the new video clip is completely stand-alone and requires none of the component parts to be played on another system or in a multimedia production.

Many other features are common to both Lumiere and Premiere (and other such applications), and you will begin to see more of the similarities as you delve deeper into this chapter.

THE TIMELINE/PROJECT WINDOW

As you can see in Figures 11.1 and 11.2, both Lumiere and Premiere use a multi-track timeline editing window (shown as the Project window in Lumiere and the Timeline window in Premiere) on which to drag and drop the content components for your video project. In both programs the imported content is shown in a content library window (the Media Catalog window in Lumiere and the Project window in Premiere). Any video or audio clips, still images, and in the case of Premiere, titles, can be dragged from the content library window to the Timeline/Project window.

TRACKS

In both Lumiere and Premiere, you use a visual timeline with multiple video and audio tracks to assemble your project. Lumiere provides two primary video tracks, A and B, with a transition track T between them to mix (transition) video from one of these tracks to the other as required. Premiere also has two primary tracks, Video 1A and Video 1B. These tracks also have a transition track between them. Figures 11.1 and 11.2 show the video tracks in use and the transitions between them.

This Timeline/Project window interface is a visual assembly place for your video project's intended content and enables you to graphically "map" how you would like your final video piece to look before you actually compile the final clip. In Premiere, the Navigator floating panel almost looks like a map, giving an overall schematic of your project layout (see Figure 11.1). You can move, edit, and manipulate the content as much as you like until you're happy with the layout. You can also use any clip or component over and over until you're satisfied with it.

TRANSITIONS AND SPECIAL EFFECTS

When it comes to special effects and transitions, both Premiere and Lumiere come equipped with many to choose from. In either application, transitions can be dragged from the Transitions window and dropped between the two video tracks you wish to merge. Figure 11.3 shows a transition in Premiere as it looks in the Transitions window, in the Timeline window when in use, and in the Monitor window as it shows the effect of the transition.

The best way to familiarize yourself with the many transitions available in these two applications is to test them between two test clips. Drag and drop a selection of transitions between the two clips and preview the results (as described

USING TRANSITIONS

You need to watch for two important factors when you use a transition. First, check that the ends of the transition (as shown in the Timeline/Project window) are aligned with the ends of the clips you are transitioning between (as shown in Figure 11.3). Second, make sure that the "direction" of the transition is correct, meaning that it is transitioning from the final clip to the next clip. Double-clicking on the transition, as shown in the transition track, will provide you with the settings you need to check on the direction.

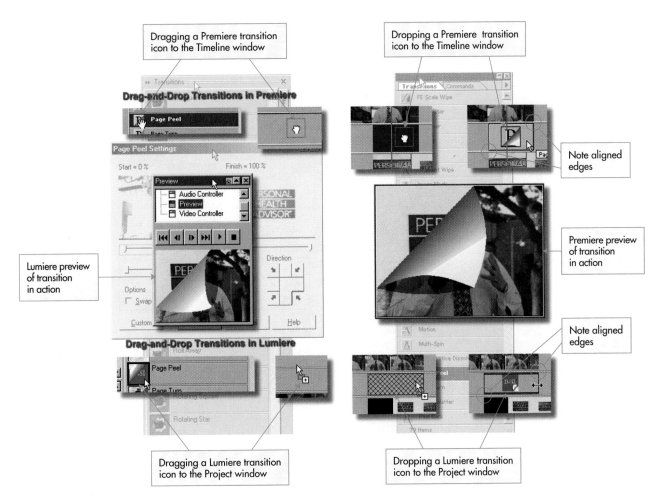

Figure 11.3

Creating a smooth and professional transition between two video clips is a simple drag-and-drop process in both Premiere and Lumiere.

later in this section). Double-click on the transition when it's displayed in the Timeline/Project window to invoke a transition settings control panel. Use the control panel to adjust the transition parameters, as shown in Figure 11.4.

Special-effect filters provide you with a multitude of special effects that you can apply to your video clip. If you want to apply a lens flare, change your clip to black-and-white, bend and distort the clip, or emboss the video, you can do so by applying the appropriate filter. Additionally, these filters can be "stacked" upon each other, so that you can combine the special effects of multiple filters on any clip. For instance, a sci-fi clip may have an image pan effect combined with a lens flare and an emboss filter. Just remember that each of these special-effect filters takes quite a bit of computing horsepower to achieve, and you may find your project taking an inordinate amount of time to render. Figure 11.4 shows some of the special effect filters available in both Premiere and Lumiere, though it's difficult to really appreciate their impact in a static image. My suggestion, as with the transitions, is to play with them for a while until you get comfortable with their operation.

To apply special-effect filters to each clip, select a clip, select a suitable filter, and adjust the filter parameters to suit. In both Premiere and Lumiere, you apply filters to the selected clip by choosing Filters from the Clips menu, which invokes the Video Filters selection panel for both applications. Also, both applications use the Ctrl-F keyboard shortcut, and on a PC, right-clicking over the clip displays a shortcut menu that includes the Filters command.

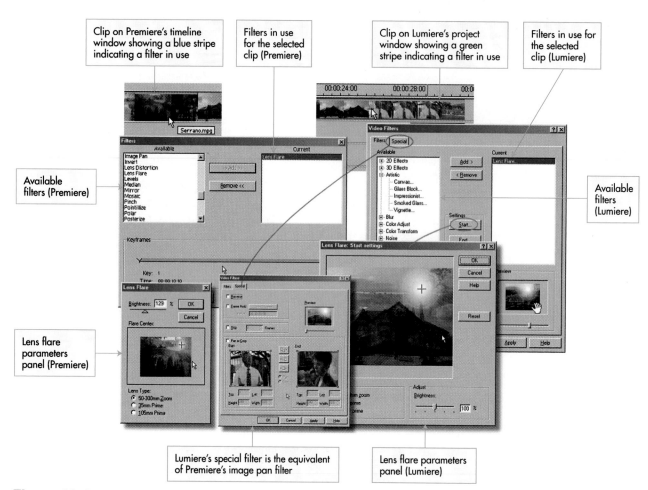

Figure 11.4
Both Premiere and Lumiere offer a large selection of filters (the lens flare filter for each is shown here), as do most digital video editing software applications.

PREVIEWING YOUR WORK

In Figures 11.1 and 11.2 you can see the Workspace bar (in Premiere) or the Control bar (in Lumiere) at the top of the Timeline/Project window. This bar indicates the section of your project that you are selecting either for previewing or for building into a new video clip. Rather than having to compile all of your work just so you can preview or output a specific piece, the bar allows you to indicate that specific section for rendering.

When you wish to preview the section of your work identified by the Workspace/Control bar, choose the Preview command from the Project menu in either application. Pressing the Enter key in Premiere and pressing the F9 key in Lumiere will also create a preview. Once you have told the application that you want to preview your selected section, it will compile all of the media content and apply the transitions, special effects, transparencies, and sounds that you have specified in the Timeline/Project window. It will then automatically create and play a temporary video clip of that section for you.

Another way to preview your work is to scrub through the timeline. Scrubbing is a simple and effective way to see, frame by frame, the results of your work. To scrub, simply drag your mouse pointer (which will show up as a time marker) in the timeline in the Timeline/Project window; as you do so, the application displays your edited video at the pointer location. Note that as you

scrubbing

The method of reviewing edited digital video in the digital video editing application by dragging a scrubbing control backward and forward on the project timeline.

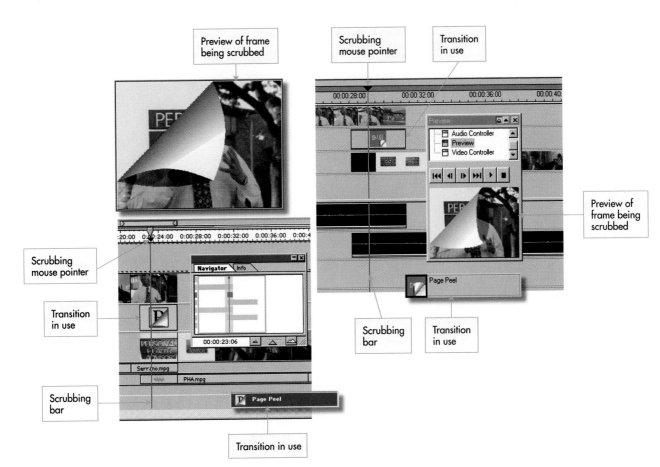

Figure 11.5
The scrubbing technique in any digital video editing application is a valuable way to review your work on a frame-by-frame basis.

scrub (see Figure 11.5), a vertical line follows the mouse cursor. What you are previewing when you scrub is the combination of all media components, edits, transitions, and filters that lie directly beneath that line. So if you scrub to a specific position or frame that you would like to edit, that line indicates the precise location of that frame and all of the components that combine to create the final frame image.

Also shown in Figure 11.2 is Lumiere's jog control. This feature is unique to Lumiere and allows you to move back and forth along your video project with precise speed control so that you can analyze a clip in normal or slow speed. Premiere allows you to drag the Set Location slider in the Monitor window, but this does not provide the neat scrolling effect of Lumiere's jog control. If you have an opportunity to do so, try this feature in Lumiere to get a better feel for how it works.

jog control
Dragging this control right or left will play or rewind, respectively, a video clip.

WHEN SCRUBBING DOESN'T SHOW YOUR EDITS

In Premiere you may find that scrubbing through a transition or special effect section of your project will not show you the results of that work in the Monitor window. Why? In Premiere 5.0 and higher, you must first build a preview of that section of the project before Premiere will show that effect when you scrub through it.

When creating a preview of your work, the digital video editing application creates a temporary video file of the section of your project you indicated with the Workspace/Control bar and plays it back so you can see the results of your work. Usually this preview video file is smaller in size and of a lower quality to facilitate a quick rendering and viewing of your work. However, this preview file does take up significant disk space. You could find your preview files taking up a large chunk of your drive space if you're not careful to monitor this.

In the case of Premiere, these preview files are created in a subfolder in the location on your hard drive where your project file is stored. You will notice a folder entitled "Adobe Premiere Preview Files"—guess what that's for?

In the case of Lumiere, you can specify the location of this temporary preview file. You will find this setting in the Temporary Files tab of the Project Options control panel. You can view this panel by choosing Options from the Project menu.

These previewing techniques will help you view the results of your editing and enable you to precisely review your work on a frame-by-frame basis so you can pinpoint changes you may want to make.

THE VIDEO PROJECT

Up until the point of building the final movie piece, your video project is really just an assembly of a lot of media components with an assembly plan. Therefore, it is very important to be well organized when you start to assemble your project components. If you work on more than one computer system, it is vital to make the component media transportable from one editing system to the other.

COLLECTING, ORGANIZING, AND ASSEMBLING YOUR DIGITAL VIDEO BUILDING BLOCKS

As you learned earlier in this chapter, the digital video editing application is, in effect, a sophisticated map builder for your final video piece. It provides a graphical layout of the edits you perform, but until you build the final digital video product, it simply references the component clips wherever they may be located on your system or on the network connected to your system. Therefore, it makes sense to collect these media components into one place so that they're both organized and transportable.

The best method for organizing your files is to store them all in subdirectories within one project folder. Figure 11.6 shows the directory structure of a recent animation and video project I did for Intel Corporation. The Intel folder structure is highlighted, and among the folders is Premiere's preview file storage folder, also highlighted.

By using such a simple organizational structure, you gain two primary advantages. First, you can easily locate the file of your choice, and when you get into sophisticated projects you will amass a multitude of small files that are crucial pieces in your work. The Intel project structure shown in Figure 11.6 contains 136 media files to support a 33-second animation short.

Second, if you need to transport your project to another system (this is particularly important if you are working with an external video production studio or bureau), then your project is still intact if you copy the project folder and all of its subfolders. Imagine trying to assemble a complicated video project if your components were scattered all over your system and perhaps even all over your network!

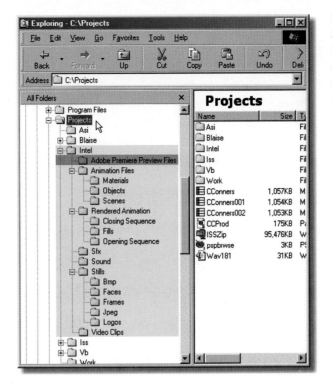

Figure 11.6
Storing your project components in subfolders is a great way to stay organized and to help move the project between editing systems.

When moving your video project to another system, watch out for those large preview files. You may want to leave them behind if you're having trouble fitting everything onto your transport disk. You can always rebuild them on the other system, but leave yourself time to do so.

Also, make sure to get *all* the pieces. It can be very disheartening to arrive at the other system to find that one crucial clip is not on the transport disk and you have to go back to the original editing workstation to find it.

EDITING YOUR MOVIE

In this next section you will create your own digitally edited video piece. To do this, you will have to install a digital video editing application, such as Premiere or Lumiere. Refer to the introductory section of this book for instructions on how to locate demonstration versions of these products through this book's Web site.

You will also find the component media clips required to complete this exercise on your book's CD-ROM. They are located in the Samples\Video folder on the CD-ROM. You will be instructed to locate these media clips in this location.

In this same location on your book's CD-ROM you will find a completed Premiere project file, and in the Samples\Video\Completed Sample folder you will find the finished product movie file, called MediaQ.avi (MediaQ.mov if you are a Macintosh user) to compare to your own work. Even though you can simply load the completed version, it is far better to follow the steps and create your own version of this project from scratch. That way you'll be more likely to remember the techniques and processes used to create this movie, and you will have the satisfaction of having created a new digital movie yourself.

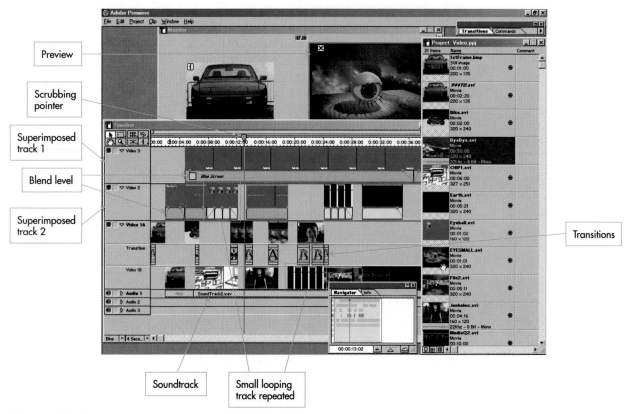

Preview
Scrubbing pointer
Superimposed track 1
Blend level
Superimposed track 2
Transitions
Soundtrack
Small looping track repeated

Figure 11.7
A finished project in Premiere, ready to export to a new digital video piece.

Figure 11.7 shows a similar (though more complex) completed project in Premiere, which is ready to export to a new digital video piece. You can find this Premiere project file and a similar Lumiere project file in the Samples\Video folder of this book's CD-ROM. Use it for reference and examples of how to apply more complex transitions and special effects.

Before you start, you can adjust the appearance of content as it appears in the tracks of the Timeline/Project window. In Premiere, use the Timeline Window Options command on the Window menu to change settings to suit (make sure the Timeline window is open first). In Lumiere, use the Options command on the Project menu to invoke the Project Options control panel, and click the Display tab. The illustrations created for this book were done with display parameters set in both applications to show frame images of a medium or large size. You can select the settings that suit your tastes. Just beware that it can often take longer to redraw the Timeline/Project window when it's set to show frame images throughout.

To begin you must first fire up either Premiere or Lumiere and import the media components supplied. You can, of course, follow along using your own media clips, but if this is your first time, it is recommended that you use the supplied clips. That way your work will be in sync with the file names and clips being described.

STARTING THE PROGRAM

When you start Premiere, you will see a dialog box asking you some initial questions about your project settings. Click OK to accept the default settings. You can change these settings later if you need to. With Lumiere, the choices are much simpler, as shown in Figure 11.8.

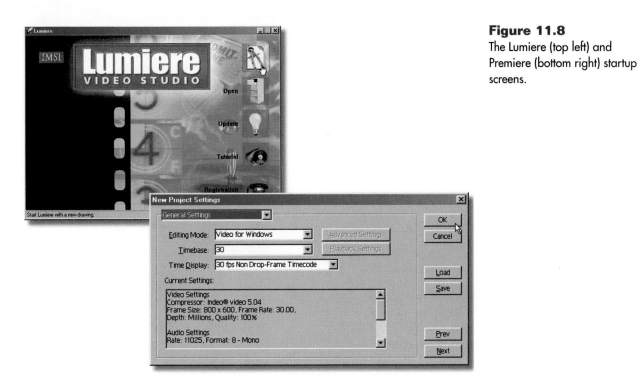

Figure 11.8
The Lumiere (top left) and
Premiere (bottom right) startup
screens.

IMPORTING MEDIA

To import your media components into either Premiere or Lumiere, you will choose Import from the File menu. In Premiere you also can import individual files or a folder containing your content, or capture video through a video capture interface.

1. For this exercise, choose Import from the File menu, then choose Folder in Premiere to import the Samples\Video folder from your book's CD-ROM. In Lumiere, you will need to import the files located in the Samples\Video folder on your book's CD-ROM one at a time.

2. When importing with Lumiere, change the Files of type: setting to All Files, so that you can see the different file that you should import from this folder. The Premiere (*.ptl) title files will not import into Lumiere, so select the bitmap files (*.bmp) of the same name. Your Project window (Premiere) or Media Catalog window (Lumiere) should look like those shown in Figure 11.9. Note how in Figure 11.9 Lumiere shows the first and last frame of each clip, and how both Premiere and Lumiere each indicate that the clip has a soundtrack attached to it.

EDITING MEDIA CLIPS

To begin editing your video piece, you will start with a title screen.

1. In your Project/Media Catalog window you will find a series of title bitmap images and Adobe Premiere title files. In Premiere, these Premiere title files can be edited by double-clicking the title. You can tell whether you're looking at a title file in the Project window by checking for .ptl extension on the file name.

2. In Lumiere, titles are created using a graphics application like Photoshop, Paint Shop Pro, or Corel's PhotoPaint; the latter is supplied with Lumiere when purchased. These images are saved to disk and imported as a still

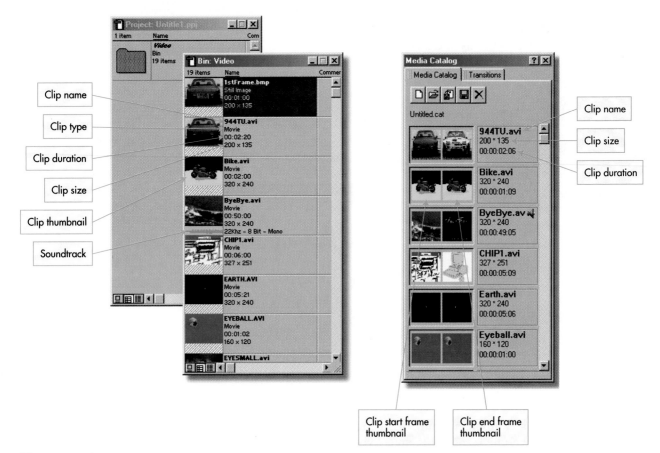

Figure 11.9
The contents of the Samples\Video folder imported into both Premiere (left) and Lumiere (right).

image into Lumiere. For the moment, you can use the preproduced titles that appear as bitmaps showing text on a blue background, which are listed in your Media Catalog window.

3. Drag the TitleIntro title (TitleIntro.ptl in Premiere, TitleIntro.bmp in Lumiere) into your Timeline/Project window and drop it onto the start of video track A for Lumiere and video track 1A for Premiere. The default video duration for a still image/title in both applications is one second, so you will see that title shown over a one-second length as indicated by the timeline ruler of the track you dropped it into.

4. Adjust your scaling settings (refer to Figures 11.1 and 11.2) to get the best view of your work. If you wish to lengthen or shorten this clip, simply grab the right-hand edge of the title (the mouse pointer will change shape over the edge) and drag the right-hand edge of the clip to the point where you want it to finish. For this exercise, drag the right-hand edge of this title out to a two-second duration. In either application, you can also right-click (hold down your single Macintosh button for a second) and choose the Speed command from the shortcut menu. This allows you to type in the precise required duration of the clip.

PREVIEWING AND THE WORKSPACE/CONTROL BAR

1. Drag the morphing video clip called 944TU.avi (944TU.mov on the Macintosh) and drop it onto video track B/1B in the Timeline/Project window.

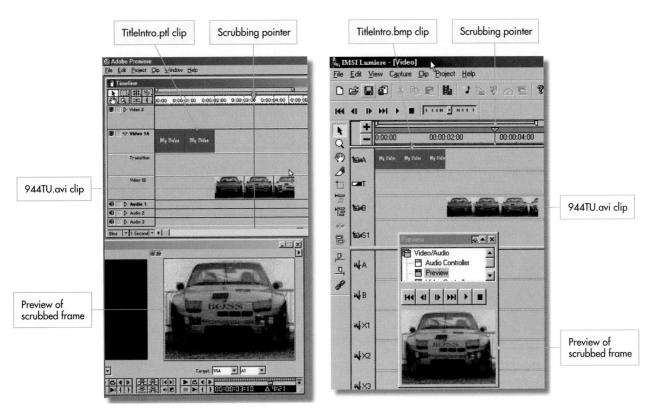

Figure 11.10
The beginning of your project, showing the first two clips in the Timeline/Project window in Premiere (left) and Lumiere (right).

2. Slide the clip so that the left-hand edge of the clip is directly beneath the right-hand edge of the first title.

3. At this point, drag the right-hand edge of the Workspace/Control bar at the top of the Timeline/Project window so that it stretches across the extent of the project you have created so far.

4. Figure 11.10 shows how the Workspace/Control bar "covers" the entire project up to this point. From the Project menu in both applications, choose Preview and you will see the results of your work so far. Impressive, no?

TRANSITIONS

1. Locate still image 1stFrame.bmp in your Project/Media Catalog window, drag it into the Timeline/Project window, and drop it under the last second of the TitleIntro clip, as shown in Figure 11.11. The reason you are dropping it onto the opposing track to the title in the same time frame is that you will use a transition to blend the title into the image, which requires overlapping track data to mix together frame by frame.

2. Locate the Cross Dissolve transition from the Transition window in either application. Drag and drop it into the Transition track (in Premiere) or T track (in Lumiere) and if necessary, pull its edges to fit the section of Transition track or T track in between the 1stFrame.bmp image and the last second of the title.

3. Preview your work. You should see a smooth dissolve from the title to the still images, which matches the first frame of the morph video (with the exception of the "license plate" logo).

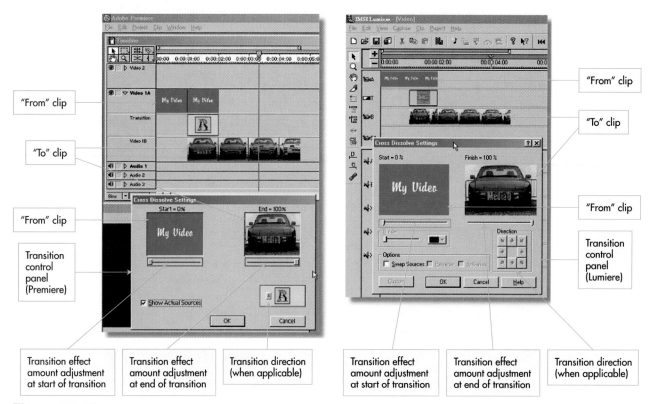

Figure 11.11

The two video tracks are joined together by a cross-dissolve transition. Premiere is on the left and Lumiere is on the right.

SCRUBBING

This is a good time to try the scrubbing technique in the Timeline/Project window. In Figure 11.12 you will see a small black triangle at the top of a vertical line in the Timeline/Project window. This is the location in that window where you should drag your mouse pointer left and right.

1. Click and hold on the triangular pointer at the top of the frame location line.
2. Drag the pointer right and left. Notice how the Preview window shows the video being scrubbed through.

Remember that in Premiere, you need to create a preview of your work before you will be able to see the effects of transitions and special effects when scrubbing. If you scrub through a section of your work and it seems as if your transition doesn't appear, this indicates that you have to render a preview of your work. Also, if you make any changes to this section of your work, you'll have to preview it again to be able to see results when scrubbing. Note that (as shown in Figure 11.12) Premiere shows a thin gray line beneath the Workspace bar to indicate the sections that have been rendered for preview.

ADDING MORE CONTENT

Now it's time to add another video clip and transition between it and the rest of your project.

Figure 11.12
Scrubbing through your project is a terrific way to see your work on a frame-by-frame basis in Premiere (left) and Lumiere (right).

1. Drag the Merglass.avi (Merglass.mov for Macintosh users) video clip and drop it onto the opposing video track to the 944TU clip in the Timeline/Project window.

2. Select a transition and place it between the overlapping ends of these two video clips, as shown in Figure 11.12.

3. If they do not already overlap to facilitate a transition, slide the last one in the timeline so that there is about a second of overlapping video clip.

SPECIAL-EFFECT FILTERS

1. Add a special-effect filter to the Merglass clip by clicking the Merglass clip on the Timeline/Project window to select it, and then choose Filters from the Clip menu to bring up the Filters dialog box, as shown in Figure 11.4.

2. In Premiere, find the Lens Flare filter and click in the upper right-hand corner of the frame shown to locate the lens flare, as shown in Figure 11.13.

3. In Lumiere, double-click the Lens Flare listing in the right-hand panel of filters in use, or click the Start button (shown in Figure 11.4) to see the Lens Flare control panel (see Figure 11.13).

4. Click your mouse pointer in the top right-hand corner of the frame to locate the Lens Flare effect. Click the OK button to apply the filter to this

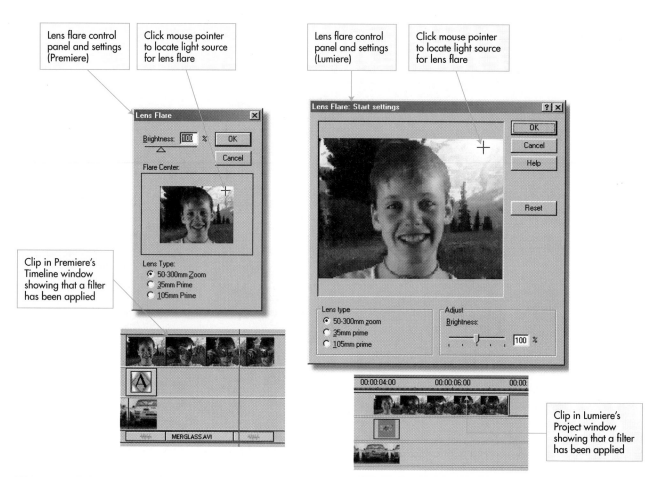

Lens flare control panel and settings (Premiere)

Click mouse pointer to locate light source for lens flare

Lens flare control panel and settings (Lumiere)

Click mouse pointer to locate light source for lens flare

Clip in Premiere's Timeline window showing that a filter has been applied

Clip in Lumiere's Project window showing that a filter has been applied

Figure 11.13
The lens flare filter at work in both Premiere and Lumiere. Notice the similarities between these two applications.

Note how even though the girl in this example is not actually in the mountain scene (she was superimposed over it), the lens flare overlaps the image of her face. Since the glare seems to be coming from the sun in the background, it helps the illusion (somewhat) of her being in the actual scene. Compare it to the original raw clip.

chroma key

When applying a superimposed video track you will choose the method of Transparency called a chroma key to use for the superimposition.

clip. You will see a colored line at the top of the clip as shown in the Timeline/Project window (see Figure 11.13). This is an indication that you have applied a filter to this clip.

5. Preview your project so far and see the results of the special-effect filter you just applied.

SUPERIMPOSING AND TRANSPARENCY

Now it's time to apply a superimposed track into your project. The technique you will use will be a chroma key, called blue-screen transparency, and it is quite easy to accomplish. You must drag the clip that you want to superimpose on top of your project into an appropriate track that supports creating transparency.

1. Locate the Title3 file in the Project/Media Catalog window (Title3.ptl for Premiere, Title3.bmp for Lumiere) and drag it onto the Video2 track (in Premiere) or the S1 track (in Lumiere).

2. Slide the left-hand edge of this title to align it with the right-hand edge of the first transition, and drag out the right-hand edge of this clip to align it with the end of your last clip in the project, as shown in Figure 11.14. Note that while the project layout now looks quite a bit different in Premiere compared to Lumiere (see Figure 11.14) because of the different location of the superimposing track, they are basically identical to this point.

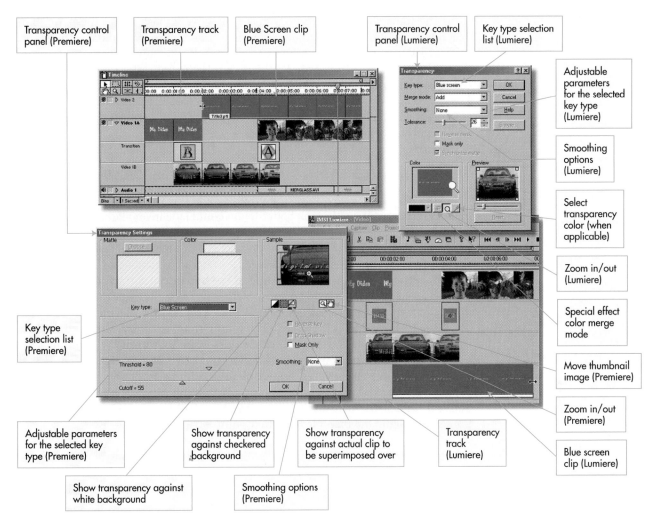

Figure 11.14
Using transparency in both Lumiere and Premiere provides the digital video producer with many creative options.

3. In Premiere, select the clip, choose Video from the Clip menu, and then choose Transparency to invoke the Transparency control panel.

4. In Lumiere, select the clip and then choose Transparency from the Clip menu to invoke the Transparency control panel.

5. In the Transparency control panel, select Blue Screen as the chroma key type option (since you want to make the blue of the image transparent, leaving behind the text overlaid onto the image).

6. Using the visual thumbnail preview for reference, adjust the available parameters until you get as clean a transparency around the text as you can. There are no "dial-in" settings for these parameters, which is why they are provided in the form of linear slider controls. "Tweak" them until you're pleased with the preview results and then click the OK button.

For a more in-depth explanation of the workings of each setting, refer to the help file supplied with either product. Lumiere's Tolerance setting is similar to Premiere's Threshold setting. Both determine how blue the transparent color should be to become transparent. Increasing this value results in making more and more shades of bluish colors transparent until all colors become transparent. Somewhere there is a setting here for you that works. The Mask Only setting turns the transparent image into a mask, effectively masking off the parts that become transparent. With Lumiere, you have many more additional settings for each of its transparency Key Types to play with, but not as many Key Types themselves to choose from as in Premiere. But both applications provide the digital video editor a vast range of transparency options.

7. Preview your work so far. Figure 11.14 shows the Transparency control panel at work in both applications.

FADING IN AND FADING OUT SUPERIMPOSED CLIPS

Your superimposed text should look pretty cool at this point, but it comes in and exits too strongly. It would look better if you could fade in and fade out the superimposed text. Well, as it happens, you can, without using transitions. The superimposing tracks in both Lumiere and Premiere have a blend-level adjustment line that allows you to adjust how opaque the track is, independent of the transparency settings. To adjust the blending of the transparency track contents, both Premiere and Lumiere provide a small blend-level line that you can move up or down, depending on how opaque or how blended you want the track to be.

To access this line in Premiere, click on the small triangular arrow to the left of the track name. The arrow will rotate downward and open the blending settings of that track. In Lumiere, clicking on the small line at the bottom of the superimposed clip brings up a similar blend-level line. In Premiere, clicking on the line will create a small control-point joint, which can now be dragged up or down to adjust the blend level. The line that "rubber-bands" between these points represents the blend level at that point during the clip.

1. Using Premiere, click on the line to introduce two new control points. Drag the endpoints down to the completely transparent level and leave the majority of the line up in the opaque level, as shown in Figure 11.15.

   In Lumiere, the process of adjusting the line to indicate the blend level over the duration of the clip is the same, except that Lumiere provides buttons for tools to add or delete control points, adjust control points, and a fade control to automatically fade in and out. A very nice feature of Lumiere is that it previews the frame to which you are applying the control point as you move that point.

2. Adjust the blend line, as shown in Figure 11.15, to give a nice smooth fade-in and fade-out in the application you are using. Preview your work. Quite a difference, don't you think?

SOUNDTRACKS

Remember how easy it was to drag and drop a video clip, still image, or title into the Timeline/Project window? Well, adding sound to your project is just as simple.

1. Locate the SoundTrack2.wav (SoundTrack2.aiff for Macintosh users) and drag it onto an available soundtrack in the Timeline/Project window. In Premiere this will be Audio 2; in Lumiere it will be the B audio track (showing a small speaker icon).

   Notice that you cannot use the Audio 1 or Audio A track, as it already has a soundtrack in it from the Merglass video clip. If a video clip has a soundtrack, it will occupy an available soundtrack beneath the video clip. You will need to delete the obstructing soundtrack. The location of the soundtrack is not really

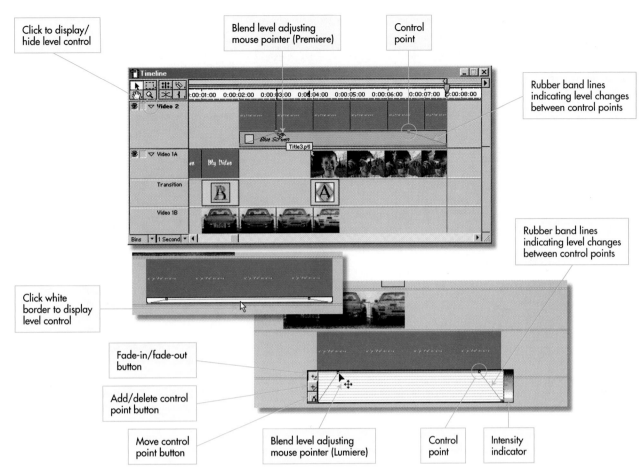

Figure 11.15
In both Lumiere and Premiere, the blend level of the superimposed tracks can be adjusted by the level line at the bottom of the superimposed clip.

important. As with the video and image clips, several soundtracks are provided in both applications so that they can overlap as you edit them together into one complete production. Since the soundtrack associated with the Merglass video clip is of little value, you can remove it from the video clip by simply selecting the soundtrack by clicking on it, and then pressing the Delete key on your keyboard. It's gone! Remember that there is always an Undo command on the Edit menu, just in case.

2. Preview your project so far, and see what a difference a soundtrack can make.

FADING IN AND FADING OUT SOUNDTRACKS

As with your superimposed clip, the sudden stop on the soundtrack at the end of your video project is not very satisfying. It would be better if you could fade out the soundtrack to coincide with the clip's end. Adjusting the sound level is as simple as adjusting the blend level of a superimposed clip. In fact, the process is almost identical.

1. In Premiere, click the small triangle to the left of the audio track name and it will rotate as the sound volume level adjusting line is revealed.

2. In Lumiere, click on the white strip at the bottom of the audio track and a level adjusting panel will appear.

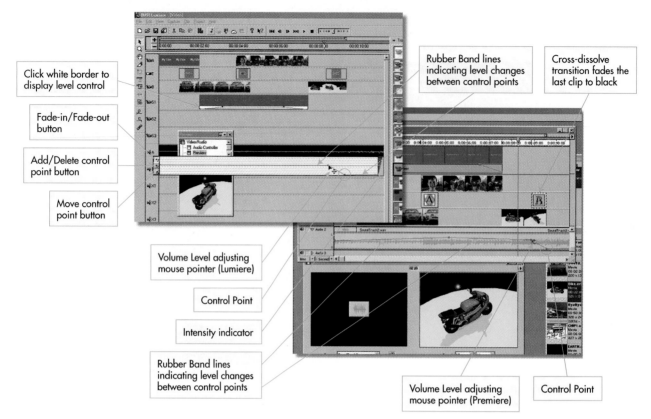

Figure 11.16

In much the same way as you adjust the blend level of a superimposed clip, you can also adjust the volume level of the soundtrack.

In both applications, adjusting the audio levels to create a fade-out is done in the same way as adjusting blend levels.

3. Adjust the sound levels to create a fade-out as shown in Figure 11.16.

Note in Figure 11.16 that an additional clip has been added and a cross-dissolve transition has been added to dissolve to black (no clip) to end the movie. The music fade-out coincides with the video fade-to-black. You should know from the previous steps how to replicate this last fade-out clip technique.

BUILDING AND EXPORTING THE FINAL MOVIE

Once you are satisfied with your edits, you are ready to make one complete new digital video clip. In Premiere, you export a new digital video file from the application, and in Lumiere, you build your project into a new digital video file. Though named differently, the process is the same for both applications. They will render a new digital video file, in the codec and format of your choice, to a new file name of your choice. This step requires you to make a myriad of decisions related to formats and settings for both the video and audio components of the project. These choices will be detailed in the next section, "Exporting Your Movie." For the moment, simply follow these simple steps to create a new digital video from your project.

The following instructions are for Premiere.

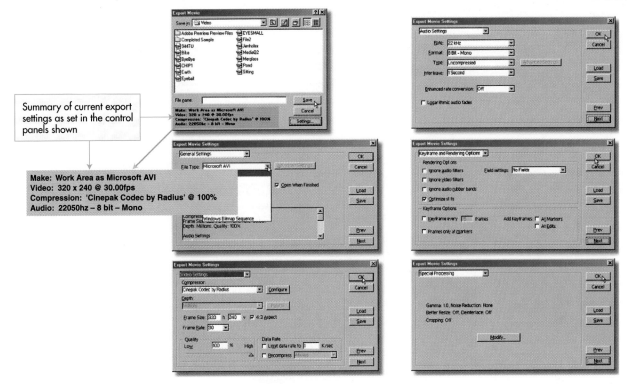

Summary of current export settings as set in the control panels shown

Make: Work Area as Microsoft AVI
Video: 320 x 240 @ 30.00fps
Compression: 'Cinepak Codec by Radius' @ 100%
Audio: 22050hz – 8 bit – Mono

Figure 11.17
Premiere provides quite a large and often complex range of movie settings when exporting your final movie.

1. In Premiere, make sure that the section of your project you want to export to a new video clip is indicated by the Workspace bar.

2. Choose Export from the File menu, and then choose Movie to invoke the Export Movie dialog box.

3. Type in a suitable name for your movie, and then click the Settings button to review the movie format and codec parameters.

Figure 11.17 shows the series of settings screens that are available to you when you're ready to export your completed movie.

4. Accept the default settings with the exception of the Compressor (codec) setting, for which you should choose Cinepak at 100% quality. (Refer to Figure 11.17 for settings.)

5. Click the OK button, then click the Save button. Watch Premiere create your new movie for you. When it is complete, Premiere displays your new movie in a window for you to play.

The following instructions are for Lumiere.

1. In Lumiere, make sure that the section of your project you want to export to a new video clip is indicated by the Control bar.

2. Choose Build from the Project menu. The Export dialog box appears. Enter the file name of your choice.

You can save your project video as uncompressed or compressed video. If you select compressed, the Video Compression control panel will appear, as long as the Suppress filter dialog checkbox is unchecked (refer to Figure 11.18).

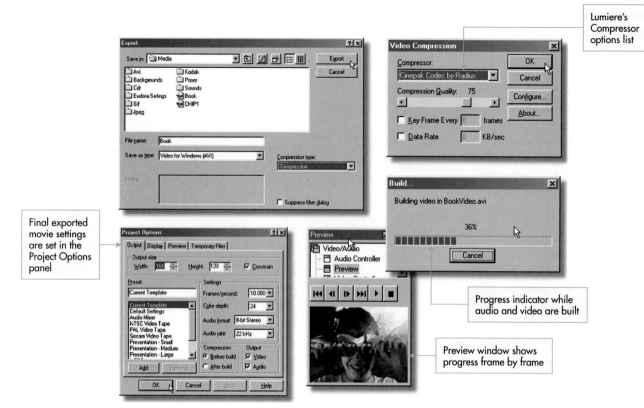

Figure 11.18
Lumiere offers a myriad of compression, movie, and audio format options.

3. Choose the Cinepak compressor (codec) and set the quality slider to 100%. Your audio settings for your video project are set in the Project Options control panel, as shown in Figure 11.18.

4. To get to the Project Options control panel, choose Options from the Project menu. This panel is also where you set the movie size parameters.

Lumiere provides several sets of parameters for specific usage, which is quite convenient. Once you click OK in the Video Compression control panel, Lumiere creates your new video file on disk.

Congratulations on creating a complete digital video project! Don't forget to save your project file so that you can edit it again in the future.

EXPORTING YOUR MOVIE

As you have just learned, you must make a complex and large selection of choices when deciding what digital video file format to use. (These choices are shown in Figures 11.17 and 11.18.)

In Chapter 10 you learned about codecs and were provided with a fairly in-depth explanation of each video file format and its uses. In this section, you will learn about the specific settings that you need to decide upon, above and beyond your choice of codec and file format.

PRINTING TO VIDEO

Most digital video editing software applications can "print" your work out of a video port on your video digitizing interface (if you have such an interface with such a port). You then record that video signal on your VCR or camcorder, which is connected at the other end of the cable. In the absence of hardware that will support a video-out signal, the Print to Video command simply displays your work on your computer monitor in full-screen mode. Print to Video provides a full-screen rendition of your work without the need for the editing interface. It enables you to see your work as a video project, outside the small editing windows the digital video editing application provides.

In Premiere, once you have built your movie, exported it to a video file, and can see it in the left-hand video panel of the Monitor window, choose Export from the File menu, and then choose Print to Video. In Lumiere, choose Print to Video from the File menu. If your video-digitizing interface in your computer has a Video Output port, you should be able to record the printed video onto videotape.

In both applications, simply choosing the Print to Video command displays the video clip on a black background in its original size, or scaled to full screen if you choose that setting. If you have a video capture card that supports a video-out signal, you must first build your video project as an exported file in the codec that is supplied with the video capture card. Once compiled, choosing the Print to Video command should send a video signal to the video-out port on your video capture card. You can view your work on a monitor or TV attached to that port. If a VCR is attached, simply pressing the Record button on the VCR will record that signal for you on videotape.

VIDEO SETTINGS

In any digital video editing application, whether Lumiere, Premiere, or another brand, there are several key settings that you should become familiar with to be able to produce high-quality, efficient digital video. The following universal settings are central to any digital video file format. Time taken to experiment with these settings will be time well spent.

- *Compressor/codec.* Select your compressor according to your own needs and tastes and the comparison between the codecs in Chapter 10.

- *Image size.* The size of the output video clip is your choice, but for "broadcast" work (anything that will end up on videotape) you should not use a size smaller than 640 × 480 pixels which is used for NTSC format video (NTSC stands for National Television Systems Committee, which is the body defining the television video signal format used in the United States). If you wish to record PAL format video (PAL stands for Phase Alternate Line, the television broadcast standard throughout Europe), you will need a 768 × 576 pixel size to conform to PAL format. For computer use, digital video files can be whatever size you specify. Keep in mind that the bigger you go, the more difficult a time the computer will have in playing back smoothly.

- *Frame rate and quality.* Typically you will select 30 fps as the appropriate setting. You may need to reduce that rate down as far as 12 fps if the digital video file you're producing is having difficulties playing. When you record to videotape, your frame rate should be at 30 fps (29.97 fps is the actual NTSC frame rate). The Quality slider allows you to sacrifice a little visual quality for performance considerations. This is a subjective call on your part, and it's recommended that you build a few small test clips at different quality settings to see what quality is acceptable and compare file size savings. Typically, noticeable quality depreciation appears only below an 80 percent quality setting, though this can vary with different codecs.

- *Data rate.* You will need to set the data rate for digital video created for CD-ROM or Web playback. In these cases, you will have to figure out the

NTSC

National Television Systems Committee; the body defining the television video signal format used in the United States. The term NTSC is used to describe the U.S. video signal format defined by this body. (Also, humorously, "Never Twice the Same Color.")

PAL

Phase Alternate Line; the television broadcast standard throughout Europe (except in France, where SECAM is the standard). This standard broadcasts 625 lines of resolution, nearly 20 percent more than the U.S. NTSC standard of 525.

Figure 11.19

Premiere's Movie Analysis window showing the movie clip's data rate, and Premiere's Properties window and Data rate graph window.

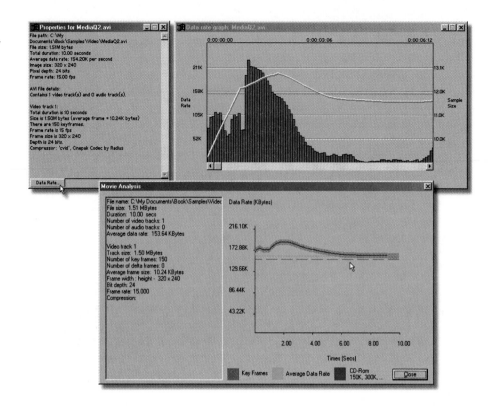

lowest possible rate at which your users can access your video work, and then set that as the data rate. In effect, you are "telling" the application that it is to compromise the other settings for the video piece to ensure that your video clip never requires more than the data rate you specify to play. This can sometimes result in grainy quality and/or dropped frames so you will have to experiment with this. Figure 11.19 shows the Movie Analysis windows in Premiere, including a graph of the data rate of the movie over its elapsed time. You can see this analysis screen by right-clicking on the movie playing window that appears when Premiere has finished building your movie and selecting this option.

• *Recompress.* If you want to force the settings you have made throughout the video piece, then choose the Recompress command. When you're working with digital video clips, the clips will doubtless be in different formats and use various codecs. Choosing Recompress conforms all clips to your settings. However, you may lose some quality on some clips in the process especially if you are using a lossy codec. Again, do a test run first.

MOVIE ANALYSIS

When you are playing back the new video clip you created in Premiere, right-clicking the clip in the left-hand panel of the Monitor window opens a menu from which you can choose the Get Properties command. At the end of the extensive analysis listing for that clip is a button called Data Rate. When you click this button, you'll see an analysis chart for the data rate of your movie over its duration.

In Lumiere, the Movie Analysis command on the File menu allows you to load a video clip and analyze it. The average frame rate value is the first value to aim for when considering a limited data rate for your movie.

- *Audio settings.* Audio settings are given the same consideration as described in Chapter 3 and in Part 5 of this book. Keep in mind that you want the lowest values possible without compromising the sound quality. Be aware that a perfectly good video project can often develop performance problems when an audio track is applied. Remember to do a movie analysis and check the data rate. If necessary, force a data rate that you know you can live with. Premiere provides many audio codecs. See Part 5 of this book for more details on audio compression.

- *Keyframe and rendering options.* The codec you're using can create keyframes on a set interval or at set markers throughout the project. Usually, setting the keyframes to the suggested interval for that codec works best. You may notice pixelation and artifacts (blotchy bits) at sudden changes of scene when you render your movie. If this occurs, you may want to place a marker on the first frame of the new scene and instruct your digital video editing application to use that marked frame as a keyframe source. In the Rendering Options dialog box, you can switch off audio and video filters and audio volume level "rubber bands." This can help eliminate all of these factors in one place so that you can check to see whether doing so eliminates the problem you are trying to rectify with the final product. In Premiere, the Optimize Stills setting does just that. When you have a still image for a duration in the movie, there is no point in storing the same image over consecutive frames. Optimizing Stills allows Premiere to grab the first still frame as a keyframe and ignore the rest until the still changes. This can greatly save on the storage space required for your video file. When using the Print to Video command, check your video output hardware's field rendering requirements and make sure that you set these options to suit. Field rendering (see Chapter 10) is a broadcast video/videotape issue. When you're creating digital video for multimedia application content, use the "both fields" or "no fields" rendering (whichever your digital video editing software provides) to effectively eliminate field rendering in your digital video clip.

AVOIDING PITFALLS

Digital video editing applications such as Premiere and Lumiere locate and record pointers to the media components you are editing together to create your final video masterpiece. However, such applications allow you to locate those media components anywhere on your system, including a network if you are connected to one. By keeping all of your media components in one folder, you can easily transport all your content to another system without breaking links to files that cannot travel with the project file. Keep all your content in one folder, along with the project file that you are working on.

There is a tremendous temptation to use all of the digital video "toys" when you discover how creative you can be. You run the risk of your video looking amateurish and too busy. At the same time, you will be making your computer system work overtime, trying to render multiple layered special effects, transitions, and transparency clips. Keep it simple, and incrementally add special techniques and effects as the project warrants it. Note how the best ads on TV are those that are elegantly sophisticated. The cheesy ones have too much glitz for the sake of glitz.

When creating transparencies (titles often being the most common use), create an image or title that uses a clear primary blue or green as the background color. Use contrasting colors for the titles or superimposed image. In this way you can choose Blue Screen or Green Screen as your chroma-key type. These transparency methods are clean and easy to adjust. Be sure to get bright, uniformly lit primary blue or green as your background color. The better the background color, the cleaner your transparency effect will be.

Before you invest a lot of money in a digital video editing application, check out demonstration versions of the product and see which works best for you. In my multimedia development studio we do a lot of digital video editing—it's one of our staple components. We use three different digital video editing applications and several utilities to get the job done. We use each for its strengths and avoid its weaknesses. Until you can afford multiple applications, check out the less-expensive products. Often you can create very professional work on a product that costs one-tenth the price of the "industry leader."

Preview your work frequently to judge the effects of your edits. Applications such as Premiere provide a Preview from RAM option; use this feature to save time rendering the preview file (Lumiere previews on the fly). By previewing often, you can avoid a mistake that can be compounded by later edits and that could end up impossible to fix once discovered.

Chapter Summary

- The fundamental basics of digital video editing applications are essentially the same. A step-by-step comparison between Lumiere and Adobe's Premiere shows just how closely related such applications are.

- The techniques used to apply special effects, build superimposed clips, generate titles, create professional transitions between clips, and apply and edit soundtracks are all straightforward and quite easy and intuitive (once you've done it a couple of times).

- The organization and collection of the components that make up your digital video project are very important, especially if you're working on multiple workstations.

- When you finish your digital video editing, you must choose from many different output formats, each one with many parameters and choices.

- When creating a video project for broadcasting or for use on videotape, you must take special care to use the correct settings required of NTSC- or PAL-format video.

- The process of printing to video requires your digital video capture hardware to have a video output port to which you can connect a videotape recorder.

Key Terms and Concepts

Checking Your Knowledge and Skills

1. If you do not have access to the full versions, install the demonstration versions of both Premiere and Lumiere, available via links on this book's Web site. Create an identical video project on both applications; while doing so, make a list of features you like and don't like about each product. Create a features comparison chart for both products and locate the current price for either product on the Web (if you're a student, don't forget educational prices). Try www.creationengine.com or www.dvdirect.com. What do you conclude from your comparison?

2. Having created a digital video project using a digital video editing application, create your final rendered digital video in an uncompressed format. Without changing the screen size of the video, but being free to adjust all other parameters, including audio compression, what is the smallest file you can achieve for this project? Go to the point where you still are happy with the quality of the smallest clip. As a percentage of the original uncompressed clip, how small is the smallest you achieved?

3. After creating the smallest possible video file, compare the performance on your system of the original and the small file. Do a movie analysis on both video clips and see how the data rate has been affected. Does limiting the data rate of the movie help or hinder its performance?

4. Use a digital video editing application to reformat one of the sample video clips provided into another codec of your choice. Set the data rate to meet the bandwidth needs of a 4X, a 16X, and a 32X CD-ROM, and those of a 28.8 Kbps and a 56 Kbps modem for Web use. You should end up with five identical video clips, with the exception of their forced data rates. You will find the information you need to determine what these data rate requirements are in KB per second in a previous chapter, but part of this exercise is finding that chapter!

5. After completing exercise 4 and viewing the resulting clips, determine what difference in quality, if any, is apparent in these clips. Which would you recommend to your client for a CD-ROM multimedia product and for a Web-based multimedia product? What implications would this recommendation have on the range of users who could use this product?

Critical Thinking Challenges

1. Create a digital video piece using a digital video editing application like the ones described in this chapter. Without adjusting the video compressor parameters, build your project into three digital video files using 11 kHz, 22 kHz, and 44 kHz audio, respectively. Use the movie analysis tools to examine the performance of each file. Which audio format would you choose for your project and why? Are there projects where the audio quality would be more important than others?

2. Review a selection of CD-ROM or DVD-ROM multimedia applications (at least four) and list the digital video used in each case. Demonstration CD-ROMs from software manufacturers are very useful for such critiquing. Find the video files on each CD-ROM or DVD-ROM and copy them to a folder on your hard drive. Use the movie analysis tools to determine what codec and compression parameters were used to create these clips. Can you import any of these clips into your digital video editing application and create a better-performing, smaller digital video?

3. Find a selection of images from the Web and import them into your digital video editing application. Using the special effects and transitions provided, create a fast-paced digital video with a soundtrack to tell a story about Web content. Use filters such as Image Pan and Camera View to add motion to still images. In the Samples\Video folder on this book's CD-ROM is a video entitled ByeBye.avi (ByeBye.mov for Macintosh users) that I created some time ago from images downloaded from the Web. What does this exercise tell you about the creativity tool that a digital video editor represents?

Hands-on Exercises

BUILDING A DIGITAL VIDEO PROJECT

In the previous chapter's Hands-On Exercises you prepared a storyboard and assembled the content to create a digital video project. Now is your opportunity to turn that plan into reality!

Now that you've read this chapter, determine whether you need to make any changes. This is a good time to make those changes.

Using your digital video editing application, build your video project, remembering to constantly preview your work, and export a finished digital video file. How close is your final product to your original storyboard?

Master Project

CREATING YOUR VIDEO CONTENT

So far you should have created a binder for the project that includes your project concept, a project plan and timeline, and your sketches and visuals for your design. You should also have begun the process of building your content and storing it on disk.

Using the storyboard and content collection from the previous chapter, build your digital video content for your multimedia digital portfolio. Remember that these video segments are intended to promote you, so take the time and be patient with the process. That way you are most likely to create video segments that you can be proud to showcase in your multimedia portfolio.

Save your work to a Zip disk (or equivalent) and keep it with your project binder.

PART

Five

DIGITAL
SOUND
AND MUSIC

CHAPTER

12

MULTIMEDIA BUILDING BLOCKS: SOUND AND MUSIC

Chapter Outline

Chapter Objectives

After completing this chapter, you will be able to:

- Distinguish between analog and digital sound and describe how to convert between these forms of sound
- Distinguish between digital MIDI sound files and recorded digital audio sound files
- Describe how sound files are used on the Web and list their various formats
- Describe the function and capabilities of the digital sound hardware and software used in your computer system
- Distinguish between the sound file parameters that affect the quality and the performance of the digital sound file
- Describe how digital sound is recorded
- Determine whether copyright considerations need to be addressed when using a digital sound file
- Describe how digital MIDI sound files are recorded
- Discuss the inverse correlation between sound file quality and sound file performance in a multimedia application or Web site, and describe how to manipulate these factors

Chapter Overview

Sound is the heart and soul of a multimedia product. Music stirs the emotions, narration can make digesting large volumes of information easier, sound effects give reinforcing aural feedback to the user's actions, and video components come to life with an accompanying soundtrack.

You'll doubtless agree that a multimedia application without a good dose of sound effects and/or music is lackluster. It's like being entertained by a mime instead of a movie, or watching a TV set with a broken speaker. You can watch the silent entertainment for just so long, but with the full-blown experience you can completely lose track of time. Although sound (hearing) is one of our most important senses, it is so ubiquitous that it is often both overlooked and neglected. This is especially true in multimedia applications.

In this chapter you will learn about sound files and their many formats. The following chapter offers hands-on instruction on how to massage and manipulate those sound files to suit your multimedia needs. You will learn how to distinguish among the many different formats available and how to determine the best one for your application.

You will learn that the quality-versus-size relationship applies to digital sound as much as to any other media component. You will also learn why Web-based sound needs very special attention and formatting to enable it to play over that tiny delivery pipeline we call the Internet.

One thing to remember is that the audience for your multimedia piece will often tolerate an occasional visual glitch, a staggering video, dropped frames, a momentarily stalled interface reaction, or a lethargic animation. But there is little forgiveness for bad audio. It can be intolerable. A perfect visual presentation can seem ruined by a soundtrack that misses a beat, while a visually flawed project can often be carried by good audio.

OVERVIEW OF SOUND AND MUSIC FILE FORMATS

This chapter will cover how to edit, format, and use digital sound and music files. However, to fully understand digital sound requires an understanding of how it differs from analog sound.

ANALOG VERSUS DIGITAL

Sound travels in waves. The vibrations that travel through air particles and other materials (just as waves travel through water particles, only you can see the effect in water and not so easily in air) vibrate your eardrum and you perceive this vibration as sound.

A waveform is represented by a continuous line that looks like a wave. If you were to draw a graph of such a sound wave, plotting the height of the wave to represent the volume of the sound, you could pick any location along that waveform and read the volume value at that instant. Because a waveform is continuous, there are, theoretically, an infinite number of such locations along that line. This simply means that no matter how much you were to zoom in on that waveform line, you would always see a line, and could always choose a point from

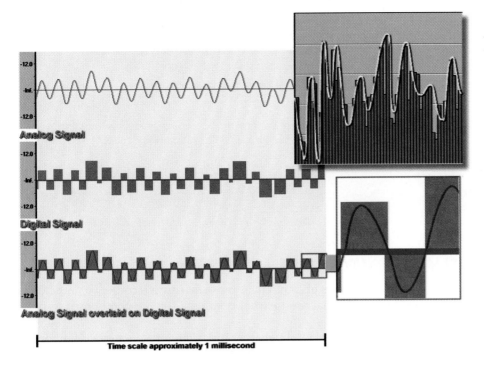

Figure 12.1
Analog audio versus digital audio.

analog

The name for an electronic signal that carries its information/sound as a continuously fluctuating voltage value.

digitizing

The process of converting an analog signal to a digital one.

sampling rate

The frequency, or rate, at which a digital value is taken from an analog signal.

frequency response

The range of frequencies a sound device can respond to or work within. For example, the human ear is said to have a frequency response of 20 Hz to 20 kHz—however (with the possible exception of young children), most of us cannot hear reliably over this range. A telephone, by comparison, has a frequency response of 200 Hz to 4 kHz.

which to read a value. This continuously changing level format is called analog. In the world of music, *analog sound* refers to a nondigital tape or vinyl record recording of sound. The process of converting an analog signal to a digital one is called (for both sound and video) digitizing.

A digital signal, however, is a series of discrete values in quick succession, as opposed to the continuous curve of an analog signal (see Figure 12.1). Instead of a continuously changing value, the *A-to-D (analog-to-digital) converter* of a digital recording device takes frequent samples of the continuum and stores the value it finds at that instant in time as a digital value. This frequency of sampling is referred to as the sampling rate. By taking enough of these samples every second, the sound can be stored digitally with sufficient clarity for the human ear not to notice the "missing" levels between the values sampled. For an audio CD, the sampling rate is about 44,000 samples per second (44 kHz). In Figure 12.1 you see an analog signal represented as a curve. At a set sampling rate, the digitizing process collects a stream of individual numbers (shown as red bars), which, when played back, sound like a faithful reproduction of the original sound. In Figure 12.1, the final digital recording would look like the bar graph while the analog sound would follow the line graph.

Even though CD-quality sound is considered high-fidelity, you can see from Figure 12.1 that even at 44 kHz, sound information will be lost in the conversion to a digital format. That is why the most elite audiophiles still have analog equipment, and still collect vinyl records and high-quality tape recordings.

Furthermore, the frequency response of a digital audio file is about half that of its sampling rate, or about 22 kHz for a sound sampled at a CD-quality 44 kHz. The human ear has a frequency response of up to about 20 kHz, meaning that sounds whose pitch is above the 20 kHz range become too high-pitched for the human ear to pick up. That is the realm of dogs and other animals with this ability. So a digital sound file recorded at a 44 kHz sampling rate should be within the entire frequency range of the human ear.

For our purposes, we are more than happy with CD-quality sound and will often have to degrade this sound quality in an effort to reduce sound file size and enhance performance.

When you reduce the sampling rate of a sound file (when trying to reduce its file size), you also reduce that file's frequency response, and are therefore "chopping off" those high-frequency sounds that give a recording its richness. You will perceive the sound becoming a little flat, but this may be an acceptable trade-off for a smaller, better-performing sound file.

While the highest fundamental frequency available on a piano keyboard is less than 5 kHz, it may have far higher harmonic and overtone frequencies that give it its full-bodied feel. These often-imperceptible characteristics are sacrificed when reducing the sound file's sampling rate. You notice them only when they are missing.

TABLE 12.1	Comparison of Sound File Formats	
Feature	**Recorded Sound Audio**	**MIDI Music**
File format	WAV, AIFF, AU, RA, MPG, MP3, SW	MIDI
File size	Large (10 MB/minute for CD quality)	Very small (often 10 KB will store two minutes of music)
Sound fidelity	Depends on settings. Excellent at top-quality parameter settings.	Very good. However, often considered "tinny."
Ability to record sound events	Yes	No
Instrument control data	No	Yes

MIDI VERSUS WAV OR AIFF

There are two primary types of sound files: those that are a recording of an actual sound event, and those that are instructional data for the computer's sound interface to play.

Recordings of an actual sound (whether it's a slamming door or a symphonic masterpiece) are recorded at a high-frequency digital sampling and can thereafter faithfully reproduce that sound repeatedly. This sound file is often large in size to facilitate the storage of all those data points required to reproduce the sound. Common formats are WAV (PC) and AIFF (Mac). Other formats, such as RA (RealAudio) and MP3 (MPEG-3) are used in specialized circumstances, such as audio streaming over the Net. MP3 music in particular is increasingly popular as a high-fidelity format for personal digital music players.

Digital music files, most commonly MIDI files (pronounced "mid-ee"), simply store music data that is read by the computer's sound hardware (or an electronic keyboard attached to it) and is played back as per those instructions. MIDI stands for "Musical Instrument Digital Interface," and the format was originally designed for communication between digital musical instruments. Since it is instructing another device to generate the appropriate sound, it does not need to record that sound, just the instruction to the instrument or sound card to reproduce it. As a result, the file size can be tiny.

To record the actual sound of a single note for one second (perhaps from a flute) will require storing 44,000 data points in a WAV or AIFF file. However, in a MIDI file, one instruction to your computer's digital sound hardware to play the note for that duration is all that's required to reproduce the desired sound.

MIDI files can be used to create attractive music with tiny file size and performance overhead for a multimedia application, but often these files create music that sounds "synthesized" and "tinny." MIDI files cannot support the recording of actual sound events, such as speech or a car engine.

There is a balance to be found in the pros and cons of each file type. Table 12.1 compares the two basic sound file formats.

SOUND ON THE WEB

As with any other multimedia application, sound on a Web page falls into one of two categories. There is extended sound that is played in its entirety, such as background music, or a sound media component, such as speech for the purpose of entertainment or information. Such sound is initiated by the user and plays to the end unless interrupted. In addition, there are sound effects that are played in response to a user action, and whose purpose is to provide interface feedback. Button clicks and other interface sound effects would fall into this category.

Adding extended sound to a Web page is not too difficult, as a sound file can simply be embedded in, or linked to, a Web page, waiting for the user to play it. However, a Web page is not a technology format that is conducive to quick-response sounds to users' actions. For this, you will have to create multimedia applets to package the interface into a program that can provide these sound effects. Technologies such as Macromedia's Shockwave are excellent at providing this.

While all sound file formats can ultimately be used on the Web, some formats are specially optimized for playing over the Internet. Such files are very tiny in file size to facilitate slow connection speeds to the Internet, and also support audio streaming. In the same way that video files stream over the Web, audio streaming allows the audio file to start playing the beginning of the sound file while the rest is still downloading in the background.

Perhaps the most well known Internet-specific audio file format is RealAudio from RealNetworks (www.real.com). This pioneering streaming format is widely used throughout the Internet and offers some advantages over other formats, such as being able to select the best version of the audio data stream to suit your connection speed. More sophisticated versions of this format can scale themselves to adapt to your connection speed. Figure 12.2 shows the RealNetworks Web site and the pop-up window that your users will see if you send them to the RealNetworks Web site to download the free RealPlayer plug-in for their browser application. Also shown is the logo that you would use to direct users to this site.

Current versions of applications such as Adobe's Premiere (Chapter 11) and Sonic Foundry's Sound Forge (Chapter 13) can encode audio files in RealAudio format, making it easy to develop sound content for the Web.

Other formats include the most up-to-date versions of both Apple's QuickTime and Microsoft's NetShow audio formats. Others such as Bamba (IBM), Beatnik (Headspace), Crescendo (LiveUpdate), Liquid MusicPlayer (Liquid

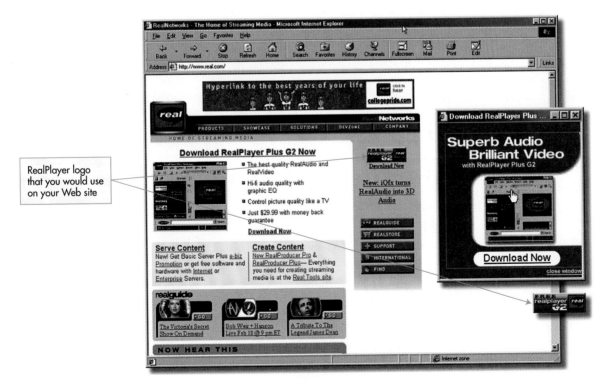

Figure 12.2
The RealNetworks Web site.

Audio), MidiPlug (Yamaha), RapidTransit (FastMan), and WebTracks (Wildcat Canyon Software) provide high-quality sound over the Internet at relatively slow connection speeds. Before committing to one of these formats, be sure to check what plug-ins your user will need, and what you, the developer, will need to encode in these formats.

In Chapter 16 you will learn how to implement these audio files in your multimedia Web pages.

UNDERSTANDING COMPUTER SOUND HARDWARE CAPABILITIES

A brief technical overview of your computer's sound capabilities will help you understand the appropriate use of digital sound in your multimedia application or Web page. Knowing the capabilities of your computer's (and your users') sound system will help you avoid under- or overspecifying the correct file format.

The basic function of your computer's sound hardware is to convert analog sound to digital sound data, and vice versa. Figure 12.3 describes this process. When inputting audio from an analog source, such as from a microphone or stereo line feed, your computer digitizes that signal to create a digital sound file that can be then saved to disk. That disk-based digital file can later be played by the computer's sound hardware to an analog line connected to a speaker (which is an analog device). So your computer sound interface has quite a lot of work to do.

When a MIDI instrument is connected, the process of storing the MIDI data and later playing back to the MIDI instrument is a simple one, as there is no conversion between digital and analog signals. It all remains in digital format. However, if that MIDI file is played by the computer's sound hardware so that the resulting music is heard over the computer's speakers, then it is being converted to an analog signal for the speakers to use, as shown in Figure 12.3.

Figure 12.3
Analog and digital audio connections through the digital sound card and the personal computer.

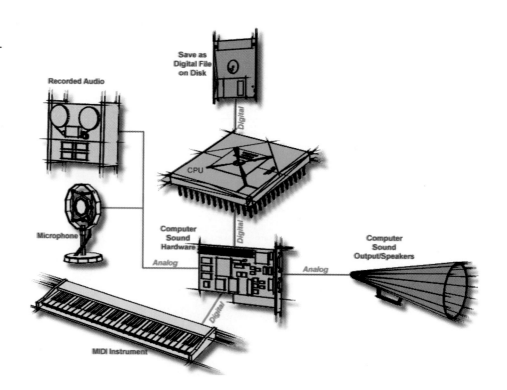

However, when a microphone or hi-fi system is connected to the computer's sound card and that sound is recorded, then that analog signal must be converted to a digital one to store it in a file on disk. This process uses an analog-to-digital (A-to-D) converter (sometimes also called ADC) to transform the analog electrical fluctuations that are created by the microphone or audio device sound into a series of digital bits and bytes. The reverse process is true when that digital sound is played back through the computer's speakers. A digital-to-analog (D-to-A) converter (sometimes also called DAC) translates the stored digital sound file back into those electrical fluctuations that cause the speaker to also fluctuate and generate sound. This conversion process can be tracked through Figure 12.3.

In the 1980s, digital storage of sound became a big hit when Sony Corporation and Philips Electrical jointly developed compact disc technology and standardized the format we know so well today. This was an inexpensive way of storing high-quality sound in a format that was not as prone to dust, scratching, and damage through physical contact as were vinyl records. With CD players, the sound is permanently stored in digital format on an inexpensive plastic disk and converted to an analog signal to accommodate the headphones, speakers, or stereo system the CD player is connected to. Another advantage of CD technology is that no contact with the disk is required to play the music. A laser light beam "reads" the digital signal from the reflective layer inside the disk. Therefore, there is no wear and tear associated with playing CDs. They wear out only when users mistreat them.

Digital sound provides the following benefits:

- There is no tape or vinyl record to wear out.
- Digital sound format does not add any artifacts or noise/distortion to the sound (as does tape).
- There is no loss in signal introduced when you make copies of the sound. You can make successive duplicates of a digital file thousands of times over and the last sound file will provide the same sound quality as the first.
- Digital files are random-access, meaning that any point along the soundtrack can be accessed instantly. On tape the sound has to be played sequentially.
- Digital sound files can be used with other digital media easily and can be integrated and stored in an application executable file. Digital sound can be added to digital video, for instance.
- In a digital format, your personal computer can become a sophisticated sound editing workstation. It can be used to record (digitize) sound from your tape deck and play back again to the same deck to create a master copy of the edited work with little or no loss in quality from the source sound. This process is often referred to as *digital remastering*.

DIGITAL SOUND FILE QUALITY FACTORS

When you are digitizing sound, two factors determine the quality of the resulting digital sound file: the sampling rate and the resolution.

SAMPLING RATE.   The sampling rate is the rate at which ADC samples the incoming analog audio signal during the conversion to a digital format. The sampling rate also determines how much digital data describing that sound is crammed into each second of its duration. The more data stored, the higher the fidelity of that recorded sound in reproducing the original. It also follows that the more data stored, the larger the resulting digital files will be.

analog-to-digital (A-to-D) converter

A hardware and/or software product that converts an analog signal to a digital data file. When recording sound on your computer through a microphone, you are using the A-to-D converter of your computer's sound interface.

digital-to-analog (D-to-A) converter

A hardware and/or software product that converts a digital data file to an analog signal. When playing a digital sound file through your computer's speakers, you are using the D-to-A converter of your computer's sound interface.

TABLE 12.2 Quality Comparison of Sound Files of Different Sampling Rates		
Digital Sound Sampling Rate	Comparable Sound Quality	Approximate Size of a One-Second Digital Sound File
44,100 Hz	CD audio quality	175 KB
22,050 Hz	FM radio quality	87 KB
11,025 Hz	Telephone quality	43 KB

Table 12.2 shows what quality differences are represented by the various sampling rates.

Notice in both Table 12.2 and Figure 12.4 that as the sampling rate for these sound files is halved, the file size for the sound is also halved. For the multimedia producer, the objective would be to reduce the sampling rate as far as possible while preserving an acceptable sound quality. This will ensure the smallest and best-performing sound file possible.

SOUND RESOLUTION. As with other digital media file formats such as images and video, the sound resolution of a sound file refers to the number of bits used to represent the sound signal level for each sample during the digitizing process. The *bit depth* of a sound file determines the dynamic range of the sound, usually described in terms of decibels (dB) in analog sound. Each bit of sound resolution provides an additional 6 dB of sound volume. Therefore a 16-bit sound file has a *dynamic range* of 96 dB, meaning that the sound file has the capacity to pump out 96 deafening dB of volume.

By converting the bit depth of a sound file to 8-bit, which has the effect of changing the dynamic range to 48 dB, you create a file that is half the size of its 16-bit counterpart, but has the dynamic range of an average cassette deck. The bit-conversion process often introduces hissing and static that can be considered unacceptable quality.

sound resolution

In sound terms, the bit depth of a sound file. This factor determines the volume and dynamic range of the sound file.

Figure 12.4
Reducing the sampling rate of the sound file correspondingly reduces the file size and increases the performance of the multimedia application.

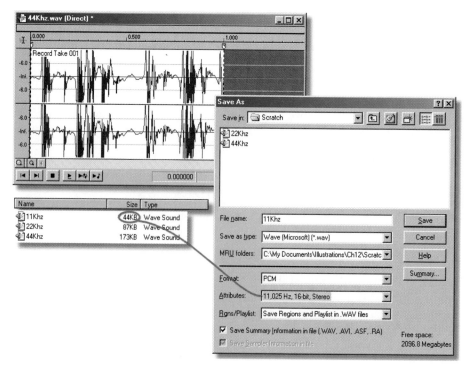

When you consider that the human ear finds sound levels above 96 dB unpleasant, it's surprising to note that currently available 32-bit sound cards for computers have the potential to produce 128 dB of sound. This is well into the permanent-eardrum-damage range. While the potential to create such literally deafening sound is there, this available dynamic range allows for very-high-fidelity sound at those lower pleasant levels, with premium high-resolution quality.

While the sampling rate and the resolution of a sound determine its quality, file size, and performance characteristics, it is always best to capture or digitize at the best possible quality for editing and manipulation purposes. Working on a 44 kHz, 16-bit stereo sound file provides you with the maximum amount of data to manipulate and play with. You can always save your final file at whatever rate best suits your product's needs. Typically the lowest-quality sound file acceptable is an 11 kHz, 8-bit mono format. However, the appropriate sound file format and quality settings will be determined by the needs of your application and on how the resulting sound file actually sounds to your ear. This is an area of digital media manipulation where your senses can be more important than arbitrary selection of preset values.

RECORDING SOUND FILES

Recording sound files is usually as simple as clicking the Record button in your sound editing application and either talking into the microphone or pressing play on your audio deck, which is connected to your computer's audio line-in socket. This audio line-in socket is usually found on the back of your sound card or is clearly labeled on your CPU case. Figure 12.5 shows some of the many sound recording applications available for Windows 95/98/2000.

When recording, be sure to capture your audio at the best possible quality rate you can. You can always edit the quality factors to best suit your needs, but when starting with a medium-to-low-quality sound recording, you have no recourse but to accept the quality, whether it's suitable or not. As with image editing, the more data contained within the image file, the more data you have to manipulate. You may want to add special effects or process the sound some way. To do this effectively and still achieve quality sound, you must begin with an

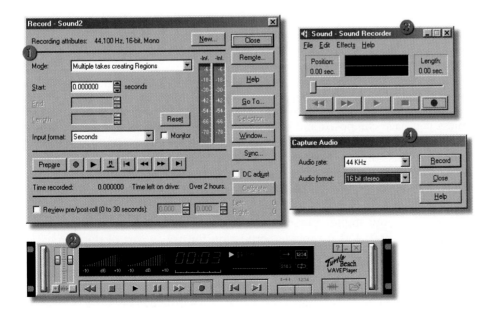

Figure 12.5

Shown numbered in order of sophistication: (1) Sound Forge; (2) Turtle Beach Wave Player; (3) Windows standard Sound Recorder; (4) Lumiere's Capture Audio utility.

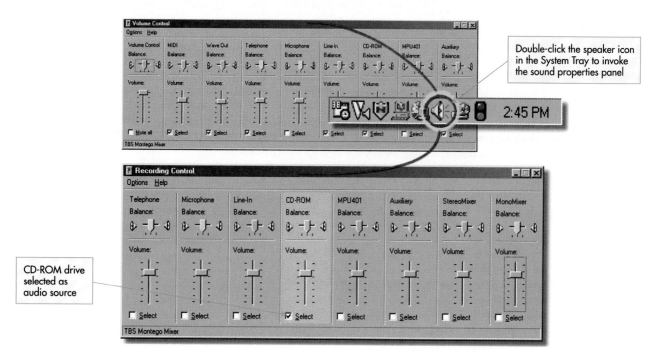

Double-click the speaker icon in the System Tray to invoke the sound properties panel

CD-ROM drive selected as audio source

Figure 12.6
Audio recording options available in Windows 95/98.

excellent-quality sound to work on. In Figure 12.5, both Sound Forge (1) and Lumiere's Capture Audio (4) show the quality setting of the sound they are about to digitize. The other applications require you to set those parameters in a settings section.

Most multimedia-capable computer systems include a CD-ROM drive that can play audio CDs and a software application (such as the Windows CD Player) that plays them through your computer's sound hardware. If this is the case for your system, then you should be able to simply run your sound recording application and click the Record button while the CD is playing to record the CD audio. Figure 12.6 shows the Windows 98 sound recording control panel, which you can access by double-clicking the small speaker icon shown in the Windows system tray (at the bottom right of your screen). By checking the Select checkbox underneath the level controls for CD-ROM, you can now record from CD audio with any of your Windows sound recording applications.

In Chapter 13 you will work through step-by-step instructions on recording your digital audio.

COPYRIGHT CONSIDERATIONS

Unless you have composed and created the audio you are recording or already own the copyright to the sound, you probably cannot use or record that sound without permission. The consequences of copyright infringement can be very severe if the copyright holder pursues it. You could find your multimedia development business very quickly tied up in legal wrangling and expenses.

The safest way to adhere to copyright requirements is to either generate original music and sound yourself, pay someone to do it for you, or purchase music/sound libraries that provide permission for use as part of the purchase. You will find sound libraries in most computer stores. The packaging should clearly state that you have royalty-free permission to reuse the contents. Some permissions specify that if you create a product for commercial gain, the permission does not extend that far and you must contact the owners for a license to use the audio. Read the fine print.

Some new products, such as Sonic Foundry's ACID (www.sonicfoundry.com), allow even the most musically challenged person to create professional sounding, unique music.

There will always be talented musicians or music students who, for small consideration and prominent mention of their name in your product's credit, will create original music for you. Not only do you avoid copyright hassles and licensing fees this way, but you stand to develop a relationship with someone who can fulfill this need again and again. Incorporating custom music in your multimedia application or Web site is of tremendous benefit to you and to your customers—and quite a selling point.

In short, the best way to avoid any problems associated with copyright is to follow this rule: If it's not yours, don't use it.

RECORDING MIDI FILES

MIDI files can be generated in two ways: first, by recording the MIDI data from a MIDI instrument (such as an electronic keyboard) as it is played, and second, by using a MIDI sequencer software application.

MIDI sequencing software has completely changed the music industry. It places the ability to conduct a veritable orchestra in the hands of the individual. By selecting the instrument to use, and the track upon which to play that instrument, the MIDI musician can layer instrumental track upon track to achieve a full-band effect.

The musician records the MIDI data for each track of the composition and selects the instrument that the MIDI device, synthesizer, or sound card in the computer will play. While playing back those tracks already recorded, the musician can add additional tracks and edit the existing ones. MIDI sequencing software is sophisticated enough to help the musician precisely synchronize tracks and auto-generate fill-in tracks if required. Figure 12.7 shows a screenshot from a very sophisticated MIDI sequencing program called Cakewalk. This application not only allows you to compose and edit MIDI music on your desktop computer, but also works with your MIDI instrument and can read and

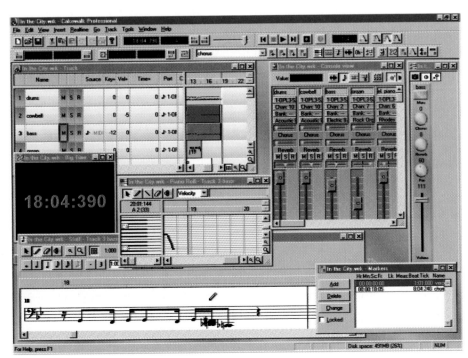

Figure 12.7
Among the more sophisticated MIDI sequencing applications is Cakewalk for both Macintosh and PC.

Figure 12.8

TekknoBOX is a simple MIDI sequencer (once you become familiar with it).

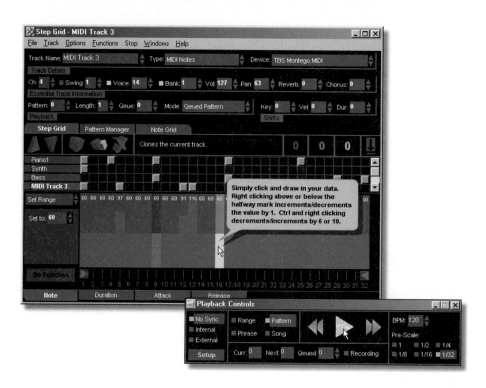

write musical notation as shown. There is even a version of Cakewalk for guitar players that includes a digital fret board to demonstrate what strings and chords to play.

For the more musically challenged, there are applications like Jon Gilkison's TekknoBOX (see Figure 12.8). TekknoBOX is a simple MIDI sequencing application, once you become familiar with its operation. A comprehensive tutorial and help file is provided for this purpose.

Simple MIDI sequencer applications like TekknoBOX allow MIDI music composers to select the instrument of their choice, tell it where in the bar of music it should play a note, what pitch that note should be, and how that note should behave (duration, attack, and sustain). With a few simple mouse clicks you can create quite sophisticated MIDI music.

You can find links to downloadable versions of both TekknoBOX and Cakewalk at Web sites such as www.xs4all.nl/~rexbo/pc_midi.htm. Cakewalk and TekknoBOX can be downloaded from Web sites that provide shareware and demo applications, such as www.shareware.com and www.zdnet.com. Simply do a search for "MIDI sequencer."

MANIPULATING SOUND FILES FOR EFFECT AND SIZE

As with all digital multimedia content, the objective is to create a media component of suitable quality for your application in the smallest file size possible. Sound files are no exception. While MIDI files are, by definition, very small, recorded sound wave files can be enormous and will often have to be reduced in size to be effective. The additional bandwidth overhead of a large sound file can often send an application over the acceptable performance threshold.

You learned earlier about how to reduce the file size of a wave sound file by reducing the quality parameters until you begin to dip below an acceptable quality level. In addition, the codec you select for your sound file can provide additional compression and file size savings that will help this size/performance equilibrium.

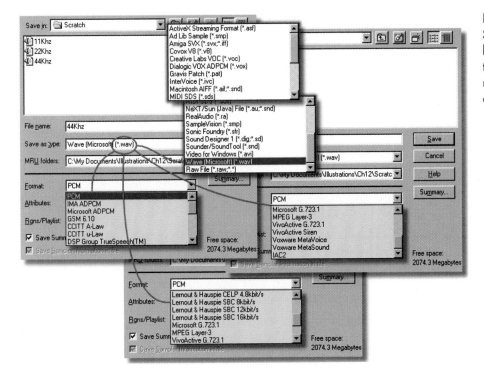

SOUND FILE CODECS

Audio codecs, such as Adaptive Delta Pulse Code Modulation (ADPCM), offer file size savings in the order of 2:1 and 4:1 compression (the compressed file will be one-quarter of the original uncompressed file size). But often, such codecs (including ADPCM) are lossy compressors, so you will have to experiment and see whether the quality loss incurred in the compression is acceptable for your project. Figure 12.9 shows nineteen of the sound file types available when saving a wave file from Sound Forge. For Microsoft WAV, twenty-one different codecs are available. The sound file type you choose depends on how you will use the sound file. Which compressor you use on that sound type depends on which offers the best file size with the best quality and which codec will be available on your users' systems.

While using an audio codec to compress sound files can provide tremendous performance benefits, there may be drawbacks:

1. Most audio codecs are lossy and will therefore degrade the quality of your resulting compressed sound file. The degree of degradation depends on the codec you choose.

RESEARCH YOUR CODEC

Research the codec you choose, as codecs may differ in functionality from system to system even though they may use the same name. You may end up using a codec on your development system that is incompatible with the codec of the same name on your users' systems, causing your multimedia application to be silent or not work at all. For instance, Microsoft's ADPCM codec is not compatible with the International Multimedia Association (IMA)–approved ADPCM codec. Check the documentation that comes with your sound editing program for details on using the codecs supplied.

> Your edited sound file will doubtless end up as a media component in another application—maybe as a digital video soundtrack or a sound effect in a multimedia application. Be sure to check out whether that media development program compresses audio as part of its final compilation of the multimedia product. Some authoring tools do compress their own audio and embed the audio data internally in the final multimedia executable product. In this case, you are often better off using the best-quality sound file you can achieve, and let the development tool optimize the compression at the final stages of creating the application.

2. Your users must have the same audio codec you've used installed and available on their system. Without the correct codec, they will be unable to hear your audio and may be prevented from running your application. Research the standard codecs found on your target audience's typical system to prevent this from happening.

3. Compressing audio requires more computer processing time than working with uncompressed audio. The amount of processing time depends on the codec, as well as your audio workstation setup. Opening and saving compressed files will usually take longer than with uncompressed files.

Saving compressed audio files can be as simple as choosing the appropriate codec in the Format drop-down list of your sound editing application's Save As dialog box. Keep in mind that your ear will be the most useful tool in determining whether you are still working in the acceptable-quality range for your sound file. Experimentation is probably the most important step in deciding whether to use audio compression for your projects.

As mentioned earlier, special audio file formats are purpose-made to give extremely high compression, tiny file sizes, and streaming capabilities. These formats, such as RealAudio, have been developed for Web deployment of sound content. Recently, there has been a vast improvement in the quality of the sound these formats can achieve at high compression rates. The quality is getting so good that these specialized codecs are being used in mainstream non-Web multimedia applications. They can offer quality sound with very small file sizes. Among the Web streaming technologies being brought into the mainstream multimedia development arena is Shockwave technology from Macromedia. You will learn more about Shockwave in Part 6.

AVOIDING PITFALLS

When recording digital audio, it is best to record your source files at the best possible quality you can. You can always edit them later and save the files in an inferior format. But if you need to revisit the project again and apply digital processing or perhaps create several versions of the sound file, then it is best to have the full-quality files to work from. If you record an inferior-quality source file, you will never be able to improve the quality above the levels at which it was captured.

A little planning can go a long way. By determining the intended purpose of the sound file you are working on, you can best massage and format it to fit those needs. Using sound in a Web page or in a CD-ROM–based multimedia project can result in two dramatically different formats to deliver what are in essence the same sounds. This planning phase should also incorporate an analysis of your audience's sound capabilities. This is far more relevant when publishing to the Web. Using a sound file format and/or codec that is not available to your users could compromise your entire project.

There are many software applications for editing and creating both digital audio and MIDI files on your desktop system. Most of these applications are available in demonstration or shareware format, allowing you to install and evaluate them before investing in them. It is worth taking some time to assess a good software application for your needs. Seek recommendations from people in the field you trust and read independent magazine reviews and product reviews before making a decision.

Before using sound files, make sure you have permission to use them. Seek out source audio and music that explicitly gives you permission to use it in the way you intend as part of the usage license you purchase. It may take a little longer up front to determine this, and it may cost a little more to purchase sound/music with such a license. This initial effort and cost will be invaluable to prevent your entire project being stopped by a court injunction brought by an angry producer.

Rely on your sense of hearing to determine the effectiveness of the sound file you're editing. If you don't trust your own ear, have someone else give his or her opinion. It is usually easy to determine whether a sound has passed the point of an unacceptable quality level, and you can then back up a step to return to the last acceptable setting. All sound editing applications have an Undo button for this very purpose.

As with an editing application, be sure to save often and keep backups of your work. There's almost nothing in life quite as demoralizing as losing hours, or even days, of work when your computer or editing application crashes.

Chapter Summary

- Digital sound files are a computer's representation of a sound and are stored in a digital format. To convert an analog sound that your ear can hear into a digital sound file that your computer can process requires special hardware called an analog-to-digital converter and appropriate sound editing software.

- Digital sound files fall into two basic types: digital recordings of an actual sound event, and digital musical instructions to the computer's sound synthesizer. These are analogous to a tape recording of a symphony (the recording captured the event when the musicians played) and the sheet music (instructions) the musicians read to play the music. MIDI files contain instructional data for the computer's synthesizer, while a digital sound recording faithfully reproduces the sound event as it occurred.

- When it comes to using audio on the Web, the sound data file used must be as small as possible for receiving over the Web. It usually has to be a streaming format so that users do not get bored waiting for the sound file to download before they can listen to it. Web-specific sound file types are used to cater to these special needs.

- A multimedia-ready personal computer usually comes complete with the basic hardware (and sometimes software) needed for a basic digital audio editing workstation. This hardware and software combination converts analog sound into digital file formats and then back to analog sound so that you can hear it.

- The required application of the resulting digital sound file determines your choice of sound file types. Thereafter, that file type can be compressed using an audio codec. The codec you use will be determined by the required file size and quality parameters for the application and whether the intended users of the application have the chosen codec on their system with which to hear the results of your hard work.

- When creating and manipulating digital sound files that you didn't originate yourself, you must address the copyright considerations. Be sure to determine your copyright situation for all media you use.

- Recording digital audio files and MIDI files can be a fairly straightforward task, given the right combination of hardware and software. Often the correct software is more of a determining factor in getting quality recordings.

Key Terms and Concepts

analog, 267
analog-to-digital (A-to-D) converter, 271

digital-to-analog (D-to-A) converter, 271
digitizing, 267

frequency response, 267
sampling rate, 267
sound resolution, 272

Checking Your Knowledge and Skills

1. Locate and run the standard sound recording utility that comes with your computer system. Put your favorite music CD into your computer's CD-ROM drive. If the utility to play your CD doesn't automatically pop up, locate and run that too. While playing your favorite track on the CD, click the Record button of the sound recording utility and record the CD audio to a digital sound file. When done, play back the sound file and hear how well it compares to the original. Then look at the sound file size and format. How much disk space would it take to record the entire CD?

2. Using a digital sound editing application, load a sound file or use the one you recorded in exercise 1, and note the sound quality parameters and file size. Using the tools provided in your sound editing application (you will have to find them unless you read ahead to the next chapter and use the applications described therein), see how much smaller you can get the sound file while maintaining an acceptable quality. You can do this by reducing the sampling rate and the bit depth and converting to mono before you begin to find the resulting quality unacceptable.

3. Locate a source of MIDI files (a simple Web search will result in a gazillion downloadable files) and find one you like that is longer than one minute in dura-

tion. Record a comparable digital audio file from an audio CD in your CD-ROM drive, and compare file sizes and quality of both sources of music. Which is better quality and which would be a better bet for use on a Web page?

4. Locate a demonstration or shareware MIDI sequencing application on the Web and download and install it. Spend a little time becoming familiar with this application and learn how to create your own MIDI composition. Create a MIDI soundtrack for a multimedia application.

5. Using a microphone connected to the microphone port of your computer system, take a tall empty drinking glass and dangle the microphone on the end of its cord in the glass. Record on your computer the sound of the microphone "tinking" against the sides of the glass. When you have several of these sounds in a sound file that you can edit, use a sound editing application to select one of these "tinks" and crop the file to just this one sound. Using tools and processes such as echo and reverb in your digital sound editing application, edit the sound until it will work for you as a button sound for your multimedia application. Save it as the smallest possible sound file.

Critical Thinking Challenges

Given the prevalence of digital audio in all aspects of multimedia, answer the following questions to the best of your ability:

1. Find a Web site that uses sound, perhaps as a background sound or as sound effects in an applet's interface. Use the Web page as the developer intended, and then use it again with your computer sound turned off. What difference, if any, does the sound make? Locate a Web page that is not really affected by the

loss of its sound, and then locate one whose usage is severely compromised by the loss of its sound. Why is this the case for each example Web site?

2. Review a selection of CD-ROM or DVD-ROM multimedia applications (at least four) and list the digital sound used in each case. Demonstration CD-ROMs from software manufacturers are very useful for such critiquing. Locate the audio files on each CD-ROM or DVD-ROM and try copying them to a folder on your hard drive. What format are they and how small has

the multimedia developer made them? If you cannot do this (because they could be embedded into the program itself and not accessible to you), see whether by running your computer's sound recording application you can record the sound as it is being played by the multimedia application.

3. Either in a computer software store or on the Web, find a source of stock digital audio that can be used in a multimedia application under the license acquired with the purchase. Look at other sound libraries and compare the apparent quality and quantity of those sound files. If there are any sound libraries that you would like to use that do not come with an unlimited-use license, then find out what the licensing terms are and what impact those terms would have on your multimedia project.

Hands-on Exercises
BUILDING A DIGITAL AUDIO PROJECT

Design a multimedia application that uses a narrated soundtrack. This could be a multimedia story, a description of a product, or a multimedia-based course on some topic. Write a script for the narrator that coincides with and refers to the project's storyboard.

Find a suitable narrator and use your computer to record this person reading the script you designed. Save the narration in small sound bites, each containing the narration for one section, or screen, of your application.

When done, review the combined duration of all of your narration sound bites and their file sizes. How will the recordings affect how you would plan the remainder of your project?

Create a prototype using an application such as Microsoft's PowerPoint, MetaTools's ScanSoft's Kai's Power Show, or any other multimedia authoring application you're familiar with. If you have no experience with any such presentation tool, then simply gather the sound bites together on a disk and present the narration to your audience while they read the storyboard.

Play back your narrated presentation (or just the narration) to an impartial audience and invite comments and critiques of the narration itself and how it fits into the presentation.

Master Project
DETERMINING SOUND CONTENT FOR YOUR MULTIMEDIA PORTFOLIO

So far you should have created a binder that documents your project concept and includes a project plan and timeline as well as your sketches and visuals for your design. You should also have begun the process of building your content and storing it on disk.

Using the storyboard and content collection from the previous chapter, determine your digital sound content for your multimedia digital portfolio. Use sound to bring but-tons and controls to life, narration to add additional information to the mix, music to set the mood, and soundtracks to enhance your video segments. Add sound references to your storyboard and get ready to create these planned sound components in the next chapter.

Save your work to a Zip disk (or equivalent) and keep it with your project binder.

13

HANDS-ON DIGITAL SOUND EDITING

Chapter Outline

Chapter Objectives

After completing this chapter, you will be able to:

- Navigate sound editing software applications such as Sound Forge

- Describe the process and parameters for recording digital sound on your desktop computer system

- Identify the processes and special effects used in editing digital sound data

- Choose the most appropriate sound file format and compression codec that best suit your eventual multimedia needs

- Discuss how sound data is implemented in the multimedia application and Web site development process and describe how to prepare for that task

Chapter Overview

Editing sound is a straightforward process once you learn the principles behind digital sound technology as detailed in Chapter 12. Thereafter, it becomes a question of what digital sound editing process or special effect to apply, and how to do so. Your own ear will be the best judge of the result.

In this chapter you will learn how to manipulate digital sound files using a superb sound editing application called Sound Forge. While this is a Windows-only product, the techniques used apply to all sound editing applications. They all represent the sound data as a sound wave image and allow you to apply special effects and editing processes to selected sections of the sound file.

Another feature-rich sound editing application is Goldwave. It is a shareware product, meaning that you can download it for free and begin using it immediately. If you feel the product is worth the price, then you buy it. Check out this book's Web site for a link to download this product.

For Macintosh users, the sound editing application of choice is Macromedia's SoundEdit 16. The techniques and processes you will learn here are also apply to SoundEdit 16. If you have any difficulties translating the techniques to SoundEdit 16, or cannot locate a specific process, technique, or special effect, simply refer to SoundEdit 16's online help file, which will quickly help you locate the feature you are looking for.

The hands-on creation and editing of MIDI files is not explicitly addressed in this chapter. To create, edit, and manipulate MIDI music is a science in itself, and one that greatly benefits from the digital composer having an established knowledge of music theory and composition. Many fine publications are available specifically on this topic, many of which are larger than this book! They are your best source of information if you want to get into digital music composition. In the meantime, your best bet is to invest in a few "clip media" CD-ROMs that provide MIDI music content for your multimedia application or Web site.

INTRODUCTION TO DIGITAL SOUND EDITING USING SONIC FOUNDRY'S SOUND FORGE

Figure 13.1 shows a screenshot of the Sound Forge interface. Spend a few minutes familiarizing yourself and playing with this product's controls and features. This will help you a lot later on.

Sound editing can be terrific fun. However, because you're often dependent on your own sense of hearing to determine the best outcome of your editing process, it can also be very frustrating. Sometimes there is no discernible difference between different sound effects or formats. In these cases you must use your best judgment and have patience and persistence.

In the remainder of this chapter you will learn how to perform the primary processes used to edit digital sound. Thereafter, you will depend on your hearing to tell you how many, or what parameters, of the processes to apply. Fortunately, products like Sound Forge allow you to preview the effects of the process you are adjusting as you make incremental changes.

Once something sounds good to you, click the OK button to commit to the edits and move on to the next task. Avoid the temptation to board the perpetual editing train. It's a nonstop track to project overruns and missed deadlines.

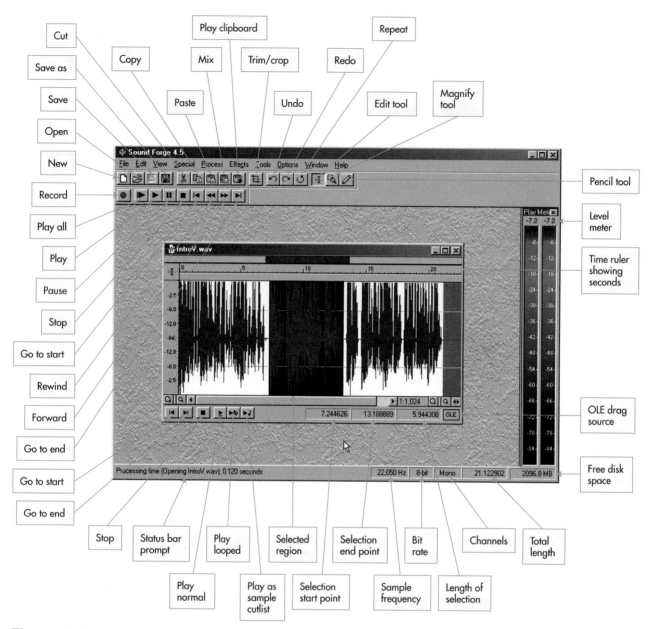

Figure 13.1
Sound Forge's interface and controls.

DIGITAL SOUND EDITING CONSIDERATIONS

mono sound

Monophonic sound, as opposed to *stereophonic sound,* plays all sound data in one channel. Stereo sound spreads the sound over two channels (one for the right speaker and one for the left speaker).

In Chapter 12 you learned about digital sound formats. You also learned that by reducing sound quality factors such as the sampling rate, the bit depth, and converting to mono (monophonic) sound, you can greatly decrease the required file size of the digital sound and enhance the multimedia application's performance. The degree of file size reduction and performance improvement you can tolerate depends on your hearing. You must decide when the audible quality of the sound is beginning to suffer and must be improved.

For the editing process you will want to start with the best-possible-quality sound file you can obtain. This will result in your editing a large sound file which would doubtless, without some weight reduction, compromise your multimedia application's performance. However, you can always apply the file size reduction techniques as the final step before implementing the sound into your multimedia product. For the editing process, you will need the best-quality file (that is, having the most data) from which to work.

For instance, when you apply a digital sound special effect, the more sound data in the file you're editing, the more data the special-effect process has to work with, and the better the resulting quality of the edit. If you start with poor, scratchy sound, you will get a poor, scratchy sound effect. As with digital video or digital images, always start with the best-quality raw materials and reduce for performance from there.

For example, if you were to start with an 11KHz, 8-bit mono sound file, and wanted to improve the audible quality to that of a 44KHz, CD-quality sound, it would be impossible. While you can promote the sound file format parameters to match those of a 44KHz, 16-bit stereo sound file, you will succeed in increasing the sound file size without improving the audible sound quality. What you hear is what you get, despite the file parameters.

Starting with the best-quality sound file you can obtain will ensure that at the very end of the editing process you can intentionally apply whatever file size and quality reductions you deem acceptable. You will not have to accept a sound file of an inferior fidelity unless that's what you intended.

RECORDING DIGITAL SOUND

Sound recording is an often-overlooked feature available on most multimedia-ready computer systems. All computer sound cards have a microphone input socket that allows you to plug in your microphone and record sound to a digital file using appropriate software. Should you choose to record your own audio, as opposed to using clip sounds, then you'll need to be aware of several considerations and tips.

As you learned in Chapter 12, there are three sources of digital sound wave files that you can record from on your computer:

1. *Microphone-in socket.* Connect an analog microphone to your computer system, click the Record button in your sound editing/recording application, and thereafter edit the recorded digital sound file as required.

2. *Line-in socket.* Connect an analog sound source from a personal stereo, such as a Discman, or from the line-out socket of your hi-fi system. Typically this requires a cable with the appropriate connector on each end to connect your computer to the audio device. Again, simply click the Record button in your sound editing/recording application, and thereafter edit the recorded digital sound file as required.

3. *CD-ROM drive.* An often-overlooked source of superb-quality sound for your multimedia application is your own CD-ROM drive. Most of you know that an audio CD can be played through your computer sound system. I'm listening to a Sarah McLachlan CD in this way as I type this book. However, few realize that if you click the Record button of your sound recording application, such as Sound Forge, you can record what you hear to a digital sound file. No cables, no fuss, and superb quality.

When recording sound on your computer system, make sure that your sound input device is correctly selected in your system's Sound Recording settings. In Windows, simply double-click the small yellow speaker icon in the bottom corner of your Windows 95, Windows 98, or Windows 2000 computer. Figure 13.2 shows the Windows sound recording control panel. Ensure that the device you are recording from is the one selected, otherwise you could lose considerable time checking volume levels, cables, and connectors trying to figure out why your sound recording software is recording silence.

Figure 13.2

The Windows 95/98 sound recording Properties panel.

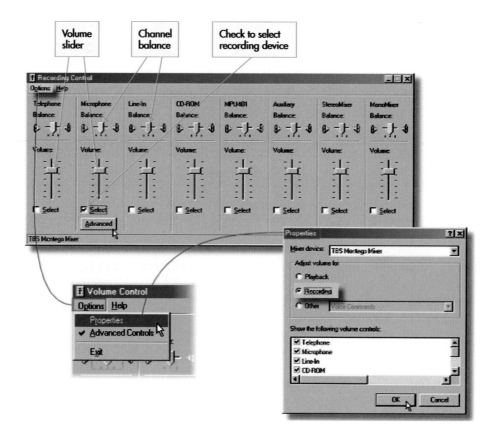

The process is quite simple. Follow the subsequent steps to record digital audio on your desktop computer system.

1. Ensure that the device you intend to record from is securely connected to the correct sound card socket as appropriate.

2. Check that the correct device is selected as the source of your sound in the sound recording control panel.

3. Make sure you can actually hear the sound you want to record coming through the computer's speakers. If you're using a microphone as the input device, don't place it too close to the speakers. This will produce a high-pitched squeal called feedback. In extreme cases, this squeal can damage your sound system and/or your ears.

4. Run your sound recording software and test sound recording levels. Some applications will allow you to adjust these levels within the application. More primitive applications, such as the Windows Sound Recorder, have no such controls, but you can make the same adjustments directly in the system's sound recording Properties panel.

5. Set your sound recording application to record at the best-possible-quality data parameters. Specify recording to a 44KHz, 16-bit file, and select stereo or mono as appropriate to the device being recorded from. In Sound Forge, for instance, when you click the Record button, and can see the Sound Recording panel, the New button provides you with a sound attributes panel with which to change these settings (see Figure 13.3).

6. Once you are happy with your settings, click the Record button and press the appropriate Play button on the sound device, or speak into the microphone as appropriate.

7. Click the Stop button when you have finished recording, and don't forget to save the file for later editing.

feedback

Audio amplification systems can produce a high-pitched squeal when the microphone is brought too close to the speakers. The microphone picks up sound that is played back on the speakers, which in turn is picked up by the microphone if too near, and further amplified, and further picked up in an amplification loop that results in a deafening squeal. Modern amplifiers have special circuitry to eliminate this phenomenon.

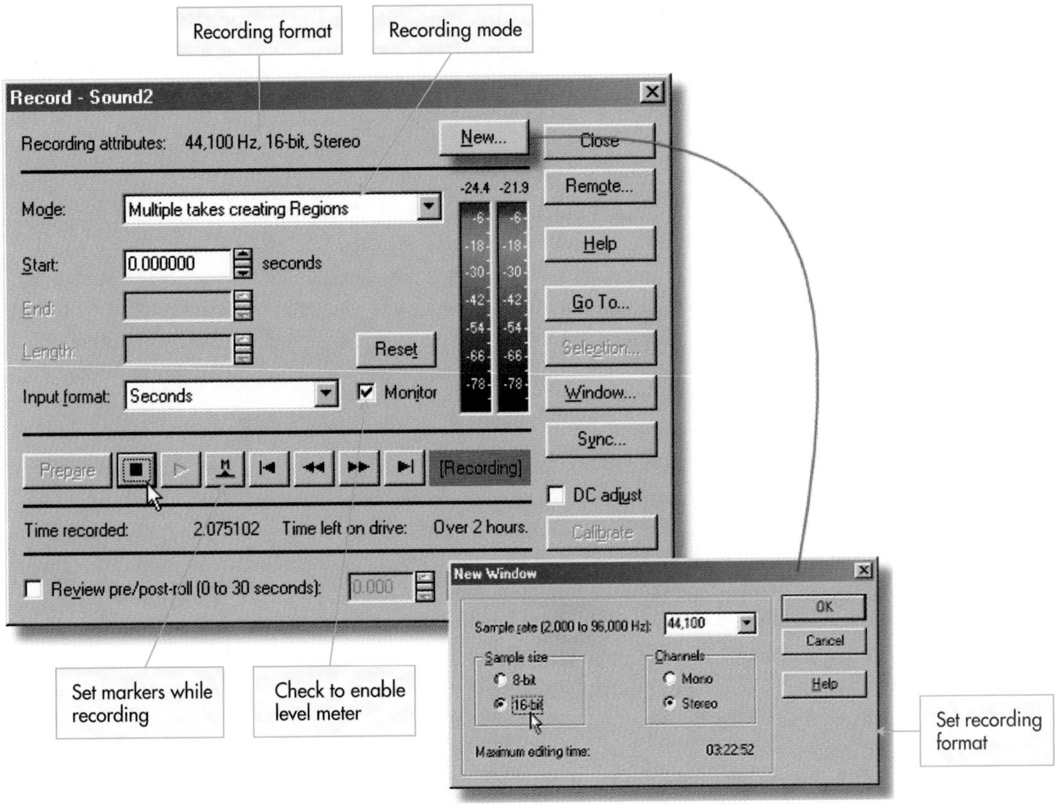

Figure 13.3 contains labeled callouts:

- Recording format
- Recording mode

Record - Sound2

Recording attributes: 44,100 Hz, 16-bit, Stereo   New...   Close

Mode: Multiple takes creating Regions   Remote...

-24.4 -21.9

Start: 0.000000   seconds   Help

End: Go To...

Length: Reset   Selection...

Input format: Seconds   ☑ Monitor   Window...

                                                     Sync...

Prepare ■ ▷ ♯ |◄ ◄◄ ►► ►| [Recording]

                                                     ☐ DC adjust

Time recorded: 2.075102   Time left on drive: Over 2 hours.   Calibrate

☐ Review pre/post-roll (0 to 30 seconds):   0.000

New Window

Sample rate (2,000 to 96,000 Hz): 44,100   OK

Sample size   Channels   Cancel

○ 8-bit   ○ Mono   Help
● 16-bit   ● Stereo

Maximum editing time: 03:22:52

Callouts:
- Set markers while recording
- Check to enable level meter
- Set recording format

Figure 13.3
The Sound Forge sound recording panel.

8. Play back the recorded file to ensure that you captured the intended sound in its entirety.

Figure 13.3 shows Sound Forge's sound recording controls as just described. The panel for setting the captured sound file quality parameters is invoked by clicking the New button as shown. Once the sound is recorded, Sound Forge displays the wave trace for the recorded audio, ready for you to play back and edit your recording.

EDITING DIGITAL SOUND

Selecting the precise section of the graphical waveform that you want to edit is the primary technique for mastering digital sound editing. You do this by simply clicking and dragging the mouse pointer over the required section of the waveform. Or you can click the beginning of the section required and, with the Shift key pressed, click the end of the required section. Figure 13.1 shows a section of the sound waveform selected in this manner.

1. Click your mouse pointer at the starting point of the sound waveform section you wish to select.
2. While holding down the Shift key on your keyboard, click the end of the sound waveform section you are selecting.
3. The sound waveform range selected should appear highlighted.

In products like Sound Forge, you can drag the ends of the selected section to increase or decrease the range of the selection. This is very beneficial when you need to finesse your selection to a specific point in the sound. By zooming in on the waveform and dragging the ends of the selection, you can exercise extreme precision in selecting the section of the sound file to edit, crop, process, or delete.

Once you've selected a section, you can apply your process or special effect to that section of the sound file. You can delete it from the rest of the file, or crop the entire file to the selected section. You can also copy and paste the selected section. In the absence of a selected section of the sound file, the special effect, process, or edit will be applied to the entire sound file.

The following sound editing processes can be applied to a selected section of your sound file. Whatever editing process you choose, remember that you can always use your application's Undo functions to reverse an unsatisfactory edit.

CROPPING

sound file cropping

A process in which the unselected sections of a sound wave are trimmed from the sound file, leaving only the selected section behind.

Instructing the sound editing application to remove the part of the sound waveform that is *not* selected is called sound file cropping. What remains of the sound file is only the section that was selected before applying this process. This technique is particularly handy when editing recorded sound, as most likely you will have leading and trailing sections on the sound file you will want to remove. Figure 13.4 shows "before" and "after" views of a cropped sound file.

In Sound Forge you will find the cropping process as a menu option on the Edit menu, or you can simply select the Trim/Crop button from the toolbar, as shown in Figure 13.4.

1. Select the section of the sound wave that you wish to remain after the cropping process.

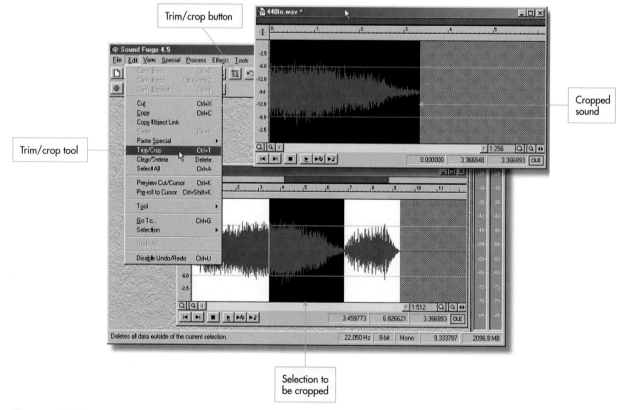

Figure 13.4
Before and after views of the cropping process.

2. Click the Trim/Crop button in your sound editing application.

3. Only the selected region of the sound wave will remain. The unselected ends will have been removed.

4. Click the Save button to record your changes to the sound file.

If the cropping is not to your satisfaction, you can always click the Undo button to restore the file to its original state.

CUTTING, COPYING, AND PASTING

To cut, copy, and paste sound file data, first select the section of the sound waveform you want to cut or copy. Then either select the Cut or Copy option from the Edit menu, use the Cut or Copy button on the toolbar (as shown in Figure 13.1), or use the standard keyboard shortcuts (Ctrl+C to copy, Ctrl+X to cut, and Ctrl+V to paste).

Once sound data has been cut or copied to the system clipboard, you can use one of the application's many pasting options to paste the sound clip. To fully appreciate their effects, you should take the time to practice with these techniques. In Sound Forge, the pasting options are as follows:

- *Paste*. This option pastes the copied or cut sound data at the position of the cursor as an insert. This process "pushes" the sound data represented in the waveform diagram out to the right to make room for the pasted data.

- *Paste Special>Crossfade*. This option pastes the copied or cut sound data over a section of another sound file and mixes the pasted data with the data it is being pasted over. This process has the effect of blending both the pasted data and the sound data it is pasted over while maintaining a uniform volume level.

- *Paste Special>Mix*. This option is similar to Crossfade, except that the resulting merge of the pasted and underlying sound data is an addition of their amplitudes. The net result is that the pasted file multiplies the volume of the underlying sound while mixing with it.

- *Paste Special>Overwrite*. As the name suggests, this menu option overwrites a selected section of a sound waveform. If no section of the destination sound file is selected, this menu option will be unavailable. Overwrite is a valuable function when you wish to replace silent sections of a sound file with additional sound, such as background noise.

- *Paste Special>Replicate*. This function replaces the selected section of the destination sound waveform with as many repeating copies of the pasted data as will fit. You will have the option of accepting the pasting of the partial section of the pasted data (that is, if the repeated pasted section doesn't fit exactly into the selected target area, the last repeat will be truncated to fit into the selection). Alternatively, you have the option of replacing to the nearest whole pasted clip (that is, if the repeated pasted section doesn't fit exactly into the selected target area, the selected section is expanded to accommodate the last repeated paste).

- *Paste Special>Paste to New*. You will probably use this pasting function more than the others. This option allows you to create a new sound file from the copied or cut sound data in the system clipboard. This means that you can select a section of an existing sound file, copy it, and create a new sound file from that selection. You can extract a new sound from an existing larger one. Just remember to save it when you're happy with the outcome.

Figure 13.5

Sound data processing options available in Sound Forge.

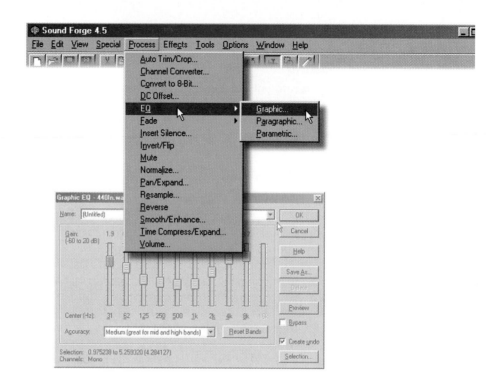

APPLYING PROCESSES

It is in applying processes and special effects where you will most value your sense of hearing. Your ears, rather than any set of dial-in numbers, will determine whether you have achieved the correct effect. Figure 13.5 shows a list of the processes available in Sound Forge, and also shows the control panel for the graphic equalizer process.

While a detailed description of each of these processes is beyond the scope of this book, a few processes are worth special mention. Of special note are those that are used to reduce your sound file's size to enhance your multimedia application's performance (as discussed in Chapter 12). For those not mentioned explicitly, a few minutes spent experimenting with the process and listening to the results will be the easiest and most beneficial way to learn the capabilities of your sound editing application. You can also rely on the sound editing application's own help file. By moving your mouse pointer over the process you are interested in and pressing the F1 key on your keyboard, you will invoke the application's help file topic on that item. Figure 13.6 shows the help file for the Resample process.

For most sound editing processes, Sound Forge provides preset settings for each process as a drop-down list at the top of the process control panel. Using these presets initially can help you apply the process effectively until you

graphic equalizer

Supplied on some hi-fi systems, a graphic equalizer provides individual level adjusters for sections of the sound frequency range. Each level can turn up or down the volume level of that part of the sound's dynamic range.

OOPS! NOW WHAT?

When you are applying processes to your digital sound file, it's important to remember that you can always click the Undo button if you do not like the results of the process or its settings. Sound Forge provides multiple-undo so that you can reverse changes made several steps back. Also, there is no substitute for trying out the process and then listening to the results. No amount of text can adequately describe the changes to a sound made by most processes (with, perhaps, the exception of the Mute process).

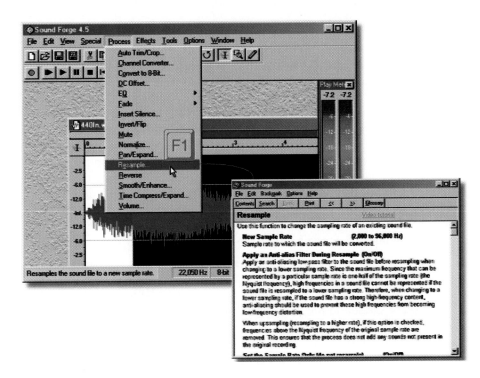

Figure 13.6
Pressing the F1 key while your mouse pointer is over a menu item invokes help on that topic.

become familiar enough with the process parameters to customize the settings yourself.

To apply any of the following processes, follow these steps:

1. Select the section of the sound waveform you wish to apply the process.

2. Click the process menu option of your choice in your sound editing application.

3. Only the selected region of the sound wave will be affected.

4. Click the Save button to record your changes to the sound file.

> Sound Forge provides you with a short description of the function your mouse pointer is over in the status bar at the bottom of the window. This is highlighted in pink in Figure 13.6. Keeping an eye on this prompt will help you choose the best processes and special effects.

- *Process>Channel Converter.* This process converts your stereo sound file to mono, and vice versa. Recall from Chapter 12 that simply converting a stereo sound file to mono is one of the processes that will effectively halve the sound file size and greatly enhance performance. This process also allows you to alter the volume levels of each stereo channel individually.

- *Process>Convert to 8-bit.* This process reduces your 16-bit sound file to an 8-bit sound file, effectively halving the sound file size. When reducing the bit depth of the sound file and reproducing the fidelity of a 16-bit sound in 8 bits, the conversion process must average out the bit data so that the 8-bit data matches the 16-bit data as best it can. To accomplish this, you can use truncation (arbitrarily chops off the 16-bit data that doesn't directly match 8-bit values), rounding (round down the 16-bit data to the nearest 8-bit value), or sound dithering (a smoothing process to even out the converted 8-bit sound and reduce conversion-introduced noise) methods to reduce the sound to 8 bits. The dithering process will usually result in the best quality. Increase the amount of dithering and preview the results using the Preview button until you achieve the desired effect.

- *Process>Fade.* While this process requires little explanation, it is still worth mentioning. You will doubtless use this fading process again and again to fade-in/fade-out the start and end sections of your sound file. The standard fade-in/fade-out provides a linear fade over the duration of the section of the sound file currently selected. The Graphic fade enables you to define the

truncation

If the amplitude of the sound file exceeds a certain level limit, the part of the sound above that level is chopped off and set to the limiting level.

rounding

Similar to truncating, if the amplitude of the sound file exceeds a certain level limit, the part of the sound above that level is averaged with the rest of the lower sound levels to keep it within the limiting level.

sound dithering

A rounding process that uses a random mixing of the parts of the sound file that exceeds a certain level limit to keep it within the limiting level (not to be confused with digital image dithering, as described in Chapter 4).

fade-in/fade-out curve so that you can control the degree and progression of the fade.

- *Process>Resample.* Sound resampling the sound file is how you reduce the sample frequency, and in doing so reduce the sound file size and enhance performance. Of course, you can expect to take a quality hit if you do this, and that is where your ears come in as a way to monitor quality and to indicate when you've reached the point beyond which the quality is no longer acceptable. The easiest and best way to apply a resample is to use the provided presets in the drop-down menu at the top of the Resample setting panel. Straying from these standards may cause compatibility difficulties later when you use the sound file in another application. Video editing applications are particularly prone to this, as some video codecs are fussy about the soundtrack format and will not accept a sampling frequency outside the standard ranges offered by the presets.

- *Process>Time Compress/Expand.* Often you will find that your soundtrack duration does not match the video, animation, or sequence of events in your multimedia application. The easiest way to remedy this is to change the duration of the sound file by using the Time Compress/Expand process. Be careful, though, as too much compression will turn speech into Munchkin voices and too much expansion will create a more sinister-sounding voice. Again, use your ears to judge. If the time expansion or compression is small, the distortion to the sound will not be significant enough to consider.

- *Process>Volume.* As its name suggests, this process lets you raise or lower the volume of your sound file to suit your needs. Use this process to explicitly set the volume levels of all sounds used in your multimedia application to the same volume level.

APPLYING SPECIAL EFFECTS

As with processes, you will most value your sense of hearing when you apply special effects. Your ears, rather than any set of dial-in numbers, will determine whether you have achieved the correct effect. Figure 13.7 shows a list of the

Figure 13.7
The sound special-effect options available in Sound Forge.

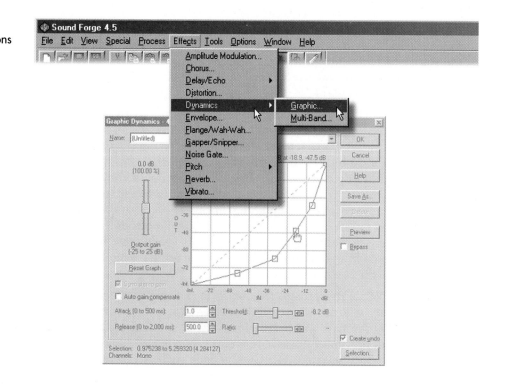

special effects available in Sound Forge and also shows the control panel for the Graphic Dynamics process.

The only real way to discover what each special effect does and to learn how it affects your sound file is to try it out. With very little time investment you can develop an invaluable understanding of and sense for these special effects.

The following tips will help you in this process:

- Use the Undo function to reverse the undesirable application of a special effect.
- Use the provided presets first, then experiment with your own settings. If you establish a good set of parameters for your project, save them as a preset for later use.
- Use the Preview button to hear the effect. When it is correct, lock it in by clicking the OK button. Remember to use Undo if you need to.
- You can layer special effects by applying them in succession. However, the order in which they're applied will affect the final outcome. Therefore, you have an infinite number of special-effect possibilities. Remember to experiment, as you can always Undo.

CREATING PLAYLISTS

Playlists are very useful when composing your own unique sound from a previously recorded sound clip. Playlists are especially useful for remastering music to suit your needs. Say a track on a CD had a wonderful instrumental intro and great instrumental segues between choruses. You may want to use the instrumental sections without the sections of the artist singing.

If you wanted to take your favorite artist's track and rebuild it to suit your multimedia or video application, you would have to copy and paste the sections you wanted into a new sound file. This is a very tedious and sometimes impossible task. To copy sections of the sound file so that they start and end on the precise beat and play back smoothly when reassembled end-to-end is extremely difficult and requires a lot of trial and error to get it right. Again, not only will your ears tell you when you get it right, but also your sense of hearing can notice a beat that is out by just a fraction of a second. It stands out like the proverbial sore thumb.

Playlists enable you to select and name sections of the original master track, and then place them in a list to be played in the new order—hence the name *playlist*. Once the sections are selected, named, and listed in the new order, the start and end points for each section can be changed and finessed to match the other sections in the list. In this way you can adjust the clips until the beat and the flow is seamless.

A *regions list* is similar to a playlist in that it shows a list of selected regions. It differs from the playlist in that the regions are shown in order of selection, while the playlist shows the regions in the new order of play that you have specified. Think of the regions list as your box of regions that you can reuse and reorder into your unique playlist. The regions are the pieces of the puzzle, while the playlist is the assembled puzzle.

When you are satisfied with the results, you can then save the file as a new sound file and incorporate all of your edits.

Figure 13.8 shows a regions list and playlist created from a recorded soundtrack and used to reorder the sequence of play. Note the small handles at the end of the selected region, which allow the ends to be tweaked to provide the precise start and end points for the clip.

To create your own unique playlist from a recorded soundtrack in Sound Forge, follow these simple steps:

playlist

A list of selected regions in a sound file that can be arranged, ordered, and repeated at will. A playlist allows the sound editor to create a new reordered version of a sound file and tweak it to get the desired results.

remastering

The task of building a new or improved version of a sound file from the original sound file data.

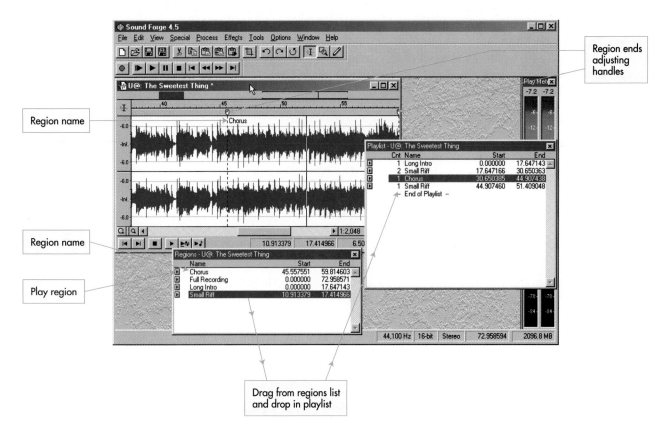

Figure 13.8
Creating a regions list with which to build a playlist.

1. Load the soundtrack you want to revise.

2. Choose Regions List and Playlist/Cutlist on the View menu to display the regions list and playlist windows, as shown in Figure 13.8.

3. Select a section of the soundtrack you want to use in your new version.

4. From the Special menu, choose Regions List and then Add. This adds the selected region to the regions list.

5. Repeat steps 3 and 4 until you have a master regions list of the sections of soundtrack you want to use.

6. Drag and drop the regions from the regions list to the playlist in the order that you want to play them. You can have as many copies of each region as you want, and you also can set the number of times each region repeats.

7. Click the small Play button to the left of any of the playlist entries and that region will begin to play. Play will continue without interruption or hesitation into the next item on the playlist. Most likely the clips you chose will not play end-to-end without a noticeable hiccup at the transition point between regions.

8. Move the end markers and test the change by playing the playlist until you achieve a seamless flow from clip to clip. You may have to do a lot of this "tweaking" before you are happy with the results. This part may seem tedious, but the reward of your own unique soundtrack at the end is well worth it. If you do this so often that you can no longer tell whether your changes are getting closer to or farther from the desired effect, take a break, make and enjoy your favorite beverage, come back with a fresh look, and try again.

SAVING YOUR FINAL WORK

While it is very important to continually save your work, there will come a point where your job is done and you need to save the final version of your sound file. At this point, you will need to determine the correct file format for your application. The file type and codec you employ should be determined by what format best suits your intended usage.

For CD-ROM-based multimedia applications, most standard sound file formats, such as WAV, AIFF, and QuickTime work well. The help file for your multimedia authoring application will tell you which formats are acceptable to your project. If you are creating a cross-platform CD-ROM product, then an audio format, such as AIFF, that can play on both Macintosh and Windows systems will be required. Again, your authoring tool will have specific requirements for you to follow in this regard.

For Web-based applications, the choice is more critical. Because of the narrow bandwidth of Internet communications, you must select a format that offers high compression and results in small files (and small packages of data to transmit) or choose a format specifically formulated for the Web.

APPLYING CODECS AND COMPRESSION

After deciding on the required file format, you will need to select a compression codec for that format. Most sound file editing applications provide extensive codec options at the point of saving your work.

In Chapter 12 you read details of the various file formats and codec options available and their implications. Based upon this information and the requirements of the next application in which you will be using the resulting sound file, you will use the file format and type options available in your sound editing application's Save As dialog box. Figure 13.9 shows just some of the file formats

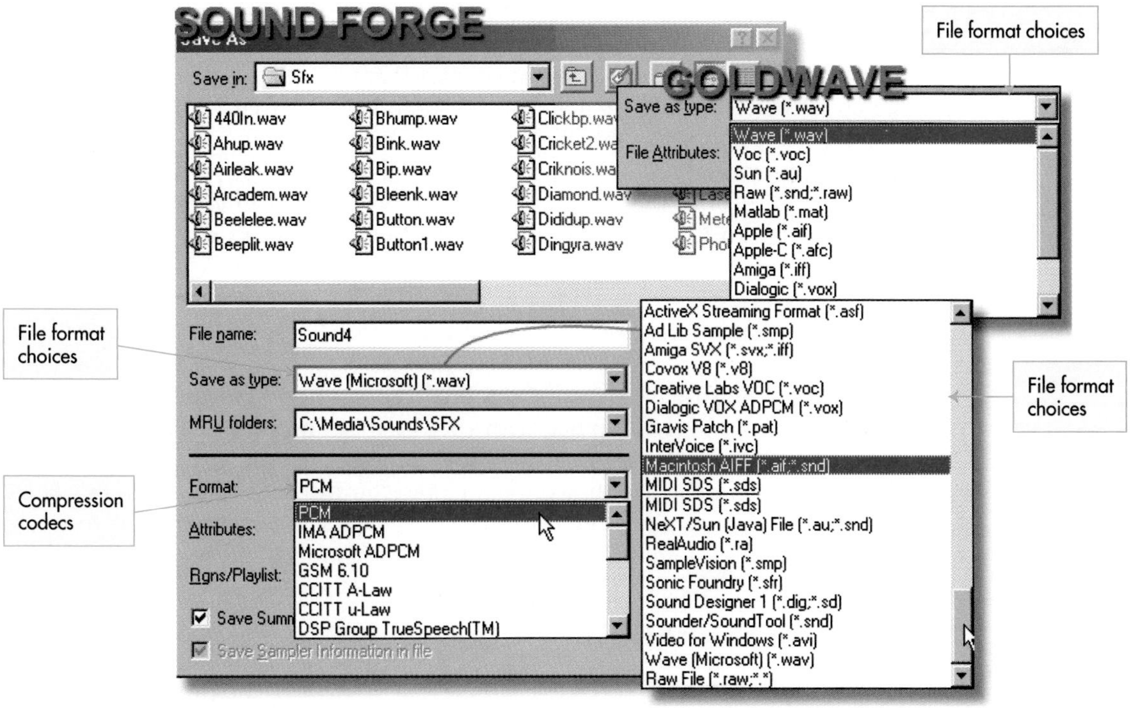

Figure 13.9
Typical file format choices for saving your sound data file.

and codecs supported by both Sound Forge and Goldwave in their sound Save As dialog boxes.

At this stage, make sure to consider the future in your project development cycle. Where the sound file will end up (does it need to play on different computer systems?) and how it will be used (does it need to stream over the Web?) will both determine, and be affected by, the file format choices you make now.

You can always save your sound editing work files, and if the format turns out to be incorrect, you can resave the file in the correct one. The main problem arises after you have passed the sound data through several applications on the way to the final destination, only to find that the format is incompatible with your project's requirements. A little planning and foresight can save you a lot of grief later on.

APPLYING YOUR EDITED SOUND FILE TO YOUR MULTIMEDIA APPLICATION

Later in this book, you will learn how to apply sound to your multimedia project. At this point a few general considerations should be noted when preparing your sound files for later integration into your multimedia project. Sound data can impose quite an overhead on any multimedia project, whether it be CD-ROM-, Web-, or video-based. Often, a perfectly good product can be crippled by the demands of large sound data files.

Most multimedia applications *internalize* sound. This means that they store the sound data in the application itself when you make the final stand-alone multimedia program. In doing so they can extract better performance (no need to locate and load an external file on disk) and better sound format consistency for the application. It is for this latter task that you need to take care when formatting sound files for integration into your multimedia project.

Most multimedia authoring and development tools reformat sound data internally to one consistent set of parameters. The highest-quality (and "fattest") sound file used in the product usually determines these parameters. Let's say you spent quite a lot of effort formatting all of your sound effects to 11KHz, 8-bit mono sound format to keep your sound overhead low and performance high. If you then added one important music clip that you felt needed 44KHz, 16-bit stereo for better quality, then all sound would be converted to match that file—the highest-quality format used. All that work massaging the sound files to squeeze out maximum performance is negated by one rogue fat sound file.

Keep an overall eye on the project as a whole. Use an application such as Sound Forge to format all sound files to the same set of acceptable quality standards.

If you intend to use clip sounds and/or music, be aware that you are accepting whatever internal file format is determined by the best-quality file in the project.

If you have to have that one top-quality file but don't want to drag down your application's performance with the other sound files being reformatted, then set that file as an external file (sometimes called an "external cast member"), and link to the disk-based file directly. You will learn how to do this later. Otherwise the only way around this issue, should you encounter it, is to reformat the offending sound file to match the other, more efficient sound files.

WEB CONSIDERATIONS

Thankfully, sounds embedded in a Web page are linked as external files, and each can have its own format as required without adversely affecting other sound files used in the Web page. However, in the case of multimedia-enhanced

Web pages, sound can cause tremendous performance problems, especially if your users are using a slow dial-up modem connection.

The sound file formats and codecs used for audio streaming and for use on the Web have been designed to enable the best possible performance from your Web site and should be used whenever possible.

Audio streaming further enhances your users' listening experience. Audio streaming enables them to hear, and benefit from, your sound content while it is downloading. Be aware that some streaming formats, such as RealAudio, require special server-based software to provide usable performance to your users, and such applications can be quite expensive. There are often serverless versions and free server applications for these formats, but usually the performance is not up to the caliber of the expensive full-blown version. Your users may also have to download and install a plug-in application for their browser before they can hear anything.

Another form of sound for the Web is embedded into an application used in a Web page. Typically, such *applets* are developed in much the same way as other multimedia applications. In some cases, especially for Macromedia products and for Multimedia Fusion, the same tool that creates CD-ROM-based multimedia applications can create Web-based multimedia applets for streaming over the Net. While this greatly simplifies the process (and learning curve) for creating Web-based multimedia, the old problem mentioned earlier of "normalizing" internal sound content applies.

In Chapter 16 you will learn more about how to create impressive Web-based multimedia.

AVOIDING PITFALLS

Remember to use the Undo function of your sound editing application as often as you need to. In this technology there can be a lot of trial and error involved before the final product is deemed satisfactory. In such circumstances the Undo function can be invaluable. Most good sound editing applications provide settings to determine how many steps back you can Undo and how much memory should be allocated to preserving this historical data. Make familiarizing yourself with these settings and features a top priority when first using any sound editing application. Doing so may save your neck and your project at the most opportune time.

Use the processes described in this chapter to reduce your sound file size to the point where your ears tell you that you have passed the point of acceptable quality. Always get to that point, and then take one step back to end up with good-quality sound with the best performance and smallest file size.

Be sure that you have permission to use someone else's sound data. Without explicit permission you may be violating the sound's copyright conditions. Similarly, when buying clip media, do not presume that the purchase conveys a right to use these sounds in your multimedia product. Look for the explicit wording that describes the permissions requirements. Often such permission is restricted to personal use, in which case that awesome new multimedia CD-ROM brochure you have almost finished for your best client is unlawful.

Chapter Summary

- Become familiar with your sound editing application's features and tools. This application will be used again and again to manipulate your sound data to produce the best-quality sound for your application at the lowest possible file size. This can require a lot of trial and error, especially when you rely on your hearing to judge the outcome. This is why familiarity with your application is essential.

- Recording sound files requires connecting the appropriate sound source device and setting the computer system's recording parameters to suit your configuration. Thereafter it can be as simple as clicking the sound editing application's Record button and saving the resulting digital sound file.

- To edit digital sound, select the section of the sound waveform to be edited, and then apply the edit, whether it be a cut, paste, crop, process, or special effect. By using the Preview button and your ears, decide when the edit settings are giving the best results and commit to the changes. There's always the Undo button.

- When selecting the appropriate format and compression with which to save your sound file, you have myriad choices. The final destination of the sound file will determine the most appropriate choices.

- When preparing your sound media components for your multimedia project, ensure that the sound file quality parameters are consistent across the board and uniform.

Key Terms and Concepts

feedback, 286
graphic equalizer, 290
mono sound, 284

playlist, 293
remastering, 293
sound dithering, 291

sound file cropping, 288
sound resampling, 292

rounding, 291
truncation, 291

Checking Your Knowledge and Skills

1. To create a button sound effect from scratch, connect a microphone to your computer system and run your sound editing application. Record the sound of a computer or typewriter keyboard in use. Select the sharpest of the "click" sounds in the waveform (multiple "clicks" will be evident) and crop the file to just that one sound (or copy it to a new sound file window). Using special effects such as reverb, echo, and vibrato, and using processes such as fade out, modify the sound until it's suitable for your multimedia application's button click effect. Save this file for later.

2. Using a digital sound editing application (if you do not already have one, download one from the Web), load the sound file called Narration.wav from the d:\media\sounds folder on this book's CD-ROM, where d: is the drive in which the CD-ROM is located. This is a professional narrator recorded to a 44KHz, 16-bit stereo sound file. Using the channel conversion, resampling, and bit conversion processes of your sound editing application, reduce the file to an 11KHz, 8-bit mono format. Compare the resulting file size of the reduced file, and then listen to both identi-

cal files in different formats. At which point would you have stopped the reduction process to preserve acceptable quality of the sound file?

3. Following the processes detailed in exercise 2, create from the original high-quality Narration.wav file three versions of an 11KHz, 8-bit mono file. All versions will have the same end specification, but change the sequence in which you apply the processes. Create the three files according to the process steps in the following table, and in the indicated order.

Process 1	Process 2	Process 3
Resample to 11KHz	Reduce to 8-bit depth	Convert channels to mono
Reduce to 8-bit depth	Convert channels to mono	Resample to 11KHz
Convert channels to mono	Resample to 11KHz	Reduce to 8-bit depth

Play back the three resulting sound files and compare them for audible quality. Are the file sizes different? If so, why? Do they sound different? If so, why?

4. Using your favorite artist's CD, select a track and record it to a digital audio file. Using a playlist, remaster the track to the point where it is a familiar piece, but a distinctly different song. Play it for several unsuspecting associates, and see how long it takes them to recognize the piece. Record their reaction to it.

5. Using a sound editing application such as Sound Forge, record yourself reading a section of text at 44KHz, 16-bit stereo (if you have a stereo microphone; otherwise mono will suffice). Save the file at full quality, and then save it again as RealAudio format. Finally, convert it to the smallest file possible and save it as a standard WAV/AIFF format. Use your browser to load the RealAudio file (use the Open menu option, located on the File menu), and compare the audio quality to the other two "standard" versions you saved. Rank them on a comparable-quality scale, and then assess how the resulting file size would influence your choice in file format.

Critical Thinking Challenges

Given the prevalence of digital audio in all aspects of multimedia, answer the following questions to the best of your ability:

1. Locate the technical specification for a multimedia development tool such as Macromedia's Director, Asymetrix's ToolBook, or ClickTeam's Multimedia Fusion. If you do not own such an application, perhaps your school computer lab, office, library, friend, or colleague will have a copy that you can look at. If not, check out the manufacturer's Web site for these details. Using the product manuals and/or online help file, determine the sound data specifications for this application and what sound data formats it accepts or requires. If you were developing a multimedia application for this product, how would this knowledge affect your sound editing tasks?

2. As in exercise 1, locate the technical specification for a multimedia development tool such as Macromedia's Director, Asymetrix's ToolBook, or IMSI's Multimedia Fusion. Determine how this product handles multimedia for Web deployment and whether it supports sound streaming. Does the product require users to install a special plug-in, and if so, how easily available and easy to install is it? How does this application handle Web sound, and does it provide you with any tools or capabilities that you would find beneficial for your Web site development projects?

3. A good source of multimedia application music is TV commercials. Some commercials, especially those for fast cars, have upbeat and energetic music that could be used to tremendous advantage in your next multimedia or video project (permissions granted, of course). Describe how you would record, digitize, edit, and remaster such a commercial soundtrack to suit your multimedia development needs.

Hands-on Exercises

BUILDING A DIGITAL SOUND LIBRARY

This exercise is best done with a colleague or fellow student. If this is not possible, you can also accomplish this task alone.

Find a small but good-quality audio recorder and carry it with you for a full 24-hour day, recording small sound bites of events and noises you encounter. The objective is to build a small library of sound effects from your everyday activities. Clink the recorder against your soda can when you're through with it (or before you're done for a different sound). Record elevator doors, car doors, traffic noise, animal noises, crowd hubbub, electronic noises, or a family member snoring. Most important, have fun with this project.

The next day (or as soon as is practical) swap sound recordings with your project partner. Independently connect your partner's recording to your computer system and record the fruits of his or her work. Using your sound editing tool, edit these sound bites into separate files and save them with appropriate file names to identify their sound. Try to give each sound bite a name that best describes the sound, as opposed to the action or object that caused the sound. For instance, *cracking thud* is more informative than *bowling ball*. Save these files into folders that classify them as different sound types, such as Animal Noises or Vehicles. If a sound file could be in more than one category, then place a copy in each folder.

When done, return the "collection" in digital form to your partner and retrieve your own from him or her. Listen to the files that your partner digitized for you, and see how your partner renamed and classified them.

Keep a copy of each of these libraries, as they will prove invaluable later in your multimedia development career.

Master Project
BUILDING YOUR PROJECT'S VOICE

So far you should have created a binder for the project that documents your project concept and includes a project plan and timeline and your sketches and visuals for your design. You should also have begun the process of building your content and storing it on disk.

Using the storyboard and content collection with sound content references from the previous chapter, create, record, and collect sound data to match the storyboard requirements. Now that you have a better idea of what's involved in manipulating sound data, would you like to change your storyboard sound specifications? Build a sound library for your Master Project and ensure that all sound files are correctly and uniformly formatted, with comparable volume levels and of suitable audible quality.

Save your work to a Zip disk (or equivalent) and keep it with your project binder.

six

MULTIMEDIA INTEGRATION, AUTHORING, AND APPLICATION DEVELOPMENT

14

MULTIMEDIA INTEGRATION AND AUTHORING

Chapter Outline

Chapter Objectives

After completing this chapter, you will be able to:

- Identify the characteristics of a multimedia authoring tool
- Describe the multimedia application and Web site development process
- Determine which multimedia application metaphor is best suited to meeting your project's goals
- Determine whether an authoring tool or computer programming is the best solution to your multimedia development needs
- Determine which type of multimedia authoring tool is best suited for your project
- Plan and manage your next multimedia project to ensure a successful and timely outcome within your budget

Chapter Overview

Imagine you're Dr. Frankenstein, in the lab on a stormy night. All your dedication and months of hard work building and gathering together parts and components will now come to life as one living, breathing entity we call a multimedia application. When done well, the finished multimedia application is always perceived as being greater than the sum of its parts.

There is a little paradox here that can often work against you, especially when you're dealing with a somewhat difficult client. When done well, a multimedia product is a smooth, seamless integration of many diverse media components. Each media component, whether a sound bite, a video clip, a paragraph of text, or an interface image, is but an individual musician. Each in its own right can create a wonderful melody, but when you bring them all together as an orchestra, they create a harmony that can take your breath away.

You are the conductor. It is your task to blend these diverse media types so that they all work well together, complement each other, and combine seamlessly. And therein lies the paradox. The more professional and the more refined your product, the less obvious is the work that went into its production.

Think of yourself as George Lucas, creating the next episode of *Star Wars*. The more mastery his production company, Industrial Light and Magic, has over the technologies it uses to create special effects, the more those effects seem a natural part of the movie. The line between realism and special effect is becoming indiscernible. As you hone your multimedia authoring skills, so too will your work become more refined and "smoother" to the eye.

This chapter introduces you to the concepts, tools, and techniques used to build that seamless multimedia application. You will learn about several different modes of authoring and how different applications use different methodologies to build multimedia presentations. In the next chapter, you will have an opportunity to use these tools, and see firsthand how well your media components work together.

media component

Each piece of media imported and used in a multimedia project, such as an image, a video clip, a sound bite, and so on, is considered a media component.

WHAT IS AUTHORING?

Authoring is the assembly and synchronization of all the media components that you have prepared for your final multimedia application. This is done in a software application called an authoring tool. Much as you would use a word-processing application to create a document, or a financial report, or a book on multimedia, you use an authoring tool to create a multimedia software application.

You could, of course, use a programming language to create your multimedia program; after all, the end result is a software application. But not only is the learning curve for any programming language very steep, the amount of work required to code every aspect and function of a multimedia product can be extensive and labor-intensive. Thankfully, some bright individual came up with an innovative solution and designed a program that allows multimedia developers to drag-and-drop their media components and content into a design structure. With little or no programming required, the program generates a new multimedia software application. Such software tools integrate the media components and allow you to focus on design and performance issues, and leave the rest of the under-the-hood stuff to the authoring tool. Figure 14.1 shows a

authoring tool

A computer application that allows the user to develop a software product, usually by dragging-and-dropping various media components, without the need to know, use, or understand a programming language.

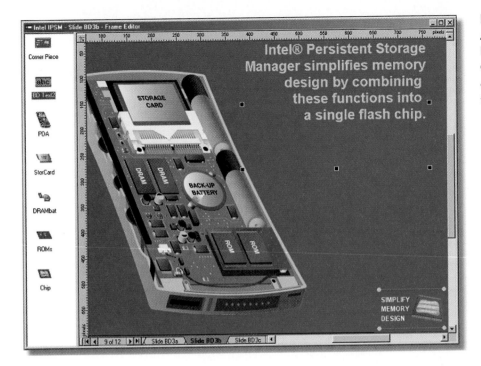

Figure 14.1
A frame from a Multimedia Fusion project for Intel Corporation shows the media components used in that frame of the presentation.

frame of a Multimedia Fusion project showing the media components used; they are the icons lined up in the Object Library panel to the left of the Frame Editor window.

For Web-based multimedia applications, the tools used are also referred to as authoring tools. Again, the program does the technical nuts-and-bolts code writing for you, allowing you to focus on the product's functionality and visual design. Web authoring tools allow those who know little or nothing about HTML programming to create sophisticated Web pages. Some multimedia authoring tools can produce a final product in either a disk-based program or a Web-based applet version. The ability to produce your work in either format is a powerful option that opens up an infinite number of possible applications you can create. You will learn more about these tools and their functions in Chapters 15 and 16.

Once you have designed your multimedia piece using the simple rules and procedures provided, the authoring tool will preview your program for you and compile a completely stand-alone software product for you on your command. For nonprogrammers, these authoring programs can be very powerful creative tools. For those with programming experience, these programs can be tweaked, pushed, and customized to obtain that extra special bit of performance or special effect that makes their work stand apart.

TARGET PLATFORM AND DELIVERY PLANNING

From the outset, it is very important to determine where your multimedia product is expected to perform and on what computer system. The following are just a few of the questions you need to answer at the initial design phase of your project, long before production begins.

- Will this be a CD-ROM–, DVD-ROM–, Web-, or intranet-based product, or perhaps a hybrid combination of some of these?
- Will it be a self-sufficient, "idiotproof" CD-ROM or a manually operated presentation?
- Will it be a stand alone information kiosk?

- Will it form the basis of a multimedia-enhanced Web site?

- How technically sophisticated is the intended audience?

- What is the least-sophisticated computer system that will be used to view this product, and what implications does that impose on its design? For example, do I need to accommodate 8-bit, 256-color display systems, or do I have the freedom to design for 24-bit, 16-million-color systems?

- Will my users need any special driver software or browser plug-ins to view my product? Do I have or can I obtain a license to distribute such drivers or plug-ins?

- Is it a PC-only application, or does it need to run on both Macintosh and Windows systems?

The purpose of target platform and delivery planning is to define the specification of the typical user's computer system, and how you are going to get your product to such users. Until this specification is determined, you will not know whether all the work you invest in your project will perform as intended for all users.

CREATING MULTIMEDIA FOR CD-ROM/DVD-ROM

A large part of the initial development process of any multimedia application, and especially the media content processing and collection phase, varies little from application to application. For instance, the graphic design techniques used to create an interface for a Web page or a CD-ROM–based multimedia application are the same. Both could use images with soft drop shadows, and the way this effect is created doesn't differ depending on the image's intended use. It's the format and the specification of the final output media piece that differs from application to application.

CD-ROMs and DVD-ROMs offer large storage capacity and relatively fast data access for your multimedia application. This means that incorporating large, full-screen video segments into your product is quite possible. Such "fat" media content can perform comfortably when delivered from a CD-ROM or DVD-ROM. However, distributing your multimedia application on such a device requires a lot more planning and preparation than is required for Web deployment, simply because there is no option to modify the product once it is produced.

To get a sense for the access speed of a CD-ROM or DVD-ROM drive, consider the "X-factor." For CD-ROM drives, each X represents a data transfer rate of 150 Kb/sec. Therefore a 40X CD-ROM drive has the capacity to deliver 40 times 150Kb/sec, or 6MB of data per second. For DVD-ROMs, each X approximately equals a 10X CD-ROM drive rate, or about 1.5MB/sec. This rate must be correlated to the data rate of your intended media components, especially that of digital video clips, to ensure that your media piece will work on your user's CD-ROM or DVD-ROM drive. If, for instance, you determine that your most basic user will have at least a 16X CD-ROM drive, then you must ensure that the most demanding data rate of any of your media components will not require more than 2.4 MB per second to play smoothly.

A CD-ROM-based application can better tolerate large image files, in terms of both screen size and file size. Better-quality audio and video files can be used. Often full-screen, full-frame-rate video can be incorporated into your multimedia application. So what's the downside?

Once the content is burned onto a CD-ROM, whether that content is good or bad, new or old, it is forever set in stone. This means that there is no reversing that production run of six thousand CD-ROMs if later you find a typo or a bug in your application. If your application is an electronic brochure and the supplier raises prices, then a rebuild and another production run is in order. The responsibility to create a "bulletproof" application and thoroughly test it is far greater than for Web-based multimedia development.

For cross-platform applications, the CD-ROM will have to incorporate Mac sectors and PC sectors on the same disk. While each format can share data space, the applications must be separate and be created separately for each "flavor" of computer. Catering to both platforms on one device can eat up valuable CD-ROM space. The authoring process for creating both Mac and Windows versions of your product is also complicated and severely restricts your choice of authoring tool to the few that can support cross-platform development.

At the end of the day, your CD-ROM project must be completely self-sufficient and the disk must be licensed. The disk also should include the drivers and applications your users will require to fully appreciate your product. To further complicate matters, once the shipment of six thousand disks arrives on your doorstep, there is the distribution to worry about. With any luck, this will be your client's headache, or perhaps the disks are intended for a trade show where they will distribute themselves!

With CD-ROM and DVD-ROM development you trade flexibility for performance.

DEVELOPING MULTIMEDIA APPLICATIONS FOR THE WEB

In contrast, multimedia development for Web deployment is far more forgiving if you don't get it exactly right the first time. If you spot a typo, you simply edit that Web page or multimedia applet, and repost it to the server. However, the very nature of the Web makes the online multimedia developer responsible for forcing every possible extra iota of added performance out of each and every image and media component.

Web multimedia development requires more front-end work massaging media components into their smallest acceptable state, and allows you more time to edit and test on the back end when publishing your creation on the Net.

Quite a few technologies are specifically designed to narrow the gap between disk-based and Web-based performance. With advances in data compression, data streaming, server capabilities, and digital communications technologies, connection speeds are improving while the technology can cope better with the slower speeds. Eventually they will converge to the point where communication speeds will match the delivery technology to match the level of performance enjoyed by CD-ROM and DVD-ROM.

Most Web page authoring tools analyze the overhead imparted by the combination of media components being used in the edited design. They can then warn you if your design exceeds the performance capabilities of a given system and connection speed. Here again the authoring tool provides you with the technical expertise to create these applications. Figure 14.2 shows how Macromedia Dreamweaver provides Web page developers with their design's current file size and download time required.

In Chapter 16 you will learn more about developing multimedia for Web deployment.

MULTIMEDIA AUTHORING VERSUS PROGRAMMING

You will often hear multimedia authoring products referred to in terms usually reserved for full-blown programming languages. While both authoring tools and programming languages can result in the creation of a multimedia software application, the primary difference between the two is the path taken to get to that point. As you have learned, authoring tools produce awesome software

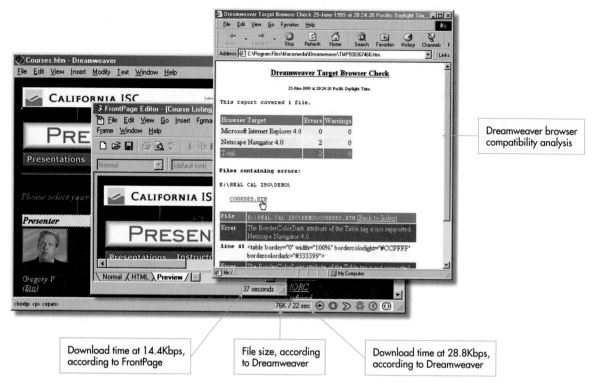

Figure 14.2
Products like Macromedia Dreamweaver and Microsoft FrontPage provide the developer with valuable information such as file size, download times, and browser compatibility.

object-oriented

A type of computer programming language in which self-contained sections of code can be treated as individual objects, and called whenever needed by the program. In this way, a software application can be created by assembling a suitable collection of these preprogrammed building blocks and making them perform the required tasks in unison throughout the program.

controls

In some programming languages, such as Visual Basic, the object-oriented programming components are referred to as controls.

MCI (Multimedia Control Interface) control

A programming language object used to control the multimedia functions of the operating system. In this way a program can instruct this control to play a movie, a sound, or a piece of MIDI music, for instance.

applications or Web pages without requiring you to know anything about programming. But what about creating multimedia applications using a programming language if you are (or want to become) a programmer?

As with any software product designed to make a task simpler, any authoring tool introduces constraints and compromises in what the multimedia developer can achieve. However, most multimedia developers will never reach those limitations and can work quite comfortably within the confines of their authoring tool of choice. Other developers usually resort to a programming language to achieve their goals—and in so doing, raise the bar on multimedia application design standards.

Practically any programming language can be used to create multimedia applications, but some do it better (and easier) than others. Most of the visual-type languages offer multimedia capabilities that harness the multimedia playing capabilities of the computer. Languages such as Visual Basic and Delphi excel at this. These programming languages take an object-oriented approach to software development that allows media controls (ready-made programming components) to be dropped into the application with ease.

For instance, Visual Basic provides an MCI (Multimedia Control Interface) control that can be configured to play many media file formats in your software application, such as WAV or MIDI sound, digital video, animation, and audio CDs (see Figure 14.3). Such controls allow the programmer to send a bunch of property values and parameters to this control when the program is running and have it respond accordingly. In this way the programmer doesn't have to invent the basic functionality of the MCI control from scratch, but instead customizes the basic operations of the control to perform the required tasks. Figure 14.3 shows the MCI control in operation, surrounded by the code window into which the programmer types the commands to control the MCI object and the

Properties control panel in which the properties affecting the operation of the MCI control are entered.

So what should you use to develop multimedia applications—an authoring tool or a programming language? There are pros and cons for both. Usually the development time required for a programming language is longer. However, applications developed directly with a programming language are usually smaller in file size and almost always perform better, because they are written specifically for the task at hand. Multimedia authoring tools carry a considerable standard operational overhead and produce (relatively) large executable files. Authoring tools simplify the development process and have a much shorter learning curve to overcome before proficient development can be achieved. However, programming languages offer no-compromise control over the nuts-and-bolts of the computer system. With a programming language you can instruct the computer system to perform almost any task you can think of. With an authoring tool, you get to choose a command to the computer system from a limited set. In this regard, authoring tools provide a subset of these features and abilities, but usually furnish more than enough multimedia-specific capabilities to do a good job.

If you're already a computer programmer and loathe giving up control over the details, then a programming language that is fine-tuned for multimedia development, such as Visual Basic, may be ideal for you. Such modern languages are well supported by sizable tool-developer industries that can provide a multitude of add-on capabilities and controls to make your development task all the easier. Some such developer toolkits can almost turn the programming language into an easy drag-and-drop authoring-like development environment.

If you're new to multimedia development, or neither know how nor want to program a computer, then an authoring tool is probably best for your needs. Quite a few multimedia development tools enable you to write programs within

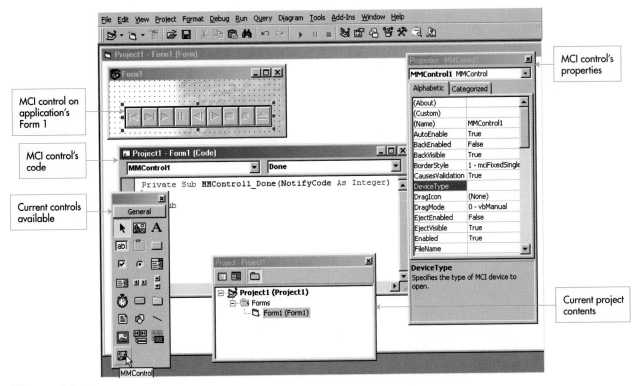

Figure 14.3
Microsoft's Visual Basic provides the programmer with a multitude of multimedia-ready controls.

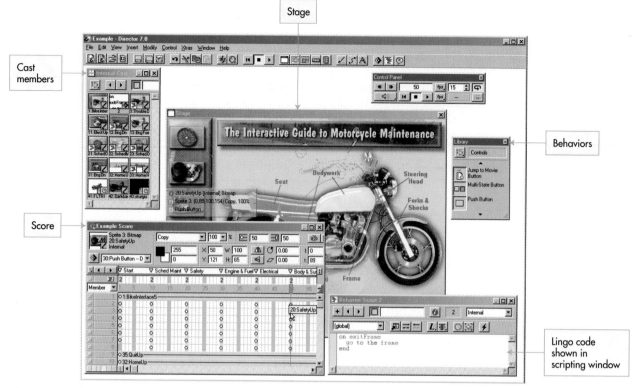

Figure 14.4
While Macromedia Director is a multimedia authoring tool, it also provides a programming language called Lingo, which gives the multimedia developer greater flexibility and control.

the application. Products such as Macromedia Director provide a programming language (also called a *scripting language*) that you can use to customize the actions and events of your multimedia program. Figure 14.4 shows the scripting window in Director, where the developer can enter code related to any element of the application he or she is developing. If you don't ever want to touch programming in your development tasks, then an authoring tool is most suitable for you.

The best multimedia developers can live comfortably in both worlds, using authoring tools to create visually spectacular applications, while resorting to programming to make up the distance between the authoring tool's limited abilities and their project's needs.

MULTIMEDIA CREATION CONSIDERATIONS AND DECISIONS

Probably the most important consideration for the creation of a professional and effective multimedia product is good planning. It is vital that you take the necessary time up front to scope out the project, define the nature and characteristics of the intended product, research the intended audience, and make sure you identify and set as a primary goal the product's intended outcome and effect on the user.

The following sections on application metaphors, development metaphors, and multimedia project planning will assist you in your planning. They will help you define your product, choose the best authoring tool for the job, and plan the development process.

APPLICATION METAPHORS

There are several "standard" types of multimedia product, whether the product is disk- or Web-based. Chances are high that your project will fall into one of these categories. Of course, you are free to forge your own way and develop new and unique formats. There are no laws preventing you from stretching your creative wings here. At some level, you will most likely find even a partial match to one of the following formats. Keep in mind, though, that hybrid formats combining the features of more than one of those listed here, such as an interactive slide show that has an automated play mode (making it a digital movie format), are also possible.

SLIDE SHOW

This is perhaps the most simple of all multimedia presentations. If you have ever used a computer-based slide presentation application, such as PowerPoint, then you will be familiar with this presentation. In this format, the user simply advances from screen to screen, forward or backward in sequence. This is a linear presentation, shown one screen at a time, much like a conventional 35mm slide show. Figure 14.5 shows a PowerPoint presentation as a linear series of slides.

These days, even the most conventional slide show applications have become very sophisticated. They offer quite a range of nonlinear interactivity options and multimedia features. PowerPoint now enables you to jump out of sequence to any slide in the set. You can also embed special effects and multimedia content in the presentation. This additional sophistication narrows the gap between slide show presentation applications and multimedia presentation authoring tools.

One such application that straddles this boundary is Kai's Power Show. This product provides video-quality transitions, text animations, and sound effects in a simple-to-use interface. Figure 14.6 shows a Power Show presentation in the making and gives a good impression of the unique interface that is now a hallmark of products from the Kai/MetaTools team. Aimed at PowerPoint users who want more pizzazz in their presentations, Power Show provides an option

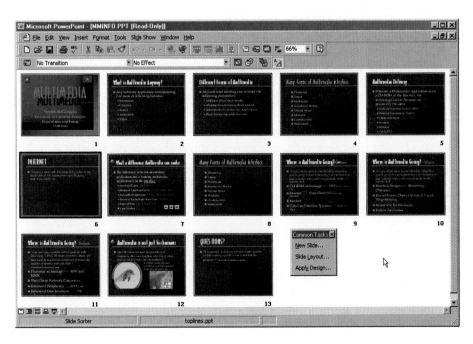

Figure 14.5
Microsoft PowerPoint, probably the standard application in this field, provides the presenter with a vast array of options with which to impress an audience.

Figure 14.6

Kai's Power Show provides a very sophisticated set of special effects with which to wow a crowd.

to import an existing PowerPoint presentation and convert it to Power Show format. With a suggested retail price of about $49, Power Show is a must-have tool for the multimedia developer. I recently created a $2,500 presentation for a client using Power Show, which provided a very comfortable return on my modest investment in this product.

Even products such as Macromedia Director now give you the option to import existing slide shows or create simple yet sophisticated presentations for business users. The intent here is to offer an easy upgrade path for PowerPoint users in the hope that they can be tempted to invest in the more elaborate product to take advantage of more advanced features.

If your product falls into this sequential screen-at-a-time category, then you are most likely looking at a slide show format design for your project. For an example of a slide show format using Kai's Power Show, check out the History folder on this book's CD-ROM. The readme file will provide you with instructions on how to install the Power Show player and view the presentation.

One thing to remember about these slide show creation tools is that almost all of them provide an option to package the presentation into a format that streams over the Internet, once viewers install the appropriate plug-in in their browser. This option can be very beneficial for travelling presenters. Someone back at the head office can update and upload the presentation to the company's Web server, and the presenter needs only an Internet connection to present the most up-to-date information to his or her audience. This Web-enabled presentation technology also offers an excellent way to provide attendees access to the presentation long after the event is over.

DIGITAL MOVIE

The digital movie motif is a noninteractive, passive multimedia experience for the user. It presents the content in a software application format that may as well be on videotape. Whether it's an actual digital movie that's playing, or a sequential multimedia application that works without user intervention, the format is the same. It's the digital commercial versus the digital brochure.

This format is commonly used as an introductory piece for an interactive multimedia product later on. A digital movie can be very effective in entertaining users and setting the big picture and mood for the information that follows. Often such a technique can set users in the right frame of mind to be more receptive to the core material, especially if that material is somewhat boring and dry.

Products such as Macromedia Director are particularly suited to this format, as they use a frames-over-time method of assembly and authoring. There will be more discussion on that in Chapter 15.

BRANCHING

A branching application provides users with a choice over where they would like to go in the presentation and what they would like to view. This format organizes the application's content in a hierarchical format, providing topic selections and more detailed subtopics. Figure 14.7 shows a schematic of the formats discussed to date so that you can compare their overall structures. In this illustration you can see how a branching application organizes its content into logical groups. In this format you can easily cross-reference information by providing links from one topic to related topics within your application. Typically the information is arranged in this flow-chart-like fashion, though there is no restriction on designers as to where they can have their users "jump" to in the program. However, to avoid confusing users too much, a simple, clearly defined structure is the best approach. It can be very easy to lose your users in an overly complicated navigation structure.

branching

A type of program processing in which at specific stages (screens) of the program, the option to jump to any one of several possible destination screens is determined by the user's interaction and input.

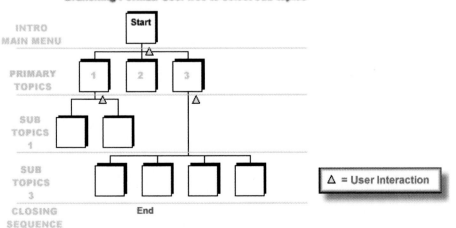

Figure 14.7

A schematic comparison of three common multimedia application and presentation format structures.

Key to a branching structure multimedia application is your ability to branch to whatever element of the application you want your users to go to. Therefore, it is vital to design this skeletal navigation "map" of the intended application at the beginning of the planning stage. A flow chart much like the one seen in Figure 14.7 can be an invaluable document with which to begin the planning of your project. It clearly defines for all involved the project's intended operation and its scope and size. Also, it clearly indicates where the media content will be required.

This is the most common structure used for Web sites. By providing a home page linked to primary topics, each with their own subtopics, you effectively create a branching structure not too different from the one shown in Figure 14.7.

A common set of controls, available at all times to aid navigation, is a requirement. These can be in the form of menu options or links back and forth within the application. Typically these controls enable users to move back up a level in the hierarchy, to return to the main menu, and/or to quit the application. Such navigation options are shown in Figure 14.8. This illustration depicts the various navigation options for a demonstration CD-ROM product I recently developed for a client. Once the video clip ends, or if users interrupt it, then the program reverts to the last-seen screen, from which users can jump to the previous screen or back to the main menu as they please. In this example, only the main menu screen offers an option to quit the application. In this application, users can select whatever content they want, when they want.

In such a hierarchical structured application it is important not to go too many layers deep, as you run the risk of losing your users. If you go beyond three layers to reach the actual content, then you will likely disorient your users and perhaps irritate them in the process. Keep it simple and elegant.

Multimedia development applications conducive to this form of application structure are Macromedia's Authorware, Clickteam's Multimedia Fusion, Asymetrix's ToolBook, and Allen Communications Quest. Each of these tools

Figure 14.8
This demonstration CD-ROM for Blaise Media shows conventional and typical controls provided for easy navigation throughout the large quantity of material presented.

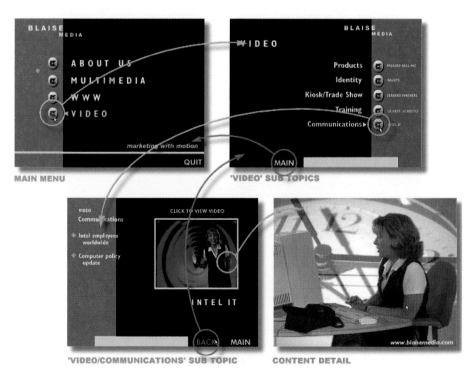

Figure 14.9

From the mTropolis demonstration CD-ROM, this electric motor assembly tutorial depends on an object manipulation format to achieve its goals.

provides a design format conducive to identifying specific screens and content modules and linking arbitrarily back and forth between them.

OBJECT MANIPULATION

While not as common as the aforementioned structural formats for multimedia applications, object manipulation formats are usually the domain of games, educational multimedia applications, and simulations. These products allow users to drag-and-drop elements of the program on screen. A jigsaw application that allows users to drag-and-drop jigsaw pieces into place to solve the puzzle is an example of such a design motif.

Figure 14.9 shows an example of such a multimedia application. This object manipulation design format allows users to learn the assembly process for an electric motor by dragging-and-dropping the motor components in place in the correct sequence.

Enabling users to manipulate onscreen elements in your application requires an object-oriented development tool capable of changing properties of the objects your users are manipulating and responding to user interactions. Multimedia authoring tools such as Director, Multimedia Fusion, Authorware, mTropolis, Quest, and ToolBook can all support such object-oriented designs, but some can do it better than others.

Programming languages excel in this arena and can often provide more flexibility and power to the developer than an authoring tool. That said, however, many excellent simulations developed with products like Authorware and Multimedia Fusion provide seamless and smooth user interaction. This is one of the areas in multimedia development where you don't need to be a programmer, but it can certainly help if you are and want to develop "out of the box."

SPATIAL ENVIRONMENTS

Spatial environments simulate the three dimensions of real-world environments with which we are familiar. By clicking or dragging the mouse in a picture of this

object manipulation format

A software application's interface that provides the user with the ability to freely drag-and-drop individual onscreen objects. This form of interface is called object manipulation. An interactive jigsaw application would be a good example of such an interface.

spatial environment

An interface in a software application represented by a virtual 3D environment, often visually representing a familiar place or a building. With a spatial-environment interface, users are empowered with intuition as to the intention and the outcome of their interaction with the software, as users expect the interface to respond as a real-world environment would, given the limitations of the software application.

Figure 14.10

Games like Trespasser provide free 3D virtual movement in realistic scenes and interaction (whether you like it or not) with ferocious virtual monsters.

3D engine

Used frequently in the gaming industry, a software 3D engine is used to render 3D objects and scenes in real time as the user interacts with and navigates through the application. Flight simulators are prime examples of this real-time rendering of a 3D onscreen environment.

simulated environment, you can navigate to another picture, giving the illusion of movement through this virtual world. The gaming industry has excelled in this arena, creating vivid 3D simulations of all sorts of fantasy worlds from Riven to Quake. Figure 14.10 shows a game called Trespasser in which you have to avoid and kill dinosaurs in the Lost World Jurassic Park to survive and get across to the other side of this 3D island.

Applications that use true 3D engines to provide free movement through their virtual environments (such as Quake) and their development are well beyond this book's scope. However, using a simulation of a 3D environment as a "container" for your multimedia application's content is well within our grasp. Such applications need not be overly complicated, and when done well with seamless transitions between scenes, they can be an impressive way to present your multimedia message.

The simplest and easiest-to-use 3D spatial environment interfaces are simply a slide show of images that are displayed according to user interaction. Figure 14.11 illustrates the concept of a virtual environment when presented as a series of interactive images. In Figure 14.11, each screen is shown as a freestanding panel positioned in relation to where the user, shown in the very center, perceives it to be. Look closely at the screenshots shown, and you will see that they are a series of images taken on a journey through this 3D environment.

Within a 3D spatial environment, clicking the cursor in the center shows the next slide in the "move forward" sequence. You can see this in the bottom left of the illustration. The user clicks on the door when the mouse pointer shows a "go forward" cursor. Successive clicks display a sequence of slides, each showing further progress in the direction indicated by the mouse pointer. Clicking in the right-hand sector of a scene displays an image of the right-hand view, as if the user actually turned in the direction that he or she clicked. Likewise, clicking left gives the illusion of rotating about 45 degrees to the left. The user has the viewpoint of the person standing at the center of the illustration. By clever design and the presentation of a sequence of "closer," "right," and "left" images in response to the user's clicks, an illusion of movement can be achieved.

Figure 14.11
By placing the user in front of a 3D image, and by displaying subsequent images in response to the user's clicking in the middle, right, or left of the image, the multimedia developer creates an illusion of a 3D environment.

There is a practical use for spatial environments. As humans we can store and retrieve objects and information (on paper) quite effectively in our 3D world. We can also make good sense of this world, as our brains are wired for that purpose. By simulating a 3D environment to store large amounts of information, you can make the process of disseminating that information, and the user's task in comprehending and remembering that information, much easier.

Compare a museum to an encyclopedia. You can retain a lot more knowledge and enjoy the process a lot more at a museum or exploratorium than you can from reading the equivalent amount of information in a printed book. Similarly, if you provide a 3D environment to "house" the choices and informational content for your users, they will have an easier and more enjoyable time comprehending it and will retain it for longer.

In such a 3D virtual environment, when your users navigate to a position similar to that shown by the figure standing at the center of the virtual conference center in Figure 14.11, they are viewing onscreen the image shown inset in the bottom right. Notice how this depiction of five conference rooms, each offering a multimedia presentation on the subject posted above the door, is really a straightforward menu option. Users can select from five menu choices, just as they do in the more conventional format shown in Figure 14.8.

The interface becomes an optical illusion. The software mechanism for offering a menu option and responding to the user's choice is the same in both cases, but the 3D spatial environment wins hands down for engaging ease of use and ability to present large quantities of information to users comfortably without their getting lost.

DEVELOPMENT METAPHORS

You have just read about the commonly used metaphors and structures for multimedia applications. The authoring tools you will use in this development process have their own metaphors, which make them more or less suitable for your project as the case may be.

LINEAR APPLICATIONS

In the same way that slide shows are linear in presentation, so too are the majority of the tools designed to create them. Products such as PowerPoint and Power Show, which are specifically designed to create linear presentations with token accommodations for nonlinear jumping and branching, use a linear design motif.

Linear applications, including DemoIt! and DemoShield, provide a development format that creates a series of screens that will be seen in sequence unless the developer specifies otherwise. This assembly method can be seen in Figures 14.5 and 14.6. Such applications can provide multimedia content and often sophisticated special effects and transitions, but their capabilities are quite limited compared to a full-blown multimedia authoring tool.

However, for a quick-turnaround multimedia presentation, these applications are hard to beat. Often the complexity of the other tools available can get in the way if the project itself calls for simplicity.

TIMELINE/MOVIE METAPHOR

Some multimedia authoring tools use a design motif analogous to creating a movie. The multimedia developer designs each frame of the movie that will play back at a set number of frames per second (typically 15 fps). Once started, the basic presentation will play through to the end at a set frame rate, unless instructed to do otherwise. This is the methodology of Macromedia Director, more of which you will see in the next chapter.

This concept of creating a movie carries through in the terminology used for the various components and features throughout Director (even the product's name is a movie-making designation). The media components you collect for assembly are called *Cast Members*. They are arranged in the *Score* and displayed on the *Stage*.

Director provides a programming language called Lingo that gives the developer an opportunity to directly instruct the multimedia application to break out of Director's linear tendency. Director also provides behaviors that can be applied to elements in the project to make them interactive. These behaviors are really prepared, canned Lingo segments, but they can certainly help the novice extract better interaction from the project without the steep learning curve required to master Lingo. In Figure 14.4 you saw illustrated the movie design motif used by Director. In the next chapter you will have ample opportunity to experience this method of multimedia creation firsthand.

OBJECT-ORIENTED TOOLS

As mentioned earlier, there is a collection of very powerful multimedia development tools that are object-oriented. These tools address each component you include in your application as a separate programming object. Each object has its own collection of properties that you can change and inquire about and actions that the object can perform and respond to that you can also address in your program. Changing the object's properties to suit your needs, telling it what to do in response to a specific event, and having it perform actions in your application uses a set of development tools that provide a powerful way to precisely develop impressive multimedia applications.

For example, an image of a ball could be imported into such an authoring tool and given the name *Ball*. It is now an image object called Ball. The Ball object can then be given the movement property of bouncing. Reaching the perimeter of the screen is an event to which the Ball object is told to react. The Ball object can react to this event with a change-in-direction-bounce action.

behaviors

In a multimedia authoring context, behaviors are a set of actions or code that is given to an object to determine how it will respond to user interaction and programmatic events. These behaviors are often supplied with the authoring tool as a library of reusable instruction sets that can be applied to specific objects. For example, a button graphic can be given a button behavior that changes what was a lifeless flat button graphic into a responsive, interactive functional control on the interface.

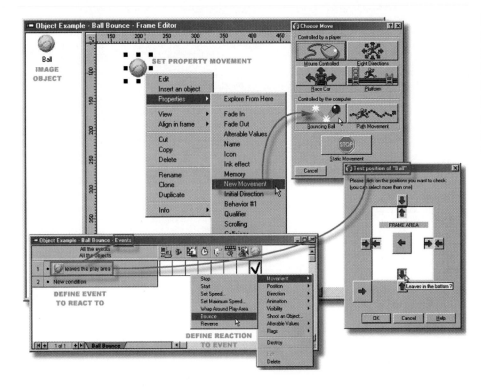

Figure 14.12

By setting movement properties for the Ball image object, defining an event that you want the Ball to react to, and then defining that reaction when the event occurs, you can quickly and simply create a bouncing-ball object as shown.

Once the program is run and the ball is given initial direction and speed, the ball will appear to bounce around the screen until the program is stopped. Figure 14.12 shows the process of creating a bouncing-ball application in Multimedia Fusion by assigning properties and actions to suit. You can view this example application on the CD-ROM that accompanies this book. You will find the Ball.exe application in the Examples folder. Note the small file size of this application.

Two programs that use an object-oriented methodology are Multimedia Fusion and mTropolis. In addition, Multimedia Fusion uses a storyboard motif for the organization of its frames in a multimedia application. You will learn more about Multimedia Fusion later in this book.

ICONIC AUTHORING

Some multimedia authoring tools use a series of icons to represent various elements and features of the application. The position of each icon on a flow-chart-like diagram indicates their position and function in the application. Among these types of applications are Macromedia's Authorware, M-factory's mTropolis, and Allen Communications Quest. Figure 14.13 shows how Authorware uses a flow-chart motif to arrange various application elements and functions represented by icons on the flow line.

Iconic authoring tools enable the developer to see the big picture when authoring and to make large-scale changes in links and direction at will. Such applications are usually good at organizing and presenting very large amounts of data and content, and their flow-charting methodology assists the developer in keeping track of where all the content is and how it is displayed.

This way of building an application also allows the developer to focus on one discrete element of the application, as represented by that icon, at a time, knowing that it will all hang together in the end. It is therefore a good way to organize your development efforts and to trace the logical flow of the application's operation.

iconic authoring

The method of authoring in which the navigation and interaction processing of the multimedia application can be controlled by assembling a series of icons along a processing path. Each icon represents a different function or capability of the program, and by assigning these functions specific properties, and by specifying their order and circumstance of appearance, the developer can create a complex multimedia application.

Figure 14.13

Macromedia Authorware uses an iconic authoring method allowing the developer to drag icons that represent features of the application to the timeline.

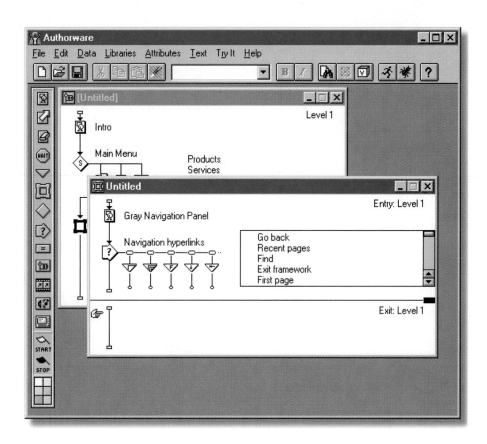

MULTIMEDIA PROJECT PLANNING

Multimedia project planning, in general, conforms to the same guidelines and regulations applied to any software project planning exercise, but with a complexity factor of 10 thrown in. To manage a multimedia project, you have to manage not only a software development project, but also several parallel media creation projects as well. Before serious authoring or programming (as the case may be) can begin, the content has to start lining up and being delivered to the developer. Graphic design must be ready, sound recordings must have been done and the resulting sound files edited, animation must be completed and post-processed, and video must be digitized and massaged into the correct format for the project. Can you see the need for tight planning of such a project to ensure a successful outcome by the deadline?

The strong temptation with development is to jump into the deep end and start developing. The allure of the satisfaction that comes from being creative often overrides all reason and patience. With a little foresight and planning, you can save yourself lots of time, resources, and grief later on in the project. When working with a team, or with a client who insists on being kept close to the development process, such planning is absolutely essential. Without a plan there is no hope of keeping everyone on the same page, much less focused on the same goal.

Here is a simple checklist to apply to your next multimedia project:

✓ Define, in writing, the scope and purpose of the project and have it signed off on by all involved.

✓ Define, in writing, the intended users and their technical capabilities. This will determine your project performance baseline and platform issues.

✓ Determine the project due date. From that date, work backward to set project milestones throughout the intervening project timetable. Allow for manufacturing/production time; thorough testing of the final product; final editing; client review; and content, media, and script approval. Once an agreeable timetable is derived from the subdivision of the available time, have all parties sign off on it.

 Assign initial project preparation tasks. Assign the storyboard creation, the media inventory management, and the creative direction.

 Have all parties sign off on the storyboard and assign development tasks.

✔ Develop, review, and revise according to the project plan and storyboard, and ensure that review milestones are kept on time.

✔ Ensure that the CD-ROM/DVD-ROM manufacturer, or the ISP, or whatever external company you are depending on to launch the new product is in line with your timetable and is paid, and that all documents and forms are signed and in place.

✔ Should there be any technical issues such as drivers required, plug-ins required, or platform-specific formats, assign an individual early on to define these issues and secure the appropriate installation file sets and the appropriate licenses required to use them.

Remember the story about the three blind men who encounter an elephant? One finds the elephant's leg and declares he has found a tree, another finds the trunk and declares it to be a snake, and so on. Without a plan with which to articulate and share the project's big picture, each team member will derive his or her own concept, which will be very difficult to shake later when it is discovered that everyone is working toward a different goal.

The following topics will assist you in developing that plan and using it to manage your multimedia development project.

EFFECTIVE MULTIMEDIA PRODUCT STORYBOARDING

Probably the most valuable project management tool that a multimedia developer can use is the storyboard, which you learned about in Chapter 3. Here are some pointers and specifics for you to use in your own multimedia project planning.

While storyboards can be developed with simple pencil and paper, the advantages of using a software application to develop and share the storyboard around a team are enormous. First, you can attach a digital file to an e-mail message and instantly update the team with a revised storyboard (and there will always be a revised version). Second, editing the storyboard becomes a snap (as opposed to redrawing the paper version).

A good product for developing a storyboard is Microsoft's PowerPoint. It offers a screen-by-screen format that can incorporate pictures and some drawing, and it can be easily edited and distributed. Figure 14.14 shows such a storyboard from an actual project I worked on recently. With the illustrations imported from the graphic artist, and text describing the sequence of operation and the required animation and effects, this format provides a good, easy-to-follow map of the planned project.

Some multimedia authoring applications, such as Multimedia Fusion, use a storyboard motif for organizing their content and visualizing the project's flow and sequence of operation. Figure 14.15 shows Multimedia Fusion's storyboard representation of the project resulting from the PowerPoint storyboard of Figure 14.14. You get to see the "before" and "after" versions. In this case the thumbnail image shown for each frame represents the opening appearance of that screen. To the left of the project storyboard is a hierarchical list of all the frames in the storyboard. Here all of the multimedia and animation content and

Figure 14.14
PowerPoint is a very effective product for creating project storyboards.

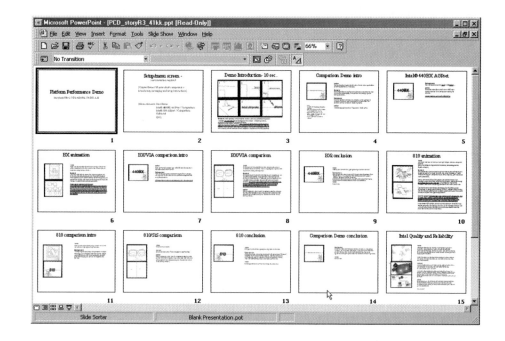

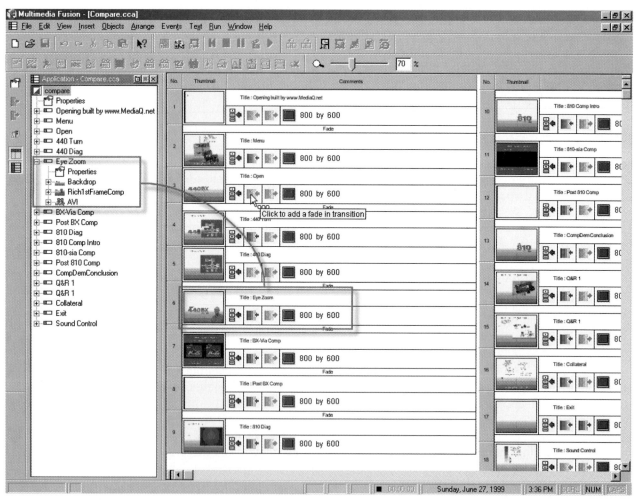

Figure 14.15
Multimedia authoring applications such as Multimedia Fusion use a storyboard format to organize and visualize the project.

each frame used in the project can be listed as shown. The frame labeled "Eye Zoom" is expanded in the list to show its subcomponents.

Whatever tool you use, make sure that you develop a storyboard for your project and use that storyboard to gain the buy-in of all those working with you on the project, including the client. Once you get approval for a storyboard and then develop to that road map, you will not run into "feature creep," where the client or other team members disregard the project's deadline and budget and start to add additional features and scope to the project. All those who sign off on a storyboard have committed to a format and a plan, and you are now free to bring that plan to life.

PLANNING MULTIMEDIA APPLICATIONS FOR THE WEB

The issues associated with project planning and storyboarding apply to Web-based multimedia projects the same as for disk-based ones. However, the Web developer faces some additional issues, primarily in the realm of collecting all of the collateral media components and external files; making sure that they are the latest and correct version; and ensuring that all links to files and pages, both local and on the Net (using URLs), are valid and active.

Some excellent applications can assist you with these project management issues. Microsoft's FrontPage is one such application that takes a sitewide view of the Web site development process. FrontPage automatically organizes your files for you, checks for correct links, monitors versions and final edits, provides a to-do list in its task manager, and flow-charts the whole process for you. FrontPage provides smooth automation of the development process without restricting more technical users from getting under the hood and tweaking their Web pages for best results. Figure 14.16 shows such a project flow-chart in FrontPage; you will learn more about FrontPage in Chapter 16.

If your Web page authoring tool does not have such features, then it's your responsibility to ensure that all the many pieces that have to come together to form a Web page in your users' browsers are current and where they are supposed to be.

MEDIA COLLECTION

Media collection refers to your ability to organize your project's media components and the files that are used to create those components. When you're developing a multimedia application, it is easy to lose track of all the different-format images, sounds, digital video clips, animations, and applications that you are building for assembly into the final product. You may go through several versions of any component until you have the right one for the job, and all those previous versions will most likely be kept until the project is completed to ensure that you can go back and edit an element again if needed.

Some excellent media management tools are available that will catalog and locate your media files for you during the development process. Go to a Web site that provides downloads of shareware applications (www.shareware.com, for example) and you will find many such applications. However, these programs will not replace simple and effective organization of your media components in their own grouped folders. Figure 14.17 shows some of my project folder structures. As you can see, I try to organize my files by type and differentiate between source files and active working files. Such a simple organizational method for keeping your files together will save you lots of time and grief when you try to locate your files for your project (which tend to be missing at the most inopportune times).

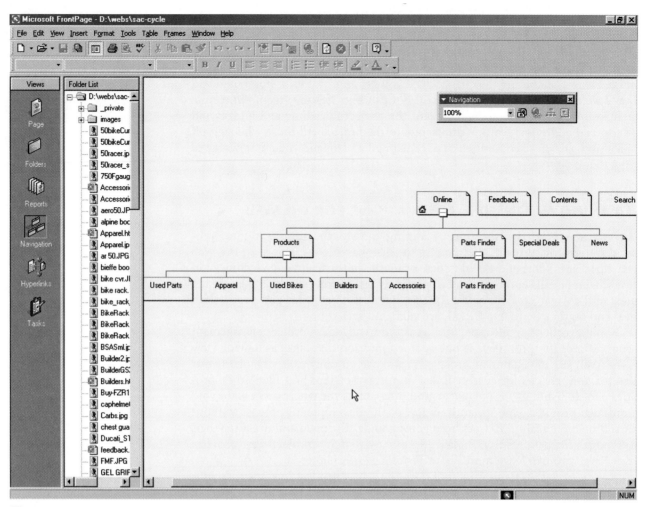

Figure 14.16
Microsoft's FrontPage provides integrated project management for smooth Web site development (a project for www.sac-cycle.com is shown).

When the time comes to package up the final production to run off a CD-ROM or from the Web, or to be installed on the user's hard drive, you will be grateful for such a folder structure. You should be able to easily locate all the components you need to publish, and if they're organized correctly, ensure that only the correct and final versions get shipped.

Once the dust has settled and your very happy client has paid all your invoices and you need to free disk space for additional work, then you will be grateful once again for this file folder structure. Once the files from that project are archived to CD-ROM, Zip disk, tape, or whatever method you use, you will most likely need to access them in the future. Perhaps you want to reuse a button set, or you need a copy of your own logo for the credits. Maybe the client wants an updated version. Either way, being able to zero in easily on the file you need because it is stored in a logical folder will save you time and frustration.

AVOIDING PITFALLS

It cannot be overstated that good up-front planning will save you time, money, and grief. Take the time early on to avoid the problems associated with poor or nonexistent planning.

Name	Size	Type	Modified
Banner.psp	59KB	Paint Sho...	6/3/99 11:49 PM
Banner2.bmp	110KB	Paint Sho...	6/3/99 11:43 PM
Banner2a.bmp	100KB	Paint Sho...	6/4/99 7:21 AM
BlueBlok.bmp	98KB	Paint Sho...	5/31/99 8:36 PM
ChipDiag.bmp	204KB	Paint Sho...	6/1/99 9:26 AM
Corner Piece.bmp	42KB	Paint Sho...	5/31/99 9:50 PM
DRAMbat.bmp	64KB	Paint Sho...	6/3/99 7:36 PM
Flash Chip.bmp	13KB	Paint Sho...	6/3/99 11:34 PM
Flash ChipGlow.bmp	13KB	Paint Sho...	6/3/99 11:36 PM
FullChip.bmp	237KB	Paint Sho...	6/4/99 12:02 AM
GreenBlok.bmp	53KB	Paint Sho...	5/31/99 8:36 PM
Help.psp	139KB	Paint Sho...	6/4/99 9:44 PM
HelpPanel.bmp	502KB	Paint Sho...	6/4/99 8:16 AM
HelpPanel2.bmp	544KB	Paint Sho...	6/4/99 9:34 PM
PDA.bmp	718KB	Paint Sho...	6/1/99 11:57 AM
PDA2.bmp	459KB	Paint Sho...	6/3/99 11:31 PM
PDA2no chip.bmp	459KB	Paint Sho...	6/3/99 11:34 PM
PDAhl1.bmp	718KB	Paint Sho...	6/1/99 12:01 PM
PDAhl2.bmp	718KB	Paint Sho...	6/1/99 12:02 PM
PDAhl3.bmp	718KB	Paint Sho...	6/1/99 12:03 PM
pspbrwse.jbf	126KB	PSP 5 Bro...	6/5/99 10:02 AM
RedBlok.bmp	53KB	Paint Sho...	5/31/99 8:36 PM
ROMs.bmp	44KB	Paint Sho...	6/3/99 7:35 PM
Ruler.bmp	258KB	Paint Sho...	6/4/99 12:56 AM
Ruler.psp	330KB	Paint Sho...	6/1/99 11:15 AM
Small Bloks.psp	275KB	Paint Sho...	5/31/99 9:21 PM
StorCard.bmp	40KB	Paint Sho...	6/3/99 7:36 PM
StrataBox.psp	54KB	Paint Sho...	6/1/99 8:34 AM
Titles.psp	130KB	Paint Sho...	6/5/99 9:22 AM
ZoomPlate.psp	331KB	Paint Sho...	6/1/99 9:21 AM

Select your authoring tool wisely—you will have to commit a considerable amount of time and effort into it to achieve your project's goals. Thoroughly research each authoring tool's options, their features, and their suitability to your project's format. Practically all of these products have downloadable demonstration versions that will let you get a taste for how they work and what your comfort level will be. Remember, the best multimedia developers are those who are expert in many development tools and are not locked into any one tool.

Make sure you define your target platform, your end user's capabilities, and the delivery system your project will use.

Chapter Summary

- Authoring is the process of developing a multimedia application using an authoring tool. Authoring tools allow the user to create software products without needing to learn a programming language.

- There are many kinds of authoring tools, and all have their strengths and weaknesses. Some are more difficult than others to learn, and some have different development methodologies than others. Be sure to research the options and choose the tools best suited for the nature of the project.

- Whether developing multimedia applications for CD-ROM, DVD-ROM, hard drive installation, or Web deployment, the basic principles and development paths taken to get to the end result are remarkably similar. However, the devil can be in the details, and the differences among the target delivery systems can make quite a difference in the development effort if they are not defined correctly at the outset.

- Certain multimedia usage metaphors are common to all multimedia applications on some level. Sometimes a multimedia application can use a combination of these metaphors in its operation. However, knowing what these metaphors and modes of operation are can help you develop a more suitable design for your final product.

- Multimedia applications use development metaphors that are aligned with the usage metaphors of such applications. Generally the development metaphor that matches the intended application's mode of operation is the development tool that's best suited to get the job done. However, the more sophisticated multimedia authoring tools can often cater to several operational methods.

- Multimedia project planning is quite similar to conventional software project planning, only more complex. A little time and effort spent at the beginning of the multimedia project can often save a tremendous amount of time and stress later on.

Key Terms and Concepts

Checking Your Knowledge and Skills

1. By using the evaluation copy of Multimedia Fusion authoring tool on this book's CD-ROM, and by downloading other multimedia authoring tools from links provided at this book's Web site, compare and contrast at least three authoring tools for features, ease of use, and suitability to the different multimedia user motifs listed in this chapter. Create a comparison chart for these products, and score their performance in the areas you, as a multimedia developer, believe to be important. Which product seems the best and why?

2. By downloading evaluation copies of Web authoring tools from links provided at this book's Web site, compare and contrast at least three authoring tools for features, ease of use, and suitability to the different multimedia user motifs as they apply to the Web. Create a comparison chart for these products, and score their performance in the areas you, as a multimedia Web site developer, believe to be important. Be sure to evaluate these tools for their ability to integrate multimedia content into a Web page. Which product seems the best and why?

3. Create a comparison chart listing the five main application metaphors, and use this chart to rank at least five multimedia applications of your choice. Be sure to choose one definitive or dominant motif for each product. List those multimedia products that cross motif boundaries and use multiple-user metaphors to get the job done. In your opinion, which methodology is most effective in achieving its goals and why?

4. Using PowerPoint or a similar product, develop a storyboard for a multimedia brochure for your choice of one of the following clients:
   a. BMW automobiles
   b. Suzuki motorcycles
   c. GMC trucks
   d. Macy's jewelry department
   e. NASA Space Program Surplus
   f. Warner Brothers Studio's used props
   g. American Airlines
   h. Walt Disney World in Orlando, Florida
   Use the Internet as a source of media content to enhance your storyboard.

Critical Thinking Challenges

Given the importance of authoring tools in the development of multimedia, answer the following questions to the best of your ability:

1. Locate the technical specification for a multimedia development tool such as Macromedia's Director, Asymetrix's ToolBook, or Clickteam's Multimedia Fusion. If you do not own such an application, perhaps your school computer lab, office, library, friend, or colleague will have a copy that you can look at. If not, check out the manufacturer's Web site for these details. Using the product manuals and/or online help file, try to determine the amount of time it would take you to complete a multimedia project based on the storyboard from exercise 4 or an equivalent storyboard. Would the outcome of this analysis affect your decision to purchase this authoring tool for general multimedia purposes?

2. Using the storyboard from exercise 4 or an equivalent storyboard, assume that you have ten weeks in which to deliver ten thousand copies of the final product to your client (or open the site to the public, if it's a Web-based project). Research the turnaround time (from the time the client receives your master copy) and cost requirements for the CD-ROM manufacturer to manufacture and deliver to your doorstep the ten thousand CD-ROMs. Working backward, divide the remaining time of the project into the planning and development phases, allowing for content creation and editing; authoring; early, midpoint, and final client review milestones; and a thorough testing of the finished product and revision phase. Counting in terms of a forty-hour work week, develop a project plan and timeline. How much you would have to charge per hour to make this project worthwhile for you?

3. Research some leading multimedia development firms in your area. The Web is a terrific place to find such companies. Contact them and ask them about their production team, how they allocate workload, what application they use for storyboarding and project planning, and what authoring tools they recommend and why. You'll find that most companies are willing to answer your questions, though finding individuals in the company with sufficient time to do so may be difficult. If they are pressed for time, suggest that you could send them the questions via e-mail if they would take a few minutes to help you out. Let them know that you're a student doing an assignment and not a competitor digging for competitive data (at least not yet). Chart your findings and see how they compare from company to company and to your own opinions.

Hands-on Exercises

REAL-WORLD MULTIMEDIA PROJECT PLANNING

This exercise is best done with a colleague(s) or fellow student(s). If this is not possible, you can also accomplish this task alone.

As with exercise 4, chose a storyboarding project and develop a detailed storyboard. You have a ten-week development time allotment from your client.

Determine how you would assign the various requirements and tasks for the project among your colleagues, and assign those tasks starting with determining the project scope and definitions. Appoint a visual design manager, an animation and/or digital video manager, a sound manager, a development/authoring manager, and an overall project manager. If you have fewer people than tasks, then allocate multiple tasks to individuals to spread the workload.

Have each individual plan out the time required for his or her task(s), ensuring that any tasks that are a prerequisite for a subsequent task cannot hold up that task and jeopardize the project. Agree on the time required and its allocation over the ten weeks, allowing for production scheduling as described in the second critical thinking challenge.

Ask each team member what his or her required payment rate is, and determine whether this includes overhead costs such as taxes, benefits, premises, utilities, insurance, telephones, software, and hardware. You may determine that the team members are all freelancers and therefore look after their own overhead costs in their required fee.

Use this information to develop a budget for the client, and divide the amount you will charge the client into progress payments that coincide with your progress milestone meetings.

In your opinion, does this look like a good deal for your client? Will the client agree to this proposal? Can you develop a convincing return-on-investment (ROI) case for this project? Do the benefits to the client outweigh the costs? How does your team's cost compare to what you can learn about the going rates for such multimedia development?

Master Project

PREPARING FOR YOUR AUTHORING

So far you should have created a binder for the project that documents your project's concept and includes a project plan, a timeline, and your sketches and visuals for your design. You should also have begun the process of building your content and storing it on disk.

Using the storyboard developed earlier in this project, determine which application metaphor your project fits into. Feel free to take this opportunity to change your storyboard if you feel the need. Having studied your storyboard, determine which multimedia authoring tool is best suited for the task of completing the job. Since the next chapter will focus on Director and Multimedia Fusion as typical development tools, it may be advantageous to see whether one of those applications will meet your requirements for an authoring tool.

15

HANDS-ON
MULTIMEDIA
AUTHORING

Chapter Outline

Chapter Objectives

After completing this chapter, you will be able to:

- Create a complete, though rudimentary, interactive
  multimedia application

- Describe the process of media component assembly and
  importation into a multimedia authoring tool

- Apply the methodologies and techniques described in this
  chapter to build a multimedia application

- Apply multimedia programming techniques

- Optimize and fine-tune your multimedia project

- Create a stand-alone executable interactive
  multimedia program

Chapter Overview

In this chapter you will learn how to build a multimedia application using two very different multimedia authoring development tools: Macromedia's Director and Clickteam's Multimedia Fusion.

These products use different approaches to what amounts to completing the same job. Each uses a different methodology and different techniques. Each organizes the design and development process differently and requires a completely different learning process to master it. Each has its strengths and weaknesses.

Despite these differences, the media components and elements that you have learned to create are equally acceptable to either authoring tool. The final multimedia products they produce can perform and look almost identical, no matter which tool is used to develop them.

So how will you decide which tool to use, and which is the better product for your ongoing multimedia development needs? This chapter will help you answer that question. Many factors, such as cost, platform compatibility, ease of use, level of complexity, and built-in special effects and capabilities, will influence your final decision. At least you can make an informed one.

Director and Multimedia Fusion are just two of a large number of such multimedia authoring products. Each represents a "class" of development tool. Director uses a timeline on which to build your application; elapsed time is the primary and default modality used to determine when changes occur in the program. Multimedia Fusion uses an object-oriented approach in which the developer specifies what should occur in response to a specific event with a specific object. By following the examples and instructions in this chapter, you should be able to develop impressive multimedia software applications with either or both of these authoring tools.

You also should develop a good sense of how each of these products works and be able to quickly learn another multimedia authoring tool, such as Macromedia's Authorware, Astound, and Asymetrix's ToolBook, among many others. The really successful multimedia developers are masters of several development tools.

Please be aware that to do justice to teaching comprehensive multimedia development with either of these complex software tools would require a dedicated book about the size of this one. The objective here is not to make you a complete Director or Multimedia Fusion developer or expert. The objective is to give you a good start in the learning process, and to help you produce rudimentary multimedia applications with these products. How much further you take this will be up to you and how much time and practice you spend on either product.

WORKING WITH A TIMELINE OR WORKING WITH OBJECTS AND FRAMES

Although Director and Multimedia Fusion are two multimedia authoring tools that use different modes of operation, both refer to the displayed screen of the resulting multimedia application at any given time as the *frame*. Both use this frame as the "window" that the user sees when the final product is running. Both authoring tools provide the multimedia developer with a full-featured set of development tools.

Director is representative of multimedia authoring tools that use a timeline as a basis for assembling a multimedia application or presentation. Conversely, Multimedia Fusion is more like a very sophisticated slide show development tool, and as such, represents applications known as event-driven, *object-oriented,* or *icon-based* authoring tools. In such applications, each frame of the final product could be a complete multimedia application in its own right, and the final multimedia product jumps to whichever frame is appropriate based on the user's input and the developer's embedded instructions. When creating your final multimedia application, both products create an executable program that can operate independently of the original authoring tool. Both Director and Multimedia Fusion can create Web-ready streaming media applets for use in Web pages. For Director, such Web applets are called Shockwave applets. For Multimedia Fusion, they are called Vitalize applets.

THE MOVIE METAPHOR

Director uses a movie motif to describe its methodology, and for good reason. Recall that movies are linear time-based media pieces. They have a start, a defined duration, and, unless interrupted, stop at a defined end time. Director uses a similar timeline to assemble its frames and to change over time what is presented in those frames. In this way Director can animate and synchronize your multimedia presentation by controlling what is displayed at what time on the timeline.

Unless you introduce specific instructions to Director's movie to jump to a frame out of sequence, Director will play all frames in your newly designed application, in turn, from the beginning through to the end at whichever frame rate you specify. To create an out-of-sequence frame jump requires a specific instruction in Director's own programming language, known as Lingo. You can create terrific multimedia pieces with Director with little or no Lingo programming, but when you begin to program instructions in Lingo, Director can become a very versatile development tool, and also quite a complex one. Figure 15.1 shows the Director interface, and in this illustration you can see how the movie motif carries through Director's naming of its primary features and tools.

THE STORYBOARD METAPHOR

Multimedia Fusion uses a storyboard motif to convey the order and layout of its frames. However, while Director uses frames much like the sequential frames of a film or of an animation, Multimedia Fusion uses its frames more like the frames of a storyboard or of a comic strip—simply as a holder of a specific screen design or segment of the story. The developer then determines which frame plays in which sequence and in response to what event. In Multimedia Fusion, you can develop quite an elaborate multimedia application using just one frame by timing the behavior and interaction of the objects onscreen. Each frame can support a complex set of actions, and jumping to another frame is usually done because of a need to change the scene or interface to another format. Figure 15.2 shows the primary Multimedia Fusion development interface and its components and tools. Notice the storyboard editor and how it lists the frames (screens) used in the application.

Multimedia Fusion uses an events matrix in its event list editor. The developer can select any event (such as the timer reaching the two-seconds-elapsed

event-driven

Event-driven applications can trap events (such as user mouse clicks) in the program and respond to them with code provided by the developer to react to that event.

events matrix

In Multimedia Fusion, events and the response to those events are represented in a gridlike chart called the events matrix.

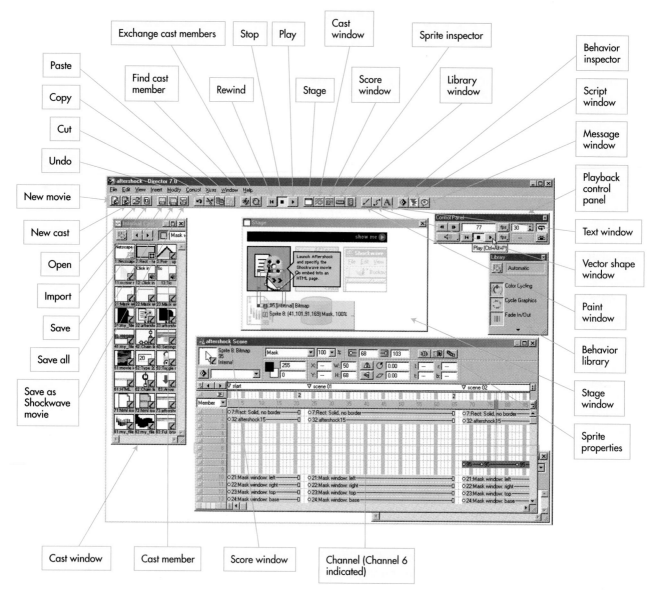

Paste
Copy
Cut
Undo
New movie
New cast
Open
Import
Save
Save all
Save as Shockwave movie

Exchange cast members
Find cast member
Stop
Play
Rewind
Stage
Cast window
Score window
Sprite inspector
Library window

Behavior inspector
Script window
Message window
Playback control panel
Text window
Vector shape window
Paint window
Behavior library
Stage window
Sprite properties

Cast window
Cast member
Score window
Channel (Channel 6 indicated)

Figure 15.1
The Director multimedia application authoring environment.

point or a moving object reaching the end of its path) in the frame and use this "cue" to pass an instruction on how to react to the application or an object used in the frame. For instance, for an opening title sequence, each letter of the title could be created as a separate active object and be given a fade-in transition. At specific timer interval events (say each half-second starting at two seconds elapsed since the frame started), each letter of the title could be instructed to respond to that timer event and appear at a specific location in the frame. The result would be a very effective opening title sequence in which each letter spelling out the title fades in quick succession.

Figure 15.3 shows such an event list creating this effect. In this illustration you can see how each time the timer reaches another second, it causes the creation of the letter at a predetermined location on the frame. In this same illustration the timeline editor shows the creation of each letter in the word *DNA* at its assigned coordinate location at its appointed time event. This is a good example of Multimedia Fusion's event-based operation.

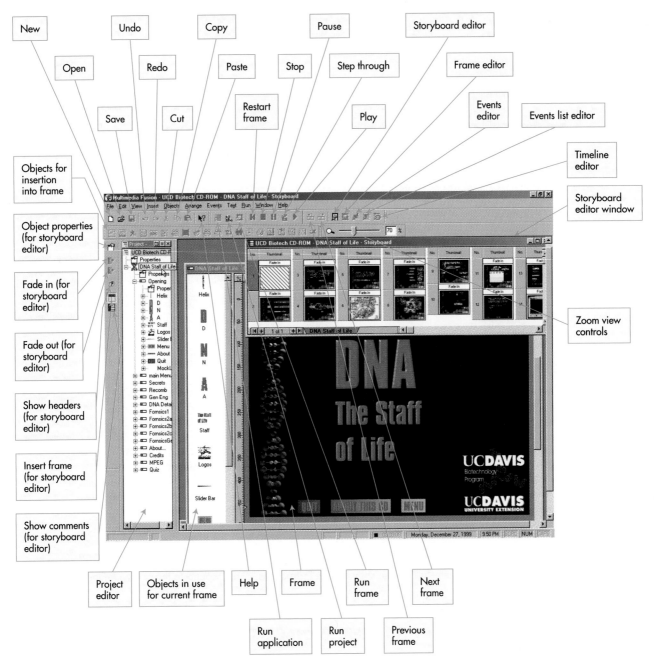

Figure 15.2
The primary Multimedia Fusion multimedia application authoring environment (some editors are not shown).

In this chapter you will learn how to use each of these modes of operation to your best advantage.

THE DIRECTOR INTERFACE

As shown in Figure 15.1, Director provides an imposing interface and selection of tools to choose from. If you spend a little time with this interface, familiarizing yourself with the location and function of its elements, you will make your learning process all the easier. Once you get a feel for this product, your work can become very efficient and fluid.

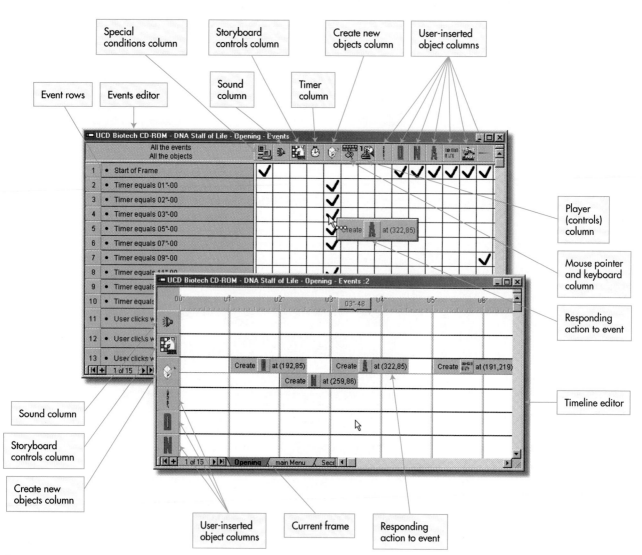

Figure 15.3

Multimedia Fusion's event list editor and timeline editor, showing the instructions set to respond to the chosen timing events.

CASTS AND THEIR MANAGEMENT

cast

In Director, the collection of media and programming components that are used in a given multimedia application developed in Director.

internal cast members

In Director, cast members that will be stored in the final compiled executable program.

compiling

When developing a software application, whether with a programming language or with an authoring tool, the final step of building a stand-alone executable file containing all of your work for final release and distribution is called compiling. An executable file is referred to as a compiled program.

The first step in building a Director application is the importation of your prepared media components as cast members for the project.

When you import your media components into Director, they are assembled and displayed in the Internal Cast window, as shown in Figure 15.4. Each cast member listed in the Internal Cast window shows a small icon in the bottom corner of the thumbnail image of the cast member. This icon indicates the type of cast member.

Figure 15.4 also shows the internal cast used as building blocks for the Interactive Guide to Motorcycle Maintenance project developed in Chapters 4, 5, and 6 of this book. An internal cast consists of those media elements that are embedded in the final product. When the final *projector* (executable file) is created, these internal cast members are compiled as part of the executable file. External casts exist as a separate cast file after the projector is created. Using an external cast enables the developer to change cast members even after the projector has been compiled.

To import your media component into a cast, choose Import from the File menu, or right-click a vacant cast member slot, or simply drag each file for

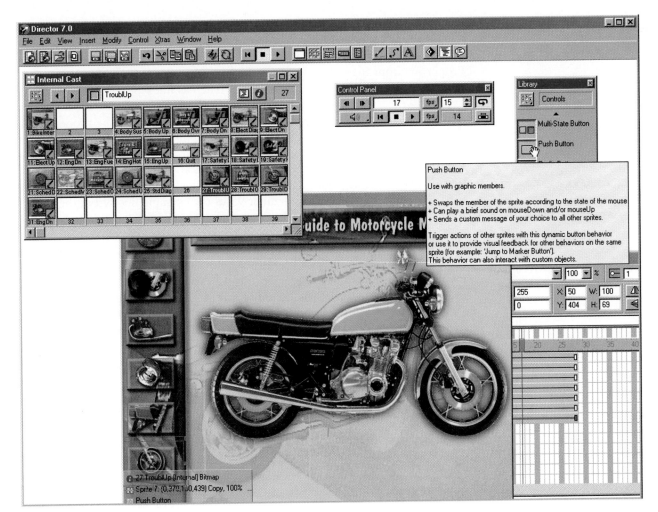

Figure 15.4

The internal cast for the Interactive Guide to Motorcycle Maintenance project started in Chapters 4, 5, and 6 (note the pop-up prompt for the button behavior used to create the interactive button bar to the left of the screen).

import from the system desktop or Windows Explorer and drop it into the cast window.

When importing cast members, you will be asked some questions. If you click the Internet button in the import dialog box, you can type in the URL for a media component located on the Web. Director can use a local drive (or local area network) path name, or a URL to locate a file. Once you have specified the files to import, you can use the Move Up and Move Down buttons to reorder the cast members into the sequence in which you wish to see them listed in the project. You can always drag them to a new cast slot if you want to rearrange them later.

Next you will be asked to choose some color depth and palette options. The default color depth Stage is usually the best color option. Choosing this option will remap the media element to the stage's color depth. If you are importing a batch of media components you may want to check the Same Settings for Remaining Images option so that you will not be asked this question for each file imported.

Once imported, cast members can be dragged directly to the Stage or to the Score (discussed later) as required to use them. Note that reusing an existing cast member does not add any size overhead to the final application. You can use a cast member as often as you wish, and still only one cast member copy is stored in your final program. A used instance of a cast member in the project is referred to as a sprite. Therefore a sprite is really a specific use of a cast member. While

external cast members

In Director, cast members that are files outside of the compiled final product and that are used in the final presentation are called external cast members. Some media components, such as digital video, cannot be stored inside the compiled application, and will always be external cast members.

sprite

A given instance of a cast member used in the application.

you only have individual cast members, you can use as many sprites of any cast member as you please throughout your project.

You can change the properties of a cast member by choosing Cast Member Properties from the shortcut menu that appears when you right-click a cast member. When you change the properties (such as ink type) of a cast member, every instance (sprite) of that cast member throughout your project will be affected by your change. However, if you just want to change the properties of the specific instance of the cast member, then right-click the sprite onstage and choose Properties from the shortcut menu. You can also change a sprite's properties by selecting it on the Stage or in the Score and changing any of the properties for that sprite displayed at the top of the Score window. Figure 15.1 shows the properties of selected cast member 95 in the example, located at the top of the Score window. In this way, when you change the sprite's properties, the properties of the source cast member are preserved while you get the benefit of the property changes required at that time of use.

Double-clicking any cast member, or on a sprite onstage for that matter, invokes that cast member's editor. In this way you can alter your cast members on the fly. Furthermore, if you are designing graphical elements as you work in Director, you can copy your edited work from Photoshop, Paint Shop Pro, or any image editing application, right-click an available cast member slot, and choose Paste Bitmap from the shortcut menu.

You can also use this method to change a cast member. Right-click the cast member and choose Copy Cast Members from the shortcut menu, paste the image into your graphics editing program, edit the image, copy the changed image, and paste it back over the old cast member. All instances of that cast member throughout your project will be changed instantly.

When developing a Director project, you can move and resize the cast window to suit your workspace needs.

THE STAGE

Shakespeare wrote, "All the world's a stage," and that's not far from the truth in Director's world. As you recall from the previous chapter, this is where it all happens. The Stage is a Director project's face to the outside world when the application is completed. The actual size (in pixels) and background color of the Stage represent the actual size and color of your final product's window (unless you instruct the Stage to be full-screen, in which case the Stage size represents the used area of the full screen).

The Stage window, as seen in Figures 15.1 and 15.4, is the presentation space for your application. You can use your sprites here by dragging them to the Stage or to the Score window. The Stage represents how each frame of your application looks. By clicking any given frame in the Score window, you can see the appearance of that frame, and its collection of sprites, in the Stage window. When you scrub through frames, the Stage changes to reflect the appearance of your application as it goes through those frames.

The Stage is also where you place and adjust your sprites to suit your design. You can place them, scale them, and select them to change their properties. Much as a sprite is an instance of a project's cast member, a frame is an instance of the project's Stage. Likewise, you have Stage settings that make changes in your project's Stage and appearance across the board, and frame settings that can change the Stage's appearance for just that one instance.

You can adjust the properties of the Stage and frame by right-clicking the Stage itself, as shown in Figure 15.5. This illustration shows the Movie Properties dialog box that changes the Stage properties for the entire project. By clicking on the small color square you invoke the color picker box, shown to one side for clarity. Stage size, color palette used and how (if applicable), and program information are all set here.

Score

In Director, the timeline matrix where all controls, components, and coding are organized and arranged over time.

Stage

In Director, the visible interface of the final application.

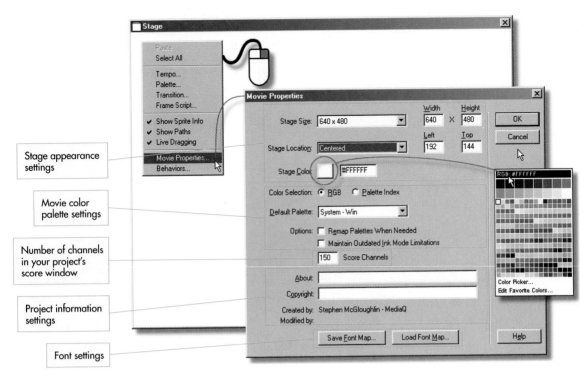

Figure 15.5
The frame and Stage property options available by right-clicking the Stage.

The font mapping features provided allow you to determine what fonts will replace those you originally select if they are not present. If you use a nonstandard font, your application is run on a different platform, or it's run in a country using a different character set (such as Japan), then this feature allows you to predetermine the way Director deals with font substitution. This provides for a better outcome than the arbitrary (and always wrong) automatic font substitution that the system will do if unassisted. Table 15.1 shows the typical font mapping used for applications running on both Windows and Macintosh platforms.

THE SCORE

The Score is a matrix-type diagram that describes and determines what happens on each Director frame and how. As you can see in Figure 15.6, columns numbered 1 and up represent frames. Every sprite, script, sound, transition palette instruction, and tempo instruction (timing controls for each frame) in each column is summed to represent the collective effect of the frame at that moment. The rows (called channels) represent the content of the frames over time. The point of intersection of any row and column is called a cell, and it is where a sprite occupying that channel, used in that frame, is shown.

CAST MEMBERS AND SPRITES IN THE SCORE.

You have met the cast and seen them perform on the Stage. Now meet their choreographer—the Score window. In Figure 15.6 you will notice that cast member 1 (BikeInterface5) is used in channel 1 for all frames from 1 through 60. As mentioned before, a cast member in use is called a sprite, and as such will appear on the Score occupying one or more cells. Each sprite occupies at least one frame/channel cell, and the number of cells occupied on any channel indicates the duration onscreen of that sprite. When first dragged from the cast window to the Score or Stage, a sprite will be automatically given a specific number of frames' duration. You can adjust this

font mapping

Since it cannot be determined what fonts are used by the end user's computer system, some multimedia authoring products, such as Director, provide the developer with the ability to map any fonts found to be missing to alternative fonts when the product is run. This deliberate compensation for missing fonts prevents the computer system from making the arbitrary decision of what fonts to substitute, which invariably does not fit with the intended design.

tempo

In Director, the control used to alter the timing of an individual frame.

channels

In Director, each sprite is provided with a timeline track on the Score window, called a channel.

TABLE 15.1	Standard Font Mapping between Windows and Macintosh Platforms	
Standard Windows Fonts That . . .		**Map to These Macintosh Fonts**
Arial		Helvetica
Courier		Courier
Courier New		Courier
MS Serif		New York
MS Sans Serif		Geneva
Symbol		Symbol
System		Chicago
Terminal		Monaco
Times New Roman		Times
Standard Macintosh Fonts That . . .		**Map to These Windows Fonts**
Chicago		System
Courier		Courier New
Geneva		MS Sans Serif
Helvetica		Arial
Monaco		Terminal
New York		MS Serif
Symbol		Symbol
Times		Times New Roman
Palatino		Times New Roman

default number by using the Sprite Preferences dialog box, available by choosing Preferences from the File menu, and then choosing the Sprite command.

In addition, channel numbers indicate the layering of those channels. Channels with smaller channel numbers are layered behind those with larger channel numbers. For instance, the background image for the Interactive Guide to Motorcycle Maintenance, shown in Figure 15.6, is placed in channel 1. Any sprite occupying channel 2 or higher will be shown on top of the interface background. This prevents the backplate from obscuring any of the other Sprites.

You will notice in Figure 15.6 that a red rectangle and a red vertical line are positioned on frame 30. This is the *playback head,* which indicates the frame currently displayed on the Stage. You can drag the playback head back and forth and scrub through your project's frames.

Any sprite on the Score can be moved by dragging or by cutting/copying and pasting. In this way you can alter the layering of your sprites and their position on the timeline. You can do this with multiple sprites by holding down the Ctrl key to select other individual sprites, or the Shift key to select a range of sprites at once. Dragging the small rectangle handle at the right end of the sprite indicator bar can also change the duration of sprites. You can also simply change the end frame number for the sprite at the top of the Score window. In this way you can stretch or shrink the frame duration of any sprite.

To edit a sprite, simply double-click the sprite as it appears on the Score. Note in Figure 15.6 the Score expander button. This button allows you to show or hide the nonsprite channels to provide you with more room to maneuver. Above this section of the Score, just beneath the properties section, is a white margin called the marker channel that displays your project's markers. In Figure 15.6 you can see the markers used to identify the primary locations in

marker channel

In Director, a channel Score window that is used to place markers on the timeline. These markers serve as reference points to aid the developer in navigating through complex constructions. They can also be referred to in Lingo code by name.

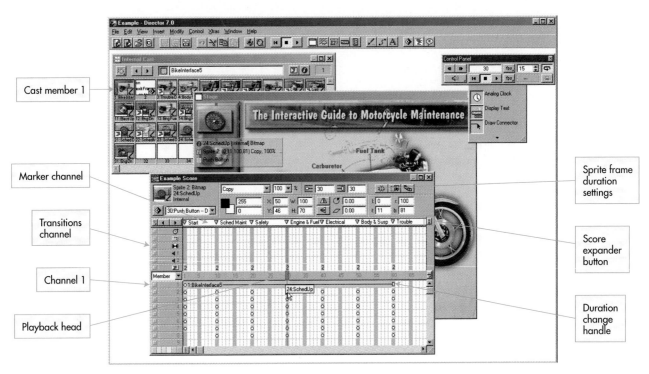

Figure 15.6
The Score window showing channels (rows) and frames (columns).

the Score for the Interactive Guide to Motorcycle Maintenance. You can use these markers in your Lingo coding, and refer to a frame's marker name as opposed to the frame number.

TRANSITIONS.   To add pizzazz or a sense of professionalism to your product, you will often want one frame to blend into another. Sometimes a transition can be a critical part of an animated sequence. Applying a transition to a frame is a relatively simple process.

To add a transition to a frame, double-click the transition channel for that frame, and select the appropriate transition for the desired effect. Once selected, run your Director project again, and when your program encounters that frame, it will apply the transition selected and use that special effect to update the new frame. When you double-click an existing transition, the settings dialog box appears, and allows you to make changes. Figure 15.7 shows the transition properties panel and the many types of transitions available to the Director developer.

INK MODES.   When a sprite is selected (on the Stage or in the Score), its properties appear in the sprite properties area at the top of the Score window. Clicking the color-effect drop-down selection list provides a range of ink effects available for use with a sprite, as seen in Figure 15.7. By selecting various color effects, the range of special effects available with image sprites is almost limitless.

TEMPOS.   Director's frames are displayed on the Stage at a specified rate of frames per second (fps). You may interrupt this progression by implementing Lingo commands to pause on a frame or divert the sequential progression to another frame number. You may also change the tempo of any given frame, allowing you fine control over the timing and playing of each frame. You could, for instance, decide to hold for two seconds on a given frame before moving to the next.

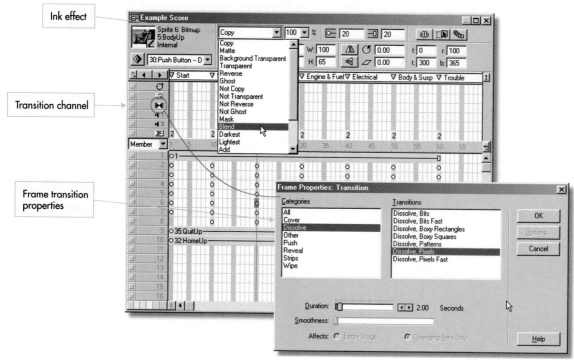

Figure 15.7
The Score window showing the transition properties panel and the drop-down list of ink effects available for a sprite.

A very beneficial use of a frame's tempo setting can be for establishing how a frame with a sound or video segment plays. To use a digital movie or sound in Director, you need to multiply the duration of the media piece (in seconds) by the frame rate used in Director. This gives you the number of frames over which the movie/sound sprite must be stretched to allow it to play to its end. This can be a very cumbersome and awkward way to play a linear media clip, and a difficult one to debug later if the other elements of your movie do not synchronize correctly with it. Instead, consider placing the movie/sound sprite on one frame, and select that frame's Wait for Cue Point tempo setting. In this way you can instruct Director to wait on that one frame until the movie or sound has completed playing and then continue its progression at the original tempo setting.

WATCH FOR THE LOOP PLAYBACK BUTTON

The Loop Playback button on the Control Panel enables your project to loop back to frame 1 after the last frame has played. You will often use this feature to bring the user back to a main starting-point screen after the last chosen task or presentation has completed. However, the Loop Playback button works only in design mode. When you finally create your stand-alone projector or Shockwave application, the program stops at the last frame, as there is no Loop Playback button to instruct it to return to frame 0. To compensate for this, you must insert the following Lingo instruction in the *on exitFrame* event in the script channel of the last frame:

go to frame 0

Then your program will return to the beginning once it has finished displaying the last frame.

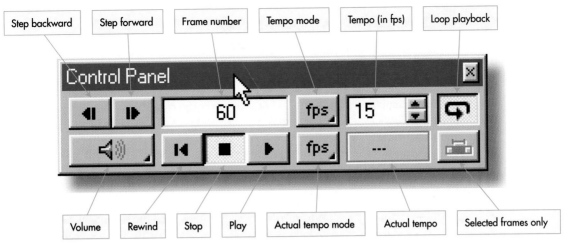

Step backward | Step forward | Frame number | Tempo mode | Tempo (in fps) | Loop playback

Volume | Rewind | Stop | Play | Actual tempo mode | Actual tempo | Selected frames only

Figure 15.8
The Control Panel and its functions.

THE CONTROL PANEL

The Director Control Panel primarily provides the developer with a VCR-type set of controls with which to control the playing of the Director project in design mode. Figure 15.8 labels those controls and their function.

The Control Panel provides the developer with the ability to run and test the project, to advance and back up one frame at a time, to alter the sound volume, and to change the playback speed rate of the project.

THE TEXT WINDOW

The Text window is where you can enter, edit, format, style, and color text used in your Director application. Figure 15.9 illustrates this process.

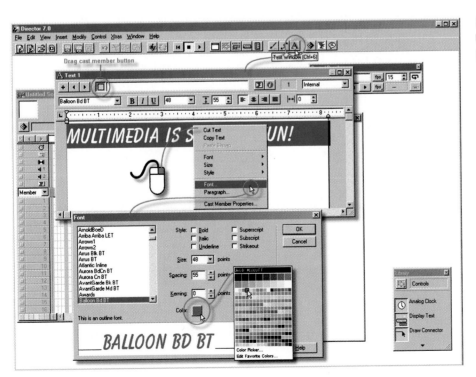

Figure 15.9
Using and editing text in Director.

When entering text in Director, you will most likely choose a font that matches your project's visual style. However, you must ensure that your end users have that font on their system for the text to look exactly as you designed it. Otherwise the end-user's computer will substitute what it thinks is the closest font in its collection to the one you specified. It could look hideous, as the computer has, without your personal assistance, no sense of style whatsoever.

Two options are available to you to ensure that the desired font will look exactly as you designed it to look. First, you can create an image in your image editor and place the section of text as a bitmapped graphic, as opposed to an editable text element. This graphic will always display as designed, ensuring fidelity to your design. However, there is a considerably larger data storage overhead when using a bitmap in place of text data (which takes practically no data space in your application).

You can also embed the font. This allows you to store the font data within your Director project so that the font displays correctly even if end users don't have that font installed. By choosing from the Insert menu, and then choosing Font, Media Element, you can select the desired fonts from the resulting dialog box and they then appear as embedded font cast members.

To enter text for placement on your Stage, click the Text Window button (see Figure 15.9) to invoke the Text window, in which you can enter the desired text. Editing and formatting of the text thereafter is done as you would format text in a word-processing application. To change font attributes and color, simply select the text to change, right-click the selected text, choose Font from the shortcut menu, and select the changes you want to make from the Font Properties dialog box. You can also use the font style commands, such as Font, Size, or Style, which provide shortcuts to those specific font attributes. You will need the Font Properties dialog box to change font color.

You can place text onto the Stage by dragging the Drag Cast Member button to the Stage, as shown in Figure 15.9. Once placed on the screen, the text you entered shows up in the cast window as a text cast member and as a text sprite onstage. To edit the text thereafter, simply double-click it in the cast window to invoke the Text window, or double-click the text on the Stage to edit it in place.

THE PAINT WINDOW

If you want to create an image in Director from scratch or edit an image imported into Director as a cast member, you can use Director's Paint window. It is invoked either by clicking the Paint Window button at the top of Director's screen, or by double-clicking an existing cast member image.

Director's image editing facilities are not very sophisticated by today's standards when compared to products like Photoshop or Paint Shop Pro. However, the Paint window is easy to use and readily available within Director for simple image editing and drawing tasks. You will most likely use the method of copying and pasting image data back and forth from Director to your image editing application as mentioned earlier, as this method provides you with far more flexibility and control over your product's appearance.

Spend a little time playing with the Paint window just to familiarize yourself with the available features. The tools, their symbolism, and their function will already be familiar to you from using products such as Photoshop, Paint Shop Pro, and PhotoPaint.

THE SCRIPTING WINDOW

At the heart of Director is a powerful scripting (programming) language called Lingo that allows more sophisticated multimedia developers and programmers to take far more control over the operation and performance of the final product they're developing. Anything beyond a very rudimentary look at Lingo is beyond the scope of this book. If you would like to delve deeper into Lingo, check out references to the books in the bibliography section of this book's Web site.

You can provide lingo instructions for a frame, a *behavior* (a prepackaged Lingo routine), a cast member, or a sprite. In this way you can ensure that the Lingo commands you type in will be executed in the right place for the right purpose at the right time. Lingo commands are entered into the Scripting window, which is invoked by clicking the Script Window button, by double-clicking in the scripting channel on the Score to enter commands for the frame that you double-clicked, or by right-clicking a cast member or sprite and selecting the scripting option of your choice.

Figure 15.10 shows this process. In this illustration, the Script window is used to enter the Lingo command *go to* to send users back to the frame labeled Start when they click the Home button in our application. In this illustration, cast member 33 is selected, and you can see it in the title bar of the Script window. Notice that cast member 33 has a small scripting icon in its bottom corner, indicating that this cast member has Lingo associated with its operation.

Note that the Script window allows you to enter code for a specific event associated with a frame, cast member, or sprite. In this way, you can choose what event in your application triggers the execution of your code, and you can write Lingo code to respond to whichever event happens while your program is running. The event you choose will be determined by when, in your project's operation, you want your Lingo code used. In the illustration, the code entered is for the *mouseUp* event. This is the event used to trap a mouse click. Since a mouse click is really two events (*mouseDown* and *mouseUp*), you want to have your code executed when the user completes the click action. If you used the *mouseDown*

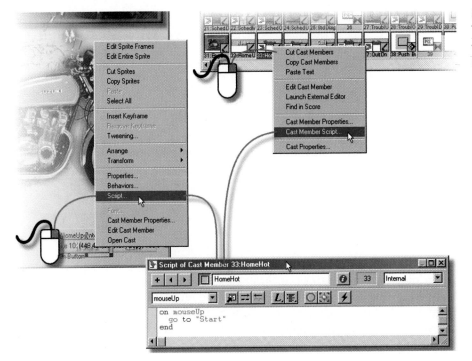

Figure 15.10

Two ways to invoke the Scripting window for a cast member or sprite.

TABLE 15.2 Useful Examples of Lingo and Its Use

Example Number	Lingo Command	Purpose
1	on exitFrame pause end	Hold the playback head on the frame using this command. As the playback head attempts to continue to the next frame, it is told to pause. This command pauses everything, including animations and button effects.
2	on mouseUp continue end	To release a paused frame, use the "continue" command.
3	on exitFrame go to the frame end	This command tells the playback head to loop back on itself, playing the frame over and over until it receives a command to branch elsewhere. This command gives the stopped-on-a-frame effect of example 1, but allows the operation of any animated or interactive sprites in that frame.
4	on exitFrame go to frame 3 end	This command provides for branching to another frame anywhere in the Director movie, referenced by that frame's number. To replay the movie, frame number 1 would be used here. The playback head resumes playing frames from the specified point.
5	on exitFrame go to frame "framename" end	This command has the same function as example 4, but using a marker label instead of a frame number. This can be very helpful when tracking your project's processing of Lingo commands and branching, as you can more easily identify the marker labels than obscure frame numbers. Lingo doesn't mind whether you use numbers or markers to locate a frame.
6	on mouseDown play frame "framename" end	Examples 4 and 5 show how to branch and send the playback head to a different starting point. The "play" command does the same, but once the "play done" command (example 7) is reached, the playback head jumps back to the point from where it was branched and resumes play there.
7	on exitFrame play done end	This is the syntax for the "play done" command referred to in example 6.
8	on mouseUp exit end	This command tells Director to quit and exit the movie. When running your movie while still editing in Director, this command will try to shut down the entire Director application. Be sure to use this command last in your programming.

event, then your code would be confused with a drag event, in which the mouse button is held down during the dragging process.

Table 15.2 provides a few very basic examples of useful Lingo commands.

Director's built-in help files provide a wealth of additional information about Lingo programming. You will read more about Lingo in this chapter as you work through a hands-on exercise. Check this book's Web site for references on where to find out more about Lingo programming.

BEHAVIORS AND XTRAS

For the less-skilled Lingo programmer, Macromedia has provided a library of prepackaged Lingo routines, or *behaviors*, that you can use in your project. These behaviors are listed in the Library window. You can use them by simply dragging the chosen behavior and dropping it onto the sprite or cast member that you wish to use this behavior. For instance, in the Interactive Guide to Motorcycle Maintenance example, the Push Button behavior provides button

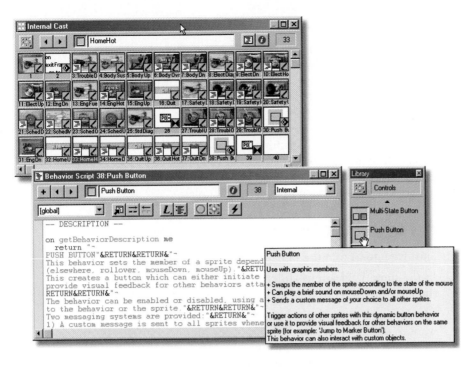

rollover and mouse click visual changes to make the button "respond" to the user's interaction. Figure 15.11 shows the behavior script for the Push Button behavior along with the pop-up description that appears when your mouse pointer rests over the behavior listing in the Library window.

While behaviors can be very beneficial in providing nonprogrammers with a canned approach to adding interactivity through Lingo, it also restricts the use of the sprite or cast member thereafter. If the canned Lingo does not accommodate the desired effect, trying to add your own Lingo commands to the behavior can be both intimidating and quite difficult. However, the behaviors supplied do provide extensive comments and assistance for the customizing of their operation.

Xtras are to Director as plug-ins are to Photoshop or Paint Shop Pro. They are additional programs that provide enhanced capabilities and features for the Director developer. They can also be developed by third-party software companies and can often provide Director with the ability to use media formats or provide special visual effects beyond the standard set supplied with Director out of the box. In the same way that a downloaded plug-in for your Internet browser can enable you to view a new media format, so too can Director's Xtras provide similar enhanced capabilities. To the developer, this means that for as long as there are companies creating enhanced features for Director, its capabilities as a multimedia development tool will expand and grow. Should you purchase an Xtra for Director, be sure to follow the installation instructions exactly as stated by the manufacturer.

Xtras

Similar to plug-ins for Web browsers and for products such as Photoshop and Paint Shop Pro, Xtras are small helper applications that can be used to provide additional features and functionality to the original Director product.

CREATING A DIRECTOR "MOVIE" IN TEN STEPS

While there is a lot more to learn about Director, the following exercise will show you how to build a working multimedia interface and the beginning of a complete multimedia application. While this exercise requires you to use prepared media content that you will have seen earlier in the book, you can always substitute your own media components and create your own custom example.

STEP 1: ENTERING YOUR PROJECT SETTINGS

Using the Properties command (choose Movie from the Modify menu, then choose Properties), it is always good to set up your overall movie attributes to match your design at the very beginning of your project. In this way your backplate image and components will correctly fit into your product's window.

In the Movie Properties dialog box, make sure that the Stage size is set to 640 × 480, and enter your own information in the fields provided for "About" and "Copyright" text. The remaining settings can be left at their default values. Since you will be using a backplate image (BikeInterface5.jpg) that is the same size as the project window, the background color is immaterial, as the background will always be hidden behind the backplate.

STEP 2: IMPORTING YOUR MEDIA CONTENT

1. Start Director. From the File menu, choose Import.
2. In the Import Files into "Internal" dialog box, select the entire contents of the IGTMM folder in the Examples folder on this book's CD-ROM.
3. When you click the Import button, you will be asked to decide whether you want to use Director's color depth or the imported image's color depth. You should select Director's, which will be listed as "Stage (24 bits)" (or 16-bit in Version 8). You can ignore the palette setting, but do check the Same Settings for Remaining Images option so that you do not have to answer this question for each individual image imported.
4. Click the OK button, and in a few seconds your cast window should be populated with the sample media components for the Interactive Guide to Motorcycle Maintenance sample project.

STEP 3: PLACING YOUR CAST MEMBERS ONTO THE STAGE

You are now ready to start using your media components. To place your media components onto the Stage, simply drag them from the cast window to the Score or Stage.

1. Starting with cast member 1, which should be the project's background graphic (BikeInterface5.jpg), drag this cast member and drop it into sprite channel 1, frame 1 on the Score. You drop a cast member onto the Score, instead of the Stage, if you want the resulting sprite to be automatically centered on the Stage. Since this is our background image, this is a desired effect.
2. Once you have placed the background graphic, stretch the duration of the sprite out to frame number 60 by dragging the right end of the sprite indicator on the Score.
3. In turn, drag each of the Up button image cast members onto the Stage in Frame 1. Place each one on the left-hand button bar and match its location to that shown in Figure 6.17 and 15.4 (the Chapter 6 figure is clearer).

Each of your button state graphics must be perfectly positioned on top of each other, and on your background, to give the illusion of a mechanical button. You can make sure that the sprite using the button image is positioned correctly by making it appear and disappear with the channel on/off button shown in Figure 15.12. Using this technique of blinking the sprite on and off, you can see whether the button sprite image "shifts" against the background indicating that it is not in register with the background image. If you can blink the button image off and on in quick succession, and all that appears and disappears is the

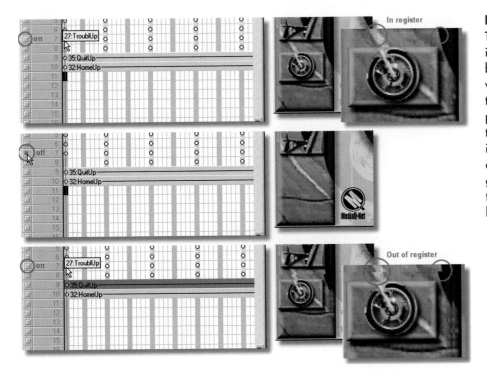

Figure 15.12
The top image shows the button image sprite placed above the background image in register, while the bottom image shows the result of the same sprite placed out of register (note that the part of the background used in the button image is not aligned with the matching background). The center image shows the sprite hidden to reveal the background.

button itself (and the background is unaffected), then you have the button Sprite in perfect registration with the background image. This is illustrated in Figure 15.12, where the TroubleUp button sprite is switched on and off to show the developer the shift in background image resulting from the button image not being in register with the background. After trying this a few times, this technique will become more familiar to you, and an indispensable one in each Director project you pursue.

STEP 4: ADDING BEHAVIORS

You will notice that this example has a set of three images for each button: an Up button (normal state), a Hot button (rollover state) and a Down button (clicked state). To animate these images in response to the user's actions you can apply the Push Button behavior to each of the images already placed on the application's toolbar, which will incorporate the remaining button state images of the set.

1. Select the Push Button behavior in the Library window and drag it onto the first button image on the Stage, as shown in Figure 15.13.

2. When the Parameters for "Push Button" dialog box appear, choose the appropriate cast member image for the Standard (Up), Rollover (Hot) and MouseDown (Down) state. You will notice that the media components provided for this exercise have been named in such a way that you can tell from the file name whether the button is the Up, Hot, or Down state image. You can leave the other settings at their default values. Complete this task for each of the buttons in turn.

STEP 5: ADDING A LITTLE LINGO FOR INTERACTIVE FLAVOR

If you click the Run button now, your project will act rather strangely and uncontrolled. Watch the playback head; it runs at the prescribed frame rate across all frames. Once it is past the end of your button sprite duration lines, the button images disappear.

Figure 15.13

Dragging a behavior to a sprite gives that sprite the functionality of that behavior and automatically opens the behavior parameters dialog box, as shown.

To remedy this, and to give the first stage of control to your application, you want the first frame to remain in play until users click one of the project's control buttons you just developed. Once users click a button, you want the program to take them to the appropriate part of the program (that step comes a little later in this exercise).

To make the first frame loop onto itself until told to do otherwise, you must type a Lingo instruction into the frame script. Double-click the first frame's Script cell and between the *on exitFrame* and *end* commands, type in the following Lingo instruction:

go to the frame

You have just created a Lingo procedure telling the program that when it is exiting the frame, instead of following its natural tendency to go to the next frame, you want it to loop back to itself. It will do this indefinitely for you until it receives an instruction that sends the playback head elsewhere in the application.

If you run your project now, you will see that two important things have occurred. First, note that the playback head is stopped on the first frame and will

USING RELATIVE FRAME POINTERS

You could have entered *go to Frame 0* and have achieved the same results. The Lingo term *the frame* refers to the frame on which the playback head is currently positioned. When you use this reference (as you will see later), that piece of Lingo can be copied and used on other frames and work equally well there. If you had stated the frame number in the command, then you would have to change that number when using the same code on other frames later in this exercise.

not move on. This is as intended. Second, because the playback head is actively looping on this frame, the behavior that you developed for the buttons should now work very nicely. Try them out and see how they work for you. You should see the Hot image appear as the mouse pointer moves over the button, and the Down image appears briefly as the mouse button is depressed over the button. You are now ready to develop those parts of the application that the program will jump to when one of your new buttons is clicked.

STEP 6: USING MARKERS TO ORGANIZE YOUR PROJECT

In this stage you are going to place markers in the marker channel at ten-frame intervals, as shown in Figure 15.6, and name the markers as shown. The purpose of these markers is to locate the position of the target frame you want the program to jump to when the user clicks the appropriate button. Now that you have markers in place, you can use the marker name in your Lingo commands to jump there, rather than having to remember the required frame number.

STEP 7: ADDING A NEW SCREEN FOR EACH SECTION

Because your backplate Sprite has been extended out to cover frames 1 through 60, you will see the blank background with or without buttons as you scrub through the Score window. The next objective is to copy a fresh set of buttons for the interface under each marker, along with the new illustration related to that button choice. For instance, you have designated frame 10 as the scheduled maintenance ("Sched Maint") stopping point. On this frame you will need a complete set of navigation buttons and the scheduled maintenance diagram so that when users are sent to that frame, they see the information they are looking for.

1. In the score, select the top button sprite and, holding down the Shift key, click the last button in the frame. This will select all of the button sprites at once.

2. Change their end frame number in the sprite properties section, located at the top of the Score window, to frame number 1. This will cause all of the button sprites to be just one frame long.

3. While the sprites are still selected (if they are not selected, select them now), right-click them and choose Copy from the shortcut menu to copy the sprite information from the Score.

4. Right-click frame 10, channel 2, and choose Paste from the shortcut menu to paste a complete set of buttons into frame 10 to be used for the Scheduled Maintenance section of our program.

5. Repeat this same pasting process for each of the remaining marked frames. You should end up with a complete interface for each marked and labeled frame.

STEP 8: CUSTOMIZING THE MARKED SCREENS

You will need to allow your users to click on the application's interface buttons. In our simple example this benefit is a diagram that serves as a next-level interface for specific details and information in a completed application. For now, our mock-up stops at the diagram level.

1. In your cast window, locate each of the diagram cast members (they have "Diag" as part of their name). Drag each diagram to its frame as marked earlier.

2. Use the same channel on/off blinking technique to register each diagram over the background image. When blinked on and off, only the overlaid schematic and text should seem to appear and disappear. Make sure that when you hide the schematic image that the background doesn't "shift."

3. When each diagram is positioned, shorten the sprites' duration to just that one frame. Since they occupy different frames, you should be able to place all of the diagram sprites in the same channel.

4. Once you have the sprites all placed, use the frame scrubbing technique to check that the correct diagram is in the correct target frame, and that all diagram images are placed in register with the background image.

To enable the target frames to operate like the first frame, you will need to select and copy (Ctrl+C) the first frame's script sprite from the Score and paste (Ctrl+V) it into the Score channel for each of the target frames.

STEP 9: PROVIDING BUTTON DIRECTION

Now that you have a skeletal application assembled, you will have to provide the appropriate commands as a response to users' clicking any of the interface buttons. When your users click the Safety button, you want them to be jumped to the Safety frame of your project and held there until they click an alternative button.

There are two ways to tell Director what to do in response to a mouse click on one of your interface buttons. First, the button behavior provides a detailed description on how to modify its canned Lingo to achieve this functionality of the button. Right-click the button onstage and choose Script from the shortcut menu. You will find many comments and details throughout the behavior's Lingo to guide you to the most appropriate way to place your commands.

Second, you can give the Down and Hot button cast members the simple Lingo command to go to the appropriate frame label in their *mouseUp* events. Wherever these cast members are used in the project, they will carry with them the instructions to jump to the frame specified by your code whenever users click on them. When you're using the Push Button behavior, this Lingo command must be placed in both the Down and Hot images to trap the *mouseUp* event and execute your command. Placing the Lingo in just the Down button cast member (or just the Hot button cast member) will not suffice.

1. For the Safety button, locate the SafetyDn cast member and right-click it. Choose Cast Member Script from the shortcut menu and in the *mouseUp* event procedure in the Script Window, type in the command *go to "Safety"*. This action tells Director to jump to the frame labeled *Safety*.

2. Locate the SafetyHot cast member and do the same. Now if you run your program from frame 1, clicking the Safety button jumps you to the Safety target frame and displays the safety diagram.

3. Repeat this procedure for the remaining buttons using the marker name, taking care to remember both the Down and Hot cast members.

Once you have created the Lingo for each button, run your program and test each button's operation. If you followed each step accurately, you should have a fully operational button bar for your application. Check out the exercises at the end of this chapter for how to create a Home button and a Quit button.

STEP 10: CREATING YOUR PROJECTOR (EXECUTABLE FILE)

Director can produce a completely stand-alone executable file that performs exactly as you have designed it without requiring users to install a copy of Director. This final executable version of the program is called a projector, in Director terminology.

1. Make sure that you have saved your project. From the File menu, choose Create Projector.

2. In the Create Projector dialog box, locate the project Director (.dir) file you just saved.

3. Once it is selected, click the Create button. Director prompts you for a file name for your projector. The name you provide will be the filename of your project's executable file. Once you click Save, Director compiles your final project file.

4. To test this executable version of your project, locate it on your hard drive, and double-click the projector file. It should run as a stand-alone application and perform exactly as you designed it.

Figure 15.14 shows the final product as it should also appear on your screen (with the exception of the Home and Quit buttons), showing the result of users clicking the Safety button.

The CD-ROM that accompanies this book contains a more elaborate example of this exercise. Load this example into Director and use it with what you have learned in this exercise to discover how to use additional media components in your Director project.

Figure 15.14
The completed Director project, showing the Safety screen.

ANIMATION AND TWEENING IN DIRECTOR

There are many ways to build animation in Director. You can create the animation in another application, such as Painter, Premiere, trueSpace, Carrara, or Flash and import it into Director. In these cases, you would be importing the digital movie output from such an application. You could create a 3D movie in trueSpace, for instance, and import this movie into Director as an AVI file. In the case of Flash (though Flash can also create AVI digital video) you can directly import your Flash project into Director and use it as an integral part of Director.

You can also use Director's built-in animation features to create dramatic animation. The simplest of Director's animation techniques is called *tweening,* as described in Part 3, in which a sprite's position, scale, rotation, and ink effect can be altered over frames by determining the starting frame state, changing these attributes of the sprite in the last frame of the intended animation sequence, and then instructing Director to "tween" the intervening frames. Director calculates all of the intervening animation states to animate the sprite's appearance smoothly from the first frame to the last.

To do this, simply drag the sprite to the first frame of your intended animation sequence. Make sure that the sprite stretches on the Score across all the frames over which you want to create the animation. Go to the last frame of the animation, and change the location, scale, rotation and/or ink effect of the sprite. Director will automatically tween the intervening frames to provide a smooth animated transition from the first frame to the last. In this way you can set your animation keyframes, much as you did for other animation applications in Part 3.

FILM LOOPS

Before there were animated GIF files, Director provided a simple way to use a continuous looping animation as an individual cast member. This single cast member with its own animation is called a *film loop.*

The advantage of this type of animation built into one cast member is that you can place the animation on any frame you want it to appear and it will simply loop forever. This is especially good for animated logos. Without the availability of an animated cast member you would have to plan your animation over many frames and determine the appropriate frame rate of play and how many frames to allow for it. Since this is all built into a film loop, the cast member itself provides the animation.

The easiest way to create a film loop is to import an animated GIF and let Director convert it into a film loop. Then you can drag it to whatever frame you want to see it in, and treat it as any other cast member. Let's say you want to create a film loop from a sequence of images, import them into Director, and place them temporarily on the Score in the same channel, but in sequential frames, making sure that each image only is one frame in duration. Select the group of frames in the Score and drag it to a vacant cast slot, as illustrated in Figure 15.15. Director automatically creates a film loop from the sequence for you, asking you to name it as shown in Figure 15.15. This new cast member can then be used as an individual animated element wherever you please. You must remember, however, not to delete or modify any of the cast members that were used to create the film loop, as Director expects them to remain in the cast for use in creating the film loop sprite when required.

The next section of this chapter gives you a brief overview of Multimedia Fusion, explains its primary functions, and guides you through the initial building of a multimedia application using this development tool.

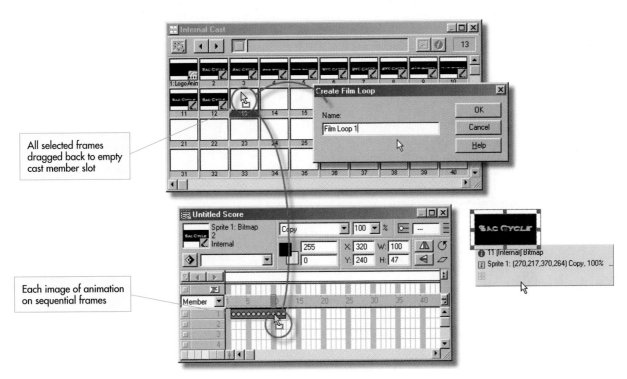

Figure 15.15
Creating an animated film loop in Director.

INTRODUCTION TO MULTIMEDIA AUTHORING USING CLICKTEAM'S MULTIMEDIA FUSION

Multimedia Fusion is a very sophisticated product offering the multimedia producer immense power and flexibility. There are far too many aspects of Multimedia Fusion to give most of them adequate coverage in this book. In addition to Multimedia Fusion's comprehensive multimedia product development tools are a versatile game development engine and a screensaver development engine. These aspects of the product are well beyond the scope of this book.

Multimedia Fusion comes with a sophisticated multimedia tutorial that guides you through the process of creating interactive applications in Multimedia Fusion. It is perhaps the quickest way to become familiar with this tool and learn the basic steps. Please check out this book's Web site for links and references to more information about Multimedia Fusion.

THE MULTIMEDIA FUSION INTERFACE

As shown in Figures 15.2 and 15.3, the Multimedia Fusion interface comprises a series of windows, each offering a different aspect of the multimedia product development process. Please refer to these two illustrations as a guide to the primary functions of the Multimedia Fusion interface.

Figure 15.16 attempts to illustrate the primary development tool windows in Multimedia Fusion, and the keyboard shortcuts used to invoke them. By becoming familiar with these keyboard shortcuts, you will be able to jump between tool windows in midtask—which, as you will soon find out, can be a very beneficial talent! When developing a large-format (800 × 600 or larger)

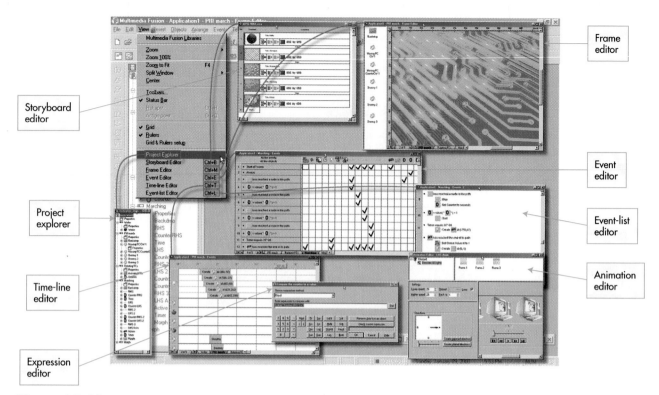

Figure 15.16

The primary windows in Multimedia Fusion, showing the keyboard shortcuts available for quickly switching from one window to the other.

multimedia product, the frame you are working on can often take up all the screen area you have, obscuring the other windows that you need to build and track your work. Use the keyboard shortcuts to skip back and forth between all aspects of your work.

There are a couple of very important aspects of Multimedia Fusion you should keep in mind as you're learning how to use this product. First, because Multimedia Fusion is an object-oriented development tool, you can drag-and-drop elements and components of your project wherever you please. You can drag a media component or graphic from one frame to the next, or from a previous Multimedia Fusion project to the current one. You can even drag object properties to ensure that two objects have the same properties as the one you dragged from. Second, Multimedia Fusion makes extensive exclusive use of the right mouse button to provide shortcut menus and options. Whereas most applications provide these shortcut menus as an alternative way to get to a feature or process, Multimedia Fusion sometimes provides this as the only way to reach that command. When in doubt, right-click an object and you may find the command you're looking for.

Refer to Figure 15.16 as you read about the specific aspects, windows, and tools of Multimedia Fusion.

OBJECTS

Multimedia Fusion's power as an interactive application development tool comes from its object-oriented roots. All aspects of the development process can be viewed in terms of objects and their use. Multimedia Fusion provides the developer with a rich toolbox of almost forty objects. By placing these objects onto a frame, you can then check for specific events that will occur in your program, and have your objects respond with an action of your choice.

To view the primary objects available in Multimedia Fusion, you can do one of the following:

1. Check out the list of commonly used objects available from the objects toolbar (as seen in Figure 15.17).

2. Choose Object from the Insert menu and see a more comprehensive list of objects provided from that menu.

3. Choose Insert an Object from the Insert menu to invoke the Create New Object dialog box, which lists all available objects.

Once an object is added to your frame, you can set that object's properties, such as its name, its fade-in/fade-out characteristics, and its movement characteristics by right-clicking it and selecting them from the shortcut menu, or by double-clicking the object's expanded properties icon in the Project Explorer. The method you use to access the object's properties is up to you.

You will notice that the new object now appears in the Event Editor with its own action column (as described next). This allows you to control what this object does when you want it to do something for you.

Some of these objects are especially noteworthy.

- The **Quick Backdrop Object** provides a way to set a color, gradient, or tiled pattern backdrop quickly and with little memory overhead.

- The **Backdrop Object** is for placing image files as a backdrop for a Frame.

- The **Active Object** is perhaps the most important object in Multimedia Fusion. It can be used to simply display a picture, store and display an animation, provide an object whose direction changes with its movement, function as an interactive button, and much more. You will read more about the Active Object later; it is specifically referenced in the Animation Editor section that follows.

- The **Counter Object** can both display and store numeric data for you. For instance, if you were to set a timer event that triggered every second, and set that event's action to set the counter to the timer's seconds value, you would have created a seconds display for your application.

- The **Button Object** is very useful for creating a plain gray button, a graphical button, a checkbox, or an option button.

- The **AVI**, **MPEG**, and **QuickTime Objects** all work in the same way and provide a convenient and easy way to place digital video in your Frame. Use these objects to put digital video in your application.

- The **String Object** and **Formatted Text Object** display anti-aliased text on your frame.

- The **ActiveX Object** allows you to insert an ActiveX control into your application. ActiveX controls are readily available programming tools that allow programmers to plug in additional functionality into their programming projects. This add-on technology works very well in Multimedia Fusion. For example, if you wanted to include Macromedia Flash animation in Multimedia Fusion, simply add the Flash Shockwave ActiveX control and set the appropriate parameters. Presto! You have just extended Multimedia Fusion's capabilities to include Shockwave! Pretty amazing, don't you think?

- The **Netscape Object** enables you to use browser capabilities in your multimedia application.

ActiveX

A technology from Microsoft that packages small programs or program components in a format that can be easily embedded in another program or Web page and used by a Web browser or another software development tool. ActiveX components can provide special capabilities and features to a browser application, much in the same way a plug-in extends the capabilities of the browser. An ActiveX component is integrated and used as you view the Web page using the component, whereas a plug-in has to be installed separately into the browser.

Using digital video in Multimedia Fusion is a simple process. Simply place the appropriate digital video object (AVI, QuickTime, FLC, or MPEG) onto the frame and select the required settings from the properties settings panel that appears.

Unlike digital sound, digital video is not embedded into the final executable file, and therefore the actual digital video file must accompany your application's final executable file. If you delete the path reference in the digital movie's "File to play" properties and simply enter the filename alone, Multimedia Fusion expects to find the digital video file in the same directory as the executable itself.

Objects can be given behaviors. Much as in Director, each object can have its own list of events and actions, which are set in the Event Editor window. This window appears when you choose the Properties command, then the Behavior command from the shortcut menu you see when you right-click an object. If you want a group of your objects to have a certain behavior (such as a rollover effect for a group of buttons), then you can create an object with the appropriate behaviors and clone that object. The behaviors are also cloned. To clone an object, select it in the frame, right-click on it, and choose Clone from the shortcut menu.

Your object can also be given a movement. These movements allow you to animate your object with a high degree of precision. With a new movement, be sure to set an event that checks the object's position on the screen and takes action if it gets to the edge. Otherwise your object will run off the screen and continue ad infinitum. Try setting an object's movement to "bouncing ball" and accept the default settings. When setting an event for the object (you will read how in the section on the Event Editor), choose the Position command, then choose the Test Position of "object" command from the shortcut menu. In the dialog box that appears, click the arrows pointing toward the inner edge of the screen. Then, as a response action for this event, set the object's movement to "bounce." When you run your application, the object moves smoothly to each edge of the screen, and upon hitting the edge, bounces back into the screen area. You can use this quite effectively as a terrific animated logo.

As with frames, each object can be given a fade-in or fade-out transition, which will be seen when the object is first created in your frame and when it is destroyed. Multimedia Fusion provides the best available special-effect transitions available in a multimedia authoring tool. Its fades are splendid.

Spend some time checking these object and frame transitions, and be sure to check out this book's Web site for links to more downloadable objects and fade effects for your multimedia projects.

THE FRAME EDITOR

The Frame Editor is Multimedia Fusion's equivalent to Director's Stage. In Multimedia Fusion you build your multimedia application and its interface. You build your Multimedia Fusion application as a series of frames constructed in the Storyboard. Each frame can be designed and assembled in this window. Figure 15.17 shows the Frame Editor in use, highlighting its primary features.

You will notice that on the left side of this window is a panel that lists the objects used in this frame. Every element used in this frame will be shown here, with the exception of sounds (which appear in the Event Editor). This same list of objects also appears in the Project Explorer, shown at the left edge of the program in Figure 15.17. Objects from another frame can be dragged to the frame showing in the Frame Editor at will.

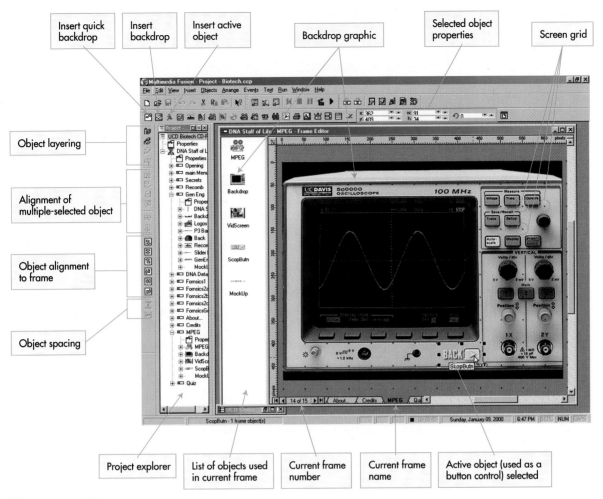

Labels around the figure:

Insert quick backdrop
Insert backdrop
Insert active object
Backdrop graphic
Selected object properties
Screen grid

Object layering
Alignment of multiple-selected object
Object alignment to frame
Object spacing

Project explorer
List of objects used in current frame
Current frame number
Current frame name
Active object (used as a button control) selected

Figure 15.17
The Multimedia Fusion Frame Editor is where each frame of the multimedia application is designed and assembled.

In the Frame Editor you can insert objects; adjust their properties, position, and appearance; and navigate from frame to frame in your application. Note in Figure 15.17 that there are a series of tabs on the bottom of the Frame Editor window. You can use these tabs to move back and forth between frames with ease. Figure 15.17 also shows a regular series of small dots on the surface of the frame. These dots are the grid dots that have been turned on. They can be very useful for aligning objects and their animation. You can toggle the grid visibility on or off by choosing Grid from the View menu. You can use the Grid & Rulers Setup command on the View menu to adjust the grid spacing and turn grid snapping on or off.

To add a backdrop to your Frame, simply click the Quick Backdrop or Backdrop button as required. The Quick Backdrop button provides a rectangular object that you can stretch to suit the size of your frame. It can generate a solid color, gradient color, or tiles bitmap background. In this way you can use a small image file and tile it over your frame background with little file size impact. The Background button allows you to import a bitmap as your background image. Simply place a Background Object onto your frame, double-click it to open its image editor window, go to the File menu and choose Import, then choose Bitmap to load the background graphic. You can always copy your background image in your image editing application, such as Paint Shop Pro, and paste it into the Background Object's image editor window. Figure 15.17 shows

Figure 15.18

The Multimedia Fusion Frame Editor properties dialog box is invoked by double-clicking the properties icon in the Project Explorer, or by right-clicking the frame in the Storyboard Editor.

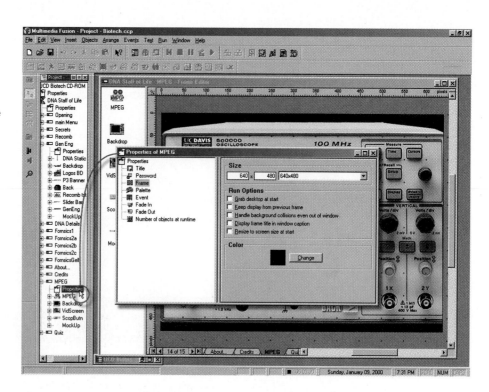

a picture of an oscilloscope used as a background and, when running, as a frame for an MPEG movie, which appears on the oscilloscope screen.

To add one of the many objects to a Multimedia Fusion frame, simply click the appropriate object button (or use the Insert an Object command on the Insert menu for even more object choices) and move your mouse pointer to the frame. Notice that the mouse pointer changes to a crosshair shape, indicating that your next click will position the requested object on the frame.

Most of the properties for the frame are best set in the Storyboard Editor. You can also double-click a frame properties icon in the Project Explorer window, usually located to the left of the Multimedia Fusion interface. Figure 15.18 shows the frame properties dialog box invoked in this way.

When you want to test your frame and see whether it's behaving as designed, click either the Play or Run Frame button at the top of the screen. The F7 key is a keyboard shortcut for this function. You also can click the Play button in the Event Editor window. To test the entire application's operation from the beginning through the frame you are working on, simply click the Run Application button, or press F8 on your keyboard.

In the next section on the Storyboard Editor, you will see how to add, move, and delete frames; name them; specify their properties; and set their in and out transitions.

THE STORYBOARD EDITOR

In the Storyboard Editor you get the "big picture" of your application. You can view a thumbnail image of each frame and its relevant details. Figure 15.19 shows the Storyboard Editor with the comments section visible beside a version of the same storyboard with the comments section hidden. The Show Comments button on the left-hand toolbar will show or hide this extra information for each frame. Right-clicking the frame thumbnail image invokes a shortcut menu, as shown in the illustration. To add another frame, simply click the numbered button to the left of the word *More,* as shown in Figure 15.19, and select from the add frame panel the type of new frame you want to add here.

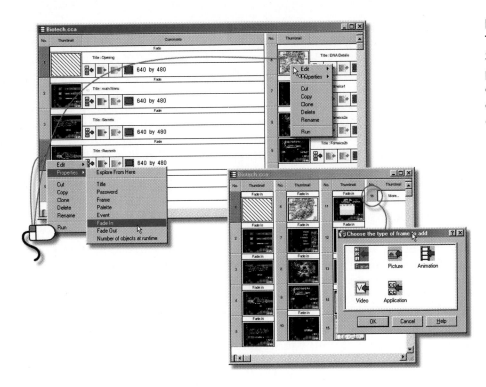

Figure 15.19
The Multimedia Fusion
Storyboard Editor shows the
pop-up options available by
clicking or right-clicking sections
of the frame information
displayed.

In the Storyboard Editor you can drag the thumbnail images to reorder them as desired. This makes the task of changing and adjusting your application relatively easy.

To view a specific frame in the Frame Editor, simply click the numbered button to the immediate left of the frame thumbnail image. Be aware that doing so opens a copy of the Frame Editor every time you click this button. It is best to launch one copy of the Frame Editor, and then use the navigation controls in the bottom margin of the window to get to a different frame.

To replicate a frame, simply right-click the frame thumbnail image and choose Clone from the shortcut menu. This creates an identical copy of the frame that you can then customize to suit your application needs. When developing a Multimedia Fusion application, it is a good idea to create one template frame and then clone it for as many frames as you need to create.

Usually you will bring up the Storyboard Editor when you want to see your application's overall plan, or to adjust some of the frame properties. When not in use, it is a good idea to minimize the Storyboard Editor and then bring it back whenever you want by pressing Ctrl+B on your keyboard.

THE EVENT, EVENT-LIST, AND TIME-LINE EDITORS

The Event Editor is where you control the actions called in response to events in each frame of your application. In this window you see an event/action grid to which you add event rows and response action columns. Each row represents

MULTIMEDIA FUSION PREFERENCES

If the Frame Wizard appears, the Create a New Frame checkbox is marked under the Wizards tab in the Preferences control panel. You can change this and many other Multimedia Fusion options by selecting Preferences . . . from the File menu.

an event. Response actions are set in the columns beneath the icons. The specified event controls anything placed as an action in any cell in the row located beneath an action column. To determine what event should trigger what action, choose the event, and then choose the action it triggers.

To select an event with which to associate an action, click the New Condition button, and as instructed at the top of the New Condition dialog box that appears, right-click the icon whose event you want to trap, as shown in Figure 15.20. In the illustration, the event being selected is the pressing of any key on the keyboard. Once selected, this event shows as a row heading, waiting for you to choose the action you want to follow the key press.

Figure 15.20 shows such a typical list of events and the responses to each one. The Event Editor is used to set and edit these events and actions. The Event-list Editor provides a sequential list of these events in order of appearance, broken out into individual actions for you to more clearly read them. The Time-line Editor shows these actions as they occur over time in the frame. You can use these editors to view your designed interactivity event/action combinations from many perspectives.

You can tell Multimedia Fusion to respond to any event in your project. Perhaps when an object has reached the end of a movement path that you have assigned to it, you would like to jump to the next frame. Maybe when the user clicks an image of a button, you would like to replay the application. As an example, you could decide that two seconds into the frame your program should play a sound effect. The timer reaching the two-second point is the event, and the action you choose to happen at that instant is the playing of the sound file (this would be located in the Sound column). All of these events trigger an action. By building a list of events and responses to these events, you can create a sophisticated interactive program. Because of the object-oriented nature of Multimedia Fusion (responding to an object's events by giving objects action commands), you can specify exactly what you want to occur exactly when you want it to happen without having to worry about frame rate or keeping pace with the rest of the program. If you do want to fine-tune timings you can do so in the Time-line Editor, as shown in Figure 15.20.

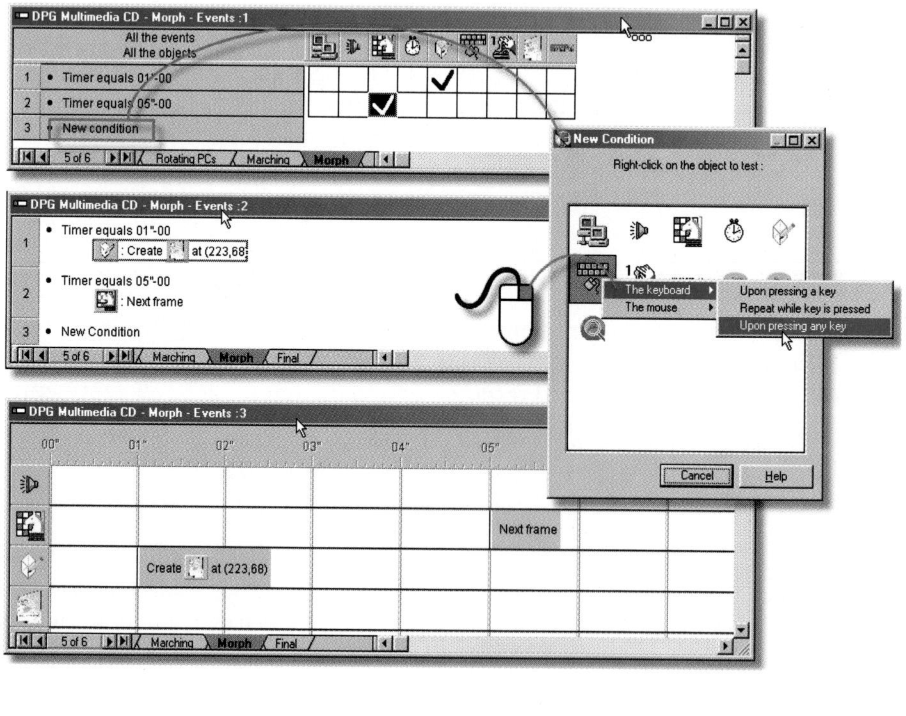

Figure 15.20

The Multimedia Fusion Event Editor, Event-list Editor, and Time-line Editor windows (top to bottom) showing the same series of events and actions in their respective views.

Using sound in Multimedia Fusion is a simple process. Simply set an action to play any sound data by choosing the appropriate action from the shortcut menu that appears when you right-click the Sound column in the Event Editor. This action can be triggered by many possible events. If you want the sound as a background sound to your application, simply use the start frame as the trigger and set the sound to loop forever. The sound could be a button-click sound, in which case the same event of clicking the button that is used for navigation can be used to play the button sound.

Once a sound is used in Multimedia Fusion, it is embedded into the application and is available for use elsewhere in the application without having to reload it. Be sure to use the lowest possible sound settings that you can while still retaining an acceptable quality level (see Chapters 12 and 13). Unused sounds are not embedded, so if you load a sound and don't use it, it will be discarded when Multimedia Fusion builds your stand-alone executable version for you.

In the Event Editor, the first seven action columns in the grid are for setting standard action responses. You can set actions for Special Conditions, Sound, Storyboard Controls, The Timer, Create New Object, Mouse Pointer and Keyboard, and Player by right-clicking the column beneath the appropriate heading. These columns are indicated in Figure 15.3.

The easiest way to learn how to create Multimedia Fusion events and actions is to try them out. Take some time to explore the large number of options available to you when you assemble your events and corresponding actions for your application. Right-clicking the action cells invokes a shortcut menu listing your available options for that object or function column. By spending a little time with the Event Editor, you will become familiar and conversant with Multimedia Fusion's way of building interactivity.

Later in this chapter you will build an interactive program and learn how to assemble these event/action groups.

> In Multimedia Fusion, if you pause the mouse pointer over an action cell in the Event Editor, a pop-up panel lists details of the actions set in that cell. The information shown is similar to that shown in the Events list Editor.

THE ANIMATION EDITOR

The Animation Editor is an integral part of the Active Object you've read about. It allows you to import and/or build an animated sequence of images that become an integral part of the object. These animations are conceptually and in practice very similar to animated GIF files in that the animation data is stored in the object to be placed and used in whatever context you decide. You can invoke the Animation Editor by double-clicking the Active Object.

Notice in Figure 15.21 that the Animation Editor shows a pair of Directions for that Active Object. You can set quite a few Directions for an Active Object, and each Direction can store a complete animation of its own. If you would like to change that animation later, simply select an event that will trigger the action of that Active Object changing to a specified Direction.

Don't let the word *Direction* confuse you. Think of it more as a different image that can be stored in the object and is on call for whenever you want to change the object's appearance to the other image. You can simply view Active Object Directions as storage slots for different animations. Later in this chapter you will see how to use these Directions to build simple and effective animated buttons. In Figure 15.21 you can see the many frames of the animation for the first Direction. Double-clicking any of these thumbnail images invokes the image editing window, as seen on top of the Animation Editor. Using this window, you

Directions

In Multimedia Fusion, a Direction is an image stored in an object that will be displayed when that object travels in the "direction" specified. For example, an object that represents a car would have an image of that car facing right in the "Right" direction, and one facing left in the "Left" direction. When the car is moving onscreen in the application, the image showing the car facing in the correct direction of travel will be displayed. Direction images can also be used as storage slots for multiple pictures of a stationary object, such as the three button state graphics.

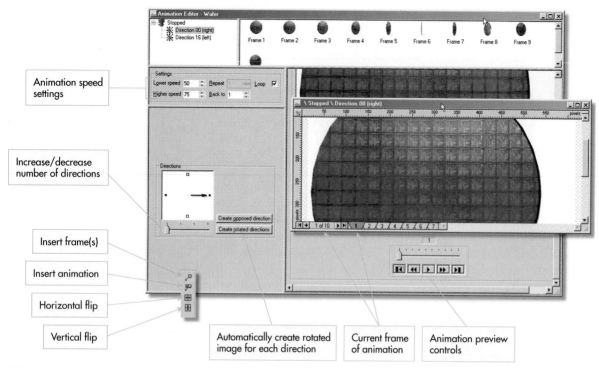

Animation speed settings

Increase/decrease number of directions

Insert frame(s)

Insert animation

Horizontal flip

Vertical flip

Automatically create rotated image for each direction

Current frame of animation

Animation preview controls

Figure 15.21

The Multimedia Fusion Animation Editor, showing an animation of a revolving disk in Direction (00).

can edit each and every frame of the animated Direction. Using the slider beneath the Directions indicator, you can specify how many directions (and therefore how many different images) you would like to have for this object.

IMPORTING AN IMAGE OR ANIMATION. You can import an animation into the Animation Editor. If you have an animated GIF, AVI, MPEG, or QuickTime file, you can convert it to an animated object by opening the animation editor and selecting the file for import (on the File menu, choose Import, then choose Animation). In this way you can quickly import an animation loop you created in your 3D animation application (refer to the chapters in Part 3) and use it as a media component in your new project. Then, this Active Object will display your imported animation everywhere you use it.

The Animation Editor is also where you will import static images into Multimedia Fusion. There are several ways to do this. When you place a new Active Object in your frame, the Animation Editor automatically appears,

When referring to these multimedia creation tools, the word *frame* is often used in similar circumstances but referring to entirely different things. With Multimedia Fusion, do not confuse the frame on which you build your project to a frame of an animation in the Animation Editor.

CREATING AUTOMATICALLY ROTATED DIRECTIONS

If you have an animated spacecraft pointing right in the default right-pointing direction, clicking the Create rotated directions button automatically copies the animation to each new Direction slot and recreates the animation for you with rotated images already in place. If you were to create a racing car game, for instance, it would be quite handy to use this feature to turn a single image of your car into a complete set of rotated images that show it running in whatever direction it is assigned.

Before you import an image, you may want to set the Picture Editor Zoom settings in the Preferences control panel so that imported images are scaled at their normal size and not zoomed to fit. Do this by invoking the preferences control panel (choose Preferences from the File menu); on the Picture/Animation Editor Preferences tab, select the Fixed Picture Editor Zoom option. Specify 1:1 as the desired scale.

showing the default teal diamond image as a single frame of the right-pointing Direction.

THE IMAGE EDITOR

Double-click the frame in the Animation Editor to invoke the Image Editor. You can paste a new image from the clipboard into this Image Editor, or, while it's open, choose Import from the File menu, then choose Bitmap and select the image you want to import. On importing you will be allowed to set the image's transparency color and specify whether this is the first image of an animation you are building. You can also use one of the buttons that appear in the left-hand toolbar when the Animation Editor is active. These buttons are shown in Figure 15.21. The Insert Animation button also enables you to create a morph effect between any two animation frames in a Direction. Experiment with this tool to see how it can be useful as a special effect in your multimedia project.

IMAGE TRANSPARENCY.   You can set many colors of an image as transparent in Multimedia Fusion. When the Image Editor is visible, you will see a selection of image editing tools on the left-hand toolbar. The small color wheel icon enables you to select the colors you wish to make transparent. Use the eyedropper to select colors for transparency, and when you're done, the remaining visible image will have a selection marquee surrounding it. Choose Invert Selection from the Edit menu, which will invert the selection marquee to select the background. Then you can press the Delete key on the keyboard to remove it. To end your image editing session, click the Close button in the top right corner of the Image Editor and select Yes when asked whether you would like to save your changes.

To close the Animation Editor, click the Close button again, and click Yes when asked to save changes.

You will read later in the worked example that you can choose a Direction to store different button state images in one object, and then use the button's behavior to change Direction (change button image) when the mouse pointer is over the button object.

THE EXPRESSION EDITOR

The Expression Editor is where you can do some calculations and math and design command statements to complement Multimedia Fusion's already comprehensive catalog of standard functions. It automatically pops up when needed and when appropriate, so you don't have to worry about when to use it—it will be there for you. You can see what it looks like in Figure 15.16.

If you want to set a Global Value (a variable that can be used to store or transfer data across frames), choose Change a Global Value, then choose Set from the shortcut menu that appears when you right-click the Special Conditions column in the Event Editor. This brings up the Expression Editor, where you can specify the value. The Expression Editor allows you to fetch a value from an object. In this way you can use values such as the current frame number to make decisions in the Event Editor. As you become more familiar with Multimedia Fusion you will see how the Expression Editor can be a very useful and versatile tool.

CREATING A MULTIMEDIA FUSION PRODUCTION IN TEN STEPS

The following exercise will show you how to build a working multimedia interface and the beginning of a complete multimedia application. While the exercise is designed to use prepared media content that you will have seen earlier in the book, you can always substitute your own media components and create your own custom example. By working this exercise you will get a better feel for how the many features, tools, and techniques available to you in Multimedia Fusion all come together to help you develop awesome multimedia products.

STEP 1: CREATING YOUR PROGRAM'S FRAME

When you start a new application in Multimedia Fusion, you are provided with a Storyboard Editor with a default frame size (640 × 480) and color (white). You can use those defaults for this exercise.

1. Select the frame's title (which should read "Untitled Frame" until you change it) and type in "Start".
2. Click the button (numbered 1) to the left of the frame thumbnail image in the Storyboard Editor to open the Frame Editor. You can also right-click on the frame in the Storyboard and select Frame Editor from the Edit menu available at the top of the shortcut menu.

STEP 2: BUILDING THE FRAME BACKGROUND

To start you will need to import our application's backdrop image.

1. Click the Insert Backdrop Object button in the Multimedia Fusion object toolbar or select Backdrop from object menu list, available under the Insert menu, and then move the mouse pointer to the frame.
2. Click with the mouse pointer crosshairs anywhere in the top left corner of the frame. This places an icon representing an empty Backdrop Object and shows the Image Editor for the Backdrop Object.
3. On the File menu, choose Import, then choose Bitmap, and select the BikeInterface5.jpg file.
4. Click Open in the import image dialog box when the image appears in the panel.
5. When your imported image appears in the Image Editor, click the Close button.
6. Click Yes when asked to save the image. The backdrop image and the frame are both the same 640 × 480 pixel size.
7. Use the object positioning buttons shown in Figure 15.17 to place the backdrop to the left and top edges of the frame.

STEP 3: BUILDING BUTTONS—IMPORT BUTTON UP STATE IMAGE

You will use an Active Object as a button control. Once you have built one, you can clone it and change its stored images to quickly build the remaining buttons required.

1. Click the Insert Active Object button in the Multimedia Fusion object's toolbar.

2. Click with the crosshair mouse pointer in the frame (it doesn't yet matter where you place this object).

3. The Animation Editor should pop up. Double-click the default animation frame to invoke the Image Editor for that frame.

4. With the Image Editor showing, choose Import from the File menu, then choose Bitmap and select the first button Up state (SchedUp.jpg) file.

5. Click Open in the import image dialog box when the image shows in the panel.

6. When your imported image appears in the Image Editor, click the Close button and click Yes when asked to save the image.

STEP 4: BUILDING BUTTONS—IMPORT BUTTON OVER STATE IMAGE

1. Add another Direction by right-clicking the "Stopped" animation and choosing Insert new direction from the shortcut menu.

2. The Insert New Direction dialog box appears, as shown in Figure 15.22. Select the left-pointing Direction, as shown.

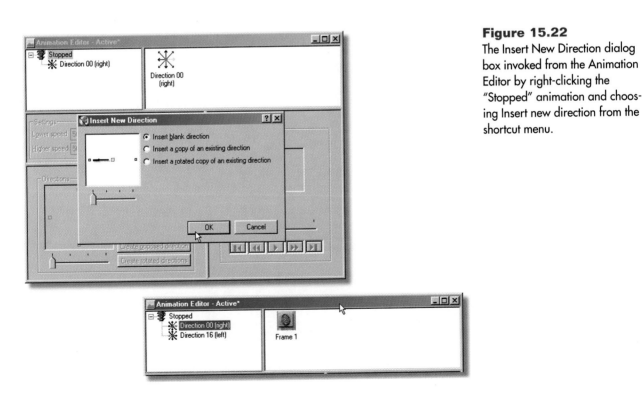

Figure 15.22
The Insert New Direction dialog box invoked from the Animation Editor by right-clicking the "Stopped" animation and choosing Insert new direction from the shortcut menu.

3. Click OK and the Animation Editor shows a new Direction 16 (left) as shown in Figure 15.22. Click on the new Direction 16.

4. Double-click this new Direction's default frame to invoke the Image Editor. From the File menu, choose Import, and then Bitmap and select the Hot button (SchedHot.jpg) image for the new Direction. Click Open in the import image dialog box. You should now have two directions; Direction 00 shows the Schedule button at rest, and Direction 16 shows the rollover state for that button.

5. Click the Animation Editor's Close button. Click Yes when asked to save your work.

STEP 5: BUILDING INTERACTIVITY WITH A BEHAVIOR

1. Right-click the Active Object as it sits in the Frame.

2. From the shortcut menu, choose Properties, and then choose Behavior #1 to bring up the Event Editor, which allows you to build events and actions for this Active Object to give it its custom behavior.

3. As shown in Figure 15.23, click the Words New Condition and then right-click the mouse-pointer-and-keyboard icon in the New Condition dialog box.

4. From the shortcut menu, choose The mouse, and then choose Check for mouse pointer over an object, as shown in Figure 15.23. Select the object showing in the Check for mouse pointer over an object window, as shown in Figure 15.23. This results in the "Mouse pointer is over" event line in the Event Editor. Now you're ready to decide on the appropriate action to be triggered by this event.

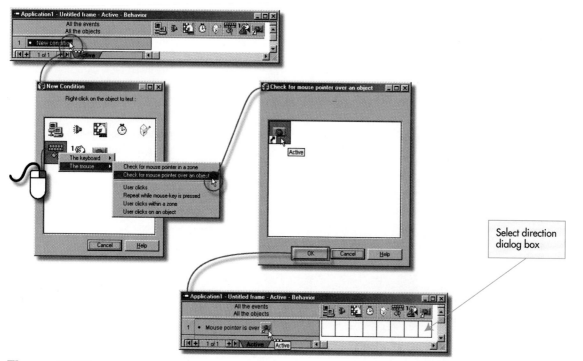

Figure 15.23

The clicking and option-selecting sequence used to add a new event condition to catch when the user moves the mouse pointer over an object.

5. Right-click the row for this event in the column beneath your Active Object button, as shown in Figure 15.23.

6. From the shortcut menu, choose Direction, and then choose Select Direction to invoke the Select Direction dialog box as shown in Figure 15.23.

7. Click to select the left direction box (16) and click the right (00) direction to deselect it. Click OK. You have now instructed the object to change to a different Direction image when the mouse pointer is over it.

Now that you have provided the commands required to change the image of the button (Active Object) when the mouse pointer is over it, you will have to tell it to change back to the normal image when the mouse pointer has moved away. Create a copy of the event you have just built and "negate" it to invert its operation. This will catch when the mouse pointer is *not* over the object. This is simple to do.

8. Click the button numbered 1 in the event editor (indicating that this is the first event) to select the entire event row. The row darkens.

9. Right-click the selected row and choose Copy from the shortcut menu. You have now copied the entire event.

10. Click the New Condition row starter.

11. When the New Condition dialog box appears, click Cancel. You don't want to start a new event condition—you just want to place the blinking cursor on that row for the next step.

12. Hold down the Ctrl key and press V on your keyboard. This is the universal Paste keyboard shortcut (any Windows keyboard shortcut for Paste will work fine, as will the Paste command on the Edit menu). Pressing Ctrl+V pastes an identical event/action row as event condition row 2.

13. Right-click this event and choose Negate from the shortcut menu. By doing so you have turned this condition into "When the mouse pointer is *not* over the object."

Now that you have set an event that will catch the mouse pointer no longer hovering over the object, you need to edit the change direction instruction so that the original image is put back.

14. Right-click the checkmark already occupying the action cell in your objects action column, and choose Edit from the shortcut menu.

15. In the Select Direction dialog box, click the right Direction box (00) to select it, and click the left Direction box (16) to deselect it. Click OK.

16. Test the behavior of your button by clicking the Play button in the top tool-bar and moving your mouse pointer over the Active Object. It should change appearance to the Hot version when the mouse touches it. Click the Stop button.

STEP 6: ADDING INSTRUCTIONS

Right-click your new Active Object button in the list of objects in frame or on the Frame itself. Choose Rename from the shortcut menu, and then type the name "Schedule" in the box provided. You now need to add to the button behavior what should happen if the user clicks on it.

Go back to the Active Objects behavior Events Editor window by right-clicking on the object, choose Properties, and then choose Behavior #1. Click the New Condition row starter button, and in the New Condition dialog box, right-click the mouse-pointer-and-keyboard icon as previously shown in Figure 15.23. This time you will choose The mouse, and then choose User clicks on an object menu option. Click OK in the next dialog box (as you are only catching a normal left-mouse click) and from the User Clicks On An Object dialog box, select the newly named Schedule object. Click OK. You will now have a new event row for the user clicking on the Schedule object.

Right-click the Storyboard Controls column where it intersects the new event row (shown where the mouse pointer is located in Figure 15.24) and choose Jump To Frame. From the Choose A Storyboard Frame dialog box, click the Use a Calculation button and in the Expression Editor type in the number 2. Click OK. Close the event editor window. Since you have yet to create any other frames, you must reference them by number. Later, when you have cloned the first frame, these numbers will match the navigation function of the buttons.

STEP 7: CLONING MORE BUTTONS

Thankfully, you do not have to repeat steps 3 through 6 for the remaining buttons, although that was not a lot of work to build a cool button. Simply right-click your Schedule button in the frame, and choose Clone from the shortcut menu to create an independent replica of the Schedule button. Notice that it is named Schedule 2. If the new button is created on top of the original, you may want to drag it to one side for easier use. Your first step in making this a new button is to rename it to "Safety" as you did for the Schedule button in step 6.

Double-click the Safety button to show the Animation Editor for the button, and then double-click each of the button Direction frames, and import their appropriate images (the Safety button images) as you did with the Schedule button in step 3. You should now have the SafetyUp.jpg and SafetyHot.jpg images in their appropriate places (remember that you are using the right Direction (00) for the normal state image, and the left Direction (16) for the rollover state image).

When you are done replacing the button images with the correct ones for the Safety button, right-click it and choose Properties, and then choose Behavior #1. Notice that this button already has its behavior in place, because it inherited it from the Schedule button. Right-click the Jump to Frame 2 action in event row 3, and choose Edit from the shortcut menu. In the Expression Editor, change the number 2 to 3. You have now created your Safety button.

Repeat all of step 7 for the remaining four buttons, and for each button change the number of the frame that it jumps to. You can set any number you wish for the frame that each button will jump to as long as you make sure the appropriate frame is in that position for it to jump to when you're done.

STEP 8: ALIGNING YOUR BUTTONS

You should now drag the Active Objects you have built as buttons to their positions on the toolbar. Once dragged to their rough location, you can use the arrow keys on your keyboard to move them into alignment with the background. Your application should now look like the example in Figure 15.24. Run the frame by clicking the Play button and test your buttons for their rollover effect.

STEP 9: CLONING THE MASTER FRAME

Now that you have designed and created the master frame, you can now clone as many copies of it as you need for your application (or you could create new frames as your project requires). Your last button, "Troubleshooting," is set to jump to frame number 7, so this indicates that you will need a total of seven copies of this frame.

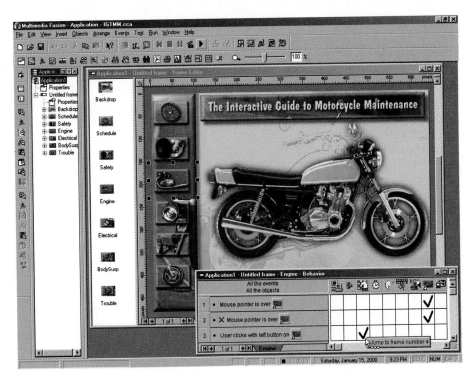

Figure 15.24
The Interactive Guide to Motorcycle Maintenance coming to life in Multimedia Fusion (first frame shown).

In the Storyboard Editor, right-click the start frame and choose Clone from the shortcut menu. Repeat this until you have seven identical frames including the start frame. Name each frame to coincide with the button that will be jumping to it. All that is left is to place on each specific frame its changed diagram to coincide with the topic of the frame.

Bring up the Scheduled frame in the Frame Editor, and place an Active Object onto the backdrop. Double-click the default frame in the Animation Editor when it appears. Import the image file SchedDiag.jpg into the Active Object, click open and close the Image Editor and Animation Editor, answering Yes when asked each time to save changes. Rename this Active Object "Diagram." Position the new Active Object "Diagram" on the backdrop. Use the frame navigation buttons at the bottom of the Frame Editor to flip back and forth between this frame and the next. If the Diagram is not aligned properly, it will show up as a shift in the diagram image. Move it using the keyboard arrow keys until there is no visible shift between frames. Make a note of this object's X and Y coordinate values, as shown at the top of the screen when the object is selected. You will be able to re-use these coordinates for subsequent frames.

Right-click the Diagram Active Object and choose Copy from the shortcut menu. Go to the next frame (Safety) and choose Paste from the Edit menu. Move the crosshair mouse pointer onto the frame and click where you would like to paste this copy of the Diagram Active Object. Use the same import image technique to load the SafetyDiag.jpg image, and then type in the Active Object's X and Y coordinates as recorded from the last diagram. Note that you could, if you prefer, drag the Diagram object from the Project Explorer onto the Safety frame to create a new copy on that frame, and so on for subsequent frames.

Repeat this process to insert the correct Diagram images into each of the remaining four frames. Note that while the Diagram object is still resident in the clipboard, you can simply go to each frame, choose Paste from the Edit menu, and type in the correct coordinates to position it. You can then go back and import the correct image for the frame.

Once this is done, run the entire application by clicking the Run Application button (see Figure 15.2) or by pressing F8 on your keyboard. Test each button

Change the name of your application by right-clicking its primary icon in the Project Explorer and choosing Rename from the shortcut menu, as shown in Figure 15.25 (you can also hold down your mouse button on the default name until it changes into editable text). This name will appear as the application's title in its window's title bar.

Use only 16-color images for your application's icon. Although Multimedia Fusion allows you to place any type of image as the application icon, as shown in Figure 15.25, they will be changed to 16-system-color images and it is best for you to do this manually beforehand to ensure the final outcome.

If your application is running slowly, you can optimize it by forcing your application to use a palette of 32,768 (16-bit) or 256 colors by choosing the appropriate setting in the Graphics Mode section of the application's properties panel. Multimedia Fusion's default color depth is 24-bit. Doing this will reduce the size of all graphics in your application to give better performance and require shorter loading times and less file space. You can always optimize the number of colors in individual images in your application through your image editing software if you don't want to do a complete conversion. Be aware that you cannot undo this step, so be sure to save a copy of the "fat" version before you take this overhead reduction step.

for correct operation. If you followed each step accurately you should have a fully operational button bar for your application. Check out the exercises at the end of this chapter for details on creating a Home and a Quit button.

At this point you will want to check out the application properties in the Project Explorer, as shown in Figure 15.25. These properties determine the appearance of your application, its icon on the Windows desktop, whether it plays in its own Window or full-screen, and so on. These settings will carry over into the next step, which is building a stand-alone application.

Figure 15.25

Multimedia Fusion's application properties control panel, showing window appearance settings and application icon settings.

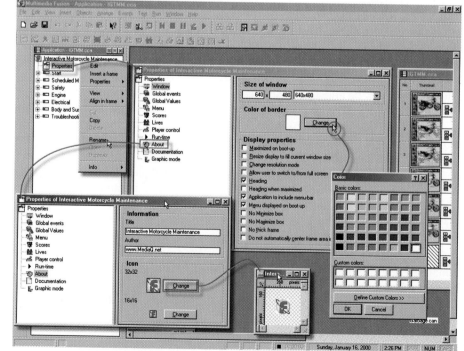

Figure 15.26
The completed Multimedia Fusion project, showing the Electrical & Ignition screen.

Congratulations! You have completed the first phase of your Multimedia Fusion project. The final working product should look something like Figure 15.26 (compare to Figure 15.14).

STEP 10: CREATING THE FINAL STAND-ALONE EXECUTABLE FILE

To finalize your project and build it as a stand-alone piece of software that can be freely distributed to your end user, simply choose Build from the File menu, and then choose Stand-Alone Application. Specify the name you wish to provide your executable file, and click Save. Multimedia Fusion creates an executable file for you to place on your distribution CD-ROM, DVD-ROM, or diskette. It really is that simple.

You will notice that you are provided with four Build options: Project, Stand-Alone Application, Screensaver, and Internet Application. Table 15.3 describes how they are used.

DON'T FORGET THIS FILE!

Unlike Director, Multimedia Fusion's executable does require another file to be present for it to run. This file, CNCS232.DLL (CNCS216.DLL if your application is intended for Windows 3.x), needs to be in the same directory as your executable file, and once it is provided, all will run well. Be sure to include this file with your final product. If you build a Project, which will include an installer for users to install your program to their hard drive, this file is automatically included for you.

While Director can be more convenient in including everything that's needed in one executable, Director applications are usually twice as large as an identical Multimedia Fusion application—and sometimes larger. There are always pros and cons when choosing your primary multimedia authoring tool.

Build Option	Purpose and Comments
Project	Building a Project allows you to combine multiple applications as one whole and to create an installer for your final product. To use this option, you must open a Project and drag your application into it. A Project is a holder for one or more applications. When you build a Project, you are asked all the questions of the application builder, plus questions about the installer. This installer creates a program setup routine for users to install your application to their hard drive. The installer also installs files required by the program to their appropriate location. See the Multimedia Fusion help file for more details about using the installer settings.
Stand-Alone Application	Building a Stand-Alone Application creates an executable file that performs exactly as you designed it without your users needing a copy of Multimedia Fusion itself. Be sure to provide the file CNCS232.DLL in the same directory as the executable.
Screensaver	Building a Screensaver does just that—it creates an SCR Windows screensaver file that can be set as the system's screensaver just as any other screensaver would. If you build your screensaver as a Project, Multimedia Fusion installs and sets your screensaver as the default screensaver on the user's system.
Internet Application	The Internet Application option builds a CCN file that will be capable of running in end users' browsers, over the Internet, if they have installed the Vitalize! plug-in. You will read more about this in the next chapter.

MULTIMEDIA APPLETS ON THE WEB

You cannot have any meaningful discussion about multimedia without direct reference to the Internet and the provision of multimedia content and applications over the Web. To provide the necessary format and technologies to achieve multimedia application delivery over the Web, almost all multimedia authoring applications, including Director and Multimedia Fusion, provide some way by which you can present your work from a Web server.

The potential for such technology is extraordinary. Your end users, connected to your server using nothing more than a Web browser and perhaps a suitable plug-in, can now run your multimedia application completely and fluidly. With this step you have opened the door to a phenomenally large user base that would be very difficult to reach on CD-ROM or DVD-ROM through the mail or from a storefront.

Such Web-based products are called *applets* for two primary reasons. First, they have to be very small in file size to be usable on a slow dial-up line to the Internet. Second, the use of plug-in technology provides the browser application with the larger percentage of the program as a permanently installed feature of the browser. Therefore only the content parts and minimal instructions need be sent to the plug-in for it to assemble and run the program as designed on the user's computer. Hence, the term *application* would be incorrect, as this small incomplete part of an application is best referred to as an *applet*.

In this chapter you have already seen how to build an Internet application from two leading multimedia development tools. In the next chapter, you will learn how to use such Web-based multimedia applications, as well as how and why they work.

AVOIDING PITFALLS

Many issues are covered in this chapter, and with them come associated traps that you should avoid. Most of them have been addressed in this chapter, but the following is a summary of the most important ones:

Be prepared. Before you step into the multimedia authoring and programming phase of your project, be sure to have all of your content and media components ready and organized. Even though you will most likely find yourself editing and creating components on the fly as you build your project, taking time to assemble all of the pieces of this puzzle before assembly will help ensure that you have one homogenous product. It is easy to spot a multimedia product that is developed on the fly—it's the one that shows few or no signs of consistency, takes twice as long as it should to develop, and includes changes in appearance and/or user methodology as you delve deeper into its content.

There are pros and cons to the timeline and object-oriented approaches to multimedia development. Take time to evaluate which tool is best suited for the job. The best developers are conversant in several diverse tools and decide which is best-suited to the project's requirements.

Be prepared to test your final product on the target system, and be prepared to find some performance gains in your project through optimizing of your content and media components. It may take several attempts before you have the optimally performing final product, but it will be worth it.

Find a good Web-based users' group that you can subscribe to. Get to know the top performers and experts in this development field. Find developers whose livelihood depends on correct and optimal production from the authoring tool you have chosen to use. You will find that these enthusiasts are willing to provide invaluable advice and guidance when the manuals and tech support lines have failed you. You can't beat the experience of those who have solved the problems before you. You may even make some good friends along the way.

Chapter Summary

- Multimedia authoring tools can be broadly categorized into two camps: those that use a timeline on which to base development and assembly of the multimedia project, and those that use an object-oriented approach.

- Macromedia Director is a powerful multimedia authoring and development tool that uses a movie metaphor for the many tools and components it has to offer the developer.

- Macromedia Director has a built-in programming language called Lingo that can be used to provide interactivity and control to Director's standard and continuous frame-by-frame playing mode.

- Multimedia Fusion provides a storyboard motif for developers to assemble and organize the frames (screens) of their project. Its object-oriented approach offers high performance and many unique features.

- Multimedia Fusion applications are built by identifying events that happen to the application or to the objects therein and defining what actions should be taken in response to those events.

- Most multimedia authoring tools can produce a version of the multimedia application that is optimized for delivery over the Web.

Key Terms and Concepts

Checking Your Knowledge and Skills

1. Using the ten-step process for Macromedia Director, create the following application. Using the additional media components provided on this book's CD-ROM, add interactive Home and Quit buttons to the application. These buttons should bring the user back to the first frame of the project (Home) or kill the project altogether (Quit). Use the Lingo provided in Table 15.2 to make the buttons execute these required actions. Build a projector (EXE) file and test it for complete operation.

2. Using the ten-step process for Multimedia Fusion, create the following application. Using the additional media components provided on this book's CD-ROM, add interactive Home and Quit buttons to the application. These buttons should bring the user back to the first frame of the project (Home) or kill the project altogether (Quit). Import the button graphics into your Multimedia Fusion project. Using Multimedia Fusion's Event Editor, add an event to check for, and in the button object column, provide the button object with the desired action to have the buttons execute these requirements.

3. Having completed exercises 1 and 2, create a pros-and-cons comparison chart to assess the benefits and capabilities of both Director and Multimedia Fusion. In your opinion, which product is most effective in getting the job done, and why? Compare your notes to those of your classmates. Do you agree on which product is better?

4. Search the Internet for examples of Internet-based multimedia delivery systems. Be sure to check out Shockwave, RealNetworks, and Vitalize!. Develop a list of such technologies and establish a features grid that will compare the benefits and deficits of each technology.

Critical Thinking Challenges

1. Using what you know about Director and Multimedia Fusion, choose a typical multimedia project, such as a digital brochure for a car company or a virtual tour multimedia CD-ROM of a new conference center/hotel, that you would like to develop. Formulate separate project plans based upon the use of each of these authoring tools. Would the outcome of this analysis affect your decision to purchase this authoring tool for general multimedia purposes? Which tool would get the project done sooner? Which product would be easiest to develop with?

2. Put yourself in a client's shoes. You want an awesome multimedia presentation piece for a fast-approaching conference and you want it fast. Try to determine what amount of reporting and feedback you would like to have during the project, and what information you would like to see to determine progress. Given these client needs, would you choose one authoring tool over the other? Why?

3. Research additional multimedia authoring tools available to you. You could find competing products in your local computer software store, or at a Web site such as www.egghead.com, www.microwarehouse.com, www.creationengine.com, or www.maczone.com. Build a comparison matrix, comparing the features that you know Director and Multimedia Fusion provide. Can you find a product that appears to offer better tools, value, price, performance, and flexibility? Be sure to check out products such as Asymetrix's ToolBook, Astound, Microsoft's PowerPoint, and Macromedia's Authorware, among others. Has this made any difference to the way you have evaluated Director and Multimedia Fusion in this chapter?

Hands-on Exercises
BUILDING A DIGITAL CATALOG

Pretend that you own a flower shop. You have the world's best floral and plant products (especially those exotic orchids that are unavailable elsewhere), along with planting supplies and special delivery services. You have a complete department dedicated to creating custom arrangements and bouquets, and they do the best work for the money available anywhere in the country.

Your marketing campaign calls for a mailable CD-ROM digital catalog. You have decided to develop this product in-house, as those pesky multimedia developers don't seem to understand your business (they don't listen!) and they cost too much.

Using content that you find and "borrow" from the Web (such as pictures of flowers), develop an easy-to-use and inviting digital brochure that allows users to categorize and browse through your products and services and to jump to an order form when they have decided what they want.

Build a simple (six products, two services) digital catalog mock-up. This mock-up version will be presented to the board in two weeks time as a proof-of-concept piece to persuade the board to invest the needed funds. Provide the board members with printed handouts of the most important screens so that they may take away with them a teaser sample of the potential final product.

Master Project
BUILDING YOUR DIGITAL PORTFOLIO

So far you should have created a binder for the project that documents your project concept, includes a project plan and timeline, and includes your sketches and visuals for your design. You should also have begun the process of building your content and storing it on disk.

Having determined in the previous chapter which authoring tool seemed best suited to your Master Project, reevaluate this decision based upon your new hands-on experience with both of these products.

Assemble your work on the Master Project to date, and using your project plan and storyboard as a guide, build your Master Project in the multimedia authoring tool of your choice.

Solicit the input of others as your work progresses. A fresh look at your work to date from someone not involved with the details can often be very helpful. This could help you avoid pitfalls and design flaws.

16

CREATING AWESOME MULTIMEDIA APPLICATIONS ON THE WEB

Chapter Outline

Chapter Objectives

After completing this chapter, you will be able to:

- Enhance a Web page to display your multimedia content, such as digital sound, digital video, images, Shockwave movies and interfaces, and Java applets

- Create simple Flash animation and interactivity

- Create simple animated Java applets using 3Space Publisher

- Use simple HTML to embed multimedia components in any Web page

- Determine the best delivery system for your multimedia products, whether it be online delivery, CD-ROM, DVD-ROM, or installation to the end user's hard drive

- Market and promote a Web site on the Internet

Chapter Overview

In this chapter you will learn how to use your new multimedia content development and authoring skills to build a multimedia Web site.

You may not realize this yet, but you already have most of the skills required to develop online multimedia. The media components you have been creating, the background and button graphics, even multimedia application authoring all have a place in multimedia Web development. All you need to know now to bring all of that together is how to create Web pages and how to embed multimedia in them.

Thankfully, several excellent software products can assist you in achieving this without having to return to the basics and learn a new technology all over again. There is a common myth that you have to learn HTML to create Web pages. It is the same myth that states you have to learn QBasic (an old text-based version of the BASIC programming language) before you can learn to program in Visual Basic (a modern Windows-based version of BASIC offering a visual mouse-driven interface and many drag-and-drop features). In principle, you may be a better programmer if you are familiar with the older technology tools, but that knowledge is certainly not necessary to start learning with the more modern tool set.

The same holds true for HTML. Though many expert Web page developers started coding HTML in simple text editor applications (such as Windows Notepad), almost no professional Web developers would exclusively use this method to create Web sites. It can be beneficial to be able to "get under the hood" and tweak the HTML code in this manner to suit your needs, but you will see in this chapter that having never used HTML before need not hinder your success in this field.

In this light, you will be introduced to several Web development tools. These products will help you create your Web page and develop Web-specific media content to place therein. At the end of this chapter you will learn how to publish your creation onto the World Wide Web, and how to find the best approach to attracting traffic to your multimedia-enhanced site.

WHY THE WEB?

It is arguable that the Internet is the single biggest communications technology revolution since Gutenberg invented the movable-type printing press in 1450. Because of that technology, the number of books in Europe grew thirtyfold in the following fifty years, from some 30,000 handwritten manuscripts to over nine million publications. Like the movable-type printing press, the Internet places mass information–publishing ability in our hands—but on a far greater scale, of course. Furthermore, the Internet revolution has just begun.

The Internet is a vast communication tool for information sharing and publishing, which has its pros and cons. On the plus side, you can instantly provide information to anyone and everyone online throughout the planet. On the minus side, your information becomes a minor speck in the information superhighway cosmos. Multimedia online has become an effective, essential way to enhance Web content to the point that it stands above the crowd and attracts attention.

When publishing on the Web (at least for commercial Web sites), there are five primary goals:

1. Attract visitors to your site.
2. Entice visitors to stay.
3. Motivate visitors to bookmark your site.
4. Attract repeat returns from visitors.
5. Inspire visitors to refer others to your site (which takes you back to goal 2).

While there are several strategies to achieve all of these objectives, multimedia enhancement of a Web site provides effective solutions for goals 2 through 5.

There is another misconception about the Net. Many think that their Web site is like a billboard on the information superhighway. Unfortunately, even if you create the most awesome and breathtaking multimedia-enhanced site, your product will never be seen unless Web surfers know the exact address (URL) or can link there from another site or from a search engine site. Web sites are not automatically promoted on the Web. You must promote your site yourself and be quite proactive about this. Later on you will learn how to achieve goal 1.

HOW BROWSERS WORK

As you learned in Chapter 9, a Web browser's primary function is to follow a Web page's HTML instructions to find and display all of the components of the described Web page on the user's computer system. A Web browser "builds" a copy of the Web page on the viewer's computer. It is this "local assembly" of the page that can sometimes take so long, and why it is so easy to right-click a Web page graphic and save it to your hard drive. The neat trick is that the image you are saving is already on your hard drive, in your browser's data cache folder.

When you have a free moment, use an image browsing application such as Paint Shop Pro (Chapter 5) to view the contents of your browser's cache folder. If you use Internet Explorer, it should be in C:\Windows\Temporary Internet Files, and the subfolders therein. If you're using Netscape (version 4 and later), your cached files should be in C:\Program Files\Netscape\Navigator\Cache. On a Macintosh, do a Find for the Cache folder. You will most likely recognize the images stored in this location as pieces of recent Web pages that you have visited. This is where the browser stores the elements of any Web page it creates for you while processing the HTML instructions of any Web site you visit.

The important concept here is that when surfing the Net, your browser's job is to assemble the Web page you're viewing on your computer system. This means that every piece of text, image, and video clip has to be downloaded for you to view it. An exception would be for some media formats that allow for streaming, but even here the data you are viewing has to be transferred from the server you're addressing to your system via whatever connection you use to access the Web. Therefore, optimization of your media components is essential for good performance, especially when it comes to those fat multimedia files. You must always be aware of the overhead imposed on any Web page by the use of each and every media component. You learned about such optimization in the early chapters of this book as you learned how to create each media type for your project. Later in this chapter, you will learn how the Web page development tools you use can identify the performance criteria (usually, time to download) of your design at various bandwidths.

Web browsers use a technology called *plug-ins*. You have read about this many times before in this book. It is essential that you know which plug-ins are required by visitors to your site in order for them to view your multimedia content. You should always take great care to provide a link to the download site for the required plug-in for visitors who do not already have this installed.

cache folder

The location on your computer's hard drive where the browser application temporarily stores the components that make up a Web page while viewing it. The process of storing data temporarily while it's in use is called *caching*.

surfing

Browsing or searching on the Internet with a browser application.

For instance, if you built your Web site to incorporate Shockwave content, and perhaps a few QuickTime VR elements, then your visitors would need the plug-ins for both these technologies installed before they could view your work. Enabling them to fetch these plug-ins quickly is not just a courtesy on your part. It is a way to keep them attached to your site while they go through the plug-in installation process. Without this service, they would most likely not bother finding and installing the appropriate plug-in. Even if they did, what is the likelihood that they would return to your site? It's better for you and them if you foresee the need for any required plug-ins.

Microsoft's Internet Explorer uses ActiveX technology as well as conventional plug-in technology. You learned about ActiveX technology in Chapter 15. This technology allows the browser to recognize the need for an additional capability to view content of a type not seen before, and automatically download and use that ActiveX component to meet that need. This can be tremendously beneficial to users, especially less-technical users who do not want to go through a plug-in installation process. However, ActiveX works only with Microsoft Internet Explorer. Visitors using Netscape Navigator will need to find a suitable plug-in, if available. Be sure to cater to both browser brands whenever possible.

QuickTime VR

A variant of the Apple QuickTime digital media file format that can store and display 360-degree panoramas of a scene or 360-degree rotations of an object.

AUTHORING FOR THE WEB: DO I HAVE TO LEARN HTML?

To create Web pages viewable by a Web browser, do you have to learn HTML? The answer is no, though knowing something about HTML can help your task. Modern Web page authoring tools, such as Microsoft's FrontPage, Macromedia's Dreamweaver, Adobe's PageMill, and many others provide a graphical-design approach to Web page design. Figure 16.1 shows a Web site designed in FrontPage. In this illustration you can see both the visual page design and the HTML screen, selectable by tabs at the bottom of the interface. With products such as FrontPage, the HTML code required is generated automatically by the application in response to changes you make in the visual design. Figure 16.1 shows you the HTML code automatically generated by FrontPage to support the visual design work shown.

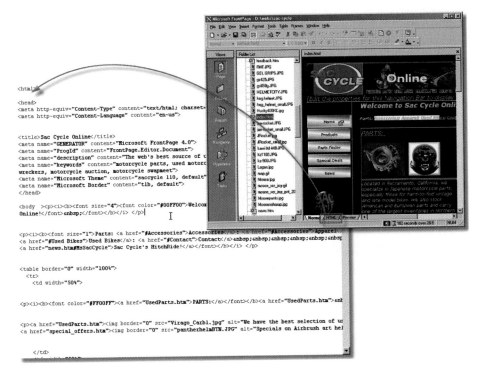

Figure 16.1
FrontPage provides the visual designer with an automatic generation of clean HTML code.

PROJECT FILE LOCATIONS

When creating multimedia Web pages, you will be using quite a few image and media files that will be used by the Web page to display your product for end users when they view it. It is important to keep a complete set of these files in the same directory as your HTML document. If you create a new directory for each project, then you can always copy/publish the entire directory contents in one step, knowing that everything in the directory is a necessary component of the Web page.

If you want to organize your media and content files in their own directories, then it is advisable to use subdirectories beneath the one that houses the Web page using these components. In this way, all references to those files will be describing locations relative to the one in which the Web page lies. With such a directory structure, you can then copy/publish the contents of the Web page's directory, including subdirectories, and retain an intact set of file references in your HTML.

The primary focus of these types of applications is to enable visual designers to create awesome Web pages without having to learn any HTML. Since HTML is almost a programming language, the task of learning this text-based coding would be an impossible prospect for most designers. Products such as FrontPage place the creativity of Web page design back in the hands of the designers.

In previous chapters you learned about multimedia authoring. In the same way that products such as Director and Multimedia Fusion do the programming for you and create a final product based upon your visual design, so do FrontPage, Dreamweaver, PageMill, and many other similar applications.

In this chapter you will create Web pages without using HTML. If you can sustain a faith that learning HTML is not necessary, and follow the instructions provided, you will soon be creating impressive multimedia Web sites. Please note that if you learn HTML coding, you will further empower yourself with skills that allow you to get "under the hood" and go that extra distance in your Web creation. You can always learn HTML later.

CROSS-PLATFORM CONSIDERATIONS

One of the best benefits of Web-based content, applications, and multimedia is that they're mostly platform-independent. Unlike CD-ROM–based multimedia, Web pages can, by and large, be viewed on a PC, a Macintosh, or a Unix system with a browser and a connection to the Net. The beauty of this technology is that it is so universal. Because of this universality the technical considerations that have to be made in determining whether end users can view your work is made in relation to browser versions and plug-ins, not on the brand of computer system used to browse the site.

With few exceptions, it is nice to be able to focus on your Web project's appearance and performance, and not worry about the make of computer used to view it. You can use this built-in benefit to your advantage.

INTERNET/INTRANET DELIVERY COMPARED TO CD-ROM/DVD-ROM

There are many pros and cons among the forms of product delivery available to multimedia developers. You may be approached by clients who can articulate their needs in terms of a final outcome, but cannot determine the nature of the final product. For example, the request for a digital brochure to showcase a new

TABLE 16.1	Comparison of Multimedia Delivery Formats				
Characteristic	Internet	Intranet	CD-ROM	DVD-ROM	Hard Drive Installation
Performance	Slow	Fast	Faster	Faster	Fastest
Data storage capacity	Very high	Limited	650 MB	Up to 14 GB	Limited
Special hardware required	Connection to the Internet	Connection to the LAN	CD-ROM drive	DVD-ROM drive	None
Video delivery	Poor	Fair	Good	Very good	Excellent
Content revisability after publication	Instant updates possible	Instant updates possible	Fixed at publication date	Fixed at publication date	Changeable, but on a very restricted basis
Revision costs	Small	Small	Large	Very large	Large (must deliver new application and installer)
Ongoing management and maintenance required	High maintenance	High maintenance	Distribution only (not counting tech support)	Distribution only (not counting tech support)	Distribution only (not counting tech support)
Need to include suitable drivers and installers	Provide links to plug-ins and installers	Provide links to plug-ins and installers	Provide driver installer applications on CD-ROM under license	Provide driver installer applications on DVD-ROM under license	Provide driver installer applications with product installer
Postdevelopment manufacturing costs	None	None	High	Very high	Not applicable
Custom interface and controls	Limited to the functions and capabilities of the viewer's browser	Limited to the functions and capabilities of the viewer's browser	Complete control: custom design	Complete control: custom design	Complete control: custom design

line of women's summer wear tells you that you are asked to create a digital multimedia catalog for the client, but on the Web, CD-ROM, or DVD-ROM? Often you will have to guide the client in making this determination. Table 16.1 will help you weigh the pros and cons of one delivery system over the other.

Table 16.1 should give you an idea of the relative pros and cons of the delivery systems listed. You can also consider hybrid delivery methods, in which, for example, you publish your Web page content on a CD-ROM or DVD-ROM. In this format you have the benefits of browser interface control and some platform independence, but you forgo the ability to make changes to the application after its release date.

By developing a project checklist from Table 16.1, you can create an excellent client questionnaire that will help you and your client determine the best product solution.

MACROMEDIA SHOCKWAVE

In Chapter 15 you were introduced to Macromedia Director and the concept of Shockwave technology. Shockwave has become the standard multimedia delivery technology for the Web, with millions of users benefiting from "Shocked" Web sites daily. It is such a standard that long-established companies in the design applications field, such as Adobe, are providing their Web content development applications with the ability to create Shockwave products.

The main benefits of Shockwave technology include the following:

- Very high data compression, results in small data files to transfer to end users.
- All the benefits of disk-based multimedia applications are embedded in a Web page.
- Streaming technology allows the application to run before having been completely downloaded.
- With most of the operational programming in the plug-in, the data to be downloaded can be very small.
- High-level interface design and user interaction incorporate sound and graphic effects not available with the common browser.

In particular, all Macromedia's multimedia authoring tools, such as Director, Authorware, and Flash, can output Web-ready Shockwave applications that can easily be embedded into a Web page. To further this development, Macromedia provides additional Web page creation and authoring tools, such as Dreamweaver and Fireworks (Web graphics design) to fully round out the Macromedia family of digital development applications.

Of special note is Flash, which combines the benefits of a vector graphics drawing program with animation and multimedia authoring in a format that works exceedingly well as a Web-based Shockwave development tool. While Flash can, like Director, create stand-alone executable software products, its primary strengths lie in its ability to add tremendous pizzazz and animation to the Web. It has become a very popular tool and a much sought-after form of Web page multimedia enhancement.

The following section will introduce you to Flash and set you on the road to learning more about this amazing product.

A QUICK LOOK AT MACROMEDIA'S FLASH

Figure 16.2 shows an animated diagram being built in Flash for later viewing on the Web. In Flash each element is drawn using a selection of shape and line drawing tools. They can be filled with gradated colors and shapes much like using an illustration tool such as Adobe Illustrator or Corel Draw. The zoomed inset in Figure 16.2 shows both examples of gradated fill and another of Flash's terrific features. Because the image is effectively "drawn" every time it's viewed, you can also zoom into the image as far as you want and the image still retains its fidelity.

By adding animation capabilities to the mix, Macromedia has produced an awesome product for creating animated Web imagery. Flash uses a frames-over-time concept similar to that of Director for creating animated presentations. By defining the position, size, orientation, and appearance of a symbol at a beginning and end frame, Flash can automatically tween the intervening frames to produce a smooth animation. In Flash, animation is performed on Flash symbols, which are whatever elements of a drawing or text piece you group together and tell Flash to convert to a symbol. Symbols are then treated as objects that can be manipulated as a whole and are stored in the library for that project. While you can edit symbols at any time, they become components of a Flash movie, in a similar way to Director cast members, to be reused as needed. You will see how this works in the exercise that follows.

To best illustrate the capabilities of Flash for your Web site project, the following exercise will guide you through the process of creating an animated banner and toolbar for the top of your Web page. To work through this exercise, you will need a copy of Flash installed on your computer system. If you do not already have this installed, you can download a working trial version from the link provided on this book's Web site or directly from Macromedia at www.macromedia.com.

embedded

When a file is embedded in a Web page, it becomes part of the Web page design and is viewable as part of the Web page. It is displayed in the Web page alongside all the other elements of that page. If not embedded, media components would either appear in their own separate window or be downloaded by the browser for independent viewing.

Flash symbols

In Flash, any drawn element or parts of a drawn element can be selected and converted to a symbol by pressing F8. Once made into a symbol, this now-independent drawing is added to the symbol library and can be animated in a Flash movie.

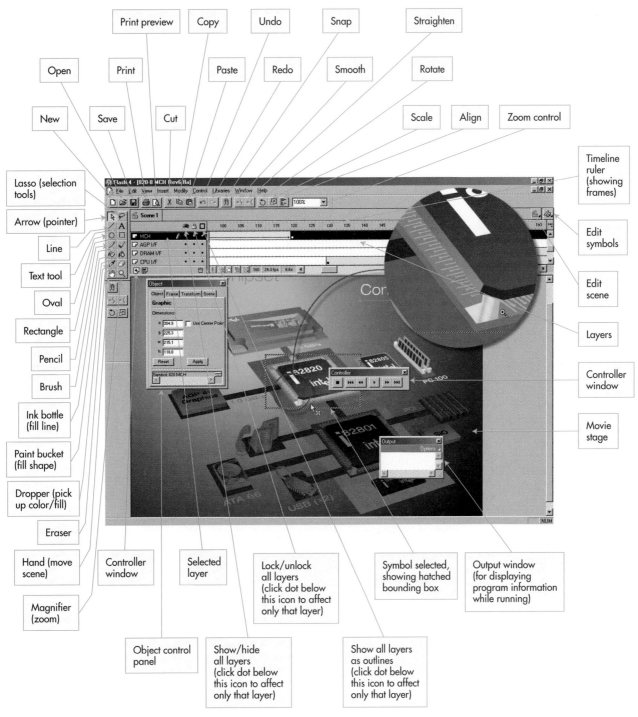

Figure 16.2
Macromedia Flash at work, showing an animated diagram for Web viewing being built.

You are about to learn a set of specific tasks in this product. The intention is not to provide you with a deep knowledge of this software tool, but to give you a sense of Flash's capabilities. Once you have completed this exercise, you will be capable of creating many more similar animated banners in Flash. Flash itself comes with a superb set of animated interactive tutorials on creating animation and interactivity with Flash technology. It is essential that you work through those tutorials to build upon the short introduction you will read here.

To presume that this exercise summarizes anything close to the many capabilities of Flash is to miss a tremendous opportunity to explore one of the most creative Web content development tools available. You can pursue this further by visiting this book's Web site and linking to more information about Flash.

STARTING YOUR NEW FLASH PROJECT

1. Start Flash and if a blank new document is not apparent, click the New button to start one.

2. To resize your document to a size more suitable for a Web page banner, choose Movie from the Modify menu.

3. In the Movie Properties dialog box (see Figure 16.3), type 640 for the width and 75 for the depth of the new document size. Set the Background color to black, as shown in Figure 16.3. Click OK. Make a note of the width and height of your Flash banner for later exercises.

DRAWING IN FLASH

4. To create a circle shape, first select the Oval button (as indicated in Figure 16.4), and when the color tools for oval shapes appear below the toolbar, select a bright green outline and a no-fill inside (refer to Figure 16.4).

5. Holding the Shift key down (for uniform scaling), drag out a circle (starting at the top left corner dragging down to the right) that looks like the one shown in Figure 16.4.

CREATING A SYMBOL

6. To animate this circle, you must convert it from a simple drawing to a symbol. Using the Arrow tool, drag a selection rectangle over the circle to select

Figure 16.3

The Macromedia Flash Movie Properties dialog box.

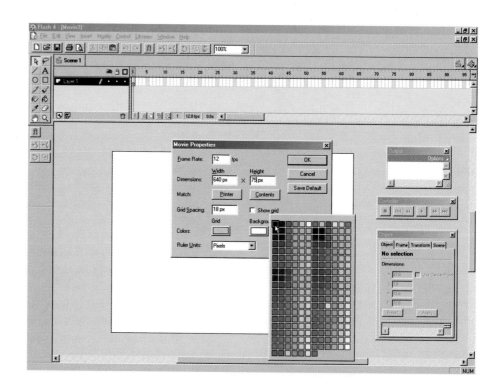

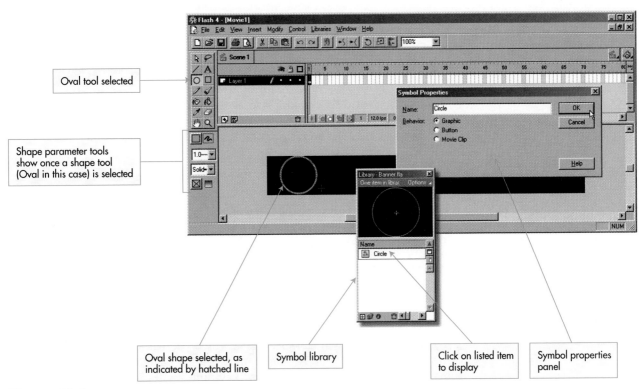

Oval tool selected

Shape parameter tools show once a shape tool (Oval in this case) is selected

Oval shape selected, as indicated by hatched line

Symbol library

Click on listed item to display

Symbol properties panel

Figure 16.4
Macromedia Flash drawing a green outline circle.

it all. Once selected it will become hatched in appearance, as you can see in Figure 16.4. This means that it is selected.

7. To convert the selected shape into a symbol, choose Convert to Symbol from the Insert menu and type "Circle" in the Name field in the Symbol Properties dialog box. Click OK. The circle should now have a rectangular selection box around it and a small crosshair in the center. It is now a symbol that can be animated.

8. To verify that you have created a new Circle symbol, choose Library from the Window menu to view your project's library of symbols. There should be just one, and you should recognize it as your circle, as shown in Figure 16.4.

USING LAYERS IN FLASH

9. Double-click the layer name (Layer 1) and change it to "Circle Animation." Naming your layers in Flash will help you find elements of a complicated animation later.

ANIMATING IN FLASH

At this stage of the exercise you will build a short animation. You will do this by inserting keyframes on the timeline, setting the scale of the symbol to be small at the first keyframe and large at the last keyframe, and then instructing Flash to tween the scaling on intervening frames.

10. Right-click frame 40 and choose Insert Keyframe from the shortcut menu. The playback head should now be positioned on frame 40.

11. Click the Scale button (handles should appear around the symbol) and, holding down the Shift key, drag a corner handle of the symbol until it is about three times larger than the original.

12. Click frame 1 to reposition the playback head to frame 1 and click the Scale button again. This time, holding down the Shift key, shrink the circle to about one-third its original size. If you now click the Play button in the Controller window, you will have 39 frames of the small circle with a sudden larger version showing on the last frame.

13. To tween the animation from frame 1 to keyframe 40, simply right-click any frame between these two frames and choose Create Motion Tween from the shortcut menu.

14. Click the Play button again and watch the smooth animation as your circle grows in size.

VISUAL EFFECTS IN FLASH: FADING

15. To add fading to enhance the symbol animation, right-click frame numbers 5 and 30 and choose Insert Keyframe from the shortcut menu each time.

These keyframes will mark frames at which you will change the alpha properties of the symbol. The Alpha properties of a Flash symbol determine its transparency. Tweening between these keyframes will create a smooth fade-up (from Alpha 0% to Alpha 100%) and fade-down (Alpha 100% to Alpha 0%) effect.

16. Click frame 1 to place the playback head there. Select the Circle symbol, right-click it, and choose Properties from the shortcut menu, as shown in Figure 16.5.

17. In the Instance Properties dialog box, click the Color Effect tab, and choose Alpha from the drop-down list of color effects. Move the slider down to 0%. Notice that the thumbnail preview image of the symbol also fades as you move the slider. Click OK. Repeat this same process for frame 40.

You should have the following Alpha setting sequence: Frame 0 = 0%; Frame 5 = 100%; Frame 30 = 100%; Frame 40 = 0%. You didn't have to set the Alpha value of the symbol on frames 5 and 30, as they have the original Alpha value of the object at the time you set the keyframes, which was by default 100%.

18. Click the Play button to view the resulting animation.

REUSING ANIMATED SYMBOLS IN FLASH

Your Circle animation can be reused to give an illusion of ripples. To do this, you will have to add additional layers to your project.

19. Right-click the Circle Animation layer title, and choose Insert Layer from the shortcut menu, as shown in Figure 16.6.

20. Repeat this process so that you have a total of three layers. Rename the two new layers "Circle2 Animation" and "Circle3 Animation."

21. Click the first frame of your "expanding circle" animation and, holding down the Shift key, click frame 40 to select the complete set of animation frames in the Circle Animation layer.

22. Right-click the selected frames and choose Copy Frames from the shortcut menu.

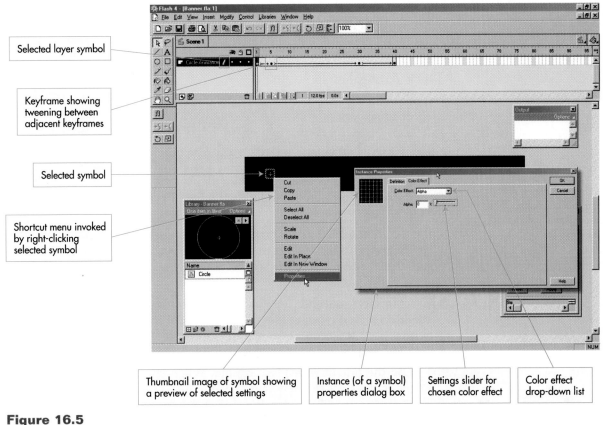

Selected layer symbol

Keyframe showing
tweening between
adjacent keyframes

Selected symbol

Shortcut menu invoked
by right-clicking
selected symbol

Thumbnail image of symbol showing
a preview of selected settings

Instance (of a symbol)
properties dialog box

Settings slider for
chosen color effect

Color effect
drop-down list

Figure 16.5
Changing symbol properties in Flash.

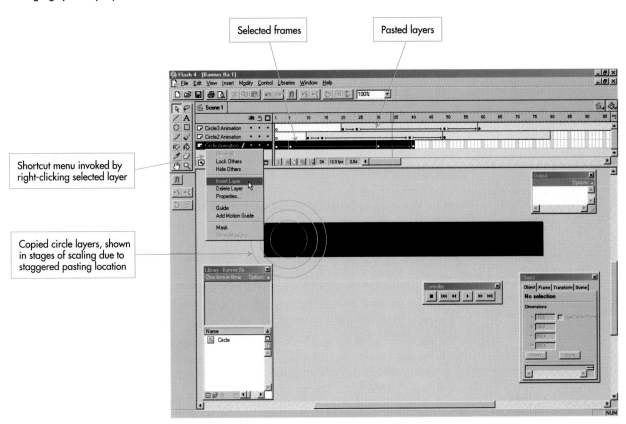

Selected frames

Pasted layers

Shortcut menu invoked by
right-clicking selected layer

Copied circle layers, shown
in stages of scaling due to
staggered pasting location

Figure 16.6
By copying the animation sequence and pasting it into new layers, offset by a few frames, you can create
a pleasing ripple effect.

23. Right-click frame 10 in the new Circle2 Animation layer and choose Paste Frames from the shortcut menu.

24. Right-click frame 20 in the new Circle3 Animation layer and again choose Paste Frames from the shortcut menu. Your animation project should now look like Figure 16.6.

25. Click frame 1 and then click the Play button to view a very pleasing ripple effect animation.

USING AND ANIMATING TEXT IN FLASH

26. To add some banner text, right-click the Circle3 Animation layer title and choose Insert Layer from the shortcut menu. Rename this new layer "Main Text."

27. Right-click frame 10 in this new layer, and choose Insert Keyframe from the shortcut menu. Click this frame to place the playback head in it, and make sure that the new Main Text layer is currently selected (as indicated by the small pencil icon).

28. Select the Text tool and click the center of your circle as it appears at frame 10. Select a bold typeface (such as Arial Black) and a large size, such as 48 points, from the drop-down selections provided. Select a suitable color, such as blue, for your text.

29. Type in the title of your Flash banner. When you are finished, select the Arrow tool, select the new text element, and choose Convert to Symbol from the Insert menu. Give this new symbol the name "Title." It should appear in the symbol library window.

30. Using the Scale tool, drag the right- or left-hand handle and squish the text symbol as shown in Figure 16.7. Drag the text so that it is centered vertically in the banner and the left-hand edge of the first letter is in the center of the circle. This will be the starting point for our next animation.

31. Animating our text is as simple as animating our circles. Right-click frame 59 in the Main Text layer, and choose Insert Keyframe from the shortcut menu. You can see this keyframe already inserted in Figure 16.7. Click frame 59 to place the playback head there, if it is not there already.

32. Select the Scale tool, and use this and the Arrow tool to expand the width of the text back to what looks like the original proportions, and reposition the left-hand edge of the text to about where the center of the circle should be.

33. Right-click any frame between 10 and 59 in the Main Text layer and choose Create Motion Tween from the shortcut menu.

FADING TEXT IN FLASH

34. To add a fade-in, click frame 10 in the Main Text layer to place the playback head at that frame. Select the Title symbol, right click it, and choose Properties from the shortcut menu.

35. As before, set the symbol's initial Alpha value to 0% to make it invisible by clicking the Color Effect tab, selecting Alpha from the drop-down list of color effects, and moving the slider to show a 0% Alpha setting. Click OK. Since all frames are tweened from 10 through 59, the new color effect information becomes part of that tweening, and Flash animates a nice smooth progressive fade from frame 10 through 59.

36. Click the Play button to view your work so far.

If your text is looking a bit jagged around the edges, you can choose Antialias from the View menu to smooth out appearances.

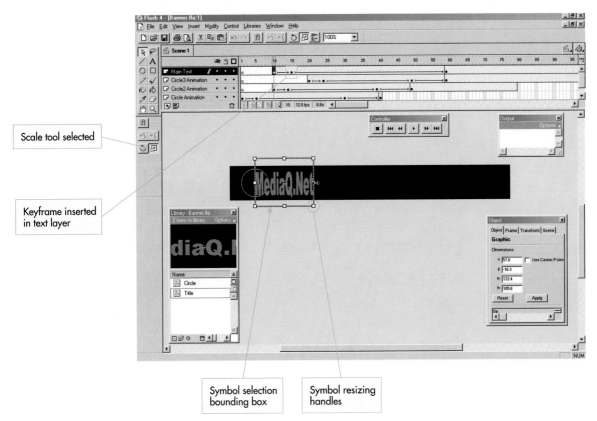

Scale tool selected

Keyframe inserted
in text layer

Symbol selection
bounding box

Symbol resizing
handles

Figure 16.7
By converting your text to a symbol, you can now scale it at various keyframes and tween the resulting animation.

ADDING INTERACTIVITY TO FLASH

To make this a functional banner requires interactivity. Now it is time to add buttons.

37. Choose Buttons from the Libraries menu to show the extensive button collection that comes with Flash.

38. Rightclick the topmost layer title, and choose Insert Layer from the shortcut menu. Rename this layer "Buttons."

39. Click frame 1 in this new layer, and make sure that the pencil icon indicates that this layer is the one currently selected for editing.

40. From the Buttons Library, select the Ping Pong button as shown in Figure 16.8 and drag it onto the banner.

41. The button will be far too big, so use the Scale tool to resize it to match those shown in Figure 16.8. Once you have one in place, select it, right-click, and choose Copy from the shortcut menu. Now right-click in a different area and choose Paste from the shortcut menu. This method is a quick and easy way to replicate this button symbol.

42. Align three copies, as shown in Figure 16.8. Choose Enable Buttons from the Control menu to view the buttons in action.

Creating your own custom buttons is easy in Flash, but you will have to check out the excellent tutorial provided with Flash for more details, as that is beyond the scope of this book.

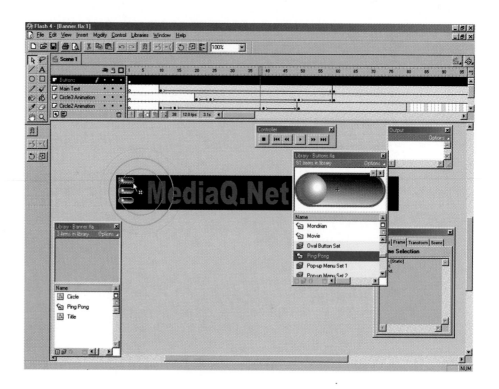

TESTING AND PUBLISHING YOUR FLASH MOVIE

Now it's time to test and create your Flash banner. At any time you can test your movie by choosing Test Movie from the Control menu to run the project at a performance rate similar to the final stand-alone product.

43. To create a stand-alone Shockwave file, choose Export Movie from the File menu and type in the name "Banner" and click Save, and then OK on the Export Flash player window that appears. Flash creates a Shockwave file called Banner.swf, which you can then double-click to view separately from the Flash authoring environment. In this very short exercise, you were instructed to accept the default settings in the Export Flash player window. Take some time to experiment with these Shockwave file settings using the Help button to guide you. You can make changes to the settings that will significantly alter your Shockwave movie's performance on the Web.

44. Choosing Publish from the File menu creates a Web page with the appropriate HTML code in the directory where you last saved your project. You

BUILDING A STAND-ALONE SHOCKWAVE EXECUTABLE FILE

Shockwave files are very small. The final Shockwave file for this project weighs in at a measly 5.53 KB. The Web page to support it, when published, is only 1.83 KB. At a combined total of only 7.36 KB, you can see why Shockwave technology is so popular for use over the Web, especially for those with slow dial-up connections.

Note that one of the File menu commands for the stand-alone Shockwave (.swf) version is Create Projector. Choosing this command creates a transportable, self-sufficient executable file that looks exactly like the Shockwave version, but doesn't need Shockwave installed on the end user's system. However, the file size for the projector (.exe) version of the file jumps to 285 KB because this independent version needs to carry with it all of the software required to run a Flash file. Even so, this is still a very small program.

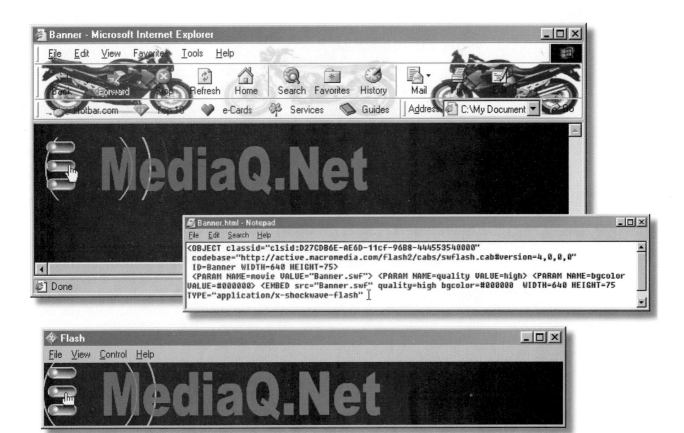

Figure 16.9
The published version embedded in the Web page generated by Flash, and the stand-alone Shockwave/projector version (note that Internet Explorer is shown with a custom "skin" graphic installed).

can view this page in your browser, and also use it both as a template for further enhancement and a source from which to copy and paste the correct HTML code (see Figure 16.9) into an existing Web page. Figure 16.9 shows the stand-alone Shockwave version as well as the published version.

You have barely scratched the surface of Flash and Shockwave capabilities, but perhaps you can see their potential and how easy it is to start creating amazing animations for Web usage.

CREATING GRAPHICAL JAVA APPLETS WITHOUT LEARNING JAVA

You already know that it's possible to create terrific multimedia-enhanced Web pages without becoming an expert in HTML. Likewise, it's possible to create stunning Java animation applets without knowing much about Java programming.

Because a Java applet is a small program, it can be downloaded and run quickly and easily by the browser application. Most special-effect Java applets use a source image with which they apply those effects. In this way you can often achieve stunning animation with just the download overhead of one small applet and one image. In the exercise you are about to work through, you will see how to make the Java program create an animated special effect in real time, as opposed to using more conventional animated content, which would require streaming a video clip or building a large animated GIF image.

Java

A programming language developed by Sun Microsystems for Internet use and applications.

applets

Small programs that are tiny in size for quick download and are designed to run in a browser.

CREATING AND USING ANIMATED JAVA APPLETS WITH 3SPACE PUBLISHER

You encountered 3Space Publisher in Chapter 9 when you created 3D content for Web site use. 3Space Publisher also does a terrific job of generating animated Web content by applying preprogrammed Java applets.

The full version of 3Space Publisher comes with an additional program called 3Space HTML Helper. You will not be able to complete this exercise with the free downloaded version. This program takes images and applies them to a prepackaged Java applet. It automatically sets the parameters the applet requires to animate the image and generates an HTML Web page including the animated Java applet embedded. This Web page can be used to further build the rest of the Web page around the applet, or as an example from which to copy the Java applet operation. 3Space HTML Helper also provides a way to copy the HTML fragment that's needed to embed the Java applet into your Web page.

As with Flash, there is a lot more to this versatile application than we have time to cover here. Check out this book's Web site for more information about 3Space Publisher. Refer to Figure 9.6 for an overview of the 3Space Publisher interface and features. If it's been a while since you have read Chapter 9, you may wish to briefly revisit it to refresh your memory.

1. Start 3Space Publisher and if a blank new document is not apparent, click the New button to start one.

2. Select the 3D Clip Art gallery, and from the Animals tab, select one of the fish (DV13809 or similar, shown in Figure 16.10) and drag it into the perspective view.

3. Click the Display a Floating View button and, in the Floating view, use the Change The Camera's View tool (hand icon) to move the fish so that it is pointing upward out of the bottom of the window. Remember from Chapter 9

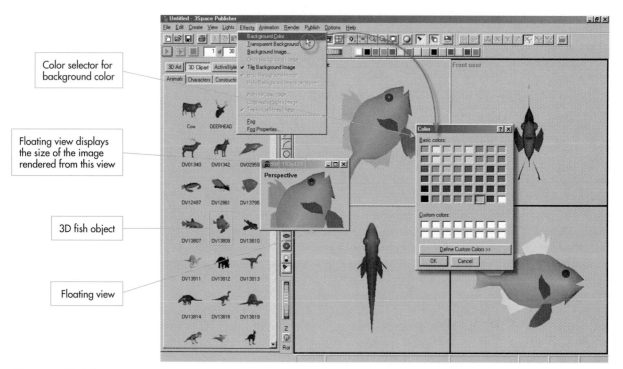

Figure 16.10
Position the fish object in the Floating view so that it points up from the bottom of the window.

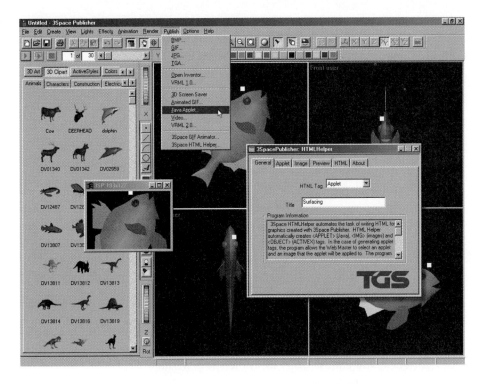

Figure 16.11
Once you're pleased with your 3D scene, use the command on the Publish menu to select your final output. In this case, we select Java Applet.

that in 3Space Publisher, the Change The Camera's View tool provides additional scene-moving functions when used with the Shift and Ctrl keys.

4. Resize the Floating view and Zoom in/out on the fish to achieve the effect shown in Figure 16.10.

5. As shown in Figure 16.10, choose Background Color from the Effects menu and, from the color selection panel shown, select black as the background color. You will want to use black against a black Web page background to hide the edges of the image. This will make the fish and the Java special effect appear to float on the Web page.

6. Choose Render Preview from the Render menu to see what your 3D scene will look like photo-rendered. This is a good time to add to the scene any lighting you desire to enhance the rendered image.

7. Once you're happy with your scene/object arrangement, choose Java Applet from the Publish menu (see Figure 16.11). 3Space Publisher first renders and saves the image before applying it to the Java applet.

8. Select the High Photo-Realistic option and specify the image file location and name. If you do not want the default settings, make a note of the file location (you will need this later for step 15) and click OK. 3Space Publisher renders and saves the image and passes the image name and location to 3Space HTML Helper, which then appears automatically.

9. The 3Space HTML Helper screen should be visible. Type "Surfacing" into the Title box (see Figure 16.11) and click the Applet tab.

The "Lake" applet should be showing by default in the drop-down selection of applets. You will be using this one, so no changes are needed here. The applet width and height parameters are derived from the size of the image you've just rendered, so they should be correct as defaults. Note that for this applet, the height will always be twice that of the image's. You can guess why later when you see the end results. Left alignment on the Web page is also good, and later you may wish to change this to suit your needs. Once you have completed this exercise and have become more familiar with Java applet publishing in 3Space Publisher, try the other applet choices and see how they look. Make a note of the width and height value shown for later exercises.

10. Click the Image tab and the Preview tab. The image shown should be the one you've just rendered. This is a confirmation only, or an opportunity for you to change images if you want (remember to change the width and height parameters to suit if you do).

11. Click the HTML tab. You can choose between viewing the HTML ready-made for a complete document or just the fragment you need to paste into an existing Web page project.

12. After you type in a name for the HTML file (see Figure 16.12) and check the Test on Save option, clicking Save brings up your browser with the new Lake Java applet embedded in a Web page, loaded and running as seen in Figure 16.12.

13. To quickly place this Java applet in the Web page you created in the last exercise with the Flash banner, use a text editor (such as Notepad for Windows users) to open the Banner.html file you created.

14. In 3Space HTML Helper, make sure the Tag Fragment option is checked in the HTML tab. Drag your mouse over the HTML code shown to select it, right-click, and choose Copy from the shortcut menu.

15. In your text editor, right before the </BODY> tag in the Banner.html code (see Figure 16.13), right-click and choose Paste from the shortcut menu to insert the new HTML that embeds the Java applet you just created into the Banner.html page. Don't forget to save it.

However, before you view the results, make sure that a copy of the image you created in step 12 and the file "lake.class" are located in the same directory

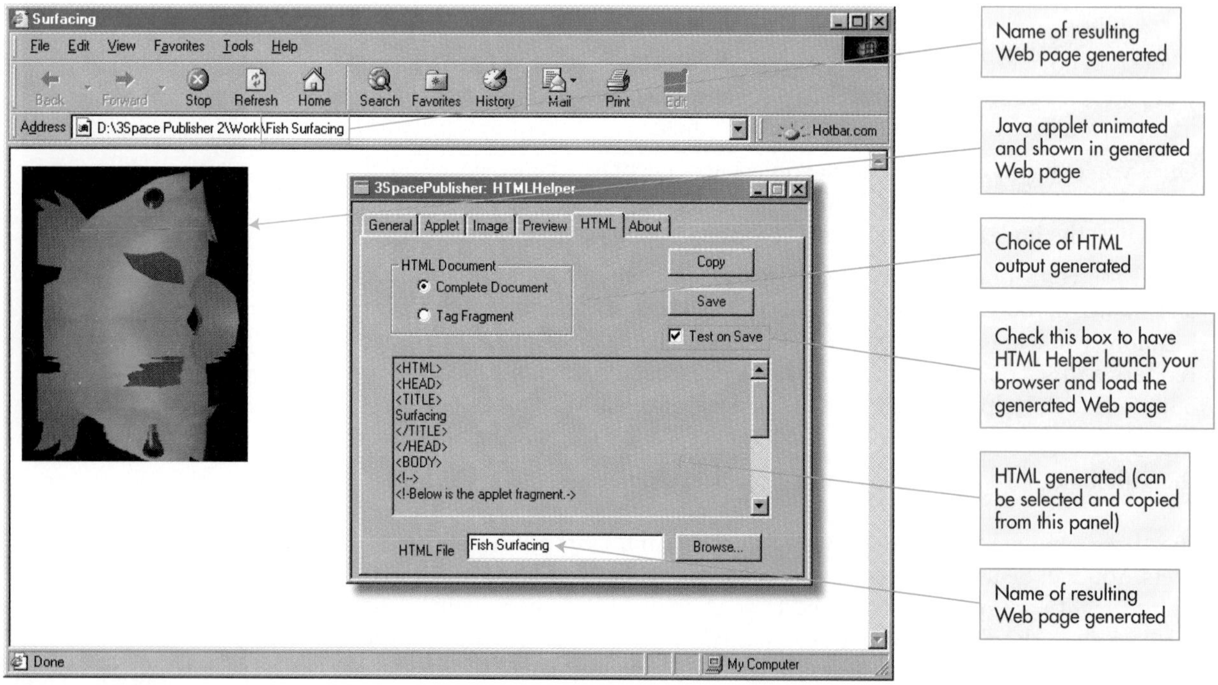

Figure 16.12
The HTML tab settings in 3Space HTML Helper and the final product shown in Internet Explorer.

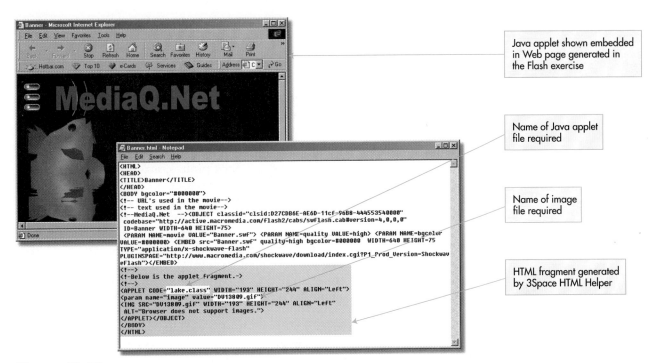

Java applet shown embedded in Web page generated in the Flash exercise

Name of Java applet file required

Name of image file required

HTML fragment generated by 3Space HTML Helper

Figure 16.13
Your Java applet embedded in the Web page created earlier in the Flash exercise. Note the highlighted inserted HTML fragment and the file references indicated. Yours may be slightly different depending on the names you used to save your files.

as the modified file Banner.html. If you were impatient and jumped ahead, you will see a blank space where you should see the Java applet. You should have made a note of the image location in Step 8, and the file lake.class will also be in the same location. Figure 16.13 shows the new Java applet code highlighted, indicating the references to the files that need to be located in the same directory as the Web page itself. Drag copies of these files to your directory containing the newly modified Banner.html. Double-click Banner.html to view your animated page. It should look pretty cool.

BUILDING A MULTIMEDIA WEB SITE

In this book, you have learned how to create interface graphics, optimize images, create 3D imagery, create computer animation and digital video, and create and edit digital sound. What's more is that you have brought all of these media components together in a multimedia application. In this chapter you have expanded your knowledge further by creating simple Shockwave applets and animated Java applets for Web deployment. Now it's time to learn how to use and deliver these media components in a multimedia Web page.

This section of the book will not refer to nor teach you about design layout and visual appropriateness of any Web site design. That is the domain of any one of the many books you will find on Web page design. Instead you will be asked to concentrate on the steps you will need to know to present multimedia on a Web page. You will learn about bandwidth, Web server considerations, and technical design issues, irrespective of visual design issues.

In that light, the presumption is that you already know, or can easily find out, how to create a fundamental Web page. In the following examples you will be jumping in at the deep end and going straight to the meaty multimedia implementation steps. You can follow the steps provided even with no prior knowledge of Web page creation, but it will help you to learn more about this fun and highly creative technology.

A BRIEF LOOK AT MICROSOFT'S FRONTPAGE

There are many Web page authoring applications to choose from. Microsoft's FrontPage is among the most versatile and capable of such products. It is also a product suitable for beginners and seasoned professional Web designers alike. Some products, such as Macromedia's Dreamweaver, are a little more sophisticated than most beginners would start with, but are excellent tools for skilled users. For our purposes of demonstrating the ways to embed media components in a Web page, FrontPage is ideal because it shows the HTML for the page under construction evolving as each new component is added. There are also quite a few free Web page and development authoring tools available for download from the Web, along with a considerable amount of content such as images, Java applets, and media pieces. Check out this book's Web site for links to such online goodies.

Take a little time to study Figure 16.14, which shows the FrontPage interface and functions. It also shows our Flash banner page from earlier in this chapter (note that button graphics have been added to show the image editing toolbar at the bottom of the FrontPage interface).

In FrontPage you can visually design and create a Web page in the main document section of the interface (in Page view—see the section titled "Views" that follows), while viewing the HTML as it grows in the HTML source window. Figure 16.15 shows the Flash banner with the Java applet page you created earlier in this chapter, in FrontPage's Normal, HTML, and Preview modes.

As a complete Web site development and management tool, FrontPage includes Web publishing tools (using the Publish Web button, shown in Figure 16.14), allowing you to quickly and easily publish your work to your Web server and easily maintain it thereafter, without having to be an expert in file transfers on the Web, or having a separate FTP client application. To do this, the server you are publishing to (or the ISP providing you with server space) must have FrontPage server extensions installed. Check with your Webmaster or ISP to ensure that these are in place.

In the absence of FrontPage server extensions, FrontPage can still function well as an excellent Web site development tool, but some of the more sophisticated features available to your Web page design will not work and will have to be omitted. Check Microsoft's FrontPage Web site (www.microsoft.com/frontpage) for more details.

FTP client

FTP stands for *file transfer protocol.* An FTP client is a software application that allows users to transfer files between their desktop computer and the remote Web server.

server extensions

Support programs running on a Web server that assist the process of publishing Web content and the operation thereafter of that published work. While they are not exclusive to Microsoft's FrontPage, its server extensions are the most commonly used server-side support extensions for any one Web page authoring and publishing product.

SMART MENUS IN FRONTPAGE

FrontPage, like other members of the Microsoft Office family of applications, uses "smart menus." That double-chevron symbol you see on some menus indicates that more functions are hidden from view to declutter the feature-rich menus. Clicking the double-chevron symbol or double-clicking the menu heading expands the menu to reveal the less-used choices. Once selected, those choices are then added to the visible set of primary menu options.

If you come across a menu command in this book that you cannot found, identify the menu title and double-click it to reveal the command you are looking for.

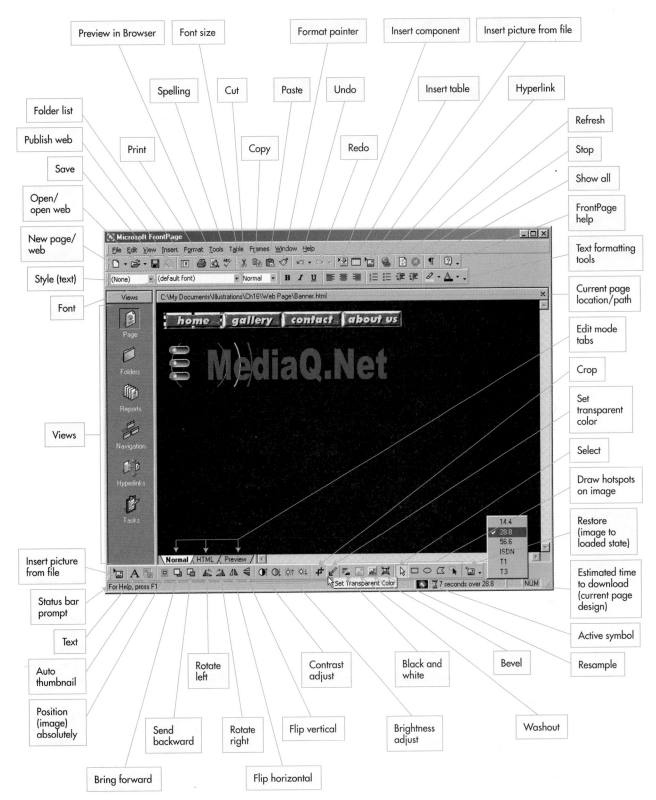

Figure 16.14
The FrontPage interface. Take a few minutes to familiarize yourself with its features.

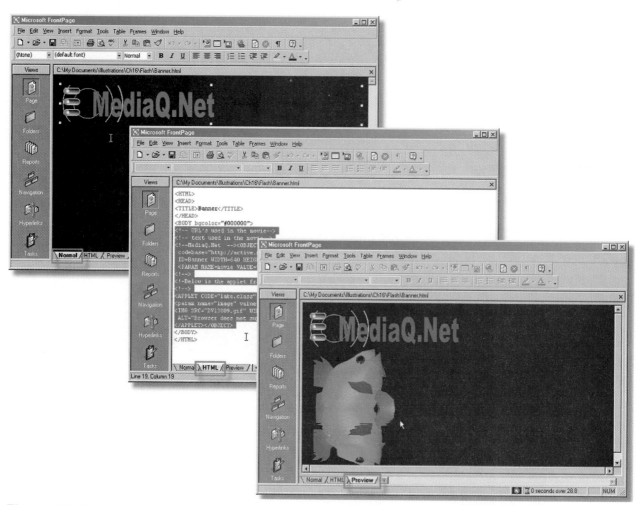

Figure 16.15
The Web page example you created earlier in this chapter shown in FrontPage's Normal, HTML, and Preview modes, as selected with the tabs provided at the bottom of the screen.

WEBS

FrontPage uses the term *FrontPage Web* or sometimes simply *Web* to refer to an integrated Web site (multiple interlinked Web pages) developed in FrontPage. This is analogous to a complete Web site development project. FrontPage can track, monitor, debug, organize, and publish complete Web site projects with relative ease. One of FrontPage's particular strengths is the organization of a Web site and the ease with which you can later make changes and have FrontPage track and automatically make required modifications to your Web site.

For instance, in Navigation view you can see a nicely organized flow chart of your Web site. If you decide to move your News page from beneath your Home page and place it under your Contacts page, you can do so by simply dragging-and-dropping the flow chart symbol for the News page to its new position. This capability is remarkable enough on its own, but when you do this, any FrontPage navigation bars affected automatically modify all button links and button titles to accommodate the change. To do this manually would require a tremendous amount of work on the developer's part.

When working with FrontPage Webs, remember that you are working with a project comprising a set of Web pages. Be sure that when you open, close, save, and publish through FrontPage that you do so for the entire Web, as opposed to the individual page currently being edited.

To start a FrontPage Web, click the New Web button, and if the New Page button is showing in its place, click the small down arrow to the right of the New Page button and choose Web from the drop-down menu. When starting a new Web, FrontPage offers a selection of templates and Web wizards to choose from. Take some time to experiment with the wizards, especially the Corporate Presence wizard, and become familiar with them. The next time a client needs a Web site on a quick-turnaround schedule, you will find that the FrontPage wizards could save you many hours, if not days, setting up your client's site.

VIEWS

Though most development and design time in FrontPage is spent in the Page and Navigation views, the Folders, Reports, Hyperlinks, and Tasks views are all very useful. The Hyperlinks view enables you to check the integrity and correct connection of all of your hyperlinks leading to and from your Web page. The Reports view provides an immense amount of management information about your Web and is especially useful for checking for and locating broken links.

The Page view is where your Web page is designed and built. The Page view offers three "modes," as indicated by the tabs at the bottom of the screen (see Figure 16.4): Normal (visual editing of the page), HTML (text editing of the page's HTML code), and Preview (a close approximation of what the page will look like in a browser). Note that in the Page view, a very important piece of information is displayed near the bottom right corner of the screen: the estimated time it would take your user to download your Web page given the stated connection speed. By clicking this small panel, you can select different connection speeds from the shortcut menu that appears, as shown in Figure 16.14.

THEMES

FrontPage Webs can use visual design templates called Themes, which are prepared image sets for backgrounds, buttons, banners, dividers, bullets, and other design treatments. FrontPage comes with a set of about a dozen of these design packages, and allows you to customize any of them to suit your own needs. These Themes provide button graphic sets to accommodate button rollover effects in FrontPage navigation bars. If you are designing a corporate identification package for a Web site, FrontPage Themes provide an excellent way to edit and maintain it; applying a new or changed Theme to a Web is as simple as clicking a button.

As shown in Figure 16.16, choose Theme from the Format menu and spend some time playing with the Theme options, getting a feel for how they work. With Themes, the techniques you learned in Chapter 6 for creating button and banner images can be put to good use. Just remember to create blank button and banner graphics and save them in GIF format, because in a FrontPage Theme, the text label on any piece of a Theme (such as a button face) is added for you. Then use the buttons beneath the "What would you like to modify?" label in the Themes control panel. This process is illustrated in Figure 16.16. In this figure you can see how to invoke the Themes control panel and how to modify the graphics used in any Theme.

To modify any particular piece of a Theme, simply double-click that element in the Theme preview in the Modify Theme window, or select it from the drop-down list of components. Using the Browse buttons provided, you can load your new Theme element with ease.

The following exercise will take you through the process of placing and/or embedding in a Web page an image, your Flash Banner, your Java applet, your animated GIFs, your digital sound, and your digital video.

Figure 16.16
FrontPage provides complete
Web site–wide visual design
templates called Themes (a
custom client Theme is shown).
Your list of themes may differ
from those shown.

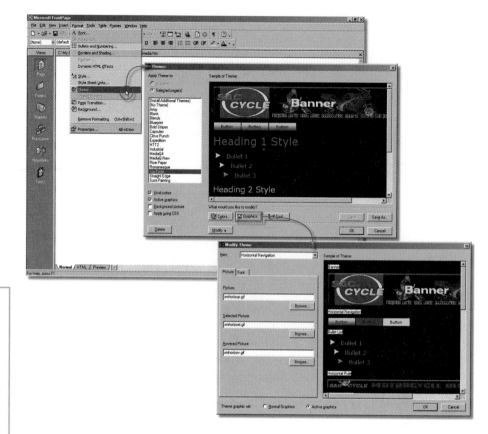

A hyperlink to a Web page
opens that Web page in the
browser. In addition, any
media file can be hyperlinked
to a Web page by setting the
hyperlink of an image or
piece of text to the media filename. Your browser will then
play the media file separately
from the Web page itself (in
the case of an unrecognized
media file type, your browser
will prompt you to download
the file from your hard drive
or ask you to specify an
application with which to
open it). When you embed a
media file in a Web page, you
are instructing the Web page
to play that media file in the
HTML document itself so
that it plays on the surface of
the page. This technique will
become more apparent when
you work through the exercises that follow.

Auto Thumbnail

A feature in Microsoft's FrontPage
by which large image files can be
converted to a smaller thumbnail
image on the Web page, with an
automatic hyperlink to the original
large image file. This allows users to
view the small image and choose
whether they would like to go
through the long download to view
the entire large image.

PLACING AND EMBEDDING MULTIMEDIA CONTENT IN A WEB PAGE

Let's start with images on your Web page. Placing images in FrontPage is a very
simple process. You can either click the Insert Picture From File button, or simply drag the image file onto your page from Windows Explorer or from your
computer's desktop. Once placed, the image will appear as placed, and will be
available for editing with FrontPage's image editing tools in the Normal view.

Once the image is on your page, FrontPage provides tools to size, crop,
brighten, darken, mirror, rotate, convert to grayscale, and bevel. Figure 16.14
shows these image editing tools. Of course, you can use any image editing tool,
such as Photoshop or Paint Shop Pro, to edit your images outside FrontPage,
and then place them into your Web page. However, FrontPage's own image editing tools can make those tasks much easier when the image is already placed on
the document.

Of special note is FrontPage's Auto Thumbnail tool. The button for this
feature is also located among the image editing tools, but is active only when
larger images are selected. This tool creates a thumbnail version of the placed
image and automatically hyperlinks the thumbnail to the original large image
file. The result is that the small thumbnail image loads quickly and invites the
user to click it to view the larger, slower-to-download version. The appearance and size of the automatic thumbnail are set by using the Page Options
command on the Tools menu and clicking the AutoThumbnail tab to view and
change settings.

While Web pages are restricted to the use of JPEG and GIF image file formats only, FrontPage allows you to drag-and-drop other image file formats,
which FrontPage then converts to an acceptable GIF or JPEG file.

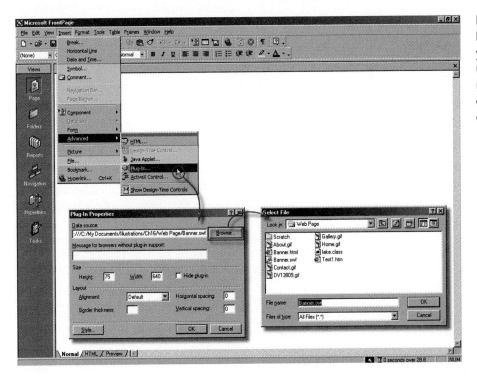

Figure 16.17
Embedding a Flash movie into
your Web page using FrontPage
(note that you will have to
remember the width and height
of the Flash banner from the
earlier exercise to enter here).

EMBEDDING YOUR FLASH MOVIE

1. Create a new directory in which you are going to build this Web page.

2. Copy the Flash banner file you created earlier (Banner.swf) into this directory. When you save your Web page from this exercise, you will save it to this directory.

3. Click the New Page button in FrontPage. A blank white document appears, ready for your multimedia creations.

4. To embed a Flash movie, choose Advanced from the Insert menu, and then choose Plug-In, as shown in Figure 16.17.

5. In the Plug-In Properties dialog box, type in the width and height of the Flash banner you created. These dimensions were 640 width by 75 height if you were following along, and if not, you can always look at the HTML of the original Web page you created to play the Flash banner, where you will find width and height specified (shown as "ID=Banner WIDTH=640 HEIGHT=75").

6. Use the Browse button to locate the Banner.swf file, and click OK. Click the Preview tab at the bottom of the screen to preview the embedded Flash banner.

Embedding of your Flash movie was achieved by the HTML code (automatically generated for you by FrontPage)

<embed src="Banner.swf" width="640" height="75"></embed>

as can be seen by clicking the HTML tab.

No matter what Web page authoring or editing tool you use, even if you code straight HTML in a basic text editor, this simple piece of HTML, the EMBED tag, will always work for you. You can type it straight into any Web page, and as long as the file referenced as the source file (src="filename.ext") is in the same directory as the Web page (or in the location specified between the quotes after the SRC tag if a file path is used), this code displays your Flash component.

7. Click the Save button, and save your new Web page to a file called FlashMultimedia.htm in the directory you created for this project.

To view your work in a browser, double-click the file you just saved to invoke your default browser application and automatically load your Web page. You can also use the Preview In Browser button provided by FrontPage.

EMBEDDING YOUR JAVA APPLET

1. Create a new use folder in which you are going to build this Web page.
2. Copy your Java applet file (lake.class) and your fish image (DV13809.gif, or whatever you named it) into this directory. When you save your Web page from this exercise, you will save it to this directory.
3. Click the New Page button in FrontPage. A blank white document appears, ready for your multimedia creations.
4. To embed a Java applet, choose Advanced from the Insert menu, and then choose Java Applet, as shown in Figure 16.18.
5. In the Java Applet Properties dialog box, enter the name of the Java applet (lake.class) in the text box labeled Applet source, as shown in the illustration.
6. Next, type in the width and height of the Java applet that you recorded when you originally created it using 3Space HTML Helper.

The dimensions shown in Figure 16.18 will most likely differ from yours, as they depend on the size of the image you rendered for this applet. You can always find the width and height of the image you rendered earlier for the Java applet exercise by using your image editing application, or simply refer to your

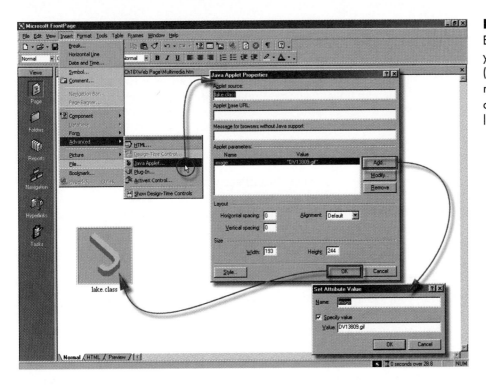

Figure 16.18
Embedding a Java applet into
your Web page using FrontPage
(note that you will have to
remember the width and height
of the Java applet from the earlier exercise to enter here).

notes from that exercise. Then enter the actual image width and twice the actual image height. You can always look at the HTML of the original Web page you created to play the Java applet, where you will find width and height specified.

7. Click the Add button in the Applet parameters section of the Java Applet Properties dialog box, and in the Set Attribute Value dialog box, enter the Name (Image) and Value (your image name) settings, as shown in Figure 16.18. Be sure to enter the full filename, including the .gif extension. When you click OK, this parameter will be passed to the Java applet lake.class as shown in the parameters listing in the Java Applet Properties dialog box.

8. Click OK to show the Java applet symbol on the Web page.

9. Click the Preview tab at the bottom of the screen to preview the embedded Java applet.

Embedding of your Java applet was achieved by the following HTML code (automatically generated for you by FrontPage).

```
<applet width="193" height="244" code="lake.class">
<param name="image" value="DV13809.gif">
</applet>
```

as can be seen by clicking the HTML tab.

As with the HTML used to embed the Flash movie, no matter what Web page authoring or editing tool you use, even if you code straight HTML in a basic text editor, this simple piece of HTML, the APPLET tag, will always work for you. You can type it straight into any Web page. As long as the file referenced as the code file (code="filename.ext") and any other file referenced in the parameter listing for the applet is in the same directory as the Web page (or in the location specified between the quotes after the CODE tag if a file path is used), this code displays your Java applet.

10. Click the Save button, and save your new Web page to a file called JavaMultimedia.htm in the directory you created for this project.

11. To view your work in a browser, double-click the file you just saved to invoke your default browser application and automatically load your Web page. You can also use the Preview In Browser button provided by FrontPage.

EMBEDDING VIDEO AND SOUND

First, let's look at the automated "FrontPage way" to do this.

 VIDEO.   You will find sample video files on this book's CD-ROM in the samples folder. There are two automated ways to embed video into a Web page using FrontPage:

1. Choose Picture from the Insert menu, and then choose Video.

2. Drag your video file from Windows Explorer and drop it onto your page.

FrontPage uses the DYNSRC tag to embed the video content in the Web page. The resulting HTML looks like this:

```
<img border="0" dynsrc="file:///C:/Media/BookVideo.avi" start="fileopen" width="160" height="120">
```

SOUND.   There is one automated way to embed a sound file into your Web page, and only as a background sound (there are no visible player controls for your user, which is not a good idea, in case users don't agree with your taste in music and wish to turn it off). Be aware that not all browsers can support background sound. You set a background sound for your Web page as follows:

1. Choose Properties from the File menu (or right-click the page, and choose Page Properties from the shortcut menu).

2. Click the General tab in the Page Properties dialog box. In the Location text box in the Background sound section, type in the name of the sound file you want to play, or click Browse to locate the file.

3. To play the sound continuously, check the Forever checkbox. To play the sound a fixed number of times, uncheck the Forever checkbox, and enter the number of times you want the sound to play in the Loop box.

FrontPage uses the BGSOUND tag to provide background sound. The resulting HTML looks like this:

```
<bgsound src="file:///C:/Media/Sounds/POScar.wav" loop="-1">
```

Now let's take a look at how to embed video or sound in a Web page using any Web page authoring tool or HTML text editor. You have already seen the EMBED tag used to embed a Flash movie into your Web page (if you wish, you also can use the FrontPage Insert Plug-In method to achieve the same results, exactly as used to embed the Flash banner earlier). Use of the EMBED tag is very simple.

1. To embed a video file in any Web page, simply enter the following HTML into the page (for a video file called MyVideo.avi that is 320 pixels wide, by 240 pixels high):

```
<embed src="MyVideo.avi" width="320" height="240" autostart="true"
loop="true"></embed>
```

The AUTOSTART parameter tells the video clip to begin playing as soon as it is loaded, and the LOOP parameter tells the video clip to repeat playing forever. Both of these parameters are optional. All you need is the EMBED tag and the WIDTH and HEIGHT parameters.

For different video formats (such as QuickTime (.mov), RealVideo (.rm), MPEG (.mpg), and so on), simply insert the file name and let the browser figure out what plug-ins or drivers to use to play the media piece.

2. To embed a sound file in any Web page, simply enter the following HTML into the page (for a sound file called MySound.wav):

```
<embed src="MySound.wav" autostart="true" loop="true"></embed>
```

The AUTOSTART parameter tells the sound file to begin playing as soon as it is loaded, and the LOOP parameter tells the sound file to repeat playing forever. Both of these parameters are optional. All you need is the EMBED tag.

In the case of sound files, there are no actual WIDTH and HEIGHT parameters. However, if you do specify width and height, and depending on the sound file format, you will be specifying the visual appearance of onscreen controls for your user to play, stop, and review the sound file. You will have to experiment with these parameters, as each sound file player will have a different control size, and each browser version will also use different size settings. You will have to experiment with this. With a little trial and error you can determine the appropriate size to provide your user with sound controls to accompany your sound file.

For different sound file formats (such as sound-only QuickTime (.mov), RealAudio (.ra), MPEG3 (.mp3), Macintosh sound (.aiff), and so on), simply insert the file name and let the browser figure out what plug-ins or drivers to use to play the media piece.

QUICKTIME VR MOVIES

Apple's QuickTime digital media format comes in a variant called QuickTime VR (VR stands for *Virtual Reality*). QuickTime VR movies provide the user with 360-degree panorama images that provide an illusion of being right in the scene. Users can drag their mouse pointers around in the image to make it pan throughout the surrounding view. QuickTime VR Objects are QuickTime-format files that allow users to seemingly rotate a picture of an object by dragging their mouse pointer across the image.

Both formats are widely used on the Web, especially by automobile manufacturers who provide 360-degree views of car interiors and rotatable views of car exteriors (see this book's Web site for links to such examples). These media components are popular for their incredibly small file size, and therefore quick download times, and for their ability to bring picture-quality 360-degree experience to the Web.

Several products are available for QuickTime VR authoring. Macintosh users can use Apple's own QuickTime VR Authoring Suite (www.apple.com), and Windows users can use products such as Pictureworks's Spin Panorama (www.pictureworks.com/dphome.html).

Once you have created these QuickTime VR files, simply place the file name and size parameters in the EMBED tag as shown for other digital movie formats, and watch the magic unfold. Be sure to install the Apple QuickTime drivers, and provide your visitors with a link to Apple's Web site.

Figure 16.19
A Web page using images and
embedded multimedia content.
"Buttons" shown are simply
images on the Web page.

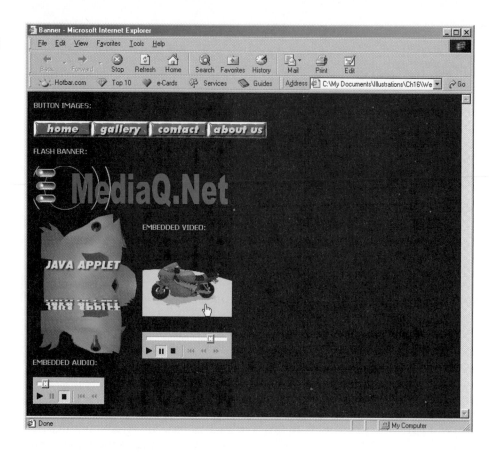

MULTIMEDIA ON THE WEB

While you have just scratched the surface of creating multimedia-enhanced Web sites, you have discovered how to embed into a Web page the various multimedia components you've learned about throughout this book. The rest is now up to you. How creative are you?

Figure 16.19 shows a completed Web page showing our placed images, embedded Flash Shockwave movie, Java applet animation, and digital video and audio. You would not normally create such a "cluttered" Web page, but rather use each of these media components individually as best suited to your project's needs.

WEB SERVER/INTERNET SERVICE PROVIDER CONSIDERATIONS

As you know, multimedia files are fat bandwidth consumers. It would be incredibly easy to overload a Web page with too much multimedia content. While one solution is to spread your multimedia components over several pages, there may be Web server or ISP restrictions to consider. Most ISPs and Webmasters provide their customers with a limited amount of space, so be sure to determine at the outset just how much server space you have to work with, and use it carefully.

Some products, such as FrontPage, require special support applications running on the host server. These *server-side applications* provide easy-to-use features that make FrontPage so attractive, especially to the beginner or the less technically inclined. Features such as hit counters, site search engines, automated tables of contents, discussion groups, information request forms, and the like require FrontPage extensions installed on the hosting server.

hit counters

A digital numeric display provided on a Web page to show the number of times a Web page has been visited.

discussion groups

A service provided on a Web site in which a program allows users to publish questions or comments. Subsequent visitors can publish their own questions or comments, respond to a previously posted question or comment, or reply to someone else's response. The original discussion topic and all responses are displayed in a list that usually indents each response under the topic listed above it. In this way a debate can be held on the Web over time, and anyone visiting the discussion group can review the "conversation" to date and follow the discussion.

These extension applications also provide communications between the copy of FrontPage on your computer system and the server when publishing your FrontPage Web. They enable FrontPage to initiate a file transfer connection to the server and to determine what special components are needed and configure them. They also enable FrontPage to determine what files have been changed compared to the published set on the server and transfer only those files. This cuts down unnecessary connection and file transfer time that's otherwise wasted on transferring copies of files already present on the server.

If, for some reason, your server administrator/provider cannot provide FrontPage server extensions (as is the case if you publish to server space provided as part of America Online membership, for example), you can still transfer the complete FrontPage Web to your server space using an FTP program. Many such programs are available for free download from Web sites such as www.shareware.com and www.zdnet.com. Once you become familiar with your FTP application, simply transfer the contents, including subdirectories, of the FrontPage Web folder (set up by FrontPage when you named your Web site, and given the same name as you gave your Web site) to your server account. Most features, such as button rollovers, will work. Refer to the FrontPage help file for a list of components that will not work without FrontPage extensions. You should avoid using these features in the absence of a FrontPage-compliant Web server account.

Note that none of the multimedia embedding techniques described in this chapter requires FrontPage extensions.

Any Web server will have a set name for the default home page. When Web surfers visit your Web site, they do so usually by typing in, or linking to, your URL. The URL doesn't specify a home page by name, nor does it have to. Your Web server software has a predetermined home page name that, when present, is provided to visitors to the URL who don't specify a specific Web page by name. This convention allows for one of three standard home page names. Your home page will have to be named default.htm, index.htm, or home.htm. Your Webmaster will tell you which one your server requires, and you will use that name for your site's home page. There are no exceptions to this rule, so homepage.htm will not work. Any other Web page must be addressed using its specific name—for example, www.myURL.com/contacts.htm.

Some servers require the use of an HTML file extension, some require HTM, and some simply don't care (as long as your Web pages use one or the other). Some UNIX systems must have the full HTML file name extension. Older versions of Windows NT support only HTM. The safest solution is to use the shorter HTM version, as this is the most universally accepted. However, a simple check with your Webmaster will remove any uncertainty.

When discussing these issues with your Webmaster, it is important to determine whether the server you will be publishing to is case-sensitive in its handling of filenames. Current-version Windows NT servers don't care about case and will match uppercase and lowercase versions of the same file name. Some UNIX servers, such as Apache, must have matching case in filenames to locate referenced files and perform hyperlinking. To such servers, a hyperlink to the Web page contacts.htm will never link to the intended file if it is named Contacts.htm. Some very old (in computer years) server applications use only uppercase filenames.

Check these issues out in advance. If there are filename case restrictions, use all uppercase or all lowercase naming for consistency (except in a situation where lowercase is unrecognized). Be aware that some FTP applications have a nasty habit of changing file name case on the server end once the file is transferred. You may have to experiment with a test Web page or two on the server to ensure that all is hanging together well.

MARKETING AND PROMOTING ONLINE MULTIMEDIA PRODUCTS

Promoting your Web site is a proactive task. It requires considerable effort and attention to do correctly. In the absence of promotion, no one will visit or link to your Web site, no matter how well it's designed, and it will languish undiscovered indefinitely in an Internet version of Limbo.

To actively promote your Web site, and to provide it with the best possible chance of a high ranking on the primary Internet search engines and directories, do the following:

1. *Design each and every Web page such that the page title, its meta tags, and its textual content reflect the primary topic of the page.* Check out this book's Web site for information and links about meta tags. These sections of a Web page's HTML have no visual effect to the design of the page; they are provided as a method to store informational text about the page. In particular, the "description" and "keywords" meta tags provide information that feeds a search engine's classification and ranking of the page. Figure 16.1 shows a Web page with extensive use of meta tags, including the "description" and keywords" meta tags.

2. *Submit your URL to the primary Web search engines and directories.* Never do this until you have completed step 1. It is very difficult to change your submission once it is established, so take time, be patient, and complete the meta tags, title, and text content review for each and every Web page in the site. Most search engines, such as Altavista (www.altavista.com), Lycos (www.lycos.com), Excite (www.excite.com), DirectHit (www.directhit.com), and Google (www.google.com) have a small link at the bottom of their home pages, usually called "Add a URL," that provides a form to fill out to submit your new Web site to their search database. Web directories, such as Yahoo (www.yahoo.com) and Go (www.go.com), have similar "Add URL" sections. Register your Web site with as many of these sites as you can find. It is tedious but worthwhile. Most quote a lag time of two weeks to two months before your site begins to filter up in searches. There are also companies that will do this for you on all search engines and directory sites for a fee. They can be found by doing a search for "web listing services." If you can't find such a company in this manner, that would be a good indication of their ineffectiveness in this field.

3. *Give people a reason to visit.* Provide added value on your site—some sort of service or entertainment. Perhaps you provide a cool downloadable screensaver. If your business is automotive finance, provide online loan calculators or parts-locating services. Maybe your business is health care, in which case doctor referrals or discounted supplies or research information may be the draw that entices visitors to use your site and bookmark it for repeat visits.

4. *Give people a reason to come back again and again.* A Web site is, and should be, a dynamic medium. Changes made to a Web page are instantly available throughout the planet. That is an awesome thought! However, if visitors who have bookmarked your site return to find nothing changed and the same information that they have already viewed, then the likelihood of them returning again is next to none. You will need to provide a management regime that includes ongoing updating and maintenance of the Web site.

5. *Exchange links.* There will likely be many other Web sites in your area of business or field, and they would benefit, as would you, from some mutual cross-referencing. Often a simple introductory e-mail with an invitation to visit your site and an offer to exchange links will suffice to gain agreement and cooperation. The Internet is all about hyperlinking and exposure. This

can be a way to leverage some of the traffic your partners (or competitors) in the field have established, and likewise for them.

6. *Seek out Web rings.* Web rings are organized cooperative links among Web sites that share a common focus or interest. For instance, if your Web site sells accessories for four-wheel-drive vehicles, then you could find a 4x4 Web ring, add your site to the ring, and place the Web ring link and logos at the bottom of your primary pages. You will find Web rings by surfing the Web in your topic of interest and watching for the Web ring references at the bottom of the pages you visit.

7. *Monitor your site's performance on the Web.* After the initial period of a couple of months that the search engines and directories have taken to digest your Web site, start a program of random searches to monitor your site's ranking among your competitor's listings. Examine sites that rank higher than yours, and borrow their performance tricks (their HTML is available for all to see). Revise and resubmit your site and monitor its performance. Repeat as necessary until you achieve the ranking and listing you desire. It's also a good idea to ask others to search for you, as you will usually tend to test for search patterns that are particular to your personal way of thinking—which may or may not match the thought patterns of your typical customer. Once you achieve your search engine goals, remain vigilant. Thousands of other sites on the Net are also vying for those top-ranking slots. If you become complacent, you may find yourself slipping off the listing screen.

AVOIDING PITFALLS

Many issues were covered in this chapter, and with them come associated traps that you should avoid. Most have been addressed in this chapter, but the following is a summary of the most important ones:

When building Web sites, especially multimedia-enhanced sites, keep accurate and complete logs of all files used and their location. Wherever possible, create a designated directory or directory structure for each project to keep all of the many individual files of your project together in one place. Then if you encounter a broken link or an inoperative media file, you know where to start looking for the problem.

Determine before you start your Web site project what filename parameters are required of the server application. Your ISP or Webmaster will tell you this. These parameters are not issues you should stumble across later after extensive development work has been invested in your project.

Of all the delivery vehicles available to you as a multimedia producer, the Internet presents the most challenges in optimizing multimedia content to perform well over low-bandwidth connections. Determine your lowest-common-denominator user at the project outset, and ensure that your Web site's performance meets this criterion. Thereafter, any user who has the advantage of a faster connection will only benefit from an enhanced experience at your site. By planning your content overhead in this manner, you ensure the viability of your Web site to the largest possible audience.

Practice, practice, practice. There is no substitute. The more exposure time you get to any of these applications, the more familiar you will become with their operation, and the more quickly and fluidly you can get the job done. One definitive thing that technology and the Internet have done to business and society is to accelerate the pace at which we achieve. Clients for online multimedia (in my experience) have increasingly shorter project schedules and require quicker completion and delivery. The better and more adept you become with your chosen tools, the more quickly you can meet the needs of your client, and the greater the likelihood that you will benefit from repeat business.

If you have the opportunity to learn HTML, take it. While not essential for the creation of multimedia Web sites, it is essential if you want to stand apart from the many other individuals making a cottage industry of Web content development. If you have the skills to "pop the hood" and manipulate the nuts-and-bolts HTML code of your Web creation, you can extract that extra bit of performance and creativity that sets you apart from your competing developers.

Chapter Summary

- Multimedia authoring tools can be broadly categorized into two camps—those that use a timeline on which to base development and assembly of the multimedia project, and those that use an object-oriented approach.

- The Internet is one of the all-time most significant communication developments in human history. We have only just begun to see its full potential. On the crowded World Wide Web, you can use multimedia to enhance a Web site and make it stand out from the crowd.

- While you will benefit from knowing how to code using HTML, such knowledge is not essential for creating multimedia Web pages. It is important to understand the pros and cons of the multimedia delivery methods available for your end product. If you're using the Web as a delivery vehicle, then it's important to know how a browser application works so that you can design your online multimedia product to cater to each browser's way of displaying your work. Web page authoring tools create the HTML code required to describe your Web pages and allow you to concentrate more on the visual design of these documents.

- When you use Flash and 3Space Publisher, it is quite easy to create Shockwave movies and Java applets to enhance Web pages and bring true interactivity and multimedia capabilities to the humble browser. Follow the exercises in this chapter to learn how to create Flash movies and Java applets.

- A Web page authoring tool such as Microsoft's FrontPage makes the job of creating Web pages, and even entire Web sites, easier than ever. Embedding multimedia into a Web page is a simple affair. Using the EMBED tag in HTML, you can use any Web page authoring tool to display your media content.

- When publishing your multimedia Web site to the Net, it's important to make sure that the server that will host your work can support the technology elements you choose to use. A little preparation will save you a lot of revision work later.

Key Terms and Concepts

Checking Your Knowledge and Skills

1. Using the skills you learned in the exercise for creating a Flash banner, create an introductory animation for your Web site. This is a promo piece. It should entertain your visitors, entice them to watch the remaining animation, and encourage them to explore your Web site. Sound can be imported easily into Flash and placed in a keyframe. Look up and follow the instructions for this in the Flash help file and tutorials. Use a looping soundtrack to enhance your animated intro. Be sure to provide visitors with a link to Macromedia's

Web site and the download page for the Flash Shockwave plug-in. Don't forget to provide a button that users can press to enter the rest of your site.

2. Using the skills you learned in the exercise for creating an animated Java applet with 3Space Publisher, create a "shoreline" animation from an imported image. Find a suitable digital shoreline image, such as the New York City skyline or a picturesque image of a mountain lake. Locate the image using an Internet search engine, such as Altavista (www.altavista.com), that can search for pictures as well as Web pages. Crop the image to the shoreline, so that all you have is the top of the image from the water's edge upward. Convert the image to GIF format and record the image dimensions. Launch 3Space HTML Helper (located with 3Space Publisher in the 3Space Publisher group in the Start menu) and specify this image as the one to use to create the Lake Java applet. Don't forget to specify the height of the applet to be twice that of the image. Once you have the desired results (a rippling reflection of the shoreline/city), place this Java applet animation into a Web page and create a fictitious site that relates to your animation.

3. On the Web research reviews of the main Web page authoring tools available to you. Find feature comparisons and develop a pros-and-cons comparison chart. Computer magazine Web sites, such as www.zdnet.com, are always a good source of such information and provide search features to aid your research. In your opinion, which product seems most effective in getting the job done and why? Which is, in your opinion, the best value for the money, and why? Which product seems to be the most widely used? What features would you value most in making a decision among these products? Compare your notes to those of your classmates. Do you agree on which product is better?

4. Search the Internet for examples of online multimedia. Web sites such as Macromedia (www.macromedia.com), Microsoft's multimedia showcases (www.microsoft.com/windowsmedia), Real Networks (www.real.com), and others showcase many examples of multimedia content. View the source code HTML for these pages and find the EMBED tag usage. If there is no EMBED tag, can you determine how they embedded their multimedia?

Critical Thinking Challenges

1. Select an industry that you believe could put your Web multimedia talents to good use. For example, perhaps a local real estate agency could use a Web site enhanced with multimedia presentations of key properties. Perhaps a local veterinary clinic could use a little multimedia help showcasing their animal hospital. Pretend that such a client wants you to create a multimedia Web site for them. Research their clientele and the level of computer sophistication and connection speeds that would be typical of such customers. Use these data to determine for the client what degree of multimedia content they should have and generate a proposal for such a Web site, citing your market research for your multimedia choices and recommendations.

2. Download and evaluate free Web development tools (see the links available on this book's Web site).

Compare and rank them with the purchased tools you have been using. How do they compare? Would you use any instead of or in conjunction with your current Web page authoring tool? Why?

3. Using Web server space available to you, or available free on the Web (at sites such as www.geocities.com or www.xoom.com), build an informative Web site about your favorite topic, hobby, business, or talent. Develop a Web marketing campaign for this site. Make it your goal to have this site come up as one of the first three hits of a Web search on the main search engines/directories. Implement your plan and build a daily log of your progress. How soon did it take for your site to reach your intended goals? Which search engine/directory was the first to feature your site?

Hands-on Exercises
BUILDING AN ONLINE DIGITAL CATALOG

In Chapter 15 you developed a multimedia digital catalog for a hypothetical florist business that you owned. This time, pretend you own an automobile dealership. You have a terrific stock of cars, especially those trendy sport-utility vehicles for the active-lifestyle customers that are difficult to locate. You also have an accomplished service department, with many awards to prove it, and an excellent body shop.

You need a fully multimedia-enhanced showcase Web site. You have decided to develop this product in-house,

as those pesky Web developers don't seem to understand your business (they speak another language!) and they charge too much. Sound familiar?

Using the Web as a source for competitor sites and of content (such as pictures of your cars) that you "borrow," develop an easy-to-use and inviting showcase Web site for your dealership. Design it so that it allows users to categorize and browse through your products and services and to jump to an inquiry form when they have decided what they want. Be sure to include features that you have identified as enticements for your users to linger at your site, and features that will attract them back.

Build a simple (six products, two services—auto service and body shop) digital showcase mock-up. This mock-up will be presented to the board in two weeks as a proof-of-concept piece to persuade the board to invest the needed funds. Provide the board members with printed handouts of the most important screens so that they may take away with them a teaser sample of the potential final product.

Hint: If you are using Microsoft's FrontPage, start with the Corporate Presence wizard to save a lot of time and energy.

Master Project
PUTTING YOUR MASTER PROJECT ON THE WEB

So far you should have created a binder for the project that documents your project concept, includes a project plan and timeline, and includes your sketches and visuals for your design, along with a completed CD-ROM–/disk-based multimedia product.

Determine which Web page authoring tool is best suited to your Master Project.

Assemble your work on the Master Project to date, and using your project plan and storyboard as a guide, build a support Web site for your Master Project using the Web page authoring tool of your choice. Be sure to showcase excerpts of some of the multimedia content available on the CD-ROM.

Solicit the input of others as your work progresses. A fresh look at your work to date from someone not involved with the details can often be very helpful. This could help you avoid pitfalls and user design flaws.

PHOTO AND SCREEN CAPTURE CREDITS

Chapter 1 Figure 1.1: Courtesy of Gateway; Figure 1.3: Courtesy of Macromedia; Figure 1.6: Courtesy of Adobe; Figure 1.7: Courtesy of Cyan Inc.; Figure 1.10: Photo courtesy of Intel Corporation.

Chapter 2 Figure 2.7: Courtesy of Dorling Kindersley; Figure 2.15: Courtesy of Intel Corporation; Figure 2.16: Courtesy of Reality Interactive; Figure 2.19: Courtesy of Wall Data; Figure 2.20: Courtesy of Intel Corporation; Figure 2.22: Courtesy of Intel Corporation.

Chapter 3 Figure 3.1: Courtesy of Boston College; Figure 3.2: Courtesy of TeleVideo; Figure 3.11: Courtesy of NASA.

Chapter 4 Figure 4.17: Courtesy of Dorling Kindersley.

Chapter 12 Figure 12.2: Courtesy of RealNetworks.

INDEX

A

ACID (Sonic Foundry), 275

Active Object, 353

ActiveX *A technology from Microsoft that packages small programs or program components in a format that can be easily embedded in another program or Web page and used by a Web browser or another software development tool. ActiveX components can provide special capabilities and features to a browser application, much in the same way a plug-in extends the capabilities of the browser. An ActiveX component is integrated and used as you view the Web page using the component, whereas a plug-in has to be installed separately into the browser,* 353, 377

ADC, 267, 271

ADPCM (Adaptive Delta Pulse Code Modulation), 277

AIFF, 268

Airbrush tool *A painting tool, available in most image editing and graphic design software applications, that is used to simulate the use of an airbrush, providing a fine, faded painting effect,* 100

Alias Wavefront object, 150

Alien Skin, 138

Amiga computer, 8

Analog *The name for an electronic signal that carries its information/sound as a continuously fluctuating voltage value,* 267

Analog-to-digital (A-to-D) converter *A hardware and/or software product that converts an analog signal to a digital data file. When recording sound on your computer through a microphone, you are using the A-to-D converter of your computer's sound interface,* 267, 271

Analog vs. digital sound, 266–267

Animated GIFs, 148–149, 150, 200–201

  spinning-logo, 204–209

  video vs., 202

Animated text, 386

Animation. *See also* 3D graphics and animation

  in Director, 350, 351

  in Flash, 383–386

  in Java applets, 389

Animation keyframe *A milestone frame in an animation sequence that sets the animation parameters that the 3D modeling and animation application uses to extrapolate the required animation over the previous frames leading up to that milestone frame,* 153

Animation Shop (JASC), 203

Antz (film), 145

Apple Computers, 5, 228

Applets *Small programs that are tiny in size for quick download and are designed to run in a browser,* 297, 389

  authoring for the Web, 370

  Java, 389–393

  Shockwave, 329

  Vitalize, 329

APPLET tag, 401

Area lights, 191

Artifacts, 261

Aspect ratio *The ratio of an image's width to its height. A 640 × 480 image has an aspect ratio of 1.33:1, or 4:3—its width is 1.33 times its height. 4:3 is the same ratio in round numbers. When scaling an image, if you maintain the aspect ratio, you prevent distortion of the image as it is scaled,* 97–98

Asymmetric compression *A codec that compresses the video data in more time than it takes to decompress it for playback uses asymmetric compression. Asymmetric compression usually provides greater compression, resulting in smaller file size,* 219

Atari, 4

A-to-D (analog-to-digital) converter. *See* Analog-to-digital (A-to-D) converter

Audio. *See also* Sound

  codecs for, 277–278, 295–296

  embedded in multimedia product, 278

  settings, 261

Audio streaming, 297

Authoring *The process of creating a software application or Web page without the need to use, or even understand, computer programming. An authoring program provides the user with an intuitive design tool that will do the work of programming the end product to match the visual design of the author*, 44, 301–373. *See also* Director (Macromedia); Multimedia Fusion (Clickteam)
  applets on the Web, 370
  avoiding pitfalls, 322–323, 371
  branching applications, 311–313
  for CD-ROM/DVD-ROM, 304–305
  defined, 302
  digital movies, 310–311
  of disk-based application, 197–201
  frame-based, 328–329
  iconic, 317–318
  linear applications, 316
  movie metaphor for, 316
  object manipulation formats, 313
  object-oriented tools, 316–317
  programming vs., 305–308
  project planning, 318–322
  slide show applications, 309–310, 311
  spatial environments, 313–315
  target platform and delivery planning, 303–304
  with timelines, 316, 329
  for the Web, 201–202, 305, 377–378
Authoring tool *A computer application that allows the user to develop a software product, usually by dragging-and-dropping various media components, without the need to know, use, or understand a programming language*, 302
  icon-based, 329
  object-oriented, 329
Authorware (Macromedia), 317, 318
AutoDesk file formats, 150
Autorecord *When autorecord is turned on, all changes made to a scene are automatically recorded as keyframe animation instructions unless*

the current frame number is 0, 183
Auto Thumbnail *A feature in Microsoft's FrontPage by which large image files can be converted to a smaller thumbnail image on the Web page, with an automatic hyperlink to the original large image file. This allows users to view the small image and choose whether they would like to go through the long download to view the entire large image*, 398
AVI format, 148, 150
  for digital video or animation, 199–200
  feature summary, 219
  video capture card support for, 228
  video streaming support in, 218
AVI Object, 353

B

Backdrop Object, 353
Background image, 85, 86, 126, 127, 192
Background (stage), creation of, 126–132
Bandwidth, 214
Banner graphics, 126, 127
Beanie Manager, 86
Behaviors *In a multimedia authoring context, behaviors are a set of actions or code that is given to an object to determine how it will respond to user interaction and programmatic events. These behaviors are often supplied with the authoring tool as a library of reusable instruction sets that can be applied to specific objects. For example, a button graphic can be given a button behavior that changes what was a lifeless flat button graphic into a responsive, interactive functional control on the interface*, 316
  applied to images, 345
  applied to sprites, 346
  cloning of, 354
  Lingo and, 341, 342–343
  objects with, 354

Bezier curve *A method of drawing a smooth, curved line on a computer screen. Bezier curves provide draggable handles on the ends of the curve to allow the adjustment of the degree of curvature*, 81
BGSOUND tag, 402
Binary system, 68–69
Bit *The smallest piece of computer data available. In the same way that letters are used to make words, which are used to make sentences, bits (binary digits) are assembled to make "words" of eight bits, called bytes, and multiple bytes are used to form the instructions used by computers to get their work done*, 68
Bit depth, 272
Bitmapped images *An image displayed on a computer screen as an array of colored dots, called pixels. When viewed at normal viewing distance from the computer screen they give an impression of an image*, 71, 80–81
Blaise Media, 312
Blend-level adjustment line, 254
Bluescreening technique, 31, 223
BMP (Windows Bitmap), 150
  3D scene stored as, 148
  as uncompressed, full-quality format, 81, 198–199
Boolean object combination procedures *A process of adding, subtracting, and finding the difference between two 3D objects. Unlike gluing, when two 3D objects are added together in this way, the resulting object becomes a new single object without any of the information stored that would allow for a reversal of this process or a separation of the original two objects. A boolean object combination process results in one object*, 176
Boston College Liberal Arts Career Network Web site, 43
Branching applications *A type of program processing in which at specific stages (screens) of the program, the option to jump to*

Graphic equalizer *Supplied on some hi-fi systems, a graphic equalizer provides individual level adjusters for sections of the sound frequency range. Each level can turn up or down the volume level of that part of the sound's dynamic range,* 290

Greenscreening technique, 223–224

H

Hard drives, 49–50, 60
  IDE, 229
  SCSI, 229
  of video editing workstations, 229
Hardware. *See also* Tools of the trade
  for multimedia producer, 44
Head-mounted display *Used in virtual reality applications, a computer screen display in a device that is worn on the head. Because of its proximity to the wearer's eyes, the display fills the user's complete field of view,* 6
History of multimedia, 3–11
  Atari, 4
  mouse, 5–6
  1980s, 6–8
  1990s, 8–11
  PC revolution, 5
  Pong (game), 3–4
Hit counters *A digital numeric display provided on a Web page to show the number of times a Web page has been visited,* 404
Home networks, 15
Hot button *Similar in function to a hot spot, this is a button image (or state) that changes dramatically when the user passes the mouse pointer over it, to emphasize its importance to the user, sometimes also referred to as a "rollover,"* 124
Hot spot *An area of a software application's interface that visually changes when the mouse pointer moves over its surface. This visual "reaction" draws attention to that screen*

area and indicates intuitively to the user that this is an important element of the interface that should be clicked, 31
  in interfaces, 126
HTML, 377–378
HyperCard, 8
Hyperlink, 398

I

IBM, 5
Icon-based authoring tools, 329
Iconic authoring *The method of authoring in which the navigation and interaction processing of the multimedia application can be controlled by assembling a series of icons along a processing path. Each icon represents a different function or capability of the program, and by assigning these functions specific properties, and by specifying their order and circumstance of appearance, the developer can create a complex multimedia application,* 317–318
IDE hard drives, 229
Image(s)
  background, 85, 86, 126, 127, 192
  bitmapped, 71, 80–81
  capturing, 229–230
  creating, 122
  scaling, 361
  16-color, 368
  sources for 2D graphics, 82–83
  still, 197–199, 202, 229–230
  vectored (line art), 80–81
Image dithering *A process of displaying images using a random dot pattern to give the viewer an impression of more detail and colors than the file format or computer display can actually support,* 75
Image resolution *The number of pixels used to display an image—usually given by pixel width times pixel height (such as a 640 × 480 image). The greater the number of pixels used to display an image, the better the image detail*

definition will be, but the file size will also increase, 71–72
IMA (International Multimedia Association), 277
IMAX theaters, 215
Importing media, 247, 248
  into Director, 198, 344
  into Lumiere, 247, 248
  into Multimedia Fusion, 360–361
  for nonlinear video editing, 48, 247
  into Premiere, 247, 248
Indeo codec, 221
Infini-D (Metacreations), 161–172
  background images in, 192
  Command floater in, 165, 166
  image format options, 200
  Information, Navigation, and Animation floater in, 165–166, 167
  interface of, 162
  keyframing in, 193
  lighting tools in, 191
  mouse operations in, 170
  navigation and learning aids for, 164
  Object Info panel of, 186–187
  Render Mode in, 169–170
  scene views in, 167–169
  Sequencer panel in, 166–167, 168
  SplineForm Workshop in, 170–172
  3D text in, 188
  tools groups in, 164–165
  trueSpace compared with, 161–162
  virtual floor in, 185
Infinite light, 191
Information overload, 25
Ink modes in Director, 337
Input device, resolution of, 72–73
Intel Corporation, 7, 32–33
  3D technology Web site, 34–36, 37–38
Interactive kiosk *A self-contained multimedia application provided in a public-display case in a format that users can interact with. Interactive kiosks usually take the appearance of arcade video game consoles or automated teller devices,* 4
Interactive video, 222

Working in the industry, 62–63
  career paths, 42–43
World Wide Web (WWW) *A
    version of the original Internet
    that supports graphics and
    multimedia technologies to
    enhance user experience and
    ease of use on the Net,* 8, 9, 59.
    See also Internet; Web site
    development
  authoring for, 201–202, 305,
    377–378
  branching structures of, 312
  browsers for, 10, 60, 376–377,
    400
  codecs specific to, 221

images from, 83
marketing and promoting online
    multimedia products,
    406–407
planning multimedia
    applications for, 321
sound on, 268–270, 296–297
video over, 214, 217–218
Wozniak, Steve, 5
.WRL, 150

X

Xerox Corporation, 5
Xtras *Similar to plug-ins for Web
    browsers and for products such*

*as Photoshop and Paint Shop
    Pro, Xtras are small helper
    applications that can be used to
    provide additional features and
    functionality to the original
    Director product,* 341,
    342–343, 345

Z

Zero-offset drop shadow, 138
Z-Soft Paintbrush, 150